The Bells Ring No More

by

JOHN TSCHINKEL

The Bells Ring No More

Reviews from the Slovene press.

"There is little in the recent past that moved me as much as the tale of John Tschinkel, revealed in his book The Bells Ring No More. Of the Gottschee Germans who for six long centuries lived a part of southern Slovenia we know very little. It is therefore even more precious to read the revelations of one who describes his early life there, his roots and the fate of his family in such a simple and sensitive manner. He left behind him a trail that can not be erased".

ZLATICA KASAL, *PRIMORSKE NOVICE, OKTOBER, 2010*

"The bells in Tschinkel's book, in addition to ringing historical and ethnographic melodies, above all ring a melody of the tragic destiny of over twelve thousand members of a people who had surrendered to the ideological fanaticism of Nazi youths. Youths, who were assigned the task of convincing their own people to give up their homes and way of life for nothing more than a promise".

MILAN VOGEL, *DELO, NOVEMBER, 2010*

"The author grew up in a self sufficient village in Slovenia until its entire population surrendered to the pressure to resettle in 1941. Not 'Home to the Reich' as promised, but to another part of annexed and ethnically cleansed Slovenia from where they were expelled in 1945 to become homeless refugees. He settled in America in 1950.
The book is a merging of at least four aspects of a story running in parallel: history, politics, cultural awareness and personal narrative. Because of this intertwining, the tale never gets boring. The expressive power of the book has several peaks. The last is the description of how the family is trying to outrun the Communist Partisans".

PROF., DR. MARJAN KORDAŠ,
SLOVENE ACADEMY OF SCIENCES AND ARTS, DECEMBER, 2010

"With his memoirs, intertwined with historical facts and data, John Tschinkel has made certain that the fate of the Gottscheer will not be forgotten. With the critical distance of an educated American immigrant, one who can not get rid of a burning sense of permanent loss, he has assembled a coherent mosaic of a vanished community".

MOJCA RAMŠAK, *VEČER, JANUARY 2011*

Excerpts from the Foreword

"Most serious historians would estimate that at least 40 million people perished in the death camps and on the killing fields of World War Two. In the face of such a figure, it should cause no surprise that they received more attention than the millions who 'merely' lost their homes, were uprooted or ethnically cleansed ...

John Tschinkel's autobiographical history deals with a small and relatively unknown group of such persons, the Gottschee Germans.... . For six hundred years this former enclave in Slovenia survived and even prospered under the generally benign sovereignty of Habsburg Austria ...

Fundamentally, the Gottschee Germans, like countless other ethnic German groups in the Balkans and Eastern Europe, fell victim to Third Reich blandishments, entreaties, threats and downright coercion to 'return home'. When they voted overwhelmingly to do so, they were resettled not within Germany proper, but in a nearby part of Slovenia that had been annexed and brutally cleansed of its Slavic population on Himmler's orders. ...

In their new land they were surrounded by hostile elements, including the ethnically cleansed Slovenes whose homes had been seized and given to the Gottscheer. Of these 37,000 Slovenes, a large number never returned from forced labour in the Reich. As the war came to an end, the Gottscheer found themselves deprived of ancestral territory to which they could return. ..

They finally set off on foot and in horse-drawn wagons; not to their former homes but to exile ...

Tschinkel is an American immigrant of mixed parentage, with an ethnic German father and a Slovene mother. Brought up to be both bilingual and bicultural he is able to draw on many sources to buttress and lend substance to the historical framework and scope of his chronicle, for he sets off his personal recollections against a broad canvas depicting what this ethnic island was in the twentieth century and how it had arrived there".

PETER FOULKES
Former Professor of German Studies, Dean of Humanities Stanford University, California. Emeritus Professor, University of Wales.

John Tschinkel

The Bells Ring No More

an autobiographical history

THE BELLS RING NO MORE

First published in Slovenia in 2010 under the title "Zvonovi so umolknili". This English edition was printed in the United States by CreateSpace, an Amazon Inc. subsidiary.

Foreword: Peter Foulkes
Editors: Marko Vidic, Anne P. Wall
Layout: Brigitte Tiszauer
Cover illustrations: Vesna Vidmar
Maps: Mateja Rihtaršič
Photographs: Norbert černe, Tone Ferenc, Mitja Ferenc, Mirko Oražem. Archives of the Republic of Slovenia, Museum of Contemporary History of Slovenia, Bundesarchiv Koblenz, Germany, Archives Modrijan Založba d.o.o., Family Archives.

On the cover are the bells of the parish church of St. Primus and Felician in Grčarice (Masern) in Slovenia. They fell to the ground when the church was destroyed by fire during the battle of September 1943. Photo: Slavko Felicijan, 1943, Museum of Contemporary History of Slovenia.

Copyright © 2010 by John Tschinkel. All rights reserved, including the right to reproduce this book or any portion thereof in any form whatsoever.

ISBN: 1478274743

ISBN 13: 9781478274742

The original English manuscript was translated into Slovene and published by Modrijan založba, d.o.o., Ljubljana, Slovenia.

Editor: Marko Vidic

Translation by: Maja Kraigher, (English text), Nataša Peternel, (German quotes)

Copyright © 2010 Modrijan Založba, d.o.o. and John Tschinkel

CIP - The book is listed in the catalog of the Slovene National University Library in Ljubljana.

This book is dedicated to the two Marias. To my mother Maria Tschinkel who was the rock of our family and to Grandma Maria Ilc who taught me to read and showed me the way.

But it is especially dedicated to my wife Anne. Without her encouragement, patience and never ending support this book would not have been written.

Content

Chapter	Page
Introduction	xvii
Foreword	xxi
1. The Fire Pump	1
2. Return to the Past	19
3. The Enclave	39
4. A Village through Time	83
5. The Church on the Square	115
6. The Gypsies	141
7. The Railroad	147
8. My Family	161
9. Aunt Johanna's Roof	179
10. The Seasons	193
11. Mattl	211
12. Assignment and Preparation	223
13. Completing the Task	255
14. Our Ingathering – their Deportation	291
15. Mission Accomplished	317
16. Veliko Mraševo	333
17. The Rabbit	357
18. Settling In	367
19. Twilight by the River	385
20. The Road to Exile	417
Bibliography	459

Author's Note:

Throughout the centuries, the formal names of places described in this book reflected the nationality of their rulers. Under the Romans Ljubljana, the capital of today's Slovenia, was known by its Latin name Emona. The Germans under Charlemagne changed Emona to Laibach the name used by the governing Hapsburg Empire until 1918 when Laibach became the present day Ljubljana.

During their 645 year rule, the Hapsburg overlords added a German equivalent to all places under their control, including Slovenia, German being the administrative language enforced in all provinces of the Empire. The indigenous population everywhere was, however, free to use the ancient place-names among themselves in their daily lives.

In Slovenia, the duality of formal place-names flipped in 1918 when the administrative language became Slovene. In the ethnic enclave of Gottschee, where German place names had been used for centuries the habit continued. All residents were, however, required to use only Slovene in their dealings with the new State.

In this book, place-names are in Slovene followed by their German equivalent in parenthesis. The prime example is Grčarice (Masern), the village where I was born. During my time there we used only Masern while our Slovene neighbors, only a few kilometers away, called it Grčarice. Such duality was prevalent throughout the enclave.

I use the Slovene place-names in deference to the State and for the benefit of the new generation who are no longer aware of the now anachronistic German equivalent, found only on archaic maps and in buried archives. The German name in parenthesis is however, provided to accommodate those of my generation and their descendants who continue to cling to a period that was ended by the forces of racial nationalism.

JOHN TSCHINKEL

Vero Beach,
June, 2012

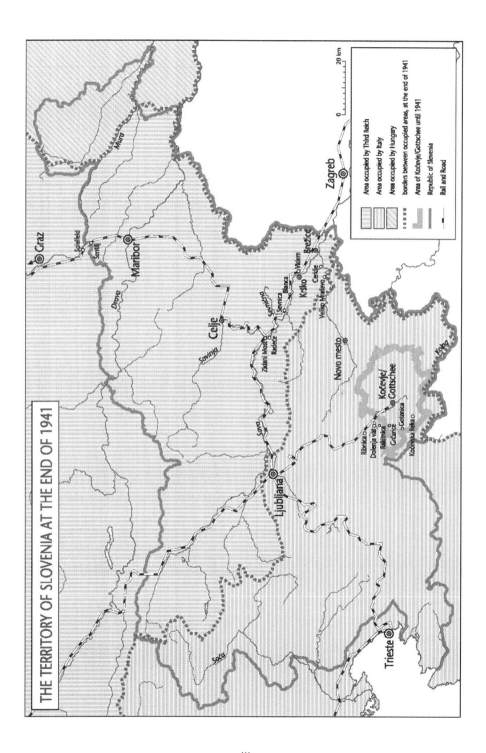

Nationalism:

"A society united by a common error as to its origins and a common aversion to its neighbors".

J.S. Huxley & A.C. Haddon.
"We Europeans" Oxford Encyclopedia 1940

Author's Introduction

My writing is the result of a decade long effort to recount a period before and during WW II that ended in millions becoming homeless refugees in 1945 as the result of Hitler's ingathering policy of "Home to the Reich". A small part of these millions were the descendants of people that had settled an empty forest in Slovenia in the middle of the 14th Century. Among them was the entire population of my village including my family and myself.

The book tells my story in two parts, each with its own beginning and end.

The first part looks back on my first years in a pastoral village into which I was born in 1931. A self-sufficient community for six centuries, it was insignificant in history but not to the inhabitants of this village at the edge of the world. As one of them, I was fortunate to be able, even after six decades, to recollect my first ten years there; to describe the daily and seasonal rhythm as well as the roles and actions of its main characters and protagonists. I write about the two sides of my family that were separated not only by a geographic and linguistic, but eventually also by a national divide. Also be able to describe my father's house in which were born at least seven generations and in which, as a product of a racially mixed marriage, I lived through the racial tensions of that decade.

I also describe in detail the events that persuaded my village and the entire Kočevje (Gottschee) enclave to leave their homes and their lands and turn their backs on the soil from which they extracted a meager if adequate livelihood for six centuries; move to a place in a near yet foreign land from which all residents had been driven out to make room for us. I describe how the people of this enclave were persuaded to return "Home to the Reich" in 1941 during a war whose successful outcome, even at that time, was no more than an uncertain hope.

The second part describes the four years after the coerced resettlement in 1941 into another part of Slovenia from which the resident Slovene were expelled. It tells of a life of apprehension, unrest and terror and the tragic end of the entire community in the spring of 1945. All traumatic events in which I was destined to participate and only by the grace of providence managed to survive.

THE BELLS RING NO MORE

The "Home to the Reich" program was part of the plan to enlarge the Third Reich, a plan in which German nationals living outside the boundaries established after WWI played an important role. Most of these Germans, including the Gottscheer, now lived in territories that had been awarded to other Nations by the Versailles Peace Conference; Germans who, even in the 1930's still resented their new subservient status and actively resisted the requirements of their new sovereign State. This resistance was mainly due to the mandated learning and use of another language; one that replaced German as the formal language of the State. This, above all else, was seen as the loss of the cultural marker that identified them as Germans, as part of a superior race. Now no longer part of the ruling class, all were therefore hoping for an eventual return home. To reach its objective of enlargement, the Reich actively exploited this resentment and with an ever more radical interventionist agenda, the Reich worked actively to inflame their resistance into confrontation thereby getting the reason it needed to intervene.

On October 6, 1939 Hitler gave a speech at the Reichstag justifying his occupation of Poland as an effort to free the German nationals there from oppression. In this speech he also announced his intention to bring "Home to the Reich" all ethnic Germans still living outside the now expanded borders of the Reich. And on the following day he gave Reichsführer-SS Heinrich Himmler the directive to perform the task. In 1940 the order was formulated into a set of ideological guidelines which specified that the non-German population in the recently annexed lands be removed and the land resettled with German nationals brought back "Home" from other parts of Europe. The guidelines also ordered that after their return, the former ethnic concepts of the ingathered be, "in the shortest time", wiped out and that the new citizens submit fully to all requirements of the Reich.

The brunt of this "Ingathering" was to fall on the roughly ten million Poles in the annexed Poland, the main part of the grand plan to gain the "Lebensraum" for the Germans of the Third Reich. Nearly one million Poles were expelled, while 600,000 Germans from Eastern Europe and 400,000 from the Reich were settled in their place.

The "Home to the Reich" program was enthusiastically received by all those who wished to again become part of the German nation. This was the case also with the Gottschee Germans. Here, the Reich counted on a group of Gottscheer leaders, young men who had been converted into fanatical adherents of National Socialism and who in 1938, with the full weight of the Third Reich behind them, took over the leadership of the enclave.

The Gottscheer of the 1920's had, however, begun to accept their role as an ethnic minority subservient to the Slavic Yugoslavia. Cooperation with the new State, after an initial period of conflict and resistance, began to take hold. The State was,

AUTHOR'S INTRODUCTION

if gradually, again allowing the Gottscheer to function as a German enclave in their land. But the re-emergence of the new Germany under National Socialism soon brought this cooperation to an end and renewed confrontation, so essential to the plan of the Reich, was actively encouraged and financially supported after 1933.

On April 6, 1941, the Reich and its Axis allies invaded Yugoslavia which surrendered after sixteen days. This nation had emerged as a sovereign State from parts of the Austrian Empire and its creation had been sanctioned at Versailles. The conquered country was now divided among the Axis partners, except that Croatia became a Puppet State and Serbia a protectorate administered by the Reich. Slovenia, a former Crown land of the Austrian Empire and after 1918 a part of Yugoslavia, was split into two. The northern half was annexed by the Reich. The southern part that also contained the Gottschee enclave, (until 1918 under the protective umbrella of Austrian aristocrats) was, for strategic reasons occupied by Italy.

This was a great disappointment to the youthful Gottscheer who had actively lobbied that the enclave be attached to the Reich in the event of a takeover of Yugoslavia. Since this was not to be, these leaders were informed by Hitler personally of their "Return to the Reich" while simultaneously he also promised that the entire Gottschee population would be resettled as the closed ethnic group it had been for centuries. That the latter was false and entirely contrary to his policy was to become clear to them only after they accomplished their assigned mission. What was true, however, was that their destination in the "Reich" was not to be the annexed Poland but a part of the annexed Slovenia, only a short 70 kilometers away, a place from which the resident Slovene were to be expelled.

The assignment to the unknowingly betrayed Gottscheer was to now persuade their own people to resettle. Both the SS and their Gottscheer surrogates knew that coercive persuasion was required to get the population to agree. They certainly would not agree to leave for a place from which the Slovene population had been expelled to make room for them. To succeed in their mission, the young Gottscheer fanatics, now fully committed to the objectives of the Reich, decided to keep the resettlement destination a top secret from the population. At least until the deed was done. With this decision the betrayed became the betrayers. They managed to keep the secret and with their effective tactics of persuasion during the remainder of 1941 the mission was successfully completed in February 1942. But soon after that, in line with ingathering guidelines, they were relieved of their former leadership role by their SS masters and sent off to the various fronts.

After the resettlement, the book recounts life in the annexed Slovenia, in a village emptied of its rightful owners, a place full of ghosts. The former ethnic group was no more; the former Gottscheer, as citizens of the Third Reich, were now forbidden to speak their ancient dialect. Its small bourgeoisie was dispersed; its youthful ideological leaders stripped of their former role. All in line with the strict guidelines of Hitler's "Home to the Reich" objective as was formulated by the SS staff of Heinrich Himmler.

Here we lived a life of diminishing hope, of terror and increasing fear. Of terror that came to us in the form of ever more frequent nightly raids from safe places by former residents or the Partisans as had been promised us before we left the enclave. Then the dawning knowledge that the Reich that betrayed us was soon to collapse and with it our once hopeful future. And above all the realization that in only a short while we would become homeless refugees, providing we were to survive what was sure to come.

Survive we did, if just. And homeless refugees we did become after seventeen terror-filled days and nights in May of 1945 on the way to our Exile in Austria and beyond. At first, amid the collapsing army of the Reich and its allies, all feverishly trying to outrun Tito's Partisans. And after that in the terror caused by the non-too-gentle liberators who identified us as part of the former occupier and treated us accordingly. But in spite of what at times seemed hopeless and seemingly insurmountable hardships, we did reach our exile after we crossed the border into Austria on May 25, 1945.

Ours was a destiny no different from that of millions of German nationals who became victims of a nationalism that evolved into the lethal version of the Third Reich. We all paid bitterly for succumbing to the siren song of "Home to the Reich". And after its collapse, we were tarred as a willing part of the occupier and became targets and recipients of the rage of victors. As part of this rage, between 10 and 14 million Germans were expelled from countries of Eastern Europe, including 2.5 million from Czechoslovakia, 3 million from Poland and 500,000 from Yugoslavia. The expulsion had been authorized under the terms of Article XIII of the Protocol of the Potsdam Conference, which however, stipulated that the expulsions were to be conducted in a humane fashion which, particularly in the early phases, was far from being the case.

Other millions had fled in time to escape a similar treatment. We, the former Gottscheer tried to do this, but our attempt was futile and far too late.

Foreword

Most serious historians would estimate that at least 40 million people perished in the death camps and on the killing fields of World War Two. In the face of such a figure, it should cause no surprise that those who died in that terrible conflict have received more attention than the millions who 'merely' lost their homes, were uprooted or ethnically cleansed, fled before invading armies, secret police, shells and bombs. Sometimes people fled through fear; and sometimes they were driven by a sense of guilt about what had been done in their name. In some cases they were driven out of their homes by a native population bent on vengeance after years of servitude and terror. Others were deported en masse because they were considered to be a threat, while some moved because they themselves were deemed to be threatened. Although World War Two ended in Europe in May 1945, for months and years afterwards there were still floods of refugees, or Displaced Persons as they were called at the time, seeking to rebuild their shattered lives amidst the ruins of destruction.

John Tschinkel's autobiographical history The Bells Ring No More deals with a small and relatively unknown group of such persons, the Gottschee Germans. Gottschee is an area of around 400 square miles in the south of Slovenia. In the early 14th century this heavily forested region of Carniola, then owned by the counts of Ortenburg, was settled by Germans from the north-west, who cleared and worked the land, built towns and villages, and mostly lived in peace, strained at times, with their Slavic neighbours. For six hundred years this German language enclave survived and even prospered, first as an outpost of the heterogeneous Holy Roman Empire and later under the generally benign sovereignty of Habsburg Austria. Throughout this period they retained their culture and their antiquated German dialect. Following World War One and the dissolution of the Austro-Hungarian Empire, Gottschee was incorporated into what would become Yugoslavia, and is today the municipality of Kočevsko in Slovenia, which has been a member of the European Union since 2004. The city of Gottschee has reverted to its Slovene name of Kočevje.

In the late nineteenth century Gottschee had a population of some 23,000, and although a steady stream of inhabitants left to seek their fortunes in the New World over the years, the area was still a thriving and viable German language enclave in the twentieth century. At the beginning of World War Two there were around 12,500 ethnic Germans left in the region, the others by then having settled in the USA. Today, however, there are scarcely any traces of these people still to be found in their traditional homeland. Their German dialect, already an anachronism centuries ago, is now virtually extinct in its ancestral home.

Whole villages have disappeared either through destruction as part of fierce battles between the defenders and occupiers, be they Italian or German, or by being allowed to fall into ruin; churches have suffered the same fate, and even graveyards have been obliterated and stripped of German inscriptions. The thick carpet of forest, laboriously cleared over the centuries to make room for crops and animals, has returned and again covers much of the area.

How and why did this happen? There are no straightforward answers to this question, and John Tschinkel, in making his own personal contribution to an ongoing debate, is well aware that he is stepping into a realm in which history, memory, propaganda and deceit mingle and coexist in an uneasy and constantly shifting relationship.

The disappearance of the Gottschee Germans is by no means a mystery, however, for numerous archives, personal accounts and historical studies have dealt with the events from various viewpoints; the basic sequence of events is not in question. Hans Hermann Frensing, building on the pioneering work of the eminent Slovenian historian Tone Ferenc, provided a sober and meticulous history (1970), which examines in detail the relevant archives covering the final years of the Gottschee community. Frensing's study constitutes a balanced and well documented description and analysis of the events in the 1930s and early 1940s that led to the dissolution of a culture that had endured for six centuries. His account is valuable mostly as a step by step analysis of the archival material, detailing the methods and subterfuges, intentions and effects of National Socialist policies that created turmoil and upheaval in Gottschee as they did throughout Europe.

Fundamentally, the Gottschee Germans, like countless other ethnic German groups in the Balkans and Eastern Europe, fell victim to Third Reich blandishments, entreaties, threats and downright coercion to 'return home'. When they voted overwhelmingly to do so, they were resettled not within Germany proper, but in a nearby part of Slovenia that had been annexed and brutally cleansed of its Slavic population on Himmler's orders in order to make room for the newcomers, whose task was to strengthen 'Germanness' on the southern flank of the newly expanded Reich.

As World War Two ground on to its inevitable conclusion and the total destruction of the Third Reich, the hapless transplanted Gottschee people found themselves adrift in a limbo over which they had little control. They had given up their ancestral lands and homes, voting to return to a Germany that had not merely betrayed them in several ways, but had in fact managed to contrive a situation in which they would

FOREWORD

themselves be subject to intolerable pressure by Yugoslav Partisans and the expelled Slovenes, some of whom had vanished into the parts of Slovenia occupied by Italy and were eager to return. As ethnic Germans, moreover, the Gottscheers were associated in the eyes of many in Yugoslavia with the brutalities and atrocities perpetrated by the Nazi occupiers and their accomplices, and it comes as no surprise that they fled into neighbouring Austria, from where many of them moved to Germany or emigrated to the US, Canada and other countries.

So while there is no dispute concerning the major events that culminated in the dissolution of the Gottschee community, every stage in its dissolution has been subject to acrimonious disagreement concerning the causes and interpretation of those events, and these disagreements persist to the present day. The inhabitants of Gottschee, for example, did indeed vote in 1941 for resettlement, but when they cast their votes, they were under the mistaken impression that they were 'going home' to the Reich, whereas their leaders and Himmler's functionaries knew that they were to be resettled within a nearby part of Slovenia.

Nor can the vote be regarded as free in any normal sense, since the Nazis deployed their full arsenal of persuasion, deception and coercion, tactics already well rehearsed in Czechoslovakia, Poland and South Tyrol, in order to guarantee the vote they wanted. Agitators were sent in from the Third Reich, and local people were recruited, trained and given the task of softening up the voters. Dissenters were vilified as enemies of the people and vermin ("Volksschädlinge"). They were threatened with imprisonment in concentration camps, and at the same time intimidated by rumours claiming falsely that the Italians, who had been allowed to occupy part of Slovenia, including Gottschee, intended to ship to Sicily or even Abyssinia all those who refused to sign up for resettlement in greater Germany.

In their new land they were surrounded by hostile elements, including the ethnically cleansed Slovenes whose homes had been seized and given to the Gottscheers. Of these 37,000 Slovenes, a large number never returned from forced labour in the Reich, another reason for the growing enmity and desire for revenge. As the war came to an end, the Gottscheers, who had voted to give up their Slovenian citizenship and homes in exchange for citizenship of the Third Reich thus found themselves deprived of ancestral territory to which they could return.

They finally set off on foot and in horse-drawn wagons to achieve what had been promised to them in 1941, the return 'home', a home from which their ancestors had departed six centuries earlier. This nightmare journey across a collapsing and war-torn corner of Europe has been represented variously as a flight from Tito's Partisans, an expulsion carried out by vengeful Slovenes, or as a conscious intention to escape from an Eastern Europe that looked likely to fall into the orbit of the communist Soviet Union. To some extent, it contained elements of all these things, but it was also an attempt to escape from the knowledge of monstrous crimes and self-deception on a massive scale, one further stage in the development of a national repressed memory syndrome, a problem that has beset Germany in one form or another ever since the 1930s.

These arguments are still taking place at meetings, in newspapers, chat rooms and on websites around the world. Like many disagreements concerning the interpretation of historical events, the rhetoric used is at times intemperate and heated, reminiscent of the scurrilous language used by the Nazi supporters of resettlement in the early 1940s. Some of the people commenting on the events were in fact Nazi supporters of resettlement at that time, and ironically they have used the current debate in order to obfuscate matters and to create confusion about their own role.

John Tschinkel's book is primarily a deeply personal and at times painful contribution to the ongoing debate about Gottschee. The bells that no longer ring, featured in his title and front cover, are those of the Roman Catholic chapel in Grčarice (Masern), the Gottschee village where the author was born in 1931 and where he spent the first ten years of his life. His aim in writing the book, he states, was to make a permanent record of experiences and memories that would otherwise slip into oblivion. This initial intention was later supplemented by a desire to set the record straight in the face of a resurgence of the strident and deceitful rhetoric first used by the National Socialist supporters of resettlement. One example of this was the 1955 renaissance of the *Gottscheer Zeitung* in Klagenfurt, Austria, under the editorship of the person who had edited it in Gottschee in the late thirties and early forties, when it was beating the drum for Hitler's Third Reich and the desirability of resettling there.

Tschinkel's focus is on his own experiences during these years, and his major contribution to our knowledge of the events is the series of vividly recalled incidents, anecdotes and memories, recounted with a powerful narrative skill and an authorial voice that is at times wry, ironic, angry and frustrated, but always deeply humane and striving for a balanced vision. Unlike most of those who have commented on the events, Tschinkel, an American is of mixed parentage, with an ethnic German father and a Slovene mother. In his early years he was brought up to be both bilingual and bicultural, and he is able draw on many sources to buttress and lend substance to the historical framework and scope of his chronicle, for he is determined to set off his personal recollections against a broad canvas depicting what Gottschee was in the twentieth century and how it had arrived there.

FOREWORD

And above all, what was being lost forever when the Gottscheer Germans fatefully embarked on their journey just three and a half years before Hitler's Thousand Year Reich came to its ignominious end. The bells that 'ring no more' become powerful and recurrent symbols marking the phases and cycles of a vibrant culture, with its births and deaths, dangers and ecstasies, past and future. They are the 'blue remembered hills' of a narrative permeated by an aching sense of loss and a growing consciousness that the collective future is slowly but inexorably blurring into nothing.

The author is too skilful a narrator to lay claim to having witnessed personally all the events described, even those where he was clearly present. He deals with this adroitly in his second chapter in which the details of his own arrival, filtered through the memory of his older sister Mitzi and his own later experience of his younger brother's birth, are used as focal points for a gradually enlarged picture placing his home village within its historical and geographical framework. This frame is further marked out between two central points in time: December 7, 1941, when the family set off on their fruitless resettlement to what village leaders had been calling the land of 'milk and honey', and a return trip in 1974, when he was able to see that while 'much had changed . . . much had also remained the same.' Slovenian relatives of his mother had prepared him what to expect: 'It still snows as it used to and the basin still fills and overflows in the spring when the snows melt in the hills. But the cistern in the basin behind the church, once the main watering place for the livestock and the fire pumps, is no longer used and is crumbling away. Weeds cover the ruins'.

The plangency and power of Tschinkel's narrative spring in part from this tension between remembered past and present experience, in which vividly captured moments of childhood and adolescence blend with historical and cultural knowledge to form a coherent mosaic of a vanished community. All is pieced together with affection and ruefulness, and illuminated further through the prism of the author's post-war emigration to the USA, where his education and professional life as an engineer provide new contexts of interpretation and evaluation for his earlier life.

It is, however, these lively and compelling snapshots of the author's first fourteen years that represent the essence and enduring quality of Tschinkel's contribution, for they bring a welcome human dimension to the necessarily drier and more dispassionate historical studies. As such they offer a lively and at times grimly humorous correction to other personal accounts, which are mostly flimsier and more narrowly focused than Tschinkel, and are sometimes tendentious and self-serving to the point of caricature. An early image of the narrator as a boy, surrounded by an ocean of brilliant chamomile flowers, gives way to the picture of his mother holding the head of the ailing family horse Yiorgo so that his father could pour a soothing and medicinal chamomile extract into the animal's mouth. The wiser and older boy then makes a brief appearance in order to impart the insight that chamomile tea was 'the standard cure for most ailments of man and beast . . . especially if fortified with a generous portion of slivovitz.' Later we witness the youthful Tschinkel falling in a faint in his Hitler Youth uniform on parade one stiflingly hot summer day. His emotions were shame and despair that his weakness might be attributed to his mixed racial heritage.

There is a good deal of humour in Tschinkel's account, and on one level it could be placed in the genre or tradition of amusing pictures of village life. The humour, entertaining though it is, is also a foil that etches out with greater clarity a darkness, a deep sense of foreboding that runs through the narrative. Sometimes this is achieved literally, as in the passages describing the Tschinkel family's arrival in their new home during the resettlement. The villages and houses are strangely empty, and when the bus passes the walls of the village cemetery, the author adds, 'in which, in the very near future, were to be buried two of my best friends.' A few minutes later the parents and their three children are dropped off in front of a house, while 'the bus backed out and returned to the centre of the village, leaving us standing in the few inches of newly fallen snow.' Inside the bitterly cold house there awaited more ominous surprises, for it was clear from the unwashed dishes and unmade beds that its previous occupants had departed in haste and probably fear, the realization of which brought Tschinkel's father to tears, which he sought unsuccessfully to conceal from his children by stepping outside to inspect the stable and barn.

And then there is the chapter entitled The Rabbit, in which humour and horror are played out against a growing sense of historical understanding that takes years to develop into a full awareness of what had happened. The chapter is devoted to the author's close friendship with a boy from school, Josef, whose Gottscheer family had been allocated a farm some distance from the village. In addition to spear fishing, the two friends shared a passion for rabbits, which they prized as pets but also raised as a supplement to the families' meat ration. Josef was the proud owner of a dominant male, a 'beautiful rabbit with smooth and shining grey fur twice the size of any other in the stables of the village'. He was called Adolf, and was greatly admired by John who was allowed to take him home for a few weeks, where he created havoc by attacking John's own male rabbits and by impregnating the females too quickly for the planned sequence of meat supplies.

In the autumn of 1943 Josef arrived at John's house in an agitated and breathless state. He had run two kilometers from his home, in order to tell his friend that

FOREWORD

he and his family were being forced to leave the village immediately, and to request him to look after Adolf for the time-being. John went back with Josef, where he found his friend's mother and sister in tears and his father loading suitcases on to a truck under the gaze of the Gestapo. After a hasty handshake Josef was made to join his sister and parents in the back of the truck, and they were driven off leaving John 'standing alone in the middle of the courtyard.'

He returned home with Adolf, and a few weeks later received a postcard from Josef saying that the family were happily settled in their new home, which a local Nazi official had explained to the uneasy villagers was situated in the old Reich and that the family had been sent there since they were deemed too unreliable to serve as guardians of Greater Germany's southern border. The card contained no return address, and had been mailed from Poland. John discovered later that Josef's mother was a Gypsy. Later still he discovered what was happening to Gypsies, Jews and other 'undesirables' during and after those idyllic summer and autumn months of 1943 that he had spent in the company of Josef.

Adolf, with a fine sense of historical irony, survived until the spring of 1945, when he was shot and eaten by a group of thuggish SS men who took over the Tschinkels' home and beds for a night as they fled before the advancing Partisans. Years later John Tschinkel suffered from a recurrent nightmare in which 'Josef merged into the body of the dying Adolf dragging himself across the dirt'.

The Bells Ring No More ends on a note which encapsulates the whole narrative and could serve as a chilling reminder of how the National Socialists betrayed the people of Gottschee as well as their ethnic brethren within and outside the Reich. Shortly before they complete the final steps of their journey across the border into Austria, the Gottscheer pass an embankment bearing four words written in huge capital letters:

WIR DANKEN UNSEREM FÜHRER

Tschinkel comments, 'Plain for all to contemplate, in silence, the four words of now bitter irony, words we had been made to utter so often in mass rallies during the summer of 1941 and the years after that without really knowing why'.

Peter Foulkes
Former Professor of German Studies,
Dean of Humanities Stanford University, California.
Emeritus Professor, University of Wales.

Chapter 1

The Fire Pump

Father came home very late that night.

He had left for the meeting after the evening meal in an already foul mood and Mother said that he would be back late. She knew that unless he finally convinced the others, he would return angry, his anger inflamed by pints of the watered down wine served at the pub where the meetings were held. So she kept us up late into the evening hoping that the presence of his children would ease his frustration, but finally could wait no longer and all three of us went to bed. She sent Mitzi to her room, but kept me with her in her bed. Worried, she wanted me near to deflect and soften his anger when he came home.

That evening in 1939 they were going to decide on the fuel powered fire pump for the village. The manual one, purchased after the big fire in 1882, was not powerful enough to get the water to the outlying buildings, which had been added to the village in the last century. It would not even serve the buildings near the center since it took much too long to get the pump to the cistern, hook up the hoses and manually pump the water to the fire.

The majority of the villagers living near the center of the village were arguing for the smaller pump, mounted on a platform to be carried by a group of firemen from the firehouse to the cistern. To this group, cost was the professed reason but they were accused of duplicity by those living at the edges of the village. The charge was that they opted for the smaller and therefore cheaper pump, knowing that it would do for them.

Father, who sided with the minority and was their most vocal supporter, argued for a more powerful and therefore more expensive version. This infuriated the central villagers who accused him of breaking ranks, since his buildings, like theirs, were near the center just behind the church and the parsonage. Father's argument was that only a more powerful pump could deliver water to the most distant buildings. This heavier pump would have to be on a rubber wheeled cart which could quickly be rolled to the central cistern, the only real source of water. Naturally, it cost more but according to his argument, the smaller pump would not serve the entire village and therefore was not a fair choice.

THE BELLS RING NO MORE

The meetings started in late fall after all the big farming chores were out of the way. Most of them ended in heated arguments. They were held in the Jaklitsch pub and went on for months, no doubt to the benefit of Franz Jaklitsch, the village leader and owner of the pub, since Father and all others consumed a lot of wine and returned home drunk after each meeting. My sister Mitzi and I would retrace his steps the following morning and count the number of rest stops his bottom impressed in the usually new snow on the way home.

But on that night, the final decision was to be made after another round of animated discussions. Mother knew from her friends that he was losing the battle and that the prospect of convincing the opposition this evening was very small. He was going to be very late and angry and she wanted me near her to help calm his anger and divert it from being directed at her when he finally returned home.

She woke me when he was still fumbling with the front door. But instead of coming to the bedroom, he went into the kitchen slamming the door behind him. Then there was silence and after a while, a mighty crash that shook the walls.

"Go see what he did", she ordered. When the kitchen door opened he expected Mother, but seeing me, his expression changed to a friendly grin. "Go get the shoe and then back to bed".

He had taken off his shoe and thrown it against the wall. He was relieving his frustration. I did as he asked and left the kitchen to report to anxious Mother. Not long after that there was another crash. Again I was sent to the kitchen and again I was ordered to fetch the shoe. This time I was told to go to sleep and not come back.

How mother coped for the rest of the night I do not remember. But that was the evening when they had decided to buy the wrong pump. The only concession to the minority was a rubber wheeled cart for the smaller pump.

There were some meetings after that but he stayed away. His supporters came to his shop to talk about the coming vindication. Their moment came when the new pump arrived and was put to the test.

The fire of August 2, 1882 destroyed fifteen houses and their adjacent barns and stables. It was started by lightning and there being no organized fire fighting and all the buildings being close together, the fire could not be stopped. Flying embers carried the flames from roof to roof; easy prey for any home, barn or stable covered with home made wooden shingles. All owners could do was to rescue the contents of the main house and the adjacent structures before the unstoppable and all consuming flames took hold. The fire stopped on its own accord only when the embers could no longer ignite the more distant structures.

What was left were the badly charred stone walls of the single story structure, upon which a new set of roof beams could be constructed. And, instead of wood shingles the new covering was reddish-brown terra cotta tile which had long been the roofing material in other parts of Slovenia.

Most, except one of the destroyed houses, were rebuilt within a year or at least covered with a new roof and therefore habitable. But it was the first winter following the fire that brought discomfort not only for the victims but also for the relatives and neighbors who put them up. Fortunately, the livestock was saved and the crops, vital for survival until next fall and essential for seeding the new growth in the spring had not yet been harvested and a future food shortage was thereby avoided.

The exception to the reconstruction was the house at Number 30 which was rebuilt into the first village school that opened in October 1884. It contained one large school room and a separate apartment for the teacher in the other half of the house.

It was this fire that convinced the villagers to appoint a fire chief, establish a fire brigade and purchase the manually operated pump, mounted on the platform of a horse drawn cart. This was also the time when they built the cistern, to collect and store an abundant supply of water for the pump. Unfortunately, none of this was put to the test until the succession of three fires in the 1930's.

The fire on March 10, 1931 destroyed the barn and part of the main house of the fire chief Karl Schaffer only a short distance from the firehouse across the square. Total destruction of the house was prevented only because the firehouse was so near and the pump was put to work quickly after the big bell brought the firemen to the scene.

But it took two more fires, and five more years of urging by Schaffer to get the new pump and modernize the equipment in the firehouse which had been built together with the first village school. Both buildings as well as the cistern in the village bowl for storing the water for the pump, were completed in October 1884 and the fire brigade, formed after the big fire in 1882, took possession of the firehouse the following spring. The fire brigade, which included all able men in the village, was trained by Karl Schaffer, the first Fire Chief of Grčarice (Masern) and father of the present Karl, who took over when his father died.

The meetings to do with the new pump started after the fire in the early fall of 1938 burned to the ground Katharina's small wooden house on the hill at the southeast end of the village. Katharina's fire was the third in seven years and I remember it well. The second fire, two years before in the summer of 1936, partly destroyed the barn of Ferdinand Tscherne, at the southwest end of the village, equally remote from the center, as was Katharina's house.

Father attended the meetings of all tax paying landowners in the village. But regardless of how much land you owned if any, Franz Jaklitsch never turned away anyone who had money for wine. Women were not allowed to attend.

The meetings filled the public room of the Jaklitsch tavern with the men smoking and drinking quantities of wine from quarter liter glass pitchers with a line scratched into the glass to show the quarter liter mark. There was no electricity in the village and the light from the single kerosene lamp in the center of the ceiling struggled through the thick smoke. The lamp was a marvel and the only one of its kind in the village. Its light came from a silk membrane kept glowing-white by kerosene vapor from the chamber of the lamp. During the long meetings, the pressure had to be maintained with a built-in small hand pump which, if not carefully used, would fracture the delicate pear shaped membrane that could not be replaced very quickly.

In that case, standard wick burning kerosene lamps were brought to the tables. In the dimmer light, the blotches of spilled wine and misdirected aims at the spittoons were no longer visible in the sawdust from the village sawmill covering the floor.

Young women hired for the occasion served the wine from two barrels in the adjacent room, which also contained the small dry goods store. The barrels were behind the counter and the wine in one of these was diluted and used only when the drinkers could no longer tell the difference.

Wine, tobacco and cigarettes were dispensed by Regina, the wife of Franz. The ever-attentive Regina, always on the look out for empty pitchers and short cigarette stubs, carefully recorded replacements while her husband kept the heated meeting under reasonable control. He had considerable standing in the village in part because he was the most popular innkeeper of three by providing easy credit. But most of this standing was because, even in 1938, he was already chief of our branch of the "Kulturbund", the illegal association whose mission was to convert the ethnic Germans of Slovenia to the Nazi cause. But more on that later.

The undisputed origin of the Schaffer fire was spontaneous combustion of freshly mowed grass left on the wooden floor of the barn. According to Schaffer, the grass had been left there by his much abused second wife Maria, whom he publicly blamed for the accident.

But according to Mother, who was very friendly with Maria, a Slovene born Miklitsch and who like Mother was a village outsider, the grass was left there by Schaffer himself only months after he purchased an insurance policy on the house and the adjacent structures including the barn. The fire was deemed an accident by the insurer and the payment was sufficient to rebuild the barn and repair the parts of the damaged house. This included a new roof for the house and a complete refurbishment of the outside walls, and with these improvements the Schaffer house became the most attractive on the square in the village center.

Karl Schaffer was a huge man with a rascally upturned thick mustache and an imposing presence. In his frequently drunken state from the wine of the Jaklitsch pub, at times during a workday and certainly on weekends, he not only terrorized his wife and two teenage sons from a prior marriage, but also anyone near him.

On the way home from the pub, drunk and stumbling, the boys of the village, myself included, would tease him from a safe distance and woe to those who were caught. And some of us, the littler ones, were. The older boys would hold us until he came near then let us go at the last moment. When he caught one of us, his hand was heavy on the behind and hurt quite a bit. Another thrashing came afterwards from our parents for not leaving the man alone. We, of course, had said nothing but they heard it from the big boys who ran to tell.

He also took liberties with the ladies who had not learned to give him a wide berth when they saw him coming. Once home, he would beat his wife who, after escaping his grip, would come to Mother and stay until he slept off the wine.

But when sober, he projected a commanding presence and his volunteer firemen jumped to his booming orders during their frequent practice. Their brass helmets with purple braiding and chain chinstraps, normally hanging on hooks below brass nameplates in the firehouse, were always polished to a gloss, as were the brass insignia on their uniform jackets. So was the brass enclosure and the other trimmings of the fire pump on top of the horse drawn carriage with its large, steel rimmed, red painted wooden wheels. In action, the pump was operated, see-saw fashion, by four husky firemen, two on either end of the actuating bar and who were replaced with rested mates when they tired.

These practices were always a great show for all, especially for us kids. On such events we were allowed into the firehouse and to climb on to the pump carriage with even the fire chief forgetting our former taunts. After such practices, Schaffer and his closest buddies all went to the Jaklitsch pub to unwind and get drunk all over again.

According to Mother, on the day of the Schaffer fire, the Chief and his team performed magnificently. The fire alarm bell of the church, the largest of three, was rung, the trumpet was sounded and most of the firemen assembled quickly. The burning barn was only 200 meters from the main water cistern and an equal distance downhill from the firehouse and with most firemen on hand, they quickly pulled the pump carriage into place. Since the barn could not be saved, they concentrated on keeping the fire under control to prevent it from spreading.

Father, Mother, my sister and my paternal grandmother were watching from our neighbor's back yard, which had a clear view of the adjacent Schaffer property. Watching with them was our neighbor, Mathias Primosch, a bachelor who lived in the house of the brother who, like so many others in the village, had left for America in the early 1910's for the better life. Later on in the 30's Mathias, known as Mattl, who in his perpetual solitude welcomed my frequent visits and had taken a liking to me, told me stories of his youth and of events in the village. And in 1941, after one of our many times together, a serious lapse of judgment on his part nearly caused my death. But this is also part of another story.

Both Father and Matthias were of prime age for being volunteer firemen were it not for their physical handicap. Father was 37 and Mathias was 51. Mathias had a perpetual sore in his lower left leg, which made him limp badly and walk only with the help of a cane. The sore started in his youth supposedly after wading in flood waters of the overflowing cistern which happened every spring as a result of the melting snow.

Father had only one leg, having had the right one amputated after a freak accident in 1918 at age 25. He cut himself in the knee; the wound festered and the leg was amputated in the military hospital in Ljubljana. This happened at the end of WW I, after spending years in the trenches of the Northern Italian front where he had been a battlefield soldier in the Imperial Austrian Army.

As the firemen struggled to prevent the fire from spreading to the main house, they were forced to pay less attention to the ever more fiercely burning barn. In no time the draft created by the fire carried glowing embers high into the sky only to let them drop on the various nearby roofs. Fortunately, most of them were now tiled except the roof of our barn, which was still covered with wooden shingles. And since the roof was not pitched enough, some embers lay in place instead of rolling off. It rapidly became apparent that unless something was done quickly, our barn would also be burning soon.

THE FIRE PUMP

There was, of course no chance of diverting the firemen and their water hoses from the burning Schaffer complex. But calls for help from Father's small group did divert others from the main attraction and they came with ladders and buckets. Father, whose lack of one leg was no hindrance to his agility, was soon on the roof with a broom, sweeping off glowing embers. With water from buckets that were handed to him from down the ladder, he doused areas about to start burning. While he was struggling on one side of the roof, Mattl, in spite of his troubled leg, was busy on the other.

When after several hours, the fire finally subsided and the embers stopped flying, the two exhausted but victorious invalids came down from their rooftop battlefields. Mattl made it down unscathed, but Father slipped on the ladder. He came tumbling down, breaking the fall by trying to cling to the rungs of ladder. At the bottom he brought down Mother who tried to catch him. But apart from two broken ribs and badly bruised hands he and Mattl saved our barn and very likely, the spread of the fire to the main house and other neighbors on our side of the Schaffer disaster.

Similar heroics were performed on roofs of buildings on the other side of the fire chief's barn; however, no building with a thatched or wood shingled roof was as near the fire as was Father's barn. And no one was hurt.

Schaffer's fire smoldered and kept his firemen on guard for several days. But it took two more fires and four more years of the chief's urging before the assembly of villagers was persuaded to modernize the fire department and get a modern, fuel powered pump. And in this, as became apparent later, the village had made the wrong choice.

The Tscherne fire, two years later in 1936, was started midday by a bolt of lightning during one of the summer storms that frequently came at great speed across the hills to the south. According to Tscherne, when lightning struck the barn, it came as a ball of fire through the shingled roof, spinning across the floor and out the wide open barn door, leaving fire in its wake. Fortunately, the heavy rain extinguished the burning shingles, while Tscherne and his sons managed with buckets of water from a nearby rain barrel to put out the catching fire left by the spinning ball on its way out of the barn.

Had it not been for the heavy rain and the presence of Tscherne and his sons, his barn and nearby house would have burned to the ground. The fire brigade of the village would have been unable to save either his barn or his house.

Katharina's house was the last of the three fires and the one I saw with my own eyes. The fire happened in the middle of the night and was already burning brightly when I was shaken awake by Mitzi, my eight years older sister, with whom I shared the bedroom and bed.

She too, had heard the bell and the trumpet, but was told by Mother to stay in her room. When she shook me awake, the room seemed unusually bright and she said she wanted me to see the fire. She lifted me up because I was frightened and carried me to the window. The flames licking the sky were blinding my sleepy eyes, making me cry out and wriggle to get away. But only for a short moment. This was a spectacle not to be missed by this seven-year old as an experience to embellish on when telling it to my playmates as soon as I had the chance.

We watched until Mother came in and sent us back to bed. She and Father had walked the short distance up to the village square to join others watching the firemen in action. They, like the others, had been awakened by the church bell and the trumpet blown by Karl Schaffer, calling his men into action. This included getting the heavy wagon with its pump and hoses to the village water reservoir, directly across from the window at the back of our house from which Mitzi and I were watching the fire. But by the time all of this came into our view, the roof of Katharina's house was beginning to cave in and the flying embers were like fireworks in the sky. In the lit surroundings of the house there were the moving figures of what must have been Katharina and Alois, her husband, her two young sons and neighbors. Schaffer and his firemen were still struggling with the much-rehearsed task of getting their equipment in place when the entire structure collapsed.

The new pump arrived in late spring of 1939. Word came via a messenger on a bicycle that the pump was sitting on the platform at the railroad station in Gottschee city. Plans for the festive reception of the pump had been worked out in advance by Jaklitsch and Schaffer and were now expeditiously put into action.

Jaklitsch cycled to town to finalize the arrangements for taking possession of the pump. After he returned, he organized a wagon with a team of horses and driver that was to leave the village early on the following morning on the two hour journey to the station and return with the pump around noon.

Meanwhile, Schaffer labored all day in organizing the reception. Young women decorated the archway entrance to the village with flowers. It had been created from slender willows especially for this event. Jaklitsch made sure that the wagon and horses were also suitably decorated. The lookouts, in the church steeple long before the expected arrival, were to ring the alarm bell at the first sighting of the wagon. The firemen, in full formal dress were to take up their assigned position on either side of the street entering the village and follow the wagon in parade step to the firehouse. There they were to unload the engine and both Jaklitsch and Schaffer were to give a short speech. Father Rozman, our village priest was to say a prayer, bless the pump and sprinkle it with holy water.

The bigger boys agreed to beat the lookout by waiting for the wagon way out of line of sight from the openings in the steeple. We, the little ones were, as was usual, forbidden to join but were tagging along nevertheless, albeit at a safe distance.

All worked as planned except for a false alarm. Another wagon was making its way toward the village and was mistaken by the big boys for the expected vehicle. Their yelling galvanized the little ones who ran toward the village and the steeple lookout, not to be outdone, started ringing the bell. The firemen and the others of the reception party hurried into their assigned positions but their hustle became only another drill when the wrong wagon came into sight. After that, the steeple lookout was instructed by Schaffer to ring the bell only after the correct vehicle was positively identified by him personally.

Eventually, all came off without another hitch. The entire village had assembled for this momentous event, momentous if for no other reason than giving everyone an excuse to interrupt the daily routine in the fields and stables. Of course, the schoolchildren were given the day off. After the reverend Father Rozman blessed the pump and sprinkled holy water, the pump was moved behind closed doors of the firehouse and the crowd dispersed. The women went home but most of the men joined the firemen at the Jaklitsch inn to celebrate the arrival with wine at half price for the occasion. Josef Primosch was invited by Jaklitsch to play his accordion. his reward was all the wine he could drink, which shortened his playing considerably since he got drunk very quickly even on the watered down stuff and fell asleep. Schaffer used the time to instruct his firemen on the sequence of events for the coming Sunday after Mass when the new pump was to shine in a premier performance.

First, however, it needed to be checked over and tested out. This was scheduled for the following Saturday.

THE BELLS RING NO MORE

Since early morning on that day, the firehouse was kept open with a fireman keeping a watchful eye on the new pump in the middle of the floor. The carriage with the old pump had been moved outside and we, the little ones, were no longer prevented from climbing all over it.

More firemen and others kept arriving, all waiting for Schaffer who was late sleeping off last night's wine. Finally, the pump was moved outside the firehouse where its stainless steel parts gleamed in the morning sun and where the villagers were now crowding and pushing each other, all eager to inspect and admire the awesome machine. Everyone came except Father. He wanted nothing to do with it.

The first part of the test was to start the engine. Schaffer made some adjustments and then ordered his firemen to turn the starting crank but the engine would not start. Crank it faster, crank it slower, turn up the choke, turn back the throttle yelled Schaffer, who finally sent for Jaklitsch who proved to be of no help. The firemen kept the crowd at a distance but being small I watched the progressively more animated scene up front from in between the legs of grown-ups.

Finally Jaklitsch said, "get Tschinkel". Schaffer agreed and spotting me among the legs, ordered with what to me seemed the sweetest of words; "get your father".

Out of breath I found him in his shop and proudly conveyed the chief's request. He asked some detailed questions but finally sent me back with a firm "No".

I reported to Schaffer who yelled some obscenities and they took up the cranking with renewed vigor, again without results. Once more, he yelled at me: "get your father". And again Father sent me back with the same "No".

"He does not want to come", I stammered, disillusioned that my father kept rejecting a lifetime opportunity to make his son truly proud. Jaklitsch conferred with Schaffer and finally announced "let's get him ourselves". A small crowd followed the two of them.

I ran ahead to tell him they were coming. When the two of them entered his shop he told me and the others to wait outside and closed the door.

We heard fragments of a heated discussion including some pleading, boisterous from Schaffer but calmly persuasive from Jaklitsch. Father said very little. Finally, the door opened and Jaklitsch announced "he is coming".

I walked next to him, holding on to the longer of two crutches as always when I was with him. But this time was different. He was called on to do what no one else in the village could and I was basking in the glory of my father.

I was allowed to be with him while he worked. It did not take him long. He looked at the manual, adjusted some knobs and gave instructions to Schaffer, while the surrounding crowd, except for some snide remarks from those not friendly to

THE FIRE PUMP

him, was quietly watching. When he finally ordered cranking, the engine responded after a few turns and finally revved to high speed, ejecting a cloud of black smoke. The crowd responded with cheers and I proudly looked around, gripping even more tightly his longer crutch.

He played with the speed, finally turned the engine off and nodded to Schaffer as if to tell him "it's yours". Jaklitsch and Schaffer shook his hand and Schaffer insisted that he show him the starting procedure. After a few successful tries, Father said, "let's go home".

I really wanted to stay, but willingly I went with him. After all he had just done what no other father could do. Back in the shop, he saw me fidgeting. When he finally said, "you can go", I ran as fast as I could.

The Saturday test was much more than just a rehearsal for the Sunday performance. At the firehouse, surrounded at a respectable distance by villagers of all ages, Schaffer shaped his team by assigning new duties and changing existing ones. He worked out a new signaling procedure using his trumpet together with hand signals, now that his booming voice had to compete with the roar of the engine. He appointed a team responsible for engine operation and the handling of levers and valves controlling the pump. Another team was assigned to the pump cart and its brake, needed due to the almost frictionless rubber wheels. This was particularly important since most of the way from the firehouse to the cistern was downhill. The hose team was assigned pairs of younger men, capable of connecting and rolling out each needed hose reel at great speed.

When Schaffer was satisfied he gave the order to start live testing at the cistern. The carriage team did well and the brake kept the downhill speed under control. The big hose from the cistern to the pump was connected quickly as was a length of hose with the nozzle at the end. On Schaffer's signal, the engine was started and on another signal, the lever engaging the pump was pulled. The engine slowed a bit as it began pumping and all watched the water progressing down the hose toward the nozzle. When it emerged, it surprised the two nozzle holders who had to struggle with its willful stream. The men had never experienced such force.

The roar of the engine and general commotion brought out much of the village and Schaffer proudly demonstrated the performance of his new equipment. The nozzle was directed straight up and it seemed the stream reached the height of the church steeple. It was directed into the slope of the ground surrounding the cistern where it dug a deep hole the depth of which we little ones tried to measure with sticks the next day. The test was meant to establish the force of the stream to break down obstructions to get the water to where it was needed. All the onlookers were delighted in the overwhelmingly superior performance of the new pump.

Schaffer practiced with his team by shutting down and testing with some additional reels of hoses. After that, he ordered a retreat to the firehouse and a full rehearsal of a fire drill starting at the beginning. His firemen, thrilled with their new power, performed with great enthusiasm. Schaffer was satisfied and certain of the success of tomorrow's performance. So was Franz Jaklitsch and together that Saturday evening, without Father, they celebrated in advance with many quarter liter pitchers of wine the glory they would reap the following day after Mass.

The church on the following morning was packed. This was markedly different from the usual Sunday service when the benches were only half filled and then mostly with womenfolk and their young.

But as was usual, the husbands, fathers and grown sons, even on this occasion, insisted on staying in the graveled courtyard in front of the main doors where with muffled voices they conducted important discussions. During Mass, they would pause only for the sermon, barely audible through the open doors, and when the sexton Michitsch announced the transformation of bread and wine into the Holy Host, by sounding the small bell. Three solemn single strokes, each about three seconds apart, followed after a short pause by another set of three strokes.

Then, they all would kneel on one knee and with bowed heads patiently wait for the moment where they could continue where they left off. Father, leaning on his crutches stood with bowed head. It was too difficult to kneel on his only knee. Father Rozman could not break this habit of the men regardless of how hard he tried on those days when bad weather drove them all inside. He had to console himself with the knowledge that at least every able villager attended Mass whether this attendance was under the roof of the church or the open sky.

On this eventful Sunday, the male half of the village filled the courtyard while the women and their small charges filled every bench seat inside. The outsiders included the firemen in work uniforms who were bunching around Schaffer in his parade uniform with its ribbons and polished helmet, all eager to receive last minute instructions for the demonstration drill, which started immediately after the end of the Mass.

Schaffer blew his shining trumpet and the firemen ran the 100 yards to the firehouse, up the slight hill from the church. The church emptied quickly and everyone rushed to find the best spot between the firehouse and the cistern from which to view the performance about to commence.

Schaffer and Jaklitsch had agreed on a three-stage demonstration to best impress the viewers, including the remaining skeptics. The first stage was from the pump at the cistern to the opposite end of the square furthest from the pump. This would show that all the houses surrounding the center were within easy reach of the new pump. The second stage was to move the pump from the cistern to the drinking well at the other end of the square. The hose direction was toward the Tscherne property and his barn, which he and his sons had saved from destruction with their quick response and help from the massive rain. The third stage was to return the pump to the cistern and run the hoses in the opposite direction toward what was Katharina's house, the most distant place away from the center. In each stage, Schaffer was to take note on how many hoses were needed to reach each property in the village.

At the start of phase one, the pump was at the cistern in no time, the big suction hose dropped into the large reservoir, the coiled hoses reeled out by pairs of firemen and connected together along the way. Schaffer blew his trumpet and the engine started effortlessly with a roar that was lustily taken up by the crowd. The firemen, encouraged by members of their families at each step along the way, performed superbly to Schaffer's signals.

At first, there was only a whistling sound as the air was pushed out through the nozzle pointed upward by two firemen in the end of the square. After a few squirts, the full stream emerged and traveled way into the sky, as high as the cross on top of the steeple. It was obvious that after a re-laying of hoses, even the most distant houses around the square could be reached by the impressive stream. Their owners beamed and cheered with satisfaction, but I heard Father, standing separate with his family and some of his supporters, say "just wait".

Then Schaffer blew the trumpet, the engine was shut off and new hoses were connected in a succession of trumpet blasts to reach houses beyond the square in the direction of the Tscherne barn. The crowd followed Schaffer and the nozzle as did Mitzi and myself. With each addition, however, the force of the stream diminished and eventually, came to a sad trickle long before the hoses reached the Tscherne property and barn. I ran to tell Father who had not moved from his spot.

Then Schaffer signaled the start of the second phase. The fire pump was wheeled from the cistern to the drinking well at the other end of the village square cutting the distance toward Tscherne in half. The pump was connected and more hoses were added toward the village end. On another signal from Schaffer, the pump was started again and very soon a stream, as strong as the one in the middle of the square emerged from the nozzle.

Schaffer and Jaklitsch beamed but only for a short while. The stream suddenly dwindled and after a few more squirts stopped altogether. Very soon thereafter a fireman came running, shouting on the way "the well is empty, the well is empty".

Schaffer shouted obscenities including "damn Tschinkel" as if Father were responsible for the lack of water. Jaklitsch remained silent and avoided the stare from Tscherne and other neighbors who were again on their own. As I ran to report to Father I heard murmurs from the crowd "Tschinkel was right".

It really had been pretty obvious that the stored water in the drinking well would not last very long and would not replenish as quickly as it was sucked away by the powerful pump. The well was in a cavity behind a fifteen-foot rock wall with an opening at hip height just large enough to reach inside with a pot with which to scoop out the water into a bucket outside. The cavity was large but shallow, at most two feet deep. Nearly always full, it was prevented from overflowing by a small v shaped trough which led the water into a large wooden basin outside below the opening. The slow runoff, which had cooled many thirsty lips, was nearly always constant indicating that the inflow to the well was about the same as the outflow into the trough; obviously inadequate for the pump after the stored water was used up.

The well was a gathering place for the women who came to get the pure drinking water and gossip. They carried the water home on their heads in wooden buckets,

THE FIRE PUMP

using rolled up kerchiefs, formed into a doughnut as a cushion to ease the pressure and pain. For some, home was quite a distance, in some cases nearly a kilometer. Young girls were not allowed to fetch water in this manner, the reason being that their backs were not yet strong enough. The real reason however was that their ears were still too young to hear the intimate gossip of the older matrons.

By contrast, the cistern at the bottom of the 300-foot wide bowl, the low point of the village, itself in a valley of surrounding high hills, contained an inexhaustible supply of water. The water gravitated to this place from the hills through the porous limestone underground, characteristic of the Karst region of Slovenia, only to reemerge from several holes at the bottom of the bowl. For centuries this bowl stored the water, its size depending on the severity of the rain or the amount of snow melting in the surrounding hills.

After the big fire in 1882, the municipality provided funds to build a concrete structure around the exit holes in the ground, which allowed the containment of a large amount of water in one central area. When that large container overflowed, the water spilled into the surrounding depression cutting off access to the cistern. But this happened mostly in springtime when the water from the melting snow came rushing in.

There was nothing more to be done at the Tscherne end of the village and Schaffer ordered that the pump be moved back to the cistern. The hoses were rolled up and reeled out again from the cistern toward Katharina's house according to the established plan of phase three. This the firemen did with less than the initial enthusiasm since they knew that the distance from the cistern to Katharina's house was greater than the distance from the cistern to the Tscherne barn. Some of the crowd dispersed and even Father and his friends stopped their grumbling and went home. He did not insist that I come along but told me to come back with the details of what was to transpire next.

Schaffer ordered his men through the prearranged steps of that part of the plan. As additional hoses were connected he made his notes for future reference and as was anticipated, the powerful stream turned to a trickle way before the end of the village and a long distance from the ruins of Katharina's house.

But Schaffer had an ace up his sleeve. The house of Katharina's in-laws near that end of the village had a large and deep well, which they and some of their neighbors used for drinking water. The pump was moved to this well over the protest of the owner who sensed that his well, like the drinking well at the other end of the village, would also be emptied in no time. Sure enough, Shaffer's ace turned out to be another joker and very soon after the pump was turned on, the initial burst from the nozzle turned to a spurt and then stopped altogether.

There was no celebration at the Jaklitsch inn that Sunday night.

The events of the day had proven Father right, but many of the villagers on both sides of the pump issue would only grudgingly, if at all, acknowledge his vindication. Only Jaklitsch, arguably the most astute man in the village, offered his congratulations and as a result, their already very friendly relationship improved even more.

Most of those who had wanted the larger pump blamed Father for not more effectively arguing their cause. Only his small circle of supporters and friends, among them the sexton Michitsch, the invalid neighbor Mattl, his good friend Johann Krisch, a few of the firemen and some buddies from either end of the village came to his carpenter shop to congratulate him and themselves for their foresight. I moved among them basking in the glory of my father and becoming ever more certain that he was the smartest man in the world.

There were no more fires and the pump was never used, at least not during the next two years until the winter of 1941/42, when this 600 year old village was abandoned by most of its residents for a promised brighter future in another land. Only the fire pump and a few families of mixed marriage at each end of the village, loyal to their heritage and successfully resisting the enormous pressure of Franz Jaklitsch, stayed.

The pump was, however, used in September of 1943 when the "Plava Garda" (Royalist Chetniks) was making its final stand in Grčarice (Masern). The cannon bombardment of the Tito Partisans who had encircled the village, set the Jaklitsch inn, the Rudolf Tschinkel house and the church on fire. The Garda had used these buildings, as well as the prince Auersperg hunting lodge, as defensive positions in their ultimate battle for survival.

THE FIRE PUMP

The small pump obviously was not up to putting out all the simultaneously burning fires. But it did save the Jaklitsch house from collapse. Much of the inside was burned out but not the beams that held up the roof, thereby preventing its total destruction.

The fire also destroyed a large part of the Rudolf Tschinkel tavern on the square. It fully destroyed the adjacent house that was Ivanka's general store and of course, the church. Both burned to the ground leaving only charred walls. The Auersperg lodge, the command post of the Garda did not catch fire and survived.

No attempt was made to save the church. The victorious Partisans had no desire, nor intent, to preserve this symbol of their ideological adversary, the Roman Catholic Church. And so the bells came tumbling down as their supporting beams, weakened by the flames, gave way. Their impotence was captured for posterity by Slavko Felician from nearby Rakitnica who took the photograph on 9/9/1943. They had served the village well but now, with their purpose for being at an end, they were silently awaiting their ultimate fate of being melted down in a not too distant future.

Chapter 2

Return to the Past

Mitzi remembered that Friday in the winter of 1931 when grandmother Gera sent her into the new snow to get the midwife Josefa Kresse from across the square at number 52. Mitzi, my older sister aged seven, knew what was about to happen, whereas seven years later when brother Paul was to be born in the summer of 1938, I had not the fraction of a clue.

On the way back, Mitzi and Josefa stopped at the Schaffer house to ask mother's friend Maria to come in case more help was needed. After the three of them came back to the house and in the hallway stomped the clinging snow off their boots, Mitzi was ordered into the kitchen while the two women disappeared behind the door to the large bedroom of my parents. In the kitchen, Gera was heating extra water in pots on the stove and feeding, through the arched opening, the fire in the massive tiled oven in the bedroom on the other side of the wall in which Mother was bravely struggling to open a way out for me. Her panting, interrupted by screams did not bother Gera, no friend of her son's wife, but frightened Mitzi who clung to the step-grandmother and tried to seek refuge under the many layers of her billowing floor length skirts. No longer able to control the little girl, Gera climbed into her snow boots and dragged her to the parsonage next door where she was left with the housekeeper.

When Gera returned, I had been born. Sometime later Maria Schaffer, on her way home stopped at the parsonage with the news and told Mitzi to return home. At the door of the centuries old stone house of my father's family in Grčarice (Masern), the little girl saw Gera tossing out water from a basin, leaving a pink cavity in the white snow which renewed her fright. But in the bedroom of the parents she saw her brother for the first time, red, crinkled, and ugly.

I got to know these details years later when Mitzi and I were again reminiscing about the place we used to call home. She recalled that Friday morning of February 28th, 1931 after I reminded her of the afternoon of June 29, 1938, when she came to fetch me from the square saying that I had to come home for a surprise.

THE BELLS RING NO MORE

Earlier that warm summer afternoon, the holiday of St. Peter and Paul, Father and I were lying on a blanket spread out in the shade of one of the apple trees in the orchard behind the house. Some of the blossoms had already given way to little balls, the first evidence of the fruit to be, while others, lagging the cycle, were being visited by noisy bees. I had dozed off and when I woke up, I was alone with no one in sight. Being hungry I wandered into the house but in the hallway on the way to the kitchen I heard voices from the parents' room. As I opened the bedroom door, Josefa, known as Zefo, her hands bloody, flew toward me and motioned me out of the room saying mother was very sick and that I should go to Mattl, our neighbor. He would give me something to eat.

Outside the house I climbed on to the bench underneath the window to the parents' room and through the panes watched Mother being sick. She was on her back on the bed, alternately screaming and whimpering with her legs held high by Father and Maria Schaffer while Zefo was somewhere in between. I soon got bored; Mother had been sick before and always got well again. Mattl assured me that Mother would be well soon and, after some bread, I went to seek playmates on the square. Mitzi found me on the stone benches under the big linden to bring me home for a surprise which turned out to be a tiny baby next to my recovered and smiling Mother. Sitting on the bed near her was the grinning Father who insisted that I put a finger into the curled up hand of brother Paul, born that afternoon.

With such auspicious beginnings, my brother and I arrived in a village settled sometime in the 14th Century with people who were part of a group that came from a distant land. For over six centuries thereafter, they maintained their uniqueness and resolutely clung to an unfriendly earth which they loved but nevertheless abandoned in the winter of 1941/42. And throughout these centuries, they were part of a tribe that struggled to maintain its identity until its ultimate dissolution in the spring of 1945.

For ten years after Mitzi fetched the midwife from across the square, I was a part of a place called Grčarice (Masern), insignificant in history, but not to the inhabitants of this village at the edge of the world. It is on the western edge of the Kočevje (Gottschee) forest of Slovenia, south and east of Ljubljana, the capital of the country. It can be found on the map about half way and slightly south of a straight line between Trieste and Zagreb, ancient cities in the neighboring countries of Italy and Croatia.

In spite of its proximity to the three cities - 51 kilometers to Ljubljana, 80 to Trieste and 90 to Zagreb, all in existence before the Middle Ages - Grčarice (Masern) was bypassed by time. And even in the early 20th century, most of its 260 or so inhabitants lived isolated from the world since few, excepting the desperate or ambitious, seldom ventured beyond a radius of twenty kilometers.

The German settlers arrived there in the early 14th century. They came from the north-western part of Europe at the invitation of Count Ortenburg, the local noble and landlord of the region. At the time of the initial settling, Grčarice was a hamlet or perhaps only a clearing in a dense primal forest and a collection point for lumber used by builders in the lowlands of Carniola, the present day Slovenia. The hamlet and its surrounding forests belonged to the Ortenburg counts who were pressed by their Germanic king for more taxes. To attract settlers, the count offered ownership of parcels of the forest which could be cleared and made into arable lands, in exchange for taxes which would help him to satisfy the needs of his monarch.

Long before the arrival of the settlers, the Kočevje forest and the surrounding land was part of the "Land of the Slavs" (Provincia Sclaborum), which was settled by heathen Slavs who had arrived from the East. Out of this land emerged, among others, the area described as Carniola which the Slovene called Kranjska. Later on Carniola expanded into Upper Carniola (Gorenjska), Middle Carniola (Notranjska) and Lower Carniola (Dolenjska) which, together with other parts populated by Slovenes, merged into the present Slovenia. Grčarice was and still is part of Lower Carniola.

In Carniola, all formal names of settlements, be they towns such as Ljubljana or smaller and lesser settlements were initially in Latin, later in German and after the establishment of the Kingdom of Yugoslavia in 1918 in Slovene. Ljubljana was Emona to the Romans and Laibach to the Germans. Over the years, however, the Slavs of the local population continued with the names established by their ancestors when they arrived in the area over 1,500 years ago.

Grčarice is a Slovene name derived from Grča, which describes a piece of gnarled wood. The initial German settlers arriving in Grčarice changed the name to Masern, hardly a coincidence since the German equivalent for a piece of gnarled wood is Maser. Most likely therefore, the settlers simply translated the already existing Slovene name into German. They also brought with them a curious German dialect which they kept alive for the next 600 years.

But the Slovene in the neighboring Rakitnica, four kilometers on the other side of the steep hill that was the divide between the linguistic enclave and other parts of Slovenia, continued to use Grčarice. The new inhabitants of Masern on the other hand used Rakitnitz, the official German name for Rakitnica when they talked about their neighbor. The two villages and their inhabitants coexisted peacefully for the next seven centuries. And they continued to do so even after 1918, when Slovenia became part of Yugoslavia and the official name of Masern reverted to Grčarice. But the village and the enclave continued to use Masern, a name that had long ago become an established habit.

Topographically, Grčarice (Masern) is in a clearing at 519 meters altitude in a valley surrounded by a dense pine forest. In springtime when the sap begins to flow, the pollen that appears on the pinecones produces a heavy fragrance that dominates the village, a fragrance that is captured in a thick whitish honey, harvested by swarms of busy bees. In my time, the village was home to 260 souls living in 63 houses. It had a church and an adjacent parsonage for the resident priest and his housekeeper, a one-room school, a general store, a saw mill, three pubs and a cemetery. It also had its own smithy and smith, a midwife, a shoemaker, a saddler, a seamstress, a game warden and a fire brigade instantly ready to respond. And high up in the church tower, a slowly rusting clock announced the time of day by striking two of the three bronze bells suspended on wooden beams.

This self-sufficient village however lacked a mill for grinding the grain and a bull for fertilizing its cows. But all were within easy walking distance as were the occasionally needed doctor or dentist.

The church stood at one end of the village square, its portal in the bell tower facing the open space in front. The parsonage was behind the church next to the adjoining stable and barn, all at the level of the square. And behind these three structures was a sharp drop off leading to the lowest level of the village and the cistern bowl.

Opposite the bell tower, at the other end of the square stood the ancient village linden tree, surrounded by a circle of stone benches. From the base of this tree one could see, through the open double doors in the tower, the altar at the far end of the church.

While the portal in the bell tower dominated the square, the big linden at the other end attracted with fragrant blossoms in the spring and a welcoming shade on hot summer afternoons. Its circle of stone benches invited villagers for a cool evening of gossip and occasionally the tunes from the Primosch harmonica emerging through the open windows of the Jaklitsch inn. Some women and older men brought cushions to soften the seat. Younger men usually stood in groups and when not talking, carefully rolled their cigarettes for the next smoke.

The square was the main intersection of all roads, be they from neighboring villages, remote houses or surrounding fields and forests. The main road from Dolenja Vas entered the village at the linden end of the square through an opening between two houses, one of them the Jaklitsch tavern at number 11. It skirted the canopy of the big tree and crossed the open space toward the church. After passing the church, it turned right toward the Kren tavern and the cemetery beyond and left Masern toward Gotenica (Göttenitz) and other villages in the deeper forest.

Two other roads entered and left the graveled square at different points. The church, the square, the roads through it and the houses surrounding were all part of a symmetrical arrangement except that the houses on one side of the square were at a slightly higher elevation than those on the other.

The early priests of the eighteenth century were supported financially in part by the parish in Ribnica (Reiffnitz) and in part by the villagers through the mandated annual tithe. Apart from that, they were self sufficient, maintained their livestock and cultivated the land allocated to the parsonage. In this the priest had help from a live in housekeeper and the villagers whenever he was in need of it.

The inner village houses were clustered around the large square whose perimeter resembled an open ended rectangle. Most of these houses were elongated boxes, close together on narrow but deep parcels of land. They stood next to one another, with the narrow part facing the square. The main entry door to each house was on the long side facing the back wall of the neighbor's house and in between was adequate space for passage of a carriage or wagon to the courtyard in the rear. Usually, another door in the rear of the house also led to the stable, barn, vegetable garden, orchard and other structures further in the back. All were built with local materials, stone walls three feet thick with hand crafted pine shingles resting on roofing beams hand hewn in the local forest and left there to dry out until ready for use.

Three pubs in a village of 63 houses was certainly excessive during the final years of the community when modern transport in the form of fuel powered trucks came of age. But in past centuries they all were welcoming places for the drivers of columns of horse drawn wagons who needed a place to eat and rest, water and feed their horses and even spend the night before continuing a journey lasting several days. And the same was the case in reverse when they passed through again for their next haul of lumber, all part of a non-ending cycle in which the tireless forest was forever a willing participant. In the thirties, two of the three pubs were idle except for the occasional traveler, the annual local festivity or the occasional wedding. But not the Jaklitsch tavern which, due to the increasing prominence of its owner Franz in the 1930's, became a magnet not only for the locals but also for visitors from foreign lands, particularly the new Germany, the Third Reich. These visitors passed through the village with increasing frequency in the late thirties to stay for the night or for a few days.

My father's house at Number 15 was adjacent to the church on the other side of the road leading from the square to the cistern basin behind the parsonage. The road sloped gently downward to the cistern level passing on its right the church grounds that used to be the cemetery prior to its being moved to the end of the village. Our house was already at a lower level and therefore, our courtyard gate faced the embankment across the road. Embedded into this embankment was a narrow footpath leading diagonally up to the front of the church. This path shortened the otherwise much longer walk to the church via the square.

Similar to other houses in the village, the narrow wall of our rectangular house was along the sloping road while the long part, containing the entry door, faced the large and level courtyard. Along the courtyard wall of the house was the long wooden bench, part of which was under the window through which I watched the birth of brother Paul.

Dominating the left view from the bench was the bell tower of the church. Each of its four walls had its own Roman numeral clock face above the opening to the chamber of the bells. The view of the clock face from the bench was up so high it strained the neck.

I sat on this bench when my milk teeth started to loosen and waited for the clock to strike while holding the end of the sewing thread Mother had tied to the loose tooth. I was determined to pull the string at the stroke of the next quarter. Usually by then the will had weakened and the action postponed for another fifteen minutes. Many quarters passed, and the tooth, loosened by constant checking and wiggling, usually fell out by itself.

I often climbed the steep narrow stairs that hugged the inside of the tower wall, up to the bells in spite of the concern of sexton Michitsch who was worried about my safety. But ever since I became an altar boy, I had access to the church and getting into the bell tower was, in spite of the sexton, not difficult at all.

On the way up, after entering the tower at the choir level of the church, I had to pass the storage space of burial implements of picks, shovels, ropes and stretchers used in funeral services. Leaning against the wall was the black cross, its intersection painted with the white skull and crossbones, carried high by the sexton in front of a funeral procession from the church to the cemetery. Small openings in the thick stone walls of the tower allowed only a little light, adding to the eeriness of the place.

Getting past this part in the tower always gave me a fright. Climbing the narrow stairs, past the suspended stone weights of the clock, past the platform that held the clock with its greased and slowly rusting wheels was also scary but once up there with the bells, the view from any of the four openings in the belfry made it all worthwhile.

Staying up there had to be timed so as not to be there when the hammer of the clock struck the large bell to tell the hour. The intensity of the sound was unbearable. The quarter hour ring from the smaller of the three bells I could just bear, but only if I covered my ears.

The sound of the bells telling time was heard in the remotest part of the village and the surrounding fields. It was loud on the square and at our house so near the church especially so, but years of conditioning had long ago desensitized our ears.

News from the municipality in Dolenja Vas was delivered to the village by an employee on a bicycle. It was read to the villagers on Sundays after Mass when they had assembled under the big linden tree at the village square opposite the church.

The municipal authorities required that the village select an elder fluent in Slovene who could read the announcements and translate them for the villagers. They did not require that this person be a village official. Normally, the resident priest, when we had one, would perform this function. In the 1930s after Father Klemenčič died in 1934, this elder was Albert Tschinkel, a distant relation and one of few villagers who spoke Slovene. In the later '30s, the village official was, if informally, Franz Jaklitsch the tavern keeper at Masern No 11 but he did not know Slovene well enough to meet the requirement of the municipality.

Albert Tschinkel read the notices and decrees, all in Slovene. He stood on the stone bench surrounding the linden and with a raised voice proclaimed "Official

Announcement". After he finished reading in Slovene, he gave a summary translation in the dialect of the Kočevje (Gottschee) enclave, the only language the villagers understood well. He explained the essence of the notice and answered questions. Throughout the year, he made these "announcements" in all kinds of weather since this was the required way for bringing official information to the public.

Mail was delivered twice a week by Jula Bojčeva, on foot from the post office in Dolenja Vas. The middle aged postwoman brought the post in a leather bag strapped to her shoulder which she took to the house of the village smith at Number 7 where she also picked up the outgoing mail. Afterwards, she took what looked important or official directly to the address where she asked if she could rest a bit and perhaps even learn what was in the mail she delivered. She often came to our house even if there was nothing to deliver and exchange gossip with Mother over a cup of chamomile tea.

But Jula came only if there was mail to be delivered and if the road was passable. Often during the winter months, the village was cut off from the outside for days if not weeks by the snow, which fell regularly from early December through late March, at times up to three feet high.

And there also was no mail in early spring when the water from the melting snow in the surrounding hills found its way through underground channels to the cistern, overflowed the basin and searching for lower ground, covered not only arable and sometimes already planted fields but also the main road to Dolenja Vas. Again there was no mail, sometimes for many days until, eventually, the waters drained away.

The only item of mail that came regularly, absence of snow or water permitting, was the enclave newspaper, the weekly Gottscheer Zeitung. The newspaper was in German and published in Kočevje (Gottschee City), 15 kilometers away.

There was no electricity, no telephone and until 1936 not even a battery operated radio. The Jaklitsch tavern on the square had a wind up record player with a huge horn and about half a dozen records, most of them with grooves long robbed of their original melody by overused steel needles. In one of the songs, a melancholy female reminds her lover that the raindrops knocking on the window pane are a greeting from her.

"Regentropfen, die an das Fenster klopfen, daß merke dir, sie sind ein Gruß von mir".

RETURN TO THE PAST

Some 600 years after Grčarice was settled and became Masern and then Grčarice again in 1918, the villagers, my family and I, now ten, traveled the road out of the forest, for the last time on the 7th of December 1941 . The destination was a place in the Third Reich where, as Franz Jaklitsch the new village leader promised, "milk and honey" freely flowed.

I returned more than a quarter of a century later in 1974 to see that much had changed while much had also remained the same. I was accompanied there by Janez Pahulje the husband of Angela, my maternal aunt. He and his family lived in Dolenja Vas, the birthplace of my mother 6.5 kilometers away, the second Slovene village on the road to Ribnica.

A short summary from him the day before prepared me for the return.

"It still snows as it used to and the basin still fills and overflows in the spring when the snows melt in the hills. But the cistern in the basin behind the church, once the main watering place for the livestock and the fire pump, is no longer used and is crumbling away. Weeds cover the ruins.

"The mail now comes regularly in spite of the snow. Engine powered plows clear the way over the improved road from Dolenja Vas across the hill. It was rerouted away from the steep parts to gentler slopes and on lower grounds it was moved out of the way of the water overflowing the basin collecting the melted snow from the hills. Diesel powered trucks have replaced horse drawn wagons hauling lumber to distant mills. The gravel paving you walked as a boy is now buried permanently under black asphalt.

"The church is no more and green covers the ground where it stood. The parsonage is neglected and empty, aware of its lost purpose for existing. The church was destroyed in the fall of 1943 during the three-day battle between the Partisans and their opposition, the Plava Garda, the Blue Guard. The ferocious battle included howitzers and other weapons left behind by the retreating Italians who, until the collapse of Mussolini in the summer of 1943, had been the occupier of Kočevje and a large part of Slovenia. The church was the main hold-out of the doomed Garda, the local opposition to the Partisans of the National Liberation Front.

"Many of the houses around the square, including those of Schaffer, Jaklitsch and the Auersperg hunting lodge were extensively damaged during the battle in 1943. Most of them have been renovated with attractive improvements made by the new occupants.

"The ancient linden tree in the village square, opposite the Jaklitsch tavern still blossoms with luscious fragrance every spring. But the stone benches surrounding it in a continuous circle which once encouraged the gathering of the young and provided the old with a shady place to rest and gossip, are no longer there.

"Your centuries-old family house at number 15 still stands and has changed very little. The present occupants, Slovene made homeless elsewhere during the war, would be glad to let you see the house. They now call it their home, but know little of its centuries-long history.

"And the ghosts of your ancestors are waiting for your return".

We set off in the morning and after leaving Dolenja Vas, I was about to make a right, a turn the settlers made some 600 years ago and get on the road which the settlers and their descendents used until their departure in 1941. But Pahulje directed me further along the main road toward Kočevje to another fork to the right and on to a very modern asphalt road now leading toward Grčarice (Masern). He explained that this more direct route, bypassing Rakitnica was built by the Slovene government in Ljubljana in the early 60's as a high speed highway into the mountains beyond Grčarice where the state government had created an underground complex to be used by its officials in case of war.

Thus, instead of the arduous trek up and down the steep hills on the winding graveled dirt road I walked as a boy, we sped comfortably toward Grčarice which we reached in a few short minutes.

Pahulje stopped at the former Jaklitsch house, now no longer a tavern or an inn. The house had suffered badly in the 1943 battle between the Plava Garda and the Partisans, being directly on the village square but had since then been fully restored. It still housed the small grocery store that used to be part of the inn and since the door was open Pahulje bought a bottle of wine. With that we walked the 200 meters toward the house which I called home for the first ten years of my life.

The house, with its three feet thick stone walls and slate roof, resting on one-foot square beams hand hewn from local lumber, received little damage in spite of being only a short distance from the church. It is the place in which Father, Paul, I and most, if not all of my ancestors were born. Entries in the parish books, now in the archives of the Dolenja Vas parish, prove this to the beginning of the 18th century. Records of earlier dates were kept in Gotenica (Göttenitz), the parish further into the forest, but were unfortunately lost or destroyed during the heated battles between the occupying Italians and the Partisans in 1941 to 1943. Nevertheless, later on I discovered a good many of these ancient dates in the archives of the Archdiocese in Ljubljana.

After an introduction and having presented the wine, the new occupants willingly let us see the inside of the house.

It was with suppressed emotions that I walked through the rooms that revived so many dimming memories.

Nothing significant had changed in 30 years except that the furniture was different and no longer occupied the familiar spaces. The house was not yet electrified and kerosene lamps still hung from the ceilings. Wood still fired the ancient tiled masonry kitchen stove with its six cooking spaces of overlapping concentric rings. The rings, from the smallest to the largest, were for lifting off successively with a handle to accommodate the bottom of different size pots and to expose them directly to the heat and soot of the flame. In addition to heating the kitchen, the stove also heated the built-in copper water boiler, the only source of hot water in the house.

Most of our indoor living had taken place in the spacious kitchen, while the other three rooms were used mainly as bedrooms. Our meals were taken on the heavy pine plank table in the center of the room. The soft parts of the planks were worn away by generations of scrubbing, excepting the harder knots which protruded from the otherwise smooth surface like the moles on grandmother Gera's face. We would usually eat from a common central bowl except on high holidays and some Sundays when individual plates and bowls were necessary to deal with slices of smoked ham and vegetables and to begin with, the soup made from the liquid used to boil the ham. This is when the protruding knots really got in the way.

The weekday meal was from a common bowl in the center of the table, made and glazed by the potter in Dolenja Vas. The large bowl was heaped with Ganzallein, cornmeal boiled in water on the stove. After most of the water was boiled away, the cooked cornmeal was stirred to a fluffy consistency and transferred into the center of the terracotta bowl. There, the mountain of yellow was liberally covered with cooked sauerkraut, itself covered with melted drippings, including the tasty cubes of pre-cooked pork from the vats in the adjacent below ground cellar. Finally, boiled milk was poured into the bowl to surround the heap in the center which now resembled an extinct volcano sticking out of a sea of white.

There were many variations on this; mashed potatoes or other grain substituting for the cornmeal. And as the year progressed toward the next harvest and the stores of sauerkraut and solidified drippings neared the bottom of the barrels, the peak in the center of the bowl got less and less of a covering; in lean years, very little of anything or nothing at all. Then, there was only the island in the center surrounded by milk.

The word Ganzallein has a curious origin. It comes from joining two German words 'ganz' and 'allein' meaning all and alone which, when joined together, aptly describe a solitary dish devoid of any enhancement. This, most likely, was the daily fare of older settlers for centuries; the fluffy consistency being an easy meal for the folks who in their mid forties had already lost most, if not all of their teeth.

On special occasions, when Joseph Kren, the village butcher and owner of the Gasthaus near the cemetery, slaughtered a cow, mother would buy some beef, providing the cow was not too old or too skinny or too muscular. She ascertained this from Johann Krisch, a neighbor across the square, a bachelor, good friend of the family and a particularly close friend of Father. He was also a neighbor of Kren and helped him with the butchering. After that, he revealed to Mother, under promise of secrecy, the quality of the beef.

Anyway, when mother did buy the meat, she would produce the most delicious boiled beef known as Tafelspitz. It translates from the German into 'peak of the table'. She learned to make it in her mother's gostilna, or Gasthaus in Dolenja Vas. I accidentally recognized Mother's dish many years later in Vienna where it is known as a delicacy. The version at the Haas Haus restaurant there was nearly as good as Mother's, even with nostalgia pushed aside.

Johann Krisch continued to play a major role in our family, even after the resettlement to Veliko Mraševo where in 1943 he asked father for permission to marry the now eager twenty year old Mitzi, a request denied since both parents believed that Johann, with his forty four years, was too old for the tender girl. In spite of this, the friendship continued undisturbed into the traumatic days of May 1945 when he stood by his friend's family during its most trying times and on the morning of May 12 twice saved my life.

The old table is still in the center of the kitchen, under the flypaper spiral suspended from the ceiling, but now serving other diners. It was too large and too heavy to be taken with us when we left in 1941.

RETURN TO THE PAST

The metal gates next to the stove still cover the waist high vaulted opening to the large cavity deep in the masonry oven in the large room on the other side of the wall, nominally the bedroom of the parents, but which, especially in wintertime, doubled as our living room. Inside the cavity of this oven, on its glazed clay baking surface, also at waist height, Mother would feed a lively wood fire. The smoke, like the smoke from the stove, escaped up the central chimney or, when required, was diverted by a gate in the attic, to the smokehouse to cure the hams, sausage and sides of bacon placed there after the slaughter in late fall. When this was the case, the usual pine firewood gave way to seasoned oak, kept separate for this very purpose.

When the oven was sufficiently preheated, she swept aside the glowing embers with a long handled broom to expose the terra cotta slabs on which she baked the large round loaves of bread in quantities to last for days if not weeks. She deposited the soft loaves, their knife scarred round raised by sour dough and brushed with egg white, on to the smooth surface with a long handled wooden spatula and retrieved them after they showed a uniform light-brown crust. The loaves cooled on the shelves of the ground cellar where the crust hardened to keep the inside of the loaf soft and moist for weeks. This cellar, behind the heavy door on the kitchen wall directly opposite the stove, also stored in large vats the fat, melted into liquid during the seasonal slaughter of pigs. The fat solidified into a white paste preserving in it the floating but now captured small cubes and random bits of cooked pork, to be scooped out with a spoon and melted on the stove for the tasty drippings that were part of most meals. The paste was also scooped for spreading on slices of bread which together with cool spring water made for a hardy and satisfying lunch in the shade after a long morning's labor in the fields. In addition, the frost free cellar stored, in large barrels the indispensable sauerkraut and in separate bins, all the farm and orchard harvest, essential for survival and hopefully adequate to last the year.

In the depth of winter, the oven was fired continuously, heating the "Big Room", the largest room of the house, and with the doors open, even the two smaller adjacent rooms, one of which was the room of grandmother Tschinkel. This big room, while also the bedroom of my parents, became the main family room when the activities in the kitchen had slowed, its stove cooled and no longer a source of comfort. The primary attraction was the warmth from the oven in the corner, banishing from the "Big Room" the subzero of the howling wind outside that was driving the direction of yet another foot of large flaked snow, being released from the seemingly unlimited supply above.

The oven was a five foot cube stuck to the inner corner of the nine foot high room. It was flat on top and along each of the two sides there was a wooden bench, firmly fixed to the base of the oven. The backrest of the benches was the oven wall, tiled with glazed squares with a blue design on a white background, tiles that had radiated comforting warmth to the backs of many generations.

But the special attraction was the smooth and flat masonry top, covered in its entirety with a wooden platform of narrow planks, slightly separated to let the warmth through and over which were spread layers of woolen blankets. The top was accessible via a narrow stepladder and used at any time of the day not only by the three siblings but the grown ups as well. Often, and on especially cold evenings, when moving to a cold bed was a particularly unpleasant prospect, Mitzi and I would spend the night up there in spite of reservations from Mother who was worried that we might roll off in our sleep and get hurt.

Late in the evening, the fire would receive a final batch of wood spread apart to burn slowly and last deep into the night. After that, the embers remained glowing until morning and required no more than a little kindling to light the new armful of wood from the shed.

Other parts of our former home were less emotional than the main house except for Father's workshop opposite the main house across the courtyard, now used as a storage shed.

Gone was the six inch thick wooden work bench with the wooden vise that held the planks he cut, planed and nailed into coffins for departed villagers which he and I measured for size, with me holding the other end of a folding rule. This was also the vise that young Karl Schaffer used to cut frames from curved shapes of lumber around which he constructed, as village saddler, the softer parts of a horse's harness he was commissioned to make. I helped him with the cutting by pulling on the two handled saw until the time when I nearly lost the index finger of my left hand when he pulled the saw toward him and I let my finger get in the way. Karl was (in 1939) the twenty eight year old second son of the fire chief and my very best friend, even then already marked by a tragic destiny which, in only a few short years, was to end his life.

It was also the vise that held the drum of Mattl's Italian revolver into which I was trying to force an oversize cartridge until it exploded. It was the vise that held the boards I was shaping into a box including knobs and a dial to resemble a radio which I had promised to build for the dim witted fourteen year old live-in helper of the wife of the village smith. All in return for lifting her skirt for me to see what

I had never seen before. It was the vise that held the bits of wood I shaped into the small ships I would launch into the floodwaters that flowed past the lower parts of the house and under the raised barn and beyond every spring.

This and much more, all with tools too large and difficult to handle with my small hands, tools Father had brought with him on his return from America in 1914 when he answered the call to join the Austrian Imperial Army or else lose his inheritance.

The shop was also a warm place where men of the village came to gossip for a few hours during the idle and cold days between late fall and early spring. Congregate here and avoid spending precious coins for wine at the Jaklitsch tavern; an unwritten requirement for congregating there. Here they were always welcome; their only task feeding the potbellied cast iron stove with the leftover bits that had come off the workbench. Here I heard many a story, but much resented being sent outside by Father when he sensed that what was coming was not for my ears. So I went into the adjoining frosty cold woodshed and listened to most of it as it came through the knotholes of the planked wall.

And finally, it was the place where Father made the crates for those items of our household that we were allowed take with us to our future home in the Reich.

The stable, part of the main house beyond the living space, restored visions of Yiorgo, our unforgettable, above average horse, an intimate member of the family, the engine of our transport. Yiorgo shared the space but had nothing in common with the two cows who went through their predictable annual cycle of the bull, calving and giving milk. Now the space was empty, the new residents using a small car for transportation and getting their milk from other sources.

Yiorgo was a small good-natured Siberian pony with a Greek name, conjuring up an ambiguous origin and interesting past. Father had bought Yiorgo from a band of Gypsies that had stopped in the village on their periodic trek through the region.

Father acquired Yiorgo in the spring of 1919 to pull a very light four wheel hackney seating three on its front bench with a small platform in the back, bordered by an eight inch high railing to keep any cargo in place. Both Yiorgo and the hackney cab became a necessity after he lost his right leg in the fall of 1918. It was the only way for him to get around.

Now, Yiorgo was past middle age, had infinite patience, most of the time in good humor and incredibly smart. He knew us all and followed all commands, be they from Father or any other member of the family, myself included. And when in the middle of a wet night in 1937 he was forcibly pulled out of the stable by a Gypsy horse thief, he made enough of a fuss to wake up both Father and Mother. At the front door they saw the thief ride Yiorgo out of the courtyard. When Father yelled his name, Yiorgo bolted and shook off the Gypsy who ran off to join his accomplices who were rallying the few other horses in the village.

Next morning, the gendarmes from Dolenja Vas examined the footprints left by the barefoot thief in the mud of our courtyard. They also found the trail of the stolen horses in the soft ground leading southwest into deeper forest toward the Italian border. The gendarmes formed a posse to follow the trail and recovered all three horses two days later. When the thieves heard the approaching gendarmes, they abandoned the horses, disappeared into the forest and escaped. The grateful owners of the recovered horses treated the proud but tired Gendarmes to a decent meal at the Jaklitsch pub. That Gypsy column, one of several that came through the village every year, however, did not come back again.

As I said, Yiorgo was smart. On the way home from the market in Kočevje or Ribnica, Father would stop in Dolenja Vas at the tavern/gostilna of his mother-in-law, Grandma Ilc. While Father would have a few quarter liters of her wine, Yiorgo would munch on hay in the courtyard outside.

When it was time to go, Father was usually wobbly and soon asleep after he, with Grandma's help, maneuvered the horse and carriage on the road home. But Yiorgo knew the way, even in the dark. He managed the light carriage safely up and down the steep hill, avoiding the treacherous embankments along the way. At the stable door, he would bang a hoof against the door signaling the arrival to Mother who came running to take care of the two tired travelers.

At one time in the summer of 1940, when for some undetermined reason no one else was around, brother Paul and I, aged two and nine respectively, decided to visit Grandma in Dolenja Vas. An obliging Yiorgo allowed me to lead him from the stable, mount the harness while standing on a stool and couple him to Father's carriage. As we rolled toward Dolenja Vas, curious villagers working the fields became alarmed seeing the two small boys on a carriage pulled by a lone horse on a tricky road. To my great annoyance, they turned us around and brought us back home. Of course, Father was angry at me but even more at Yiorgo for participating in such a foolish adventure.

There were times when Yiorgo's coughing woke the family in the depths of the night. He was colicky and asking for help. But it took a while for Mother to brew up the cure: chamomile tea.

First, a fire had to be lit in the kitchen stove and water with a generous amount of dry chamomile flowers and a helping of sugar was brought to a boil and allowed to steep. After cooling, a soft drink bottle was filled with the brew and while Mother held the head of Yiorgo high, Father helped the horse drink the liquid from the bottle inserted into the side of the mouth away from the teeth. Not that Yiorgo would have crunched the bottle. He knew what the drink was for and did not resist.

Chamomile tea was not only the medicine for Yiorgo but also the standard cure for most ailments of man and beast. It was also reputed to prevent ailments especially if fortified with a generous portion of slivovitz, the brandy of Slovenia and other parts of the Balkans. For the children, a spoonful of sugar had to suffice since, according to Mother, slivovitz only worked for adults.

Harvesting the chamomile flower was an important spring event when the meadows were an ocean of white and yellow. The flower was clipped off where it joins the stem and ample quantities, large enough to last the year were dried in the sun on wooden trays, a process that required frequent turning and care for several days. When dry, the "tea" was stored in round wooden containers resembling a hat box but made of thin sheets of wood, a specialty of lower Slovenia, and kept in the dry attic among other similar items required throughout the year.

All the other buildings were as we had left them. There were no pigs running about, but there were some chickens, including a rooster demonstrating with obvious pride his reason for being. In the orchard, the blossoms of the apple trees were again giving way to tiny balls of the new crop and in the fenced in vegetable garden, the lettuce was bulging and the budding strawberries were showing their first blush.

What had changed, however, was the outhouse. The rickety wooden convenience, attached to the end of the house beyond the stable, had been replaced by a brick structure of uneven and irregularly placed brick oozing mortar from between the joints, displaying the amateur in the mason. The door, made of coarse planks, was neither square nor plumb, but the latch was lockable on the inside, guaranteeing privacy as did the cardboard strips covering the large gaps between the unevenly edged boards.

THE BELLS RING NO MORE

Pahulje and I sat on the old bench in front of the house, hand hewn from a tree trunk and after a while, emotion gave way to answer questions posed by the anxious new occupants. Were we planning to return? Clearly relieved by the answer, we were asked to visit again, anytime.

For much of the remainder of the day, Pahulje and I wandered slowly through the village, stopping occasionally to allow past events to emerge from buried memories. Many of the less central houses were empty and turning into ruin. We stopped at the cemetery where all the old gravestones, reminders of those who found their resting place there before being abandoned by their descendants in the winter of 41/42, had been removed and replaced by markers for those who died since. We did locate our family plot, now the resting place of others, only because I remembered the surrounding concrete border poured in place by Father in the late thirties.

Returning from the cemetery we passed the house that once was the Kren Tavern. Pahulje was not pleased when I began to talk of his confrontation with Father in the public room over 30 years ago and he became visibly angry when I mentioned his broken thumb. But when I tried to pass off the episode as a humorous remembrance he soon recovered. I did not mention Aunt Johanna's still empty house, the upheaval it brought to our lives and the split it produced in Mother's family. Neither did he. But much more about that later.

We passed the school house now empty and no longer used. It brought back memories of the day when I carefully repackaged, again, the new little rucksack, given to me by aunt Grete on her visit that summer, with notebooks, pencils and erasers, leaving room for the little sandwich Mother was going to give me in the morning as lunch for my first day. The school house also reminded me of the three children of Alojzij Dežman, the last teacher in the village. All three were special playmates with whom I shared a common language, they being children of not only one, but two Slovene parents. Dežman and his family, in the village since 1933, left in 1941, driven out by the animosity of the villagers now fully conditioned to be hostile to anything Slovene. The description of the Slovene as "inferior humans of an inferior race" was a useful tool in the arsenal of the self appointed young Gottscheer leaders who had been promoting Hitler's racial ideology throughout the enclave since 1938.

Using the trail that skirted the village behind the houses, we continued in the westerly direction, passing the drinking well which was still delivering a lively overflow from the cavity in the rock wall. A well, which in 1939, had led to the major embarrassment when the new fire pump was being tested.

Continuing toward Masereben, we stopped at the abandoned smithy, its interior no longer illuminated by the white hot coal in the hooded forge kept at high heat by the air from the leather bellows being pumped by the foot of the smith wearing his blackened leather apron. Also the space no longer lit up by flashes of sparks flying off the anvil in all directions as he was shaping the cherry red metal into a shoe for the horse waiting outside.

This done, he ran outside to fit it on to the previously shaped hoof held up by his helper. As the red iron burned itself into the hoof for a proper fit, it produced a cloud of pungent white smoke and rapid coughing from those who could not get away from it. And when after several such fittings, the smith slowly lowered the still hot shoe into the bucket of water; it produced a lively sizzle and a cloud of steam.

After 1939, Father discouraged me from lingering at the smithy, the reason for which I discovered only years later. Apparently the smith, who lived next to the smithy at number 7, had accosted the lone sixteen year old Mitzi while she was working in the fields. But she struggled and got away from him. Father and Mother immediately took her to the gendarmerie station in Dolenja Vas to report the incident. I do remember two gendarmes coming to see Father whom they found in his shop. But since I was not to hear the details, he sent me outside out of hearing. I also remember how shortly thereafter, the then pregnant wife of the smith came to see Father carrying one of her two children above the swollen belly with one arm while with the other holding the older boy. Apparently to plead, but I discovered the reason why only much later. There was a hearing in the Ribnica courthouse later on, the results of which remain a mystery even after asking Mitzi who never wished to talk about the event.

We continued past the house of the village shoemaker who made robust footwear for all the villagers, be they men, women or children. As he was making my first pair I visited him daily, watching him cut the various parts from piles of pleasant smelling leather which he then stitched, glued and nailed together on the metal last in between his legs. His thirty something son had an eye on Mitzi and in 1940 came to ask Father if he would allow her to marry him. The answer was no, the first of such replies to the same questions as years went by.

We walked to the house of the game keeper who with his family remained in the village after we left in 1941. After he died, it had become the house of his son Norbert Tscherne who now keeps a small tavern in the large room of the house. He gave his account of the battle in 1943 which I will describe in a later chapter.

On the way back to the square we walked by the house once owned by Rudolf Tschinkel a distant relative and the owner of the local sawmill, the major employer in the village. The house, once the second tavern on the square, was used as one of the defense posts of the Plava Garda during the battle in 1943. It was damaged extensively but is now fully restored. An engraved plaque of polished black marble commemorates the event. It is mounted on the wall facing the square and reads:

> V SEPTEMBRU LETA 1943
> SO V TEM KRAJU ENOTE NOV
> UNIČILE ZADNJO UTRDBO
> PLAVE GARDE V SLOVENIJI

> In September of 1943,
> in this place, units of the NOV
> destroyed the last stronghold of the
> Blue Guard in Slovenia.

This visit of Grčarice (Masern) was followed by many others, over many years. Endless urging from family and friends, always eager to hear yet another tale from another time convinced me to put them in writing. In this I was helped by vivid recollections, renewed by these returns into a succession of scenes, not unlike the pictures at an exhibition. For decades, these scenes continued to emerge from memory scraps of less than 14 years into the mosaic of a distant past.

This mosaic is however part of a larger picture, one that represents centuries of history within which this village illustrates typical fragments. The following chapters describe the fragments of this and other villages and how they jointly evolve into a canvas that traces the six centuries of its being.

A summary overview, helpful in comprehending the overall historical evolution of the enclave, its progress through time and its final destiny, is contained in the following chapter.

Chapter 3

The Enclave

595 - 1809

The region of Slovenia now known as the county of Kočevje is reached via the road from Ribnica in a south-easterly direction. The western boundary of the county starts a few kilometers beyond Dolenja Vas, the last village in the fertile valley of the Ribnica plain.

At the end of the plain, the road climbs a hill and after a flat stretch, it descends into a narrow but broadening valley to continue toward Kočevje City, the center of this southeastern part of the country. From there it leads further east toward the border of the State of Croatia. All along the way, small villages line either side of the road which runs through what was once known as the "Mainland" part of the former linguistic enclave of Kočevje or Gottschee in German.

Before the hill and a short distance beyond Dolenja Vas, the main road toward Kočevje has a branch to the right leading toward the village of Rakitnica. And just beyond Rakitnica, the road, like the road to the "Mainland", also climbs a hill which after a flat portion descends to Grčarice (Masern), the start of the "Hinterland" part of the former enclave. The Hinterland, like the Mainland is a series of small, forest enclosed valleys, except each at a higher elevation.

The two "Lands" are separated by a mountain range, on top of which are the remains of castle Friedrichstein, the administrative seat of the enclave until the middle of the 17th Century. But in the 1930's, this dividing range of hills was bridged only by a few narrow footpaths, used mainly by goatherds and poachers.

In both instances, the hills beyond Dolenja Vas mark the beginning of the former Kočevje (Gottschee) enclave with its center in the small city having the same name. And over the centuries, ever since the arrival of the Germanic settlers in the late 13th and early 14th century, the hills were a natural boundary that encouraged a linguistic separation lasting more than 600 years. In this separation, Grčarice was culturally bound to the enclave.

The French, during their presence in Carniola, (1809 to 1813), reorganized the conquered lands into districts, cantons, townships and municipalities. On 15 April 1811, they made the Gottschee area a canton including, among others, Ribnica, Dolenja Vas and Grčarice. A subsequent modification on 7 January 1812 established

Ribnica as a separate canton under which were moved the municipalities of Ribnica, Rakitnica and Dolenja Vas. (Grčarice was placed under Dolenja Vas as a sub-municipality remaining as such until the present day). With this re-apportionment, Grčarice was, at least administratively if not culturally, moved outside the enclave. [1] From then on, Grčarice and Rakitnica, the Slovene village on the Ribnica side of the divide shared the post office, the roads, the weather and the air of Dolenja Vas. Except that the air in Rakitnica lacked the heavy fragrance of the pines in the vast forest surrounding Grčarice which in springtime, when the sap began to flow, dominated our village.

Life in the villages on either side of the divide was identical, but it was the lack of a common language that kept them apart. On the Ribnica side of the hill, the language was Slovene, whereas on our side, only 4.5 kilometers away, the language was the ancient German dialect the settlers brought with them but no one outside the enclave understood.

The main reason for this linguistic separation was the way this part of Slovenia and the Kočevje forest was settled.

Records show that the lands of present day Slovenia, the adjacent Carinthia and other surrounding areas were first settled by heathen Slavs who had arrived in the region from the East, where they owed allegiance to the Avar Khans. By the middle of the 6th Century, the area had become a powerful Slavic principality known as "*Provincia Sclaborum*". This name is mentioned for the first time by Paulus Diaconus (720 – 799) who writes ca. 783 in his *Historica Langobardorum*, (Biblioteca Laurenciana, Florence), that in 595 AD, the Bavarian Duke Tassilo I. made an incursion into the "*Provincia Sclaborum*".

Out of this "*Provincia Sclaborum*" emerged, in the early part of the 7th Century on the north side of the Karavanke mountains and beyond, the principality known as "*Carantania*" which included, roughly, the areas now known as Carinthia and Styria. And on the southern side of the Karavanke, in the Sava valley emerged "*Carniola*" the forerunner of the present Slovenia. "Carniola was a further Slavic principality in the eastern Alpine area, alongside that of Carantania". [2]

---

1   Kočevski zbornik. Razprave o Kočevski in njenih ljudeh, Ljubljana 1939, pg. 127, 128, later: *Kočevski Zbornik*.

2   P. Štih, V. Simoniti, P. Vodopivec, *Slowenische Geschichte*, Graz 2008, pg. 39. Later: *Slowenische Geschichte*.

THE ENCLAVE

Štih, on pg. 39, also writes that it was Paulus Diaconus who first used the term *"Carniola"* in 740 AD and that another early use is in the Royal Frankish Annals dated 820 AD. Further "all early medieval sources that actually mention Carniola, clearly distinguish between two separate Slavic communities north and south of the Karavanke Mountains".

Due to continuing raids by the Avars deep into their territory, the princes of Carantania, in 745, asked their Bavarian neighbors for help. After that, they paid for such continuing assistance with progressively higher dependence with the ultimate result of losing their independence to the Bavarians in the later years of the 8th century. And when Charlemagne campaigned against the Avars in 791 and 799, Carantania was annexed to the Frankish Kingdom and placed under the dukes of Bavaria. According to Štih on page 40 "during the Frankish-Avar wars, Carniola recognized the Frankish overlords perhaps as early as 791".

After 828, the Frankish concept of earldom was introduced into the Slavic territories. With this, foreign counts received land leases from the Frankish kings, thereby replacing the Slavic princes as rulers of the region. And from that time forward until the independence of Slovenia in 1991, the center of administrative authority was always located outside the territory of Carniola.

Peter Štih writes further: "In this way there was formed in the Slovene territories, until the end of the 11th century, the basis of an ownership structure which, however, was continuously changing. In this time there have been historical developments within the Slovene area which have been labeled Colonization, Germanization, Assimilation and also Feudalization of the community". [3]

The annexation of Carantania to the Frankish Kingdom effectively started the Christianization of the pagan Slavs. Up to that time ecclesiastic control over Carantania and Carniola was ambiguous, with both the Bishop of Salzburg and the Patriarch (bishop-prince) of Aquileia vying for control of the area. The Patriarchy solidified, gradually, its hold over the pagan Slavs in the later part of the 8th century and Patriarch Paulinus II (787-806), set up parishes and other administrative centers of the church. In the same century, missionaries also came from Ireland via the Bishop of Salzburg (himself Irish) to convert the Slavs and teach them to pray in their native tongue. But Charlemagne, who actively encouraged and supported Christianization of the heathen Slavs, eliminated competition for control by Salzburg and Aquileia by fixing responsibility for the area south of the river Drava to Aquileia and the northern part to the Bishopric of Salzburg in 811.

---

3   *Slowenische Geschichte, pg. 62*

THE BELLS RING NO MORE

For two centuries after the death of Charlemagne in 814, the ongoing struggles within the Holy Roman Empire slowed the Christianization and less attention was paid to westernize the Slavs. And when in 936 Otto I became the East Frankish (German) king, he recovered control over northern Italy, Lombardy and Aquileia and Pope John XII crowned him Emperor in 962.

Otto I enhanced the Patriarchy and granted it extensive political privileges and feudal rights. With the Patriarch of Aquileia as Bishop-Prince, now fully in charge of Carniola (as well as the other parts of the present Slovenia), he established, in AD 1082, Ribnica (Reiffnitz) as a major parish of the Patriarchy in the region. This made Ribnica responsible for the spiritual well being of all of Lower Carniola including the training of its priests. Ribnica was also the seat of the Counts of Ortenburg, major landowners in Lower Carniola. The ruins of castle Ortenburg still stand. Other local monastic and diocesan centers were established which injected western European culture into the Slovene population.

The settling of German stock among the Slavs started effectively after Otto I became Emperor in 962. German settlers, mostly aristocratic and clerical lords with their dependent peasants began to arrive and lay claim to large parts of the land as their fiefs, with the resident Slavs becoming their serfs. The settling had, in part, the objective to flesh out the sparsely populated Slavic areas of Carinthia, Carniola and Styria with stock from the north and northwestern parts of the German Empire and thereby increase the tax revenue from the land. The use of German spread through the area and in the northwestern parts of the former Carantania became the prevalent language.

The arrival of German settlers continued gradually for centuries after the death of Otto I in 974. And when the Habsburg prince Rudolf I became Holy Roman Emperor in 1273, all of the area once known as "*Sclaborum*" was divvied up into a hierarchy of fiefs each ruled by increasingly higher ranking German aristocrats.

In summary, the initial colonization of Lower Carniola was a gradual shift of Germanic stock from the northwest of Carniola and beyond to the end of the Ribnica plain and into the fringes of the Hočevje forest. The shift occurred at the beginning of the 10th century and started to peak in the last half of the 13th century.

During this process, the already resident Slovene of Lower Carniola absorbed these new arrivals into their communities as they had absorbed the German settlers who had been arriving gradually during the past three centuries. The settlers also adopted the Slovene dialect as they became integrated into the local population.

THE ENCLAVE

When his wars with Ottokar II of Bohemia ended in 1278, Rudolf I was weakened and he began to pressure his estates for additional tax revenues. This included the Counts of Ortenburg, one of the biggest land owners of Lower Carniola.

The pressure for additional taxes in the 13th century started the first wave of a greater settlement process in which German residents of upper Carniola and Carinthia were invited by the Ortenburg counts to move into the forest of Lower Carniola beyond the fertile area of the Ribnica plain. An increase in productivity and improved tax revenue was expected from a more densely populated land.

Limited settling of the area beyond the Ribnica plain had started in the early part of the 13th century, but mostly by Slovene from the Ortenburg domains of Lower Carniola. They cleared parts of the forest and started villages with Slovene names.

One such village was called Hoče, the area surrounding it – Hočevje. [4]

To attract more settlers into the forest, an inhospitable place that until now only few had been willing to clear and wrestle a livelihood from its unproductive soil, Count Otto VI of Ortenburg promised personal freedom and ownership of parcels of land in return for an annual tithe. The promise to become free men, free of the bonds of serfdom was a powerful attraction for many near and far away. And the prospect of becoming landowners enticed the peasants of the Germanic kingdom to travel great distances to reach their promised land.

The resulting first wave of settling of the still mostly empty Hočevje forest started at the end of the 13th century. The colonizers came from Tyrol, Carinthia and other parts of the German kingdom. They came in groups large enough to be linguistically self-sustaining at their destination and as such were able to absorb the thinly settled Slovene already living in the forest. These earlier arrivals had done some of the initial clearing and thereby provided the basic settlement features for the new waves of settlers. In addition the hills, isolating the newly expanded settlements from the Slovene of the Ribnica plain, assisted the separation by providing a natural barrier to being linguistically absorbed into the Slavic (Slovene) language.

The certainty that the settling of the forest started near or at the end of the 13th century comes from the fact that a resident chaplain was appointed to the chapel of Mahovnik (Mooswald) in 1339, just on the inside edge of the forest along the road to the inner "Mainland". Count Otto VI of Ortenburg had requested permission for this appointment, permission he received in 1339 from Bertram, the then Patriarch of Aquileia.

---

[4] E. Petschauer, *Das Jahrhundertbuch; Gottschee and its People Through the Centuries*, New York, pg. 50. Later: *Das Jahrhundertbuch*.

THE BELLS RING NO MORE

It appears that in the past few decades preceding the request, the population of Mahovnik and its surroundings had grown to a number where the Ribnica parish could no longer effectively tend to the spiritual needs of the parishioners living there. Even if only thirteen kilometers from Ribnica, Mahovnik was too far away for parish priests to travel to their flock on the marginal roads of those days.

Twenty four years later, in 1363, the count also received permission from Patriarch Ludovicius I, the second successor to Bertram, to elevate five additional villages to parish status. The villages "Gotsche, Pölan, Costel, Ossiwniz et Gotenitz", were to be under the main parish of Ribnica, the Archdiocese of Lower Carniola since 1082. Permission from the Patriarch came in a letter dated 1 May, 1363 and it is in this letter the name "Gotsche" (the Slovene Hoče) appears for the first time.

As the new arrivals moved into the thinly settled villages and gradually absorbed its Slovene local population, they also changed the village names to their German equivalents. The Slovene Hoče became Gotsche, as spelled out in German by the Patriarch in 1363. Phonetically the two names are nearly identical. The area surrounding Gotsche became Gottschee while the Slovene changed Hočevje to Kočevje, a minor change. Other such examples exist. On the other hand, Grčarice became Masern, phonetically different but in their distinctly different language each describing a piece of gnarled wood.

It is of interest to note that the early German settlers did not come to the forest as "Gottscheer"; the name having developed from the Slovene "Hočevje" only after their arrival. The proof of this and the fact that the Gottscheer are of a mixed racial make-up is clearly documented by Erich Petschauer who cites Professor Balduin Saria as his reference. [5]

The main part of the first wave occurred in the middle part of 14th century. This was when large groups of self-contained settlers started to arrive from the Germanic kingdom further to the west and the north. In his "Glory of the Duchy of Carniola", Baron Johann Vajkard Valvasor (1641-1693) the historian of the 17th century, a Carniolan nobleman of Italian origin, scholar and member of the Royal Society in London, reports on one such group.

Valvasor writes that a group of settlers, 300 men with their families, passed through Ljubljana in the middle of the 14th century on their way toward Ribnica,

---

5   *Das Jahrhundertbuch, pg 50.*

THE ENCLAVE

Dolenja Vas and the forest of Lower Carniola. Valvasor claims he found this information in the archives of Skofja Loka (Bischoflak) near Ljubljana. The entry into the archives was made by Bishop Thomas Hren in 1590 who stated that he found the information in the diary of Bishop Paul who lived in Ljubljana in the 14th century and had made the entry in 1363.

According to Bishop Paul, this group came from the Franconia/Thuringia part of the German Empire of Charles IV. Friderick, one of Otto Ortenburg's relatives, who was aware of Otto's difficulty in attracting settlers to the forest, appealed to Emperor Charles IV for help. Charles, who had recently subdued the peasant rebellion led by Günther Schwarzenburg, agreed to make available to Friderick 300 of the vanquished and their families instead of punishing them for their rebellion. Friderick sent the rebels to Lower Carniola where Count Otto VI had promised to make them independent landowners of one full unit of land (Hube) in return for clearing the forest.

They made their way there in oxen drawn wagon columns via Carinthia, Upper Carniola, Ljubljana and Ribnica, the seat of the Ortenburg. The journey was long and arduous particularly since throughout Carniola in 1349 raged a cattle plague which forced the weary travelers to avoid the established and well traveled normal routes.[6]

Since the offer of one Hube (Hide in English) per family was available to all, it is reasonable to assume that not all those who settled in the forest came from this group. Others may have come from elsewhere in similar or smaller groups.

The German dialect these waves brought with them thus became the language of the ethnic enclave of Kočevje or Gottschee, which was to remain a linguistic island until the early part of 1942. The inhabitants preserved this dialect while being surrounded by Slavs ever since their ancestors were invited by the Ortenburg to cultivate the forest.

The Gottschee dialect with its Germanic origin has very little in common with the present day German language. In the 19th century, after public schools were established, it even had its own adaptation of an old Germanic alphabet. A modern German would not understand it and no one but a Gottscheer could read it. Conversely, the average Gottscheer villager did not know German until he learned to read. The dialect has no commonality with the Slovene language which has a Slavic as opposed to a Germanic base. It is, however, the only cultural marker that, over the centuries, differentiated the Gottscheer from the surrounding Slovene; all other cultural characteristics being similar, if not identical.

---

6   *Kočevski Zbornik, pg 56 - 58.*

In Grčarice we spoke only Gottscheer and the Slovene inhabitants of the adjacent Rakitnica, 4.5 km away and other villages west of the hill had, except for a few expressions, little knowledge of what we were saying. Likewise, at least until after WWI, when the Gottscheer had to learn the new official State language, few Gottscheer understood them. Of interest, however, is the fact that more than half of the names of the inhabitants of Rakitnica and many in Dolenja Vas have names which are phonetically equivalent to those within the enclave including Grčarice.

There were later settlement phases. One labeled as the second wave was from 1547-1618, when the Gottschee leasehold was given to the Croatian Count Blagay. He brought with him Croatian settlers who were absorbed into the Gottscheer German villages, especially in the eastern end of the enclave. Also, some of the Turks who invaded Carniola over the many decades left behind pregnant women. Names abbreviated from the Turkish Skenderbeg hint of this.

The 20th century Gottscheer of the enclave resisted the notion of a mixed origin because they wished to preserve the illusion of being of German nationality as opposed to a mixed racial makeup of German, Slovene and Croatians. This illusion began to develop in the 19th century when the Slovene pressed the imperial monarchy ever more strongly for autonomy, self-rule and freedom from the germanization drive of the Austrians. The Gottscheer, in turn, sensed in these Slovene aspirations a threat to their presumed ethnic German identity, an illusion reinforced by the radical nationalism of Hitler's Germany.

A personal experience made me aware of the complex origin of the Gottscheer and their dialect. On a tour of Greece with my wife in 1972 we stopped overnight in Naplion on the Peloponnesian peninsula. At breakfast, with no empty tables available, I sat down at a table already occupied by an elderly couple speaking French. Attempts to communicate with my limited French soon stopped but resumed when my wife joined us shortly thereafter. Since she speaks French fluently, I resigned myself to listen only.

I asked her to inquire where they were from. When I heard Strasbourg in Alsace, France - in the 13th century part of the Germanic kingdom, I addressed them in German to which they responded fluently and we chatted happily in that language for a while.

THE ENCLAVE

I asked how they communicate among themselves at home. Oh, we speak in a very old German dialect, which is now dying out. When I asked them to demonstrate, they started to speak a language virtually identical to that of the Gottscheer and when I replied likewise they were as astonished as were my wife and I. This incident confirmed that my forefathers had come to Grčarice and the enclave from far away indeed.

While in the existing villages outside the forest the German language or dialect of the new arrivals during the initial settlement phase (10-13th Century) was absorbed into Slovene, the phonetics of the family name of the arrivals remained unchanged. Conversely, the groups settling the forest during the 14th Century were large enough to be linguistically self-sustaining and able to absorb the thinly settled already present Slovene into their German dialect. And since the offer of land was available also to settlers already living in the area outside the forest, residents of other parts of Carniola, of both Germanic and Slovene origin, also took up the offer to resettle into the forest. They too were absorbed.

It is this phonetic commonality of family names that preserves the evidence of the mixed origin of people on both side of the divide since in either language, the pronunciation of the name remained the same. This is evidence that the intermingling of Slovene and German residents and their integration into the respective communities inside and outside the enclave started already in the 10th century and continued long after the first wave of settling the forest in the 14th century was concluded.

Austria acquired Carniola in 1335 and it is from this date forward that the long identification of Carniola with the Habsburgs of Austria begins. Carniola became Krain, Upper Carniola Oberkrain and Lower Carniola Unterkrain. Austrian administrators referred to the Slavic inhabitants of Krain as Krainer or Windische. Under the Austrians Gotsche became Gottschee, a market village in 1377 and in 1393 an independent parish but subservient to Ribnica. In 1471 the market town of Gottschee, was granted City status. The spiritual control over the land, however, remained in Aquileia until the establishment of the archbishopric in Ljubljana in 1461.

Throughout the centuries after 1335 until 1918, the "Amtsprache" (administrative language) of Carniola/Slovenia was German, the language of the Austrian empire, the language of the educated and upper classes. However, in the villages in and outside the enclave, all communication was in the local language, be it Gottscheer or Slovene or any other. Spelling did not play a role throughout this time, since most Slovene and Gottscheer learned to read and write only after the establishment of state primary schools in Carniola during the last half of the 19th century, long after the universal education act of Maria Theresa in 1774. "The population as a whole had no education and, prior to the introduction of the mandatory schooling law of 1775, the majority in the land had no knowledge of how to read and write."[7]

All official records were in German until the 19th century and Slovene family names were spelled to fit the German alphabet. It was only after Slovene was formalized that their phonetic names were gradually absorbed into the spelling of the Slovene language at the end of the 19th and the beginning of the 20th century. German speaking residents living in predominantly Slovene speaking areas kept the German spelling of their names. The phonetic names of the residents within the enclave however, be they of German or Slavic origin, had already been taken into the long established German spelling and remained as such. On either side of the linguistic divide, the absorption and integration of the phonetics of the names into the spelling of the respective German or Slovene language made the separation complete.

One example among many is that of my Slovene grandmother whose married name was Ilc. I traced this name and lineage to 1615. But her maiden name was Zbašnik, in German spelled as Sbaschnig. It was pronounced Zbashnig on either side of the ethnic divide.

But in 1941 there were also four land-owning Gottscheer families called Sbaschnig in Grčarice (Masern). Their names appear for the first time in the Therezijanski Kataster of 1752. But there were Sbaschnigs in Dolenja Vas before then. Likewise, there are many present-day Slovene and Gottscheer-Germans with my family name, pronounced in all languages as Chinkel. But it is spelled Činkel in Slovene and Tschinkel in German.

And in the Slovene Rakitnica, four kilometers away, more than half of the inhabitants have names which are phonetically equivalent to those within the enclave, including those in Grčarice. Records in the National Archives of Slovenia verify this.

---

7   *Slowenische Geschichte, pg 219.*

THE ENCLAVE

1809 – 1918.

Cooperation between the people on either side of the ethnic divide was unhindered by nationalistic awareness until the start of 19th century. Until then the Slovene and Gottscheer lived peacefully side by side, each loyal to the Kaiser and the Austrian monarchy. The first disruption to this peaceful coexistence between the evolved and accepted language separateness surfaced with the arrival of the French under Bonaparte in 1809. Already years before, the French revolution in 1789 and the subsequent Napoleonic wars brought unrest and revolts to other parts of Slovene lands.[8] Consequently, the farmers were not hostile to the French when they arrived in 1809.

The Gottscheer of the enclave, however, did not welcome the French. They viewed them as foreign invaders and as loyal supporters of the Vienna monarchy they were duty bound to resist. Already in 1797, the order came from the Austrian military command that fortifications were to be erected on the boundary to the enclave between Ribnica and Kočevje. Five strongholds were erected by 4,295 local laborers of which 2,892 were Gottscheer at a total cost of 650 Florin. The entrenchments were be manned by the Gottscheer militia to prevent the French from entering the enclave.[9]

In May 1809 the French occupied Ribnica and Kočevje. The fortifications manned by the Gottscheer militia did little to stop them from occupying the enclave.

Some Slovene intellectuals, among them a handful of Slovene nationalists, however, welcomed the French as liberators from the Austrian effort to Germanize the Slavs of Carniola. To this writes Joachim Hösler: "So kursierte bei vielen Intellektuellen zu Begin de 19. Jahrhunderts die diffuse Idee einer illyrisch-sudslawischen Einheit und Autochtonie. Diesem Geschichtsbild suchten die Franzosen entgegenzukommen" (There circulated among the many intellectuals at the beginning of the 19th century the diffuse idea of an illyrian-southslavic autonomous union. This perspective the French attempted to accommodate.)[10]

---

    8   *P. Vodopivec, Od Pohlinove do samostojne države, Ljubljana 2006, pg 12, later: Od Pohlinove slovnice ...*

    9   *9 Kočevski Zbornik, pg 127.*

    10   *Slowenien. Von den Anfangen bis zur Gegenwart, Regensburg 2006, pg. 69, later: Slowenien.*

Consequently, Napoleon Bonaparte in 1809 caused the formation of the "Illyrian Provinces" which the French had deliberately designed to make into a Slovene national state. (These "Provinces" encompassed part of Carinthia and Tyrol, Carniola, Gorizia and Gradisca, Krain, Istria including Trieste, Croatia south of the river Sava, Dalmatia and Ragusa).

C. A. Macartney in *The Habsburg Empire* comments on this:

"... they [the French] had drawn up blue-prints for an advanced system of general education with an elementary school for boys in every commune and one for girls in every Canton, twenty five gymnasia and a lycée and a High School of university standing in Ljubljana. Instruction was to be in the 'local language' in the elementary schools; in the secondary and higher schools, partly in that language, partly in French and Italian."[11]

Macartney continues:

"There had been, as we said before, no instruction at all in Slovene, and very little in any other language (when they [the French] took over Carniola and Istria, where they found that only 3,000 of the 419,000 inhabitants of the two lands had attended, or were attending, school) and hardly any printed literature in Slovene existed except one or two devotional books including a Bible, which had been printed in Germany in the sixteenth century."

Macartney continues by writing that after the French left: ".... the Austrians in 1817 restored the *status quo* in almost every respect, including instruction in German in the schools. However, the French had left behind them a new interest and pride in their nationality among the younger Slovenes, and, incidentally, had settled what had until then been an undecided question, what the Slovene language was to be. They [the French] had at first thought of making the language of instruction and public life the *Što* dialect of the Southern Slavs spoken in Ragusa [Dubrovnik]. But a Slovene philologist named Jernej Kopitar, the Keeper of Slavonic Books at the Court Library in Vienna, who was generally regarded as the leading authority on the subject, persuaded them to adopt the 'local language'. [Kopitar had published the first grammar of the Slovene language in 1809 which contributed to the ongoing development of the Slovene language.] Later intellectuals thought of reversing the decision, but were never able to do so and Slovene remained thereafter a separate language; it may even be true to say that the decision settled the question whether the Slovenes were to remain a distinct people".

---

11   C.A. Macartney, *The Habsburg Empire, 1790-1918" pg.216*, Macmillan, NY 1968, later: *The Habsburg Empire*.

THE ENCLAVE

The French encouraged the use of the still evolving but not yet fully formalized Slovene as the official language. Maréchal Marmont, the Governor General of the Illyrian Republic told a Slovene deputation that: "the Slovene do not know how to defend and love their language and because of the German colonizer, they learn his language and neglect their own. It is therefore not surprising that they are an awkward, subservient nation, which the colonizer does not respect".[12]

But some Slovene were not discouraged either by the above remark or the Austrian restoration of the status quo. "In spite of all this, the establishment of the 'Illyrian Provinces' awakened great hopes in some members of the Slovene 'Rebirth' movement in Krain."[13]

The Gottscheer in the enclave, however sensed that their ethnic independence was, for the first time in centuries, actively threatened by a Slovene state based on the projected French reforms. Such a state would grant them only a dubious minority status, their autonomy no longer assured by the protective power of the Austrian nobility. They decided to resist.

This resistance was brought into the open by the oppressive economic and political policies of the occupier which rapidly alienated the Slovene aristocratic and bourgeois upper classes as well as the rural population. "The French especially disappointed the farmers whose lot had with certain measures, actually been improved." writes Peter Vodopivec on page 228. However, on July 7, 1809 the French imposed an annual tax of 15,260,000 Florin on the Illyrian Provinces which included Lower Carniola. Part of this levy fell on the Gottschee enclave. On 10 September 1809, six hundred landowners, mostly Gottscheer who refused payment, assembled in the square of Gottschee town to protest. However, when faced by a battalion of heavily armed French soldiers commanded by General Souchy, the protesters dispersed. The Gottscheer persisted with their rebellion and started an enclave-wide general uprising. In this process, they killed many of the French. They also killed Venceslav Gaspari, the French district commissioner of Novo Mesto and threw his dismembered body into a crevasse.

---

12   Kočevski Zbornik, pg 361.
13   Slowenische Geschichte, pg. 231.

The French reacted severely by killing many of the rebels, burning a number of villages and parts of the city. They captured the organizers of the rebellion and executed five of the main leaders in the town square on October 18, 1809. After that, the hopeless resistance to an overwhelming opponent crumbled and a systematic mop-up campaign by the French brought the ill fated uprising to its inevitable end.[14]

But with their rebellion in 1809, the Gottscheer announced for the first time, that their aspirations were different from those of the Slovene.

After Austria regained control of Slovenia, German was reestablished as the "Amtssprache" of Slovenia. While, as before 1809, basic primary schooling could be conducted in Slovene, knowledge of German was essential and required for communicating with provincial or municipal officials. All higher education was again exclusively in German and taught by mostly Austrian professors as it was before the arrival of the French. All civil, administrative and governmental functions were again conducted in German and all official and formal documents had to be in that language. The Austrian administration was staffed mainly by Austrians or Germanized Slovene who made sure the rules of the Habsburg Monarchy were adhered to and enforced.

Before and after Napoleon, all villages and towns everywhere in Slovenia had dual names, the German being the official administration version. The original Slovene names had, over the centuries, been given a German equivalent which was used in all "official" documents and communications. The German version for Grčarice was Masern, Kočevje was Gottschee, Gotenica was Göttenitz, Dolenja Vas was Niederdorf, Ribnica was Reifnitz, Ljubljana was Laibach, etc. as it had been before 1809. Among themselves, the locals used their own version, be it either Slovene or German. However, mail addressed for delivery to Grčarice, or any other place identified by its Slovene name, was recognized only at the discretion of the post master.

Before and again after Napoleon, the germanization of the Slovene was according to the Imperial politics of Austria. In this, the dominating position of the German language in the governing institutions and academia promoted the desirability of a German identity. Such identity automatically indicated a higher education including

---

14　*Zbornik, pg 127.*

the cultivation of cultural values and liberal thought. All Slovene could attain a level of Germanness through proficiency in the German language. Fluency in German was vital for financial and social achievement and a crucial prerequisite for any upwardly-mobile Slovene seeking higher social status in government service or in commercial and academic circles. Austrian as well as Slovene liberals all accepted the notion that the better educated Slovene identify themselves as Germans and thereby become more successful. Language was no longer only a means for communication but it had become a status symbol and proof of being part of the elite. However, even in the middle of the 19th century, it was mostly the elite Slovene, educated in German secondary or higher schools that knew how to read and write even though more and more of the country population was becoming literate. Aggressive germanization, however, evolved into the politics of the Austrian ruling parties only in the second half of the 19th century.

Despite their frequent opposition to enforced policies, the Slovene Liberals had never questioned the legitimacy of the Monarchy. They viewed the central state as an instrument which might help them transform Slovene society into one equaling that of the German, albeit as Slovene nationals.

The exposure to national independence introduced by the French, however, caused progressively more of the educated Slovene to forgo their being accepted by the Austrian dominated elite and turn instead to the emerging national awareness and politics at home. Germanization, for centuries a path to class status and financial achievement, gave way to increasing political mobilization. The Slovene activists, defining national identity as more significant than class position and acceptance by the Austrian administration, argued that occupational, business or bourgeois interests had to be secondary to the emergence of the Slovene nation. And these nationalists worked hard to prevent the Slovene from continuing to serve Austrian political and class interest.

After the French left and Slovenia was restored to Austria, the Austrians hardened their opposition to the emerging nationalism, not only in Slovenia but throughout its multiethnic empire, leading to the revolutions throughout their lands in 1848. In Slovenia, the special relationship between state institutions and the now suspect German-speaking Slovene bourgeoisie started to deteriorate and even some Slovene who had graduated from Austrian universities were excluded from civil service jobs. One example is France Prešeren, a university trained lawyer, who in the years 1832-1845 was denied a license to practice five times for this very reason. Prešeren, (1800-1848) who became Slovenia's greatest poet, had expressed his country's desire for national and political independence while advocating equality and friendly coexistence among nations. He complained bitterly that German was privileged in contrast to Slovene, but, nevertheless, he had no aversion against the Germans.

The position of the Slovene nationalists was in opposition to the liberal elite who, like their liberal counterparts in Austria championed a more gradual evolution of a Slovene state, albeit within the structure of a united Germany.[15] Such a Germany was contemplated in Frankfurt in 1848 as a result of the uprisings throughout Europe mainly due to the suppression of liberal thinking that was sparked by the French revolution. This united Germany was to include the states of the Austrian empire severely shaken by the uprisings that forced Emperor Franz Ferdinand to abdicate on December 2, 1848 in favor of his eighteen year old nephew who became Franz Josef I, and caused Prince Metternich to flee to England. Metternich, as the foreign minister of the empire, had been the architect of the post Napoleonic policy which was attempting to restore the old order and suppress the emerging nationalism now spreading throughout Europe.

The Gottscheer appeared to see in this spirit of equality and friendly coexistence, as advocated jointly by the Slovene and Austrian Liberals, a continuation of their comfortable status quo. They found their champion in Count Anton von Auersperg, a respected poet known as Anastasius Grün who represented the Slovene at the Frankfurt meeting. Grün, like his friend Prešeren, believed that the Slovene would be able to develop better and fully within the framework of united Germany, a position rejected by the Slovene nationalists advocating independence.

The Frankfurt attempt to produce a unified Germany failed mainly due to the reluctance of Austria to surrender its centuries-old dominant position as an empire. Greatly strengthened, the Slovene nationalists saw in this Austrian stance an affirmation of their politics and were, therefore, driven to pursue even more vigorously their quest for independence. And in the decades following 1848, these nationalists made huge inroads into the Austrian controlled civil service and commercial interests, especially in the larger Slovene cities where the German nationals dominated. This effort was made easier by an imperial government now severely weakened by uprisings and the push from the many non-German parts of its multiethnic empire for self rule and independence. Assisting this weakening was the struggle of the Austrians to prevent the unification of Italy, the independence drive of Hungary and the war with the unified Germany of Bismarck in 1866.

---

15   B. Požar, Anastasius Grün in Slovenci, Maribor 1970, pg 270.

THE ENCLAVE

The enclave, however, saw in the erosion of power of the dominating Germanic bourgeoisie in the large cities of Slovenia a danger to their own regional control. After the failure of Frankfurt and until WWI, the Gottscheer made every effort to strengthen their ties to the monarchy. Much help in this came from the Auerspergs who were close to the center of imperial control in Vienna and who, as the largest landowner in the region, had their own private reasons for preserving the enclave. They were the recipients of all the taxes collected there. The Gottscheer became progressively ever more aware of their increasing vulnerability as a weak minority within a strengthening Slovene majority, itself a subordinate minority within Austria. Already in 1854, the Slovene provincial administration succeeded in reassigning two linguistically mixed border areas of the Gottschee district to the fully Slovene districts of Novo Mesto and Črnomelj.

The efforts of the Auerspergs in Vienna on behalf of the Gottscheer did not, however, go unnoticed by the emerging Slovene nationalists and the divisions, planted as seeds by the French during their tenure in Slovenia, began to grow into a progressively increasing polarization throughout the 19th century. This not only between locals at the linguistic boundaries of the enclave, but more importantly, also at the municipal and higher state levels where more and more of the Germanic administrators were being replaced by Slovene under whom the Gottscheer were beginning to receive less and less of the formerly preferential treatment.

The Gottscheer in the enclave reacted to the growing power of Slovene nationalism, the increased settling of Slovene within the enclave and the resulting erosion of their privileged minority status by actively seeking funds to build private schools in the enclave. These schools were to teach the German language, and thereby help to maintain their linguistic identity, the only marker that separated them from their Slovene neighbors. While very limited elementary education was available through the church since 1690, the first German private district school was opened in 1818 and by 1856 another eleven such private schools had opened in private houses. But attendance at these village schools was extremely low, the reasons being the lack of teachers and the tuition charged the parents to cover salaries and supplies.

This changed when the *Educational Reform Act*, decreed by Empress Maria Theresa in 1774, became effective as the Universal Education Law in 1867. This law required school attendance of all youths starting at age six for six years (6-12) throughout the multi ethnic lands of her Empire. The costs were to be borne by the local community.

The Imperial Primary Education Act of 1869, created a uniform basis for the entire system and compulsory school attendance was increased from six years to eight years. (6-14). The control of the schools until then in the hands of the Church was taken over by each land or province of the multi-ethnic monarchy and every local community had to erect and maintain public elementary schools and attendance was required. Privately funded schools were accorded the validity of public primary schools and certified, providing they fulfilled the legal requirements.

But the Act of 1869 brought with it further polarization in ethnically mixed areas throughout the Austrian monarchy including Slovenia. Since the language of instruction was required to be that of the nationality prevalent in the school district and since private schools meeting the legal requirements were allowed, private organizations with a nationalistic agenda, interested in preserving or absorbing ethnic minorities became quickly established. These organizations collected funds for building private schools in what they considered critical areas to promote their nationalistic ideology. In the past the Church had no such nationalistic objectives.

One such organization was the "Deutscher Schulverein" (German School Association). This private association was established in Vienna in May 1880 to assist ethnically mixed areas with starting and operating German education and thereby prevent further erosion or loss of the "German character" of communities, such as Gottschee, by assimilation into the surrounding, non-German majority. This highly nationalistic agenda was in reaction to the dwindling control of the Germanic Austrian monarchy over its many multiethnic parts, Slovenia included.

According to "*Mittheilungen des Deutschen Schulvereins,* # 5, November 1882", pg. 1, the motto of the Schulverein in soliciting funds for its objective was: "we will never accomplish our mission until all social strata of the people take an active part, until those who inhabit the German palaces, as well as those who inhabit German peasant huts, make a claim to their Germanness".[16]

The drive of the Schulverein to collect funds for this objective was highly successful.

The appropriate behavior for prevent assimilation and maintaining Germanness was embodied in the "Ten Commandments of the German Farmer":

---

16 Peter Judson, Class, Ethnicity and Colonial Fantasy at the Margin of the Habsburg Monarchy", Department of History, Swarthmore College, Feb 1993.

1. Thou shall honor thy mother tongue and believe that all Germans are thy brothers.
2. Thou shall read only newspapers sympathetic to the German cause.
3. Thou shall honor Emperor Franz Joseph as your liberator and hang his picture in your living room.
4. Thou shall sign no promissory note.
5. Thou shall marry thy daughter only to a German.
6. Thou shall not go to court over every small issue.
7. Thou shall make certain that thy children diligently attend school.
8. Thou shall not complain about bad times but shall bravely persevere.
9. Thou shall be a good Christian, but never fall into excessive piety.
10. Thou shall join the German School Association.

The Schulverein enabled the establishment of German private schools throughout ethnically mixed areas of the Austrian Monarchy, including Slovenia. In this manner it tried to prevent the German minorities from being absorbed by the non-German population. Conversely, since instruction in these schools was required to be exclusively in German as the condition for continued funding, the "Germanic character" would be maintained and the encroaching non-German minority attending these schools absorbed.

The Slavic minorities throughout the monarchy reacted to the "Deutscher Schulverein" by forming similar organizations of their own. One of them named "Družba sv. Cirila in Metoda" was formed on July 3, 1885.[17] This organization built schools in villages where the ethnic-German population was a minority. Since Austrian Imperial law, via the Provincial School Council, determined that the teaching language in primary education was to be in the majority language of the community, absorption of the minority in such a community was a foregone conclusion. Similar organizations were set up in other ethnically mixed parts of the Monarchy, including Slovenia. But already in the 1840's a member of the circle of Janez Bleiweiss, revered as "the father of the [Slovene] nation", actually writes: "From now on, let no Slovene maiden give her name to a German husband, unless to draw him over to her nationality".[18]

A wealthy Gottscheer merchant living in Prague donated a large sum to the Gottschee branch of the "Deutscher Schulverein" to prevent such "erosion" in the

---

17 T. Ferenc, *Nacistična raznarodovalna politika v Sloveniji v letih 1941-1945*, Maribor, pg 73-79, later: *Nazistična*.

18 *The Habsburg Empire*, pg. 300.

enclave. These funds made possible the erection of nine such schools in the villages of the enclave between 1881 and 1888, including the one in Masern in 1884. (Since Masern was on the very edge of the ethnic enclave and as such considered as an endangered village, it qualified for financial support from the Verein). By 1918, this number of village schools had increased to thirty three. Reporting on this, *"Das Jubiläums Festbuch der Gottscheer 600-Jahresfeier 1930"* (The book of the 600 year jubilee in 1930) states: "So war der Deutsche Schulverein der größte Wohltäter des Gottscheer Landes". (Therefore, the German School Association was the largest benefactor for the Gottscheer land).[19]

The primary target of the Schulverein (and of the already germanized Gottscheer living in the city of Gottschee) was the population of the villages, the place of residence of the bulk of the Gottscheer living in the enclave. Here were virgin people of "German character" who needed help in bringing their "Germanness" in line with the motto of the Schulverein. These were people whose everyday language was the centuries old dialect which, in spite of its German origin, was not understood by a person speaking German. A place where few if any of the villagers spoke German (in Masern more likely Slovene, the language of our neighbors) and where German teachers could not communicate with their pupils.

This led to the establishment, in 1872, of a private secondary school (Untergymnasium) in a private home in Gottschee city, to produce teachers knowing the Gottschee dialect necessary for communicating with their pupils in the village schools. The Austrian Government provided books and funds. To allow these homegrown teachers to teach the first few grades, special permission was obtained from the Ministry of Education in Vienna.[20] In spite of this, teaching German was difficult since the pupils reverted to the dialect as soon as they left the classroom and their parents were of no help since they had little, if any understanding of German themselves. And even in the 1930's, the dialect was used exclusively throughout the villages of the enclave, Masern included.

But not in Gottschee city, a place consisting mainly of shopkeepers and small time merchants who, driven by higher ambition had, over the years, escaped the limitations of village life. German only was spoken here, a status symbol and the sign of achievement that signified their achieved elevated status. Though all understood the Gottschee dialect, it was used only to accommodate county folk in town for business or relatives from the farms, but then only when absolutely necessary. And in this, the town population aided the objectives of the Schulverein in educating

---

19   *Zbornik, pg 358.*

20   *Das Jahrhundertbuch, pg 76.*

THE ENCLAVE

the villagers and force them to "claim their Germanness" by learning the language superior to the dialect now disdained by the Germanic "elite" of the City.

An even greater disdain by this "elite" was directed toward the Slovene, labeled by the Gottscheer leader Dr. Arko in his "Gedächnisschrift" of 1942 as a people "intellectually inferior" to the "German" folks in the Gottscheer villages. For centuries, all being on neighborly terms with those across the ethnic divide, folks who were, in all respects no different, except that they spoke a different tongue.

1918 – 1933

The seeds of alienation between the residents of the enclave and the Slovene, which started to germinate with the rebellion of the Gottscheer against the French in 1809, were helped to grow throughout the 19th century by the rising nationalism of the Slovene. This nationalism reached yet another plateau when the Austrian multi-ethnic monarchy ceased to exist with the signing of the armistice in the Villa Gusti near Padua on November 3, 1918. (The armistice with Germany was signed on November 18 ending WWI.) In anticipation of this, the Kingdom of the Serbs, Croats and Slovene (SHS in short) was agreed upon on October 29, 1918 at the National Council of Habsburg South Slavs meeting in Zagreb during October of 1918. And on December 1, 1918, this new Kingdom came into existence.

The Slovene, who had increasingly resented their "colonial" status under the Austrians (see Peter Štih, pg 62) and particularly after the departure of the French in 1813, asserted their new-found independence in no uncertain ways. They acted by transferring on to the Gottscheer the "minority" status the Austrian monarchy had for so long imposed on them. With this turning, the submissiveness required of the Slovene by the Austrians was now demanded by the Slovene of the Gottscheer in the enclave in spite of much futile protest.

The tide had turned. To the "elite" Gottscheer of the city and in the villagers, only recently awakened to their German roots, this new role as a subservient minority was an unacceptably bitter pill. And the Gottscheer Bote, the bi-weekly newspaper of the enclave, lamented on November 11. 1918:

THE BELLS RING NO MORE

"The humbling of the German people brought painful tears. It is hard to be burdened with such a destiny, but we must not despair over the terrible ruin which has befallen the German nation. This will, however, not take away our hope that after the present Golgotha, there will emerge a new day".

The Gottscheer, until now unblinkingly believing in an Austrian victory had, in spite of their outward optimism, started to prepare for an unspeakable outcome of WWI. Already in 1917 they formed the "Deutscher Volksrat" (German Council), tasked to protect the nationalistic interests of the enclave in case Austria lost the war. Toward this, the Council developed various strategies to be pursued, including annexation by Austria, autonomy as an independent state similar to Monaco or Andorra or an autonomous Republic under the protection of the USA. Nothing came of this and in March of 1919, the new state of the SHS dissolved the Volksrat and nationalized its property.

Nearly a year before the armistice was signed, the Gottscheer had started to lobby for an autonomous state. Already on February 2, 1918, the Gottscheer Bote (renamed to Gottscheer Zeitung in 1919) published a Resolution, signed by ten priests and the director of a school district, in which they proclaimed:
1. their love for and faith in the beloved Austria,
2. as utopian and unattainable the goal of statehood to which the Slovene aspire,
3. their rejection to be included into a possible Yugoslav state,
4. their fear that the districts and parishes of Gottschee would lose their German identity,
5. their right for self-determination and autonomy for the 24,000 inhabitants of Gottschee.

A second Resolution was published in the Gottscheer Bote on October 19, 1918, responding to Anton Korošec the head of the National Council of Habsburg South Slavs meeting in Zagreb during October of 1918. Korošec had guaranteed all foreign language minorities in Slovenia, all rights to national, cultural, economic and social-development.

The Gottscheer labeled these promises as "honorable and sincere but it is not possible to build a solid future on such promises". The only reliable assurance to maintain such rights would be "annexation to the Germanic-Austrian state, even if this would result in geographically cumbersome and difficult obstacles".[21]

On November 11, 1918, the Gottscheer Bote wrote: "Gottschee has, in number of inhabitants and geographic size, the undeniable right to self-determination and

---

21 *Gottscheer Bote, October 19, 1918*

autonomy. This is fact and we hope that our question will be resolved at the peace conference. It is right and proper that in the interim there exists in Gottschee the status quo". The signers concluded with a reminder that the Gottschee enclave, being larger than Monaco, San Marino and Lichtenstein is self sufficient and therefore entitled to full autonomy.

On November 18, 1918, Gottscheer municipalities sent to the Paris Peace Conference and the government of the SHS a request for independence in which they outlined their historical role, the administration, number and distribution of inhabitants of the enclave and repeated the comparison to the smallest principalities in Europe. They claimed that the enclave was a - "…vollkommen geschlossene Siedlung…" – (a totally enclosed settlement) of 20,161 inhabitants in spite of the fact that the census of October 1918 showed that 5,502 (27% of the total) of them were Slovene.[22] And they concluded with certainty that an independent Gottschee was capable of being self-sufficient.[23] The SHS government rejected the request partly because it was submitted in the no longer official German language.

Yet another Gottscheer proposal for autonomy foresaw an independent republic under the patronage of the USA. The proposal was presented to the Paris Peace Conference on behalf of the Gottscheer by the Italian delegation. It was also submitted to the American commission in Vienna. Here also, the Gottscheer requested a status quo ante until the question was resolved.

Within the enclave, however, the long wait for autonomy and self-determination to be granted by either the Paris Peace Conference or the American Government, produced the illusion of a status quo, never agreed to by the state of SHS. In line with this, the newspaper Slovenec on February 8, 1919 reported the following:

"And in January 1919, the city of Gottschee elected a new City Council composed of former Austrian soldiers, a large number of young people as well as members of the German Council. In this 'younger' council, the dominant role had an attorney [Dr. Hans Arko] destined to be the future Minister President of the Gottschee Republic. At the meetings, the new SHS state was severely criticized. The highlight was the attendance of Prince Auersperg [January 25 & 26] who, with aristocratic gesture, stated that all will be as they wished. As a result, there was jubilation throughout the enclave; if the prince promised, so shall it be. And the Slovene will soon be gone.

"Older and wiser moderates advocated a less confrontational approach, however, the impulsive and immature youth and former Austrian officers continued to

---

22   Wanda Trdan; *Življenje Kočevskih Nemcev med 1850-1918*, pg 95.

23   *Gottscheer Bote*, Dec. 4, 1918

malign, threaten and instigate against the new rule. But never mind; soon we will have our own State, our own currency, etc. and all will be well."

Other newspapers also reported extensively on this, with the result that the Slovene population turned even more against the Gottscheer. The weekly *Naprej*, on June 10, 1919 defined as:

".. absurd the writing in the *Gottscheer Bote* predicting an independent autonomous state. The Slovenes are not alone in characterizing the Gottscheer requests, demands and resolutions as not only unrealistic, but also utopian".

Sure enough, events did not develop according to the expectations of the Gottscheer and the promise of the Prince. Their request for annexation by Austria was ignored in Vienna; it had its own problems to deal with and the American commission there, to which the request for an independent Gottschee republic had been sent, did not respond.

At the peace conference in St. Germain where the Austrian issue was debated, the Gottscheer question did not even appear on the agenda. The conference that started on January 12, 1919, ended one year later on January 20, 1920 without the results promised by Prince Auersperg. The enclave of Gottschee now formally re-named Kočevje, irrevocably became part of the Kingdom of SHS, a state now increasingly more un-accommodating to this troublesome minority. And by struggling against the new reality, the Gottscheer became increasingly more deeply immersed in the rising tide of radical German nationalism which, in the not so distant future, was to use them as pawns and make them its victim.

While guaranteeing all minorities ethnic, cultural, economic and social-development rights, the State decreed that Slovene was now the official language to be used in official documents, records, the mails, and in all interactions with officials of the new administration. Those who did not speak Slovene, and this meant most of the inhabitants of the enclave, required a translator in all their dealings with municipalities, the provincial government and the State. Government functionaries who could not speak the language were discharged and replaced with Slovene candidates. Some of those discharged were promised re-employment providing that within one year they had learned Slovene. The Gottscheer branch of the Schulverein was dissolved; its property nationalized.

On November 16, 1918, Slovene was mandated to be the language of instruction in elementary schools. Teachers in the enclave had to submit to a qualifying State examination which showed that the majority did not know Slovene and were therefore replaced or pensioned off.

This had little effect throughout Slovenia where (as before under the Imperial Act of 1869) elementary instruction in grades one to three now continued in the language of the ethnic majority in the school district. And if there was a sufficient number of pupils of German nationality in the district, separate departments were required to teach the minority language in separate classrooms. In Kočevje city, such minority departments teaching German were established in 1919 reflecting the decreasing number of Gottscheer students in that district.

This changed with the School Decree of 25 November 1927. The Decree, Zl. 79.413, issued by the Minister of Education Dr. Kumanudi, ordered the following:

1. The German school child will, in the first four years, be instructed in German. However, in the third year and beyond, Slovene will be taught for four hours per week as a subject.

2. When the child reaches the higher levels (five to eight years), all subjects must be taught in Slovene.

3. All German schools whose pupils have completed the fifth or sixth grades in German must have, without exception, recovery instructions in Slovene for the two missed years. Three hours per week must be set aside for this purpose. Recovery instructions should be in half hour increments alternating between Slovene and German.

Secondary education, however, was mandated to be exclusively in Slovene already in 1920. Teachers who were not able (due to not knowing Slovene) or willing to comply would not be licensed and were replaced. Also, the eight grades of the gymnasium in Gottschee city were reduced to four due to a shortage of pupils, forcing all those wishing to continue to do so in Ljubljana.

And in January 1935 the Decree issued by the Ministry of Education dictated that all education be conducted in the applicable language, in our case the language of the Slovene.

With this ended German secondary education in the enclave which started in 1872. By contrast, the first Slovene (private) secondary school in Ljubljana (long demanded from the monarchy) was allowed by Austrian authorities only in 1905. And the first Slovene university was established there only after Slovenia became part of the SHS Kingdom in 1919.

THE BELLS RING NO MORE

This severely distressed the Gottschee "elite" that clung to the belief that higher education and proficiency in German would continue to provide for them an elevated status and assure their survival as Germans stranded in a sea of Slovene. They therefore challenged the new requirements and continued to operate private schools teaching German. The new state reacted by closing or nationalizing all private Gottscheer institutions believed to be circumventing the policies of the new administration.

Dr. Hans Arko, the former Gottscheer leader, reports on this in his memoirs written in 1942. "All children whose family name had a Slovene sounding name were forced into purely Slovene classes. [The Slovene believed these were Slovenes who had been Germanized.] The number of children in German classes became progressively smaller and ultimately shrank to zero. The children entered school as calves and left it as oxen. A child could no longer read or write in German". [24]

Arko, a Gottscheer attorney living in Gottschee city, provides much insight into the politics of Gottscheer-German nationalism after WWI. Instead of moving to Austria after 1918 like so many non-Slovene speaking teachers, municipal employees and other professionals, he opted to stay and learn the Slovene language claiming to be the only one remaining who could represent the nationalistic aspirations of the Gottscheer of the enclave in their contacts with the new government. (According to H. Grothe: "The only academically educated that remained were two lawyers and two physicians").

In his memoir, Arko states his belief that: "The Gottscheer have always been conscious of their Germanness, being intellectually far superior to the Slovene". (A rather dubious claim in view of the fact that the Gottscheer, in contrast to the Slovene, throughout the centuries produced no significant writers, poets, scientists or other similar intellectuals). But the remark indicates that the racial superiority concepts, the leitmotiv of Adolf Hitler, had taken root in the enclave.

Arko reflects on the activities of the Schulverein and Südmark before and during WWI, all committed to promoting their nationalistic objectives via various "cultural" associations to prevent the "erosion" or loss of the "German character" of the [Gottscheer] communities.

---

24   *Gedächnisschrift, pg 7*

After WWI, the various Gottscheer "cultural" associations, supported before and during WWI by the Schulverein, continued with their established objectives to maintain the "German character" of the Gottscheer. But the now independent Slovene state, mindful that the basic mission of these associations was to promote German nationalistic agenda, dissolved the Schulverein and nationalized its properties in 1919. And according to Arko, such activities were allowed to resume only after 1924 since until then, the Gottscheer-Germans had no representation in Parliament.

All efforts toward obtaining independence from the Slovene having failed and receiving no further support from the outside, the Gottscheer (again according to Arko) realized that they should now pay attention to their new state. And to have a united front in representing the Gottscheer of the enclave, Arko and other leaders formed, in 1919, the "Gottscheer Bauernpartei". (Gottscheer Farmer Party). This party adopted a less confrontational approach by proclaiming, at least officially: "Just as we were loyal subjects of the Habsburg monarchy, we wish to be faithful citizens of Yugoslavia". (*Slovenec*, 3/2/1919). This led to the often used, but for the Slovene unconvincing slogan of the Gottscheer: "Staatstreu und Volkstreu". (Loyal to the State and true to our [German] nationality.).

The first enclave-wide elections were held in 1924 with the objective of gaining a seat in the Yugoslav parliament. This failed since only 5,000 of the 6,000 required votes were cast for this objective.

In the village districts, the leadership was captured by the Gottscheer; in the city however, the "Bauernpartei" captured only ten of the 24 seats on the City Council. According to Arko, this defeat was due to the heavy influx of Slovene in the six years since 1918. He also stated that work on this Council: "was for the German representatives a "martyrdom" since their proposals, being written in the German language, were never included in an agenda". (The administrative language of the City Council now being Slovene). Arko was a member of this Council until 1938, except for the period between 1931-1933.

Further according to Arko: "the Gottscheer could never muster a sufficient number of votes to elect their own representative to the Parliament. However, in elections after 1924, the Gottscheer prevailed with many of their wishes but only because they compromised and cooperated with one of the local Slovene parties. And when, in 1929, the dictatorship of the Kingdom of Yugoslavia replaced the federal Kingdom of the SHS and all political parties based on narrow nationalistic objectives were dissolved (including the "Bauernpartei"), the Gottscheer joined the newly formed Yugoslav State Party. Local branches of this party were formed also in the enclave in which the Gottscheer were fairly represented".

In 1928, the Reverend Josef Eppich, the publisher of the Gottscheer Zeitung which replaced the Gottscheer Bote in 1919, was elected as the representative for the Gottschee district and Arko his deputy. The two remained the leaders of the enclave until the start of 1939. The Gottscheer population, mainly via Eppich and his deputy, had sufficient weight to negotiate with other candidates favorably on matters related to their mutual interests. And when in 1930, the Slovene Minister Ivan Pucelj was appointed Chairman of the Commission for District Affairs, Arko became his deputy. Pucelj was born in the enclave, spoke the Gottscheer dialect and effectively supported the cultural rights of the Gottscheer.

It was clear that the Gottscheer were adjusting to their lot as a minority in the new state and that the increasing cooperation and compromise produced a relatively stable and improving environment between the two sides. As a result, the Slovene allowed the re-emergence of many of the cultural associations dissolved in 1919 and in 1935 there were again fourteen elementary schools teaching German.

In his memoir, Dr. Arko states that the authorities allowed, after 1924, the re-establishment of the: "Turnverein, Gesangverein, Leserverein, Theaterverein, Kindergartenverein, u.s.w." Arko takes pride in having participated as a leader in all of them and being elected as their "Honored Member". He particularly singles out the Gesangverein (singing association) of which he had become the Choir Master in 1923 and writes: "This association had more of a political than cultural importance". The Gesangverein traveled extensively through the villages and thereby "the sung word was also the carrier for our propaganda and as a singing group, it was a good cover vis-à-vis the authorities". And after each performance, Arko urged the assembled villagers to remain faithful to their German roots.

A new horizon had opened for the Gottscheer in 1920 when the Schwäbisch-German Kulturbund was formed in Novo Mesto and Arko was elected to represent the Gottscheer in the enclave. The Kulturbund claimed it was a cultural umbrella organization for ethnic Germans in the Yugoslav Kingdom, but in reality it was a replacement for the former Schulverein to again promote German nationalism. In 1922, a local branch of the Kulturbund was established in Gottschee city and Arko was elected Chairman. At the first membership meeting there was great enthusiasm because "the Kulturbund was seen as the liberator".[25] But the Gottschee branch was dissolved by the Slovene authorities after only eight days since at this meeting "there surfaced political tendencies forbidden by the statutes".[26] In 1928, the ban on the Kulturbund was removed and Arko again became the Chairman of the Gottschee branch. And in 1929, sub-branches were formed in eighteen villages, each with its own youth group under the coordinating youth leader in Gottschee city. To demonstrate results, Arko further writes:

"At a meeting of the Sport Association in 1932 in Gottschee city, 800 youths assembled to demonstrate their training and discipline. ... and in the villages, information meetings were held on evenings and weekends in which German nationalism and the superiority of the German race was explained. News from the new Germany was heard live on radios, obtained by Arko as gifts from the Reich". The radio in the Jaklitsch tavern in Grčarice/Masern was one of them.

1933 – 1941

In 1933, Hitler became Chancellor of the Third Reich. The prediction in the Gottscheer Bote, of November 11, 1918 that ".... after the present Golgotha, there will emerge a new day", had come to pass.

To the Gottscheer as well as millions of ethnic Germans throughout Europe, this re-"emergence" brought great pride. It also produced admiration for its initial accomplishments from non-Germans everywhere. The admirers did not know that this aggressive and radical nationalism, based on racial supremacy was, in only a few short years, going to bring great tragedy to the world, disaster to most ethnic Germans in Europe and the end of the Gottscheer as an ethnic group in the winter of 1941/42.

In his memoirs, Arko states that the Gottscheer were early supporters of National-Socialism. He admits that he became a National-Socialist in 1927 and that he persuaded many a Gottscheer to adopt this new "Weltanschauung". He also explains that he personally made it possible for Gottscheer to again peddle wares in the Reich after 1933, a place where they learned this new form of German nationalism and on returning home spread it throughout the enclave. While the peddling was officially done to earn much needed monies, Arko states that the primary benefit

---

25   *Gedächnisschrift.*

26   *ibid.*

was the importing of National-Socialism into Gottschee. (Such peddling was first initiated by Emperor Frederick III in 1492 to allow all residents of the enclave, Gottscheer as well as Slovene, to recover from the damages inflicted by the Turks).

Arko continues: "Under the cover of peddling, 25 to 30 young farmers were sent annually to the Reich where they gathered in a camp during the winter months for training in Nazi ideology. The first such peddlers were sent to the Reich in 1933 and continued in the years 1934, 1935 and 1936". After 1936, passports to allow peddling were no longer issued by the Slovene authorities after they realized that more than just money was being brought back to the enclave.

In spite of the growing allegiance to the Reich, the Gottscheer under Dr. Hans Arko and the Reverend Josef Eppich claimed to remain loyal to the Yugoslav State and loyal to their German nationality. "Staatstreu und Volkstreu". All the while passively rejoicing in the new German nationalism which, according to the Gottscheer Bote of 1918 had been humbled and reduced to "painful tears" but now had reappeared in a "new day", if however in another and new form.

With this often repeated slogan, "Staatstreu und Volkstreu", the Gottscheer merely paid lip service to the Slovene and the State in which they lived. A State which they claimed had been attempting to destroy their nationality through assimilation. Arko and Eppich had been resisting this perceived attempt within all the legal means available to them by using parliamentary methods. They had been quite successful in this with the help of Ivan Pucelj, the Chairman for District Affairs who actively supported the cultural rights of the Gottscheer.

But it was this passive nationalism of Arko and Eppich, tolerated to some extent by the Slovene authorities, which ultimately brought about their end as leaders of the Gottscheer. The passive approach to accomplish their objectives within the legal system of the State did not suit a "secret student group" of young Gottscheer, who responded to the courting from the Reich in a much more radical way.

This group, which grew up in the confrontational environment after WWI and came of age in the late 1920's, became radical supporters of National-Socialism, the new "Weltanschauung" so aptly introduced into the enclave by Arko. They interpreted the "Staatstreu" part of the slogan "Staatstreu und Volkstreu" as loyalty to the Third Reich and not loyalty to the nation they lived in. This challenge to the State and their actions after 1933 put them on a divergent course with the leadership of Arko and Eppich who were pursuing their objectives in a moderate manner within parliamentary rules. In this Arko and Eppich had overwhelming support from the clerics, the only other intelligentsia that had remained in the enclave.

THE ENCLAVE

The charismatic leader of this secret group was Wilhelm Lampeter, born on January 22, 1916. In his "Die Gottscheer Volksgruppe 1930-1942" written in 1942, he states that:

"In National-Socialism, which reached the remote Gottschee only after its ascendance to power in 1933, the youth discovered its true life's purpose, the recognized signpost to their aspirations and willingness to act." [27]

Lampeter dismisses the contribution of Dr Arko as being the one who brought this new "Weltanschauung" into the enclave even before 1933. And by 1938, years before Lampeter wrote these lines, Arko and his supporters had become his determined adversaries in his struggle for control over the enclave.

The fervor of the youth group was aptly exploited after 1934, when the first wave of students from the Reich appeared in the enclave. The visitors from the Reich sponsored and conducted work and training camps in which they introduced to the Gottscheer youth a "self-help" plan while simultaneously propagating Nazi ideology. The "self help plan" appealed to the youth because it promised to lift the enclave out of its then current economic depression. The plan was developed specifically for the Gottscheer by the VDA, an organization that existed in Germany before 1933 as "Verein für das Deutschtum im Ausland". (Association for German nationals abroad). After 1933, it continued in the Reich as "Volksbund für das Deutschtum im Ausland" (Union for German nationals outside the boundaries of the Reich). This organization dealt with all matters related to ethnic Germans abroad. Such economic guidance could effortlessly be integrated into the existing youth movements that had been developed and promoted by Dr. Arko without, at least initially, exposing the underlying broader objectives of the VDA to the Slovene authorities. (The VDA was absorbed in October 1939 by the VoMi, Volksdeutsche Mittelstelle, an SS organization headquartered in Berlin. It was founded in 1937 and, under SS-Obergruppenführer Werner Lorenz, was to be in charge of all ethnic Germans living outside Germany.)

In 1935, the VDA sent in another student group to conduct further training. The concept of "self-help" promoted via the underlying ideology of National-Socialism was enthusiastically accepted and the result of this training brought most of the Gottscheer youth into the orbit of the Reich.

The relatively passive indoctrination under the cover of the "self-help" program, however, did not satisfy the more aggressive leadership in the new Germany bent on direct confrontation. The effort of the VDA was outdone by the active intervention of Hitler Youth groups sent into the enclave by the Reich. Fritz Berthold, the

---

27   W. Lampeter, *Die Gottscheer Volksgruppe 1939-1942*, later: *Die Gottscheer Volksgruppe.*

VDA official responsible for "Volksdeutsche Süd" who was in the enclave in August 1935, writes in his report:

"The Gottschee area this season was flooded with approximately 300 youthful hikers dressed in military clothing who passed through the region with their flying banners constantly singing political fighting songs. This produced great agitation in Slovene circles and can only lead to a worsening for the Gottscheer Germans".[28]

H.H.Frensing writes: "The Gottscheer youth, now firmly behind Lampeter, actively participated in all these events. The Slovene public and nationalistic organizations took notice of these activities and had begun to react. The boiling point was reached when the Gottscheer opened its first youth and culture club in Sredna Vas (Mitterdorf). Slovene students and other youths arrived from as far as Ljubljana to disrupt the celebration and it came to a wild brawl. However, this was only a telling symptom of an increasingly more poisoned climate between the Gottscheer and the Slovene".[29]

The Slovene authorities reacted by resorting to increasingly more repressive measures which ultimately resulted in the dissolution of the village chapters of the Kulturbund in 1937. The given reason was that the chapters "held political seminars and sang irredentist songs such as the Horst Wessel song, Heiliges Deutschland and other similar songs imported from the Reich".

Frensing on page 18 quotes a Slovene intellectual: "The organizations of the Kulturbund were prosecuted because they were identified by the authorities as agitation cells. No self-assured state could continue to tolerate such activity.... The two emissaries of the Reich...[Dick and Neunteufel].... have, for many months, conducted an activity which no self-respecting state could tolerate for any duration."

In the following years until 1938, the Gottscheer youth, under the leadership of Lampeter, solidified its relationship with the Reich. This was done through extensive indoctrination and training in the Reich and clandestinely in special training camps at home. Arko and Lampeter each report on this in their memoirs written in 1942, albeit each with their own perspective. Arko viewed these activities in the context of "Staatstreu und Volkstreu", whereas to Lampeter and his adherents, the loyalty part in both terms of this slogan meant loyalty to the Third Reich. Their relationship to the Slovene was fully in line with the objectives of the purposefully

---

28   D. Bieber, Nacisem in Nemci v Jugoslaviji. 1933-1941. Ljubljana 1966, pg. 111.

29   H.H. Frensing, Die Umsiedlung der Gottscheer Deutschen. Das Ende einer süddeutschen Volksgruppe, München 1970, pg. 17, later: Die Umsiedlung.

confrontational politics demanded by National-Socialism of ethnic Germans living in Slavic lands.

The 'old leadership' tried, in desperate attempts, including direct appeals to the prime minister of Yugoslavia and Austrian government officials, to cool down the inflamed nationalistic passions of the Slovene and Gottscheer and bring about a compromise. And when in March 1938 the "Anschluss" of the republic of Austria to the Third Reich took the national passions of the Slovene and their ethnic Germans to new heights, all chances toward a compromise came to an end.

Frensing, in his chapter "The failed attempts of the old leadership.." describes their efforts in detail and encapsulates the primary points:

"The Reverend Josef Eppich, a Christian-Socialist and Dr. H. Arko who embodied the national-liberal tradition of the Gottscheer, no longer satisfied the demands of National-Socialism regarding ethnic Germans. In their attempts for moderation, they lost the confidence of the now radicalized youth. To them, the slogan "Staatstreu und Volkstreu" had become obsolete. And since this was obvious to the Slovene, they were not inclined to grant further concessions".

Against this background, the now twenty two year old Wilhelm Lampeter and his inner circle, who called themselves the "Renewers" convinced the authorities of the Reich to force Arko and Eppich to resign. In November 1938 Arko was notified by the VoMi in Berlin, that he was relieved of his leadership role. Arko publicly resigned and so did Eppich on 1. January 1939. He handed the editorship of the Gottscheer Zeitung (GZ) to Herbert Erker, an intimate and inner circle member of Lampeter's VolksGruppenLeitung, the VGL.

Frensing states that: "in spite of the change of leaders in the enclave, it did not come to a public split between the 'young' and the 'old' in the enclave". This is borne out by Arko in his reflections of 1942, when he states that he continued to support the various organizations that he developed and nurtured over the years, and claims that as a result: "the Gesangverein accomplished its objectives fully and had it not been in existence, no Gottscheer would have agreed to resettle" in 1941.

The ouster of Arko and Eppich as leaders of the Gottscheer at the beginning of 1939 is in line with Hitler's comments to an intimate circle of representatives of ethnic Germans in 1934. Frensing in *Die Umsiedlung*, on page 21, quotes H. Rauschning, who reports on this in *"Conversations with Hitler"*:

"Their obedience [ethnic German leaders abroad] is the fruit of their confidence in me. Due to this, I can not tolerate in our circles any representatives of the old parliamentarian ways. These gentlemen should resign. Should they not voluntarily clear their place, you must remove them by any possible means. The politics concerning the German groups abroad will no longer be debated and considered, but will be defined by myself, and in my absence by my party colleague Hess."

After the assumption of control of the Gottscheer by the 'young' leadership, the term "Staatstreu" toward Yugoslavia, was replaced by "loyalty to the Third Reich". And, according to Frensing, "from this point on the relationship toward the Slovene people was no longer one of compromise but one of confrontation".

The parliamentarian ways of Arko and Eppich, honorable men who pursued the interests of their constituents within the laws of the State with much success, were now replaced by the totalitarian rule of the "young", marching to the drumbeat of the dictatorship of the Reich. The ways of Arko and Eppich had produced, especially during the mid and later 20's, a constant stream of improving relations with the new state. A state which was well underway to accommodate the wishes of the minority in the enclave by allowing the reestablishment of cultural associations, cultural activities and the renewed teaching of German, albeit as a secondary language.

This was now no longer likely.

After assumption of power, the "Renewers" called themselves the Volks Gruppen Leitung, (Ethnic Group Leadership), or VGL for short. And during 1939, '40 and '41, the VGL, consisting of seven inner circle members, each of them extensively trained in the Reich, converted the political structure of the enclave from an elective body to a clandestine mini-state. It was formalized on May 1, 1941 and based on the totalitarian leadership concept of the Reich. Until then, the legitimate state received lip service only when and where absolutely unavoidable.

Each of the seven had a unique ministerial type function, but their ideological leader was Wilhelm Lampeter, in 1939 all of twenty three years old. Josef Schober, an unknown older man, was given the title of Group Leader because Lampeter wanted a "much older man as a front".[30] The thirty three year old Herbert Erker, (b. 17/11/1908) one of the inner members became the editor of their main propaganda organ, the weekly Gottscheer Zeitung, until now under the Reverend Josef Eppich. Erker's assistant was Ludwig Kren, born 12/12/1920.

After the dismissal of Arko and Eppich, Josef Schober became also the head of the Gottschee branch of the Kulturbund which was re-established in 1939 after having been dissolved, together with the local groups of the villages, in 1937. (When

---

30   *Das Jahrhundertbuch, pg 118*

Milan Stojadinovič was replaced as Prime Minister of Yugoslavia by Dragiša Cvetkovič on February 5, 1939, the Kulturbund was again allowed in Yugoslavia).

Lampeter, as Mannschaft-Führer, (militia leader) took personal charge of the twenty five village groups of the Kulturbund that were formed in the villages after 1928 and which after being outlawed in 1937, had continued under the cover of the village fire brigades. In September 1939 the VGL formed the "Mannschaft"; disciplined militia units, dressed and trained in line with the SA organization in the Reich. All members of the Kulturbund between twenty one and fifty were required to be part of such a unit called a Sturm under their local Sturmführer trained by Lampeter and his group in a special school. There were twenty five such Sturms in the enclave, each identified by a number. Masern was Sturm 13 and its Führer was Franz Jaklitsch, the keeper of the tavern on the square.

The Gottscheer Zeitung, in its July 24, 1941 issue, solidified the obligation of the Sturm trooper:

"For each comrade, starting with the Mannschaft-Führer to the last Sturm man there exist three examples. The soldier as expression of the defense capability of the nation, the comrade in the SA or SS formation as the expression of a political self-consciousness and combat willingness of the nation and the worker who with brow and fist stands behind plow and desk, anvil and lathe as the expression of the social justice of the nation".

A sub-unit of each Sturm was the youth of the village. The boys unit was divided into two age groups, 7-13 and 14-21, each dressed in a uniform based on that of the Hitler Youth in the Reich and each age group having its own leader. Rigorous training prepared them for entering a Sturm as a fully trained Sturm trooper on reaching 21 years of age. The girls were organized in a similar manner. Their training in military support functions was under Maria Röthel, herself trained in the Reich. All four youth groups were under the Jugendführer Richard Lackner, (b. 8/24/1919) a member of the inner leadership circle and in 1939 twenty years old.

Training included all common military exercises used to train recruits. Clandestinely, each Sturm trooper was also instructed in the use of a rifle. The few that were available were passed on to the next Sturm after all men in a Sturm were trained. And during evenings, informational meetings, initiated originally by Arko but now reinvigorated with greater enthusiasm by the VGL, dealt with indoctrinating the mind in Nazi ideology.

Formation exercises were conducted on the village square and marching through the villages while singing the songs of the Reich. These exercises, held mostly on Sundays, were scheduled to coincide with the timing of religious services. This was the initial challenge to the clergy that still had some control over their parishioners and who let it be known that they saw in this new form of German nationalism a danger to the enclave and its culture. These were the same priests who after the end of WW I, had lobbied for an independent enclave state.

It was also an open challenge to the Slovene authorities who tried, if not very successfully, to stop these illegal activities. But the VGL would not be deterred from publicly confronting the Slovene, all of which led to a progressively increasing hostility and hatred between the two sides. Totally committed to the Nazi cause, their actions now were backed up by the full power of the Third Reich, a state that encouraged, promoted and supported confrontation for its own political purposes not only in Slovenia but also in other states throughout Eastern Europe that contained pockets of ethnic Germans.

The youth, which since 1933 had been brought fully into the orbit of National-Socialism and after 1938 organized as the cadre of a clandestine mini-state, were, at the beginning of 1941, in total control of the Germans in the enclave. The openly confrontational attitude toward their legitimate state had been increasingly emboldened by the string of successes of the Reich which included:

1. the re-occupation of the Rhineland in July 1936,
2. the "Anschluss" of Austria in March 1938,
2. the takeover of the Sudetenland in October 1938,
4. the occupation of the remainder of Czechoslovakia on March 15, 1939,
5. the rapid takeover of Poland starting on September 1, 1939, all resistance ending on October 6, 1939,
6. the invasion of Belgium, the Netherlands, Luxemburg and France, on May 10, 1940.

The conquest of all of Western Europe (except England) was completed on June 25, 1940. This impressive list was complemented by other facts that even further emboldened the VGL.

a. The Reich and the USSR sign a non aggression pact on August 23, 1939,
b. Norway, Portugal and Sweden proclaim their neutrality on September 1, 1939,
c. Spain, Ireland and the USA proclaim their neutrality on September 3, 1939,
d. The Reich invades Denmark and Norway on April 8, 1940,
e. Greece concludes armistice with the Reich on April 23, 1940,
f. The Axis, the Tripartite Pact – Germany, Italy and Japan formed on September 27, 1940,
g. Hungary and Romania join Axis on November 20, 1940,
h. Bulgaria joins Axis on March 1, 1941.

THE ENCLAVE

Of particular significance to the VGL were the actions against Czechoslovakia and Poland which were, according to then prevalent Nazi propaganda, occupied to free the ethnic Germans living there from oppression by the Slavic population. From October 1939 forward the VGL had, therefore, few restraints on its confrontational activities against the Slovene population and their state, and hoped that the resulting repressive action would produce an intervention by the Reich. In line with this Martin Sturm, a member of the VGL, sent on April 13, 1939, a telegram directly to Hitler requesting that the enclave be annexed to the Reich in the event Yugoslavia ceased to exist. [31]

In addition to the VGL, all the ethnic Germans of Yugoslavia began to clamor for annexation, now only a short distance away from the annexed Austria, an independent nation since 1273, but one that ceased to exist in March 1938 with its "Anschluss" to the Reich. (In 1941, the ethnic German population throughout Yugoslavia was approximately 700,000, according to *Projekat Rastko* by Carl Kosta Savich, 2001. This in contrast to a total population of 15.4 million.)

The actions of the Reich against Czechoslovakia and Poland and their consequences did also not go unnoticed by the Yugoslav government, itself being accused by the Reich of mistreating its German minority. Aware that the Nazis had used the excuse of ethnic suppression to invade Czechoslovakia, the new government of Prime Minister Cvetkovič, in power since February 5, 1939, tried to avoid open confrontation with ethnic Germans of which the Germans of the Gottschee enclave were only a small but vocal and aggressive part. Finding itself vulnerable, his government removed the ban of the Kulturbund in the fall of 1939, after the German invasion of Poland, lest Yugoslavia be accused of oppressing and harassing its ethnic German population and invite similar reaction from the Reich.

In a speech to the Reichstag on Oct. 6, 1939 to celebrate the victory in occupying Poland, Hitler gives the reasons for the invasion and division of Poland between the Reich and the USRR. Among his reasons, the following stand out and are quoted below:

".... minorities living in that country had to suffer what amounted to a reign of terror. I do not consider it my task to speak for of the fate of the Ukrainians, or

---

31   *Nacistična, pg 97.*

White Russian population, whose interests now lie in the hands of Russia. However, I do feel it my duty to speak of the fate of those helpless thousands of Germans who carried on the tradition of those who first brought culture to that country centuries ago and whom the Poles now began to oppress and drive out. Since March 1939, they had been victims of truly satanic terrorization. How many of them had been abducted and where they are cannot be stated even today.

"Villages with hundreds of German inhabitants are now left without men because they all have been killed. In others, women were violated and murdered, girls and children outraged and killed. Already in 1598 an Englishman - Sir George Carew - wrote in his diplomatic reports to the English Government that the outstanding features of Polish character were cruelty and lack of moral restraint. Since that time this cruelty has not changed. Just as tens of thousands of Germans were slaughtered and sadistically tormented to death, so German soldiers captured in fighting were tortured and massacred.

"The warning to suspend or at least to take steps against the unceasing cases of murder, ill treatment and torture of German nationals in Poland had the effect of increasing these atrocities and of calling for more bloodthirsty harangues and provocative speeches from the Polish local administrative officials and military authorities".

In the same speech he also announces his intention to "ingather" the ethnic Germans of Europe.

"The aims and tasks which emerge from the collapse of the Polish State, insofar as the German sphere of interest is concerned, are roughly as follows:

"1. Demarcation of the boundary for the Reich, which will do justice to historical, ethnographical and economic facts.

"2. Pacification of the whole territory by restoring a tolerable measure of peace and order.

"3. Absolute guarantees of security not only as far as Reich territory is concerned but for the entire sphere of interest.

"4. Re-establishment and reorganization of economic life and of trade and transport, involving development of culture and civilization.

"5. The most important task, however, is to establish a new order of ethnographic conditions, that is to say, resettlement of nationalities in such a manner that the process ultimately results in the obtaining of better dividing lines than is the case at present.

"In this sense, however, it is not a case of the problem being restricted to this particular sphere, but of a task with far wider implications for the east and south of Europe which are to a large extent filled with splinters of the German nationality, whose existence they cannot maintain. In their very existence lie the reason and cause for continual international disturbances. In this age of the principle of nationalities and of racial ideals, it is utopian to believe that members of a highly developed people can be assimilated without trouble".

And on the following day, October 7, 1939, Hitler solidifies paragraph 5 of his speech in a decree and appoints Reichsführer-SS Heinrich Himmler to be in charge of an organization dealing with the reordering of the ethnographic conditions. Himmler becomes "Reichskommissar für die Festigung des Deutschen Volkstums", (Reich's Commissioner for the Solidification of the German Nation), RKFDV for short. Subsequently in mid October 1939, there emerges Himmler's "Dienststelle", a multi-branched organization whose function it was to deal with all of the many facets of Hitler's directive.

"In the ethnic German groups of Eastern Europe, especially among the large German minorities in Yugoslavia, Hitler's speech of October 6, 1939 produced great unease. The German embassy in Belgrade found it necessary to calm the Volksdeutsche in Yugoslavia via the *'Deutsches Volksblatt'*, the publication serving the ethnic Germans, saying that the resettlement action for Yugoslavia is not a topic". [32]

The Gottscheer VGL however, took the topic to the German consul in Ljubljana on November 6, 1939. Frensing, on page 25 reports: "To start with, they announced their subordination. Even with regard to a re-settlement, the interest of the ethnic group must stand behind the interest of the entire German nation".

With total self-confidence, they do this on their own, without having in any way a mandate from the people they were representing and whom they had not consulted.

On April 6, 1941, the armies of the Third Reich and those of Mussolini's Italy invade Yugoslavia and 12 days later, on April 18, Yugoslavia ceased to exist as a nation.

After the destruction of Yugoslavia, Hitler ordered the country to be reduced down to "old Serbia" and allocated the adjacent parts to neighboring countries according to their demands. Furthermore, at the Vienna conference on April 18-20, 1941, in the presence of Count Ciano, the Italian Minister of Foreign Affairs, Hitler

---

32 *Die Umsiedlung*, pg 25.

set the border between Germany and Italy. Germany relinquished part of Slovenia to Italy including the Gottschee enclave, to great disillusionment of its inhabitants.

The Germans of the enclave were, however, happy to be freed from a state which, as they claimed had during its twenty three years of existence, denied them their nationality and tried to assimilate them.

The decision to resettle the Gottscheer was communicated to Lampeter by Himmler on April 20, 1941 and verified to him personally by Adolf Hitler at the Maribor meeting on April 26, 1941. Lampeter was also told that the Gottscheer would be settled on the German side of the annexed Slovenia. A place from which 37,000 Slovene were to be removed to make room for the "ingathered"; the new citizens of the Third Reich.

The destiny of the Gottscheer as an ethnic group had been decreed.

The events leading up to invasion were in line with Hitler's objectives for total control of Europe. His initial attempt was to neutralize Yugoslavia by bringing it into the Tripartite Pact. On March 4-5, Prince Paul the Regent of Yugoslavia was summoned in great secrecy to the Berghof by the Führer, to discuss the pact. And on March 25, the Prime Minister Dragiša Cvetkovič and Foreign Minister Aleksander Cincer-Markovic arrived in Vienna, where in the presence of Hitler and Ribbentrop they signed up Yugoslavia to the Tripartite Pact. The Yugoslav leaders were given letters from Ribbentrop confirming Germany's "determination to respect the sovereignty and territorial integrity of Yugoslavia at all times" .. and promising that the Axis would not demand transit rights for its troops across Yugoslavia .. "during this war".

As soon as the Yugoslav ministers returned to Belgrade, they, their government and the Prince Regent were overthrown by a popular uprising on the night of March 26-27.

According to William L. Shirer's *"The Rise and Fall of the Third Reich"*:

"The coup threw Hitler into one of the wildest rages of his entire life. He took it as a personal affront and in his fury made sudden decisions which would prove utterly disastrous to the fortunes of the Third Reich.

"He hurriedly summoned his military chieftains to the Chancellery in Berlin on March 27 and raged about the revenge he would take on the Yugoslavs. He was therefore determined "... to destroy Yugoslavia militarily and as a nation.

No diplomatic inquiries will be made," he ordered, "and no ultimatums presented." Yugoslavia, he added, would be crushed with "unmerciful harshness." He ordered Goering then and there to "destroy Belgrade in attacks by waves," of bombers operating from Hungarian air bases. He issued Directive No. 25 for the immediate invasion of Yugoslavia and told [Generals] Keitel and Jodl to work out the military plans that very evening. He instructed Ribbentrop to advise Hungary, Rumania and Italy [German allies] that they would all get a slice of Yugoslavia, which would be divided up among them, except for a Croatian state.

"And then, according to an underlined passage in the top-secret OKW (German Army High Command) notes of the meeting, Hitler announced the most fateful decision of all.

"*The beginning of operation Barbarossa*", [code for attack on Russia]," he told his generals, "*will have to be postponed up to four weeks*". It had originally been set for May 15 in the directive of December 18, 1940. [33]

Shirer continues:

"This postponement of the attack on Russia in order that the Nazi warlord might vent his personal spite against a small Balkan country which had dared to defy him was probably the most catastrophic single decision in Hitler's career. It is hardly too much to say that by making it that March afternoon in the Chancellery in Berlin during a moment of convulsive rage, he tossed away his last golden opportunity to win the war and to make of the Third Reich, which he had created with such stunning if barbarous genius, the greatest empire in German history and himself the master of Europe.

"Field Marshal von Brauchitsch, the Commander in Chief of the German Army, and General Halder, the gifted Chief of the General Staff, were to recall it with deep bitterness but also with more understanding of its consequences than they showed at the moment of its making, when later the deep snow and subzero temperatures of Russia hit them three of four weeks short of what they thought they needed for final victory. For ever afterward they and their fellow generals would blame that hasty, ill-advised decision of a vain and infuriated man for all the disasters that ensued.

"...At dawn on April 6, [Hitler's] armies in overwhelming strength fell on Yugoslavia and Greece, smashing across the frontiers of Bulgaria, Hungary and Germany itself with all their armor and advancing rapidly against poorly armed defenders dazed by the usual preliminary bombing from the Luftwaffe.

---

33 *Minutes of the OKW meeting are part of the Nuremberg Documents under: "Nazi Conspiracy and Aggression", volume VI, pp 275-278.*

THE BELLS RING NO MORE

"Belgrade itself, as Hitler ordered, was razed to the ground. For three days and nights Goering's bombers ranged over the little capital at rooftop level - for the city had no antiaircraft guns - killing 17,000 civilians, wounding many more and reducing the place to a mass of smoldering rubble. "Operation Punishment," Hitler called it, and he obviously was satisfied that his commands had been so effectively carried out".

On April 17 the hostilities were over and on April 18, the Kingdom of Yugoslavia ceased to exist.

In June 1940 the leadership staff of the "Dienststelle" of the RKFVD was integrated into the "Staatshauptamt", the headquarters of the SS organization. Frensing comments on this in *Die Umsiedlung* on page 28:

"In the spring of 1940, the following program was sketched out: From the lands annexed to the Reich, the non-German population was to be removed and taken to the "Altreich" as foreign labor or sent to the Generalgouvernment [a catch-all area in occupied Poland]. Volksdeutsche [ethnic Germans] whose cultural autonomy could not be secured are to be resettled from their homeland into the annexed lands".

And in mid 1940, one of the branches of the "Dienststelle" issues a compendium of ideological guidelines to be used in the "Ingathering" of ethnic Germans. The head of the branch designated "Menscheneinsatz", SS-Obersturmbannführer (Lieutenant Colonel) Dr. Fähndrich writes an eight point introduction of which paragraphs 1, 2 and 5 are of special significance: [34]

"1. Those Germans living outside the sphere of interest of the Großdeutsche Reich are, according to urgency and necessity, to be re-settled".

"2. The call of the Führer represents a complete revolutionizing of any prior German nationalistic policy now restructured to fit the axiom of ingathering valued German blood to strengthen the Reich".

"5. This obligates the returned Germans to subordinate themselves organically to the discipline, stock and order of the greater German Reich. Specific demands are:

    a. With the ingathering of an ethnic group into the Reich, the prior organization of the group ceases to exist, for over this group stands the Reich.

---

34   *Die Umsiedlung, pg 145*

b. The concepts of the Baltic-Germans, the Wolhynian and Bessarabian-German, [Gottscheer], etc., must in the shortest period, be wiped out".

All eight points are listed by Frensing on page 145. Paragraph 5 in effect spells out the destiny of the Gottscheer as an ethnic group.

It is likely that the principles of paragraph 5 were unknown to the VGL. This may be deduced from a directive of the SS-Gruppenführer (Major General) Greifeld, Chief of the RKFDV in Berlin to SS-Sturmbannführer (Major) Laforce, the officer in charge of the Gottscheer re-settlement authority in Marburg/Maribor, in the now de-facto annexed Slovenia.

In a letter marked "Secret" dated October 31, 1941, Greifeld directed Laforce that:

"The existing VolksGruppenLeitung [the VGL] is to be kept intact during the re-settlement since only through a tight leadership can a frictionless re-settlement be accomplished and that.

"After completion of the settlement of the Gottscheer in Lower Styria [the Untersteiermark], I ask that you make certain that the concept of the Gottscheer as an ethnic group ceases to exist and that they integrate themselves, unconditionally, into Styria and into the overall German nation". [35]

Having obtained the assurance of the highest levels of the Reich that the Gottscheer would be re-settled as a group, the VGL was convinced that they would remain the leaders of this closed ethnic group and as border-farmers defend the boundaries of the Reich. Lampeter personally challenged Gauleiter (State Governor) Sigfried Uiberreither, the head of the Civil Authority of Styria, under whose jurisdiction the new settlers were to belong, on the acreage allocated to the settlers. Lampeter believed that the farm sizes were not large enough to allow for a healthy development in the future.

Lampeter also resisted the requirement that the ethnic group be included in the "Steirische Heimatbund", a civilian political organization set up by the Reich in the Styrian part of Slovenia after its occupation. Its main purpose was to re-integrate into the German nation those Styrians who had been Slovene-ized during the 20th Century and particularly after 1918. The VGL and Lampeter in particular, resisted such inclusion since, as pure blooded Germans they did not wish the Gottscheer be placed on an equal level with the Slovenes who had been their adversaries during the past twenty years.

---

35   M. Ferenc, *Kočevska – pusta in prazna. Nemško jezikovo območje na Kočevskem po odselitvi Nemcev.* Ljubljana 2005, Pg. 138.

This, and other challenges, led to serious tensions between the Gauleiter and Lampeter. Frensing states in *Die Umsiedlung*, pg.102, that: "..the blatant, nearly arrogant ways of Lampeter produced a less than favorable climate for the plans of the VGL which could only be realized with the approval and support of the Gauleiter. In the course of 1941, the resentment of the Gauleiter became ever more obvious. In a conversation Uiberreither made it apparent that he valued the national substance of the Gottscheer no higher than that of the Slovene who for the benefit of the Gottscheer needed to be resettled". Similar observations were made by the RKFVD in Berlin, where according to Frensing: …"the willfulness of the VGL was recognized immediately".

Nevertheless, the Gauleiter promised Lampeter the position of a Kreisführer (District Leader) in the "Steirischer Heimatbund".

All this points to the fact that the now 25 year old Lampeter and his equally young VGL were totally oblivious of the hierarchical and organizational demands of the dictatorship of the Third Reich. After having run a virtual, if clandestine ministate during the past few years, they had become overconfident and arrogant and had been setting themselves up for bitter disillusionment when ultimately, and very soon, they were to come up against the unalterable - "ingathering principles" - of Hitler as spelled out by SS-Officer Dr. Fähndrich in his Paragraph 5.

Chapter 4

Village Through Time

Just beyond Dolenja Vas, there is fork in the road toward Kočevje (Gottschee) City. The branch-off to the right leads to the "Hinterland" a narrow valley nestled between mountain ranges but at an altitude higher than the plain of the "Mainland". It is not altogether unlikely that a part of the group of settlers coming from Franconia/Thuringia or a part of another such group coming from elsewhere took this fork toward Grčarice, which was to become Masern, their village for the next 600 years.

Others went beyond Grčarice toward the neighboring Gotenica which became Göttenitz. Still others went beyond Göttenitz, ever deeper into what was then a prime forest.

In 1363, the village of Göttenitz became a parish. This is indicated in a letter dated May 1, 1363 from Ludwig della Torre, the Patriarch of Aquileia, to Otto VI of Ortenburg, the aristocrat of Lower Carniola. The letter directed the Count to appoint a resident chaplain to Göttenitz and thereby raise the village to the status of a parish.

The elevation to parish status implies that Gotenica (Göttenitz) was a village for some time before 1363 and that the population there and in its surrounding settlements such as Grčarice (Masern) had grown to a point where spiritual care could no longer be effectively provided out of parish of Ribnica (Reiffnitz), the Archdiocese of Lower Carniola since 1082.

Masern, only 4.5 km from Göttenitz and until then under the parish of Reiffnitz, was transferred to the new parish. And from then on, the priest in Göttenitz took care of the spiritual needs of Masern. This priest, being closer and more easily accessible spoke their language, whereas the priests in Reiffnitz could, beyond saying their Latin Mass, communicate with them only in a limited way.

Masern remained under the Göttenitz parish until 1741 when it was returned to Reiffnitz, which in turn placed it under the Slovene parish of Dolenja Vas as a sub-parish in 1767, where it remains until now.

THE BELLS RING NO MORE

The early history of Grčarice (Masern) comes from the pages of the *Kočevski Zbornik* (Gottschee Anthology) compiled by the Slovene Association of St. Ciril and Metod in Ljubljana in 1939. It is a scholarly study of the area and its inhabitants and meticulously lists its sources, many of them recognized authorities such as Valvasor, Grothe, Hauffen, Schroer, etc.

The Zbornik states that in 1498, 135 years after the village of Göttenitz was raised to parish status, Masern appears for the first time as a village in a Register called *Das Vrbar des ambts Riegkh*. (The Land Record of the Community Rieg). The Zbornik describes the *Vrbar* on page 71.

"The Vrbar is bound in reddish colored parchment stuck to paper. At the top of the binding is written: Rieck vnd Sichelberg. /... /. The writing is on hand produced paper. It has 48 written pages, with one additional being smaller and one added later /... /. It is located in file 12 under inscription Sichelburger Lehensbriefe. 1644 - 1706."

The *Vrbar* was kept by the tax collector for the "Hinterland" who resided in "Riegkh", the present day Kočevska Reka (Rieg), another village in the forest, six km beyond Göttenitz. Now, it is in the vaults of the National Archives in Ljubljana. This *Vrbar* mentions Masern as a tax-paying village and lists twelve owners of one-half "Hube" each. It also shows how they were taxed.

The initial land awarded by the Ortenburg Count to a settler was a unit called a "Hube" or Hide in English. According to the Zbornik, the size of a Hide was not uniform; it was different in various parts of the settlement area. In Göttenitz, it was 90 hectares. In Masern a Hide consisted of 55.16 hectares or 136 Acres. The initial Hide did not include the common lands such as pastures, watering holes, or village centers. Nor did it include the forest, which remained the domain of the Count, but could be used by the settlers for needed construction lumber and firewood.

The listing of twelve owners of a half Hide in 1498 implies that the population of Masern had grown substantially after 1363, forcing the settlers to split the original Hide in half. The split in turn implies that there were six families who received a full Hide when they settled in Grčarice sometime before 1363 when Göttenitz became a parish. With 4.5 generations covering the span of 135 years (1363 to 1498) at 30 years per generation, the conclusion that Grčarice was settled by the new arrivals before 1363 can be justly defended.

That Grčarice existed in 1363 or even before is further supported by the fact that the settlement was a meeting hub of several roads out of the deeper forest, one of the main sources of lumber for the region of Lower Carniola. Due to this strategic

VILLAGE THROUGH TIME

location, all transporters of lumber had to pass, until today, through Grčarice. This strategic hub of roads may also be the reason why this small village had, even in 1941, three taverns serving as a rest and watering stop for the drivers and horses of long columns hauling lumber out of the forest.

In 1563, Archduke Carl Habsburg ordered a land survey of Lower Carniola, one of his dominions, which he mortgaged to local aristocrats. The Archduke ordered the survey to verify the reported growth in the region from which he could re-assess his taxation. This also included the Kočevje (Gottschee) enclave.

This extensive land survey produced a register named the *Urbar Register der Stadtt Gotsche, Anno 1564*. As a result of the survey, the Archduke raised the enclave taxes by 26,160 Florins, an increase that was strongly protested by the Count von Blagay, the mortgage holder since 1547, causing a reduction to 15,000 Florin. [36] This Register, also in the State Archives, shows that even in 1564 there were still only twelve owners of one half-Hide each in Masern. Its land status had not changed in the 66 years since 1498. But it appears that the population of the village had increased substantially.

Sometime after 1564, the Blagays made their own assessment to verify the findings of the Archduke and determine in which of their villages the population had increased and through such growth was capable of clearing more of the forest. The Urbar *Gottschee, Ao 1568* shows this. (Ownership of the enclave mortgage had been split among three Blagays, with Countess Elisabeth getting the Masern part).

The assessment found that the population of the village had indeed increased and consequently, five and one half additional Hides were leased to Masern residents in 1613, thereby increasing the taxation by the Blagays. The increase brought the total land in the village to eleven and one half Hides, a number that remained constant for the next 264 years.

The survey also showed that property splits elsewhere in the enclave had lowered the taxable productivity of the land. As a result, further splits of land could be made only with the approval of the Count.

---

36   *Kočevski Zbornik, pg 89*.

More information on Masern is provided by the Therezijanski Kataster of 1752.

This Register now shows seven and five eighths Hides owned by twenty three owners and three and seven eighths Hides leased to twelve renters. Together this again adds up to eleven and one half Hides. It shows that ownership increased from the original six Hides to seven and five eighths, indicating that one and five eighths released for rental had already been converted to ownership.

In 1770 Empress Maria Theresa ordered a recruiting census of all males and a count of all urban and rural dwellings. This census shows that at that time there were thirty eight houses in Masern. Unfortunately, the number of males living in the village is not listed.

The next important milestone was written by Father Johann Posnik in 1877. (Father Posnik was the resident village priest in the years between 1867 – 1884).

In his tabulation, Father Posnik lists every house in the village, including the number of the house, the formal and village name of its owner, his age and the size of the land he owned. Unfortunately, he does not list the number of residents living in each of the houses.

But Father Posnik's tabulation shows that further splits had occurred since 1752. While in 1877 total ownership is still eleven and one half Hides, the land is now split into small fractions of a Hide. There are sixty three houses in the village with thirty one of them owning the eleven and one half Hides. The other thirty two houses own no land other than the space surrounding the house and a small adjacent garden.

The heavy emigration to America that started in the second half of the 19th century and reduced the ethnic German population of the enclave from 22,920 to 10,983 also reduced the total population of Masern. [37]

Already in 1877, Father Posnik lists some houses as empty. The people who left were mostly the young who never returned after leaving their parents behind. And when these parents eventually died, the house, most of them centuries old, became vacant and started to fall into ruin. In the 1930s there were at least seven that were vacant and in yet others lived only an elderly parent or relative, the owner or caretaker of the house and the property belonging to it.

And in the winter of 1941, all except five of 63 houses became vacant as 206 residents, on December 7, 9 and 11 left, leaving behind an empty village in which they and their ancestors had lived for over 600 years.

---

37   Kočevski Zbornik, pg 148

But back to the beginning.

As already mentioned the initial Hide did not include the forest, which remained the domain of the Ortenburg Counts, but could be used by the settlers for needed construction lumber and firewood.

This arrangement, however, soon produced friction among the settlers in the later part of the 14th century and led Count Friderik of Ortenburg, the leaseholder at that time, to enact the "Forest Law of 1406". (Zbornik, pg 63)

This law divided the common pastures among the settlers, thereby enlarging their ownership. They were also allocated parcels of the forest, albeit conditionally at first. This loosely defined right to the forest eventually evolved into full ownership, which together with the divided pastures increased the size of a Hide from the initial 55.16 hectares to 84 hectares. (In 1941, my father was the owner of one quarter of a Hide, or 21 hectares. Of these 21 hectares, two and a half were arable land, seven were meadows and 11.5 were forest parcels).

The right to permanent ownership of the forest parcels was, however, linked to several conditions:

a) "The right is lost if a parcel is not tended for nine years and one day".

The intent of this requirement was to prevent the underbrush from invading the arable land. While the law assigned and defined the conditions of ownership of the individual parcels of the forest surrounding the village, it also allowed the villagers continued access to the remainder of the vast forest still the sole property of the Count. All could take from this domain, but for personal use only, the lumber needed for construction, firewood or any other purpose related to the tending of their land. The hunting rights, however, remained the exclusive right of the Count.

b) "The right is jeopardized if the obligation to report to the owner of the dominion the number of falcon nests in the parcel is missed for two consecutive years and the annual yield of falcons is not offered for sale to the lordship".

His lordship paid 60 shilling for an adult sparrow hawk, 32 shilling for a female and 12 shilling for a young male hawk. He trained the hawks for use during the hunt.

c) "The law requires from each settler the annual delivery of five Pilich".

The "Pilich" (dormouse), a squirrel-like creature living in the forests of Carniola, including those surrounding Masern, was prized by the lordships of Friedrichstein for its soft smooth fur, stitched into warm coats and blankets needed during the bitter cold winter months of the region.

The Forest Law was propagated through the centuries by word of mouth from generation to generation. Some parts of it were still resonating in Masern during my time there, some 530 years later.

THE BELLS RING NO MORE

Part "a" of the Forest Law had two sub-parts. The first, tending the forest, was no longer an imposed requirement but it was still taken seriously even in the 20th century. When there were no other more pressing chores, our entire family would make for the edges of our forests that needed to be cleared of underbrush infringing on our arable lands. The need for this had become obvious long ago. For me it was a welcome event since it always included a large fire, which Mitzi and I were tasked to feed with the cut brush.

And when the fire reduced the wood to glowing embers, we were allowed to roast in the ashes our potatoes for a hand and tongue searing accompaniment to the midday lunch or a snack before leaving for home.

The second sub-part of this law allowed the use of the Count's forest for personal needs of the settlers but it was limited to firewood only. A forest/game warden enforced this limitation for the Count and his successors up to our days. But since these forests were beyond those owned by the settlers and in many cases a long distance from their homes, those without their own forests helped themselves to firewood in nearer places. This led to many a row including one, which I remember vividly.

In the fall of 1937, a "Keuschler" named Albert Tschinkel, living in Masern No 65, asked Father if he could borrow Yiorgo and the wagon to get firewood for the winter from the forest of the Auerspergs, the successors to the Count. A Keuschler was a landless villager, one who lived mostly off the 'landed' in exchange for tending their arable lands. In exchange for such labors, the 'landed' let them use unused acreage on which they could grow their own crops. Father, a handicapped landowner, used this method extensively to farm his lands. Even though Albert was not one of his leasers, nor a close relative in spite of the similar family name, Father granted the request and at the end of the agreed upon day, both horse and wagon were brought back by a seemingly grateful Albert.

Some days later, Johann Krisch, the good friend of Father, reported that Albert was telling the villagers how he took advantage of my father by not only borrowing his horse and wagon but also using both to get firewood from his forests.

Father confronted the scoundrel with the deed. His straight-faced reply was that he knew of no boundaries and besides, the Forest Law allowed use of the forests for personal needs.

I was present when Father confronted this man and noticed his sneering reaction, which implied "So, what are you going to do about it …"? Of course, there was not much he could, nor wanted, to do.

Part "b" was still enforced by the Forest/Game Warden.

Franz Jaklitsch, the tavern keeper had mentioned to Father that Josef Eppich of Masereben (the annex to Masern) had caught a pair of young hawks and was keeping them in the mostly empty barn of Father's older sister Johanna Krisch who now lived in Brooklyn. Johanna had left Masern for New York in 1906 at age nineteen where she soon married Johann Krisch and after Johann died a few years later, married his brother Paul. Both brothers had left for America after their parents died, abandoning their half-Hide property in Masereben, leaving the ancestral homestead empty to slowly crumble into decay. However, Johanna and Paul had put Father in charge of administrating the estate and he in turn leased out the acreage to other villagers in return for upkeep of the land. He granted use of the barn to Josef Eppich, a neighbor of the empty house.

Father asked Jaklitsch if the hawks were captured with the permission of Anton Tscherne, the game warden of Prince Auersperg who now owned the gaming rights in all the forests including those owned by the villagers. Jaklitsch had asked the same question of Josef Eppich who replied that he had captured the hawks according to the Forest Law and would turn them over to the Prince on his next hunting visit to Masern. But Jaklitsch checked with the warden who said the hawks were now a protected bird and catching them was a punishable offense. Besides, the prince was not coming to Masern this year for his annual hunt.

All this got back to Josef Eppich and he quickly released the hawks. But Father had doubts and sent me, his eight year old son to Johanna's barn to see if the hawks were still there. Since the barn was padlocked, I went to the Eppich house and asked for the keys. Josef Eppich was most indignant and denied that he ever caught hawks, but after my persisting, he took me to the barn and unlocked the door. There were no hawks in the barn, but there were unmistakable signs of their former presence. Eppich insisted the droppings were those of chickens, not hawks. I, however, knew better and Father was satisfied with my report.

Part "c" had long ago ceased to be enforced. The capture of the "Piliche", however, continued through the centuries. The dormouse, known in German as a "Siebenschläfer", was a delicacy enjoyed by all residents of Slovenia and long before that by the ancient Romans who caught them alive and fattened them on walnuts. These nocturnal animals live in trees except when hibernating in underground nests during winter. When fully matured they grow to around twelve inches not including the bushy tail. They live on berries, nuts, pollen, and insects. In our forests, the Pilich prepared for the long winter by getting fat on nuts of beech and oak trees.

The capture of the "Piliche" became a major event in the fall when the beech trees were brimming with nuts. This is when the traps, a small box with a hooked end, were readied to be hung on a branch high-up in the tree by using long poles. The creatures liked nuts but had a weakness for the slice of an apple whose aroma lured them inside past the trap which snapped and clamped tight the animal trying to dislodge the lure.

The event that lasted through the night started in late afternoon by selecting an area of nut-filled trees most likely to be visited by the night feeding creatures. Nearby, but some distance away so as not alarm the creatures, a camping site was set up by a group of three or so men and a fire was lit. After setting and hanging the traps, the men took turns to stay awake to listen for the snap of the trap while the others slept off the picnic meal and the slivovitz which, in addition to the fire was meant to keep them warm. Or, if neither listening nor sleeping, carefully scouting about to empty the animals caught in traps of other groups who, including the guard, had fallen asleep. Great ingenuity was used by each group to outsmart the others, but all were on the lookout for the non-trappers who stole from all. Woe to those who were caught.

All this led to a lot of laughs or embarrassment afterwards, when the success or failure of the night, including the success or failure of the various attempts at deception, was made public over wine at the Jaklitsch tavern. Sometimes tempers flared, but Franz Jaklitsch managed, most of the time, to calm the sore and heated with another quarter liter on the house.

The Urbar of 1498 lists the taxes of each of the twelve owners of the half hide in Masern. It was: "A ten measure of millet and the sum of 82 Shilling or its equivalent in chicken or eggs. (two Shilling for one chicken, one Shilling for seven and one half eggs)". [38]

According to the Urbar, the tithe was collected by "Gregor", the village elder known as "Supann", one of the property owners in the village. He was appointed to that position by the caretaker of the dominion residing in the fortress of Fridrichstein.

---

38   Kočevski Zbornik, pg 74

This was a difficult assignment, since it required to perform both the role of enforcer and trustee of the village.

The collected tithe was delivered to "Riegkh", (later Rieg) which was the intermediate collection point for the Hinterland. Rieg, (now Kočevska Reka) is a village another ten km beyond Gotenica (Göttenitz). From there it was taken to the fortress of Fridrichstein, the administrative center of the Gottschee dominion on top of the hills that separate the two valleys. Delivered there were also the tithes from other collection points in the dominion. After 1641, the collection point was moved to the Town of Kočevje (Gottschee) when the new administrative seat was established there.

The tithing for the enclave, according to the 1498 Register, was enforced by the "Caretaker" who lived in Fridrichstein, a fortress on top of the hills that separate the "Hinterland" from the "Mainland". This mighty fortress, never conquered by the Turks, was the place where the "Supann's", (župan's in Slovene) of the Hinterland assembled to hold court over their subjects, including those in Masern. It remained the administrative and legal center of the dominion until it was moved to the new Auersperg castle built in the town of Gottschee in the middle of the 17th Century. In 1650 the only resident left in Fridrichstein was the gatekeeper.

The "Caretaker' had been appointed by the lease holder of the dominion, at that time Frederik III, Duke of Carniola, King of Austria and Emperor of the Holy Roman Empire. (Reign 1440-1493). The dominion had reverted to the Emperor when the last count of Cilli died in 1456. The Cilli Counts had been given the leasehold by Emperor Sigismund in 1420 after the Ortenburg leaseholder era had come to an end with the murder of Friderik III, the last Count of Ortenburg. According to the historian Michael Gotthard Christalnik, Friderik died in 1418 from a poisoned apple given him by his wife, Countess Margarethe during some festivities at castle Waldenberg in Radovljica (Radkersburg), Krain.

The new leaseholder, Friderik II of Cilli had the fortress built during 1422-1425. Friderik was married to Elisabeth but he fell in love with Veronika, one of his wife's ladies in waiting. After he had Elisabeth murdered in 1422, Friderik moved with Veronika into the fortress to the fury of his father Hermann II and the great displeasure of his subjects. Hermann eventually arrested his son, but Veronika escaped. She was found by Hermann's bailiffs and was condemned by the judges of Hermann's court to die and was executed in October 18, 1428. Two knights carried out the verdict by drowning.

Friderik II of Cilli died in 1454. But in the interim he had become reconciled with his father who forgave him his transgression with Veronika.

THE BELLS RING NO MORE

Friderik had one son Ulrich II. But Ulrich had no legal children and when he died in 1456, the Cilli line came to an end and the leasehold of the enclave reverted back to Frederick III, Emperor and Duke of Carniola.

After the administrative center was moved from Fridrichstein, the fortress was allowed to decay into a ruin. In the 20th century, the ruin became a favorite destination for a day's outing by the residents of Kočevje (Gottschee) city. The two hour uphill walk promised great views in many directions and a pleasant place to have a picnic. I took part in such an outing without knowing that the former hideout of Frederick and Veronika had brought such tragedy to the lovers and even after so many centuries was a place for amorous adventures.

In the summer of 1937 my father took me to the city and the large house of my father's cousin Franz for a summer holiday before I started school in Grčarice (Masern) that fall. Franz was the son of my grandfather's brother, also Franz, who left Masern for the town in 1891 to make a name for himself. In Kočevje he soon became a wealthy merchant as a trader of bicycles and sewing machines. His son Franz took over when he died in 1935. His second younger son Herbert died in 1939 when he slipped in the bathtub and hit his head against a faucet.

Grandfather's brother Franz had, apart from the two sons, four daughters, Herta, Irene, Ridi and Selma. Of the four, only Selma was still at home taking care of the house and her brother. But that summer, Herta had come to stay for a few weeks with her two sons Donald and Peter, my second cousins one year older and younger, respectively. Herta had married a Slovene merchant named Logar and was living in Ljubljana. We three had a grand time together, especially in the water of the nearby river Rinse, carefully supervised by Tante Grete, also there for the summer. She made certain we remained in shallow water. She was my grandfather's sister, a well preserved 72 year old spinster who owned a stationery store in Austria. She nearly killed me when she vacationed in Grčarice with my father in the summer of 1931 and fed me, an infant, milk straight from the cow.

Herta's younger sister Selma, then 20, had an admirer named Horst who was not welcomed by her brother Franz but they met secretly whenever they could. Horst was already one of the fanatical young Nazis, but that was not the reason why Franz did not like him.

One day, Herta, Selma and the three boys were to make an outing to the ruins of Fridrichstein. We kids knew that Horst was coming with us, but were forbidden to tell Franz. We left early in the morning and met Horst on the way.

It was a beautiful walk up to the ruins. The early sun painted, through the foliage of summer, yellow spots on the ground and we drank the clear cool waters of the brook bubbling over rocks on its way to the Rinse river. We were anxiously anticipating lunch from the rucksack of Horst, promised us when we got to the picnic place at the ruin. And a beautiful lunch it was, laid out by Horst in the clearing inside the wall of the former fortress. Afterwards, we three were ordered to go and explore the grounds outside the wall since the adults wanted to rest without disturbance. As we reluctantly went outside, Horst closed the high and heavy wooden gate in the wall surrounding the ruin behind us while reminding us not to go far.

We explored the vicinity but soon got bored and curious. Over the objection of the two brothers, I climbed a tree near the wall which gave me a view of the picnic grounds and the two sisters and Horst sunning themselves on blankets, dressed in nothing but emperor's clothing. I became frightened and came down quickly saying that I saw nothing in spite of the urgings of my playmates. We explored some more until Horst called us from the opened gate.

I begged the two boys not to tell that I had climbed the tree but they did tell their mother that evening after we got back. Herta became very angry and questioned me at length to find out how much I had seen. I lied, saying that the tree I climbed was far from the wall and I had seen nothing. She made me promise not to say anything to her brother Franz, a promise that would be hard to keep. But fortunately, he did not ask.

Decades later I met Selma in the lobby of the Stamford Court Hotel in San Francisco. In the telephone directory, I had found among several Tschinkels, the name Selma. I phoned and sure enough, it was she. And yes, she remembered me and we agreed to meet in the lobby of the hotel. She would wear a light colored rain coat to help me recognize her.

It was apparent that the once sparkling, pretty and self assured girl, now in 1978 a somewhat tentative older woman, had aged beyond her 61 years and over dinner it became clear why this was so. She talked about Horst, moving out of the comfort of her father's house during the resettlement, her times in refugee camps after the war.

Horst, whom she agreed to marry in 1941, had died on the Russian front. Later she married a man with whom she had two children but a separation left her with only one son, the other having been awarded to the father. After that, she left for America. There she was ill prepared, given her privileged background, to take roots as a newly arrived immigrant and start at the bottom. At 61, she seemed very unhappy with her lot in life.

Herta Logar whom I met years later in Austria fared worse yet. Her husband, a well to do Slovene merchant, had also been persuaded to accept the resettlement option and become a citizen of the Third Reich. After the end of the war and with Slovenia cleared of the Nazi occupier, he and his family were not allowed by the new State of Yugoslavia to return to Ljubljana. After staying in refugee camps, they also went to America as immigrants. Also unable to assimilate, they returned to Austria after a few years where it was even more difficult to make a fresh start. Herta's fate as a victim of the war was particularly tragic since her husband was a Slovene national and they all could have survived the war with their livelihood intact, had they stayed in Ljubljana.

In addition to natural disasters and the exploitation of the enclave through heavy taxation especially after the death of the last Ortenburg count, Lower Carniola including Gottschee, was ravaged by the westward moving Ottoman Turks. In 1469 they burned the district town of Gottschee and the market town of Reiffnitz. During the 22 years between 1469 and 1491 they came into Carniola 22 times, severely affecting the livelihood of the population. [39] To assist the inhabitants, Emperor Frederik III, in 1492, granted the citizens of Lower Carniola (Gottschee and Ribnica) the privilege to peddle their wares throughout his Empire. This brought much relief to the region but also exposed (for the first time) the residents of Lower Carniola to the larger world outside.

In May 1522 the Turks again swept through the valleys of Lower Carniola toward Trieste and Venice. On their return through Postojna, Cerknica, Ribnica and Kočevje (Gottschee) toward Croatia and Bosnia, they caused great damage. Between Ribnica and Kočevje they passed through Dolenja Vas and very likely went the short distance to Masern to plunder and search for booty. They came again in 1528 and nine more times after that until 1598. But after the turn of the century,

---

39 *Kočevski Zbornik, pg 136.*

they preferred the more profitable route through Hungary toward Western Europe and once again to Vienna where they were overwhelmingly defeated in September 1683.

The repeated forays of the Turks into Lower Carniola produced an organized reporting system to announce their approach. Small, easily portable cannons were cast to produce loud explosive sounds that could be heard over long distances. One explosive sound announced that the Turks were on the move; three successive explosions announced their arrival in the domain. Three blasts were also the signal for designated able men to assemble at defined places while others were to hide with women and children in the forests or caves. To the cannon blasts was added the lighting of huge bonfires on successive hills, which in combination with the cannons allowed the population to make for their hiding places. One such bonfire was at fortress Fridrichstein. Others in the vicinity of Masern were in Rieg, in Göttenitz and Dolenja Vas.

The people of Masern came to rely more on the noise from cannons than on the bonfires which could not be seen on rainy and cloudy days or nights. These cannons, known as "Böller" were still in the villages in the 1930s. There were several of them in Masern and they were kept at the firehouse, unloaded. They were used by the firemen during special occasions such as religious processions or weddings as extra loud equivalents of firecrackers which startled the praying women, scared the young and frightened the horses.

The "Böller" was a tapered cast iron cylinder about 12 inches in height. One end, flat and measuring about 14 inches across, was meant to rest on soft ground. The other end, also flat and tapered to about ten inches across, had a handle on each side so it could be carried by two strong men. From the center of this surface, three quarters into the cylinder, was a two inch hole which, at the bottom, was met by a small horizontal bore from the outside, the hole for the fuse. Most of the big hole was stuffed with powder and plugged off with clay or mortar that was allowed to harden. And after the fuse was lit, the recoil of the explosion would drive the cylinder inches into the soft flat ground on which it sat.

It made a cannon-like sound, clearly heard even in Masern when they were setting them off in Göttenitz or Rieg. "So that we would hear it when the Turks were coming", was the answer given when I asked for the reason why.

THE BELLS RING NO MORE

Still known were the places where the villagers hid after the fires, or blasts, or both told them the Turks were on their way. And there is no doubt that they were ready to run and hide, as was my family in the fall of 1940, when blasts from several "Böller" woke us one night announcing that hostile armed Slovene were approaching from the direction of Dolenja Vas to do us in. This was the time when the racial tension between the Gottscheer and the surrounding Slovene had reached its most hostile peak.

The Slovene never intended such violence. It was, however, a purposefully false alarm to test the response of the already frightened villagers. The test was part of an effort to further inflame the deteriorating relationship between the villagers and the neighboring Slovene. The fear of such violent action from the Slovene had been instilled over many meetings conducted by Franz Jaklitsch, our new village chief. Fanning this hostility was a part of the effort to convert the residents to Nazi ideology and its objectives.

Father took the alarm seriously in spite of his doubts. He knew most of the people in Dolenja Vas and could hardly believe them capable of what Jaklitsch was predicting. When the blast from the "Böller" woke us up, Yiorgo was quickly engaged and all five of us were on the wagon being trotted by the equally sleepy Yiorgo toward our "safe place" on our property known as the "Unterbinkl". But halfway there, the church bell began to ring, telling us the signal that the danger had passed and we could all return home.

Very likely, this "safe place" was also one used by my ancestors when they hastened to hide from the Turks.

The "Unterbinkl" (Low Corner) was the lowest part of the Masern bowl where the slightly downward sloping fields ended in grazing meadows and beyond that in brush and scraggy trees that covered the now flat ground. All this soon gave way to steeply rising hills on which stood magnificent pines. In this flat part, among the brush and trees were the deep fissures into which disappeared the waters that emerged every spring from the lowest point in the village - the bowl-like depression behind the parsonage and our house. These waters from the melting snow on the surrounding hills found their way through underground connections to the bottom of the depression where they emerged, filled and overflowed the bowl, and seeking lower ground through fields and meadows were swallowed by the fissures of the "Unterbinkl".

Our "safe place" was in a cavern, a short distance down the side wall of a crevasse hidden among rocks, brush and trees. The cavern, the size of a small arched room, could easily accommodate our entire family, including blankets and supplies, on its reasonably flat stone floor. It was accessible via a ladder resting on the ledge of the cavern while the other end was leaning on the opposite edge of the crevasse at ground level above. Once inside, the ladder was to be pulled down into the cavern.

Needless to say, climbing down the ladder was going to be dangerous, but Father was convinced that all of us could get down safely, even in the dark. Fortunately this never became necessary. I do not remember what Father had in mind for Yiorgo and the wagon; maybe hide both in bushes nearby. Surely those who hid from the Turks centuries ago would have done the same.

There were many crevasses in the Unterbinkl, several on our land. I got to know the location of all of them, even those partly hidden by brush. Father made it a point to show them to me believing that if I knew where they were I would stay clear of them. Most of them were quite deep, the depth tested by listening for the echo of a dropped stone as it bounced off walls on the way down to the bottom or perhaps to a ledge on the way there. Of course, the stone was dropped while lying flat on the stomach; legs pointing away from the abyss, the awesome depth too frightening for standing upright.

This posture of self preservation was helped along by Father's tale about a dog belonging to his father that fell into such a crevasse while chasing a deer. His whereabouts were discovered when whines and barks were heard emerging from the deep when grandfather was calling the dog while searching the area. Fortunately, the dog had landed on a protruding rock shelf, but too far down to be reached with ladders.

Grandfather tied a wicker basket to the end of a long rope. In it was placed a piece of juicy meat and the basket lowered on to the shelf. The now very hungry dog climbed into the basket and while chewing on the meat, the basket was pulled up by the rope to safety.

"It was lucky he landed on the ledge. Had he not, he would have fallen deeper and died. So stay far away from the crevasses, you may not be so lucky".

This cautionary tale, often told, had its effect not only on me but on the other youngsters as well.

In 1547, King Ferdinand, later Emperor Ferdinand I, (1556-1564) gave the leasehold of the Gottschee dominion to Stefan I, Count von Blagay, a Croatian lord. The King, (also Archduke of the Austrian duchies owned by the Habsburgs), gave Stefan the leasehold as a reward for bravery in fighting the Turks. In these battles, the Blagay clan suffered heavy losses and most of their castles were destroyed. As a result, the enclave adjacent to their property in Croatia became the Blagays' most important holding.

The Blagays held the lease until 1618. That year, the Habsburgs sold the leasehold of the Gottschee dominion to Baron Von Kysel who in turn held it until 1641 when it was assumed by Count Wolf Auersperg. The Auersperg family held the lease until 1918, when the Empire of the Habsburgs, rulers over a large part of Europe since 1273, came to an end.

During the 71 years of Blagay rule, the Gottschee dominion experienced its largest influx of settlers as part of the "Second Wave". The bulk of these came from the Croatian part of the Habsburg lands.

The Croatian Counts brought with them many of their Slavic subjects. This is apparent to this day in the clearly Slavic names of the many who assimilated into the enclave population and became Gottscheer i.e. "ethnic Germans" [40] An ironic but typical example of such a name is Jaklitsch, the name of Franz Jaklitsch, the tavern owner in Masern who, as a "racially pure" German became the Nazi leader of the village in the 1930's.

Due to this heavy influx and expansion of settlements, Archduke Carl, also lord of Lower Carniola, appointed a commission to verify the reported growth and increase in value of his mortgaged dominions which included the enclave. The commission was tasked to assess its value, set its boundaries, re-establish the tax levy for property owners and settle outstanding disputes.

The result of the survey is the previously mentioned document, the: *"Urbar Register der Stadt Gottschee, Anno 1564"*. This Register is the first official document defining the value of the enclave, its boundary, the number of settlements as well as the number and size of the land parcels therein.

The survey of 1564 shows there were no land splits in Masern since 1498. But a later and more detailed assessment of the population was made by the Blagays which showed the population had grown to a size capable of clearing more of the forest. As a result, an additional five and a half hides was offered to the villagers for sale or lease by Countess Elisabeth Blagay in 1613, bringing the total recorded land in Masern to 11.5 Hides. Elisabeth was the widow of Stefan II, Count of Blagay, the great grandson of Stefan I who had been given the leasehold over the Gottschee estates by King Ferdinand, also Archduke of Carniola, in 1547. Elisabeth had received one third of the leasehold that included Masern, by Ferdinand when her husband Stefan II died in 1598. The second third went to Stefan's brother Nicholas and the third to George of Blagay, the eldest of Stefan's nephews.

---

40 G. Widmer, *Urkundliche Beiträge zur Geschichte des Gottscheerländchens. 1406 – 1627*, Wien 1931, pg.10

VILLAGE THROUGH TIME

The survey also showed that property splits in the Count's dominions had been lowering the productivity of the new owners. Until then the land awarded at the time of settling could, at the discretion of the owner of a Hide, be sub-divided as the village grew in population. As a result of the survey, further splits of land in the domain of the Archduke could be made only with the approval of the local administrator of the Count. This was done mainly to prevent further erosion of the tax paying ability of the owner of the parcel, mainly in the form of farm produce.

Count Wolf Engelbert of Auersperg took over the leasehold of the enclave from the Blagays in 1641. As a Countship, the enclave became his personal domain, with all taxes collected there to be delivered to his treasury exclusively for his benefit. And by 1650 he had built a castle in the town of Gottschee into which he moved all administrative functions from Friedrichstein which he abandoned.

The reign of the Auerspergs, while largely benevolent, was not altogether free of problems produced by excessive taxation. As owners of the domain, the Auerspergs, like all other similar owners in the Empire were obligated to pay their taxes into the Imperial Treasury, taxes which they in turn had to collect from their subjects. In 1653, some Gottscheer subjects resisted what they deemed to be overbearing taxation and servitude and in 1654, a delegation of leaders took their complaint directly to the Emperor who promised an inquiry which was completed in 1661. Emperor Leopold dismissed the complaint as lies and ordered the protesters to adhere to the decrees of the Auerspergs, his intimate friends. But the petitioners were not satisfied and in 1662 they rebelled, an uprising that was forcibly put down by Engelbert Auersperg. He had the ringleaders killed and expelled the others from the domain.

The Auersperg assumption, however, brought a period of relative stability which lasted until 1918 when the Austrian Empire came to an end and Slovenia became part of Yugoslavia. After WW1, their former political role in the enclave ended, but they kept their castles and a large part of their properties. In 1945 they lost even that.

The name Auersperg has a long association with Lower Carniola. The roots of this family go back to the 11th century and they were looked upon as one of the important noble families in the region. Their seat was castle Turjak, just north of Ribnica (Reiffnitz) in which the "Bela Garda" (Slovene Catholic nationalists opposing Communism), was defeated by the National Liberation Front in 1943.

THE BELLS RING NO MORE

As owners of the leasehold of Reiffnitz (1220-1263), the Auerspergs competed for dominance over Lower Carniola with the more powerful counts of Ortenburg, who had one of their many castles only fifteen miles to the west. But the Ortenburg succession came to an end with the death of Friderik III, the last Count of Ortenburg in 1418, and with it came the expansion of the Auersperg fortunes in Lower Carniola.

In 1641, the Auersperg clans already had extensive holdings in other parts of the Habsburg monarchy and were well connected to the Emperor. The most notable of these centuries-spanning connections was Count Wolf's younger brother Johann Weikard who became Private Secretary to Emperor Ferdinand III, Conference Minister and Knight of the Golden Fleece. In 1653 he was elevated to rank of Prince. And when Wolf died in 1673, Johann inherited the leasehold and with this inheritance, the Gottschee enclave became a princely estate.

The name Auersperg had a special meaning to the inhabitants of Masern since the princely line owned the gaming rights for the forests surrounding our village. Most autumns after the onset of frost, the current Prince came to the village to hunt for bear or stag, either of which was on its last minute search for food to get ready for the severe winter.

I particularly remember one such visit in the fall of 1938, his last. The Prince arrived in a large, gleaming chauffeur driven limousine and stayed for a week in his large house on the hill across the cistern depression, diagonally opposite ours. In addition to the chauffeur, the Prince came with his gun carrier and his cook.

For weeks the village was getting ready for the arrival. The empty house, its shutters closed for most of the year, received a thorough cleaning under the careful supervision of Anton Tscherne, the local game warden of the Prince. Tscherne lived in the warden house at the western end of the village close to the forest. As warden he had an eminent position in the village, helped along by his rather standoffish demeanor and his immaculate dress; gray hunter's jacket, embroidered with green at the collar, sleeves, and elbows and button holes for buttons made of antler bone. The gray breeches, gathered and buttoned just below the knee, gave way to elaborately knit woolen stockings which ended in ankle high boots, always polished to a gloss.

He wore a gray soft felt hat, tapered and ending in a rounded off top. The band was a thick green cord into which was tucked a carefully arranged set of feathers.

And always on one shoulder, the highly polished double barreled shotgun, its wooden stock matching the shine of the brown boots.

After the Prince arrived that afternoon, teacher Dežman struggled to keep our attention and so he let us out early. We all raced to the bottom of the hill, reluctant to go near the house and particularly the garage in front of which stood the shiny Mercedes with its canvas top rolled back. And when after a noisy while, shifting from one leg to the other, we were shooed off by the game warden, we reluctantly dispersed for home.

In the weeks before the arrival, Tscherne had been making preparations in different parts of the forest where the Prince could get to shoot a bear or a stag. In either case, small fenced-in platforms with benches seating two or three were built some distance up a sturdy beech or oak that could be reached by climbing a ladder which would be pulled up after the hunters settled in for the wait. The lumber for these platforms came from the village sawmill on Father's wagon drawn by Yiorgo. Mother led the horse by the bridle along the narrow and sometimes steep paths as near as possible to the site while Father sat on the wagon and held the reins. The warden led the way while, in the back, Mitzi cranked the brake when necessary. I tagged along in the rear.

That week, the Prince shot a large stag with huge antlers counting five points. He did this while sitting on a platform in the "Unterbinkl" not very far from the crevasse that had swallowed Grandfather's dog. He also sat for several nights on a platform in the deeper forest where the warden suspected the presence of bears. But in spite of the lure of fresh horsemeat, no bear showed up.

The slain stag was dragged on to Father's wagon and taken to Josef Kren, the village butcher near the cemetery. Kren carefully separated the head including antlers from the carcass, cleaned out the inside of the skull and wrapped it in burlap for transport to the taxidermist in the city. He then butchered the carcass into sections which were, on the Prince's orders, given to the villagers. Mother roasted our portion in the big oven, already fired up this late in the season to heat the house.

While the Prince hunted and roamed the forests, the chauffeur busied himself with the huge limousine. Since he was particularly friendly with Father, he allowed me to be near him and help him polish the brass headlamps, clean the wire spokes of the wheels and wax the paintwork. And he even let me sit in the driver seat and allowed me to try to turn the wooden steering wheel.

But equally exciting, if not more so, were the stacks of illustrated newspapers and magazines this Austrian chauffeur brought with him from Vienna on the drive to bring the master to his hunting grounds. The sepia colored pictures of marching troops, flying banners, masses of smiling and cheering faces and uniformed leaders with swastika armbands standing on raised platforms, were glimpses into a yet unknown world, not only to this eight year old but also to all others living in the village. Such literature was freely available in Austria which had been annexed to Hitler's Reich in March of 1938. But it was strictly outlawed in our part of Yugoslavia. Soon all that would change.

I was unhappy to see the men of this hunting party leave. But more so the chauffeur than the Prince.

In the summer of 1939, work began on a new Auersperg mansion high on the northern hills of the Masern bowl but on the gentle slopes facing the south. Surrounded by magnificent pines, the beautiful site had great views especially of the westerly hills into which disappeared the reddening disk of the evening sun. And at the bottom of the hill, with every detail fully exposed during the bright of the day, was the picture postcard of our village.

The construction site being not far from the center of the village, we would often make for the place, after being let out of the classroom and having obtained permission at home. Progress at the site was slow since all work was manual, a great boon for the idle labor of the region, much of it in Masern, Rakitnica and Dolenja Vas. By the end of summer 1940 the foundations were in place and some structures, such as garages and servants quarters, had been built. However, in April 1941, WWII also came to Masern and with it an end to all further construction on the new mansion of this aristocrat.

In 1943, the Auersperg hunting lodge in the village was heavily damaged during the final battle in which the surrounding Partisans wiped out the last units of the "Plava Garda". (More on this later). The thick walled, two story structure was ideally located to fend off the attackers surrounding the village. At least until the expected arrival of the relief forces that never came. But even before the defenders ran out of ammunition, exploding howitzer shells, aimed through barricaded window openings killed most of the defenders and caused the survivors to surrender.

After the Auerspergs acquired the dominion in 1641, the population of the Gottschee enclave increased substantially. Part of this was due to the settling of the inner forest which became known as the "inner settlement phase", to a large extent with subjects from other Auersperg estates within the Empire. This phase ended around 1825 and soon thereafter began to reverse when many residents started to leave for America.

The increase in the population of the enclave is evident also in our village. According to the census of 1770 ordered by Empress Maria Theresa, who was in need of soldiers for her wars with Frederick II of Prussia, the census revealed that the residents lived in 35 houses, but the number of males living in these houses was not listed. However, assuming five residents living in each house puts the population of Masern at 190 persons. But this increase was due to a natural increase only and not due to arrival of additional settlers, evident from the fact that since 1613, no additional land was released to the village.

Among these 190 inhabitants were young men fit to be soldiers who were pressed to serve in the armies of the Empress. Most of these young men saw, for the first time and in numbers far exceeding those who traveled as peddlers through the Empire, the world beyond the forest. Some may have even learned to read and write during their absence lasting many years. This would have given them a significant advantage when they returned.

But their military training also prepared them for the next invader, the French. However, these preparations and fortifications erected on the hills beyond the fork outside Dolenja Vas separating Ribnica (Reiffnitz) from the enclave did little to stop them in 1809.

The French may have left in 1813, but some of the institutions and functions they had put in place remained under the "Kingdom of Illyria". The Kingdom, a province of Austria was dissolved in 1849, its area distributed among the Crown lands of the Empire.

One of the functions that remained was the Office of Surveyors which surveyed all properties in the villages. In Masern this was done by a Frenchman named Franz Colanetté who recorded each parcel of an owner in an "*Alphabetisches Verzeichnis der Gemeinde Masern im Jahre 1825*", a register now kept in the Slovene National Archives in Ljubljana.

Buried among the pages of this register was a surveyor's map of Masern prepared by Colanetté, showing each sliver of each parcel which he identified with a number corresponding to the number in the alphabetical index of owners. It was a beautiful, multi-colored document, drawn on parchment and modestly signed and dated by Colanetté. From these two documents, I was able to identify each of the 57 different parcels owned by my great-great Grandfather Johann Tschinkel who was born in 1789. I successfully resisted the temptation to put this map into my briefcase and smuggle it out of the Archives. Unfortunately, someone else had no such reservations. When only a few years later I tried to find this map where I had left it and get it reproduced, it was no longer there. But it was the effort of this Frenchman which, 114 years later, saved my father's dignity and got me my first bicycle and a new set of clothes.

Father had a sizeable parcel of forest on the hill behind the "Kuckenbichl", the Cuckoo Hill, a flat piece of grazing pasture on the easterly hill surrounding the village. It was known as the Cuckoo Hill because it was here the cuckoo was heard every year, telling the village that spring had arrived.

The adjacent forest parcel was owned by Karl Tschinkel living at Number 12, three houses away on our side of the square. Karl, the oldest of three brothers, had automatically inherited the property when his father died, the mother having died before that. Also living in the house were his two single brothers. The three bachelors were looked after by their married sisters Katharina and Jedert. Katharina's house had burned down in 1938 and she now lived, with her husband and two sons, Albert and Anton, in the house of her in-laws at the eastern end of the village. Jedert was married to Johann Sbaschnig and lived with her husband and son Karl in a house across the square next to the fire house.

The relations between Father and the Tschinkels in number 12 were far from friendly. In fact, thanks to the survey of Franz Colanetté, they were downright hostile.

The Tschinkels of number 12 were related, albeit distantly, to those of us living in number 15. It seems that some time in the 18th century or even before, there was a sub-division of property owned by the Tschinkel family, including a parcel of the forest which was split into halves. Colanetté had surveyed the split, put in place markers and recorded the division in the Land Register of 1825.

The Tschinkels of Number 12 did not agree with Colanetté; they claimed that the Frenchman had set the dividing line to their detriment. And the anger over this perceived injustice simmered over many decades and generations to the present. It came to a boil in the spring of 1939 when, after some dispute with Father, the brothers living in Number 12 secretly moved the markers to the right, 10 meters into our land and felled the lumber on the annexed part.

Father and I set out for Kuckenbichl immediately after somebody brought the news of the rape of his forest.

The devastation was heartbreaking. An entire swath of mature pines had been felled on the entire stretch along the boundary and each tree cut into sections for transport to the mill. Since it was spring and the sap in full flow, the bark had been stripped from each log making the violation even more vivid by the nakedness of the victims now sprawled helter-skelter on the barren ground.

Father ordered me to fetch his friend Johann Krisch and Franz Jaklitsch, the now unofficial head of the village. Mother told me later that he did this in part so that I would not see him cry. He had for years been tending the ground under those trees to keep the underbrush in check and allow the trees to mature unencumbered. In contrast, the land of the Tschinkels next to his was bare, its lumber having been sold off for needed cash over the years, the bareness inflaming only more their lust for the riches on the other side of the boundary.

The three agreed that only the law was able to deal with this violation. When the gendarmes arrived and confronted the perpetrators, their defense was, the markers were placed by Colanetté in the wrong place and they only took what was rightly theirs.

Karl Tschinkel and his brothers were ordered to cease any further action until the matter was put before a magistrate in Ribnica (Reiffnitz). At the hearing a few days later, this magistrate ordered a survey to verify the boundaries determined in the original survey by Colanetté and taken into the records of the county as final.

The arrival of the surveyor and two assistants, both accompanied by several gendarmes, was a village event. There had not been this many legs trampling the new spring growth of grass on the flats of Kuckenbichl since it ceased to be common grazing ground many centuries ago. The gendarmes had their hands full to keep the villagers out of the way of the surveyor and his assistants.

The outcome of the survey was, of course, predictable and the assistants moved the markers back to the original position. The fury of the Tschinkel brothers, in part over the loss of the lumber and even more so due to their public embarrassment, was held in check only by the presence of the law. But on top of it all, they were to be charged for the expenses of the court and that of the surveying team. I grinned along with Father as the three of them, together with their retinue, most of them relatives, left the arena. But my reason for grinning was different from that of my father.

In the days leading up to the arrival of the surveyor, Mother and Father, who were certain of the outcome, kept discussing the disposal of the lumber and what to do with the money from its sale. "A new horse; a new wagon; a new roof for the main house; new clothing for the kids; a bicycle for Johann", they said. I immediately verified what I heard and staked my claim; the bicycle I had been begging for, for quite a while. "Yes, if we win, you will get your bike". And win we did, and with that, my bicycle was now only days away. A very good reason to grin.

Father treated the surveying party and the gendarmes to a meal at the Jaklitsch tavern. Wine flowed freely even for those who arrived after the surveying party left and after it became known that Tschinkel was buying.

In the days to follow, in spite of the victory, Mother voiced her concern. "Is this public embarrassment of the Tschinkel brothers going to lead to even more hostility? Yes their behavior was that of bullies and we set them straight. But they had been fully convinced they were in the right, this belief having been passed down to them by their father, grandfather and others before that. And it seems that they were also desperate, even lacking the money to pay for their annual assessment, having stripped their forests bare to sell the lumber. And now they have to pay the cost of their mistaken behavior. Why don't we split this cost with them, consider it as payment for felling the trees and stripping and cutting them into mill-ready logs. There will be enough money to do this when we sell the lumber".

After several of such discussions which included our good friend Johann Krisch who believed Mother's plan was overly generous, Father went to talk to Jaklitsch who judged that it was a good idea. Father asked that he become the intermediary and take the offer to the brothers which he did.

Predictably, they insisted that Father pay all the costs since they still believed that Colanetté had made a mistake. They also insisted that he pay for their labors. But Jaklitsch was persuasive and got both sides to agree to a compromise. Father was to pay half of their fine and give them the other half as payment for their labors. Jaklitsch also convinced them to give up their notion that Colanetté was wrong.

Jaklitsch had been persuasive and the village was impressed with his diplomacy. But the full power of this ability to convince became evident two years later when he convinced most of the villagers to give up their homes, lands and heritage and resettle into the unknown for no more than a promise: "a secure future guaranteed by the full power of the all powerful Third Reich".

So the lumber was sold at a good price and new groups of wagons, ferrying naked sections of pines stopped at the Jaklitsch inn for lunch. This time the lumber was from the forest of my father, lumber that was soon to bring the cash for the bicycle I now dreamed about every night.

The day this happened found us in Gottschee city, in the store that sold bicycles, the store of Father's cousin Franz. My eyes quickly settled on a multi speed beauty with a gearshift mechanism that would help me take in stride the steep hill on the way to Grandma Ilc in Dolenja Vas. It also had very modern rim brakes for the long slope downhill on the way back, not the brake embedded in the rear axle which, after only a short distance of serious braking, overheated and failed, causing a dangerous runaway unless the rider was somehow able to stop and continue by walking downhill. To deal with this problem, riders would cut down a small Christmas tree sized pine and attach it with string to the saddle post of the bike as a brake. But this was put to a stop after it was noticed that the area around the top of the hill was becoming bare.

Franz listened attentively to my arguments but Mother prevailed. A bike like that would be more than we could afford, besides no one else in the village had anything like that and why should I be different.

I had asked for the moon, but got a distant star instead, a silvery beauty just the same. Soon after we got home, I was surrounded by all my schoolmates of both sexes who wanted to try it. I sped away but they were waiting for me on my return at the edge of the village. Unable to retrieve it from the bigger boys, I had to run home tearfully and it was Mother who finally got it back for me.

But soon the novelty evaporated and disappointments arrived.

Both Father and Mother had insisted with Cousin Franz on an adult bicycle since I was growing rapidly. I got a bike years too big for me; its saddle too high even at the lowest setting. I could sit on it only if it was adjusted so that its front pointed downward at a steep angle. And even so, the tips of my toes reached the pedals at their low point only if I kept shifting my behind appropriately from one side to the other, which soon resulted in a serious rash between my tender buttocks. Not to speak of my testicles, aching from continuously being crushed against the center bar, far too high to be comfortably straddled by legs too short for their feet to reach the ground.

My first long journey on this bike was a visit to Grandma Ilc in Dolenja Vas. This turned out to be both a joy and disillusionment. I moved with speed over even ground renewing the sores on my buttocks, and at even greater speed on downhill slopes. But at nearly every upward slope, I had to get off and push. The gear ratio was too high and my weight on the pedals too light. A gear shift or even a lesser ratio would have overcome all that. The bike was best for level ground only, something Cousin Franz omitted to explain to Mother.

Even more upsetting was the brake. It began to fade down the long steep hill into Masern and only crashing into the embankment saved me from excessive speed and a serious fall. The front wheel was twisted, the fender bent beyond repair, my face severely bruised and bleeding. The face healed and the bike was repaired, but when I next visited Grandma Ilc, I walked the bike both up and down the hill.

In addition to the bicycle there was money for many other needed things. Mother confided to Schaffer's wife Maria that she was grateful to the brothers since her husband had had no intention of harvesting the already fully grown lumber in spite of her frequent urging. And decades later with hindsight to support her, she confessed to Karl's sister Katharina: "They should have cut down even more; it only got left behind for others anyway".

There was money for clothes, including my first suit which was ill fitting and much too big. Like the bicycle, it would fit when I grew a little more. Except that I wore it out long before I got there. But that is part of another story. There also was enough money for a new wagon and a new horse.

Yiorgo was showing his age by tiring from even the easiest tasks. Father could no longer urge him into the lively trot he once so willingly fell into on the way home from Grandma Ilc. Even the measure of oats waiting for him at the trough was no longer an incentive. He resisted leaving the stable and the once so effective chamomile tea, administered ever more frequently, was becoming ineffective against his nightly colic. All this was a recurrent topic at evening meals, irrefutable logic used to overcome the objections of both Mitzi and myself, both drawn ever closer to our ageing friend who looked at us with sad but now oozing eyes as if sensing his imminent fate.

There was no warning and no tearful goodbye. And when Father and Mother came back from the city one day, a vigorous new Yiorgo trotted the wagon into the courtyard.

The new Yiorgo (we all agreed to keep the name), was a young "Schimmel". Young, "because the gray of the fur had only a few of the white spots which with age would ultimately cover the entire body", they said. He was also much bigger and stronger than his former namesake and even the harness fit better; it had always looked too big for his predecessor who, like me, also never grew into it. "But be careful, don't go near him yet, he is young and impetuous; he has to get used to you first". A trip to Dolenja Vas now took considerably less time. To make full use of the stronger horse, father also bought a bigger farming wagon with better brakes and stronger wheels. Those on the old one had started to wobble in spite of the attention annually received from the smith.

All these additions did not escape the Tschinkel brothers; still smarting over their defeat in spite of the promise to Jaklitsch, they were not letting bygones be bygones. And one Sunday afternoon when we returned from visiting Grandma Ilc, the new wagon was missing. But it was soon discovered straddling the peak of the house. The brothers had taken it apart and re-assembled it on the peak of the roof. Mother cried, Father ground his teeth and some neighbors shared his outrage, but most of the village had a good laugh.

Again, Jaklitsch came to the rescue. The next day he assembled the firemen including Schaffer, and with the promise of free wine they formed a "bucket brigade" up a ladder to the men taking the wagon apart and passed the pieces on to the ground where it was put together again. Jaklitsch even persuaded the brothers to take part, but more with a promise of free wine than an appeal for remorse. But with this prank the mutual animosity ceased and a few years later, the century old grievance was forgotten. And many more years later Karl's sister Katharina became Mother's best friend.

The plague arrived in Masern in August 1836. The disaster lasted 53 days from August 11 to October 3 and claimed 51 lives, nearly one third of the inhabitants of the village. Father Munini, the village priest who administered the last sacrament, recorded each victim in the "ledger of deaths", listing Variola, or black smallpox, as the cause. Who brought the pox, where it came from and what stopped it, Father Munini did not write. Since medical help was not available, the most likely end to the disaster was the natural resistance of those who survived.

Among the 51 victims were two members of the Tschinkel family at Number 15; Elisabeth, 50 and Gera 38. A total of ten Tschinkels died; the other eight living in houses of related families, Tschinkel being the most common name in the village.

At the height of the carnage the villagers, led by Father Munini, prayed to Saint Rockus, the patron saint for protection against diseases, to lift the pox and spare the village, which he did on October 3. 1836. They pledged to commemorate the divine trial in an annual procession to the church in Dolenja Vas dedicated to the saint. This promise was kept every year on August 16, the name day of the saint. I participated in the final procession in 1941.

On the morning of that August 16, a group of villagers assembled at the church and followed the sexton, holding high the banner of our village Saints Primus and Felizian, toward Dolenja Vas. In the procession behind the sexton was Father Gliebe in his black funeral attire and white cassock, leading in prayer the followers, mostly women in black, their heads covered with black kerchiefs, all fingering their rosaries and responding to the priest in muttered unison. Father Gliebe was the permanent priest of Göttenitz/Gotenica who became our stand-in spiritual leader after Father Rozman left in 1939. Later, Father Gliebe, like most of the priests in the enclave became a forceful advocate against the resettlement in addition to his well known hostility to the young Gottscheer leaders who were preparing the population for the move. He remained in his village when it was emptied in 1941 and thereafter served new arrivals there until 1949 when he became the priest of Dolenja Vas where he died in 1960.

In Dolenja Vas there was a lookout in the church steeple and its sexton rang the small bell when the pilgrims came into view. When they arrived at the church, the parish deacon greeted them at the open portal. He then led the procession into the church where Father Gliebe prostrated himself before the image of Saint Rockus as his tired followers slid into empty benches. During the Mass conducted by both priests, our sexton Michitsch held upright the banner of Primus and Felizian and after Holy Communion, the pilgrims were led in a final thank-you prayer to the Saint who had heard our plea in 1836.

After the Mass, the pilgrims descended from the church to tables in the shaded courtyard of my Slovene grandmother's tavern at the foot of the hill, where they ate the lunches brought with them while Mother, Mitzi and I served them liquid refreshments.

VILLAGE THROUGH TIME

The pox left its mark on the village in other ways.

To begin with, the walled-in cemetery surrounding the church could not accommodate the large number of those who died of the pox and who, as a result, had to be buried temporarily in a mass grave consecrated by Father Munini. This forced a decision to move the cemetery and all its buried contents in 1838 to a larger location at the end of the village in the direction of Gotenica (Göttenitz). Now that there was more space in the cemetery, each house in the village was assigned a larger plot and the remains from the old grave at the church were transferred there. Each house handled its own relics. A corner of the walled-in cemetery was reserved for a small charnel house and the space around it was left un-consecrated to accommodate those who did not die in grace.

The space vacated by the cemetery made possible the planned elongation of the church by adding a bell tower which also provided room for a raised choir space and eventually, an organ. The belfry space was designed to accommodate three bells to be obtained in the future. Until then, the small bell would continue to serve the village but from a higher and more effective vantage point.

Entry to the church was now through the vaulted ground level space of the tower. Holes through the vaulted ceiling provided for the long ropes to the three future bells so that they could be rung from ground level. The completion date of 1845 was recorded on an engraved stone embedded in the portal above the new entry door.

Father Munini also persuaded the villagers to erect a chapel dedicated to mark ending the pox in 1836. The memorial, called "the old chapel", was a three meter high masonry structure with a pointed, four sided peaked roof covered with wooden shingles. The structure had a recess in the wall facing the street to hold a picture of St. Rockus and, occasionally, a bouquet of wildflowers. It stood at the bottom of our side of the hill toward Dolenja Vas and the pilgrimage stopped there for a special prayer. The chapel fell apart from decay after WWII and the ruins were removed.

Another and more substantial chapel, dedicated to Mary of the Seven Sorrows, was built just outside the village toward Dolenja Vas. It was surrounded by a waist high wrought iron fence with a swinging gate. The chapel itself had a wrought iron door and inside was a small altar on which stood the statue of a sorrowful, upward looking Mary with her exposed heart pierced with seven symmetrically spaced daggers; four on her right and three on her left. Hanging on a chain from the ceiling was a small glass vessel for oil on which floated an eternally burning wick. The women of the village replenished the oil and provided the flowers that always graced the altar. Over the decades since the plague, the grateful villagers did not forget the reason for this and even today this chapel still stands.

While the pox brought about the enlargement of the church, a major fire in the village resulted in the first schoolhouse, a firehouse outfitted with a manual fire pump, uniforms and brass helmets for the firemen and a cistern to collect and store the runoff waters from melting snow and frequent rains.

The fire of August 2, 1882 destroyed fifteen houses and their adjacent barns and stables. The story of this event and its aftermath has already been told in the Chapter "The Fire Pump".

One of the houses destroyed that August was the one at Number 30. The burned out shell was rebuilt (with funds from the Deutscher Schulverein) into our first school which opened for formal education in October 1884. It consisted of one large schoolroom in one half of the house and a separate apartment for the teacher in the other half. While this schoolroom became the center for our learning, it also became the symbol for competing ideologies, not only in our village or the enclave, but also throughout many lands of the multi-ethnic monarchy where minorities such as the Gottscheer struggled for ethnic survival. In the enclave the struggle was against the encroaching majorities of the Slovene, while the Slovene in turn were struggling against the long Germanization objective of the Austrians.

The Primary Education Act of 1869 had mandated state supervision of the school system, thereby supplanting the function until then performed by the Church. And since the language of instruction was to be that of the majority of the ethnic make up of the population living in the district, the language of schooling in Grčarice (Masern) was German. The Church, however, retained the duty of supervising religious instruction.

Prior to the opening of the schoolhouse in Masern in 1884, limited education was provided in the parsonage by the village priest, teaching his pupils to read and write a short letter. The first resident priest/teacher was Anton Wallisch who came to the village in 1767 and left in 1771. For 51 years thereafter, there again was no priest/

teacher and Masern again had to rely, as before 1767, on the priests from Göttenitz and Dolenja Vas for learning and religious care.

Johann Munini was the priest between 1822 and 1837 and after he left there was again a 30 year period when there was no resident priest/teacher until the arrival of Father Johann Posnik who came to Masern in 1867.

In spite of the prolonged absences of priest/teachers, the villagers of Masern learned to read and write, even if in only a very limited way. This is evident from the ledgers of births, marriages and deaths stored in the Archives of the Archdiocese in Ljubljana, starting with the year 1773. The initial entries made by the priest who kept the records, show only crosses substituting for a signature.

Learning progress was very slow since instruction was in German, a new language for the children as well as most of the adults of the village; the language of the village being the Gottscheer dialect which had little resemblance to the language they were now required to learn. Due to this the priests, who spoke only German or Slovene, had a difficult time communicating with their parishioners.

But with the arrival of Father Johann Posnik in 1867, continuity of teaching and religious care finally came to Masern. He had come as a priest and gave limited instruction at the parsonage, but only to boys. Learning was still slow in part due to the language barrier and also because the boys could come to lessons only when they could be spared from doing farming chores and then mostly on weekends or during the winter months. Their help was desperately needed due to the large scale emigration to America of both men and women not only in the enclave, but throughout Krain, that started in the second half of the 19th century. This emigration reduced the 1857 population of the enclave from 22,920 to 10,983. [41]

In Masern all this changed when the new school opened in 1884 and all children were now required to attend class. Father Posnik gave up the priesthood to become the first full time teacher in the village, but continued to give religious instructions until 1892. As a teacher he was paid a salary and therefore was no longer required to live off the fields that belonged to the parsonage.

In 1892, Posnik was replaced by Johann Hutter who was a full time teacher for the next fourteen years. But in 1906, his teaching job was relieved by Johann Schober, a full time teacher. From that time forward all instructions were by full time teachers and priests were no longer called upon to teach the children of Masern.

With the dissolution of the Monarchy in 1918, the village school at Masern number 30, the property of the "Deutsche Schulverein", was sequestered by the State of Slovenia according to the right of pre-emption of the Kingdom of the Serbs,

---

41 *Kočevski Zbornik, pg 136.*

Croats and Slovene. On June 4, 1920, the sub-municipality of Grčarice purchased the school and its surrounding property for 700 Krone, the currency of the former Monarchy. And Masern, for about 600 years the official name of the village, reverted to its original - Grčarice. [42]

The Imperial Education Act of 1869 remained in effect until December 5, 1929, when it was replaced by the School Act of the State of Yugoslavia, the successor to the Kingdom of the Serbs, Croats and Slovene. But this Act had little effect on the school of Grčarice or other schools in the enclave or other parts of the land where primary instruction continued in the language of the ethnic majority of the principality.

This changed with the Decree issued by the Ministry of Education in January 1936, which decreed that all education be conducted in the language of the land, in our case the land of the Slovene.

When I started school in the fall of 1937, I had no problem with this. Because of Mother and Grandma Ilc, I not only knew how to read and write but also could speak Slovene fluently which put me from the beginning at the head of my class. My success was obviously not due to the inability of the others; I simply had a head start, whereas they had to struggle with the new language the way their ancestors struggled only a few decades ago when they were learning German.

But my good fortune immediately got me into trouble with my school mates. This in part because by 1937, Slovene had become the language of an "inferior race". At least according to the ideology of the Third Reich which by then had taken hold in the enclave, including Masern, a hold greatly strengthened by the Decree of January 1936. And I was part of this "inferior race", at least half of me was, a fact that caused me much agony in the days to come.

---

42 Hans Loser, *Masern in Wort und Bild*, in *Gottscheer Kalender 1931*

Chapter 5

The Church and the Square

It is likely that a chapel was erected in Grčarice (Masern) soon after the settlers arrived in the middle of the 14th century. Being God fearing and with much of their lives revolving around their religion, constructing a place of worship, which also doubled as a meeting place, would have been a high priority. Encouragement and assistance for this would have come from the regional parish in Ribnica (Reiffnitz), or from Count Ortenburg, or both.

The villagers, including the Slovene subjects of the Count living in the hamlet, dedicated the chapel to patron saints Primus and Felician. The two saints were brothers, born in the 3rd century and living in Rome. They had converted to Christianity for which they were beheaded in 305 AD, during the persecution of Christians by Emperor Diocletian. Already in 1689 Valvasor identifies the brothers as the patron saints of Masern, which proves that the chapel was erected years before that.

But even before Valvasor identifies the patrons, the chapel had a small bell which served the village for nearly seventy years. Leopold Raktelj, a priest of the diocese and the chronicler of Grčarice, wrote in the periodical Slovenec in 1936 that the bell was one of the oldest in Carniola-Kranjska. He writes that the inscription on the bell was: "IESU CHRISTE FILI DEI VIVI MISERERE NOBIS. AMEN. A° MDCXXI", fixing the year of its casting at 1621.

Raktelj also states that in 1895 there were two other bells in the tower, each of them larger than their little brother born 274 years before. All three were installed in the newly built bell tower when it, as part of the overall church enlargement, was completed in 1845. The enlargement was possible when the cemetery surrounding the church was moved to the open space along the road to Göttenitz. The existing cemetery had become too small to accommodate the dead from the pox in 1836. The freed up space not only allowed the elongation of the church but also significantly enlarged the village square.

The two larger bells were embossed with a picture of the garlanded St. Joseph and of a cross as well as the inscription "OPUS JOSEPHI REISS NOMINE HAEREDUM VINCENTII SAMASSA ANNO 1816".

According to the chronicler, a new priest (Leopold Raktelj) took up his posting in Masern on December 2, 1895 and moved into the recently refurbished parsonage behind the church. There was a formal installation event on December 17, 1895 and high religious and public officials came to the village for the event. The new priest was initiated with great pomp and there were spirited celebrations afterwards. And when the guests were leaving, the bells were rung so hard that the larger of the two developed a crack. This was perceived as a bad omen, especially since the other bell already had a crack. But it was the small bell that survived.

The villagers, eager to correct the situation, started negotiations with a caster to have him melt down the damaged bells and use the metal as partial payment for their replacements. The 3,000 Florin for the new bells were to be borrowed from the Kranjska hranilnica, the regional savings bank of Krain. Already on January 10, 1896, the two damaged bells were lowered to the ground. But the bell caster Samassa insisted on advance payment which, after repeated pleas from the villagers, was finally approved by the bank.

The new bells arrived in Ribnica on Good Friday April 3, 1896. The following morning, on Easter Saturday after Mass, a group of villagers went to fetch them from the railroad station. When the approach of wagons with the bells was announced by blasts from the steam whistle at the sawmill complex in Jelendol, a procession of all the villagers, with the priest at its head went out to meet them. "At four in the afternoon, the bells were installed and were pealing a joyous alleluia. Young and old cried aloud. All night long were they rung; the celebrations ending at five o'clock in the morning". "Resurrection!" the chronicler exclaims.

Twenty years later during WWI, the two new bells were requisitioned for the war effort to be melted down for ammunition. Again, the little bell of AD 1621 had to re-assume its former, centuries long tasks, duties which it had turned over to its larger brothers a mere two decades ago. But the war not only claimed two bells; it also took 64 able men of the village of which eleven never returned.

The wooden roof of the bell tower was replaced with tile in 1911; the roof of the church in 1921. And in 1923 the village purchased three new bells which were dedicated on October 26, 1923.

The little bell was retired after the three new bells were installed in 1923. It was relegated to passivity on a stand in a corner of the bell chamber in the tower next to the newcomers to again become a silent participant and a reminder of ancient days. To be kept in reserve, just in case. Many times I swung its clapper against the rim to hear the mellow sound which had so nobly served the villagers of Masern during the many centuries of our past.

The larger newcomers, each of a different size, were purchased in part by the villagers who for years had been collecting money for the bell and clock fund. A large part of the money had been coming from the villagers who had left for America. Seed money for the purchase had been provided by the parishes of Dolenja Vas and Ribnica. The new bells served the now much larger congregation by sounding the time of day, delivering unique messages heard in the remotest part of the village or ringing in concert on special events and joyous occasions.

On July 8, 1925, the clock in the tower again started telling time after not doing so since the new bells were installed. Two workers from Osilnica adapted the mechanism to function with the new bells for which they were paid 1,500 Dinar. And at 7 o'clock in the evening of January 1, 1926, a moderate earth quake shook the village and produced several cracks in the walls of the church and the parsonage. There was no other reported damage in the village.

The ultimate fate of the ancient small bell and its three newer brothers is tied to the battle in the village between the "Plava Garda" and the Partisans starting on September 8, 1943. This was the last stand of the Garda, also known as Četniks, adherents of Yugoslav royalists under General Mihailović. The Garda, surrounded in the village, kept fighting for 3 days until their ammunition ran out and they were forced to surrender.

(Another faction, the "Bela Garda", Slovene Catholic nationalists opposing Tito, was destroyed a few days thereafter by the Partisans in a major battle at the fortress of Turjak, 10 miles north-west of Ribnica on 13 September 1943. Remnants of both factions later merged into the Slovene anti-Communists known as the Domobranci who pledged allegiance to the Nazi occupier with lethal consequences to themselves after the end of WWII).

During the battle, the Partisans used howitzers to silence the machine guns of the "Plava Garda" firing at them through the openings in the bell tower. The bombardment set the roof of the church, the wood inside the masonry walls of the tower and the steeple on fire. The heavy wooden beams, on to which the swinging mechanism of the three bells was mounted, were last to give way and the bells came crashing down.

On one of my returns to Grčarice, Norbert, the son of Anton Tscherne the former Auersperg game warden, talked about the battle which started in the afternoon of September 8. In 1941, Anton had decided not to resettle and remained in the village.

When the shooting started, Anton moved bed mattresses against windows to stop stray bullets from entering and made the family sleep on the floor until the fighting was over. And yes, the precaution was warranted as became obvious from several windowpanes that were shattered in the following days.

The church caught fire on the first night of the battle. The Tscherne family could not see the flames, their house being at the far end of the village, but the burning enveloped the sky in a brilliant glow that lasted deep into the night.

But most memorable to Norbert was the sound of the bells landing on the stone floor and on top of each other after their respective support beams weakened and at intervals let go of their load. The sounds, louder than ever before, were strange and different, befitting a death-knell, but this time a knell for themselves. Strange and different, but by then their individual tone had already changed from the familiar ring to an unfamiliar groan, the heated metal having robbed them of their former voice.

The battle lasted for three days and nights. And when the hoped-for relief did not appear, the tired survivors of the "Plava Garda" surrendered to the Partisans and an uncertain fate. After surrender to the NOV (National Liberation Front), a court-martial in Kočevje condemned most of the 97 survivors to death and after the trial they were returned to the parsonage in Masern in the middle of October 1943. On October 24, twenty three of them were executed and buried in the forest off the road toward Glažuta. [43]

The others were executed and buried in Jelendol, the saw mill complex two kilometers away on the road to Dolenja Vas. The bodies buried in Jelendol were exhumed in the 1980's and the Register of Deaths in the parish church of Dolenja Vas records each of them by a number and the remark, "death due to a shot in the back of the head".

For six years until 1949, the bells had been lying where they fell. That year, the still standing walls of the church and the bell tower were taken down, removed and the grounds leveled and seeded. At the beginning of the clean up, all three were taken to Schaffer's barn for storage.

During the electrification of Grčarice in 1953-54, the new inhabitants of what had become a workers' village decided to contribute some of their labor to the communal good. To build a new church was, in those postwar days, out of the question. Instead,

---

43 Mirko Oražem, *Grčarice, Zgodovinski kraj*, Ribnica 2003.

THE CHURCH AND THE SQUARE

the workers' council decided to sell the bells and with the proceeds purchase the wire needed to bring electricity from the transformer station in Jelendol to the village.

The bells were offered to the municipal organization Dinos in Kočevje and when a few days later it sent an oxcart to pick them up, Dinos paid on the spot. And shortly thereafter, the two damaged bells were broken up at the factory and the pieces melted down.

The entire transaction was done without the knowledge and permission of the parish office in Dolenja Vas which took the matter to the District Court. The court decided that the still intact bell weighing 258 kilo be turned over to its rightful owner, the Dolenja Vas parish. It was kept there for many years but ultimately disappeared without a trace. The court also ruled that the funds from the other two could, as was planned, be applied to purchasing the wire for the transmission line to bring power to Masern. Details of the proceedings are in the District Court of Novo Mesto under number GZ 287/54-3, dated 15 October 1954. [44]

Whatever happened to the small ancient bell remains a mystery. It simply disappeared.

During the years the bells hung on the beams up high, they functioned as the heartbeat of the village and guided its daily rhythm. But the brain behind it was the gigantic clock, mounted on a platform on the level just below that of the bells.

Narrow steps, starting at the choir level, zigzagging upward on one of the four walls of the tower, reached the clock platform as their first stop. One more set of steps led to the bell chamber, the level from which the doomed Plava Garda fired their machine guns in September 1943. The steps to the first platform were climbed by the sexton once every week to rewind the clock. He allowed me to come along and watch him turn the cranks, being still too small to help him with this chore.

The mechanism, a gigantic grandfather clock really, was powered by two huge stone weights, each hanging from a pulley wheel for the rope whose one end was fixed to the platform. The other end was tied to a drum in the mechanism which was cranked to raise the weights, thus winding up the clock. One of the weights ran the time mechanism while the other much bigger stone powered two heavy hammers, one to strike the big bell with the hour, the other to hit the middle bell with the quarter.

---

44   Mirko Oražem, *Grčarice skozi preteklost*. Ribnica 1998, pg. 76-77.

THE BELLS RING NO MORE

It took a week for the weights to descend the tower before they had to be rewound again. But the clock never stopped, its long pendulum, swinging in the space of the tower, never taking a rest. The weekly rewind was done by the sexton before dusk and before he had rung the middle bell reminding the villagers to come to evening prayers.

After I became an altar boy I was allowed to climb the ladders on my own to watch this array of toothed wheels, levers, gears, rods, pulleys and ropes perform their timely spectacle. The most fascinating of these was at noon when the escape mechanism started a whirring of wheels and movements of levers that produced the four strikes of the fourth quarter on the middle bell, followed by twelve more on the big bell for the hour of noon. While this was happening, the big stone descended a sizable distance away from his smaller brother, which always caught up during the next twelve hours.

Unperturbed by this frenzy, the pendulum worked the escape mechanism, gearing, rods and finally the two arms of the clock face on each of four sides of the tower. Rods carried the hours and minutes from the mechanism through the bell level up to a gear box and from there horizontally to each clock face above the large openings in the tower walls. And through these openings flowed the sound of time to the remotest fields and forests beyond the village center, especially to places from which any one of the four faces of the clock could not be seen.

While the chiming of the two bells telling time was heard throughout day and night, each of the three had their individual voice according to a fixed protocol established by the parish.

Apart from announcing time, the bells could be rung from the small entry space in the base of the tower just behind the portals. From there, the ropes reached the bells through holes in the vaulted ceiling of the tower base. Normally the ropes were hung on hooks on the wall to keep them out of the way of churchgoers passing through. But on Sundays the bells were rung from the choir level above to keep the entry to the church clear.

All three bells, Big, Medium and Small were rung in unison for two minutes just before morning Mass. But 30 minutes before that, two bells were rung briefly for several minutes to remind the faithful to get ready for church. Medium and Small were rung on weekdays, but Medium and Big on Sundays, conveying a greater duty with their bigger sounds.

THE CHURCH AND THE SQUARE

Each of the three, if rung individually, also conveyed special messages on extraordinary occasions.

To the commanding voice of the Big bell had been assigned the job of sounding the fire alarm and requesting the immediate gathering of the firemen at the firehouse. I remember hearing it in 1938 when the Tscherne barn was struck by lightning. There had been the fires in '34 and '36 but they had started during the night when I was asleep. But I heard it several times when Karl Schaffer, the fire chief decided on a dry run. Being so close to the church and the firehouse just across the square, I got there with the first of his men and watched the others as they came running, some out of breath, from all parts of the village.

To let the village know that this was a dry run only, Medium was rung after all the firemen arrived at the firehouse. This procedure superseded a prior one in which Medium was rung, announcing the "all clear" as soon as some, if not all, firemen arrived. This had given those who suspected a false alarm time to wait and see. But there were a few times when Medium was sounded immediately after Big stopped when it became obvious Schaffer was drunk and had decided to have a dry run and ring the Big bell himself.

While Big sounded the alarm and Medium announced the all clear, Small was the messenger of sad news, be it at any time of day or night. Single strokes, expertly executed by the ringer pulling the rope in a way so that the clapper hit only one rim of the bell at "paused" intervals, announced that the priest was on the way with the Host to a dying villager to hear the final confession and administer last rites. All who heard, of course knew who the dying person was, given the size of the village and its ability to rapidly spread either news or gossip. And as the priest with the host walked by, those meeting him along the way dropped to their knees, crossed themselves and bowed their heads.

After that, the people were expecting the next, often inevitable follow-on sound, again from the Small bell. If the ringing was briefly stopped twice, the deceased was a man. If there was only one interruption the deceased was a woman. Thereafter, Medium and Small were rung for one minute three times a day each day until the body was buried. They were rung at eight in the morning, at noon and at four in the afternoon, the sequence starting after the interrupted ringing of Small had announced the death of the villager.

After the mid morning Requiem Mass, the "paused" tolling of Small was also the final accompaniment in the procession to the cemetery. The procession was led by the sexton Michitsch carrying high the black cross with white skull and crossbones, his clothing hidden by a white knee length smock embroidered with lace at the bottom, at the end of sleeves and the collar. Behind him the altar boy similarly dressed, slowly swinging the chain of the incense vessel to keep the embers glowing and produce the incense cloud. (When I was the altar boy, I did this). Following was the reverend Jože Rozman, (1934-39) reading aloud from his breviary. He was also in a similar smock, but his head was covered with the black biretta of the Catholic priest.

The cart with the coffin was drawn and pushed by the bearers, some of them having dug the grave on previous days. While digging, they were surrounded by us children and some adults watching the bones of the prior occupant appear on the heap of earth alongside the grave.

Behind the cart walked the family and behind them, relatives and villagers who came along for the final goodbye. Some also came in anticipation of the wake to follow, usually at the Kren inn, it being the nearest to the cemetery. There was the likelihood of sausage, ham and cider or even wine, or perhaps even a few jiggers of slivovitz; our way to celebrate the passing of a villager.

I remember several times when the interrupted ringing of the small bell started yet another event lasting several days. Among them are three that I recall particularly well.

The first of these, in 1939, was the passing of Grandma Sturm who lived by herself in number 22 in the eastern part of the village. She had one son who had left her years ago for a city in Austria where he married and had a son and daughter. The old lady had been in failing health and had notified her son and he came, but only after having been notified of his mother's death. The burial, however, could not be delayed until he and his wife arrived, so the funeral preparations were assumed by neighbors, the old lady not having nearby family for this last act. The preparations included the making of the coffin, a job always given to Father by default, he being the only person in the village with a shop and tools needed for this task.

The initial part in this was the measuring of the body. This time I kept insisting that he take me along to which he finally, if reluctantly, agreed after consulting with Mother. She had no doubts saying that it was time for this eight-year old to see a dead body at close range. "Besides, he knew her well when she was alive, had she not talked to him when he passed by her house and given him candy! She is no different now except that she is dead".

THE CHURCH AND THE SQUARE

The body was already laid out in the center of the large living room. They had dressed her in black and placed her on the bier, a platform of planks resting on two saw-horses. She was to lie there until put into the coffin when it was brought to the house. Until then and until the morning of the funeral, the body was watched over continuously by villagers who came to pay their last respects. After kneeling and bowing their heads toward the body and mouthing a prayer, they sat on benches or chairs at a respectful distance, having jiggers of slivovitz. Many stayed until the empty bottle was no longer replaced with a full one. But some alternated in staying through the night, a custom surely as old as the village itself.

As instructed by Father on the way to the Sturm house, I took the end of the unfolded carpenter rule to the toes of the body and held it there until he noted the length at the top of the head. After a little chat with those present and a few jiggers of slivovitz, we left. He had work to do and work quickly to have the coffin ready in time.

The needed materials and supplies were kept in his shop. Air dried pine planks from the village sawmill, rolls of strong black paper, boss-relieved with angels sprouting wings. Nails, screws and handles for the bearers. All within reach.

He made a form-fitting coffin, the sides wider at shoulder height but from there tapering toward head and foot. Top and bottom flat, the edges fitting the six cornered shape. All outside surfaces, except the bottom were covered with the embossed black crepe paper folded over the edges and tacked to the boards with decorative nails. The inside was lined in white cloth. I helped him with most of the tasks, finding for him the hardware or tools he needed next; holding the boards while he was cutting, planing or nailing, handing him the next nail from the bucket. When all was done, I was sent to the Sturm house to say that the coffin was ready. And when they brought it to the house, the body fit. How he got paid for this or any other coffin I do not remember. Mostly, it was labor in kind for work on his farm.

There was the time in 1936 when the deceased was Hedwig Rosa, the one year old daughter of Franz Jaklitsch, for whom the coffin had to be white. Lacking the embossed crepe paper in white, Yiorgo pulled us to a store in Ribnica to get some. And as was usual, we stopped at Grandma Ilc for a chat, a quarter liter of wine for Father, a soft drink for me and a bit of hay for the horse.

The second death, in 1940, was that of Michaela Primosch, the second wife of Josef Primosch living in number 16, diagonally across the cistern from our house. Joseph's first wife had died some years ago and he found the younger woman in another village deeper in the forest. It was a loveless and unhappy marriage, as was apparent from the violent arguments that drifted across the cistern bowl and through our kitchen window.

Josef was one of our two musicians, the other being Anton Tscherne living at the opposite and far end of the village. Both played the accordion at dances held at the Jaklitsch or Kren tavern with Josef being the preferred musician. Their music, in spite of some discordant notes, provided the rhythm which overheated the spinning couples and fired the merriment of others not already inflamed by wine. They played not only during the warm summer months as part of village festivals such as Easter, Ascension or Patrons Day when dance platforms were erected in the courtyard of the inns but also on cooler days when the dancing was done indoors in the large public room of either place. No dances were held at the Tschinkel tavern; the proprietors, Rudy and his aging mother no longer up to the hassle ever since the father and husband had died some years ago.

Josef had three sons, the youngest at fourteen, the other two a few years older. All three practiced on their father's instrument hoping to become as proficient as he was. In good weather, after the last chores of the day, they practiced outside on the bench next to the front door. Their tunes, drifting across the village square on cooling summer evenings were always welcomed by tired villagers, resting on benches lining the wall to either side of the front door. But especially welcome were the tunes played by the father.

One day the loud voices from the Primosch house across the cistern turned unfamiliar and alarming which made me run there to see the reason for the change. I was one of the first to arrive and from the bottom of the stairs to the attic I saw the three sons lifting their 40 year old dead step-mother out of the noose of the rope. Village gossip had it, according to Mother later on, that the poor woman was driven to madness by her husband and his sons. "This had been apparent in her confused speech and flashing eyes". These days, a more likely diagnosis would be clinical depression.

This time, the length of the coffin was provided to Father who made only a simple box, the raw cut of its boards not hidden by black crepe with embossed winged angels. There was minimal attendance at the vigil and there was no Requiem Mass and the usual procession from the church to the final resting place. The four men took the coffin there directly from their house and buried it in a grave dug in the unconsecrated corner of the cemetery. She had not died in grace.

THE CHURCH AND THE SQUARE

The third burial was on April 19, 1941. It was that of Hans Michitsch, at twenty seven the younger of two sons of the sexton, killed in the days following the invasion of Yugoslavia by Nazi Germany and Fascist Italy on April 6, 1941. All fighting was already over on April 14, the armistice signed on April 17 to become effective the following day. However, the news had not reached all Yugoslav units and Hans was intercepted on the way back to Masern on April 16. Riding a horse he tried to evade one such unit, but they judged him to be a deserter and shot him dead.

A Slovene from Rakitnica brought the news and Franz Jaklitsch, as head of Sturm 13 the new village chief of Masern, sent a group of his men to bring the bloated body back to the village. It was placed into the coffin on a bier of sawhorses in the firehouse, since the smell was already too strong for the house in which he was born. Father had been instructed to make a simple box only, the planks unadorned with any religious symbols. It was covered instead with the red swastika flag of the Third Reich and men of the Jaklitsch militia stood continuous guard until the day of the burial. According to Jaklitsch: "Hans was a hero because he was rushing back to join his militia in defending our German-friendly Masern from being ravished by the retreating cowardly Serbs". He was now free to say this openly, there no longer being a State from which he had to hide his subversive political activity which included the conversion of the Schaffer fire brigade into a village militia called the Sturm.

Given the tense days of April 1941 and prior months and years of progressively increasing hostility between the Reich-friendly Gottscheer and the Slavs, the possibility of a raid from the surrounding Slovene was promoted as real and the label of "Hero" was willingly accepted. But not by the Reverend Josef Gliebe, parish priest of neighboring Gotenica (Göttenitz), a vocal critic of the polarization and the young propagandists that were causing it. And so, the burial of Hans Michitsch became a face-off between Gliebe the cleric and Sturmführer Jaklitsch, our new village chief.

Since the Reverend Rozman left in 1939, Father Gliebe, like so many other priests from Göttenitz in the past, tended to the spiritual needs of the village. He came on Sundays to hear confessions and after that hold Mass, assisted by the sexton and myself as the altar boy. He also came a few days during the week to give religious instructions and some lessons at the school house after our teacher Aloizij Dežman, as an undesirable Slovene, was encouraged to leave the village in January 1941. Gliebe and Father were good friends and he often stopped at our house before walking home to Gotenica, his own parish.

The parents of Hans Michitsch, both deeply religious, particularly the father who as sexton of the church had served three priests over two decades, were very unhappy that instead of the cross, a swastika flag covered the coffin of their son. And they were incensed over the insistence by Jaklitsch that the customary funeral service be subordinated to a military one, with the swastika flag replacing the cross all the way from the firehouse to the cemetery including the requiem Mass in the church. An honor guard, dressed in Sturm trooper uniforms with swastika armbands was to accompany the coffin all along, including standing at attention alongside the casket during Mass.

The reverend Gliebe would have none of it. Either a traditional funeral or one without him! He would not be persuaded to change his mind.

This time Jaklitsch lost. He was not yet certain of his newfound power, so soon after the collapse of the hated Slavic State; the liberators, the victorious and kindred Germans having not yet arrived. He surrendered to the pressure of Gliebe, the sexton, my father and others and agreed to let his un-uniformed men carry and accompany the coffin, the raw of its boards hidden by a cross embroidered sheet. And on April 19, Gliebe held the requiem Mass, assisted by me as the altar boy and the sexton, his tears wetting the stone step to the altar on which both of us were kneeling. It ended when he and I as the chorus, provided the final 'Amen' to the priest's 'Requiescat in pace'.

On the way to the cemetery after Mass and to the "paced peal" of the small bell, the black cross with the skull and crossbones was carried high up front, but this time by someone other than the sexton who assisted his wife as they walked behind the coffin carried on shoulders by friends of the deceased. As insisted on by Gliebe: not in uniform. At the gravesite, apart from the words of the priest, there were no speeches and no "Sieg Heil' salutes as Jaklitsch had demanded and after the last shovelful of earth was dropped by those nearest to the family and the deceased, most ignored the invitation to come to his inn and went to the house of the sexton instead.

Gliebe had won this round, but it was his last. His victory over Jaklitsch made him into a bitter enemy of the new order, the young Gottscheer trained by the Reich to be devoted adherents of National-Socialism. These young fanatics, who in January 1938 replaced the much older leadership with a Catholic priest as its head, saw in this defiance of Gliebe an opportunity to attack the Gottscheer clergy, the majority of which was hostile to their cause. This clergy, with its centuries-long influence in the community, foresaw in this new ideology the destruction of their own. This

THE CHURCH AND THE SQUARE

was made evident to them by the new leaders who, freed from the prior restraint by a hostile State, announced in the weekly *Gottscheer Zeitung*, its front page now emboldened with a swastika: "Catholicism is treated in the inner leadership circle as a 'universalistic vision of the world' which must be exterminated." [*Die Umsiedlung*, pg.86].

But, in spite of Gliebe's words, Hans Michitsch did not 'rest in peace'. In this clash of conflicting ideologies, Franz Jaklitsch had the final word.

Jaklitsch as Sturmführer of the Masern militia (now called Sturm 13), insisted that the temporary simple cross bearing the name and dates of the deceased be replaced by a massive free form stone into which was inserted a marble plate engraved with a swastika. This instead of the planned slab engraved with a cross, the customary memorial at the head of graves of each family that had a plot in the cemetery. Nevertheless, the stone was installed after a few months by men of the militia over considerable opposition from the parents, many of the villagers and the Reverend Gliebe, all to no avail.

And on August 3, 1941 as part of a huge rally, 800 uniformed, swastika armbanded men and women from Masern and neighboring villages assembled in the village square and marched to the cemetery to formally dedicate the stone, representing the victory of the new ideology over the old. The 800 included the similarly uniformed youth, the Gottschee version of Germany's Hitler Youth of which I was now a part. But much more on that later on.

The bells did more than announce time and tragedy. They were rung at christenings, weddings, on high holidays during processions and other joyous occasions individually or together in various combinations of tonal mix and durations fitting the occasion. But on Thursday before Easter they became silent; a sense of quiet anticipation permeating the village. The hammers of the clock were disengaged from the mechanism and the ropes pulled up high - out of reach of an intoxicated Schaffer, just in case.

Their place was taken by the "Ratch", a mechanism with a ratchet wheel which, when cranked, produced an ugly clapping sound heard throughout the village. It was up there with the bells and operated by the sexton when the bells "were away" but only to call the believers to morning Mass or evensong at the end of the day.

But at nine thirty on the morning of Easter Sunday, the bells resumed in concert and with renewed vigor rang out the usual reminder to get ready for Mass, this time High Mass at ten.

The significant event of Easter Sunday was the Resurrection procession interrupting High Mass before Holy Communion.

Preparations for this started in the morning of Saturday and were directed by the sexton and the fire chief. The chief's biggest task was to get the route of the procession within the village lined with young birches cut in the forest and dragged into the village. There they were re-erected by placing the stems into holes made with crowbars. At each of the two entries to the village, two tall birches were tied at the top to form an arch signifying the village gate. Schaffer saw to it that this was done properly by some of his firemen. He also saw to it that their brass helmets and his bugles were polished and all uniforms in decent condition. And since they were to lead the procession, he gave them a drill just to make sure they understood his commands. All this was joyous fun for us youngsters watching the proceedings and sometimes getting in the way.

Other firemen were assigned to the sexton who had them make ready all other items needed during the procession.

Special attention was given to the baldachin, the canopy we called the "Himmel" (heaven) that was carried above the priest by poles during the procession. It was a rectangular piece of fabric measuring about two by three meters, stretched on to a frame into which, at each corner, was inserted the spiked carrying pole. The underside of the fabric was colorfully embroidered with holy figures and multitudes of angels looking down on the priest underneath. To each of the four sides was attached an eight inch wide red velvet panel, trimmed with a red velvet rope from which were hanging closely spaced swaying tassels.

Under this canopy the priest was to walk in the procession holding up the monstrance inside which rested, on a golden sliver of a moon, the holy Host. He held it high for all to see, including those watching from behind the birches. All were, however, expected to bow or drop to their knees and cross themselves as the Host was being carried by.

The baldachin was normally folded up and kept in the sacristy with the other festive items. Now it was assembled and raised up by four poles which were inserted

THE CHURCH AND THE SQUARE

into holding rings on the benches of the center isle of the church, ready to be lifted out when the priest moved under it and the procession got underway. After the procession re-entered the church, the Baldachin was returned to its place in the center of the church between the benches of the center isle.

And down from the wall behind the altar came the church banner, embroidered with the portraits of Primus and Felician, the Patron Saints. It also was mounted on to its carrying pole and made ready to be carried high by a single fireman trailing the fire brigade.

Yet other men busied themselves with the "Böller", the cannon noisemakers from the days of the Turks, placing them in the locations where they were to be set off during the procession.

Women readied the festive gold embroidered vestments of the priest and the embroidered tunics of the sexton and the altar boy, who was ordered to make sure there was adequate incense in the freshly polished burner. The women also decorated the altar and replaced the ordinary candles with the much larger and festively decorated ones used only on this and other special days.

And in the back, in the choir space above the benches, the village soprano and Franz Jaklitsch, the cello accompanist, practiced their respective talent which, when joined together, would be a substitute for our non-existing village choir during this Easter Mass. High Mass required the voices of a choir to respond to the "Dominus vobiscum" chant of the priest with a chanted "Et cum spiritu tuo". This and other responses normally came either from the altar boy or in his absence from the sexton, during weekday Mass when chanting was not part of the service.

Our High Mass, of which there were several throughout the year, the chanting response was much abbreviated mainly so as not to overtax both the struggling soprano and the uncertain cello. But she always insisted on singing an Ave Maria, an effort that normally caused the congregation to cringe and afterwards led to debates on whether or not she should be told the hard facts about her voice. But after Father Rozman left in 1940 and was not replaced, this was no longer necessary since the occasional service delivered by Father Gliebe of Göttenitz/Gotenica was no longer celebrated with a High Mass.

There was a multitude of other activities during Easter week.

Already on the Palm Sunday a week before, villagers brought to church bundles of freshly cut willow reeds, the catkins displaying their new growth with soft furry coats. The reeds, after being blessed by the priest, were believed to have the power to keep away evil. They were kept in various places on the property, on doorways and inside the house and as homage around the crucifix hanging on a wall.

And on Thursday after Mass the bells, including the little hand bell of the altar boy, were silenced, all crucifixes were covered in black and black ribbons were tacked on to the church doors.

On Friday morning after Mass, the priest prostrated himself at the altar and afterwards led the parishioners, mostly women in black, their heads covered in black kerchiefs, in prayer past the simple paintings on the wall, each showing a Station of the Cross. Throughout the day all labor ceased, fasting was the rule and the eerie silence throughout the village was interrupted only by the ugly clapping of the "Ratch" in the bell tower, a small version of which was used by the altar boy during Mass, taking the place of the hand bell, if only for a few days.

Another round of blessings took place on Saturday during and after Mass.

During the service, the priest blessed the basket of food the woman of each home had been preparing with great care for days and brought to church. The basket, covered with a white embroidered cloth, contained parts of the various foods eaten during the year. Among them were the colored "Easter Eggs" and the boiled smoked ham and grated horseradish. It was hoped that the blessed basket would continue to provide throughout the coming year. But weeks before this event, the priest, in sermons, reiterated the religious purpose of the blessing. He did this in a chiding manner because the size of the basket and the quality of its content had become overly competitive among some of the women of the village.

The blessed food in the basket was also the main part of the festive Easter Sunday meal to be eaten after Mass. Until then the Lenten fast was expected to be observed.

While the Saturday Mass was in progress, the sexton prepared a charcoal fire in a cast iron basin outside in front of the church gates. After Mass, the robed priest blessed the fire, another essential part in the life of the village, if at times a destructive force as it was in 1882 when it destroyed nearly half of the houses in the village. This done, the man of the house would ignite from this burning basin his own kindling which he took with him to light the wood in his hearth at home.

Industrious youths lit from this holy fire dried sponges on a wire and ran to take the fire to those mostly elderly who could not come themselves. In addition to ample thanks expected was also some form of more tangible gratitude.

THE CHURCH AND THE SQUARE

After Mass that morning, as every year on this day, all small kids under ten were invited to the annual Easter egg hunt on the grounds of Gertrud Hönigmann, the elderly widow living alone in her house at Masern 16, our neighbor across the cistern bowl. She had been boiling and coloring the eggs throughout the week with the help of some of the older girls of the village. The cooling eggs were dunked in warm water, colored by the powdered dyes sold at Ivanka's general store across the square. For days thereafter, Gertrud and her helpers struggled to wash the rainbows from their fingers and hands.

After gathering all of us around her and her girl helpers, she gave the signal and we all ran off in different directions. The eggs were hidden under bushes, leaves, pots, in stacks of firewood, in stable troughs, in the hayloft and other secret places not used in prior years. Some of the very small cried because they were too slow, but Gertrud showed them the few yet undiscovered spaces. Just to stop the tears.

But especially sought after were the eggs wrapped in paper that also contained a coin. This allowed the lucky ones to take part in the "Egg hacking" game later in the afternoon on the square, usually supervised by a fireman if not Schaffer himself. You offered your egg to be steadied in a depression and from a measured distance a gamer would toss a coin and try to make it stick in the egg. If successful, he got the egg. If not he had to forfeit the coin to the owner of the egg. Again there were tears because many an egg was lost to the bigger boys who had been practicing for this event. But the fireman made sure all was done fairly and those who argued were excluded from continuing.

It was Gertrud Hönigmann, a good friend of our priest, who persuaded me, nearly eight years old, to become an apprentice altar boy in the winter of 1938/39. Father Rozman was about to lose his present altar boy Albert Primosch, the thirteen year old son of the musician who was finishing his schooling that summer and refused to continue beyond that. Other boys were not interested, in large part because the anti-clerical attitude of the Reich had now reached also into Masern and being an altar boy was no longer encouraged or desired.

Gertrud was my tutor in learning the Latin liturgy with which the altar boy answered the priest during Mass. She gave me passages to memorize which I had to demonstrate when I went to see her after class. When I did particularly well, my reward was a coin and an especially large one when I finally recited a large part of the *Pater Noster*. In the spring I was prepared enough to serve the priest with some help from the sexton during weekday Mass and by Easter 1939 good enough to take part in both the High Mass and the associated procession.

As a result of becoming an altar boy I did get some ridicule and hostility from some of my schoolmates. But even more so from Albert, my predecessor who later that year became the leader of our branch of the Hitler Youth group under fourteen years of age. But when in the fall of 1939, Father Rozman was moved elsewhere by the diocese, I was the sole altar boy for Father Gliebe who cycled in from Gotenica (Göttenitz) to attend to our spiritual needs and hold Mass on Sundays, if at a later hour. I had not yet learned all my replies, but since he was somewhat hard of hearing, I just mumbled the difficult parts.

Later on Easter Saturday, the villagers lined up in front of the confessional to await their turn for the mandatory annual confession of major and minor transgressions. This was also required on other high holidays, but neglecting the purging of one's sins on Easter was a mortal sin. Final absolution came, however, only on the next day when the holy Host was laid on the tongue of the repented sinner who, as part of a long queue, finally arrived at a kneeling space before the communion rail in front of the altar. A rail crafted by Father during the major renovation of the church interior in 1937.

The procession started when the fireman brought the Patron Saints banner through the open doors of the church. Schaffer, now in his impressive uniform including ribbons and medals, had assembled his men leaving a distance between the end of his fire brigade and the church entrance. Adequate space for the banner, the incense swinging altar boy, the sexton with the holy water and finally the baldachin under which now stood the monstrance-carrying priest; in that order. With all in place, Schaffer blew his bugle and the fire brigade, with Schaffer's second in command leading the procession, got under way. The congregation spilling from the church followed the Baldachin, with some of the more eminent villagers leading the other believers.

 Its route was from the portals of church toward the linden and from there past the Jaklitsch tavern toward the chapel of the Lady of the Seven Sorrows. There it stopped long enough for the priest to bow toward the flower decorated door and offer prayers of thanks to the Lady inside. After that, the procession rounded the chapel and made its way back to re-cross the square, pass the church and walk toward the cemetery at the other end of the village. There the priest offered a prayer for the souls and resurrection of the deceased after which the procession turned and made its way back into the church where the participants returned to their seats.

With all settled, the Mass continued with Holy Communion and the final blessing of the congregation. After that, with all three bells ringing in unison, all rushed home for their long awaited big Easter meal. Later on in the afternoon the festivities continued in one of the three taverns and there was dancing late into the night, especially so since the following day was Easter Monday, a restful public holiday.

A similar procession was held on Ascension Day 40 days later, but it was a one day event, one that was not preceded by week long preparations.

There were other church festivals throughout the year, but Easter was the most prominent and meaningful. In part, because it signified both the end of the cold and the beginning of another round of planting, tending and harvesting; of giving birth and burying the dead. And in between, living with both the joys and sorrows the almighty was sending the villagers' way. Only to arrive at the end of yet another cycle that had carried them through the centuries year after year in a place they called Masern.

But the most anxiously awaited festival was "Kirtok", the day of our Patron Saints Primus and Felician. (Kirtok was the equivalent of Kirchweihtag, the German version for church consecration day). It was held on the Sunday nearest to June 9, the day of the saints. On this day the world came to the square of Masern in the form of a village fair.

There were preparations for this day also, albeit of a kind different from those for Easter Sunday. The square was cleaned, potholes filled, the droppings of horses and cows on their way to the cistern collected and disposed of. Women washed the windows facing the square. And as for Easter Sunday, two young birch trees were erected at each of the two village entrances. This time their tops connected by a ribbon on which was written in large letters 'Primus und Felician'.

There was frantic activity at the Jaklitsch tavern, both inside and out. This tavern was the best suited for the event; it was directly on the square and had a large walled-in courtyard.

In this courtyard, a raised dance floor was erected with planks from the Tschinkel saw mill. It was bordered by a railing to prevent excited spinning couples from missing the edge. The floor had, in one corner, a slightly raised part for the man with the accordion, the player alternately being either Josef Primosch or Anton Tscherne.

The space surrounding the dance floor was filled with cross legged tables and benches otherwise stored in the large barn at the far end of the courtyard. Additional barrels of beer were delivered, rolled into the ice cellar next to the main house and readied to be rolled out again to be placed on a stand and fitted with a spigot.

Inside, Regina and her women helpers hired for the day were preparing the food to be served with the beer. Krainerwurst - the Slovene boiled smoked sausage, a specialty of the region, was served with mustard and a slice of bread with both Jaklitsch and Regina hoping there would be enough for the many guests. Guests not only from Masern but also from other neighboring villages in the enclave; many of them of marrying age, each hoping to spot a dancing partner in the crowd with whom they could start a relationship that might lead to matrimony. These events offered an opportunity to the young men of neighboring villages to find a mate and over centuries led to severe inbreeding in the enclave.

The merchants arrived very early in the morning. They stopped their horse-pulled wagons around the edge of the square and immediately began setting up their covered stalls behind a temporary barrier erected by the firemen to keep the road through the village clear. Their wares were laid out on tables or hung on racks, but kept out of sight by covers or curtains until the end of Mass.

Already in the afternoon of the day before, the traveling circus had arrived on the square: several horse drawn wagons, on one the cage of the dancing bear and on another the pieces of the "Ringelspiel", a brightly painted merry-go-round that needed to be assembled in place. This task the men of the troop began immediately after the fire chief allocated a place for it. The space was quickly surrounded by the young and the erecting activity was watched intently especially by the older boys. Boys who the next day were to be selected by the operator to climb the ladder to the platform around the main mast and, at his command, push the spokes of the structure at whose end was suspended, on a chain, a seat for the customer. The boys pushing the spokes were the engine for this amusement park staple, payment for it being one ride in return for four rounds. Skirt-wearing girls were, for obvious reasons, not chosen but some were, after much shuffling, selected to serve as ballast during the

THE CHURCH AND THE SQUARE

initial tests. Free of charge. After that they had to either pay or talk one of the boys into letting her take his earned ride.

Testing began as soon as the erection of the carousel was completed; the older boys crowding the operator, begging to be selected as pushers and earn rides. Unfortunately, as one of the smaller boys, I was told that I was not yet strong enough and had to run home to beg Mother for the coins needed for rides. By the time I returned the colorful merry-go-round was ready for paying customers and I was told to await my turn in the queue.

Already on display was the dancing bear. It had been urged to climb from the opened cage in the rear of the wagon on a short ladder to the ground. There it now sat waiting for its master to be satisfied with the quantity of coins he was collecting in his cap while cautioning the audience standing behind the circular barrier to be quiet and make no drastic movements that might enrage the beast. While this was going on there was hushed talk about the adequacy of the muzzle and the strap held by the master whose skill and strength were needed to keep the beast under control.

And when no more coins were being offered, he urged the bear with a slight tug into the center of the circle and made it stand up. There was silence when the full height of the animal revealed itself and it started to turn on hind legs, its paws hanging down from its outstretched front legs. After the master led it in a number of full circle turns, another tug on the muzzle strap brought it back to its four legs and it was led up the ladder into the cage. Only after carefully bolting the door, turning back to the silent audience and bowing was there applause, the concern about an enraged beast now no longer present.

Dusk had arrived and there being no artificial light on the square most went home, but some of the men made for the tavern for a quarter liter or two and only then were they ready for bed and tomorrow. Meanwhile on the square around their wagons, the circus people were having their meal and getting ready for sleep, while at a respectful distance some of Schaffer's firemen unobtrusively kept their eyes on them. Just in case.

Mass on the following morning, while not much different from any other, seemed to be exceedingly long. And when the final "Amen" followed the "Ite, Missa est" and "Benedicat vos omnipotens ….", the doors swung open and the congregation spilled out only to merge with those who would not wait and were already milling among the stalls looking for bargains.

Women carefully examining cloth bales to be made into dresses, skirts, kerchiefs, aprons or underwear. Either for themselves if they owned a sewing machine or as barter for others who did not. Or checking out the size and weight of skillets and pots, wooden spoons, earthen bowls, rosaries and trinkets; items not sold at Ivanka's store.

Men were at stalls considering pants, jackets, shirts or hats, some of them "slightly" used. Others were looking at metal items for the farm not made by Johann Sbaschnig the village smith; rakes, scythes, whetstones, flint stones, lighter fluid, axle grease; all items for which they would have to walk to Ribnica or the even more distant Gottschee City. Some also looked at shoes since the village shoemaker was overbooked and would not make their new pair until months from now.

Some of my school mates and I, a few coins in our pockets, hung around the stalls selling fancy pocket knives but had coins only for the cheapest version which could barely cut a hazelnut twig without bending the blade. How I would have loved one with ivory covering the handle and a blade made from Solingen steel! We also wandered among the stands selling sweets, but here the candy cost more than that in the glass jars at Ivanka's store where sometimes she would drop an extra piece into the cone she expertly fashioned from a sheet of wrapping paper torn from a roll.

Others made for the "Ringelspiel", surrendered their coins and waited, safety chain in place, for the other seats to get filled. Only then would the attendant ring the bell to signal the boys on the platform to start pushing and get the spinning underway.

By early afternoon, the tables at the Jaklitsch courtyard were filled and stacks of bicycles that had brought young men and women from other villages lined the walls of the main house. Dancers spun to the three quarter beat, waitresses for the day were rushing about with filled pitchers of foaming beer and Regina was boiling yet another pot of sausages. But later, she found time for a ride on the carousel which, however, was not to be since the weight of her ample figure nearly tipped the mechanism, forcing the attendant to return her money.

Not all coins were handed out at the stalls or for rides on the carousel. Some were spent at the Jaklitsch beer stand that also sold bottles of soda pop. Yet others were saved for the ice cream man.

He arrived around noon and, surrounded by kids, was escorted into the shade of the linden where he asked for water and a few moments of time to wipe the sweat from his face. He had come a long way.

THE CHURCH AND THE SQUARE

He brought his colorful sorbets from Ribnica inside the ice filled cooler box on wheels to the sides of which were attached the two wheels of the tricycle. He pedaled from the seat over the rear wheel and steered with a bar attached to the box in front of him.

After setting up the stacks of cones in ring holders attached to the sides of the cooler, his business was brisk selling both to kids on the square and to customers drifting over from Jaklitsch. By late afternoon, however, most of the older clients preferred draft beer or wine and the few youngsters milling around him no longer had any coins.

With the containers not yet empty and the contents getting soft he resorted to exchanging what was left for eggs; two eggs for one scoop of sherbet.

Word got around fast and again he was surrounded by kids who knew where the hens laid their eggs. And with the mothers making merry at the Jaklitsch tables, getting them was easy. Soon the containers were empty. How he made his way back to Ribnica on the bumpy road without much breakage we never learned.

The last "Kirtok" was on June 8, 1941, one day before the day of the patron saints. This was ten days after the *Gottscheer Zeitung*, on May 29, announced that Hitler had decided to take us back into the Reich. The full meaning of this decision had not yet penetrated the minds of the villagers and this festival day was not much different from those in years before. While the carousel had arrived the day before, there were fewer merchants since some, being Slovene, now preferred to stay away, given the political atmosphere.

And there were fewer at Mass; the service being upstaged by a parade through the village of Sturm 13 men and youth, their marching song interfering with the service inside. And later, before the dancing got underway, Jaklitsch gave a short speech from the dance floor but made no reference to Hitler's decision. No point in interfering with the fair!

Which ran its normal course except for an alarming development; three year old brother Paul had gone missing.

A tearful Mitzi brought the news to the parents who were on a bench near the dance floor. She had been put in charge of both Paul and me but lost sight of both of us while spinning on the carousel. She soon found me but not Paul, in spite of having looked everywhere.

Father talked to Jaklitsch and Schaffer who ordered some of their men to look for the lost child. And as more and more people were searching in all unlikely places, the festivities soon became disrupted and some of the half emptied pitchers of beer were losing their head, fewer orders were being placed for sausages and it took longer to fill the seats of the "Ringelspiel". But Paul could not be found.

After getting nowhere, with many having given up, it occurred to Mitzi that he may have wandered into the fields, the most likely being the "Unterbinkl". The thought occurred because the week before all five of us had been there again to clear more of the intruding underbrush. During the day we had run out of drinking water and Father sent me with the pail to get some more from the drinking well in the village.

With all this in mind, Mitzi ran to see if Paul had gone there, fearing that, like Grandfather's dog, he might have fallen into one of the many crevasses. He did go there and she soon spotted him returning, an empty water pail in hand. With streaming tears he cried out: "I took water to Father but he was not there."

Father Gliebe conducted Mass again the following morning and gave thanks to the Almighty for protecting the child.

Since the very early years, the spiritual welfare of the villagers of Masern was looked after by a parish priest from Göttenitz who held Mass, gave religious instruction to the children and maintained the church ledgers which containing the dates on births, marriages and deaths in the village. When Göttenitz was unable to attend to Masern, other priests from the district parish of Ribnica held Mass.

This was the case for centuries before 1689, the year Valvasor mentions Primus and Felician as Patron Saints of the chapel. In 1741, Masern was transferred to the Ribnica parish and with the arrival of Father Anton Wallisch in 1767, the village, for the first time, had a resident chaplain. And that same year, Masern now at 38 houses and 160 souls, became a sub-parish subordinated to the parish of Dolenja Vas.

Father Anton Wallisch was the village priest until 1771. For 51 years after he left in 1771 until 1822, there again was no resident priest. Among others, Father Anton Namre from the Göttenitz parish looked after the spiritual welfare of Masern and during this time maintained its ledgers on births, marriages and deaths. And when these ledgers were filled, Father Namre started a new set in 1773.

Father Johann Munini arrived in Masern in 1822 and stayed for 15 years until 1837. After he left, there again was no priest for 30 years.

THE CHURCH AND THE SQUARE

Father Johann Posnik arrived in 1867. Posnik, who had given up the priesthood in 1884, became the full time teacher in the village, inaugurated that same year, but he continued to give religious instructions and maintained the ledgers. He remained in the village as a teacher until 1892.

Father Leopold Raktelj arrived in 1895 and stayed until 1908 when he exchanged roles with Father Franz Sturm from Poljanske Toplice.

The Reverend Franz Sturm remained for 16 years but disgraced himself in 1923 when it became known that he had made Leni, the spinster sister of the village smith, pregnant. The villagers stopped attending church services and openly called him "Hurenbock" which translates roughly to whoring he-goat. When they stopped paying him his wages he took legal action, but his health suffered and he died in July 1924. For the following three months, Fathers Gliebe of Göttenitz and Karel Škul of Dolenja Vas alternately cared for the parishioners.

Paul Klemenčič, the first German speaking Slovene priest arrived on October 30, 1924. He became much loved and admired in the village. Mother often talked of him with great fondness, reminiscing of the comfort received from him after she arrived from Dolenja Vas in 1930. She had come into a village unable to speak its language and which, apart from the priest, his housekeeper and a few kindred souls with similar burdens treated her as an inferior Slovene outsider. And she came into the house of her hostile mother-in-law who called her the "Kroinar", the derogatory word for a Slovene used in the enclave. And the Kroinar came, she said, with an "illegitimate seven year old cross-eyed daughter burdened so by the sin of her mother".

Paul Klemenčič christened me on March 5, 1931. Due to serious illness he left the village for the hospital on May 30, 1933 and died there the following year.

His replacement, father Jože Rozman, a Slovene who also spoke fluent German, came in 1936 but he was transferred out by the diocese in 1940 and not replaced. He had served the village well and was much appreciated, at least until the late 1930's, when the National-Socialist ideology imported into the enclave brought the anti-clerical climate also into our village and undermined his position. Rozman, one of those who for centuries had served the village, was no longer respected or much wanted by the majority of the residents. I was his last altar boy and sad to see him leave.

After Rozman's departure, Father Gliebe again looked after our spiritual welfare, including religious lessons to the children, if only sporadically. As had done many other priests of Gotenica (Göttenitz) in the past. But during 1941, in the months before our departure, Gliebe was no longer wanted.

Chapter 6

The Gypsies

The Gypsies were an undesirable but harmless lot traveling at leisure through the countryside. They moved through the enclave on horse-drawn wagons on to which was built a wooden house with tiny windows on the sides and in the back, a door and fold down steps for easy access. A stovepipe chimney poked through the pitched roof and up front the roof extended forward to cover a bench used by the driver and other members of the tribe. The scraggy horses that pulled the wagons were undernourished as was evident from the protruding bones of their ribcage.

When such a small caravan of three or four wagons pulled into our village, usually in the warmer months, they made for the square near the linden where they would camp for the next few days. Their arrival was an event and the caravan was quickly surrounded by the village kids and eventually if at a distance, by grown ups. The wagons disgorged women in billowing multicolored skirts, children in much patched clothing and from the bench up front climbed unshaven men in striped shirts and pants shining from a lack of soap and water. All of them exuded a strange and pungent smell. Some of the men immediately set out to beg for hay to feed the horses while the women and children made for the cistern to get water.

Soon Schaffer would arrive with an assistant or two, all decked out in uniform, including medals and ribbons, to discuss with the leader of the caravan the purpose and length of stay in the village. "Buy some provisions, use the communal water to wash, help with farming or other chores in return for food or money" was the usual reply, for which Schaffer allocated only the shortest number of days. He spelled out to them the rules to follow while in the village, rules which they surely heard often and were the same wherever they camped. They were discouraged from roaming the village and also asked to stay near their wagons on the square unless engaged by someone for a task. Schaffer also reminded them that they would be watched.

Later, Schaffer met to report to the villagers in a meeting at the Jaklitsch inn and assess their needs for the Gypsies' labors to get a sense of how long he was to let them stay. He reminded all present to gather up the chickens, lock up the sheds and livestock in the stables and keep a sharp eye on the uninvited guests. He also met with his firemen at the firehouse and assigned volunteers to maintain a watch through the night and raise the alarm if necessary.

The Gypsy men generally followed Schaffer's rules and stayed near their wagons, knowing the villagers would come to them to engage them for work. The women were less compliant and soon, in groups of two or three, followed by their children, were making their way from door to door soliciting their services to the woman of the house. Hardly any of them were ever let inside, but raking the yard or cleaning out the hen house or stable was a chore they were hired to perform in return for provisions or a small sum of money agreed upon after much animated haggling. But the hen house job was no longer given out after it became apparent that the chickens of the shed cleaned by the gypsies had laid fewer eggs on that day. They were still hired to clean the stable but only while carefully watched by a member of the family ever since it was discovered that without such precaution, the cows suddenly had less milk.

But the Gypsy women always found ways to divert suspicion and attract the attention of the housewives with glass beads, cheap perfume or tales of magic healing potions. One such potion had the power to heal sore and callused feet with "magic crystals" dissolved in hot water. While the woman patient was sitting in front of her house with her feet in a bucket of hot salty brine and her watchful eyes diverted by the chatter, the companions of the healer or her children looked about for easy take.

The most exciting part of their stay, however, was on evenings when some of them started to play their instruments, drawing many a villager to the benches around the linden. Their music, mostly from a flute, a guitar or a violin or even a combination of all, was usually accompanied by a pretty young dancer, shaking her skirt and tambourine at the smiling villagers. And when done, she made the rounds again; this time with a wicker basket into which were dropped the coins she coaxed from the embarrassed if reluctant village men. She had more luck with the youngish ones to which she devoted more of her seductive charms in spite of knowing that they had the fewest coins.

At least one young Gottscheer succumbed to the charm of such a young Gypsy woman whom he married and who gave him several children, one of whom became my best friend. But not for long, for fate would intervene. The full story is told in the chapter *The Rabbit*.

This was also the time Schaffer's men were on the alert and on the look out in case any of the Gypsies wandered off. But the travelers knew they were being watched and stayed in their place. And, if anything did disappear, it was usually minor, not missed for days after they left the village and soon forgiven and forgotten.

One exception to this was when after one such stay, some of the Gypsy men returned at night to steal horses, including, without success, Father's horse Yiorgo. The following morning a posse of villagers, including two gendarmes from Dolenja Vas was assembled for a hot pursuit and after following their tracks through the forest, the horses were recovered while the thieves managed to get away.

Another exception, certainly less severe than the theft of horses but definitely more humorous involved Schaffer, the ever watchful and alert fire chief and village elder.

Schaffer had contracted with the leader of one caravan to produce 50 cubic meters of gravel by breaking up large boulders of quarry stone that had been delivered to a site along the road between Masern and Dolenja Vas.

Gravel had for centuries been used to produce a firm roadbed for the heavy wagons transporting raw lumber from the forests via our village to distant mills. Due to this heavy and continuous traffic, constant replenishment of gravel was needed to maintain the solid surface. To obtain the gravel, large boulders were transported in specially designed tipping troughs on horse-drawn wagons and dumped at sites along the road where more gravel was required to restore the surface.

To get this done, the county contracted responsible villagers, in our case Schaffer, who in turn hired sub-contractors to break up the boulders with sledge hammers into smaller pieces and afterwards at roadside into gravel to repair the surface wherever repair was necessary. The sub-contractors were our own village men, otherwise idle during early spring before the plowing season. During this time they were happy to sit at 100 meter intervals hammering away at the granite to produce

THE BELLS RING NO MORE

small piles of gravel which they later shoveled into ruts in the road and wherever restoration and repair was needed.

As a middleman, Schaffer was suspected of making a hefty profit which he vehemently denied. But since many of the village men desperately needed the extra money, they were happy to be chosen by Schaffer to do the work, which he doled out as he saw fit. One spring, when to the consternation of village men, he selected a group of Gypsies camping in the village to produce 50 cubic meters of gravel he was publicly accused of lining his pocket. It was suspected that he paid the Gypsies a lot less and kept the difference himself. He forcefully denied the accusation and stuck to his decision. But in the end, his accusers had the last laugh.

At the site where a large number of boulders had been dumped, the gypsies went to work. Schaffer ordered that the gravel produced be placed in a pile so that it could be measured for the agreed upon 50 cubic meters and payment made. Schaffer monitored them often and was pleased at their progress. The mountain of boulders shrank rapidly as the pyramid of gravel grew and when he agreed that it was equal to 50 cubic meters, he paid the Gypsies who left the following day.

Later on, the gravel was transported to various locations along the road where it was needed for repair. For this task, Schaffer hired Father who had a tipping trough for his wagon and one of the two horses needed to pull the heavy load. He got the second horse from another villager as he did on other occasions whenever a team was needed, an arrangement that both horse owners used to mutual benefit. To load the gravel on to the wagon, Schaffer hired a number of other men. Unloading at the site was by tipping the trough with the crank of a lifting jack.

It took only a few loads before the perfidy of the Gypsies was discovered. Beyond the outer layer of gravel, the pile consisted mostly of the original bulky boulders which they covered with gravel whenever Schaffer or any other villager was not watching.

Schaffer was beside himself, loose with invectives. Knowing that the villagers were laughing behind his back for having been had by a bunch of deceptive Gypsies put him into a prolonged rage. When the village men asked for increased payment to complete the unfinished work, their request only added to his fury. But when he threatened to bring in Slovene from the neighboring villages to do the job, the

THE GYPSIES

men backed away from their demand for more money and went to work for what he offered.

As was usual, he tried to drown his rage with wine at the Jaklitsch inn. Unfortunately the main recipient of his fury was his wife Maria, who as many other times before, sought refuge with Mother to escape the beatings. He terrorized his two grown sons Hubert and Karl who tried to stay clear of his blows and the children of the village ran when we heard him coming. The rest of the villagers kept out of his way leaving him to be the only person in the guest room of the Jaklitsch inn since he would quickly pick a fight all tried to avoid, as he was the strongest man in the village.

It took some time for Schaffer to regain his normalcy even after he returned from a determined search to track down the Gypsies, an effort in which he got little support from the authorities. They also knew of his tricks and were as amused over the incident as were the villagers of Masern and its surroundings.

Generally, the Gypsies knew the limits to their transgression, and certainly of one that could be discovered while they were still in the village or nearby. But the group of Gypsies that made a fool of Schaffer did not return.

A part of the mosaic, the Gypsies brought a not unwelcome diversion to the otherwise uneventful existence, not only to the villagers of the Masern, but to other parts of Slovenia as well. Their arrival and departure were part of a cycle as regular as the inevitable changing of the seasons. Unfortunately their centuries-long desire to remain free spirits put them at odds with the concepts of uniformity required by the Third Reich. And all who deviated, such as the father of my friend Josef, paid a bitter price for doing so. But more on this later.

Chapter 7

The Railroad

It was the smell that was first noticeable when we pulled up to the small stationhouse of stucco walls and terra-cotta roof and Yiorgo had been slowed to bring the carriage to a stop. It was different from the smells that were familiar; be they from the frying meat or freshly baked bread in Mother's kitchen, the fresh sawdust in Father's shop, the fetid aroma steaming off butchered pork in the bracing November air or the pungent smell of the dung heap at the far end of the house.

It was different also from the fragrance of the pines when the sap was running. Or the smell of oil laden steam, hissed out by the huge engine powering the blades of the village saw mill that cut the logs into slices, not unlike the machine at a present day bakery.

The smell was strongest standing on the coarse gravel between the tar saturated ties holding the rails in place. The mixture of tar, coal and carbolic had quickly replaced the dust laden air we had been inhaling on the unpaved lane through the fields from Dolenja Vas to nearby Lipovec, the local stop of the railroad linking Kočevje/Gottschee to the capital of Slovenia.

Father and I were on the way since the early morning of that day in the spring of 1935 to take the train to Ljubljana to see Mother in the hospital where she had just survived a serious operation. Grandma Ilc had come with us from Dolenja Vas to the nearby station at Lipovec to take Yiorgo and the wagon back to her house. She would come to get us when we returned late that afternoon.

This was to be my first time on a train, my first travel to the big city. A first time for many things.

The gleaming surface of the tracks merged in the distance from where the train was to arrive. Eventually, a spot appeared above the rails, a spot that rapidly began to grow and take shape. With it came a rumbling sound outdone at intervals by the shrill of the whistle as if to tell me, the barely four year old kid, to get off the tracks.

I stood even closer to Father as the hissing of the monster locomotive brought the train to a halt and waited, huffing impatiently for us to climb the stairs to coaches high above the rails. I did not see the station attendant raise the red disk signaling the engineer to resume the journey, being far too eager to find a window seat which was easy, the coach being only half full. The whistle blew again and through the window, which Father had lowered by the two inch wide leather strap, I waved to Grandma as the train pulled away.

It took one and a half hours to get to Ljubljana, stopping on the way so often that the train never seemed to get back up to speed before it had to brake again. The longest stop was in Ribnica where there was some maneuvering to attach freight cars to the end of the train. At further stops the coach began to fill up, mostly with kerchief-covered women carrying heavy wicker baskets, on the way to the market in Ljubljana. In between the stops and open valleys, where farmers were already busy tending their fields, Father hurriedly closed the window to keep out the dense, spark-interlaced coal smoke whenever we entered one of the many tunnels. And when the conductor came, Father handed him the small cardboard ticket he had purchased at the station. After he punched a hole into it, he asked me for mine. But when he saw that his look frightened me, he started to grin. "You will need one only after you grow up".

At Grosuplje where the tracks from Kočevje joined the main line between Ljubljana and Novo Mesto, there was a lengthy stop. We had to wait for a gap between trains having priority on that line. Father leaned out the window and bought two long reddish sausages with mustard and bread from the vendor. The first and best Frankfurter I ever ate.

The next excitement was the tram ride from the station to the hospital. It was crowded but some one offered Father a seat. I sat on his leg, taking in a new world passing by outside. So many people on so many streets, along so many buildings in which were so many stores selling so many different things, paling all items that Ivanka's store in Masern had to offer. When after many stops came ours and we got out, we had to walk a short distance to the hospital behind a high wall. And as we entered, there was another new smell, the smell of disinfectant, a smell that brings back that moment whenever it enters my nostrils again even after so many years.

The first disappointment came when Father was told that I could not come with him to see my mother. Children were not allowed in the ward. I would have to stay in the lobby room. He promised to come back soon and the smiling nun in white, on her head a white cap with wings that flapped when she walked, led me to a chair as Father climbed the stairs and disappeared.

But he did not come back as promised. I soon began to cry, ever louder and without stopping. The nun in white tried to console me and when she could not, became angry; I was disturbing the peace of the lobby. Others also tried but I, who had now lost both of my parents, could not stop. I cried myself to sleep only to wake up again to freely flowing tears after I realized where I was and abandoned. Only when finally an embarrassed and apologetic Father finally appeared was my misery at an end. And it turned to joy when we walked back to the tram stop and he announced that after lunch he would take me to a movie house. I had heard about movies but had never seen one, there not being a house for showing movies in either Ribnica or Kočevje, the furthest I ever got away from home.

At a gostilna, a tavern much grander than that of Grandma Ilc, Father wanted me to have soup. But I insisted on two more Frankfurters; both nearly as delicious as the first one in Grosuplje.

In the dark room of the theater, the newsreel showed some crisis in Abyssinia. But of the film that followed, I remember only a huge ship being pushed around in a sea of big waves. Nothing like the little boats I had pushed into the floodwaters that flowed past our house in the spring after the snows began to melt. Here, the high waves that kept crashing against the sides of the ship showed a scary reality. And after a particularly high one with white foam at its tips damaged the ship which then began to sink, there appeared standing on the lopsided deck a figure in vestments; on his head a bishop's miter, in his left hand the staff of his office and at the end of the outstretched right arm a hand pointing upward to heaven. Soon it was only the bow of the ship that was pointing upward and that too disappeared into the waves. I was frightened and held tightly with both hands on to Father's arm.

The worst, however, came when I asked Father who the bishop was who just sank with the ship. It was Saint Nicholas, he whispered.

On top of all the things this tender four year old had been through this day, that remark was more than I could cope with and I started crying again; loudly if not louder than at the hospital. I had just seen Saint Nicholas drown, the very Nicholas who came to our house every December 6, bringing with him my presents that I was to get for being good the entire year. And now that he was dead, who would bring me the presents I had earned?

Father could not console me and angrily complied with the request to take me from the theatre. "Others are complaining" the attendant had said. I still cried on the tram and stopped only when we got to the train station and he bought me another Frankfurter and a ginger ale. And on the train he tried to convince me that Saint Nicolas did not drown, that movies are not for real; only shadow play. I would "see this is so when next winter he would again come to our house with presents of which there surely would be more this time". And when in the following December this was the case, my occasional nightmares stopped. I finally believed it; until then I was not convinced by all those telling me that what Father was saying was true.

Grandma Ilc was waiting for us at the station in Lipovec. I was tired and with no more surprises to come being again on familiar ground, I quickly fell asleep. But not until after I heard Father tell what happened in the movie house. Grandma was angry at him for taking me, an impressionable child to see that kind of a movie. How that conversation ended I did not hear, being fast asleep.

There were five more trips on that train to Ljubljana, each with its own story. The final one, in December 7, 1941, however had no return. Instead, it continued on the main line toward Zidani Most and beyond that to our still unknown future.

The rail line connecting Ljubljana to Kočevje (Gottschee) city was placed in service in September 1893. The line was a spur off the connection between Ljubljana - Novo Mesto and beyond, leaving the main line for Kočevje at Grosuplje, just east of Ljubljana. The 70 km single track line which brought the world to Lower Carniola and the forest had many stops along the way including the one at Ribnica and at Lipovec near Dolenja Vas. The economic benefits to this neglected part of the land were many; the major one the ability to expeditiously transport lumber and agricultural products out of the area.

Newly built steam powered saw mills, built throughout the area, cut the abundant lumber into more easily transportable building materials. Such a saw mill was put into operation in Grčarice (Masern) in 1922 and it became the main employer in the village. The production of charcoal, a village industry, received a boost since the existing demand in distant cities could now be more profitably satisfied.

It also brought industry to exploit the cheap labor and the abundance of lumber and made desperately needed medical care more available. The latter mainly due to the now easier access to the regional hospital in Ljubljana.

A prior attempt to capitalize on the abundance of wood failed due to the absence of such a transportation link. A wood powered factory built in 1835 in Glažuta near our village to produce glass products failed because sand, the raw material for producing the glass was not available nearby and had to be carted in from Croatia. It was shut down as being unprofitable 21 years later in 1856.

The new railroad also eased emigration for those Slovene and Gottscheer seeking a better life elsewhere, mostly in America. The connection to the main line between Vienna and Italy simplified the route to Trieste, the port where those leaving boarded ships to Ellis Island, most of them never to return. It eased the way there for Father's older sister Johanna and his two other siblings Paula and Frank and many others of the village and the region. It brought Father, aged seventeen to that port in 1910 for his journey to Brooklyn where he lived with the now married Johanna and complemented his knowledge of farming by learning carpentry in a furniture factory.

The same train brought him and his precious Yankee carpentry tools back to Masern in 1914 to serve in the Austrian Imperial Army or else lose the right to the inheritance of his father's estate. This was made clear in the letter from his father, forwarding the draft notice to his oldest son. Not responding to the call would have surely altered his destiny; perhaps for the better. And I would not be writing these lines. Nevertheless, this train spur to its dead end in Kočevje, accessible to Masern at the hamlet of Lipovec had a big role in our lives and in the enclave and has a sizable part in the stories I have yet to tell.

After the diagnosis that she needed surgery and before she entered the hospital, Mother prayed to Holy Mary to help her get well. She also pledged to make the pilgrimage to the church of Marija Pomagaj and thank her for hearing her pleas.

Marija Pomagaj (Mary, help) was in Brezje, approximately 40 km or one hour train ride beyond Ljubljana. The original chapel there, enlarged at the beginning of the 20th Century into a large church, had become a major destination for pilgrims long before that. This caused the priest in charge, Janez Novak, in 1875 to exclaim: "In Brezje there is a miracle-working image of Mary, of which every pilgrim can confirm the words of holy Bernard: - It has never been heard that you abandoned anyone who fled under your protection, who asked for your help and begged for your intercession. - This is certified by pilgrims from all over Slovenia, Styria, Carinthia, Trieste, Istria and Croatia."

And after the surgery mother also got well. Dr. Oražem in Ribnica, who had diagnosed a tumor in her stomach, had insisted that she have it removed immediately.

This was in the early spring of 1935, just when the annual planting was to begin. An awkward time to be spending in a hospital, but since her life was in danger there was not much choice. We were told that the surgery was to remove a grapefruit size growth from the stomach. This was accepted as fact, however she intimated decades later that it had to do with her reproductive organs but would not go further. Perhaps even she may not have been told the real facts.

The surgery was highly successful and she was in the fields again by mid summer after having spent much of her recovery period with her mother in Dolenja Vas where she would get better care than in the house of her mother-in-law. She would also be nearer to Oražem, her doctor. But the pilgrimage was postponed until after the harvest. Mother was certain that the Mother of God would not mind. I was to come along on this, my second trip on the railroad.

So when Mother and I set out in late September, all of the harvest was safely stored and most of the late season's work done. What remained was the annual slaughter of the fattened pigs but for that we needed the first frost which was still one month away.

The afternoon before, we walked to Dolenja Vas and stayed the night with Grandma Ilc to be nearer the station. Walking the entire way there and back was all part of the pilgrimage she explained. But I suspected that the stay with Grandma was meant to give me an overnight rest.

This train ride was no less exciting than the first and I also got the promised Frankfurter in Grosuplje. But even more exciting was getting on a much more impressive international train in Ljubljana. A train with a much bigger locomotive, pulling longer carriages all marked with different destinations and numerals. Mother found seats in the third class coach already filled with pilgrims as became apparent when most of them got out with us at Brezje. All making straight for the huge cathedral into which could fit several of our Masern church. It had altars on both side walls but the main one up front was the biggest and the tallest, all covered in shining gold.

I remember all this because after many years, a repeat (non-pilgrim) visit refreshed my dimming memories and assurances were given that nothing had changed in the decades since. And now as then, a long row of pilgrims, mostly black clad women with kerchief-covered bowed heads, stood in the slowly forward moving line fingering rosaries. All waiting for their turn to reach the raised platform, get on their knees and then crawl around the altar which held the image of the Holy Mary. They had come to either ask for help or give thanks for help already given. Another long line led toward multiple confessionals in which the sinners were seeking forgiveness.

Mother led me to a pew, put her bundle next to me and ordered me to stay until she came back. After I promised not to cry she joined the line and waited for her turn to circle the altar on her knees. I fell asleep and dreamed of St. Nicolas on the sinking ship. I was happy when she shook me awake saying it was time to find a place to stay overnight.

This proved to be hopeless; there were no beds to be had in this town full of pilgrims. All I remember of Mother's search for a room is that she did not find one and in the end we spent the night on the benches of a gostilna in the company of many others with the same predicament. I also remember the separation between those whose prayers had been answered and those who had come to plead. On our side of the room was gaiety but on the other there was only gloom and perhaps a wish to be across the room on their next visit. But soon I was asleep.

Next morning there was again much time on the hard benches of the church as the holy Mass progressed through its paces, interrupted only by the unusually lengthy sermon. Again, Mother left me sitting while she stood in line to receive the Host. And after the Mass was over there was lunch at the gostilna followed by the walk to the station to wait for the train, more hard benches on the way to Lipovec, and the long walk home.

For me, all of four years old, the journey to Maria Pomagaj was not only another train ride; it was proof that when you pray hard you get better. And this belief was soon to be put to the test. For Mother it was the fulfillment of a promise for prayers heard. But for her it was also a two day break from the chores which had accumulated in her absence and were waiting for her return.

I was on the train twice the following year, my third and fourth time, both times on the return home from the children's ward of the hospital in Ljubljana, the hospital where Mother had her surgery. Each time, the way there had been in an ambulance from Ribnica; specifically from the clinic of doctor Oražem who had set my broken leg in a temporary splint. Each time the same leg; the fractures on the upper right leg only two inches apart.

The first time was in the spring of 1937; a simple break that healed quickly and I was back to normal in less than two months. The second, eight weeks after the first, was a compound fracture which kept me in the same ward, in the same bed, twice as long. When I arrived there the second time, in the ward were children who remembered me from before. The recovery at home was much longer than the first and for a while I, like Father, used a crutch to get about.

The first fracture was due to a fall while running toward the back door of the fire chief's house to seek the protection of my twenty six year old friend Karl Schaffer, the fire chief's second son. I tripped and fell on the uneven dirt and gravel of the driveway while being pursued by the nine year old Albert Kresse, four years my senior.

Albert was part of the quartet of bullies forever seeking confrontation with defenseless village boys. Their taunting usually produced either a run-away of their target or a futile response such as throwing a stone at the provocateur. When this was the case, the resulting beating was justified as an act of self-defense. They did this either individually or if it suited them, as a team. But when they were confronted by a group they backed away only to get revenge for their humiliation by dealing with the individuals separately later on. While their bullying was indiscriminately heaped upon all of the defenseless, I had become their unique target for several reasons.

Albert Kresse was Katharina's older son. He and his younger brother Anton were supported by their cousins Karl Sbaschnig and Rudolf Tscherne. All were related to the Tschinkel brothers living at Number 12. Rudolf's father was a landless villager who once reneged on a verbal contract with Father and carried a grudge against him.

The brothers continued to intimate, in spite of the recent re-survey and amicable settlement negotiated by Franz Jaklitsch, that during the village-wide survey in 1825 by the surveyor Colanetté, their family was cheated of a large part of land which was awarded erroneously to the Tschinkels of Number 15. This lingering resentment was helped along by Grandma Gera who maintained close relations with the Tschinkel brothers of Number 12 and their many relatives who lived elsewhere in the village. She did this to spite her son for surrendering her house to his wife, the foreigner, the hated Slovene.

As a result of this lingering resentment, inflamed by Gera's doings, I became an object of revenge to the four nephews of the brothers at Number 12, an easy target of their bullying, most likely encouraged by their uncles and aunts. Since Father's and Mother's complaining to their parents had little effect, I gradually learned how to deal with the problem. I stayed at home, playmates were invited to our house and when in the village, I was often accompanied by sister Mitzi, a strong teenager who was my unhesitating defender. In addition, Father and Mother appealed to Jaklitsch and other friendly villagers, whose children were also, if far less so, bullied by the quartet. They, in turn began to confront the parents of the bullies and, as a result, my life gradually became less troublesome.

But until then, when playing with other children in the village, they would isolate me and chase me toward home. The leg broken on Schaffer's driveway was the result of one such chase.

THE RAILROAD

I fell partly because I was an awkward, non-athletic child. I was forever falling, as was evident from the perpetual scabs on both knees, always visible since like all boys, I wore short pants during the warm months. But the main reasons for this fall were the long stockings Mother had me wear in the cold months instead of the long pants worn by all other boys. And when, as a result of this event, she relented and finally dressed me the way all others were dressed, I still kept falling; however, the scabs were now hidden behind the patch of each long trouser leg.

Until the incident in Schaffer's driveway, the knee scabs were hidden by those long cotton stockings. (The rips at the knees always carefully re-knitted with yarn of never matching color). The stockings were held in place way above the knee by pink rubber bands normally hidden by the trousers of the knee length pants I wore all year round. But the stretch of the bands had, apart from the slippery skin, nothing to hold on to and the stockings they were suppose to keep in place were forever sliding down. And they slid down faster when I was running hard. Normally this was not serious when there was time to stop and pull up stocking and band before both settled on the ankle and became a hazard which caused me to trip and fall. As a result, I always came in last when running with other boys on either side of my age; they were not burdened with the get-up my mother insisted on. It was however, bruising to the ego when they laughed and called me a girl as they watched me struggle to pull things back in place. Apart from me, only girls wore stockings held up by rubber bands; a good reason for being perpetually and mercilessly ridiculed by my peers.

But this time, running from Albert, there was no time to stop and adjust. The stockings and bands had slid to the ankles and when the right foot caught the stocking on the left ankle, the forward fall snapped the upper bone of the twisted right leg.

My loud cries first brought Karl from his shop in the attic of his father's house where he had his saddler's workshop. Mother came running, Father followed, others came from all directions. Albert had disappeared. Father, and others who had been through a war and had seen fractures, realized that the leg was broken and asked for boards and bandages to fix the leg in a splint. The fire chief issued commands to firemen present to race to the firehouse to get what was needed. With the splint in place, I was lifted by many hands on to Father's carriage, brought to the scene by Father's friend Johann Krisch. Johann had harnessed Yiorgo and softened the flat back part of the carriage with layers of blankets and pillows for the long ride to doctor Oražem in Ribnica. Johann came along to bring horse and wagon back since both parents expected to come with me to the hospital in the ambulance. I remember nothing of this; but heard it told many times later.

I do, however, clearly remember lying on the table in the operating room of the hospital where they were about to set the leg and encase it in plaster. Then there was the nun-nurse who said she was about to place a cloth over my mouth to make me fall asleep and that I was to start counting. The chloroform made me gag and struggle, but in spite of it, I managed to count to four.

I woke up in the children's ward, on a white enameled tubular bed, very uncomfortable, unable to move.

The reason for this was a white post hanging by a rope from a pulley above the bed. The lower end of the white post disappeared in the sheets of my bed and when I tried to move I realized that the post was the plaster cast around my fractured leg.

The leg was kept under tension by a weight at the other end of the rope looped over pulleys high up on a bar attached to the center of the bed at each end. I had to live with that torture mechanism for the next four weeks; the most difficult part was learning how to perform bodily functions without making a mess. The sheets needed to be changed often at first.

The ward was a large oblong room with beds at right angles to the wall and ample space down the center for the traffic of doctors, nurses and visitors. My visitors were Mother and Father both getting up from chairs and telling a nun-nurse that I was waking up. The nurse explained that the broken leg was under tension to prevent it from becoming shorter than the other one while it healed. It would be under tension all the while I was in the hospital. "You do not want to have one leg shorter than the other, do you?"

Both parents soon left me, with Mother promising to come back later that day. When she did, she kept asking about the fall, apparently not pleased that I put the blame on the stockings. Months later she talked of her confrontation with Katharina who defended Albert by claiming that the chase was only normal activity of young boys. "And if you dressed him in long pants instead of girl's stockings, this would not have happened", she sneered.

Mother insisted that she was only following the tradition of her village where boys wore short pants and stockings until first communion. "Here boys wear long pants. Only girls wear stockings", Katharina replied. This logic made Mother surrender tradition and from that time forward I wore long pants, at least when it got cold. And I had to break a leg for this!

But even with long pants replacing stockings and garters, I kept falling if perhaps less so. There were still other parts of my dress that conspired against my agility and made me a subject of ridicule. Shoes that were too big, pants too long, jackets oversized. All clothing Mother expected me to grow into and soon. But to her disappointment, and mine, I grew very slowly and all was usually worn out before it fit.

Particularly troublesome were the oversized underpants. Being too large and having buttons instead elastic to hold on to the waist, they slid past the virtually non-existing hips and settled on the crotch of the pants. Fortunately the pants, held up by strong suspenders, had an oversized waist so I could reach inside and down to bring the underpants back up again. And hold them there when running or being chased.

But after the incident on the Fire Chief's driveway, Mother became more sensitive about my needs and appearance and began to dress me in better fitting clothing. And also more in line with what the others were wearing. This new found awareness was in part due to the broken leg, reinforced by Katharina's comment which, due to its relevance Mother was forced to accept. But it was conveyed to her also by other women in the village with whom she had, during the five years there, established contact.

But the bullying and persecution from the quartet did have, if in retrospect from a distant future, a positive side.

To escape, Mother frequently took Mitzi and me to stay with Grandma Ilc in Dolenja Vas. Grandma, very fit in her mid sixties still ran her gostilna and worked her fields. Living alone in the large house, Mitzi and I were always welcome and often we stayed for days. She loved our company and welcomed us always. But as my sister was in her early teens and was needed to help in our home and on the land, I began to walk the distance on my own.

And so Grandma Ilc became the first really formative influence on her impressionable grandson from across the divide. Stara Mati, as I addressed her in Slovene, knew why I kept coming and that she could give me what even my parents could not. But that is part of yet another story.

THE BELLS RING NO MORE

The fourth trip on the train, ten weeks after the second, was due to the second fracture of the right leg, two inches above the first. While the first was a clean break across the bone, this was a compound fracture which kept me in the hospital twice as long as the first time. And after the hospital, the recovery at home was much longer than the first and for a few weeks I had to use a crutch to learn to walk again.

This fracture was due to an accident at home, when I upset the balance of the heavy wooden slaughtering trough, propped up against the wall inside the barn. While climbing up to its top surface I changed its equilibrium, causing it to tip away from the wall taking me with it. As we both crashed to the ground, one edge of the trough fell on the upper right leg shattering the bone. It could have been worse.

The watertight trough, about eight feet long and three feet wide and deep was made of sturdy two inch pine planks held together with wrought iron bands hammered hot into place by the village smith. The uppermost planks of the sides extended on either end as handles for carrying it into the freshly swept yard, frozen to a solid surface by the November frost, for the slaughter of pigs that was done every year at that time. Our butchering done, the trough made its rounds to other neighbors who borrowed ours, not having one of their own. And when finally it came back and not having any other purpose, it was propped up against a wall inside the barn where it gathered dust until next fall.

Except one spring when the melting snow had, once again, turned the cistern depression into a lake. With the waters already receding and the tadpoles around its edges starting to hatch from the string of frog's eggs, the quartet and a few others decided to sail the lake in this trough. Over the protest of Mitzi, the parents being away, the trough was dragged from the barn along the road into the shallow edges of the lake. Mitzi ran into the village to alert adults while the trough filled with boys. Not being allowed to come along, I had to help pushing the boat away from the shore into deeper waters.

It nearly ended in disaster, had it not been for Schaffer, the fire chief who came running, trailed by our next door neighbor Mattl, limping and hopping.

By now the trough was some distance from the edge and in deep water. The occupants, standing in this highly unstable, perilously swaying, flat-bottomed substitute of a boat realized the danger, became frightened and started to call for help. None of them knew how to swim and neither did any of the grown ups now piling up at the shore. But Schaffer's thundering voice made the now frightened boys sit down and paddle with their hands to move the trough away from the deep. Some men and parents had come with long poles and ropes which they threw out. One was

THE RAILROAD

caught and the trough, with its now pale and subdued occupants, dragged to safety and deserved punishment.

Mitzi received much praise from those who came to Father's shop after the event where they talked about the foolishness of the boys. But some also reminded Father of the carelessly positioned trough that had caused the broken leg and urged him to do a better job in securing it to the wall. As if he needed reminding. Nevertheless, the trough was now kept in the deeper recesses of the barn, not only to prevent it from tipping, but also fastened to the wall with a locked chain.

The fifth trip on the railroad was another trip to Ljubljana, this time to my confirmation by the bishop. Part of this event was the promise of an engraved pocket watch, the usual commemorative present given on such occasion. But I received a promise only; Janez Ilc, my sponsor and Mother's brother, not being able to afford such a costly present. The promise was, however, fulfilled a few years later but there were few occasions when it could be worn in the pocket of a coat, the leather strap attached to the button hole of the jacket. And it was this strap which caught the eye of a young Partisan in Zidani Most. But more on that later.

And finally the sixth trip which, as part of our "Exodus" took us from the station in Gottschee City to Brežice on the cold and starry night of December 7, 1941, with people in the warm carriage softly singing *Heimat deine Sterne...* among others. Some cried. And when I was awakened by Mother, we were entering the station of our new "Heimat" in the Reich, a country that was to last a thousand years.

Chapter 8

My Family

My father's family lived at Grčarice (Masern) 15, the number of our house in the village. I was born in that house as were at least seven generations of my ancestors. The earliest on record is Mathias Tschinkel, his date of birth being 1729.

The year 1729 comes from the Book of Marriages which records the wedding of his son Johann Tschinkel and Magdalena Sturm on April 25, 1782. The wedding information, in addition to the birthdays of the couple, also shows that Mathias, the father of Johann was 53 years old, fixing his year of birth at 1729. The entry was made by the resident priest in Gotenica (Göttenitz).

The Book of Marriages, which shows the wedding date of Johann and Magdalena, is part of a set of three ledgers listing births, marriages and deaths kept by a priest in any village of a parish.

The ledgers on Masern were kept by the priest in Göttenitz after that village became a parish in 1363. The priest there continued making the entries even after Masern was placed under the main parish of Ribnica in 1741. And even after Masern became a sub-parish under Dolenja Vas in 1767 and Anton Wallisch became its first resident chaplain, the books continued to be kept in Gotenica (Göttenitz). During his four years there he walked the 4 kilometers to Göttenitz to make his entries. And after he left in 1771 there was no resident priest in Masern for 51 years until 1822. But during this time, the priests of Göttenitz and Dolenja Vas looked after the spiritual welfare of Masern and updated its records which continued to be kept in the parsonage of Göttenitz.

The previous ledgers filled up, the priest in Göttenitz started a new set in 1773 and continued to make entries on Masern until the arrival of its next village priest, Johann Munini in 1822. Father Munini brought this new set of books to his parsonage and from that year forward, he and his successors continued with entries on births, marriages and deaths including the descendants of Mathias Tschinkel. Unfortunately, Father Munini did not bring to Masern the sets of ledgers prior to 1773. As a result, they were irrevocably lost in the turmoil of W.W.II. But from 1773 forward a total of three sets of books were filled up. They cover the periods 1773-1820, 1821-1895 and 1896-1944. All are stored in the archives of the bishopric in Ljubljana.

Father Munini left Masern in 1837 and for 30 years until 1867 there again was no resident priest in the village. As before, the priests from the adjacent parishes of Göttenitz and Dolenja Vas took care of the spiritual welfare of Masern and maintained its records.

Father Johann Posnik came to Masern as its resident priest in 1867. He, however, gave up the priesthood in 1884, to become the full time teacher in the first school of the village, inaugurated that same year. But he continued to give religious instructions to his pupils and also continued to maintain the books on births, marriages and deaths.

Posnik in 1877 also made a tabulation of all houses in the village including the name of the owner and property owned by the house. He did this by starting with house number 1 and continuing in numerical sequence until he listed all 63 of them.

In 1939, the three sets of ledgers and the tabulation were transferred to the parish of Dolenja Vas when Father Jože Rozman, the last village priest left Masern. From there they were transferred to the Archdiocese in Ljubljana where they are kept in the Nadskofijski Arhiv to this day. The tabulation of 1877 however remained at the Dolenja Vas parish from which it was finally moved to the municipal District Office of the County of Ribnica. My birth on February 28, 1931 was recorded in the Book of Births from 1896-1944 by Father Klemenčič after he christened me on March 5, 1931.

In the absence of church records, family continuity may, however, be found in land records kept on the properties owned by each house in the village via the house number, in our case 15. But this was only so if the oldest son was the inheritor which automatically was the case according to the primogeniture law. And if the oldest son died without issue, the inheritor was the next oldest brother.

But continuity was lost if there were no sons. In this case the oldest daughter inherited the property. However, when she married, the property transferred to her husband. But the property and all its individual parcels continued to be listed in the Land Records under the number of the house of which the husband was now the owner.

Continuity via land records becomes unclear if the owner, be it the father or the oldest son, decided to split the property. In such a case, the land records were changed to show the new house number, reflect the division and all the parcels

MY FAMILY

involved. But unlike the church records which provided continuity via the ledgers on births, marriages and deaths, the land records do not show the origin of the new owner of the land that had been split away and therefore the connection is lost.

The search for the origin of my family, after exhausting the church ledgers, took me to the available land records and the belief that my ancestors may have been among the original group of six families that settled in Masern the middle of the 14th century. But there is proof that they did live in Masern ever since the end of the 17th Century.

The history of Masern and the extent to which my ancestors were part of it comes from five documents that record land ownership, the first being the *"Vrbar des ambts Riegkh, anno 1498"*. This document shows that in 1498 the original six Hides, awarded to the settlers on their arrival in the middle of the 14th century, had already been split into halves. The names of the twelve owners are:

1, Gregor (Supann), 2, Paule Weber, 3, Caspar Kramer, 4, Mathe, 5, Paull Liser, 6, Vrbann Wochenn, 7, Clement, 8, Paulle des Achatz son, 9, Jury, 10, Caspar Leschner, 11, Petter, 12, Fritze vnd Peter.

The *"Urbar Register der Herschaft Gotschee, Anno 1564"* 66 years later shows that the names of some of the twelve owners are phonetically still the same even if spelled differently. That some are already owned by their primogeniture is indicated by the "son of". The half Hides of Caspar Kramer and Vrban Wochenn now belong to Peter Stamphl, a new name. This is repeated four years later in the Blagay *"Vrbar 'Gottschee Ao 1568"*, a survey which induced Countess Elizabeth Blagay in 1613 to sell or lease five and one half additional Hides of her land to increase tax revenue and capitalize on the population growth there.

The noteworthy entry is for Paull Liser, (5). In 1564, this owner is listed as Gregor Luschar and in 1568 as Gregor Lusar, both spelled differently but phonetically are similar to Lisar. In the 1903's when each house was still recorded by its village number, not its family name, Lusharsh was the house name for Masern number two, its owner a Michitsch. Father had often mentioned that the Lusharsh were one of the oldest residents of the village.

The next available land document, the Therezijanski Kataster of 1752, was prepared 184 years later. Unfortunately, the Blagay tax records, showing the income from the land in Masern during this interim, could not be found. This missing link would reveal when and how the names listed in the 1498, 1564 and 1568 documents evolved into the names listed in the 1752 Kataster which now shows twenty three land owners and twelve land leasers or thirty five in all.

Among the twenty three land owners there are eighteen with one of six family names. They are:

Primosch (6), Fritz (4), Sturm (3), Parthe (2), Michitsch (2) and Stampfl (1).

These eighteen families now own the twelve half-Hides split into eighteen parts of one quarter Hide or more. This would indicate that these eighteen owners are the descendants of the original settlers of Grčarice (Masern) having arrived there sometime before 1498. The fact that all the owners now have both a Christian and family name that are different or new, may be attributed to the fact that the repeated use of only Christian names became impractical or that the property was transferred to a son-in-law as was then the practice.

Of the other seventeen new names in the 1752 Kataster, five are owners and twelve are leasers of the five and one half Hides of land made available by the countess in 1613. The name Tschinkel is among the seventeen and as such appears for the first time in land records.

The five owners are Krisch, Wittine, Schober, Tschinkel and Wittreich, their joint ownership being one and three eighths Hides of which Michaill Tschinkel owned one eight of a Hide and lived at Number 15. He either purchased the land from the Blagays after 1613 or married a female descendant of one of the other owners. The missing records of the interval between 1568 and 1752 would reveal this and show when the Tschinkels arrived in the village or if they were already residents known by another name before family names became adopted and used in records.

Among the twelve families leasing the balance of four and one eighth Hides were Mihael and Matel Tschinkel who lived at Masern 26 and 29 respectively. Matel (Mathias) was the son of the Michaill at number 15 and my G,G,G,G, (fifth) grandfather. He inherited the property when his father died.

In his tabulation of 1877, Father Posnik listed every house by its number, recorded the last and first name of the owner, his age and the amount of land owned by the house. If no land was connected to the house, Posnik listed "none". Even though each house had its own family name, he provided the house name well. Among the villagers only this house name was used; almost never the formal family name, a name not even known to some of the residents.

Posnik's information and the book on births, marriages and deaths since 1773, reveal a high degree of intermarriage, a large number of offspring, an enormous infant mortality and the longevity of those who survived. Also apparent is the fact that many of the Masern men took their wives from families having the familiar names of Michitsch, Parthe, Sturm and Stampfl.

But since these names also predominate in the neighboring Göttenitz/Gotenica, their wives may have come from there. In Göttenitz, twenty seven of the forty families have the name of Michitsch, Parthe, Primosch, Stampfl and Poje.

The similarity of names in the two villages is not surprising given their long and intimate association and only strengthens the conclusion that these families have been connected since their ancestors arrived there in the fourteenth century. In fact, Gertrude Michitsch, the second wife of Grandfather George, came from Göttenitz. They were married on August 14, 1886.

But after 1613, two new family names appear in the village. These are Sbaschnig and Knaus. They most likely came from the Slovene village Dolenja Vas just outside the enclave. The "*Therezijanski Kataster*", in "Bekanntnuss Tabellen, Unter Krain, 23. April 1752" under the: "*Mittel Wiertl der Krain Herrschaft Reiffnitz, Dorff Nider Dorff*", lists eight families named Sbaschnig and at least one named Knaus, all owning land in Dolenja Vas.

The same Kataster under: " *Dritter Viertl Herrschaft Gottschee*" shows that as part of the land released in 1613, the Blagays rented one and three eighths Hides to two Sbaschnig families. Given this, it can be assumed that the Sbaschnigs of Masern were the Slovene Zbašniks of Dolenja Vas who moved into the enclave and became assimilated and Germanized their name.

(Great Grandfather George Tschinkel married a Sbaschnig on March 3, 1853. She too may have come from a Dolenja Vas family).

Dolenja Vas, only six and one half km from Masern and for centuries a Slovene speaking village, has many other family names that have a distinctly phonetic equivalent to names inside the enclave. Zbašnik (nine families in 1877), Fric, Klun, Kromer, Schwerger, Kaplan are examples.

The Kataster of 1752 also shows that even more commonality is found in the even nearer Rakitnica. The names there are Widerwoll, Honigmann, Schober, Potschauer, Hegler and Fritz. (Both Schober and Fritz are listed as resident property owners in the Masern Kataster of 1752). The Rakitnica name Hegler is found to own property in Göttenitz. And the name Widerwoll, listed as property owners ten times in Rakitnica is recorded five times for owners in Göttenitz where it is spelled as Widerwohl, all of whom were identified as ethnic Germans and resettled as such in 1941.

The above indicates that the settlers on both sides of the enclave had much of their ancestry in common but adopted the language in their part for the sake of communication. But this was long before any nationalistic ideology entered their lives and drove them apart.

Based on the above records, the presence of the Tschinkel family living in Masern starts eight generations ago in an unknown year of the late 17th and early 18th century. This comes from the fact that "Mihaill", my ancestor lived at number 15 in the house I was born. The path between "Mihaill" and myself is clearly documented in the Kataster of 1752 and in the church records kept by the priests.

Based on the Posnik ledger, the number of Tschinkel families living in Masern in 1877 had increased from three to ten since 1752. Of the ten, six were land owners, together owning two and three eighths Hides in fractions of various sizes representing, in all, 21% of all the land in the village. As such, Tschinkel was the most populous name, together owning more land than any other name in Masern. The increased ownership since 1752 could have been acquired only through direct purchase or marriage to heiress daughters, or widows of landowners. Four of the ten Tschinkel families own no land but all owned their house and the land it stood on.

The entry Johann Posnik made for my great grandfather's house is:

"Masern 15, House Name: Sturnjacklsch, (meaning the house of Johann near the well), Family name: Tschinkel, Christian name: Georg, Age: 62, Property size: one quarter.

For the first ten years of my life I was known as Sturnjacklsch Johann of Number 15. By then the land owned by the house had increased from the 1/8 Hide listed in the "Theresianski Kataster of 1752" to one quarter of a Hide.

I, Johann, emerged as the product of a Tschinkel and an Ilc, on February 28, 1931. My parents, Johann and Maria, members of two families separated for centuries by a language barrier and a one hour walk over a few steep hills, found each other in the tavern of my Slovene grandmother in Dolenja Vas. Their language barrier was overcome, but more than anything else, it was their less than fortunate past that brought them together for life.

MY FAMILY

My father was one of the nine children of Georg and Gertrude, (his second wife), my paternal grandparents. Georg, the oldest son of Georg and Margarete, was born on April 2, 1862. He married Rosalie Sturm of Masern 20 on August 16, 1885. The twenty two year old Rosalie died six days after giving birth to son Johann on June 8 1886. Johann died fifty two days later, the cause of death listed in the ledger of deaths as "lack of mother milk".

Georg married again on August 14, 1886. His new wife was Gertrude Michitsch, aged twenty four. She was born on January 23, 1862 in Göttenitz at house number 22. Together they had nine children but only four survived. One died in birth, four others in infancy. Karl died of smallpox at one, Phillip at six of pneumonia, Maria at three of infection and Gertrude at ten of typhus. The four survivors, Johanna and Paula both lived to sixty eight while both Johann and Franz died at seventy six.

Most marriages produced similar numbers and the high infant mortality rate, the most frequent way of death in the village, was not viewed as a curse but as part of the natural selection process.

Johanna, Paula and the eldest son Johann (my father), left for America, as soon as they were grown. Johanna left in 1905 when she was eighteen; Johann followed her in 1910 when he was seventeen to live with Johanna and her husband. Paula joined them in 1914 when she was sixteen. This left the parents George and Gertrude, both fifty two, and the youngest, Franz aged nine to tend the farm.

The exodus for America was common throughout the area, the enclave included. The New World offered opportunities which most of the young, including those in the family of George and Gertrude, realized the enclave did not. The extension of the railroad from Ljubljana to Kočevje (Gottschee), placed in operation on September 28, 1893 brought not only America but also the other parts of the world to this remote place. The exodus was especially large in the late part of the 19th and the early 20th century, up to the start of WWI. It built on itself when those who had left reported their successes and started sending back part of their earnings. A large percentage of the population, most of them young adults, left during that period. There was little to keep them at home.

The land could no longer support the higher survival rate resulting from the improving level of education and better medical care. The inadequately fertilized soil, meager and unproductive to begin with, was being depleted in spite of crop rotation and barely provided for one family. Artificial fertilizer was not affordable and natural fertilizer from domestic animals was no longer adequate for the ever-increasing demand on the soil. Topping all that, frequent subdivision had reduced the available acreage to a point where further subdivision was no longer an option. The ownership of land had, over the centuries, been reduced to the minimum needed for survival.

Apart from lumber mills, there was little industry inside the enclave and other parts of southeastern Slovenia. Various attempts within the enclave at glass works, Loden mills and wood products including carving, did not prosper and expand.

Johann, the natural heir to the land, had gone to America with the intention of returning after he saved enough to allow him to have a head start when he took over. Johann was to inherit the one quarter Hide equal to 21 hectares or 51 acres encompassing two and a half hectares of arable fields, seven of meadows and 11.5 of forest.

After his return, he intended to marry his childhood sweetheart Minnie to whom he was already engaged when he left. Minnie was the only child of Joseph and Sophie Primosch, owners of one half a Hide. It had been agreed that the two properties would merge after the marriage.

But destiny would have it otherwise. It came to Johann and Minnie in the form of WWI. Specifically, it came to Johann in Brooklyn NY in an order to appear for duty as a soldier at the Austrian Imperial Army station in Ribnica. It was sent to him by his father Georg with a reminder to follow the order or else lose all rights as heir to the family property.

Johann, having no intention of losing his inheritance, his betrothed Minnie and her half Hide, bought a ticket on the next steamer to Trieste from where he took the train via Ljubljana to Lipovec, the station nearest to home.

After training as a soldier, he was sent to the Italian front. He was there for most of the four years of the war but was sent home on a short leave, the first since being sent to the front. This was only a few weeks before the final confrontation at the Isonzo on October 23 in which the Italians destroyed the remnants of the Austro-Hungarian army in the battle of Vittorio Veneto. All hostilities ended November 4, 1918 and the Austrian units dissolved seven days later with the general armistice of November 11, 1918.

At home he found his mother Gera, now 56, brother Franz, aged thirteen and a totally neglected farm. His father Georg had died of cancer in 1916 and with Gera on her own, she could do only the bare minimum necessary to survive.

With no firewood on hand and winter approaching, Johann, Gera, Franz and the team of cows pulling the wagon made for the "Unterbinkl", the nearest part of their forest to fell trees and cut them into logs. Ahead of this, Johann had filed the teeth of the saw and the cutting edges of the axe, something that had not been done for years since even before his father died. He also filed the edge of the machete, a cutting tool used for clearing the underbrush, into a razor sharp edge. With this tool he cut himself in the knee, a wound that would not heal and continued to fester. Apparently, the cutting edge of the axe had been contaminated by the file and the cut brought poison into the wound.

MY FAMILY

The file used for sharpening the machete axe had been used to clean the copper soldering iron with which he fixed the holes in the pots and pans the women of the village brought to his shop for repair. The iron was a pointed clump of copper at the end of a handle that was placed into the flames of the stove in the shop, and after being heated was cleaned with a file scraping off remnants of solder, copper and other residue. It was this residue that the file transferred on to the machete and which, through the cut, found its way into the blood stream.

At first, he ignored the wound as he had others while in the trenches for nearly four years. There, however, was usually a medic who took care of such wounds. In isolated Masern there was no antiseptic and medical care was hours away. And when the cut began to fester, he asked a woman in the village for some of her mercurochrome which she denied him saying she had to save it for her own family.

When the twenty five year old soldier finally got to the military hospital in Ljubljana, gangrene had set in. Recalling the events later he said that by the time the busy staff got around to him, the gangrene had spread and there was no choice except to amputate the leg above the knee. He talked about being aware of the saw cutting the bone and the pain due to the lack of anesthetic, which at the end of the war, was not readily available in this hospital.

But after he came back home to Masern without his right leg, the woman who denied him the antiseptic tearfully came to apologize for her selfish act.

While Imperial Austria lost the war, Johann lost not only his leg but also Minnie and her half Hide. Minnie's parents did not see a good future for their only daughter in being married to an invalid, called a "Krippl" in the enclave, a derogatory term used when referring to a physically handicapped person. Physical fitness was essential in this rural environment, the key to a productive existence, to survival. So Minnie's parents put her on the next boat to America where, after several years, she married but not for love.

Johann's fortunes declined even further when his brother Franz came of age and left to join his sisters in Brooklyn in 1926. Apparently, Franz demanded that the property of one quarter hide be split in half, something Johann would not agree to. With his leaving, Johann lost him not only as a brother but also as a helper in tending the land. However, Johann learned the art of leasing his acreage in return for labor to tend his own; there were many landless villagers willing to oblige. He also acquired a horse and carriage to make it possible for him to get around. The latter two brought him to the tavern in Dolenja Vas kept by Maria Ilc, my maternal grandmother to be.

The family tree of the maternal side of my family starts nine generations ago with the birth of Mihael Ilc in 1650. The tree was developed from dates in church records of both Dolenja Vas and Ribnica. My mother Maria was the second of six children of Alojzij Ilc and Maria Zbašnik, living at Dolenja vas 46, the house name "Venckovi".

Grandfather Alojzij was the third son of a prominent Ilc family, born on June 16, 1862 in the nearby Goriča Vas. But as the third in line for any inheritance Alojzij was a penniless bachelor, at twenty nine years having nothing except a good family name.

Grandmother Maria, born on November 1, 1869, was the second of eleven children of Johan and Agnes Zbašnik family in Dolenja Vas number 16. The house name was Pečkovi which, in addition to number 16, distinguished it from the other eight Zbašnik families in Dolenja Vas. All are listed in the *Theresianski Kataster of 1752*. The Pečkovi lineage itself has been traced to the birth of Gašper, born in 1767.

Among her ten siblings, Maria had five brothers and five sisters. One of them died at birth. Jože the eldest son had no interest in the land, went to study law in Vienna and remained there. As a result, the burden of running the estate and caring for the aging parents fell mostly on the eldest daughter. She proved to be an able administrator, destined for a sizable dowry since the family was exceptionally well off and therefore she was a sought-after match by the likes of Alojzij Ilc and his parents.

The marriage of Alojzij and Maria took place in 1891. It was arranged by the parents and was no love match. The dowry of Maria was large; a house and 52 choice parcels of fertile land. The large house in the center of the village included a gostilna, a tavern selling wine, beer and meals that were served in a large guest room; in the summer on the terrace under shade trees. The tavern was similar to the Jaklitsch one in Masern. The house at number 46, purchased for the young couple by the parents of Maria was, together with the land, transferred to the twenty nine year old Alojzij and as dowry recorded in the wedding contract. All believed that the clever and determined Maria, even if only twenty two, would be a capable partner to Alojzij in making a success of running the enterprise.

That Maria was clever was noted. Her intelligence was recorded at the end of first grade by her teacher Janez Čuk who entered her as exceptional in the Honor Book of Students in Dolenja Vas for the first time on August 10, 1877. The leather bound hard cover book with its gold embossed *"Ehrenbuch der Schüler in Niederdorf"*, (Honor book of students in Dolenja Vas) locally called the "Zlata Knjiga", the Golden Book, was kept by the parish to commemorate its brightest students. Janez Čuk continued to make similar entries on Maria at the end of each of the following three school years. But she did not continue schooling after the fourth grade; education beyond the fourth grade was not yet mandatory and in rural areas even undesirable since at age twelve and beyond all hands were needed to work the land.

Maria and Alojzij were formally introduced at a "spraševanje", a get together of the couple, their parents and the priest in the office of his Dolenja Vas parsonage prior to the wedding. At this meeting the priest questioned the future bride and groom about their commitment and the parents about the financial arrangement. My cousin Mira states that this was the first time Maria met Alojzij which may have been the case since their elementary schooling did not overlap and the parents usually kept a close watch on their daughters.

The marriage went bad very soon. Alojzij, at twenty nine suddenly thrust into a position of power, assumed control of both the tavern and the farm. Maria had no choice but to submit to his dictates. While she and helpers were sent into the fields, Alojzij tended the tavern, often winding up drunk with his loose friends who did not pay their bills. Maria protested but without results.

A son Alojzij was born in 1892, Maria, my mother in 1896 and Angela in 1899. Immediately after that, the now restless husband left for America, leaving Maria to cope on her own. This she did well and recovered most of the damage done by her husband. But he returned in 1904 and fathered, in rapid succession three sons, Franc, Janez and Jože (05, 06, 08.) He also continued in his former destructive ways, tolerating no interference from his wife whom he beat into submission. More than ever before he entertained non-paying customers and friends and in his perpetual drunken state neglected to pay his suppliers. Soon deliveries stopped and patrons stayed away. And everything the wife had recovered in his absence was dragged down again. To escape the consequences of his mismanagement he left for America in 1909, this time for good. He died in Cleveland on Jan 27, 1937.

However, the gostilna could no longer recover from the damage and a public auction on March 23, 1911 forced by creditors caused the sale of all 52 parcels of land. The auction yielded 6,113 Imperial Krone, then equal to 1,232 US Dollars, at today's valuation approximately roughly 140,000 Dollars. Maria Ilc herself bid on parcel number 40 which she got for 226 Krone.

But it was parcel number 40, together with the earnings from the recovering gostilna that helped the now forty two year old Maria to survive and raise her five fatherless children. And daughter Maria, at her father's final departure an able ten year old, became the right hand to her now single mother, helping her with the siblings, the fields and the tavern. But while the aging mother clung to the oldest daughter, she struggled to make sure that her other children were raised and educated in a manner that satisfied her pride and did not reflect the failings of her husband.

The apple of her eye was Alojzij, the oldest. He inherited her intelligence and she sent him to the Gymnasium in Ljubljana and from there to University in Vienna where he got a law degree, graduating just before the start of WWI. He became an officer in the 47th Regiment of the Imperial Army and was soon sent to the Italian front. There he was killed on August 18, 1917 during the 11th battle at the Isonzo near St. Giovanni in the Monfalcone district of the Veneto coastal area. His officer's sword and personal alarm clock were returned to his family by his orderly. The sword got lost, but I still have the clock, now one of my treasured possessions.

His death resulted in a life long hatred for anything Italian not only by his mother but also by his sister Maria, a hatred that surfaced into the open when the Italians came to Dolenja Vas as occupiers in 1941. But more on that later.

Angela, two and one half years younger than Maria, was sent off to Kočevje (Gottschee) City to learn to be a seamstress. After she finished training and returned home she used her skills to help support the family by sewing cloth into shirts and dresses, but resisted working in the fields which resulted in endless friction between her and the other two women. This friction among the three continued even after Angela married Janez Pahulje in 1928. As a builder of some standing, Pahulje was an acceptable husband to the mother, seeing in the marriage a repair of the honor to her family.

This honor, tainted at first by the sordid ways of her husband, then further damaged by a humiliating auction, was now dragged even further down when it became public that the twenty seven year old Maria was pregnant. Made pregnant by her secretly affianced lover; the affair kept secret because he was judged by the mother as being unworthy of her daughter. When the mother discovered the added shame brought home by this wayward daughter, she expelled her from the house and Maria went to live with the Zbašnik family, her maternal grandparents.

Maria gave birth to a girl on September 23, 1923 but by then the father had died of tuberculosis. My mother never spoke of him and I never asked. But Janez Pahulje, who knew him said his name was Karel Widerwoll; that he was a sickly man already terminally ill before the girl was born. A "kind man, but one without property or learning". This was not in line with the expectation of her mother and Maria was forbidden to marry him.

But the expelled Maria was missed as a helper and after the initial anger abated, her mother demanded that the dishonored daughter recover her graces by coming to the

MY FAMILY

inn as an unpaid day laborer. This she did for years starting daily at crack of dawn and performing her former duties until late into the night. As time went by, she was allowed to bring with her the bastard child, "cross-eyed by God as punishment on the wayward mother".

In the meanwhile, the three sons Franc, Janez and Jože had grown into teenagers and the mother was arranging their future. Franc became an apprentice to a carpenter, Janez an apprentice to a mason and Jože, the youngest was sent to a lawyer's office in Ljubljana to learn law.

Franc finished his apprenticeship and left for Argentina in 1925. He never came back. But before departing he mentioned to his coworkers that his mother wished him to do something about his unruly hair for a family photograph. They suggested a watered down mixture of carpenter glue which worked well and satisfied the mother and the photographer. But the glue mixture hardened and the hair became a solid mass which had to be softened and melted out with masses of very hot water.

Janez, after finishing his training worked for Pahulje, met Maria Bradač, the daughter of a landless worker and to the displeasure of his mother, married her in 1937. Shunned by her mother-in-law, she was nevertheless required to come and help with the gostilna, scrub the floors and clean up after the guests. After several years, the mother-in-law relented and in 1940 finally asked that her son and his family come to live with her. But this was only when she was no longer able to cope on her own at age 71.

As for Jože her youngest, Grandma Ilc pulled out all the stops. Recognizing his intellect, she sent him to Kočevje City where he finished the Gymnasium and from there to the university in Ljubljana where he studied law. After one year in the military in 1933, he went to work for a law firm in Ljubljana as an assistant lawyer. There he met Iva Knoll, a secretary and the daughter of yet another landless peasant. Anticipating disapproval from his mother, Jože kept the liaison secret for six years. And when he informed her of his decision to marry Iva in 1939, she not only forbade it, but terminated all contact with her son and never met his wife and children. This separation was maintained for eight years until 1947 when, on her death bed in the hospital, she finally agreed to meet Iva.

After the twenty nine year old Angela married Pahulje in 1928 and left the house, her mother, now at sixty, relied even more on her oldest daughter, her right hand for over fifteen years. Janez was of limited help being away on his job most of the time and Jože was a student in Ljubljana. And when in 1930 Maria, now thirty four agreed to marry Johann Tschinkel, her mother, for obvious reasons tried her utmost to prevent it. But Maria remained determined, surely aware that she was well on the way to spinsterhood and that this opportunity, even if hardly ideal, might be her last. Fortunately, strong support for her decision came from brother Janez and two of her aunts, her mother's younger sisters, Franca and Jula, both spinsters themselves. Maria for years remained grateful to all three, helping them whenever financial or other help was needed. In addition to the three, she had other supporters in the village and ultimately, her mother relented and gave her reluctant blessing. The fact that he was a landowner, even if an invalid from a German village, helped this proud woman with her decision.

The detractors were Angela and Jože, each of them to be impacted by the pending absence of Maria's support of their mother. Their joint effort to prevent the union was the beginning of a life long animosity between Angela and brother Janez and decades long hostility between the two sisters. In addition, the likelihood of any reconciliation was set back even further by the events related to Aunt Johanna's roof described in the next chapter.

Maria and Johann, each burdened by their handicaps, were brought together by the very handicaps destiny had imposed on them. She, a disgraced woman with a bastard child; he, a handicapped man on crutches. Both damaged goods no one else wanted. These handicaps forced them to be realistic about their choices and conclude that the union, while far from ideal, was preferable to remaining single. On top, there was the lack of a common language. But apart from their handicaps, both were young, healthy and strong; each determined to face a difficult future, one they started with a honeymoon in Bled.

It was Johann who got the better deal. He got himself a wife, a cook, a housekeeper, a worker in the field and had his ego as a man restored. In addition, he acquired a seven year old step daughter who was not only of help immediately, but in a few years would be a major contributor.

But while Maria got herself a husband, a landed one at that, she also acquired a mother-in-law Gera (Gertrude) who, for the next eight years until she died in 1938

But having learned to read early was also a burden, especially in our one room school where the Slovene teacher gloated because the "half-breed" was better than the "pure Aryans" many of whom had difficulty with the alphabet. Some schoolmates did not take kindly to this unfavorable distinction and I took extra bullying as a result.

I had learned to read in Slovene, but it was Grandma Ilc who introduced me to reading German which she knew reasonably well. She said it was important to learn it and therefore found easy to read material and helped me as I stumbled with words most of which had no similarity with the Gottschee dialect. And by 1941, I was able to read the *Gottscheer Zeitung* that came regularly and was on a table at the Jaklitsch tavern available to all including me.

I kept cycling to Grandma's even after the Italians arrived in the spring of 1941. A contingent of the Italians stayed in Dolenja Vas and their field kitchen was set up in the shaded orchard of her gostilna, much to her displeasure and disgust. She passionately hated all Italians for killing her favorite son. On my first visit after their arrival in May, she forcefully commanded me with "…don't go near them…"

I did not until I watched them prepare a meal and smelled the aroma. Tomatoes, beans, macaroni and other exotic things went into the big pot and the aroma was heavenly. I drifted nearer but Grandma saw me and yelled: "... get away from them ..." I reluctantly did, but in a little while the aroma became irresistible again. Again Grandma yelled and I withdrew, but not too far.

The Italians noticed the goings on which they found most amusing. And when Grandma was again not watching, they winked with their fingers and I crept toward the soldier who with a ladle scooped the pot and poured some its contents into a field dish for me. With this I ran behind the house, out of sight of Grandma and ate the most delicious food of my short life. I remembered this event of tasting forbidden fruit only after many years of puzzlement about my love for anything Italian. Fortunately my wife is a wonderful cook and very early discovered my culinary passion. I am certain that one of the reasons for our marital longevity is the way she excels in the various ways of preparing pasta.

Chapter 9

Aunt Johanna's Roof

It started with the visit in 1931 from America of Johanna, father's elder sister, her husband Paul Krisch and son Herbert. She had left for Brooklyn in 1905, where she married Paul's older brother who died nine years later, after fathering cousins Herbert and Ida. The determined Johanna soon married Paul, who became a model father to his brother's family. Especially since he had lived in the home of his brother as a bachelor and was intimate with the family which also included Johanna's youngest brother Franz who joined them in 1926.

Over the years the couple lived frugally, had saved their earnings and was now contemplating retirement in the empty home of the Krisch family in Grčarske ravne (Masereben), the Masern extension across a hill, two kilometers away. The hamlet was in a flat bottomed bowl of land surrounded by steep wooded hills which, due to its proximity of about three kilometers became an annex to Masern. This space of land was able to support only a small number of families and even in 1930 there were only eight houses, all owners of fractions of a Hide.

The Krisch house, a stone wall structure with a leaky roof, had been neglected by the aging parents after the departure of the two sons for the new world and empty for many years after both of them died. Father, the caretaker for the absent owners kept the house empty and locked, but he allowed the land to be used by the "landless" to prevent it from being recaptured by the forest.

The American visitors soon concluded that the house was not fit to stay in and moved into the empty room of our house for the duration of the visit.

During their stay, Johanna and Paul decided to renovate the house to make it suitable for their retirement in a few years. The house, its basic structure of thick stone walls intact, needed a total overhaul including a new roof. Father agreed to act on their behalf when they were ready. This came to pass in 1938 and Father awarded Janez Pahulje, the husband of Aunt Angela his sister-in-law, the job of general contractor. This decision resulted in deep fissures throughout my mother's family, producing a split that continued for three decades, one that even the best intentions on my part could not bring to an end.

Father and Pahulje had agreed to meet in the Kren tavern at the cemetery end of the village. Of the three public meeting places in Masern, it was the least frequented and therefore the large public room was likely to be empty in early afternoon, which was indeed the case. I accompanied Father on the way there. Pahulje had already arrived on his bicycle from Dolenja Vas, and was sitting in a corner at the far end of the room, having a beer. Father took a seat at a table near the door, the most distant spot from his wife's brother-in-law, and told me to go outside and play.

They had not spoken for months and any communication between them was only via their respective wives, sisters who took messages to their mother who in turn passed them to the other daughter. By the end of 1939, the dispute had reached a level of hostility which precluded any direct meeting between the sisters and given the existing confrontation between their respective husbands, direct talk was, therefore, carefully avoided.

But this method of communication created confusion, since the two sisters invariably managed to color the original message with their own bias. Grandmother realized that the messages she was passing on became distorted before they reached their destination. She therefore forced an end to this troublesome way of communication and brought about the direct confrontation between the principals which was about to begin in the empty guest room of the Kren tavern.

It was predictable from the beginning that this arrangement between builder and client was destined to go wrong. Pahulje was known for his underestimates, overruns and delays in getting a project to completion, and was perpetually in financial difficulties over debts which he repaid with moneys he received as advances from new customers. Nevertheless Father, being aware of all this, turned a blind eye to the habits of his brother-in-law and when Johanna and Paul decided to start the renovations, Father awarded him the job.

Pahulje was anxious to start and obviously the first task on the list was the new roof. This effort was awarded to Franz Sbaschnig of Masereben, a distant relative of Grandmother Ilc who, with his crew of sons and nephews, had for years been constructing roofs in all the villages of the area. He was the best around.

To start the project, Johanna sent Father an advance, part of which he paid to Pahulje for the roof. Pahulje in turn made a partial payment to Sbaschnig with the promise to pay the rest after the old roof was removed, the new skeleton installed and covered with clay tiles.

Sbaschnig started by selecting suitable fir in Johanna's forests, shaping the trees into beams on the spot where they fell, hauling the cut sections into the large barn on the Krisch premises and leaving them there to dry out during the coming winter and spring.

In early summer of the following year, the dimensions of the wall on which the old roof rested were measured and the dimensions reproduced on a flat portion of grass near the house. Wooden stakes were hammered into the ground in key places to become the template for the base beams of the new roof.

The construction of the roof was an event and all who could came to watch, including the children after school let out. It was great fun to see the skeleton of the new roof grow above the template under the crafty guidance of Sbaschnig yelling orders to his compliant crew. On to the horizontal beams, which were to rest on the three foot wide stone wall, were fitted the beams of the roof pitch meeting their opposites from the other side. The skeleton was held together with long wooden pegs driven into strategically drilled holes which were hammered back out after the entire structure was completed. All parts were carefully marked, then disassembled and stored so that the assembly sequence on top of the wall would flow without confusion.

The removal of the old roof and installation of the new one was during late midsummer of 1939, a time when the weather was most likely to be sunny and dry long enough to prevent rain from flooding the inside of the exposed house. Old Sbaschnig directed his crew as he had for decades and in less than a fortnight the gleaming red tiles were in place to keep out the wet for decades to come.

Sbaschnig demanded payment for the balance but Pahulje kept putting him off. He had long ago used the money Father had given him to pay off other debts.

Predictably, after not getting anywhere, Sbaschnig came to Father to obtain payment which led to bitter arguments between Pahulje and Father. Ultimately Sbaschnig appealed directly to Johanna in Brooklyn, who instructed Father to pay Sbaschnig and sue Pahulje to recover the funds.

Johanna's request was a difficult one for Father, but having suggested his brother-in law in the first place, he had no choice but to comply with his sister's request. This is when the interchange via Grandmother Ilc began but which came to nothing and finally brought about the face to face confrontation now underway in the public room of the Kren tavern.

I stayed near the entrance and gradually became aware of the rising voices behind the closed guest room door. I did try once to see what was going on but Father sternly directed me to stay outside. I noticed however that the two men were no longer at opposite ends of the large room but that each had moved closer to the center.

Soon there was a commotion and I began yelling which attracted, among others, the innkeeper Kren from the slaughterhouse that was part of his tavern. He separated the struggling adversaries and insisted they leave the premises immediately. Pahulje ran out clutching his left hand and cycled away. In the struggle, Father had broken his thumb. Pahulje explained the cast by saying that he fell from his bicycle, but the news of the struggle had spread and all knew better. Father emerged from the room shaky but undamaged and with a now unchecked will to sue his sister-in-law's husband, a conviction he forcefully vocalized to his worried wife as soon as we got home.

Grandma Ilc tried to find a less confrontational way to defuse the raging storm but without success. By now the two sisters were blind to reason and their rising fury, nurtured by many years of mutual rancor, only helped to solidify the hostility between their respective husbands. And Father, no longer restrained, filed his suit for recovery and damages on behalf of Johanna and Paul Krisch with the Clerk in the courthouse in Ribnica.

As the two families readied for a public fight, the two sisters lobbied the members of their family. Grandma Ilc was supportive of Father's cause, partly because she had never liked Pahulje as an in-law and as one who never paid for the wine he drank at her tavern. Also, she was not fond of Angela who since childhood was a perpetual source of friction between her siblings, maintained airs, was above helping with chores, and generally annoyed her mother.

Janez, the second of Mother's four brothers, was also supportive in large part because of the money owed him by Pahulje. Janez, a mason had often worked for his sister's husband who paid slowly, if at all. But Janez had ceased to donate his labors to Pahulje and was no longer on speaking terms with him or his wife Angela, his younger sister. Janez also did not speak to his mother who had cast him out because he married, without her approval, a woman she considered below the family's station. She did not come to the wedding and shunned wife and family for years. She relented years later when forced by age and frailty to overcome her pride and welcomed Janez and his family into the large house.

AUNT JOHANNA'S ROOF

But Janez remained close to his sister Maria and was a strong supporter of her husband. Other more distant relatives and friends of Mother in Dolenja Vas all sided with her husband's cause, knowing both the nature of the dispute and the habits of Pahulje. In Masern, relatives and friends of Father, while supportive, reveled in the dispute because they had advised him against awarding the work to Pahulje, a man whose reputation was well known. To them it promised to be a source of interesting gossip and welcome diversion from their daily routine.

The contrarian was brother Jože, Mother's youngest sibling. At thirty one years of age, this young lawyer agreed to take on the defense of Pahulje, his brother-in-law. Jože had also married below his station and like Janez, he and his family were banished from his mother's house. Apart from the offense that he had married a woman from a non-landed and poor family, she saw in his errant ways a lack of gratitude for her self-denial in getting him educated as a lawyer.

My own Mother's feelings toward her brother Jože and his family were similar to those of her mother and it was therefore not difficult for her to adhere to her directive to have nothing to do with them. Her reasons did not fully mirror those of her mother, but were more due to a belief that Jože, like sister Angela was avoiding her for having a child out of wedlock and marrying an invalid farmer, a non-Slovene from an alien village six and one half kilometers away. Neither Jože nor Angela came to her wedding and neither of them ever came to visit her in Masern. Pahulje did come by on his bicycle but only on business and Mother tried her best to avoid him.

Grandma's prohibition extended even to the second generation. On my way to visit her in Dolenja Vas, I had to pass the Pahulje house, but was forbidden to go near it. I sometimes passed cousins Božena and Janez, Angela's two children, on the way to Grandma's house, but we barely exchanged words. I had never met uncle Jože nor any of his family. They lived in Ljubljana, the big city very far away. When we finally met and got to know them decades later, the world was a different place for all of us.

In spite of her feelings toward Jože, Mother had asked him to be my confirmation sponsor. The confirmation was to be performed by the bishop of the diocese in the cathedral of Ljubljana. She believed it was important for me to have a sponsor of stature for this important event in my life, the formal entry into membership of the church. Jože seemed the most eminent of the family and the importance of this event justified putting aside all enmities, even if only for a short while. But by agreeing to defend Pahulje in Father's law suit, Jože renewed his lack of worth which even the size of this event would not overcome and he was dropped.

Mother asked her brother Janez to be my sponsor and he reluctantly agreed after she assured him that the event was not going to burden him financially. Grandma Ilc was persuaded to give her blessing and she even agreed to give the post-confirmation dinner at her gostilna which Janez and his family were allowed to attend.

I was not pleased with the change of sponsors, mainly because I was not going to get the pocket watch, the usual gift given to a young man by his sponsor on this special occasion. Janez could not afford such an expensive outlay and after many tears over this tragedy, I was consoled by Mother with the promise of a bicycle soon and a watch later. Both of them I got eventually, but being part of other events, are part of other stories.

Father believed that the facts were clear enough in his favor and saw no need for a lawyer to argue his case. However, very near the hearing in court before a judge, he got wind of the tactic to be used by Jože on behalf of Pahulje, which threw him and Mother into panic.

According to this tactic, "Tschinkel had agreed to let Pahulje use the money for the roof to pay off a debt, since he had outstanding receivables to cover the amount. Those receivables were delayed and as a result, he had no other funds at the moment to pay Sbaschnig. He needed more time to which Tschinkel had given his consent".

But this agreement was not documented and no independent witnesses were present to either substantiate Pahulje's claim or prove it false.

Mother reminded Father that I had been present and could testify that Father never agreed to the Pahulje claim. Father was reluctant but finally agreed to have me appear at the hearing as a surprise witness.

During the days up to the trial I was carefully coached by both on my coming role. I was to say that I was at the meeting but that I never heard Pahulje ask if he could use the money as he claimed. Of course this strategy was top secret; I was forbidden, on penalty of never getting a watch, to say a word to anyone, even Grandma Ilc.

The hearing was in the old courthouse in Ribnica, the center of our municipality for many centuries.

On the day of the hearing, all had assembled in the judge's chamber, but I had to wait outside in the dimly lit vaulted hallway of this ancient building. I listened to their voices until the door opened and Mother asked me to come inside. She led the nine year old in front of the judge sitting behind the desk on a raised platform.

"Is this your witness?" he asked. "But he is a child. How dare you bring a child as a witness into my courtroom".

Mother stammered, Father covered his face and Jože and Pahulje smirked as I was shown out of the room. I stayed near the closed door to listen to the proceedings and uncle Jože making his final points.

But Mother recovered and now kept interrupting Jože. At some point she exploded at her brother. She accused him of lying and being ungrateful to a sister who "changed your diapers and wiped your behind". The judge managed to subdue her fury with threats of eviction from the room.

The judge ruled that Pahulje had no valid excuse to keep the money any longer and ordered him to pay it back. Pahulje said he could not since he had no available assets at the moment. The judge asked Pahulje when he could expect his receivables. Pahulje said not for one year at least. The judge then offered a choice to Father. Either give Pahulje time to collect his receivables or demand liquidation of his assets. Father was not sure so the judge set a date for another hearing at which time Father had to state his decision.

On the way home the three of us stopped at Grandma's, where Mother, who was still beside herself over her public humiliation, tried to persuade Grandma to her point of view, which was to auction Pahulje's assets immediately. But Grandma, mindful of the trauma in auctioning her own property in 1911 counseled restraint, which was not lost on Father as he contemplated two equally unpleasant choices.

When he finally wrote to Johanna he recommended that Pahulje be given the time he required, with the proviso that if he missed the specified date, the auction would take place automatically soon thereafter. Johanna sympathized with her brother's reluctance to force the sale of his wife's sister's home, the only assets that Pahulje possessed and agreed with the recommendation. At the next hearing, after Father reported his choice, the judge ruled that within one year, Pahulje had to settle the debt and if not, his property would be auctioned off without further delay.

The outcome of the trial was of course a victory for Pahulje, his wife Angela and brother-in-law Jože, but a humiliating defeat for our side, especially for Mother and her failed tactic of putting me forward as a witness. Friends in Dolenja Vas sympathized, but the opposition and its friends were free with their ridicule, duly reported back to keep her anger simmering.

THE BELLS RING NO MORE

In Masern, the debates on the two alternatives in the tavern room at the Jaklitsch inn went on for days. Most patrons believed the judge was excessively lenient in giving Pahulje more time. This belief became firm as the wine heated the debate and with it the certainty that Father should have opted for public auction immediately. After several such evenings of debate, Father stayed away, at least until the novelty of the event dissipated. In the meanwhile, his few loyal friends gathered at his shop, sympathized with his predicament and offered praise for the choice he made.

But time was on Pahulje's side. He never paid, nor was his property auctioned off and my two cousins never lost their home. All this because in April 1941, Yugoslavia was overrun by the Axis powers and part of Slovenia and its civil courts became part of the military courts of the occupier, the Italy of Mussolini.

Even prior to the expiration of the deadline given to Pahulje Father, the advocate for Johanna's rights had moved to another country and she no longer had a local representative to force her claim. And by this time the courts were absorbed with issues more important that the roof of my aunt's house.

While Johanna and her husband were the financial losers, the intangible emotional losses of the local adversaries were much more bruising, especially for Mother. The decade long tenuous relationships within her family were inflamed with renewed force and remained so for decades to come. Grandma shunned her daughter Angela and reconciled with son Jože only shortly before she died in 1948. On the other hand, she softened her attitude toward son Janez and his family and finally invited them to move in with her. This was even more important now that her oldest daughter and her family had moved to another world.

One of the losers was me. In addition to the much-wanted pocket watch I lost an unknown uncle Jože, the confirmation sponsor who could afford to buy me one. Also, I had never met his wife Iva and their children Janez and Marjanca. I also lost Angela, a barely known aunt and her children, my cousins Božena and Janez.

But I met them decades later in 1974, when I returned to Slovenia for the first time since 1941. Since then they all became valued relations and dear friends.

After several visits to her family house in Dolenja Vas, now owned by brother Janez, Mother became reconciled with Angela and Pahulje but never with brother Jože. Her resentment toward the younger brother lingered for decades. And she made her feelings toward them apparent in not so subtle ways.

AUNT JOHANNA'S ROOF

Mother re-established contact with Janez during her first return to Austria in 1958 to visit her daughter in Graz. Mitzi had married in September 1950 and remained there with her family when Mother, Father and Paul left for America in September of 1952. I had left for New York on my own in May of 1950.

During this visit, Mother also went to Dolenja Vas where she was welcomed by brother Janez and family in the house of her childhood. While staying there, Janez, long reconciled with his siblings, urged her to visit Angela and Pahulje living only 200 meters away but Mother was not yet ready. Neither was her sister and the two kept avoiding one another and did not meet.

In the late 50s, living conditions in Slovenia, including Dolenja Vas, were dismal and Mother made it her mission, on her return to Brooklyn, to improve the lot of brother Janez and his family. But not the others who were not much better off.

She kept sending used clothing collected from neighbors, paid for food packages and sacks of flour to be sent regularly by various relief agencies. Grateful letters only encouraged her to do even more. In this she purposefully ignored the families of Jože and Angela who were equally in need. This evidently was her revenge, especially to Jože who lived in the city where foodstuffs were even more difficult to come by.

The zeal with which she helped Janez and his family was not lost on her other siblings who soon realized what the older sister was doing. Unfortunately this did not contribute to healing and the life-long friction between them, taken to full force by Johanna's roof, continued.

On my first return, Anne and I were met at the airport by cousins Božena, Janez and Marjanca. It was a happy meeting and a reunion with Marjanca, uncle Jože's daughter who as a teenager had visited us in New York some years before. While in Ljubljana we visited the cousins in their homes, met their spouses and children and surrounded by overwhelming hospitality, we cemented new friendships within the family members of our generation. Visiting the relatives of Mother's generation was to follow in the next few days. The most keenly anticipated of these was meeting uncle Jože and his wife Iva for the first time in their house in Ljubljana.

While Iva was welcoming and gracious, Jože appeared distant and brusque and I very soon discovered the trace of condescension and sarcasm Mother had talked about. Pointed comments, quickly diverted by his family members, made plain that he was not yet reconciled with his elder sister and by extension, her elder son. I began to suspect that with his rather unfriendly demeanor he was reciprocating for the brutal verbal attack of Mother on Marjanca when she came to visit us in New York in 1965. In this assault, mother vented upon this unsuspecting girl of nineteen all emotion pent up about Jože since the trial of 1940 and brought forth a flood of tears and frantic packing to return home which I managed with difficulty to prevent.

Anne and I ended this initial visit with an understanding that we would meet again which we did on a pleasant outing with the whole family to Bled and the foothills of Triglav, the set of three mountain peaks that are the national symbol of Slovenia. Unfortunately Jože due to business reasons could not participate.

The following day Anne and I drove the 60 km to Dolenja Vas to visit Uncle Janez and family where we were welcomed with joy and affection. As expected, Janez was happy to see us and we quickly became good friends. His wife had died some years ago and his daughter Mira was now the woman of the house. She and her sister Angelca were delightful cousins, as were their respective husbands, and we all became aware of how much family togetherness had been lost in our long separation of over one quarter century.

Knowing that they had long ago become reconciled with the Pahulje family, I asked Janez to inquire if Angela and her husband would receive us. After an enthusiastic response, Anne and I walked the 200 meters to the Pahulje house where, without much hesitation, we all accepted each other as if nothing had ever separated us. Pahulje was very welcoming and Angela more lively and bubbling than described by Mother, making me wonder why the differences of the past were not resolved in the amicable manner we now related to each other. Nevertheless, I soon detected traces of a cutting edge in Angela's manners which sensitive siblings such as Mother would soon find abrasive and lead to confrontation. I noticed no such edges in Pahulje, even after much time together in the following days, which made me realize that the difficulties with Father due to contractor business problems were driven to extremes by the two sisters and their decidedly different temperaments.

It was on that day that I conceived the notion of giving a family dinner in which all the relatives were to take part. The intent was to produce a lasting reconciliation. Testing the waters, all parts of the family appeared enthusiastic about my proposal.

AUNT JOHANNA'S ROOF

Cousin Janez Pahulje, Angela's son, an architect living in Ljubljana and his wife Anna suggested the restaurant at the Bellevue hotel, well known for its cuisine since it also doubled as a school for chefs. The Bellevue was on the slope of the hill overlooking the city and directly opposite the old fortress in the center of the town.

We inquired and yes, they would prepare a meal for 25 people on Thursday at 18.00 hrs and serve it in a separate dining room. Cousin Janez telephoned around and all agreed to come.

The dinner was to be held on the day before our departure to Istria and the Dalmatian coast. In the days leading up to the event, members of the family invited us to their homes where we cemented our re-established family ties. We had not yet visited cousin Janez who insisted that we come to his home if only for a short few minutes before the dinner. As elsewhere hospitality overflowed, the few moments multiplied and it became high time to make for the Bellevue. On the way there, Janez was to pick up his parents at the bus depot where they were arriving from Dolenja Vas and bring them to the hotel in a taxi.

Anne and I were to follow Anna, the wife of Janez, through the center of the city to the Belvedere. It was getting late so she would drive fast, but since her little car was bright red, I would have no difficulty in following her close behind.

We set out from the edge of the city and I carefully tailed the little red car. As we reached the center, the traffic thickened and for a few moments I lost sight as other cars got in between, but we soon saw the red car make a right turn at the intersection.

As I followed, the traffic got lighter and as the day darkened it became obvious that we were driving toward the outskirts. No doubt, Anna knew a shortcut to the Bellevue. The assumption turned to doubt, when she made a right turn toward the underground garage of a multi-story apartment house and once inside, stopped.

The door opened and out stepped a man. During the few moments at the intersection where I fell behind, another red car, identical to that of Anna got between us and made the turn to the right.

The frantic explanation of our predicament convinced the man to lead us to the Bellevue. No other red car coming between us we arrived there a full half hour late.

Waiting for us at the door were Pahulje and his family, all in great distress. Anna had arrived on time without us but was certain we were not far behind and would arrive momentarily.

Uncle Jože who had come early was not pleased and his displeasure turned into anger and then into rage and shortly before we arrived he had gathered his reluctant clan and left. The pleading by Pahulje and others to wait a bit longer had no effect.

THE BELLS RING NO MORE

Jože let all present know that this was an unforgivable insult by his nephew, predictable since he was the son of his forever rancorous and scheming elder sister.

All my good intentions had turned to disaster, the outcome the opposite of what I had hoped for. While the meal was as good as expected, the mood at the long but half empty table was subdued and no amount of good Slovene wine could overcome the gloom and bring the party to life. In retrospect, better planning could have averted the catastrophe, but hindsight brought no comfort except the knowledge that it could have been avoided, traffic and switched cars not withstanding.

To recover and make amends, early the following morning Anne and I went to a florist near the law office of uncle Jože in the center of the city where we bought a large bouquet of flowers. So armed, we entered his office where we were received by the startled Iva who accepted both my apologies and the flowers. Not so Jože who growled - "what do you want" - but softened a little at the urging of Iva, his son Jože and Borut, the husband of Marjanca, all of them being sympathetic to my misfortune and my attempt to correct it.

The deeper after effects of the incident became apparent later and lasted, as was the case with the roof, for years. I had started a new cycle. While not immediately obvious, it was predictable, given the ease with which members of Mother's family would remake a minor thoughtlessness into a serious slight not lightly to be forgiven, and forgotten only after much water under the bridge.

While Jože perceived my thoughtlessness as an intentional insult, it was Pahulje who, unwittingly, enlarged the incident by rushing to my defense. He was furious at Jože's precipitous lack of patience and slight toward me and my wife and his fury infected the others who stayed, including uncle Janez and his family. His unhappiness with Jože was undoubtedly reinforced by knowing the root of my good intentions which he got to know during our time together in Masern and Dolenja Vas. But with his zeal to defend me, he started another cycle of animosity lasting for years to come.

Nevertheless, there was a silver lining. The incident, while isolating uncle Jože, solidified the other members of the family, including Mother. On her next visit to

AUNT JOHANNA'S ROOF

Dolenja Vas she quickly marched the 200 meters to the house of her sister who, together with her husband, was equally eager to end the rancor lasting half a life time. After that, on future visits she would stay for weeks with Angela and Pahulje in Dolenja Vas where she, like her brother Janez, was made to feel at home. I also was welcomed there and began to wish Father were alive to joke with all of us about the follies of the past and sweep away the years of senseless antagonism and unpleasant memories. Especially those about the roof that was ultimately responsible for the loss of so much valuable time together.

Chapter 10

The Seasons

Life in Masern was tied to the seasons and the never-ending struggle for the needs of existence. Like other isolated villages in the enclave, it was totally dependent on an adequate harvest for survival. This harvest was wrestled from an infertile and unfriendly soil which had to be kept productive season after season, for over six centuries prior to my arrival. But the always willing forest supplied the firewood and the lumber to be traded at the village sawmill for cash with which to buy the other necessities.

After some four months of hibernation, the inertia of the winter gave way when clusters of snowdrops started to poke through the last layer of the now graying snow and the cuckoo was once again heard in the hills. The new cycle began when, in the warming air, the plow blade was filed to a new edge, the spikes of the harrow re-fastened or replaced, the axles of the wagon wheels greased and their hubs and spokes thoroughly wetted to eliminate any wobble due to dried out wood. If the resultant swelling no longer tightened the wheel, it was taken to the village smith to heat and shorten the metal rim and let the cooling steel force the spokes back into place. The smith also re-shoed the horses if the remaining metal was inadequate for the coming season. Harnesses were examined, the leather rubbed with oil and repaired if necessary by the village saddler Karl Schaffer, the younger son of the fire chief who also was my best friend.

And before the solidly frozen earth softened and let the wheels sink deep into the mud, the dung from the heap next to the stable was loaded on the reconditioned wagons and hauled to the fields to be spread evenly on the thinning layer of the remaining snow.

The cycle continued with plowing, sowing and planting. Cows were taken to the bull after they stopped giving milk and young pigs were bought at the market to be fattened during the summer for slaughter after the first frost of the fall. In between there was the weeding, the mowing, the hay making and reaping. And after the harvests came and went, there was the cutting, splitting and stacking of firewood to outlast the coming cold.

THE BELLS RING NO MORE

The cycle was, of course weather dependent and even more so at the elevated village of Masern, being shaded a good part of the day by the surrounding hills. If the snows lingered past the planting season, the shortened growing time prevented the produce from ripening. So did an early frost. Sometimes, the floods from melting snow washed away planted seeds. Hordes of wild boar would uproot an entire field of freshly planted potatoes.

And during high summer, when the wind was rippling the yellowing grain, when the cornstalks began to turn color and the small apples on their trees still had weeks of growing to do, the villagers apprehensively watched the sky for dark clouds, the first sign of an oncoming storm. Especially when the air was hot and heavy and the clouds began to gather into a dense, dark overcast, so low one could almost touch them. This was soon followed by a thundering sound of heavy downfall approaching quickly across the southern hills. Such sudden storms came across the mountains with unbelievably destructive power. Hail the size of small potatoes would lay flat and destroy an entire crop in a few minutes. In 1614, hail caused so much damage in the area that for three years the residents did not live normal lives.

It was claimed that after the three big bells were installed, the frequency of lethal hail storms was reduced. When clouds began to gather, the villagers rang all three bells at random as fast as they could. Apparently, the sound waves tended to break up the density of the low flying clouds and cause them to disperse.

Natural disasters decimated not only crops but also the essential livestock of cows, goats, pigs and chickens. Records show that there were two huge cattle plagues throughout the region that claimed a large portion of this livestock. The first was in 1761 and the second fifteen years later in 1776. [45] One of these also reached into Masern, but how destructive it was there is not known. In addition to the overlong winters, short summers, poor crops, hail, floods, diseases and fires there were the human inflicted disasters. Overtaxing landlords, Turkish marauders, French invaders, world wars, lethal nationalism, and Italian occupiers were all part of God's wrath. All the result of sins, as the villagers were reminded constantly by the priest in the sermons of Sunday Mass.

Within all of this, winter and summer, rain or shine and in no established order, the crowing of the rooster and the cows lowing to be milked started a new day. Season after season, decade after decade for six centuries the cycle continued, during which God always delivered a few surprises.

---

45   Kočevski zbornik, pg 126).

THE SEASONS

After their arrival in Masern in the early 14th century, the settlers were forced to adjust rapidly to the short growing season and a soil not particularly fertile and cooperative in making things grow at this altitude of 519 meters. The snows melted too late in the spring, the frost came too soon at the end of summer. But they soon learned which crops were suitable, that winter wheat was too long under snow and the summer mostly too short to allow it to mature. But rye grew and its flour produced a dark and healthy, if not particularly tasty bread. So did oats, barley, millet and buckwheat. Maize and potato also thrived after they came from the New World in the 16th and 18th century, respectively. These staples were supplemented by milk from the cow, meat from the chicken and ham and fat from the pig, providing, all together, the basic necessities for the inhabitants through the centuries until 1941.

Other crops were cabbage, turnips, carrots, kohlrabi, onion and garlic, which, together with apples and pears lasted, in cool cellars, long into next year. Most of the cabbage was shredded and matured in large barrels into sauerkraut to last until the next crop.

The short growing season notwithstanding, there was nearly always an ample harvest of plums, cherries, raspberries, blueberries and wild strawberries, most of which were turned into preserves and kept in earthen jars sealed with a layer of wax. Plums produced the necessary and powerful Slivovitz, but this was made clandestinely since the distillation of alcohol was a state monopoly.

Embedded into my memory of the annual cycle are images that were part of these seasonal events, the clarity of which remains untarnished by the decades since. Short segments observed by childhood eyes, each and all part of the mosaic of a village that ceased to be.

Planting the Earth. Spring

Some days after the melted snow and occasional rains thawed the now softening soil, the newly sharpened plow turned it into neat rows of brown earth, burying under it the evenly spread dung. Mother led Yiorgo and his companion pulling the plow, while in the rear the owner of the borrowed horse struggled with the handles. Mitzi and I were tasked to follow the team back and forth and pick up the rocks and stones which the frost and the plowing brought to the surface and take them to the wall at the edge of the field. I needed much encouragement in this since I was more interested in the long wiggling worms, the white crescent shaped larvae of the maybug on its seven year cycle upward and other creatures turned up by the plow.

Often, the plow also turned up a much larger boulder, pushed up into its path by the perpetual freeze and thaw. It was left there for stronger arms to be taken to the wall, which, over the centuries, had grown into a defining divide to the adjacent property.

The plowing and most other heavy tasks were a cooperative effort, sharing both draught animals and strong hands. Each season, the team of Yiorgo, Mother, the second horse and its owner plowed each other's fields and the fields of others in return for labor needed by their respective farms. Such labor in kind came also from those to whom Father gave permission to use some of his excess acreage. Such exchange was practiced harmoniously among the villagers throughout the year.

After the plowing, the earth was loosened and smoothed by the refurbished harrow being dragged back and forth by a sweating Yiorgo, led by a sweating Mother. This done, she spread the seed grain, carried in her tied up apron, with steady and even swings of her arm as she walked the length of the field and back. After that, she again walked the earth, raking in and covering the exposed grain with a light layer of soil to help the seed take root. In part also to hide the seed from those birds who had not yet noticed the scarecrows, with strips of multicolored cloth tied to their outstretched arms flapping in the breeze, which Mother had stuck in the soil after the seeding was done.

Maize and potato were planted in span deep grooves scratched into the loosened soil by a light but different plow specially made for this purpose. This plow was also dragged back and forth by Yiorgo, carefully led again by Mother to turn the field into an array of equally spaced grooves in the rapidly drying soil. Into the soft bottom of these trenches were pressed, two hand spans apart, either a few kernels of maize or a piece of seed potato that had been cut from a whole potato into segments, with each segment containing two or at most three 'eyes' so as to make one whole potato go further. Again Yiorgo, with Mother leading, dragged the plow back and forth, now between the grooves, covering the 'seeds' and turning the entire field into a washboard of equally spaced ripples in the brown earth.

While the scarecrow kept at least the still gullible birds at bay, nothing would stop the stealthy boar with their unerring nose for freshly planted potato. The villagers tried to put them off the scent with articles of clothing reeking with human sweat and kept watch the first few nights after the planting, most of this with limited success. Hiding in the deep underbrush and waiting for dusk, a family or herd of boar would

THE SEASONS

descend on the field and burrow with their snouts along each row finding most of the seedlings on the way.

Fortunately, this happened not too often, but when it did it was devastating. The entire planting process had to be repeated, cutting into the still available supply of potatoes needed until the next harvest. When such events occurred, the boars, still nearby and resting from their feast, would be chased by a posse of angry villagers deep into the forest. The males were dangerous and could turn on single individuals but usually ran with the others when approached by a yelling crowd swinging sticks. The pursuers were, however, always ready to run behind the nearest tree. In 1941 when the villagers, armed with rifles left behind by the capitulating Yugoslav army on April 19 pursued such a horde, the revenge was sweet and many a boar wound up as a gamey tasting roast on the tables of the aggrieved.

Spring, summer and autumn of 1941 were, with respect to wildlife, particularly bountiful. The wild boar was hunted by the villagers more out of revenge than for its tasty meat. The villagers, no longer concerned about being caught as poachers by Anton Tscherne, the game warden of prince Auersperg, freely hunted the ample wildlife of deer, rabbit and bear. Tscherne no longer patrolled the woods, partly because he was afraid of being shot and partly because he no longer knew to whom he could surrender a caught poacher, now that there was no longer a civil authority. He also was no longer getting paid by the prince. As a result, the villagers, throughout their long history, had never lived so well as during the spring, summer and fall of 1941.

All these activities were initiated by that most important event of spring, Easter. This was the time when the bells became silent. During the entire year they had announced time, joy and tragedy. They were rung at births, christenings, weddings, during Mass and processions on high holidays and other happy occasions in various combinations of tonal mix and durations. They accompanied deceased villagers on their final journey to the cemetery and rang when their replacements were baptized a few days after their birth.

On Thursday before Easter, the hammers of the clock were disengaged from the mechanism and the ropes pulled up high. All the crucifixes in the church were covered in black and on Saturday evening the villagers lined up on the way to the confessional to wait their turn for the mandatory annual forgiveness and absolution.

This was also required on other high holidays, but neglecting the purging of one's sins on Easter was a mortal sin.

And on Sunday morning, at nine thirty, the bells resumed with the usual reminder to get ready for the Mass, this time High Mass at ten followed by the festive procession.

During the entire week preceding the high Sunday, other Easter related activities kept the village busy.

The Weeding. Summer.

Planting was followed by a suspenseful and nervous period of hope and wait. Hoping for rains mild enough to moisten the seeds but not so heavy as to cause waters to emerge from the cistern to flood the fields and wash away the grain the birds did not find and the potato the boar did not dig up. Hoping for sufficient warmth from the sun to prevent a damaging late frost. Waiting for emerging sprouts to cover the dark brown earth with green and decorate the tops of the orderly rows with white-green shoots pushed up by either the kernels of maize or the eyes of the potato. Waiting also for the aggressive weeds that would have to be pulled out before they crowded out the wanted growth.

In between the waiting, there was time to pay attention to the neglected and expanding forest that was forever trying to reclaim the parts it lost over the decades and even centuries to the effort of clearing. This was particularly the case at the boundaries where the rich black soil of the forest unfairly competed with the cultivated, if marginally fertilized, earth. And, before the new and ever denser foliage of the underbrush impeded efficient clearing, our entire family made for the "Unterbinkl", our most vulnerable land. There, with razor sharp machete and small axes, we cut down the expanding underbrush and pushed the forest back into its place.

While it would be an exaggeration to say the forest resented the interference and took revenge, it is a fact that it did take part in one great tragedy and nearly succeeded in being part of another.

The first caused Father, at age 25, to lose his right leg in late 1918. A similar loss to me in 1938, caused by an identical set of circumstances, was averted by doctor Oražem only because of the quick response of Mother and Father who brought me to the doctor in Ribnica as fast as Yiorgo could trot. But that is also part of another story.

And when the weeds finally began to crowd the maize and potatoes, scores of bent over, kerchief-covered women labored back and forth in the rows and with small hoes loosened the soil to pull up the unwanted intruder. All the while checking the wanted growth and trimming away the excess that could limit proper development toward an abundant harvest. The grain, however, took care of itself by quickly rising and crowding out the weeds.

My job was to deliver water to the sweating and thirsty women. I waited for their call in the shade of nearby hazelnut bushes that kept both me and the water cool. It was kept in a small wooden barrel holding about four liters, filled in the morning at the spout of the drinking well. The water was drunk by raising the opening of the barrel to the lips and tilting the head way back. In doing this, some of the cool liquid was spilled but was welcome as it ran over heated cheeks. The barrel emptied all too frequently and I was sent away to get more. And when, finally, Mother yelled "lunch", all gathered in the shade to untie the knots of linen bundles full of sausage, bacon and bread that had been hanging on the branches of nearby trees.

This was also the time of year when one of our two cows stopped giving milk and began mounting others during the daily watering at the cistern trough. This was the sign that it was time to take her to the bull in Dolenja Vas for "bluing". Mother led the cow by a rope tied to a bridle while in the back I, with a twig, encouraged the animal to go on when it slowed for a luscious clump of grass.

The bull was in the stable of a neighbor of Grandma Ilc. It was a huge creature made even more frightening by the strong walls of the pen and the rope, one end attached to the ring in his nostrils and the other to a hole in the feeding trough. The bull sensed the cow's arrival and became agitated, adding to my fright, which was seized on by the adults as an excuse to keep me out of the stable as they closed the door. The small window was too high up to reach and so I had no idea what was the noisy rumpus going on inside. And when the door finally opened, the bull was lying down and our cow happily munching hay in a separate stall, a red cheeked Mother showed me the area under the tail of the cow that was now painted blue. After she gave the man some coins, we went to chat with Grandma who gave us lunch.

THE BELLS RING NO MORE

Harvest. Fall

It was a happy season during which the nearly empty storage bins were refilled, the stripped corncobs hung to dry and the hayloft refilled. All to last, with God's blessing, until next year. But for me, this part of the year brought afternoons full of chores seemingly designed to ruin an up to then pleasant day. I had to help with the harvest.

After Dežman let us out, I was quickly tasked to help Mitzi tramp down the dust laden straw that was forked to the loft after threshing, or to compress the hay from the wagon that brought it in from the meadows. It had been left to dry there after being cut by scythe swinging men, stopping only to sharpen the edge and wipe a brow.

Later in the fall, the potato harvest had me helping fill the wicker baskets with the dug-up clumps to be taken by stronger arms to larger wickers on the wagon. The same was the case when the solid cabbage heads were cut from their stems, the loose leaves stripped away and the hard, melon sized ball left in row after row to be picked up and loaded on the wagon. The kohlrabi could be pulled up by its ears but not the carrots which had to be dug up with forked spades. All the unwanted growth, the leaves, the ears and carrot green were left in place to be turned over by the plow as fertilizer for next year's crop. At home the produce was taken to separate bins in the frost free cellar next to the kitchen and covered with straw and old blankets. On especially cold winters, the kitchen door was left partly open to prevent freezing. But a large portion of the cabbage was destined to be sliced and placed into vats in the cellar where it turned into the sauerkraut that we could not do without.

Later still, I helped in pulling the corn cobs from their stalks and put them in baskets to be carried to the wagon, its sides now equipped with retaining boards. At home, they were emptied in the center of the large entry hall where they became part of a near ceiling-high pyramid. There to be stripped that evening with the help of neighbors encircling the heap while sitting on little stools they had brought with them. My favorite place was on top of the diminishing pile, listening to the hum of words, snatches of gossip and whispered stories until I fell asleep only to be awakened by Mother who led me off to bed.

On the naked end of the cob were left a few leaves which were pulled back and tied together to produce a loop. In the following days, these naked cobs were strung on to a strong rope, with a stick of wood at one end to keep the cobs on the rope. The other end was fed through a hook attached to the eves of the house and the assembly, about one meter long, was pulled up and left there to dry. For weeks thereafter, our house and all others in the village were decorated with brightly yellow stalactites swaying slightly in the autumn breeze. Later, the dry and now hardened kernels were stripped from the cob with a hand cranked stripping machine, sacked and stored in the cellar and attic where they waited to be taken to the mill. The cobs on the other hand, were shredded and fed to the cows.

The most memorable part of the harvest, however, was the annual slaughter of the fattened pig.

The preparations started days in advance. Knives were carefully sharpened on the great circular grindstone mounted on a bench created out of a six foot section of a split log. Round stakes, hammered into holes drilled into the round portion of the log were the legs of the bench while on its flat surface, part of which also served as a seat, the grindstone hub was mounted on risers. The stone was spun by a crank through the water trough hewn out of the flat portion of the log.

The wooden storage box in the barn was rummaged for discarded steel spoons with sides worn sharp by years of use. This side was ground even sharper on the grinding wheel.

The great wooden trough was hauled out of the barn and placed upside down, strategically near the barn in the freshly swept yard, hardened to a solid surface during the nights and sunless days of early November frost. The watertight trough, about eight feet long and three feet wide and deep was made of sturdy timbers held together by wrought iron bands made by the village smith. The uppermost planks extended on either end as handles to allow it to be carried four strong men to the place where it was needed.

Two heavy, big linked long chains, normally used to secure logs to the wagons transporting lumber to mills, were laid alongside the trough, and benches were arranged to allow hanging the carcass on the overhead beam of barn gate for butchering.

They were also busy inside. The big cellar barrels, now empty of last year's crop of solidified fat that had covered the small cubes of cooked pork, were carefully scraped clean and washed out with hot salted water. All available large pots and the copper water boiler of the kitchen stove were filled with water from the drinking well, brought home on the heads of Mother and aunt Neža, Grandma's younger sister, who came from Dolenja Vas to help out.

The meat grinder, fitted with newly sharpened cutting blades and a sausage making spout, was secured to the kitchen table and the pantry was re-supplied with salt, pepper, thyme, onion, garlic, barley, rice and other necessities, obtained well ahead from Ivanka's store.

There were also several loaves of black and white bread and a strudel baked the day before in the big oven that provided welcome warmth in the already chill autumn air seeping into the large living room which was also the bedroom of my parents.

One of my jobs was to stack the space next to the stove with choice pieces of dry firewood and keep the pile high throughout the next few days.

The preparations included, well in advance, a visit by Father and me to neighbors to get the promise of their help on the morning of the following day. At least five strong men were needed to fetch and hold down the animal to be slaughtered. To get this help was easy since the fine breakfast was well worth the short effort lasting at most one hour. A few extra helpers usually showed up but there was enough to go around and satisfy all.

The event, lasting at least two days and repeated several times in late fall, had its beginning in early spring with the purchase of one or two pigs large enough for fattening during the coming summer. They were bought at the farmers market in Ribnica or Kočevje, or from other farmers who put part of their maturing litter up for sale. Pigs were not bred by my family since the sties were not heated and the winters much too severe for the furless creatures. At home, the pigs were let run loose in the fenced-off part of the yard, but locked up every night in the sties. Being fed rich swill three times a day made them grow quickly during spring and summer and got them heavy and fat for slaughter in late fall when the cool weather arrived.

By now the field produce had been harvested and safely stored in cellar bins and enough firewood was cut and stacked to last the winter. It was the end of November; cool enough to make you shiver morning and noon and the right time to convert the pigs into hams, sides of bacon, long links of sausage and wooden vats full of solidified lard heavily laced with bits of precooked pork. Throughout the year scoops of this dripping would be heated and poured over the full communal bowl, turning the simplest cornmeal dish, covered with sauerkraut or sliced cooked vegetables, into a delicious meal.

Less than the usual urging was needed to leave the warm bed on the morning of this eventful day. This, in spite of the much needed and welcome space and peace left to me after Mitzi and aunt Neža got up hours before. I normally shared the bed with my sister, but Neža shared our bed whenever she came to stay. She was a big woman who took much of my allotted space in the large bed which sagged in the middle under all that added weight, forcing me into a crevasse between the snoring women. Both of them did it with gusto, but Mitzi was outdone by Neža in rhythmic variety and sheer sound power. My complaints were eventually listened to and I was moved to a sofa bed in the large room, but not until I got a little bigger and had to leave the bed to my eight-years-older sister.

Everyone else had gotten up when it was still dark to start events, which throughout the day were to follow one another in a long established sequence. The pigs were fed except, of course, the one selected for slaughter. It had not been fed several meals and was isolated from the others for the final night. The kitchen stove, fired to capacity, was already heating water in large pots, which covered most of its available flat surface. The little space left was heating milk which, with a slice of black bread, was the usual breakfast. The invited helpers started arriving and needed little encouragement to rid the chill of the morning with a few shots of slivovitz. By now it was light; the water started to boil and it was time to start.

With everybody at the ready, the struggling and squealing pig was dragged from its stall, lifted on to the trough turned upside down and held down by the strong men. While somebody also held the head down and the snout closed, Father shaved away the bristles at the bottom of the throat near the front legs with a long, sharp and pointed knife. This done, Mother washed the shaved spot and then stood ready with a wooden bucket and long wooden spoon.

Father carefully pushed the knife into the animal at the cleaned spot, cut the critical artery and quickly withdrew the knife to let the blood gush out from the clean 2 inch cut. The steaming flow was expertly caught by the waiting bucket and stirred vigorously to prevent clotting. This went on, spurt after spurt until the flow ceased and the animal stopped struggling. By this time the bucket was quite full and carried off to be mixed later with barley and herbs into long strings of blood sausage, delicious either hot or cold.

THE BELLS RING NO MORE

With the animal quite dead, slivovitz was passed around again. After that, no time was wasted to lift the heavy weight of 250-300 pounds by its legs on to the ground and turn the trough right side up. The two sets of chains made ready the previous day were laid into it so that they touched the sides and the bottom approximately at the one and two thirds point of the trough. Then the carcass was lifted, legs down, into the trough with the chains positioned on the inside of either set of front and rear legs. Their purpose was to allow the four men, one at each end of the chain to jointly lift and turn the dead animal in unison during and after the next step of the process.

This done, the men made for the kitchen and brought out the pots of boiling water, which they carefully poured over the carcass. This blistered the outer layer of the skin containing the bristles, which were then scraped off with the sharp sides of the old spoons sharpened the day before. The chains were used to turn the carcass to expose other parts to new buckets of boiling water from the kitchen. This process was repeated until all parts of the body and most of the legs up to the ankles were free of bristles and sparkling clean.

Now, the chains and all available hands lifted the gleaming carcass out of the trough on to clean boards on the ground along side the trough. Four strong men carefully carried off the trough and tipped the still hot contents into the dung pit next to the stable. Others brought buckets of cold water and poured it over the carcass to wash away sticking bits of skin and bristles and get it ready for the next step.

The trough was brought back, turned up-side down, with one end just under the barn door beam. The carcass was lifted on to the flat bottom of the trough, this time on its back with the head facing away from the barn. With a shorter but equally sharp knife, Father opened the belly and expertly removed its contents. The kidneys and the heart were placed into a bowl, held by Mother who disappeared with them into the kitchen where she cut them into slivers for immediate frying into an exquisite breakfast for all.

Meanwhile, the lung, and liver were removed from the carcass and put in separate vessels. The stomach and entrails, largely empty due to the recent enforced diet were placed in metal tubs for turning inside out and cleaning at the trough of the village cistern.

The opened carcass, still steaming, continued cooling in the frosty morning air. The spot behind the heels and tendons of the hind legs was pierced and the hook ends of two chains inserted and secured. The other ends of the chains were swung over the beam of the barn door and with the men jointly pulling and lifting; the carcass became suspended at a height to make its systematic dissection easy.

By now, breakfast was ready and mother called all to take a place at the kitchen table with its big pan of fried slivers of kidney harvested only a short while ago. This and freshly baked black bread dunked in the drippings was washed down with jiggers of slivovitz from the bottle that was being passed around.

The next and most urgent task of the women was to clean the entrails, which were to be used as sausage skins. The seemingly endless string of entrails had to be separated and cut into manageable sections for cleaning. This done, Mitzi and Neža took them to the pump at the cistern where the insides were first flushed then turned inside out and scrubbed clean.

At home, the dissection of the hanging carcass continued. The head was separated first and placed on the trough where it was opened with a saw and a hatchet, the brain removed and placed in a container for later use. The rest of the head was stripped of all meat by one of Father's remaining helpers and the pieces thrown into a vat for processing.

The butchering continued from the bottom up by removing the fore-legs and shoulders and trimming them into small hams by removing the legs below the knee. The two hoofs were pulled off and each leg trimmed for later reduction by boiling, with various ingredients, into a thick broth which after chilling solidified into aspic. Again, all trimmings were stored temporarily in vats for later processing.

Next was the removal of the fatty sides in sections, which ultimately, after prolonged exposure to smoke in the smoke chamber of the attic became sides of bacon. These sections, three to four inches thick, were trimmed and cut into approximately one foot squares, kept strong and intact by the remaining thick layers of skin from which the top layer with its bristles had been removed by the spoons. The thickness was reduced to about one and a half inches to permit penetration of the preserving smoke. The trimmed-away meaty portion was cut into small cubes and placed into the large pans together with the other bits of meat from the process so far.

Handled next was the exposed breast cage for spare ribs and loin. Section by section was removed and trimmed of excessive fat. The lower rib cage was cut away with a small axe and shaped into spare rib pieces, 12 inches long and six inches wide, the six inches being the length of the rib.

The loin section was cut into six inch chunks. The chunks joined the fore hams and rib sections in the vats for pickling.

THE BELLS RING NO MORE

Eventually, only the large hind sections were left dangling. They were heavy and help was needed to get them down on to the platform of the upside down trough which was the chopping and cutting block throughout the proceedings. Extensive trimming, shaping and removal of the lower parts of the legs eventually produced the prized hams that were eaten only on special events and holidays such as Easter and Christmas.

The hams, loins and ribs were taken to the cellar where they were placed in large barrels and covered with salty brine spiked with crushed garlic and various other spices. They were left in this brew for many days after which they were wiped clean and dry and hung on steel hooks in the smoke bin of the attic. And for the next few months, all cooking on the kitchen stove and fire in the house heating oven, both the source of smoke in the bin, was done by using hardwood only, since this produced the best flavor of smoked meat.

All this while in the kitchen, effort was underway to prepare the ingredients for blood sausage and liver dumplings. Mitzi and Neža had long ago returned from the cistern with the cleaned entrails and were now busy mashing the liver into a paste. The paste was mixed with breadcrumbs and spices into a doughy consistency that was spooned in lumps into the boiling soup, made from the bones that had become available earlier. This soup, together with slices of dark bread became a satisfying lunch. The soup also contained some of the barley and rice, cooked separately as ingredients for blood sausages.

After lunch, when the partially cooked grain had cooled, blood, herbs, salt and pepper were added and mixed into a paste. The large intestine, about three inches across, was cut into 12 inch lengths and one end stitched together in a looping fashion with 12 long wood splinters made earlier for this purpose. The other end was held open and stuffed with the mixture. When full, it was sewn closed with another splinter. After that, all were cooked in boiling water and hung on hooks in the cellar until reheated for eating, usually with Ganzallein and sauerkraut covered with drippings, during the next few weeks until Christmas.

The trimmings of fat and meat that had accumulated in the vats during the butchering at the barn door were also processed in the kitchen. Pieces of meat interlaced with fatty parts were selected to be ground for sausage stuffing, using the hand cranked grinder with the sharpened four bladed cutting knife. The cut and ground meat fell into a bucket under the grinder until it was judged that enough was ground to fill all available small intestines. Again, as with the blood sausages, to this ground meat were added the required ingredients of herbs, pepper, salt and a briny mixture of cooked bay leaves and crushed garlic, strained to keep out the solid bits. After a good mix with bared arms, the sausage making was ready for stuffing.

The coarse strainer on the meat grinder was replaced with a finer one and a 12 inch long slightly tapering tube of approximately one inch diameter was screwed on behind it. A one meter section of the small intestines, with one end tied with a string, was pushed and accumulated on this tube. The grinder with its spiral shaft pushed the meat mixture to the knife for cutting and then through the strainer into the tube. The meat, emerging from the tube filled the intestine which was being pulled off the tube by the forced out meat. When the long section was full, it was partitioned off by pinching and twisting it into 5 inch sausages and tied with string.

With all the stuffing done, the sausage strings were taken to the smoke bin to start a several month process of smoke preservation that made the sausages, like the hams, a treat in many lunches and dinners throughout the coming year.

This event was repeated in quick succession during late fall in our and other households of the village. At the height of this slaughtering period, the air, a mixture of smells from melted fat, hardwood smoke, spilled blood and offal emanated from every house and its surroundings and hung, like an umbrella, over the valley and lingered there for weeks. But it was noticed, like the flowing sap from the pines in the spring, only after coming home to the village from a distance where the desensitized nostrils had a chance to recover.

Hibernation. Winter

The harvest secured, the firewood cut, split and stacked, there was nothing else to do except feed the animals, milk the cows and wait for the snow. And when it came, in mid November or sooner, it stayed, sometimes at adult height, until the beginning of March or even later. There were times when it snowed for days with flakes the size of overcoat buttons, a density that made the church steeple disappear and the sound from the bells telling time barely audible. Apart from the snow driven by the wind and the swaying bare branches of our linden, nothing moved.

Nevertheless, a path from the front door to the stable and across the courtyard to the building housing the chicken coop, the woodshed and Father's shop, had to be maintained. To do this, Mitzi had to give up her perch on the flat of the oven and together with Mother they disappeared through the front door, opened only a crack to allow the bundled up women with their shovels to squeeze through. I too wanted to join them but no: I would only be a hindrance. But after clearing a small circle of stubborn crystals on the window pane facing the courtyard, I watched them, bent over and struggling with the wind and the snow, without much regret.

But when eventually the snowing stopped and visible life at least temporarily returned, the villagers were out clearing narrow trenches, in some places tunnels, across the square to the church, to Ivanka's store, to the Jaklitsch tavern and to the sawmill, its steam engine shut down for the duration of this or any other storm. They also cleared a path to Father's shop where idle men arrived to warm their frozen hands over the stove, part of it cherry red, and resume the conversations that had been interrupted by the snow.

The most highly anticipated part of winter, at least for us small children, was not Christmas but the sixth of December, Saint Nicholas day. On this day, at the onset of dusk, the Saint would knock on the door and bring little gifts, providing we had been good. Of the need for this we were reminded throughout the year. If we had misbehaved he would leave nothing but have us punished or taken away by Krampus the sinister creature that accompanied the Saint as the enforcer.

Saint Nicholas came in bishop's regalia including miter and staff, the very figure I saw sink with his ship in a violent sea in the film with Father in Ljubljana. Behind him was the devil-like creature called Krampus; horns above his black face, from his mouth hanging a long red tongue. In one hand, a sack with presents, in the other a long and heavy steel chain, the rattling of which the Saint tried to restrain.

Only after I stammered that I had been good and promised to be good the next year, with the Krampus rattling the chain, did the Saint reached into his bag for the hoped-for items, usually no more than some sugar coated ginger bread figures, candy and oranges from Ivanka's store.

Childhood illusion and suspension of disbelief did not survive the first school year when sniggers that St. Nicholas was really a dressed up Johann Krisch and the frightful Krampus one of the sexton's sons, his face blackened with charcoal, became confirmed. After that, annual presents, meager as they were, were handed out by the parents themselves on the day of the Saint. And after the resettlement, this ancient custom, like most of the others, also ceased to exist.

THE SEASONS

Apart from the decorated tree in the cold corner of the large room and the crystals of last night's fallen flakes glistening on the piled up snow outside, Christmas was different from the other religious holidays.

The fir tree, selected late in the fall, was cut and dragged home on the freshly fallen snow weeks before it was set up in the remote corner of the large room near the walls on which patches of ice crystals had been winning ground ever since the real cold arrived. The tree was decorated during the day of Christmas Eve with apples from the cellar and oranges from Ivanka's store, each suspended by twine from the branches to which were also attached multi-colored, spiral turned wax candles, tinsel and multicolored glass balls. And at the very top the star of Bethlehem, placed there by an uncertain Mother reaching up and out while standing on an uncertain kitchen stool. On the small cloth-covered table next to it stood the cardboard crèche, unfolded and lit from the rear by a candle to reveal its colorful occupants in a three-dimensional scene.

Eventually the candles on the branches were lit by Mitzi; the lighting presided over by a concerned Father aware of the highly flammable pine needles, with Paul and me watching from the top of the oven cube. But by the time our bundled-up parents left the warm house for the short midnight service in the unheated church, the candles were extinguished and all three of us were sound asleep.

The candles were lit again the following morning when the smell of the festive meal Mother was preparing in the kitchen penetrated the room only to compete with the strong fragrance of the fir and that of the apples and oranges dangling from its branches. This is when we fingered the gifts left under it by the Christ child during the night, usually various articles of clothing, mostly shirts, sweaters and knitted gloves and socks, all oversized for us to grow into, long unsharpened pencils with soft erasers to wipe out the mistakes in the accompanying notebooks to do our homework in. After the big meal, the sweaters and gloves were tested outside in the bitter cold, on crunching snow too cold to roll into a snowball for a playful fight. And when the all too short winter afternoon drove us, stiff and white, back inside we quickly made it up the ladder to the warm flat of the oven cube.

At least thirteen generations of my ancestors had, more or less, done the same.

Chapter 11

Mattl

Mother told me not to ask and during my frequent visits, he never offered to explain how it started. Mattl, short for Mathias, was our immediate neighbor, living in the house at Masern 14.

Mother said that as a young man he had a small injury on his leg and when he waded in the cold and poisonous flood waters that overflowed the basin during most springs after the thaw, the injury became infected and that is how he got it.

Mattl, as he was known in the village, had an open sore above the right ankle that perpetually oozed and never healed. He covered the sore with rags wrapped around his leg and secured it in place with string. The women of the village, including Mother, periodically stopped by to collect the rags and his laundry, wash them at the cistern and hang them to dry on the line in the rear of his crumbling house. Sometimes he would ask me to help him retrieve the dried rags from the line and I stayed to watch him redress the wound. It pained him when he limped even when using his cane, his spotted trouser leg hiding the rags but not the source of the stains. None of this however prevented him, during the Schaffer fire, from climbing the roof of our barn and helping Father to save it from the flying embers and certain destruction.

Now in his late 50's, he lived alone in the house of his older brother, the owner of sizable property who had left for America in the early 1900's, leaving Mattl and his younger teenage brother behind. The youngest of these three brothers was killed during one of the storms that came from the south across the steep hills during hot summer days, sometimes at speeds that took even seasoned villagers by surprise. Lightning found the scythe on the shoulder of the young man rushing home from mowing grass in one of the meadows, and left a blackened body.

Mattl lived from the occasional moneys sent him by his older brother in Brooklyn and on meals the villagers gave him, as payment in kind for the use of his brother's lands. He often ate with us and other neighbors. Mitzi and I ran his errands; Mother and other women helped him keep his quarters reasonably clean. More often than not, he was gossiping and swapping stories with other men in Father's shop.

I suspected that Mother's tale about the origin of his sore was her way of discouraging me from copying the annual attempt of the other boys to build a raft on which to sail the flood waters in the basin or be carried away by the swift stream flowing from it, seeking lower levels. After the thaw started, the water rising from the cistern slowly filled the basin and came up the sloping road past our house toward the village square. But just before the water reached the lower wall, it flowed into our garden and the adjacent orchard. Since the grounds on which the house stood also sloped downward to the side opposite the road, the water soon came around the corner. As it kept rising the water was eventually high up on the wall of two of its four sides.

After that, it flowed under the raised part of the barn on to Mattl's back yard, garden and orchard and then, past other houses on to lower parts of fields and roads. Eventually it disappeared into crevasses in the woods just beyond the farmland and meadows, all part of the lowest point of the bowl surrounding the village called the Unterbinkl, or the Lower Corner.

No matter what we were told, Mattl's sore was not a deterrent, neither to me nor to the other boys and girls. To all of us, the rising water was a magnet that distracted us from paying attention in our one room school and drew us to its expanding and later its contracting edges as soon as Alojzij Dežman our teacher let us go. We ran to see how quickly it flowed and how far it spread. Little boats, constructed or carved from pieces of wood, were launched and followed, retrieved when they sank and launched anew at more promising sites. I deeply resented being retrieved myself, first by my sister and when neither of us returned, by Mother, none too happy over my usually wet feet in my wet shoes and with the rest of me at least damp, to say the least. And punishment, in whatever form, was always accompanied by reminders of what happened to Mattl.

None of it to much avail. It took many days until the water stopped rising, stopped flowing and then started receding. During all this time there were many opportunities to be part of it but Mitzi was instructed to keep an eye on me and my many efforts to construct a raft and float on it came to nothing.

Some of the older boys were more resourceful. One day, when both parents were away they dragged the slaughtering trough from our barn to the waters edge to use it as a boat. And when filled with boys, if without me it was pushed into deeper parts, it nearly ended in disaster. But Mitzi fetched Schaffer who, with his booming voice, commanded them to paddle back to safety.

I visited Mattl whenever I was bored and remembered that he sometimes had candy. He bought sweets at Ivanka's store to draw the occasional youngster mainly to interrupt his boredom and shorten his day. He let me finger his knick knacks, look at the few photos he had received from Brooklyn and allowed me to rummage through the trunk containing his older brother's war time memorabilia.

Deep in the trunk, below various articles of uniform, caps, belts, clips, ID papers and the helmet belonging to Mattl's brother, I found the revolver.

Mattl said it was Italian and that his brother had taken it from a dead officer in the trenches. He must have brought it back on a furlough before the armistice on November 11, 1918, when all weapons had to be surrendered to the victorious Italians before leaving for home.

This was a real weapon and not a toy gun I held in my small hands. It was heavy and a little rusted but the drum turned into place when I pulled the trigger. However, Mattl was not concerned, knowing well enough that there were no cartridges in the chamber. The click of the hammer produced no response.

After I found the revolver, candy was no longer the main reason to visit Mattl. He let me play with the weapon, taking it apart, cleaning and oiling the parts and when it was reassembled, pulling the trigger at imaginary enemies. But in spite of all my pleas, he would never let me take it outside or even out of his sight. Also he made me promise to keep it our secret on penalty of never letting me handle it again, a promise that was difficult to keep.

The main reason for the secrecy was the martial law imposed by the occupying Italians shortly after they arrived in Slovenia in April 1941. This law demanded that all weapons in possession of the population be turned over to the military authority. A leaflet, nailed to the village linden, left no doubt about the severe consequences for not doing so. But the village men, still disdainful of the Italians they had faced across the trenches a quarter century ago, initially ignored the order, and Mattl's attitude was no different. However, these were new Italians, now allied with the Germany of which we had become so proud. According to Jaklitsch, the demand to turn in the weapons was only a formality directed mainly at the hostile Slovene, and was not meant to include the Gottscheer loyal to the Reich and its allies.

Nevertheless, all such possessions were to be kept secret. Certainly from the Slovene in the village, who were not in line with the political orientation of the villagers, and might report the violation to the Italians. No weapons had been surrendered when so ordered by the occupier in spite of the fact that the village was bristling with arms.

THE BELLS RING NO MORE

On April 17, 1941, barely a week before the Italians arrived, a unit of the Yugoslav army on its way out of the deeper hinterland, possibly ordered into a battle already lost to the Axis invaders, stopped in the village for the night. The light infantry unit, with its horse and oxen drawn wagons arrived early in the afternoon and took over the village square. They set up a field kitchen and later prepared a meal mostly from ingredients solicited from reluctant, none too friendly residents. Some of the soldiers bought wine at the two inns on the square. The hostile Jaklitsch stayed out of sight but let Regina serve the soldiers. They were more welcome at the other inn where the owner, Rudi Tschinkel, out of tune with the perspectives of Jaklitsch but sympathetic to the gloomy warriors, willingly accommodated their needs. Afterwards, some spent the night in a few tents around the wagons, while the rest slept in the barns of the surrounding houses.

In the morning of the next day they received news that Yugoslavia had capitulated and that the unit was to lay down its arms and surrender.

The soldiers, most likely relieved for not having to battle a superior enemy force, quickly began to disperse so as not to be caught by the conqueror who might be arriving at any moment. Some knocked on doors and asked for civilian clothing in exchange for anything of value in their possession including their military uniform. Others were startled to find themselves confronted by men who, on orders from Jaklitsch, emerged cautiously from their houses, but now dressed in their militia uniforms of riding trousers, shiny black boots and a swastika armband on the left sleeve of a white shirt, who urged them to surrender their weapons and go home.

While this was going on the villagers, realizing a one-time opportunity, frenziedly started to loot the no longer guarded wagons, loaded mostly with weapons, ammunition and other military gear. They hid the booty in places out of sight. Most of the horses had been taken by the officers who had disappeared on them. The horses that remained, as well as several teams of oxen, were soon being cared for by villagers overjoyed by the new livestock in their stables.

While this was going on, both Father and Mother were away. I don't remember where they had gone and why except that I was free to mingle and observe this unprecedented event. Having been conditioned never to take anything that was not mine, I struggled not to take part in the looting in which everyone participated with such gusto. Finally, no longer able to resist, I took an officer's uniform leather belt, wide and glossy with a shining metal buckle and ran, not home but under Schaffer's barn to hide it there and retrieve it later. In line with the conditioning, I was afraid to take it home.

Much to my surprise, this secret place, the wedge of open space on the sloping ground below the barn floor, was already brimming with loot. But I carefully placed my belt separate and apart from all the other stuff to prevent any mistake.

When, later that day, Father and Mother returned home, the looting was over; the wagons gone and the village square picked clean. A lone soldier from Croatia begged Father for some civilian clothing, an appeal that was difficult to accommodate given the fact that all of Father's trousers had one leg cut away and the opening stitched up. Nevertheless, a desired pair was found and together with a non matching suit jacket, the grateful soldier left his uniform behind as payment, a reasonable exchange since the uniform was in better condition than the clothes he had received.

Later during the day, it became obvious that Father was unhappy for not being around earlier when the army unit disintegrated. Realizing this, I braved the admission that I had taken the belt. But instead of displaying anger he asked me where it was and after I said that I hidden it under the Schaffer barn, he told me to get it.

But it was no longer there and neither was the other loot. Whoever moved his booty took no notice that the belt was separate and belonged to someone else. If Father was disappointed when, with an unhappy face, I reported the theft of the belt, he hid his disappointment by saying that it was not ours anyway.

When the Italians arrived a few days later we were much surprised. We had been expecting Germans, not knowing that Slovenia was to be divided between the two conquerors. Italy occupied a portion of Yugoslavia along the Adriatic coastline, much of which the French under Napoleon had called the Illyrian Provinces, including the part of Slovenia south of the Sava River and its capital Ljubljana. The rest of Slovenia including Lower Styria (except a small part in the north-east allocated to Hungary) was occupied by the Germans and de facto annexed to the Reich. But contrary to expectation and to the great disillusionment of most of its residents, the enclave was allocated to the Italians. [46]

As had been the case for the arrival of the new fire pump a few years before, lookouts were posted in the church steeple and a bell ringing sequence agreed upon to announce the approach of the expected Germans. However, this time it was not

---

46 T. Ferenc, *Vprašanje priključitve zasedenih slovenskih pokrajin k nemškemu rajhu, Prispevki za zgodovino delavskega gibanja*, 1974, Number 1–2, pg. 157–201.

THE BELLS RING NO MORE

Fire Chief Schaffer but Sturmführer Jaklitsch, the leader of Sturm 13, who was making certain there would be no mistake.

Again, as with the pump, there had been preparations. Girls readied flowers and garlands, swastika flags were hung out and when the bells sounded all, including the militia men, were to show up immediately and line up according to the Sturmführer's instructions.

But, as with the fire pump, it did not work out as planned.

When the bell started ringing on that afternoon, everyone leaped into action. However, this time it was not a slow moving wagon approaching the village but a convoy of rapidly moving trucks, followed by clouds of dust, that rolled into the village before Jaklitsch could put on his uniform jacket or his men could reach the square. The surprise was even greater when it became obvious that they were not Germans but Italians. This required some adjusting by young and old.

But what the heck, they were allies of the Reich and therefore there was no reason to hold back the welcome. Jaklitsch, having lost the initiative, was not able to give his prepared welcoming speech. And since it was in German, the Italians would not understand it anyway. The girls with their flowers and garlands were the first to climb the trucks and kiss the dumbfounded but now grinning youngsters from Lombardy, Tuscany, Sardinia and Sicily, echoing the smiles radiating from the faces of the villagers surrounding the trucks. These girls were hardly aware that barely 25 years ago the fathers of these boys were killing their fathers at the Isonzo.

The Italians too were overcome by surprise. Barely 15 minutes before, as they were rolling through Dolenja Vas, they saw only sour faces and heard only hostile murmurs. And now in Masern, smiles from everyone and hugs and kisses from the girls who had climbed the trucks. They started throwing whatever sweets they had at the kids and many a sardine can was caught by older hands.

They left as quickly as they arrived; they had another destination. But not before they nailed a poster on the village linden, announcing martial law and the order to surrender all weapons by a given date. When they were gone, Jaklitsch was again in control and called a meeting to be held at his place.

He had some explaining to do.

Some days later, Jaklitsch received instructions from the VGL to comply with the order and turn over to the Italians the weapons left behind by the Yugoslav unit. Not all, just some. Soon after that, a group of friendly Italians arrived with trucks to collect the weapons. They were received with great hospitality by Jaklitsch who invited their commander into the big room of his tavern for lunch and pitchers of his better wine.

Outside, the men of his Sturm were turning in some of the rifles they had taken from the disintegrated Yugoslav unit to the Italian soldiers who were also sipping from glasses served them by Regina, the Sturmführer's wife. But most weapons remained safely hidden when the Italian group, with their now none too steady leader and the trucks, not exactly loaded to the brim, left the village.

The Italians never again stopped in the village although they might have breezed through it on their way further into the Hinterland. It also became evident, judging from the frequent rifle shots coming from different parts of the forest, how much of that weaponry had not been turned in. There was no weaponry turned in by the residents of number 15, because we had no rifle. But later on that summer we nearly acquired one.

To keep the residents highly motivated in their support of the Reich, the young leadership invented various tasks for the residents of the enclave, young and old. One such task was assigned to the village youth by Herbert Primosch, the village Youth Leader, during one of his meetings later that spring. He tasked us to collect a certain wild flower from which could be produced a valuable medicine needed by German soldiers fighting the communists in Russia. This flower grew abundantly on various fields surrounding the village. The person bringing in the most was to receive a special prize.

I knew just the place and kept it from the others but confided in Mother who was skeptical. Nevertheless, she woke me early next morning and I wandered off toward the Unterbinkl, where we had both acreage and meadows, with patches of fog still covering the way and the heavy dew wetting my shoes. When I reached the spot that I knew was covered with the flower, I quickly started gathering and filling the basket I brought along.

Then I heard footsteps. Not to reveal my presence and the spot that was surely going to bring me a prize, I hid behind a bush and held my breath. The man I saw was Mams, known as Hanshe, a man of about 27 years.

He passed and walked toward a bush some distance away. At the bush he bent down and from among the underbrush and leaves he pulled an army rifle which he shouldered as he walked into the forest.

I returned to gathering the flowers. But after a while there was a shot which startled but did not scare me as much as what followed. It was a cry of agony that penetrated my bones. It was a cry of a mortally wounded animal, most likely a deer.

Petrified, I was afraid to move, not knowing what was to happen next. But eventually I again heard steps and from my hiding place, I watched Mams return to the bush and hide the rifle in the same place. After that he left the way he came.

I did not move for a long time. When certain that Mams would not return, curiosity drew me to the bush and from the underbrush I pulled the weapon that was the cause, only a short while ago of a frightful scare and most likely the end of an animal. After fingering this potent piece that could inflict such agony, I pushed it back into the underbrush. But I was no longer inclined to return to my task and I left for home with the basket only half full. I told no one about what happened, not even Mother, and I did not get the prize. But it did not seem to matter anymore.

I returned to the bush several times thereafter to finger the rifle and play with it. Disappointingly, there were no cartridges in the magazine which might have discouraged me from pulling the trigger when aiming at the tree. But without that, all I heard was a benign click.

Days later, the whole family was again in the Unterbinkl having lunch after working in the fields all morning. During slices of smoked sausage, crusty bread from the big oven and water from the wooden barrel, I mustered enough courage to tell Father the story of Mams and his rifle, hidden under a bush not very far away. Much to my surprise, he asked me to fetch it. As with the belt, I ran to get it, but it was no longer there.

But back to Mattl's revolver.

Some time after the arrival of the Italians, Father, Mother and Paul had again left for the market in Ribnica leaving Mitzi in charge. And again, like so many times before, I was with Mattl playing with his revolver. And yet again, I pestered him to let me take it, even if only next door. This time he said yes, his resistance finally giving way to my endless begging. Bring it back, he yelled as I ran out of his house, knowing exactly what I was going to do next. Load, aim and fire.

In a small compartment of the pull-out drawer underneath the workbench in Father's shop, I had seen, among nails, screws and such, a small brass cartridge with its blunt lead bullet firmly in place. It had never been used.

When, breathlessly, I got to the shop, it was still there. But when I tried to push it into a hole of the drum it would not fit. It was just a little bit too big, but not quite as big as my disappointment. Not too big enough to discourage me from proceeding.

MATTL

The soft lead bullet easily gave way to one of Father's files and in no time the diameter was reduced to fit the hole of the drum. But not the cartridge whose harder brass resisted the much abused file more than the soft lead. But I kept filing and after many tries and more filing much of the cartridge fit the hole. Finally, I pushed very hard, only to discover that I could not pull it back out. Now impatient, I clamped the drum into the vise on the bench and used a hammer to drive it home, oblivious to the fact that the end of the cartridge I was banging at also contained the explosive trigger capsule.

The explosion tore apart the weakened brass casing. And immediately after the brilliant flash and earsplitting sound, I sensed the warm blood running down my face.

Clutching my head and blinded by the light I staggered out of the shop and ran toward the rear of the barn. Mitzi, who was in the house came after me as did Mattl who also heard the explosion. Others followed. With my face and front now covered in blood and Mitzi howling, I was led toward the house and into the hands of Schaffer who put me on the kitchen table and forced my hands from my face.

It was not as bad as it appeared. A piece of the casing had partially embedded itself in my lip just below the entry to the right nostril. With tweezers from the first aid kit brought by one of his firemen, Schaffer pulled on the twisted brass, part of which was sticking out and removed it from the wound which renewed the heavy bleeding. But he kept the cut closed by pressing on it with gauze saturated in iodine and eventually the bleeding stopped.

By now the house, reeking with the smell of disinfectant was filled with neighbors who berated Mattl for his foolish act. Mitzi, finally in a calmer state, on request from Schaffer, found the slivovitz which was passed around after he and Mattl had a major portion. And when it became clear that all was under control and the bottle empty, the curious slowly dispersed.

But Mattl and Schaffer stayed. Schaffer cleaned my face with a wet towel and helped Mitzi change my bloodstained clothes. Mattl sat on a chair with his face in his hands composing an apology and explanation and listening for the arrival of the parents of this pest of a boy.

When they finally arrived, the air in the courtyard was still heavy with disinfectant, a first indication of trouble inside. But Schaffer quickly reduced their alarm as they came rushing in by vouching that the wound was minor and there was nothing to worry about. Mother looked at me angrily while Father ignored the stammers from Mattl and was questioning Schaffer about the size of the cut and were stitches necessary. Schaffer said no and Jaklitsch, who arrived meanwhile, said it would be unwise to drive to the doctor in Ribnica which was full of Italians who might find out and with a determined force descend on the village to search for other weapons that had not been turned in.

This ramification of the event had not occurred to anyone and was particularly troubling Mattl, whose hot seat was suddenly much hotter. It was reinforced by Jaklitsch in a meeting the next day, reminding the villagers of the need for secrecy. There was also concern that the Slovene of the village might report to the Italians but Mother, who knew them well, got them to promise to say nothing, a promise that was kept by all.

My wound quickly healed, leaving only a minor scar. What happened to the revolver I don't know except that I am certain it did not leave the village but enlarged the arsenal of somebody who may have had a supply of fitting ammunition.

Mattl's ultimate fate had nothing to do with the revolver. His destiny was linked to the resettlement later that year and he became one of its early victims.

Mattl was one of two in the village who were classified by Jaklitsch as "A", one of the categories the VGL used in the upcoming process of determining who was fit or unfit for "Ingathering" and thereby becoming worthy and productive citizens of the Third Reich. (The VGL had been granted the "right for self selection" by Hitler on April 26, 1941. More on this later.)

The other villager classified A was Josef Peinitsch, the 67 year old incontinent recluse who lived in the still safe and dry half of his disintegrating house at Masern 66. Josef was seldom seen in the village and when spotted was taunted mercilessly by the quartet of village bullies for the urine smell coming from his perpetually wetted pants.

Josef lived by hand-outs in the village. He cooked his meals from the supplies given to him by neighbors and had some of his meals in the houses of villagers who took pity on his plight. But only after he changed into dry clothes that had been washed for him by women who took turns to look after him. I remember him coming to our kitchen and a meal Mother had prepared especially for him. But he ate alone except for her presence, since in spite of his recently washed pants he still smelled a lot.

But Josef was a skillful carver of wooden crucifixes which graced the rooms of virtually every house in the village. He sold them also in other villages, usually for small coins. In the past he had received commissions which helped him survive, however the demand for his work fell to nothing in the late 1930's when crucifixes were replaced by pictures of Adolf Hitler.

Both Mattl and Josef were classified "A" to be separated during the resettlement process from their former neighbors and sent to the "Altreich". This classification brought 570 similarly classified Gottscheer to the "inner" part of the Reich. Those fit to work were placed in labor camps to help with the war effort. (More on this in a later chapter). Others who were unable to work were sent elsewhere to places where it is likely that the administrators had little sympathy for those who would only be a burden to the State. [47]

If Mattl and Josef survived the resettlement it was not for very long. I do know that neither was ever seen or heard of again.

---

[47] *Die Umsiedlung, pg 167.*

Grčarice/ Masern - 1930.

Grčarice/Masern Fire Brigade - 1925. Center front row Ignacij Merhar, head of County Fire Fighter Association. On his right is Karl Schaffer. On his left is Franz Jaklitsch. The Accordion players are: Anton Černe, right, Josef Primosch, left. In last row at the right is Johann Krisch.

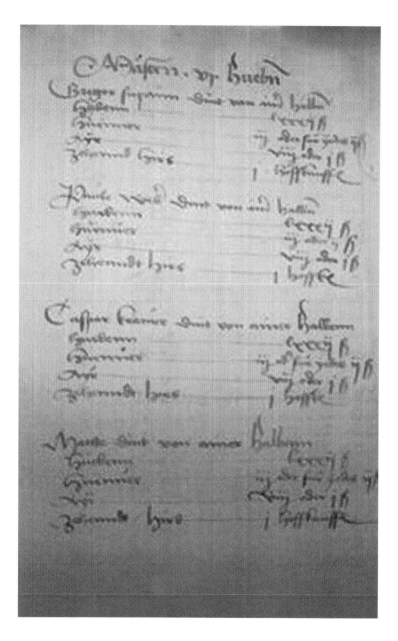

Page of 1498 Tax Records of Masern.
From State Archives of Slovenia.

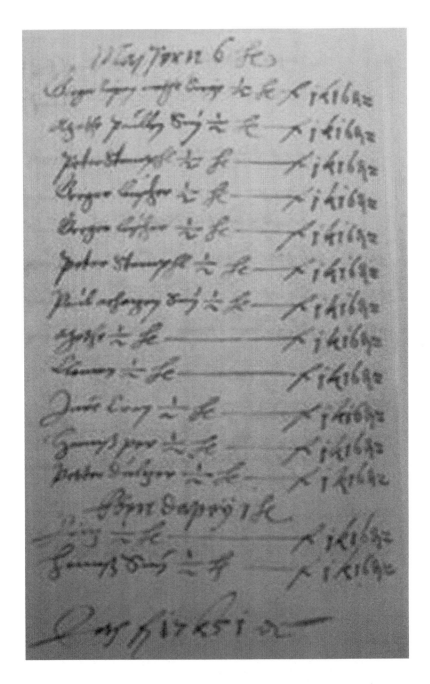

Page of 1564 Tax Records of Masern. From State Archives of Slovenia.

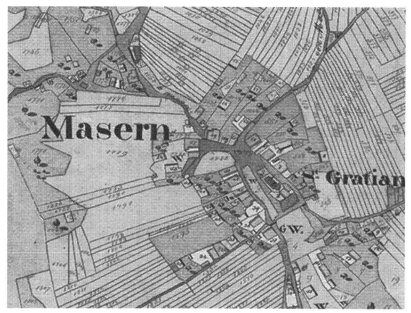

Property Map of Masern, drawn by surveyor Colanetté in 1825.
From Franciskaner Kataster, State Archives of Slovenia.

Church on the square – 1930. Village linden with surrounding bench is in foreground. Behind the tree to the left of the church is my father's house.

Back of my fathers house during 1938 flood.

Plaque commemorating September 1943 battle that destroyed the church.

Church ruins after September 1943 battle.

Jaklitsch house after September 1943 battle.

Village square in 1973. Now without church and benches around linden.

My father's house at end of road in 1973.

Grčarice/Masern village square, 2008. In center, old parsonage. At left, my father's house.

Village cemetery, 2008.

Author's father in New York City, 1911.

Author's father in Imperial Army, 1915.

Author's father as recruit, 1914.

Author in 1941. On bench surrounding village linden with Eva Tschinkel (distant cousin).

Author's father Johann, 1958.

Author's mother Maria, 1958.

Grandma Maria Ilc, 1938.

Grandma Ilc with son Alojzi, 1894

Mother's siblings, 1910: from left, Alojzi, Jože, Mother, Janez, Angela.

Author's family in 1931. From left: Paula, Mother, Father, Mitzi, Author (five months old), Tante Grete, Grandma Gera Tschinkel.

In our front yard, 1933. From left: Horse Yiorgo, Mitzi, Author, Father, Gera and Mattl.

Parade in Kočevje (Gottschee) City on 20 April, 1941.

Sturm No 1 on 20 April, 1941.

At resettlement details in summer 1941. From left: SS Major Wilhelm LaForce, Wilhelm Lampeter and Martin Sturm.

Gottscheer Zeitung

Organ der Gottscheer Deutschen Volksgruppe

GOTTSCHEE
am 17. Juli 1941

Nr. 29 — 38. Jahrgang

Wir wollen heim ins Reich!

Von verschiedenen Seiten wird mehr oder weniger versteckt Stimmung gegen die Umsiedlung gemacht. Es wird dabei immer die scheinbar große Heimatliebe vorgetäuscht. Zu all dem Treiben habe ich folgendes zu sagen:

Der Führer ruft uns heim ins Reich und wir folgen freudigen Herzens. Vaterlandslos kämpften wir auf vorgeschobenem Posten, und da der Sieg errungen, sollen wir zum großen Heer zurück. Da gibt es für Getreue kein Bedenken!

Vor 600 Jahren zogen unsere Vorfahren aus Deutschland, dem Land, das all den Generationen das Land der Sehnsucht blieb. Sie mußten Heimat und Vaterland lassen, weil sie als aufrechte und freiheitsliebende deutsche Bauern nicht die Knute der Grundherren ertragen wollten. Sie zogen aus einem unsozialen Deutschland, von Fürsten und Adeligen regiert, und erhielten eines der ärmsten Gebiete Mitteleuropas zugewiesen, woraus sich unsere Vorfahren ihre neue Heimat Gottschee schufen.

Wir haben nun das große Glück, in ein anderes Deutschland heimkehren zu dürfen. Großdeutschland von heute, das soziale Reich Adolf Hitlers, wünscht uns so hellblickend, stolz und aufrecht, wie unsere Vorfahren es waren. Die einmals verpönten und bestraften Tugenden des deutschen Mannes sind heute wiederum zu schätzen.

Uns jungen Nationalsozialisten fällt die Heimkehr ins Reich nicht schwer. Nein! Aber nicht etwa darum, weil wir zu wenig mit unserem Gottscheer Ländchen verwachsen wären, weil wir es zu wenig liebten! Wir verspüren in uns die große Liebe zu unserem Führer, den festen Glauben an Deutschland und trauen uns zu, eine ebenso schöne Heimat innerhalb der Grenzen Deutschlands neu aufzubauen. Wir empfinden es als das größte Glück, Deutsche zu sein, und dies noch in der Zeit, wo Adolf Hitler das Deutsche Reich für die kommenden Jahrtausende baut. Schwer fällt uns nur, daß wir nicht schon an den Fronten mitkämpfen können, wo heute die Entscheidungen der kommenden Jahrtausende für das deutsche Volk errungen werden.

Eine Belastung für das Reich sein und bleiben, das wollen wir nicht! Wir wollen mitbauen, mitgestalten und mitkämpfen in Großdeutschland für die Ehre und Größe des deutschen Volkes in alle Zukunft!

Jenen Gottscheern, die irgendwo in der Welt sitzen und der Heimat alle Jahre einen Besuch — oder nicht einmal den — abstatteten, heute aber den in der Heimat verbliebenen Volksgenossen von der Schönheit des Gottscheerlandes, von der Liebe zur Heimat schreiben und reden, sei gesagt: Gottschee kann nicht gehalten werden, damit ihr einen trauten Urlaubsort behaltet, wo ihr als die „gemachten Männer" bestaunt werdet. Seht euch einmal die abgearbeiteten und doch unterernährten deutschen Menschen im Walden und in der Moschn, im Unter- und Hinterlande an!

———

Wir, die arbeittragenden jungen Gottscheer, sahen besorgt den biologischen Verschleiß, den unsere Volksgruppe in ihrer Abgeschlossenheit auf dem kargen Boden, zur Gegenauslese und Inzucht verurteilt, zwangsläufig durchmachte. Wir waren aber auch entschlossen, alles — ganz selbstlos — zur Gesundung unserer Volksgruppe einzusetzen, wenn uns der Führer als vorgeschobenen Posten weiterhin gewollt hätte. Nun hat aber der Führer in seinem Weitblick einmal anders entschieden! Er sieht Großdeutschland der Zukunft vor sich. Und in dieses deutsche Reich gehören auch wir!

Den strammen Gottscheern sei es doch auf gottscheerisch gesagt: „Bir kamen von Reazoch afs Grusmöt!"

Aber nicht nur die klare Vernunft ist es, die für die Heimkehr ins Reich spricht. Die Liebe zum Führer, der Glaube an Deutschland und der Ruf des Blutes bestimmen unser Handeln.

Wir jungen Nationalsozialisten sind stolz darauf, Deutsche zu sein, und wollen Kämpfer für Führer und Volk sein und bleiben! Wer könnte es auch für sich und seine Nachkommen verantworten, nicht mehr dem Sonnenvolk auf Erden anzugehören, von dem er kommt!

Wir sind zu Kämpfern und Herren geboren und wollen keine Knechte sein!

Wir wollen heim ins Reich!

Der Mannschaftsführer:
Wilhelm Lampeter.

Vom Kirsequell zum Kulpastrand
Steht in den Wind die Fahnen,
Wir kehren heim ins Vaterland,
Die Heimat unser Ahnen.

Wir blieben deutsch trotz Haß und Not,
Trotz bitterer Knechtschaft Schande.
Es trieb das Ostertaunsgebot
Die Serben aus dem Lande.

Im Gleichschrittmarsch, der Trommel Schlag
Gibt Schritt uns beim Marschieren.
Wir rufen in den jungen Tag:
„Ein Volk, ein Reich, ein Führer!"

(Wird nach der alten Melodie gesungen.)

"We wish to return home to the Reich!"

Political rally at Hans Michitsch grave on 3 August 1941. At left is Johann Krisch.

Lampeter address at rally in Kočevje (Gottschee) City on 20 April 1941.

Leaving their homes for the new life in the "Reich", Dec 1941.

Entering train for the journey to the "Reich". Dec. 1941.

In the "Reich" in 1943. Lampeter (black uniform) reviewing Hitler Youth with Nazi officers.

In the "Reich" in 1943. Franz Jaklitsch briefing Nazi officers.

Gauleiter Ueberreiter visiting settlers in the "Reich" in 1942. Sign above: "We Thank Our Führer".

Partisan holding camp in Radeče prior to our expulsion from Slovenia in May 1945.

Chapter 12

Assignment and Preparation

"War, war, we are at war" screamed the nineteen year old Anna Parthe of house No 9 as she came crying out of the Jaklitsch house, No 11, on Sunday morning April 6, 1941, where the radio had just announced the Axis invasion of Yugoslavia. The outbreak of war was particularly distressing to Anna because Hans Michitsch, aged twenty seven and the younger son of the sexton to whom she was affianced, was a soldier in the Yugoslav army.

Also in the army was Alois Primosch, at twenty five the oldest son of Johann and Magdalena Primosch of Masern No 10. Magdalena was sitting on the bench in front of her house breastfeeding Adolf, the youngest of her eight children when Anna came running from the Jaklitsch house across the road. Adolf had been named after Hitler in a baptism performed by Father Gliebe in our church, with the sexton Michitsch ringing the bell and me as the altar boy assisting the priest.

It was a shock to most people in the village, especially since just over a week ago the *Gottscheer Zeitung* of Thursday March 27, 1941 announced with a banner headline:

"Yugoslavia in Steady Hand".

"In these destiny-burdened times, King Peter II has decided to take the fate of Yugoslavia into his own hands. Peace proclamations are being distributed in the entire land pronouncing unwavering loyalty to the King.

"Long live King Peter II !"

The headline continued:

"Yugoslavia joins the Three Power Pact".

"At a festive state act in the Belvedere castle in Vienna, in the presence of the Führer on the 25th of March, the joining of Yugoslavia to the Three Power Pact, Germany - Italy – Japan, was consummated. The Pact already includes Hungary, Romania, Slovakia and Bulgaria."

THE BELLS RING NO MORE

The next issue of the *GZ*, scheduled for Thursday, April 3rd, had not been printed due to the uncertain events that had taken place in the country during the prior week. Therefore the coup of the night of March 26-27, that displaced the government of King Peter II in Belgrade, nullified the alliance with the Axis and started a chain of events that had not yet come to the attention to the people of Masern.

April 6: Germany and its Axis allies including Italy invaded Yugoslavia. In the early morning, relays of 150 Luftwaffe planes started bombing Belgrade. The city was subjected to a continuous rain of bombs for one and a half hours which leveled the entire city, killing 17,000 civilians.

The sudden invasion took the VGL by such surprise that it allowed the Slovene authorities, on April 6, 1941, to take into custody as hostages twenty two leading Gottscheer, among them three VGL members. The remainder of the VGL managed to flee into the forest.

April 9: On this day, all hostages are released by the Slovene authorities. But during the night of April 10-11, the VGL in turn ordered all Sturm units to take up their weapons and Gottscheer Sturm troopers disarm all Slovene gendarmes in the district. They also arrest leading Slovene administrative officials, police and judges.

April 13: The twenty five year old National-Socialist Wilhelm Lampeter assumed the position of District Chief, head of the enclave. He is now head of a Gottscheer mini-state. German troops were expected momentarily. The VGL directs that swastika flags be hung from every building in the enclave.

April 17: In Berlin, the "Menscheneinsatz" branch of the RKFDV proposed the re-settling of 58,000 Volksdeutsche to the annexed Slovenia from which 130,000 Slovene are to be removed. [48]

April 18: Yugoslavia capitulated to the Axis powers and the government of the military junta in Belgrade dissolves.

On the morning of April 18, the Yugoslav army unit, having spent the night in their wagons on the square in front of the Masern church and in the hay lofts of adjacent barns, abandon their weapons, their military gear and their transport vehicles and disappear. Some of them trade their warm woolen uniforms for civilian clothing with willing villagers so as to allow them to merge into the population and not wind

---

48 T. Ferenc, *Quellen zur nationalsozialistischen Entnationalisierungspolitik in Slowenien 1941–1945*. Maribor 1980, doc. 21 later: *Quellen*.

ASSIGNMENT AND PREPARATION

up in POW camps of the conquering army, be it German or Italian. The considerable weapons cache is acquired by the Jaklitsch militia and safely hidden away.

Anna Parthe's premonition of disaster on April 6 became reality ten days later on April 16 when word came that the body of her fiancé Hans Michitsch was lying in a field near Novo Mesto (Rudolfswert). He had been shot dead as a deserter by a Yugoslav army unit on April 16, two days before the end of the war after he refused to stop on the way home. The body, covered with a blanket, was brought back to Masern on April 17 by a group of Lampeter's militia in the back of a truck on a layer of straw. Hans was buried in the Michitsch family plot on April 19 after a funeral Mass celebrated by Father Gliebe.

More fortunate was Magdalena Primosch the mother of Anton who came home on April 25, leading a pair of prize oxen which he had uncoupled from an abandoned Yugoslav army wagon and brought back to his father's stable. But the oxen were the property of a Slovene. They had been requisitioned by the Yugoslav army during the rapid mobilization shortly before the war. The owner traced their whereabouts to Masern and Anton's unhappy father was forced by the gendarmes from Dolenja Vas to return them to their Slovene owner.

Since the beginning of the war on April 6, the people of Masern, the Germans of the enclave and the VGL had been hoping that Slovenia and the enclave would be occupied and annexed to Germany. The Gottscheer are shocked when it becomes obvious that annexation of their part of Slovenia to the Reich was not to be. Now all were consumed with a burning question "what will become of us?"

But on that Sunday morning of April 6, neither Anna nor Magdalena Primosch or anyone else in the village could wildly imagine what this war would bring. Not imagine that in only eight months, specifically on December 7, 9 and 10, the residents of Masern would be leaving their homes, their properties, their way of life for nothing more than a promise. And, even more unreal, that in only forty nine months, they would be homeless refugees, victims of a failed ideology forced on them by a small group of misled young fanatics.

April 20: At the two day conference in Vienna, the distribution of the former Yugoslavia lands, including Slovenia, is decided. The ethnic Germans of Lower Styria succeed in getting their part of Slovenia annexed to the Reich. Hitler, however, relinquishes the Gottschee enclave and other parts of Slovenia to Italy

THE BELLS RING NO MORE

in an agreement with Count Ciano, the Italian Minister of Foreign Affairs. In his memoir Dr. Stier writes:

"Axis politics forced Hitler to concessions toward his partner at the partitioning of the conquered Yugoslavia". [49]

On this day, Himmler informs the VGL of Hitler's decision to resettle the Gottscheer Germans.

April 23: Italians arrive in their part of the now divided Slovenia which also includes the Gottschee enclave. But the Italian occupier has no tolerance for an independent and armed district within its territory. They dissolve the "District Commission" set up by the VGL and disarm the Sturm troopers of the enclave. The Italians also release the arrested Slovene police, judges and administrative officials, and restore to them their former offices and positions. This immediately alienates the VGL toward the Italians, a mistrust that will only increase in the coming months. The Italians in turn are, understandably if cautiously, antagonistic toward the Gottscheer who behave as if they are an independent entity, not subjects of the Italian occupier but part of the Reich.

The VGL reacts to the dissolution of the "District Commission" by forming, in turn, the "Volks Gruppen Organization" or VGO, a hierarchal structure in which all Sturm units of the enclave are under the formal leadership of the VGL. As such the VGO however has no civil function; this had been taken from them by the occupying Italians when they dissolved the "District Commission". But, unofficially, on May 1, 1941 the VGO becomes a State within a State.

The Gottscheer farmer K.R. from Slovenska Vas, (Windischdorf) comments about this period in his memoir dated March 6, 1958. It was published in *Dokumentation der Vertreibung der Deutschen aus Ost-Europa V, Das Schicksal der deutschen in Jugoslawien* [50]

On page 31, the farmer is quoted:

"At the beginning of the war between Germany and Italy on one side and Yugoslavia on the other side, we Gottscheer were convinced that within a short time our country would be occupied by German troops and that thereafter, we would

---

49 *Die Umsiedlung*, pg 26, 27

50 Düsseldorf 1961, later: *Dokumentation der Vertreibung*.

ASSIGNMENT AND PREPARATION

be made part of the German Reich. The disappointment was, however, very great when, instead of the expected German troops, Italians occupied the country."

And the Gottscheer Reverend Alois Krisch of Stari log [Altlag], in his memoir written in the winter of 1947/48, also published in *Dokumentation der Vertreibung,* (on page 9) writes:

"To be part of Italy pleased no one. Emigrate? This is also a unique reaction. Leave? Into the unknown? "

With the disappearance of Yugoslavia, the Gottscheer are jubilant since they have been freed from a State which, for twenty three years, denied them "Minority Status"; a State that forced them to learn Slovene as the official language and insisted that they adhere to its parliamentarian laws. But with the much hoped for annexation not to be the enclave is, nevertheless, once again under the jurisdiction of a 'friendly' power. Imperial Austria, the protector of the Gottscheer minority for centuries, has been replaced not by Germany but by Italy, an ally of the invincible Third Reich.

But with Slovenia partitioned and the part containing the enclave annexed to Italy, would they now be "assimilated" by the Italians and required to learn the Italian language? At this time, no one except the VGL knew yet of Hitler's decision to move the population of the enclave into the Reich.

April 26: At a meeting in Maribor, Hitler confirms the planned resettlement of the Gottscheer to a VGL delegation of Lampeter, Schober and Sturm. This decision had already been given to them by Himmler on April 20.

At the meeting, Hitler also reveals to the VGL delegation the settlement area to be adjacent to the north-west side of the Save - Sotla Rivers, a border area just inside the annexed part of Slovenia, the part now bordering on that occupied by Italy. He tasks the Gottscheer with an historic assignment to be border farmers of the now enlarged Reich.

At the meeting, the VGL members ask Hitler to allow that:
1. the Gottscheer be resettled as a group,
2. the VGL conduct its own resettlement program, and

3. the VGL be given the "right for self-selection".

Hitler grants all three requests on the spot.

The VGL makes the requests because it believes the requested items are crucial to the success of the resettlement. This conviction is based in large part on the results of the less than successful program to resettle the ethnic Germans from the South Tyrol into the Reich. That effort, which had started in 1939, was still underway in 1941 and far from completion. In view of this, Hitler fully understands the reasons for the requests of the VGL and therefore willingly agrees. [51]

On return of the three leaders from Maribor, the VGL decides to keep Hitler's decision to resettle the Gottscheer a secret. They believe such delay would soften the shock in a tense population expecting to be annexed, not resettled. As confirmed National Socialists they are prepared to execute the order of the Führer without the slightest reservation. They are also sure the entire youth of the enclave would follow Hitler's order with great enthusiasm.

They are, however, less certain about the older population and for this reason they believe it is necessary to delay the announcement. Delay it at least until after their return from Berlin, to where they have been invited at the April 26 meeting with Hitler to discuss the resettlement policy and program with the RKFDV. They believe that after their conference there they would be in a better position to present the resettlement in the best possible light.

This delay tactic, however, does not work as expected; it actually causes great unrest and encourages rumors and uncertainty. Consequently, the VGL tries to calm the population with various evasive assurances at meetings throughout the enclave. The rumormongers are attacked by an article in the *Gottscheer Zeitung* of May 1, 1941.

"These troublemakers should take note: The future shall soon teach them that they are 'Volksschädlinge' [parasites] and that this future has no place for such Volksschädlinge other than the Concentration Camp."

The same issue also announces the formation of the VGO which defines the structure of the Gottscheer "mini-state" and lists the responsibility of each member of the leadership circle, the VGL. In addition, the front page of this weekly is changed to prominently display the Nazi emblem, the swastika.

---

51   *Die Umsiedlung, pg. 62.*

ASSIGNMENT AND PREPARATION

May 2: A VGL delegation is received by Emilio Grazioli, the Italian High Commissioner for the occupied Slovenia, headquartered in Ljubljana. The VGL has requested this meeting to cement the relationship with this 'friendly' Axis power. Volksgruppenleiter Schober, the former head of the enclave branch of the Kulturbund and now the 'official' figurehead member of the VGL (being the "oldest" of the young leadership), presents to the Commissioner a *Declaration of Allegiance* to Italy. (The undisputed leader of the group remains, as before, the Mannschaftsführer Wilhelm Lampeter.)

At the same meeting, the VGL also requests special rights "from time to time" from the High Commissioner. This demand is documented in a letter to be forwarded by the Commissioner to the Duce.

May 2: Himmler appoints Gauleiter Uiberreither, the chief of the civil administration of the Styria Gau (administrative district - province) of the Reich, to also be the chief civil administrator of the annexed Slovenia. He is also appointed as the local representative of the RKFDV, the SS organization in Maribor and made responsible for the annexed area into which the Gottscheer are to be settled.

May 6: At a SD (Sicherheitdienst, SS Secret Service Police) conference in Maribor, it is announced that 260,000 Slovene are to be removed from the annexed Slovenia. The rapid resettlement of the Gottscheer into part of the vacated areas is determined to be first priority.

Three members of the VGL, Lampeter, Schober and Sturm arrive in Berlin on May 12. They have been invited, at the April 26 meeting with Hitler, to come to the SS Headquarters there to discuss the resettlement program and plans with the RKFDV.[52]

Wilhelm Lampeter, in his *Gedächnisschrift* of Feb. 9, 1942, (*Die Gottscheer Volksgruppe*) reports on the meeting:

"Deliberations were with Dr. Greifeld, SS-Brigadeführer [Brigadier General] and heads of the various branches of the Reichskommissariat. [RKFDV]. Discussed were the efforts of the VGL in the coming re-settlement. In particular, the rough details of a family questionnaire (Familienbogen) were agreed upon."

---

52   *Nazističča, pg. 585.*

Frensing[53] quotes Dr. Stier, SS-Obersturmbannführer (Lieutenant-Colonel), the resident technical adviser of the RKFDV Resettlement Office:

"The VGL welcomed the promise of 'closed settling' of all Gottscheer in the new area by not splitting them up and resettling them into various parts of the Reich. But it does ask that the following exceptions be made; mixed marriages, unfit peasants.

"Among the unfit peasants there are some who are capable of becoming full fledged farmers in the settlement area. But the majority of them are not qualified for this exception. In order to avoid conflicts between the differently handled peasants, the VGL asks that all be re-settled into another region."

"The RKFVD accepted the proposals of the VGL and is in full agreement with the request for a rapid resettlement".

Frensing adds:

"Later on, to the two groups [mixed marriages and unfit peasants] was added the group described as the 'List of the politically unreliable' ". [The list was generated by Lampeter as a secret document which he submitted to the SS on October 17, 1941]. With this simple concept, the VGL wished to make certain that only those it viewed as racially pure, professionally able and politically reliable Gottscheer reach the new settlement region.

"The RKFDV also re-affirmed to the VGL the full responsibility for the resettlement effort and the 'right for self-selection', granted by Hitler personally on April 26.

"The 'right for self-selection' had been requested by the VGL to allow it to cleanse the population of those Gottscheer [it] judged not fit to become citizens of the Reich. In addition to mixed marriage and unreliable political views, cause for rejection will be a lack of physical fitness and an inability to operate a farm or business. Exceptions may be classified as special cases and dealt with at a later date." But more on this later.

In the discussions between the VGL and RKFDV in Berlin, the resettlement of the ethnic Germans of Alto Adige (South Tyrol) undoubtedly contributed significantly in arriving at a resettlement policy for the Gottscheer. This is made apparent in Rolf

---

53 *Die Umsiedlung, pg 64.*

ASSIGNMENT AND PREPARATION

Steininger's: "*South Tyrol; A Minority Conflict of the Twentieth Century*", (New Brunswick, London 2003, later: *South Tyrol*)

South Tyrol was under the Austro Hungarian monarchy until 1918 when the south side of the Alps was allocated to Italy at the Peace Conference in Versailles. Until then a part of the larger Tyrol, the German speaking residents of South Tyrol (Alto Adige under the Italians) were now separated from their north-Tyrolean German brethren and required to learn Italian, the official language of their new government. The northern Italians, who had been under Austro-German domination for centuries, were not inclined to make such an exception. This requirement, called denationalization policy by the South Tyroleans, became even more forceful after 1922 when the Italian Fascists came to power.

The resistance of the Germans of South Tyrol to the new order was similar to that of the Gottscheer in the enclave. In both cases the state mandate for learning another language was also viewed as forceful assimilation. And as in the enclave, the Germans of South Tyrol were hoping to be annexed by the Reich. But this was not to be since Hitler had concluded that South Tyrol, like the enclave, must be sacrificed to an alliance with Mussolini.

And like the Gottscheer in the enclave, the South Tyroleans came to believe that only by resettling would they maintain their German nationality. Except perhaps for their leadership, few of the population, if any in either enclave, knew that they were no more than part of Hitler's strategy for replacing the population in conquered territories with ingathered ethnic Germans and thereby securing his enlarged Third Reich.

The Gottscheer resettlement process is striking for its use of methods that worked well in South Tyrol and the avoidance of those that did not. This was due to either the VGL being very cognizant of the details of the South Tyrol process, or to the extensive briefing it received during its visit in Berlin in the middle of May 1941. Perhaps it was a combination of both.

The facts provided by Steininger permit a side by side comparison of the methodology used in resettling the two ethnic groups. In each case, the deciding part was played by a committed local Nazi organization. In South Tyrol it was the VKS, (Völkischer Kampfring Südtirols). In the Gottschee enclave the VolksGruppenOrganization, the VGO with Wilhelm Lampeter as its ideological head.

In any event it is reasonable to assume that a discussion of tactics that worked in South Tyrol and those to be avoided took place at the conference in Berlin. This was very helpful to the fanatical young members of the VGL who were determined to succeed in the assignment given them by Hitler personally.

The 12,000 Gottscheer were to be settled as a group into a part of the annexed Slovenia from which (initially) a quarter million Slovenes were to be removed. The settlement area had been announced to the VGL by Hitler in April 1941 and the resettlement was to be completed seven months later. The destination was withheld from the population by the VGL until the trains carrying the settlers and their possessions started to leave. The first train left on November 14, 1941 carrying 40 persons, 22 animals and nine freight cars loaded with possessions. The last train completing the resettlement left on January 23, 1942. From start to finish, the "Ingathering" (including preparation) took nine months.

By contrast, the destination of the 75,000 South Tyroleans who opted for resettlement had not even been selected by Himmler when trains started to roll in November 1939.

According to Rolf Steininger, a March 1938 memorandum that became the basis for German policy, states: "Total resettlement of the South Tyroleans will be to an area made available in the future by conquest in the East". [54]

And Himmler (who had been made responsible by Hitler for planning the operation on June 16, 1939 had promised "that the South Tyrolean people will be resettled as a single unified group and that its leaders will have the opportunity to familiarize themselves with the regions that will come into consideration for resettlement before a final decision on the selection of land is made". (For reference: the occupation of Poland started September 1, 1939.)

Steininger continues: "Himmler's assurance of a unified, contiguous area of settlement was a trump card that the VKS had successfully played in its propaganda". A similar promise was made to the VGL and as with the South Tyroleans, the promise was equally false.

Trains carrying re-settlers out of South Tyrol began to leave in November 1939. At the end of 1939, approximately 11,500 had left. The largest number; 37,500 left in 1940. Thereafter, numbers began to decrease. 18,750 in 1941, 6,000 in 1942, 3,000 in 1943. [55]

---

54   *South Tyrol*, pg. 53.

55   *South Tyrol*, pg. 67.

ASSIGNMENT AND PREPARATION

Steininger claims the most important reason for the decrease was that the promise of Himmler was not kept. When the trains were leaving, the South Tyrol re-settlers did not know where they were going. Instead of being taken to their final destination, "the emigrants [according to Steininger] were housed in emergency quarters (sublet rooms, barracks, monasteries, army bases) and had to accept jobs that were often not quite what they were used to. There was no longer much mention of the grand promises that had been made in the past.

"Furthermore, there were tremendous difficulties and delays in establishing the asset value of the South Tyroleans who opted for Germany; for this reason, many delayed their departure for as long as it took to establish this value.

"By August 1942, Himmler was urging the responsible authorities in Bozen, [Bolzano] to speed up immigration and cease accepting the excuse that individuals were waiting for final selections of a contiguous resettlement territory. But even the replacement of the top man in the resettlement agency did not speed up the process".

The above makes clear why the VGL pressed to:
a. have the resettling effort under their own control,
b. perform the task as quickly as possible,
c. resettle as a group into a clearly defined area,
d. assess the property values of the re-settlers immediately.

When the VGL left the Berlin conference, the responsibility for the resettlement of the Gottscheer was totally theirs and they knew exactly what they had to do. They also took with them a page from the South Tyrol model, the "Abyssinia card". (Steininger on pages 56 and 57, talks about the "Sicilian Legend", the rumor that the Italians would deport to Sicily, Abyssinia or other regions, all those who did not opt for Germany).

The announcement that the Gottscheer will be resettled is finally made on May 22. It had been kept secret since April 20, five weeks after Himmler informed the VGL of Hitler's decision. Hitler's decision is announced in banner headlines on page one of the May 22, 1941 issue of the *Gottscheer Zeitung*:

"Gottscheer Countrymen and Countrywomen".

"The Führer is calling us home to the Reich. Accept with iron discipline his command. Prove to the final hour through work and diligence that you are worthy to be Germans of Adolf Hitler.

"The harvest of 1941 in the old homeland shall prove to the world that we, as we have for 600 years, even during this last year as ethnic Germans, are able to extract from this meager soil our bitter bread, thanks to the power of our German will. Present to our Italian ally a unique portrait of German manhood as an expression of our unshakable loyalty to the expressed policy of the Axis.

Signed: "Der Volksgruppenführer, Josef Schober. Der Mannschaftsführer, Wilhelm Lampeter."

This initial announcement of Hitler's decision to resettle the Gottscheer was brief in part because the three leaders Lampeter, Schober and Sturm had just returned from their meeting with the RKFVD in Berlin. But the May 29 issue of the *GZ* provided greater detail:

"Greater Germany takes us home".

" The decision has been made. The Führer has taken the destiny of our group into his hand. We are going home into the Reich from which we came more than 600 years ago. We look with great confidence to our own leadership which in these times has taken so much upon itself and knows that every Gottscheer these days will understand the necessity and correctness of this measure derived by the leaders of our great [German] Nation. Think not only of ourselves but of the whole of the nation, the state and its future. This is the substance of our German view of the world.

"With admirable discipline, aware of this new, beautiful and great task, our comrades accepted this decision. All, without exception, have inwardly accepted this way into the future. In meetings throughout our land, held so often by our leadership, we have been made aware of the coming duties and tasks, duties placed upon us through the honorable confidence of our nation bestowed upon us by our Führer for all future time. Our future new homeland will be better than the old one which in past centuries brought so much agony and in recent years so much pain, tears and bitterness. We will not lose much, but gain a great deal more.

"In the meetings which took place throughout the land, we all acknowledged the call of the blood, the nation and that of the greatest of German men, the Führer. The news that we will no longer be Volksdeutsche without a homeland was received with enthusiasm and uproarious joy.

"Home to the Reich."

ASSIGNMENT AND PREPARATION

After returning from Berlin, Lampeter with his staff leaders visit all village groups to announce the "Heimkehr", the homecoming call of the Führer. Lampeter, in his *Die Gottscheer Volksgruppe* of Feb. 9, 1942, writes:

"Immediately on his return, the Mannschaftsführer ordered a *'pre-option'* [to resettle] to be performed throughout the enclave [to determine the willingness of the population]. The *'pre-option'* was 100% successful because the Mannschaftsführer with his three staff leaders spoke to all village groups about the 'Heimkehr' of the Gottscheer. The call of the Reich was understood by the entire population.

"On the so called family questionnaire, distributed by the Sturmführer after these meetings, each Gottscheer German, willing to be re-settled, had to state all his personal details including a declaration that he wishes to return to the Reich.

"To the mentioned family questionnaire, signifying a *'pre-option'* was added a second sheet to be filled out fully in accordance with the guidelines provided by the Mannschaftsführer. This was to be done in detail, responsibly, objectively and in total secrecy by the Sturmführer of each village, his Deputy the Unterführer or other trustworthy individuals. As a result, we have on each Gottscheer German, a valid picture regarding his capability and character."

The Gottscheer farmer K.R. from Slovenska Vas, (Windischdorf)], reports on this in his memoir dated March 6, 1958 as follows:

"The first news that we would be re-settled by the German Reich arrived approximately at the end of May 1941. I, like most of the Gottscheer, did not believe that this would become reality. Our common and complete striving was to remain loyal to the soil of our homeland into the future.

"At one meeting with many participants, where I was also present, our 'Führers' promised that we will, in our new homeland in the German Reich, receive fine and modernly outfitted farms. We were also told that, as a result of our re-settlement, no losses will occur to anyone; the Reich is vouching for this. The farms will be equal in value and substance to the present one. We should, however, expect an improvement since the soil in our new homeland is more productive than ours. And due to the enduring persistence in our Germanness, the German Reich will place us into an improved situation.

"These were the first announcements. Because of these rosy promises by our leaders, the majority of the population was enthusiastic about the resettlement. However, in a short while this enthusiasm sank so that a large part of the population was against the resettlement. In the outlying villages all residents were against the resettlement, including myself. I often went to evening meetings where we consulted each other.

THE BELLS RING NO MORE

"And we were not told where our new homeland in the German Reich would be. Had the population known where this new homeland would be, in my opinion, no one would have joined the re-settlement, including the [young] leaders.

"At the meetings the leaders, when asked about the destination, claimed they did not know themselves and that the Führer Adolf Hitler would tell us this as soon as he believed it necessary."

And the Gottscheer Reverend Alois Krisch of Stari log (Altlag), in his memoir of 1947/48 *Dokumentation der Vertreibung*, pg. 9, writes:

"The thoughtless youth was enraptured. Mature people felt odd in their hearts, they had peculiar reactions. Abandon the homeland and all that is part of it? Is there no other escape; no other alternative?" [56]

But the ethnic Germans of the enclave remained in the dark about when the resettlement was to start and where in the Reich their new homes were to be. The fact that this was another part of Slovenia from which the resident Slovene would be forcibly ejected continues to be Top Secret.

Part of the reason for not disclosing the early resettlement date was the fear that the farmers might not continue with the planting of this year's crop, thereby creating a food shortage in the event the resettlement was delayed. This is apparent in the May 22 appeal to the "German will" to extract yet another harvest from the "meager soil". The appeal was justified, since already in May of that year there was a critical shortage of food in the enclave. This prompted Lampeter, in a letter published in the June 5 issue of the GZ, to urge the population to share existing supplies with others. It seems the urging of May 22 was taken seriously since the harvest of 1941 was an abundant one and was reported as such in the September 25 issue of the GZ.

The real reason for not disclosing the settlement area in the Reich is given by the head of the Resettlement Offices, SS-Obersturmbannführer, Dr. Stier who reports on the Berlin meeting with Lampeter and is quoted by Frensing on page 94:

"Weighing on the mood of the meeting was the demand of the VGL, at the insistence of Mannschaftsführer Lampeter, to keep the new settlement region a secret. The Mannschaftsführer explained that the new settlement region can not be made public since the majority of the Gottscheer know this region and are aware that the properties and houses are in very poor condition.

---

56 *Dokumentation der Vertreibung*, pg. 9.

ASSIGNMENT AND PREPARATION

"Responding to my position that disappointment would be worse than honest explanation of the conditions, he [Lampeter] stated that there is time for an explanation after the option is closed. Also the Mannschaftsführer was not willing to announce to the Gottscheer even the fact that the quarters are temporary and a re-planning and redevelopment is envisioned, since he feared unrest due to such announcement."

Frensing, on page 62, offers his own assessment of the reasoning of Lampeter and the VGL:

"The Resettlement Decision as well as the Settlement Region was not announced to the public. Through this the General Tactical Line, with which the VGL decided to proceed becomes clear. At first, the population shall exercise the Option, only then - when there is no return - shall the farmers be notified of the Settlement Region."

Franz Jaklitsch, the Sturmführer of Masern and the adjacent Masereben, Sturm 13, requested that all village men attend an important meeting in the large room of his tavern at 10 o'clock on the morning of Tuesday, May 27. There was to be an important announcement by high officials from the City.

The news that high officials from the City were coming spread rapidly. And long before the motorcar came to a halt that morning, the Jaklitsch tavern was filled with anxious men while a good part of the village was waiting for the visitors around the linden on the square across the street.

They came in the car owned and driven by Franz Tschinkel, my father's City cousin and Führer of Sturm No 1, the Gottschee City Sturm. (The one who had sold me the bicycle). The canvas top had been rolled back and a small swastika flag fluttered impressively from the front fender. After it stopped in front of the tavern, we kids went nearer but stopped at a respectful distance from the car as four men in their fine leather boots, black riding britches and white shirt with the swastika armband, were getting out. All four made for the tavern door, but only after Franz authoritatively ordered all kids to stay away from the car. This was difficult; such a vehicle was not often in our village. Since the meeting behind the closed doors lasted quite a while, the crowd around the linden thinned out, except for the youth which had little else to do, now that there was no more school ever since our teacher Alojzij Dežman had left at the beginning of the year.

THE BELLS RING NO MORE

The four uniformed men left as abruptly as they had arrived but Jaklitsch continued the meeting. And when the obviously agitated village men, each with a sheet of paper in hand (the pre-option form) finally started spilling out the door, they made for home without much delay, trailed by their folk emerging from the crowd around the linden.

Mitzi, Paul and I joined Father who gave the sheet of paper to me to carry so that he could walk more quickly on his crutches on the way home. He would not answer questions and remained silent until he was seated in his favorite corner in the kitchen. "We are leaving Masern and moving to the Reich" he finally said.

I remember only my own reaction, a reaction of joy to the news which promised excitement, adventure, new places in a new world about which I had gathered only glimpses in books, magazines and brief visits to Ljubljana. I do not know how Mother accepted the news and what discussions followed after he spoke those fateful words since I immediately ran out to see if the other youngsters shared my joy. All did, if perhaps for different reasons; not only in Masern but throughout the enclave.

As had been exclaimed by the Reverend Alois Krisch:

"The thoughtless youth was enraptured …".

To my deep regret, I never asked my parents about their reaction. Neither then, nor during the many years since. Then, because I was too young and overjoyed by the prospect of moving. And later on, after it had all gone wrong, I did not ask since it was difficult for them to talk about it and more so because it was irrelevant to me then; an attitude that unfortunately changed only years after both had died.

I can, however, after many years of contemplation and the benefit of hindsight, imagine not only Mother's reaction but also that of Father. I am certain that their reaction was not unlike that generalized by the Reverend.

But with my parents there was much more. Theirs was not the typical Gottscheer family.

Mother, now finally and firmly placed in her own home, on her own land, was being asked to surrender what had come to her with so much pain and suffering for a future consisting of nothing more than a promise. She was also asked to leave behind all her Slovene family and friends and all contacts she had maintained ever since she married and moved to Masern. But I am certain that ultimately she willingly accepted the bitter logic that her husband presented her with, if not then, certainly not much later.

Father's initial reaction was, most likely, similar to that of the farmer K.R. and others like him. But more than loyalty to the land, Father was burdened with more practical considerations. He had no choice.

ASSIGNMENT AND PREPARATION

No choice but to leave with the others in the village, all of whom "were enthusiastic about the resettlement", to again quote the farmer. With the village emptied out and no one left with whom to exchange the use of his lands for labor he depended on to cultivate his farm, his family could not survive. All of Mother's arguments for staying could not withstand that cruel fact.

Not wanting to remain in an empty village was the logic of even those not handicapped as was Father; unencumbered farmers who, with other able handed family members, could work the land and extract a livelihood from it. And all knew that the village itself was an interdependent family that functioned only as a unit which allowed it to exist for centuries in the past and could not continue otherwise in the future.

It was precisely this kind of thinking the VGL encouraged and counted on to successfully accomplish the mission ordered by the Führer on April 26.

And "if you don't take up the option now, you will not have a second chance" was used very persuasively.

But what Father did not know then, if ever, was that the VGL list of undesirables excluded him from being part of such a village in the new land. It excluded him because he was in a "mixed marriage" to a Slovene and for not being "fit" to become a border farmer in the Reich. He was to be resettled with the other "unworthy Gottscheer" to another place. That in his case both of these prohibitions were ultimately overlooked, is at least in part attributable to Franz Jaklitsch who, even as a committed Sturmführer sidestepped the brutal Aryan idealism of the VGL for his friend of many years. But there was another, far weightier, directive which ultimately saved Father and his family. This will be explained in the chapter called *Veliko Mraševo*.

The VGL was encouraged by the first reaction of the general population especially from the youth in which it had such a devoted following. Resistance had been expected from the better educated bourgeoisie of the city, the clergy and especially from the older generation of farmers who professed a sentimental attachment to their land and their way of life, hard as it was. These were the reasons the VGL insisted (at the Berlin meeting) that the re-settlement be accomplished at "the earliest possible date" to prevent any resistance from taking hold in the enclave.

The VGL, however, did not foresee their plans would be hampered by the occupying Italians, Axis members and close allies of the Reich. This unexpected problem became apparent very early on and is described by Frensing on page 64:

"..the VGL pressed for the earliest possible re-settlement in view of the difficulties already experienced with the occupying Italians, i.e. the disarming of their militia. Given this, the three VGL leaders sought to exploit the critical attitude of the Gottscheer population regarding the Italian position toward the ethnic group. Since this attitude had developed into outright mistrust, the VGL wished, through a rapid resettlement, to take advantage of this situation and thereby capture an unsuspecting population by surprise."

The "critical attitude of the Gottscheer population regarding the Italian position toward the ethnic group" was, in reality, the result of a campaign by the VGL to turn the population against the occupier. The VGL believed this was necessary because they had become aware that the Italians were, from the start, against removing the population from their occupied territories and wished the Gottscheer to remain in place.

Commenting on this is Dr. Heinrich Wollert, then the German official responsible for the re-settlement of ethnic Germans out of the Ljubljana province. Dr. Wollert, in his memoirs dated March 27, 1958, recalls the meeting in Vienna on April 20, 1941 between Hitler and Count Ciano, the Foreign Minister of Italy, where Hitler announced the resettling of the Gottscheer:

"The Italian side, as I remember, was reluctant to agree to the re-settlement plan. Obviously so, because the Italian side realized that this region was densely populated with ethnic Germans and, therefore, was afraid that a resettlement would produce a vacuum. Even then there were indications of Yugoslav partisan activities, and the Italians were concerned that, in an empty area such as the enclave, the Partisans would dig in and cause military difficulties for the Italian occupying army".

That the Italians were not sympathetic toward the VGL is clear from a report sent by Alfred Busbach, Stabsführer for Organization and Propaganda, to SS-Obersturmbannführer (Lieutenant Colonel) Hannes Wagner. Busbach was the head of " Der Wachsturm", (the watchgroup) an intelligence unit within the VGO to deal with reluctant or hostile elements. The group had members implanted strategically in seven of the twenty five Stürme, with each member tasked to report any deviant behavior of their comrades or the population. Busbach writes:

"In the month of May 1941 there came to us a totally German-friendly Italian Lieutenant Carlo Aglieta. His attitude is evident from the fact that he informed me of a secret letter written by Emilio Grazioli, High Commissioner for occupied

ASSIGNMENT AND PREPARATION

Slovenia, to Sisgoreo, the commissioner of the local civil authority. In this letter, Grazioli directs Sisgoreo to construct sound arguments with which to dissolve the VGO as an organization. Through timely awareness of this letter we were able to prevent Sisgoreo acting on the directive by taking the issue to the Reichsführer [Himmler]".

Frensing in *Die Umsiedlung*, on pg. 43 adds a further perspective:

"The Italians, in their handling of the re-settlement question, went even one step further. It was apparent that Italian authorities tried, in the spring of 1941, to persuade the Gottscheer not to resettle. To influence these ethnic Germans, a German-Italian newspaper was to be founded."

And to stop the activities of the Italians, "Dr. Stier informed his foreign office that this position of the Italians was viewed as an unfriendly act and should as such be presented to Italian government. Thereafter, the interference of the Italians in the preparation effort of the VGL ceased."

The differences between the Italian and German sides continued throughout the resettlement negotiations which began in Rome in the beginning of July 1941 and ended with the signing of the contract on August 31, 1941.

The effectivity date was set for October 1, 1941.

Until then [the signing of the contract] (according to SS-Oberführer Creutz.)

"the Italian side persisted in their request for a population exchange between the Gottscheer and the affected Slovene. This caused some difficulties between the Italians and the Germans. Finally, on June 18, 1941 the RKFDV ordered the German negotiators to work up a plan for a one-sided resettlement of the Gottscheer." [57]

(Hitler had never intended a population exchange. This is clear from the *Ingathering Directive of the Führer,* dated 7 October, 1939, as formulated by Himmler. It is summarized by Frensing in *Die Umsiedlung* on pg. 28.

"From the areas annexed to the Reich, the non-German population was to be moved out and as 'foreigners' either brought to the Altreich for work or pushed into the 'Generalgouvernement'. [Holding area for 'undesirables' in occupied Poland.]. Ethnic Germans are to be resettled into the annexed provinces of the Reich."

The VGL stuck to its plan of keeping the resettlement date and the destination in the Reich Top Secret. Instead, it attacked the source of any resistance with a wave

---

57   *Die Umsiedlung, pg 44.*

of propaganda in meetings and in the Gottscheer Zeitung. In a series of articles it confronted the rumors circulating throughout the villages and in the city:

"In questions regarding the resettlement, only the instructions and directions of the VGL should be believed. Utterances of others are not authoritative". [58]

"Those who continue to fall for every dumb rumor and all empty talk should take note...". [59]

"From the Office of Organization and Propaganda:

"The Roman Catholic priest Kraker of Rieg is, in the villages of the hinterland, disseminating irresponsible propaganda against the VGL ...". [60]

"As was recently discovered, our older population is becoming, through especially tenacious and fully invented rumors related to our pending resettlement, confused and frightened...." [61]

This ever widening opinion forced the VGL to make the first exception to their existing line. Seven weeks after the decision was made, the resettlement date was finally announced in the GZ of July 10, 1941.

"In line with our position and resistance against various bleak rumors, it is stated that the date for the resettlement is set for this coming autumn."

The announcement of the resettlement date was also prompted by another imponderable. It came, mid July, in the form of a pamphlet from the Gottschee Area War Council of the Communist Party of Slovenia:

"Gottscheer Worker and Farmer!

"The National-Socialistic leaders and their little Gottscheer deputies wish, prior to their own final collapse, to also bring the Gottscheer people into misfortune. They demand that you leave your Gottscheer land in which you have lived peacefully for 600 years. They wish to make a war profit at your expense.

"Many of you, who even last year believed these servants of Hitler, have recognized their criminal intention and now resist resettlement. How right you are! They wish to resettle you on the soil and estates stolen from Slovene farmers and workers whom they drove into the unknown without any of their possessions.

---

58   GZ, May 1941.
59   GZ, June 12, 1941.
60   GZ, June 26, 1941.
61   GZ, July 7, 1941.

ASSIGNMENT AND PREPARATION

"The entire resettlement is a crime against the Gottschee people!

"Rightfully, the indigenous nationals will view you as intruders, as allies of Fascist robbers, as thieves of foreign soil and the fruit of some one else's toil. They will set on fire the houses in which you settle, at every step they will slay you and haunt you incessantly. And when the German imperialism is crushed, the rightful owners of the land on which they want you to settle will drive you out. Others will have settled in Gottschee and you will be empty handed, without land, without money, without homes. Toward such a destiny your own leaders, the agents of Hitler, lead you.

"Gottscheer Workers and Farmers. This is the last moment for you to take your future into your own hands!"

The pamphlet shocked the population and generated a rumor wave which seriously damaged the credibility of the VGL while giving support to those who counseled against resettling. Shocked because the pamphlet revealed for the first time to an already skeptical population that they will not be resettled to an area inside old Germany proper, but to a place in the annexed Slovenia from which the Slovene population was to be driven out to make room for the Gottscheer. The rumor disclosed the place to be the border area surrounding Brežice, (Rann), only 40 km in a northeasterly direction.

With this pamphlet, the VGL was pressured to deviate from its dogmatic line to keep the population in the dark.

"It now realized that it did not adequately consider the psychological imponderables and had judged the national discipline of the Gottscheer too high". [62]

The following points describe the political, technical and psychological elements of the resettling task that was given to the VGL by Hitler, then the most powerful man in Europe:

1: Much of the political aspect, the conversion of the population to the National-Socialist ideology had already been accomplished prior to 1941. This effort had been started by Dr. Hans Arko in 1927, the first to bring this ideology into the enclave. [63] It was taken to new heights by the VGL in the years after 1938.

---

62   Die Umsiedlung, pg. 74.
63   H. Arko, Gedächnisschrift, 1941.

2: Many of the technical aspects of the resettlement had already been addressed by the VGL before Hitler gave them the assignment on April 26, 1941. By then, the VGL had already formed the VGO, the structure of an organization capable of running the resettlement process, since it believed that in the event the enclave was not annexed in a future conflict between the Reich and Yugoslavia, it was likely to be resettled. They had been preparing themselves for this ever since their meeting with the German consul in Ljubljana on November 6, 1939 where, according to Frensing in *Die Umsiedlung,* pg. 25:

"..they pledged their subordination to the Reich. Even with regard to a re-settlement, the interest of the ethnic group must stand behind the interest of the entire [German] nation".

3: The VGL was fully aware of the psychological aspects of the resettlement; it being the main challenge to their task. Having made the Gottscheer believers in National-Socialist ideology was one thing. But to pry them loose from their land was quite another. The challenge, therefore, was to convert the Gottscheer from love of their land to love of the Führer. And if the slogan: The Führer is calling us home to the Reich" was not followed willingly, the VGL was prepared to use the forms of persuasion that had been successfully used in South Tyrol on which they had been adequately briefed during their stay at the SS-Headquarters in Berlin. Including the Abyssinia card, which ultimately convinced any wavering South Tyrolean to submit to pressure and agree to resettle.

Having been tasked for this mission personally by the Führer, the VGL was not going to fail.

Perhaps the most pressing task of the VGL after May 22, the day the resettlement decision was made public, was to take the ideological indoctrination of the leaders of the Mannschaften and the Youth Groups to a higher level. All of the youth and most of the men and women above twenty one had already been converted to National Socialism in prior years. But now further indoctrination was necessary to arm the entire leadership hierarchy under the VGL with the ideological weapons needed to persuade the resisting and hesitant to sign the option to move.

To accomplish this indoctrination, a series of leadership training camps were held in various strategic locations in the enclave. The Sturmführers and their squad leaders were indoctrinated and trained by Wilhelm Lampeter the Mannschaftsführer;

ASSIGNMENT AND PREPARATION

the Hitler Youth leaders and their respective deputies by Jugendführer Richard Lackner. Ludwig Kren was the leader responsible for the camps.

Each of these week-long or ten day training courses spanned or ended on a Sunday when there was conducted a rally called a "Morgenfeier", a morning celebration. It was held to coincide with religious services in the local church to limit or prevent attendance at Mass, thus effectively isolating the clergy. To make it into an impressive propaganda event, Sturm units and their associated Youth Groups from surrounding villages were called in to take part in mass marches through the City and the nearest villages. [64]

The first such training course was held by the twenty two year old Youth Leader Richard Lackner (b. 14 August, 1919) during the week from June 4 to June 10 on the sports field near Gottschee City. Lackner was assisted by twenty year old camp leader Ludwig Kren (b. 17 December, 1920). A total of 120 Hitler Youth leaders took part. The *GZ* of June 12 reports on the event, the rousing speeches and the daily march led by drums and marching songs through the City. Training alternated between "Weltanschauung" and fitness training. "Much have they experienced and much was learned to pass on to their comrades" reported the *GZ*.

Another Youth leadership camp was held from August 21 to 31. Again it was conducted by Lackner, with help from the twenty five year old Lampeter and Ludwig Kren. The camp called Alttabor, was just outside the village of Moschnitze. The "Morgenfeier" took place on Sunday August 31. That camp also ended in a mass rally with Sturms 19, 20, 22, 23 and their youth groups taking part.

On June 22, 1941, Hitler terminated the non-aggression pact by invading the Soviet Union. After this day, the three million strong German army and additional armies from its Axis allies, made rapid progress deep into the Soviet Union.

The *GZ* of June 26 reports in banner headlines:

"The Reich leads young Europe in the crusade against the Jewish-Bolshevik nest of conspiracy in Moscow."

This event greatly emboldened the VGL since it now could freely include Communism as one of the "Universal Evils" confronting National-Socialism in their leadership courses.

---

64   *GZ, July 24, 1941.*

THE BELLS RING NO MORE

Lampeter conducted his own week-long leadership training course for the Sturmführers and their Zugführers (subordinate squad leaders) from July 17 to July 24. The "Morgenfeier" took place on Sunday July 20. It ended in a rally and mass march through the City.

To make the "propaganda marches" impressive, the units of Sturm 1, 2, 7 and 12 including their associated youth groups were brought to the camp for this purpose on Sunday July 20. [65] The purpose of this march and the other six mass rallies in key parts of the enclave was to demonstrate unity not only to the reluctant Gottscheer but also to the Italians and Slovene. [66]

Prior to the training, the *GZ* of July 17 printed a rousing front page appeal by the Mannschaftsführer to the population:

"Wir wollen heim ins Reich.

"The Führer calls us home and we follow with a joyous heart. .... Reason alone does not speak for our return. It is love for the Führer, the belief in Germany and the call of our blood. ... We young National-Socialists are proud to be Germans and wish to be fighters for Führer and Volk. We wish to be part of the Sonnenvolk [sun nation] on earth from which we stem. We are born as fighters and rulers, not to be servants.

"We want to return home to the Reich".

The training was to solidify the commitment of the leaders to Adolf Hitler, to the VGL and the resettlement and in turn enable them to pass this commitment to the ranks below. With this, the VGL put to use the existing hierarchal structure, developed under the cover of the Kulturbund since 1939, through which it was able to reach every member of the population in each of the villages and Gottschee City.

The training camp was purposely located on the sporting ground near the City to influence its bourgeois citizenry, the most reluctant part of the population, through a massive show of strength and determination. Lampeter writes about the success of the camp in his confidential *Lagerbrief* report of July 1941.

"Finally I mention the powerful propagandistic impression on the population created by the camp activities and the propaganda marches through the city and surrounding villages". [67]

The objectives of the leadership indoctrination were spelled out to the participants in advance by Lampeter:

---

65   *GZ, July 24, 1941.*
66   *Die Umsiedlung, pg 45.*
67   *Die Umsiedlung, pg 70-71.*

ASSIGNMENT AND PREPARATION

"The imminent Resettlement will above all, deeply affect the internal composure of our people. It is therefore especially urgent to apply everything that will solidify the inner capability of the responsible men of our national group and through thorough ideological schooling strengthen such capability or, where absent, establish one..." [68]

At the conclusion of the training, Lampeter requested that each attendee submit a report. He insisted that each participant write an essay, describing the experience and what he learned at the camp. One such reply was in his "Final Report".

"The camp gave me a 100% conviction and satisfaction that we have, in our young leadership in the Gottschee land, the right men as our leaders. Men who are capable not only to lead us in the large and important resettlement task, but who are also capable of resettling spiritually into the great ideal German Reich of Adolf Hitler".

And after he received the replies, Lampeter sent a confidential letter to the participants with objectives that he reveals in his introductory paragraph:

"From your replies I notice how deeply the experience of camaraderie at the training camp on "Weltanschauung" (worldview) has affected you. However, I also notice how necessary it is that I write you this Report; a letter which will keep the experience fresh in your minds and which you will consult whenever you wish to be refreshed about the core questions and guiding statements regarding our contemplative views of the world. I know that in these few days, so much has been forced into you, that it is nearly impossible to comprehend and keep it all. The superficial impressions and experiences, however, do not disappear so fast. I will, therefore, write little about them."

After the above introduction, Lampeter summarized the training and at the end repeated selected impressions written by the attendees. Apart from describing the superiority of the German race - "Sonnenvolk auf Erden" – (sun-race on earth) and glorifying Adolf Hitler as the foremost role model, the main aim of this indoctrination was to give the ranks the ideological weapons in the battle against "the universalistic perception of the world".

"The Propagation Theory [dissemination] is the cornerstone of the National-Socialist Weltanschauung. We see here how much the universalistic worldview - Liberalism, Communism, Catholicism - differ from National-Socialism. All these universalistic perceptions claim that all people are equal. These perceptions all have their start in a lower ranked race which attempted to conquer humanity through equalization.

---

68   *Die Umsiedlung, pg 70.*

"Until now, the creators, founders and defenders of all popular universalistic worldviews were predominantly Jews. The Propagation Theory therefore is the cornerstone of the National-Socialist worldview, since through it all other universalistic views will come to nothing as the German person learns to grasp life, nature and its laws."

By discrediting each of the three versions in his universalistic worldview, Lampeter sought to instill a fundamental strategy for battling any opposition to the resettlement. Leading this strategy was the concept of German racial superiority, hammered unrelentingly into the psyche of the Gottscheer population at rallies throughout the enclave and the weekly *Gottscheer Zeitung*. 'Was this racial superiority not evident in the successes of the Third Reich which in only eight short years transformed Germany from a defeated to the most powerful nation in Europe? And now, in 1941, was it not well underway to conquer Soviet Russia, the enemy of civilization?' Nearly every subsequent issue of the Zeitung reports yet another major battle won at the eastern front as it had reported since April 1941 on successes elsewhere.

The concept of racial superiority found easy acceptance within the enclave; it resonated there even before Hitler came to power in 1933. Dr. Arko began to proclaim it in 1927 and added to it the disdain for the "inferior Slovene" who denied the Gottscheer access to the German language and forced them to learn their "inferior language". But Lampeter and his VGL evolved the disdain into hatred as part of their overall strategy to convince the Gottscheer to move to "The Reich" and thereby forever become united with the other members of the super race.

The groups opposing the resettlement were made to fit one or more of the three versions and were attacked accordingly.

Liberalism, the major opponent in the "universalistic Weltanschauung" was associated by Lampeter with the better educated bourgeoisie, which saw itself as the cultural and social elite of the Gottscheer, having a broader and more seasoned perspective of the world than the farmers of the enclave. Included were Dr. Arko and the Reverend Eppich, the leaders the VGL replaced in 1939. This elite, living mostly in the city, resented and deeply mistrusted the young upstart fanatics with their militant ideological attitude ever since they had come to power.

ASSIGNMENT AND PREPARATION

The VGL mistrust of the "elite" was replaced by open hostility when it discovered that members of this 'liberal' opposition were conspiring against the resettlement. The conspiracy is described in the letter Alfred Busbach, the head of "*Der Wachsturm*", wrote to the SS on the resistance revealed to him by Aglieta in May 1941:

"Aglieta mentioned that he was told by the Slovene dean of the Kočevje city parish, Peter Flajnik that an action against the resettlement was in process. In the Reich, this action is led by Director Widmer in Vienna, Professor Ramor in Graz and Professor Jonke in Klagenfurt. [All of them Gottscheer living abroad.] In Gottschee the leaders of this action are the Catholic priests Schauer of Nesseltal, Kraker of Rieg and Eppich of Mitterdorf. Working hand in hand with these priests is the former Volksgruppenführer Dr. Hans Arko, the Chairman of the Savings and Loan Bank Josef Hönigmann, the wine merchant Robert Ganslmayer and the carpenter Josef Kraker. ..... .

" And when I was informed that the mentioned individuals were all preparing to travel to the Reich and on behalf of all Gottscheer submit a memorandum informing Reichsführer Himmler that the Gottscheer were against resettling, I immediately contacted an organization [?] in the Reich that this was not the case.

"What they actually did in the Reich is not clear to me. But after their return, their propaganda against the resettlement continued."

The above was sufficient reason for the VGL to start an active campaign to undermine and discredit the bourgeoisie, particularly the former leadership. It was aimed to negate and eliminate their disturbing influence. Publicly named was Dr. Arko, a committed and self professed National-Socialist since 1927, a fact which the VGL conveniently omitted to mention.

Communism, another part of the "universalistic worldview" had no direct influence in the enclave. However, Communism was now, since the invasion of the Soviet Union on June 22, described as the universal enemy not only of the Reich but of all western civilization, an enemy the victorious armies of the Reich were defeating in great victories and would soon destroy completely. This was hammered home relentlessly through the GZ and at all rallies throughout the enclave.

More directly threatening was the "negative influence of America on the Gottschee population". American capitalism, another version of the "capitalistic/

liberal universalistic worldview", which like Communism was controlled by "international Jewry", was seeping into the enclave via relatives who had emigrated there in large numbers around the turn of the century. In 1941, there were more Gottscheer in America than in the enclave, most retaining a sentimental attachment to the "homeland" and urging the family there to stay. Lampeter in his *Lagerbrief*[69] Report had this to say:

"America is the sand where German blood oozes away. Thirty million Germans moved there and in the second or third generation they are no longer German. They all became Americans. Of the 30 million, only 4 million are still aware of their Germanness. Strange world views rule in this land. The Jew has the power in his hand. It is the Dollar hunger that lured the German being to America and became his ruin. The majority of German immigrants never obtained ownership of the Dollar and had to spend a miserable life in some gray hole wishing they could return. But of these, the relatives back home do not hear."

"Any emigration through which German blood is lost must be stopped. Today the flow of German blood is in the opposite direction; no longer out from the German nation, but returning home to the Great German Reich."

Catholicism, the third part of the "universalistic worldview" was seen as the most dangerous opponent of the VGL. In his letter to the SS, Busbach describes the priests preaching (from the pulpit) against the resettlement claiming it to be an undertaking of young rascals, have-nots with nothing to lose. The settlement area land was described by them as unproductive, swampy and cursed.

Opposition by the priests to the resettlement had spread to such an extent that it forced the VGL to a direct and open attack in the June 26, issue of the *Gottscheer Zeitung*:

"The Roman-Catholic cleric K. [Josef Kraker] of Rieg has, in recent times and in various parts of the Hinterland, been recklessly disseminating propaganda against the Volksgruppenführung [VGL]...... .

"The mentioned clerical person has been insulting leading men in our ethnic group by referring to them as 'snotboys' and refers to the *GZ* as a 'Jewpage'. He produces false assertions against the resettlement and with great effort is trying to persuade members of the ethnic group not to resettle. He [Kraker] requests that the

---

69 Lampeter, *Lagerbrief,* page 5.

people wait for the outcome of the war and thereby awakens doubts about the final victory of the Axis. We await the intervention of church officials to put a halt to this peculiar doing. This even more so since through such intervention, conflicts of conscience, awakened in our pious people by this incomprehensible doing, will be stopped."

This was followed one week later with a reprint of the graveside eulogy by the Reverend Josef Eppich for the recently deceased August Schauer, also a priest resisting the resettlement:

"Come what may, we will not surrender our faith, love of home and mother tongue. These words I defend to my death. What pains me deeply is the observation that in recent times, our people began to swerve from this belief and the attachment of the younger generation to their Gottscheer homeland started to waver. From this love of homeland, I derive my position against the resettlement, a position shared by my spiritual brothers." [70]

The VGL printed the attack on Kraker and the eulogy of Josef Eppich, as a part of a campaign to advertise an open split in the clergy. By showing that the priests were not unanimously opposed to the resettlement, it aimed to negate their influential role among the population.

Support for the resettlement by the clergy was published on July 31 in the *GZ*. It came from the Reverend Heinrich Wittine:

"Why are we leaving? 'This is a superfluous question' you will say. We Germans belong together like father, mother and child; besides, the Führer is calling us and he knows why. .... What the Führer knows and is capable of he has already demonstrated.

"The thought, that an injustice will be done where we are going, is groundless; was not the Führer's hand of friendship rejected so often?"

Another supporter was the Reverend Alois Krisch. His defense was written post facto in the winter of 1947/48 and later reproduced in *the Dokumentation der Vertreibung (1961)*. His lengthy justification leaves little doubt about his position, since his opinion mirrors that of the VGL and his blinkered view denies their politics:

"No, Nazis they were not, even if they are now accused of having been such; no, of the Nazi party they knew little and understood it not. They saw only the pure part of German (without any Party coloring) ......!"

His personal justification was to follow his flock:

"I am your priest. If the majority of our people leave, so will I. And if they remain, I will remain."

---

70   *GZ, July 3 & 10, 1941.*

Contrary to his calling as a priest, he decides to follow, not lead. And he eases his and the conscience of those in his flock who questioned the forced displacement of Slovene:

"Many of the [Gottscheer] people ... had great reservation when it became known that a large part of Slovenia will be emptied for us. ..... But as their spiritual adviser I told them to ignore such scruples; the whole affair is only an exchange between two states; the individual is not responsible."

The VGL had managed to divide the clergy and thereby reduce their influence on the population. But the priests who continued in their opposition created much doubt about leaving. Their resistance, together with that of the bourgeoisie, jeopardized the unanimity of the resettlement sought by the VGL to such an extent that ultimately the SS Resettlement Authority was forced to intervene to prevent it from becoming a humiliation.

After the VGL realized that the cause of this growing resistance was the bourgeoisie and the clergy, it started an intense effort to discredit both. Defame each and thereby eliminate their influence on the farmers and landed villagers, the majority of the population of the enclave whose acceptance of the option was the key to the success of the resettlement.

"The tactics used to discredit the opposition were designed to fit each of the two groups. The bourgeoisie is unrelentingly attacked in the *Gottscheer Zeitung* and at meetings throughout the enclave as being 'philistines of a capitalistic coinage' and other similar defamations to isolate it from the predominantly rural population.

"With respect to the clergy, finer methods are applied. Within the VGL 'Catholicism' is viewed as a 'universalistic Weltanschauung' which must be eradicated, however outwardly it practiced restraint given the strong attachment of the population to its clergy. In public, therefore, the split among the clergy is exploited in line with 'divide et impera' and through this, neutralize the influence of the priests." [71]

With the indoctrination of its leadership completed, the Mannschaften trained and the opposition identified, the VGL is now in a position to systematically eliminate the spreading resistance to the resettlement.

---

71 Die Umsiedlung, pg 85, 86.

ASSIGNMENT AND PREPARATION

As a reminder of this, Lampeter issued a command in the July 24 issue of the *GZ*:

"Order of the Mannschaftsführer:"

"I have trained all Sturm and Squad leaders in Weltanschauung and Sport matters and instructed them on the subject of keeping order such that the leaders of the Stürme are, from now on, capable of performing their work at a higher level than up to now. All Sturm men have to attend to their scheduled duties, since otherwise they will have to bear the consequences."

Chapter 13

Completing the Task

After Sturmführer Jaklitsch and his squad leaders returned from the camp on July 24, they immediately started a training program for all members of the Masern Sturm. Meetings were held in the large Jaklitsch guest room or in the "Reichshaus", the abandoned house at Number 6 where the Sturmführer reiterated with fervor and conviction what he had learned at the camp. "Blind loyalty to the Führer and to follow his call to resettle home in the Reich". Parallel political meetings were held by leaders of the boys unit of the Gottscheer Hitler Youth (14-20) the Pimpfe (7-13) and their girl equivalents in both groups.

Unflinching discipline was instilled through military type training on our sporting grounds next to the cemetery, exercises which always ended in a march back to the village, past the admiring glances of the women, the older folks and the very young standing in doorways or watching the final display of formation dismissal on the square in front of the church. Such displays had been forbidden when the enclave was still under Yugoslavia, but had been done clandestinely just the same. But now, with the VGL acting on behalf of the mighty Reich, all was not only openly possible but mandated. And the occupying Italians, soon to be rid of this troublesome lot, had no desire to interfere.

The farmer K.R. from Slovenska Vas, (Windischdorf), writes in his memoir of March 1958:
"… There began an intense propaganda campaign for the resettlement which was introduced with the slogan: Heim in's Reich, [Home to the Reich]".

"This propaganda came to us from our own circles, from individuals who functioned as the so called Führers of the Gottscheer without obtaining the approval of the population. Persons who since 1939 had been occupied mainly with improving our agriculture. These Führers organized meetings in all parts of Gottschee and made the resettlement palatable to the assembled villagers."

Throughout the summer and fall of 1941, the propaganda machine of the VGL was running in high gear. A review of the weekly *Gottscheer Zeitung* of that period shows each issue with bold lettered headlines announcing new victories of the unstoppable German armies and reprints in full of the speeches of Hitler, Göring and other leaders of the Reich. All these headlines are accompanied by rallying appeals, pronouncements and speeches from Lampeter, Lackner, Busbach and other members of the VGL. The constant in all this is the reminder of the duty to the Führer which the Gottscheer, as loyal Germans, must exercise at all times.

The *Gottscheer Zeitung* (Herbert Erker, Editor) also describes in great detail the training and propaganda events held throughout the enclave. Initially, many of these events conflicted with businesses in the city and to a lesser degree, with farming activities, causing frequent absenteeism. The VGL addressed this problem in the August 7 issue of the *GZ*:

"Command of the Mannschaftsführer."

"It is repeatedly reported that many employed comrades are not standing in our formations. All German comrades, male or female, who are in some sort of employment situation, must report immediately to the local formation leader, so that they can be placed into the formations in which they belong.

"All employers are herewith notified that they do not have the right, for selfish reasons, to keep their employees out of the ranks of our units or to keep them in any way from their required service."

"The Mannschaftführer, W. Lampeter."

And, in the August 14 issue, a sterner warning:

"Command of the Mannschaftführer."

"I have noticed that some members of our nation and even members of the formations attend our larger functions and performances only after repeated and energetic urging from the comrades of the Wachzug, (Surveillance Unit). This is totally unacceptable. The Wachzug [in 1941 under A. Busbach, 211 members strong] was formed to have a Security Unit responsible for such events. It is therefore clear that orders from comrades of the Wachzug are to be followed regardless of rank or position.

"Comrades of the Wachzug carry as identification a black bordered Swastika armband and a star on their shoulder strap."

"The Mannschaftführer, W. Lampeter."

The above was a warning to the "capitalistic - liberal" bourgeoisie in the City as well as to all others to attend the functions announced in the Zeitung; all such reminders closing with "appearance is public duty", "your duty to the Führer". In addition to enforcement by the Wachzug, this obligation was also enforced by the

COMPLETING THE TASK

Sturmführer who had direct access to the men and women in the ranks and indirectly to all others living in the village.

Delinquents or resisters who continued in their unacceptable behavior were taken before the Mannschaftsgericht (Militia court) for a hearing and judgment. Of course, this court had no legal standing as such, but all defendants knew that the VGL court was now the enforcer for the Third Reich, the most powerful and seemingly invincible nation in Europe and therefore they had little choice but to comply. Besides, they had no one else to turn to. The Italian occupiers were in charge of civil administration, but had no wish to interfere. And since they had already been labeled by the VGL as hostile to the Gottscheer, they would not be sympathetic.

The Sturmführer simply sidelined the clergy by holding training exercises or information meetings during the times scheduled for church services. "Public Duty" and "Duty to the Führer" were convenient excuses now given to the priests by a cowed and coerced population for staying away.

The farmer R.K. mentions the gigantic rallies held in strategic villages throughout the enclave. The VGL called them "Morning Celebrations" and the *Zeitung* announced the date and the place and all specifics, including who must attend and when. "Attendance is Public Duty" was always added at the end.

The rallies emulated the rallies in the Reich and followed the formula that had worked so well there. The object was to demonstrate unity, strength and commitment and to persuade the uncommitted to join.

The rallies were follow-on to Lampeter's leadership training. Eight such mass rallies were held throughout the enclave during July, August and October, each attended by up to nine individual Sturm units, its Youth Groups and related village population, usually totaling around a thousand participants. All were written up in great detail in the next issue of the Zeitung, with the rousing speeches repeated verbatim down to the last "Heim ins Reich", …"Ein Volk, ein Reich, ein Führer", …"Heil Hitler", …"Sieg Heil". All with the objective of converting the population from "Love of the Land" to "Love of the Führer".

The July 24 issue of the *Zeitung* gives the specifics for the "Morgenfeier" to be held in Lichtenbach:

"The Mannschaftführer orders the holding of a morning celebration to be held on Sunday, July 27 in Lichtenbach. To this celebration, Stürme 3, 5, 8, 9, 10, 15, and 21 as well as their youth groups and women's branches must form up in ranks at 9.45 in the morning.

"The other Volksgenossen who are not in the above ranks will be in Lichtenbach at the same time. After the ceremony, there will be a comradely gathering and presentations by youth groups until late into the afternoon."

In its July 31 issue, the *GZ* devotes nearly two of its six pages to describing the event. Over 1,000 people from seven adjacent villages assemble in the village square and on command of Staabführer Busbach march to the square in front of the church where Mannschaftsführer Lampeter receives Busbach's report. The swastika flag is run up, youth leader Lackner recites a poem, a song rises high.

"The Mannschaftführer speaks:"

He speaks of "..... duty to Deutschland and its great mission. The free being thinks not about himself but about the whole; not for the moment, but for eternity. A new faith, given to us by the Führer, is waved to us by our German flag in the performance of our duty.... ."

Battle songs and the revised Gottscheer anthem ring out. The original version had been re-rhymed by the VGL to bring the new national-socialist spirit into the old melody. Key parts are: "... we are returning to the fatherland, the country of our ancestors" ...and ... we call into the young day: Ein Volk, ein Reich, ein Führer!"

The assembly in front of the church is over. The rest of the day brings sporting performances by the youth and dances and songs from the girls. And, at three in the afternoon, they assemble again at the flag in front of the church and words from Richard Lackner, the Jugendführer ring out:

".... We are on the way to a new future and one feels that a new spirit has entered the enclave. We are all of one conviction, one belief and know only: Führer command, we will follow....!

"Again, all eyes greet the flag being brought down. After short words from the Mannschaftsführer, songs of the nation rise again. [Deutschland, Deutschland über alles, ... Die Fahne hoch, die Reihen dicht geschlossen] ".

The morning celebration has come to an end.

COMPLETING THE TASK

The July 31 issue of the *GZ* also announces the next such event, this one to take place in Masern:

"On Sunday the third of August 1941 at ten o'clock, the memorial stone for the fallen comrade Hans Michitsch will be unveiled in Masern. The Mannschaftführer orders the following to attend this ceremony: Sturm and Youth Groups 1, 2, 4, 8, 13, 14 and 24. These groups are therefore excused from their usual Sunday afternoon exercises. All leaders must have their units standing in formation in the Village of Masern at 9.40."

In an article taking up the entire front page of the August 7 issue, Herbert Erker, the editor of the *GZ* reports on the event. I also took part and remember it well:

As ordered, Sturm units and Youth groups from seven villages were on time and in formation, lined up on the village square at 9.40 as ordered. At the end of four columns of 39 men of Sturm 13 was the Hitler Youth of Masern; in all 30 boys and 29 girls. Sturm 13 was named as "Sturm Hans Michitsch" to honor the comrade fallen for the Reich when in fact, he was really a deserter from the army to which he had sworn his allegiance.

I stood in the Pimpfe formation, boys aged seven to fourteen. Like the others, dressed in the obligatory long sleeved white shirt, short black trousers and white socks up to the knee. (The girls wore a black skirt covering the knees). Black belt, supported by a black shoulder strap across the chest. On the head a black cap fronting a brass swastika and on the left arm the swastika arm band, held in place by safety pins. The uniform of the Stürmer was similar except for the riding breeches and riding boots.

At Staabführer Busbach's shrill whistle, all units snap to attention. Franz Jaklitsch orders his Sturm to do a 'Right Turn' and 'Forward March' to the sports grounds next to the cemetery. Our Youth Leader, the nineteen year old Herbert Primosch does the same and we follow. The girls, under their leader Anna Dejak directly behind us. After them, in appropriate order, march the other six Sturm units, followed by their associated Youth Groups until all were lined up at the sports grounds where an armed honor guard had been receiving the formations. The field is flanked by tall flagpoles, each with its swastika flag hanging limp in the still morning air. According to Erker, over 800 comrades took part.

The parents of Hans, his brother Franz and Anna Parthe former fiancé of Hans are already at the grave site, together with Lampeter, Richard Lackner and the other members of the VGL. Absent is the Reverend Gliebe who officiated when Hans was buried in a Christian ceremony on April 19. All are standing next to the memorial that replaced the former simple cross. As described by Erker:

"... a massive natural boulder, dug from the ground in the forest by his comrades into which was set a simple marble plate. Under the Gottscheer insignia with the swastika is written: Easter 1941, Sturmmann Hans Michitsch."

"Fanfares, the song '*Listen up Comrade*' and a quotation of Hitler start the ceremony. The Mannschaftsführer speaks:

"What for centuries has been the wish and yearning of the German people has become reality: Ein Volk, ein Reich, ein Führer. For this millions of Germans have fought and also given their lives. They died for the greatness of Germany. .... And today, in victorious campaigns, thousands fall for the honor and greatness of Germany. ... . Never would the Führer have achieved the power, had the death of comrades in ranks weakened his resolve. Their blood solidified the determination of the movement.

"We Gottscheer also could not march into freedom without some sacrifice demanded from us. Four comrades sealed the way to our freedom with their blood. So have you fallen, comrade Hans Michitsch.

"You are dead but not forgotten. You will remain the example and reminder for the fulfillment of the highest duty of your Sturm.

"For us, there must be no higher duty than to work and fight for Germany and if necessary, die for it."

Lampeter had spoken. And Erker continues his report:

"The song: *Ich hat einen Kameraden* [I had a comrade] swells up. No one moved as the Mannschaftsführer placed the wreaths in front of the memorial. A quotation of the Führer is read by Jugendführer Lackner. All sing the anthems of the [German] nation.

"The ceremony is over."

All units march back to the square where they are dismissed. Afterwards, Jaklitsch does a booming business in his guest room but even more so in his large courtyard where tables and benches were set up for the event as they had been in the past for church related festivities.

However, in his *GZ* report of August 7, Erker left out a few items.

The first: - As the event progressed and the cloudless sky being no impediment, the full power of the August sun seemed now directed on to the black cap on my head which was getting very hot.

COMPLETING THE TASK

It was during Lampeter's speech, (carefully reproduced by Erker in the *GZ*), when all went black as I crumbled to the ground. Since everyone was at attention, no one came to my aid and I continued to lie there, in the first row of our unit which, as part of Sturm 13, had the privilege of being first in line to face the cemetery. Apparently not for long since Lampeter was still speaking when I came to, stood up and resumed my position.

Behind the memorial, the villagers of Masern including my parents stood at a respectful distance. And after I got up and recovered, I could not help noticing that Father and Mother were staring in my direction, but I carefully avoided their concerned gaze.

I did not notice but was told later, that there were at least two other youngsters who were felled in the same disgraceful way. Fortunately for me, the other two were pure blooded Aryans, forestalling any potential taunts connecting my weakness to having inferior blood.

The second: - Just after Lampeter had placed the wreaths, the honor guard lifted their rifles to fire a three salvo salute, their echo clearly resonating in the valley. Normally it was a fitting salute to a fallen comrade, but Erker did not mention it in his write up. For good reason.

Immediately after the occupation on April 23, the High Commissioner for the Ljubljana Province, Emilio Grazioli had issued a proclamation forbidding the ownership, by any person, of weapons, munitions or explosives on penalty of death. "The death penalty will be applied also to the head of a household in which such items are found".

Apparently, the Italians got wind of the infraction at the cemetery and during the following week a truckload of soldiers arrived in Masern where they performed a cursory check for weapons in some houses. None were found, since all weapons and ammunitions were carefully hidden in dry places under rocks in the nearby forest. The Italians, of course, knew this and were prepared to find nothing. Obviously they had to respond after some informer reported the violation of Sunday August 3.

This incident and very likely others, prompted the Italians to reissue an expanded version of the Proclamation signed by Grazioli on September 11, 1941. In addition to again proclaiming the death penalty for possession of weapons, this version also described the legal process of judgment and execution and furthermore, announced the hours of a curfew to take place throughout the Province.

The entire Proclamation was published in the September 18 issue of the *GZ*. After that date, Sturm 13 (and surely all others) no longer did training or marches through the village with rifles taken from the trucks of the Yugoslav unit that disbanded in Masern on April 18, 1941. They used wooden replicas instead.

A final, enclave-wide mass rally was held on Sunday October 19 on the sporting grounds of the City. It was a special event called "Der letzte Appell" (the last rally) attended by all 25 Stürme and their youth groups, totaling 1,910 uniformed Gottscheers. This did not including the general population standing on the sidelines. But more on this later.

For me and all the other young, and most of the older folks, these were heady times. Excitement, action and anticipation had replaced the monotony and drabness of our village life. A life in which the only entertainment came from visits by a small traveling circus with a dancing bear, or a merry-go-round, or from gypsies who stayed for a few days.

There had been church festivals during the summer when traveling merchants displayed their wares and trinkets on stands set up on the square. And in the afternoon, on a wooden platform erected on the square or in the Jaklitsch courtyard, there was dancing to the strains of an accordion, the only live music ever heard in the village and this one not improved by the watered-down wine. However, in 1941 there were no more church festivals.

Instead there was disciplined training, there were marches, rallies, sporting events and speeches about a rosy future. There were group meetings, group sing-alongs, group outings, group excursions through the enclave, readings to assembled villagers by visiting young people from other villages, amateur theatrical performances in the large guestroom of the Jaklitsch tavern by groups from other parts of the enclave - and even from abroad.

For the first time we had a very tall maypole on the square, a swastika banner fluttering at the very top. The gleaming trunk, stripped of its bark except for some spiraling bark bands, had a small pine tree fastened to it at the top by the smith who came running from his smithy with white hot iron bands that would tighten the connection between the pole and tree into an inseparable joint. With great fanfare and much encouragement from the surrounding villagers there for the event, the pole was raised in place by uniformed men from the Sturm. And after it was erected, uniformed girls circled around it to tunes of an accordion while holding hands. And there was singing followed by speeches from the youth leaders including

COMPLETING THE TASK

Sturmführer Jaklitsch himself. After that, there was as usual a lot of wine drunk in the large guest room of his place.

And for the first time we celebrated solstice. It had been ordered by Lackner and the prepared bonfire stacks on the highest peaks were to be lit throughout the enclave at an agreed-upon time so that the flames could be seen in other villages. As it had been centuries ago. Böller from the time of the Turks were loaded and set off. And when the songs diminished with the fires, the leaping over the embers proved that we were fit to face the future as part of the Sonnenvolk.

Never had there been such activity in Masern. And it was not only the young who were uplifted by it.

I was proud of my uniform, clothing that not only made me feel I was a part of my peers but also because it let me know that I was finally accepted by them as equal. And when marching with them and singing a rousing song, my crystal clear voice was heard above the others. Dressed in a uniform I treasured in part because it was clothing that finally fit, including the new shoes, custom made for me by Schuscharpasch Ate, our village shoemaker. He was very busy in those days, mostly because Jaklitsch insisted that barefooted youths were not to march in a German formation and that shoes, like the swastika, were part of the uniform. And when taking my footprint, Mother kept asking him to make the shoes larger so that I would not outgrow them all too soon, he winked at me, a secret promise which he kept. These being my first new shoes, all others being hand-me-downs, I visited him often including on the day when he cut the leather, just to make sure he did not forget his unspoken word to make them the size I truly wanted.

As the already cooler days of autumn gave way to the cold, the short pants and short sleeved shirts became inadequate even for the steeled Aryan bodies with pure German blood surging through their veins. To our joy, this was to be rectified with long pants and a long sleeved shirt, both made of tight knit black tricot material. There was elastic at the end of the sleeves and at the bottom pant legs and a string to pull the waist tight; similar to a later day sweat suit. Both to be pulled over the summer uniform when necessary, we were told. Both supplied gratis through the generosity of the Reich.

This happened when all Masern boys and girls of our youth group were taken to the Mannschaft office in the City to be outfitted with the winter uniform. Taken there on horse drawn farming wagons, sitting on improvised benches or clustered on the floor with legs dangling off the platform. Except that for some no longer known tragic reason, I was not among them. And at the next meeting of the groups, all were eagerly showing off their new black outfit, the red swastika armband contrasting the black sleeve. I was the only one shivering with embarrassment and cold.

Father would not have it and together we went to see Herbert Primosch, the leader of my troop who wrote a letter to the provisioning office. The letter gave the reason for my not being part of the initial Masern troop and said that I was worthy to be issued the outfit. Father was to take me to the City to be fitted the next day. But providence continued to play the contrarian.

In the middle of that night I woke up with an uncompromising urge to get to the outhouse and fast. I did remember, however, that the little wooden box mounted on the side wall was empty. The box was the dispenser of the essential pieces of newspaper, cut to size and folded to make the next one appear from the slit. So, in the dark and in haste, my hand flew over the kitchen table where it found a piece of paper. It was the letter.

Father was angry, but mostly at Mother and Mitzi whose task it was to make sure there was paper in the outhouse. After persuasive urging from Mother and much pleading from me, we went to Herbert again who wanted to know what happened to the letter he wrote yesterday. I no longer remember the reason Father gave, except that it was not the truth and that it was not eaten by the dog because we did not have a dog in spite of my persistent pleading over the years. Anyway, we did get another letter, if a less glowing one. And there was again paper in the outhouse to prevent another calamity.

When we finally presented the letter at the depot, there were no uniforms left. Or perhaps it was only my size. I do know that I cried a bit, something totally unbecoming for a member of the Gottscheer Hitler Youth, even if only a half-breed pretending to be a loyal pure blooded Aryan. Father argued to no avail; no more uniforms were on the way, we were told as we left.

But then he took me to a clothing store nearby which had a selection of identical items. With prudent Mother not present, I was allowed to choose the two pieces that fit. I wore both proudly on the way home where Mitzi made pleasing comments and Mother did not ask if they had a larger size.

There was another plus. The youth leader forbade the casual wearing of the new uniform, a gift from the Reich, the best piece of clothing now possessed by most of my peers including myself. The reason was to prevent it from becoming shabby and therefore unworthy of a Reich event. But since mine was not such a gift, having been purchased with my father's money, I was grudgingly allowed to wear it constantly, much to my delight.

COMPLETING THE TASK

The preliminary resettlement contract discussions between the Reich and Italy started mid July, 1941. The contract was a financial arrangement between the two nations.

The Reich wished to use the South Tyrol contract as a model for the Gottscheer project. In that contract, the South Tyrol resettler, in effect, sold his assets to Italy, except that the seller did not receive the funds. Italy used the funds, equivalent to the assets, to re-pay its national debt to Germany. Germany in turn reimbursed the re-settlers with properties in occupied lands.

With respect to the Gottscheer, the Italian side desired, among other items, a link between resettling the Gottscheer and reimbursement to the thousands of Slovene who fled from parts of Styria and Carinthia occupied and annexed by the Reich to the parts occupied by Italy. They fled there after the first big German arrest wave in which about 5,000 Slovene intellectuals were imprisoned and deported. The Slovene who had escaped to Italy now requested Italian citizenship and compensation to which the Italians reacted favorably and requested of the Germans that such reimbursement be included in the contract. To the Germans this was an unacceptable condition; they viewed the Slovene who fled across the border as political criminals.

The initial discussions however, did lead to an outline for a contract to be used in the final negotiations which started in Rome on August 6, 1941. The final Resettlement Contract, signed on August 31, 1941, consisted of 10 Articles and 27 Clarifications.

Of particular interest in this Contract are Articles 5, 6 and 9.

Article 5 states (in part): "The yield from the liquidation of Gottscheer properties, including their deposits in the Savings and Loan Bank in Gottschee City, will be deposited by Italy into Banka d'Italia and subsequently, according to the German-Italian account settlement agreement of 26 September 1934, transferred to Germany". [72]

With Article 5 the Gottscheer, by agreeing to resettle, in effect sold his property to Italy which did not pay him directly but used the funds to repay part of its national debt to the Reich. The Reich, on the other hand, promised to reimburse the resettling Gottscheer with equally valued property which turned out to be the property of

---

[72] *Resettlement Contract. See: http://www.gottschee.de (Geschichte-Dokumente). Also: Die Umsiedlung, pg 152*

Slovenes who were evicted and transferred to slave labor camps. The properties sold were all immobile assets, including personal deposits in the Gottschee City Savings and Loan Bank.

The assessment of this property, now the responsibility of the VGL had started in June with an announcement in the June 5 *GZ*:

"Directive for assessment of forest properties."

"Mannschaftsführer Lampeter gave specific instructions to all Sturmführer for assessing the lumber content of the Gottscheer forests. Since lumber is the main asset of the farmer, it is in the interest of each farmer to accurately caliper the trees. The Sturmführer has received appropriate instruction from experts as well as the blank documents on which to record this and all other property. Since the time is short, the assessment is urgent and the calipering should be made with utmost accuracy. The Resettlement Commission will make spot-checks and false assessments could lead to exclusion from the resettlement."

An announcement in the August 21 *GZ* states that any changes to the submitted assessment must be reported immediately. Any unreported reduction will result in serious consequences to the prospective resettler. (The lumber no longer the property of the resettler). The announcement was prompted by reports reaching the VGL that farmers had sold lumber after they submitted the assessment to the Sturmführer.

Some of the forest owners in Masern came to realize that there was no point in leaving all their valuable lumber to the Italians and found a willing buyer in Rudolf Tschinkel, who with his brother Albert owned and managed the Masern sawmill. The single Rudolf lived with his mother at No. 12 while Albert with wife and three children lived at No. 30. The brothers were adamantly against the resettlement and were willing to say so to anyone wanting to listen. This put them in conflict with Jaklitsch who became their bitter enemy, one who did his best to negate their influence and isolate them from the villagers. In this he was only partly successful.

The two Tschinkel brothers and their father before them had been respected employers over decades for many a villager and even the forceful Jaklitsch was unable to break the established bonds. Due to this, the lumber transactions took place in spite of efforts by Jaklitsch to stop them; he only slowed them with threats that they were jeopardizing their resettlement. But clandestine transactions continued, if now under the cover that the lumber was traded for boards from the saw mill to crate possessions for transport during the resettling. All the VGL could do was issue appeals that any reduction to previously claimed assets be reported.

Legally, the villagers were entitled to sell their property since they had not yet signed any transfer papers and believed the lumber was theirs to sell until they left. Or so they were told by the crafty Tschinkel brothers who recognized an opportunity when they saw one.

Rudolf selected the best trees in the parcel of a farmer and each tree was calipered separately by two men for its diameter. One man represented Rudolf; the other represented the farmer, a procedure suggested by Rudolf to make sure there was no error. Except that Rudolf chose two of his trusted Slovene workers to do the measuring and instructed them in a secret procedure for which he would pay them well and which in turn would produce maximum benefit for him.

As each man yelled out his number, Rudolf and the farmer separately recorded the measurement made by their own man in their own log. Often the measurements differed, especially on superb specimens. But instead of a recheck, Rudolf and the farmer agreed on an average which unbeknownst to the farmer was always to the benefit of Rudolf.

The scheme ultimately leaked out but Rudolf denied the deception. By then the farmer had no recourse and remained silent, since he also had deceived both the VGL and the Italians. But the VGL in the end had the final word.

The VGL printed an announcement in the June 12 and June 19, 1941 *GZ* which said that any Lira cash in possession of the resettlers was to be surrendered into a special account in the Savings Bank in Gottschee City. Any cash needed until the resettlement would be available if necessary. And after the resettlement, any needed cash would be provided from this account in Reichsmark. Based on this, those with newly acquired bundles of cash from Rudolf had no choice but to submit.

There was deception all around.

The Tschinkel brothers were the only two Gottscheer families who remained in the village. Together with the men from five Slovene families who also stayed, they could neither run the saw mill nor cultivate their lands for the needed harvest. And in the following year, when the ghost village became a temporary refuge for the warring factions throughout the enclave, the two Tschinkel families left for the relative safety of more densely populated Slovene lands.

Article 6 of the Contract defines the possessions the resettlers may take with them:

"…… the resettlers may, at their discretion, take with them, free of any fiscal burden, all their movable property. ….Such items include all implements necessary for the performance of the person's occupation, as well as one third of their livestock, at a minimum one horse or cow".

And Article 9 states: "…… the resettlement is to be completed by November 30, 1941".

The leader of the German delegation, ambassador Clodius reported to Ribbentrop, the German Foreign Minister, on August 13, 1941:

"Regarding the resettlement of the 15,000 Germans from the Gottscheer area, an agreement was reached which in all essential points adhered to the German demands."

The Contract was signed on August 31, 1941. The timeline was to be as follows:

October 1. The date the Contract became effective.

October 10. Himmler issues order (*Anordnung 53/I, FD 151*) to clear the Rann/Sotla (Pasavje/Posotla) area of the Slovene population and evacuate it to the "Altreich", the inner Germany. [73]

October 20. The date on which the resettling is to start is announced to the Gottscheer.

Oct. 20 - Nov. 30. This was the Option period for the re-settlers. The decision to move was to be finalized in the Ingathering Train called "Heinrich", a series of coaches outfitted into offices and medical examination rooms. The train was to be brought to Gottschee City to process the optants.

November 30. The resettlement to be completed.

The time span which began with Hitler's announcement of April 26 was to end by November 30. In only seven months all Gottscheer were to have left the enclave, their homeland for over 600 years.

(However the dates set in the Contract had to be changed soon after signing. The final resettling was extended to January 20, 1942 and February 20 was set as a terminal date for last moment optants. In actuality, the resettlement was completed when the last train left on January 22, 1942.)

But where they are going was known only from unsubstantiated rumors. The VGL keeps the destination secret until November 17, 1941 when it is finally announced in a special issue of the *GZ*. The first train left three days before on November 14. It carried 40 persons, 22 pieces of livestock and pulled 9 freight cars

---

73   *Quellen, dok.151*

loaded with possessions. And the farmer K.R. from Slovenska Vas writes on page 33:

"These first re-settlers did not, at their departure, know where they were going".

But one Gottscheer who decided to stay did know.

It was August Grill of Kočevske Poljane. In a letter dated May 8, 1996, his daughter Zofka Grill-Mirtič of Dolenjske Toplice, born in 1946, wrote to me:

"It is too late to find out how my father discovered that the Gottscheer would be resettled around Brežice. I only know that he was trying to exchange his farm with a farmer in the Brežice area. He did this because of incredible pressure from the departing Gottscheer at the behest of some of their leaders. Naturally, nothing came of the exchange. My parents stayed."

And in a letter to the GZ, reproduced in the May 1992 issue, Zofka Grill-Mirtič writes:

"To the depths of my soul I thank my parents that they did not, during the resettlement, abandon their home. We children have inherited from our parents a willingness to work, honesty, a good heart and love of our mother tongue. In our house we even today still speak Gottscheer and it pains me greatly that here with us there are only a few real Gottscheer left, only a few who still know their mother tongue; soon to be counted on fingers. What will become of our Gottscheer tongue? Here where the roots are, will in 30 to 40 years, be no more Gottscheer.....".

"PS:. Until 1965 we wrote our name with two ll's (Grill). Since then we use only one l [Gril]." [74]

Zofka's father had been in America where he saved enough to buy a substantial farm in the Gottschee area after he returned to Slovenia. He successfully resisted the pressure to resettle and give up what he had been able to acquire with the earnings of many years of hard labor in the US.

When she wrote the letter of May 8, 1996, Zofka was probably unaware of the pamphlet from the War Council of the Communist Party of Slovenia addressed to the Gottschee population which appeared July 1941 and which produced such shock among the residents of the enclave. It is very likely Zofka's father learned the destination of the resettlers from the Italians who were negotiating, if unsuccessfully, with

---

74 *Letter in possession of the author.*

the Germans for a population exchange. When the negotiations failed and it became obvious to him that for his sake Slovene were to be expelled he wanted no part of it.

In the same letter, Zofka Grill-Mirtič writes about exiled Gottscheer now living in Austria who, after WWII, visited her mother's home, her father having died a few years before. They were always welcome. But Zofka was driven to distress by an official of the *Gottscheer Zeitung* in Austria who, in 1993, called her father an Odpadnik for resisting the resettlement. (The Slovene dictionary describes 'odpadnik' as a deserter, renegade, turncoat; traitor.).

As summer gave way to autumn, the resistance against the resettlement was not abating but making headway throughout the enclave in spite of the mass rallies and the ongoing campaign by the *GZ*. (The last mass rally had been held on August 12.)

Repeating the words of the farmer K.R.:

"Because of the rosy promises by our leaders, the majority of the population was [initially] enthusiastic about the resettlement. However, in a short while, this enthusiasm sank so that a large part of the population was against the resettlement. In the outlying villages all residents were against it, including myself. I often went to evening meetings where we consulted each other. All were of the opinion it would be better if the re-settlement were postponed until after the conclusion of the war."

The VGL tried to reverse this stubborn resistance by holding its own meetings throughout the enclave at which a member of the VGL or at least a Sturmführer officiated. These events were intense and personal and dissenters were singled out for intimidation, ridicule and abuse.

Dr Arko reflects critically on these meetings in his memoir:

"It would have been more appropriate to prepare the population for the resettlement in a more soulful manner and not in a tone which was anything but pleasant. I participated in no meeting in which some participants were not addressed in an insulting manner and where the word Concentration Camp was not used."

Some Sturmführers even used physical violence. One such incident was told to me on my first return to Masern in 1974 by Mimi Morre, a young teenager in 1941, whose mixed marriage parents decided to stay. They remained in the village where she grew up, married and lived with her husband and family until her death in 2005.

Mimi described the intimidation and pressure of Jaklitsch on her parents to resettle. In reply to his question: "why not" her mother answered: "my home is here". To which the Sturmführer roared: "you are denying your German roots" and hit her so hard in the face that she fell to the ground, bleeding from nose and ear.

Rolf Steininger in his book "*South Tyrol. A Minority Conflict of the Twentieth Century*" describes in detail similar terror used by the VKR (Völkischer Kampfring Südtirols, the equivalent of the Gottscheer VGL). And the VGL took yet another page from the South Tyrol model. The Abyssinia card.

On pages 56 and 57, Steininger talks about the "Sicilian Legend", the rumor that the Italians would deport to Sicily, Abyssinia or other regions, all those who did not opt for Germany:

"We know that this rumor was the decisive factor that influenced many, if not most South Tyroleans in reaching their decision to go. Lothar von Sternbach, himself a 'stayer' conceded: 'The threat of forced resettlement to the south made more people into goers than Nazi propaganda'.

"This legend was a masterpiece carried out by Berlin. German General Consul [in Bolzano] Otto Bene was the first to speak of a possible deportation to the south of all those South Tyroleans who did not opt for Germany.

"The threat of forced resettlement to the South and the assurance of a unified contiguous area of settlement were the chief weapons in the VKR propaganda to turn the 'stayers' into 'goers".

And on the reaction of the Italians:

"No matter how many times the Prefect Mastromattei [the Italian High Commissioner] promised that 'of course, no one was going to be deported south', the denials had precisely the opposite effect.

"And on March 21, 1940, Mussolini received a delegation of those who decided to stay and assured them that they would be allowed to remain in their homeland and that no one had ever considered transplanting them to other parts of the empire".

The farmer K.R. from Slovenska Vas writes about this:

"One day there came the news which brought about the defeat of the opponents of the resettlement. From where this news came, I do not know. The announcement stated:

'The German Reich wishes to settle its borderlands with people of its own German nation. Likewise, Italy wishes to settle its borderlands with an Italian

THE BELLS RING NO MORE

population. Whoever does not wish to resettle to Germany must expect that he will be resettled by the Italian government to Sicily".

The fact that many believed it would be better if the resettlement were postponed until after the war, is also claimed by Dr. Viktor Michitsch in a letter to Frensing dated 15 July, 1965.

"My father, Georg Michitsch of Göttenitz started at the end of September, beginning of October [1941], a counter campaign. Together with several other men, among them the Reverend Joseph Gliebe, they were prepared to offer resistance to the Resettlement. Signatures were collected in the villages of Göttenitz, Rieg and Masern and submitted to the German consul in Ljubljana.

"The petition requested that the Resettlement not be undertaken during the war. This released a mighty hatred [from the VGL] against the men of the counter current. In fact the people were so intimidated that the action had no result… The people were threatened that they would be forcibly moved to Abyssinia by the Italians, should they resist the Resettlement … .". [75]

The threat of forced resettlement to the South was as effective in the enclave as it was in South Tyrol.

And according to the farmer K.R. from Slovenska Vas:

"Given this, [being resettled to Sicily] the opponents of the Resettlement reached the opinion, it would be better to live in Germany than Italy. I also joined them, but the thought remained with me that this was a questionable and risky affair."

With this comment the farmer states the prevalent fear of losing the basis for economic survival and an aversion for causing others to lose their homes.

With the use of the 'Abyssinia Card', the VGL believed it finally succeeded in persuading the population to accept the option to resettle.

In a report *The present political situation in the Gottscheer population* dated October 10, 1941, Lampeter estimated that only 600 members of the population, (5% of approx. 12,000 total), did not wish to resettle. And 360 (3% of 12,000) were not desired anyway. The report had been requested by the Eiwanderungszentrale, EWZ, (SS-RKFVD the ingathering center in Maribor).

---

75 *Die Umsiedlung, pg 84.*

COMPLETING THE TASK

One week later, on October 17, Lampeter submitted his *List of the Politically Unreliable*, a detailed list of individuals and categories to be excluded or resettled to somewhere else.

The report of October 10 was received with skepticism by the RKFVD and caused it to send Dr. Ellmer, an unofficial observer, to verify the claim. After speaking with the VGL, Dr. Elmer also talked to Dr. Arko with whom he agreed that:

"... the present VGL - apart from Ingenieur Schober, whose function is purely decorative anyway - is too young and manages the people wrongly. It is excessively abrasive and gives little consideration to the psychology of the farmers. It is feared that this will cause many not to resettle". [76]

The actual impact of the "*List ...*" was not yet apparent to either Dr. Ellmer or Dr. Arko.

To restore its now questioned credibility and to demonstrate the unity of the population to the Resettling Authority, the VGL organized a final mass rally for Sunday, October 19, 1941. It was to be held on the large sports field just outside the City. The *GZ* of October 23 reports on the event under the title, *Der letzte Appell*, (the last rally). To this enclave wide event were ordered all 25 Sturms and their youth groups, totaling 1,910 uniformed members. In addition, the general population was requested to attend and stand on the sidelines.

Sturm 13 of Masern led by Jaklitsch had marched off with his men followed by the older groups of the Youth units early in the morning, there being no transport available to bring the 120 adults to the city, 18 km away. The younger boys and girls crowded on to the few available horse drawn farming wagons, one of them owned by my father.

There was a sizeable traffic jam of marchers, wagons, trucks and buses arriving in the small town from various directions. But eventually all got sorted out and each Sturm unit marched in orderly fashion to its allocated space on the field. As Number 13, our Sturm was half way to the speaker's platform, barely visible to me, the tall men in front blocking my view.

This time I did not pass out. It was near the end of October and the sun had lost its heat. Nevertheless, standing still for over an hour was hard for this ten-year-old.

---

76 *Die Umsiedlung,* pg. 91.

THE BELLS RING NO MORE

At ten o'clock sharp, Staabführer Busbach and Jugendführer Lackner reported to VG Führer Schober and Mannschaftsführer Lampeter the presence of 900 uniformed Sturm Troopers and 1010 uniformed Hitler Youth. Off the main field there stood at least as many people from the City and the villages who had come to the event.

Schober and Lampeter received the report on the large and high stage at the head of the field, modeled after those in the Reich. In the back, high up was a large eagle standing on a swastika, huge flags to its right and left and on a raised platform behind the speakers, a row of Stürmer holding flags and trumpets. Next to Lampeter stood Dr. Heinrich Wollert, the head of the DUB, (Deutscher Umsiedlungbevollmächtigter - the resettling authority for the Province of Ljubljana) who had been invited to attend.

After the fanfare, the songs and the raising of the flag on the mast, Lampeter speaks of our return to the Reich, urging all to be determined and strong in the coming days to prove that we, Gottscheer, are real Germans worthy of our great leader, Adolf Hitler.

After a speech by Richard Lackner, directed particularly at the new generation of Germans, the units start the march through the City. Up front the trumpets and band, followed by the Youth Groups and finally by the "endless columns of Stürmer". According to the *GZ*, "the marching lasted over one hour, both sides of the street crowded with the saluting population". [77]

After the units returned to the sports field, the youth groups gave various performances until 16.00 hrs when the swastika flag was lowered for the last time in the enclave to the tune of 1910 voices singing *Deutschland, heiliges Wort* (Deutschland, holy word).

The rally ended with another speech by Richard Lackner as immortalized by the October 23 *GZ*:

"The final speech of the Youth leader, the farewell salute to our old homeland of over 600 years, pointed to our decreed task to be a participant in the securing of the foundation of an eternal Germany. A Reich, having risen from the seed of the Führer and crowned by the victorious deeds of our soldiers."

And across the field, 1910 voices shout in unison, three times in succession: "Wir danken unserem Führer".

(In just three and a half years, in May 1945, the slogan *"We thank our Führer"* was high up on a wall for us to read on our way to exile. Painted there in large let-

---

77   *GZ, October 23, 1941*

ters by the victorious liberators as a cynical reminder to all those being expelled as collaborators of the Third Reich that was no more.)

Throughout the year the SS hierarchy kept an eye on the VGL leadership and observed its performance in the enclave. In the middle of October, 1941 SS Obersturmbannführer Sievers sent a glowing report to SS Brigadeführer (Brigadier General) Dr. Scheel on the twenty five year old Lampeter:

"Joined in him is a military posture, the ability of an exemplary leader, the awareness that our world outlook is the prerequisite of the ethnic group even after the resettlement. In this respect, the Gottscheer are far more advanced than other groups scheduled for resettlement."

"Shortly thereafter, [the end of October] Lampeter is promoted by Himmler to Sturmbannführer [Major in the political branch of the SS]". [78]

Tone Ferenc writes more on this on page 604 of his *Nacistična raznarodovalna politika*. He quotes SS Brigadeführer Dr. Scheel in his letter of October 19, 1941 to SS-Sturmbannführer Laforce in Maribor:

"I received your news regarding Wilhelm Lampeter. Since then, I also received the news that the leader of the SS [Himmler] elevated Lampeter to Sturmbannführer. He also gave me permission to take into the SS, eighteen to twenty prominent Gottscheer men as SS-Untersturmführers, [Lieutenant]. They should, however refrain from wearing the SS uniform and not announce their inclusion into the SS until after their present tasks are completed".

Tone Ferenc continues:

"Lampeter soon proposed twenty one Gottscheer for induction into the SS. [nearly all village Sturmführers]. Staabführers A. Busbach and M. Sturm as SS-Obersturmführers; all others as SS-Untersturmführers". According to Ferenc, Lampeter characterized his recommended men as follows; "All comrades are politically and organizationally fit and have, throughout the years as National-Socialists behaved as is required of members of the SS. And from this time forward Lampeter signed his name followed by SS-Sturmbannführer; however, the induction of the others into the SS remained in the dark."

This was not the first time Lampeter offered manpower to the SS. In his Memoir of February 1942 he writes:

---

78 *Die Umsiedlung, pg. 120*

THE BELLS RING NO MORE

"In September [1941] the VGL quietly conducted a survey to solicit volunteers. Ninety (90) percent of all qualified Gottscheer men signed up". Many men of Masern followed the call. Most of them never returned.

Submission of the formal option papers requesting resettlement started the following morning, Monday, October 20, 1941. The requirements are spelled out in a joint announcement by the Italian High Commissioner Emilio Grazioli and the German Resettlement Plenipotentiary Dr. Wollert. The completed option papers are to be submitted in duplicate, one for the High Commissioner, the other for Dr. Wollert via the VGL. The papers must be officially certified by the local Italian municipality. Final date for submission is November 20, 1941.

Next to the Grazioli/Wollert announcement, the *GZ* of October 23 prominently displays an address by Lampeter:

"Unsere Heimkehr

"The long sought and wished-for time of our return has now arrived. The confidence of all our hearts in Adolf Hitler and Germany is unshakable. ....

"Before we start our return, the option duties must be completed. Guidance for this must be sought from the Sturmführer.

"He who neglects to turn in the option and does not show up for processing at the train, can not become a citizen of the Reich and can not return home to the Reich.

"The EWZ train will start processing on October 23."

The EWZ Ingathering train "Heinrich" had arrived on October 21 and was standing on a siding at the City station. The train, a series of coaches outfitted into offices and medical examination rooms started processing on October 23. The optants entered the train at one end and emerged as citizens of the Third Reich at the other.

Under the title *Die Heimkehr ist nah*, G. Röthel reports in the *GZ* of October 30 on the arrival of the train and the trek of old and young over sometimes poor roads to the station. She also describes, dotingly, the "Durchschleusung", the ingathering processing formality of the optants.

Excerpts are as follows:

COMPLETING THE TASK

"If one views these people more carefully, a certain anxiety is noticed. With a little mistrust, one or the other contemplates the lovely train standing on the tracks.

"Finally family Sch. is called and with pounding hearts they climb into the train. At first they enter a large room where many typewriters are clattering. Here, a friendly SS-man takes charge and leads them to the typists where they must give their name, their birthday, when they married and more. Then forward into a room where they are photographed. This causes problems since all wish to be taken as nicely as possible.

"Then comes the main item, the medical examination. These are crusty farmers who were never sick or never had time for it and therefore, have never been to a physician. Now they stand in front of a huge apparatus with tubes and glass panes and are being x-rayed. They can not comprehend that they are receiving such care, never having worried this much about themselves. These nice people are not used to such warmth.

"After being carefully examined, they continue through the lovely carriages. Everywhere questions are posed in friendly tones and if their replies at the start were agitated, their answers now are words in quiet confidence.

"The time passes rapidly and the last carriage is finally behind them. The way now leads into the City to the [hotel] "Sonne". Here they receive their transport cards and transfer their entire assets to the Resettlement Commission.

"Late in the evening they leave for home under the protection of the Italian army. To wait for the day when the entire village starts on the way home to the Reich".

Farmer K.R. writes more seriously about this on page 33 of the "Vertreibung" book:

"Without pause, over 100 families were registered each day in succession. The 50 families of my village entered the train one after the other. It took several hours in the various departments of registration until we got to the end of the train. In the order we emerged from the train we had to wait in a waiting room until we were all together. We then went in unison to the bureau of the DUT (Deutsche Umsiedlungs Treuhand Gesellschaft) where we lined up. In successive order, the resettlers gave their signature, without prior explanation as to what we were to sign. While signing, care was taken that there was no pause which would allow the signer to get a view of the content of the agreement. The resettlers were of the opinion that the signature documented only their registration in the train. Only later did it become apparent that with that signature, they surrendered also their home and everything they owned to the DUT.

THE BELLS RING NO MORE

In the signing office were a few DUT agents and two members of the VGL."

The five members of my father's family were scheduled to enter that train in the morning of Sunday, November 16. But the day before, an extraordinary event took place.

The large tub used in the slaughtering of our pigs had been dragged into the kitchen from the barn. And during that afternoon Mother and Mitzi had been filling the barrel, which normally stored runoff rainwater from the roof, with buckets of water from the cistern. This done, the water was transferred into an array of pots on the kitchen stove which had been fired to turn the cast iron surface cherry red. The kitchen itself glowed in unfamiliar warmth and the windows had turned opaque with condensation. All of us, the entire village to be precise, were going to have a bath. Jaklitsch had insisted on it.

Father and Mother went first. The glass panes on the kitchen door, normally uncovered, were hung with sheets for privacy. It was probably the first time my parents had a bath together. I stood outside and heard them frolic, envious for not being able to join them.

After they emerged steaming and smiling, it was Mitzi who gave Paul and me a good wash in the soapy water, its heat renewed by the remaining contents in the pots on the stove. That done, it was her turn and she stayed in it longer than any of us. Mother made her get out only by saying that unless she did so, the crinkles were going to become permanent.

The following morning, we and the rest of the village were brought to the station in the back of canvas covered trucks. I would be hard pressed to describe our flow through the train in more detail than described by both by G. Röthel and the farmer, but a few things I do remember.

Mitzi's crinkles had disappeared. At some point in the train, Father and I were separated from Mother, Mitzi and Paul. In the examination room we two men were asked to strip and for the first and last time, I saw my father naked.

The "Durchschleusung", the processing, had started on October 23, and was scheduled to be completed on November 20. But on November 9th, seven days before

COMPLETING THE TASK

our turn in the train on November 16, SS-Obersturmbannführer, [Colonel] Dr. Stier of the RKFDV-Headquarters in Berlin arrived in Gottschee City to investigate the reported delays on part of the population to exercise the option. He stayed for eight days until November 17. Doubts on the accuracy of Lampeter's claim of October 10, 1941, that only 5% of approx. 12,500 did not wish to resettle had already been reported by Dr. Ellmer. Now, a doubting Dr. Stier came to see for himself.

A review of the EWZ train records showed that an astonishingly low number of the population had shown up for the option. This was especially shocking to Dr. Stier when the actual tally was presented to him on November 13. Shocking since the numbers were lower than his worst expectations and three quarters of the option period had already passed.

The tally, according to Frensing, in *Die Umsiedlung*, pg. 93, showed that:

1. "Only about 40 % of the total population had shown up to exercise the option. And this absence from some of the largest Sturms! "
2. "Of the approximately 5,000 that had been processed, one tenth, or 500 re-settlers would not be permitted to join their people in the new area but were to be settled elsewhere. [A-cases]."

("Item 2 is proof that the elitist VGL had, until now, carried out the "self-selection process", granted by Hitler personally. The enforcers making sure that this was done were the "two members of the VGL in the signing office" as reported by farmer K.R.)

The above results reveal Lampeter's faulty estimate; to the RKFDV office a catastrophic setback to its ingathering objective. Dr. Stier takes immediate corrective action by canceling the entire self-selection process:

a). All mixed marriages are allowed to opt for resettlement.

b). All those opposing the VGL are allowed to opt as well.

c) All those who were excluded so far are to be re-classified according to a) and b).

Dr. Stier comments on the action of the VGL:

"It was a despotic action on part of the VGL to reject those who opposed it and those who maintained close relations with the Slovene. Through this stand of the VGL, valuable German blood would have remained in Gottschee had my forceful action not altered the position of the VGL". (see notes of Dr. Stier, Jan 24, 1942, in *Die Umsiedlung*, pg 94)

Frensing, on pages 88 and 89, describes this self-selection process as the most dismal chapter in the VGL-conducted resettlement.

"Through this process, a few young National-Socialists, (2-3%) without legitimate authority and purely according to their own elitist views, claimed the right to control, manipulate and select the other 97-98 % of the population.

"The line of Lampeter's valuation is clear. Those characterized as "unreliable" were viewed as objects that do not measure up to the morals of National-Socialism and therefore are to be expelled from the ethnic group. Whoever was identified as such has, according to the wish of the VGL, lost his right to live in the future Gottscheer community".

The extent to which the VGL controlled and manipulated the population had become objectionable even to the SS Resettling Authority. And the self-selection process, was – at least temporarily – set aside by Dr. Stier.

Frensing comments on page 95:

"Lampeter, due to overconfidence in his authority had succumbed to self delusion and caused a result in which the resettlement plans were seriously jeopardized".

To prevent a resettlement failure similar to that in South Tyrol, SS Obersturmbannführer Dr. Stier, together with Dr. Wollert takes over the control of the resettlement process. In his November 19, 1941 letter to the DUG, (Deutsche Umsiedlungs Gesellschaft), Dr. Stier writes:

"Until the conclusion of the resettlement, the VGL is granted only a limited function and with limited means".

The function of the VGL is thus reduced to a supporting role, operating under direct guidance from SS offices of the Reich. The act was a precursor to its total dissolution only a few months away.

To salvage and reverse the deteriorating situation, Dr. Stier published an appeal to the population which appeared on November 17, 1941 in a special issue of the *GZ*. It was signed both by Dr. Stier and Dr. Wollert, giving it the weight of a formal statement from the Reich. It contained no reference to the VGL.

The statement addressed, in great detail, the three specific concerns perceived by the two officials to be the main cause for the reluctance of the population to opt for resettlement. These had until now, been kept from the population by the VGL.

COMPLETING THE TASK

The answers to these concerns are loosely quoted from the November 17 issue of the GZ. [79]

Every resettler will receive equal value for the property he left behind. This means that those who drew a comfortable living from their land will be able to do the same in the new area. It also means that those with less land will receive an equal amount but will have the opportunity to better themselves.

The settlement area is announced to be the Rann (Brežice) triangle in lower Styria, a closed valley area formed by three rivers. Mountains and vineyard hills surround the area and protect it from severe winters. The prior inhabitants of this area have been resettled and are being cared for by the Reich. Apart from the assurance of full compensation, letters and reports from these people are proof that they are being well taken care of and with hope look happily to their future.

Since the assignment of properties in the new area requires careful preparation, great care is being exercised to make certain that this task, which will have an effect for decades if not centuries, is done properly. It may therefore be possible that a re-settler is temporarily given an incorrect property, one not commensurate with the one left behind. In such an event, a move during the winter months will make certain the farmer is settled on the correct property in time to start spring planting.

The doubters, reassured about their future, their guilt about being the cause of grief to others allayed, were presented with a final warning in the *GZ*:

"It is pointed out that the option period is final. Later on it will no longer be possible to become a citizen of the Reich".

With that warning, the uncommitted population was presented with a final yes or no. In view of the situation as they saw it, they had little choice.

The Gottschee population finally felt it was being addressed as responsible adults. For the first time, on November 17, they are told where they are going and their fears for the future are being allayed. But those on the trains that had been leaving in the past three days were not aware of this and knew not where they were going.

All this was now coming directly from high ranking representatives of the all powerful Reich which, according to its successes up to the winter of 1941, was

---

79 *GZ, November 17, 1941, pg. 47*

certain to win the war. Not coming from the no longer credible VGL "snotboys", now so clearly sidelined from their leadership role.

With only three days to the end of the option period of November 20, the date was extended to January 20, 1942. In the days between November 17 and December 10, another 6,747 people came to the train to be processed, bringing the total to 11,747 or 94% of the population.

The last minute effort on the part of SS Obersturmbannführer Dr. Stier, (to override the VGL and thereby prevent the failure of the Gottscheer resettlement), became a success.

The process of qualifying who was fit or worthy to resettle and live among the citizens of the Reich had started immediately after April 26, 1941. In the following months, the process evolved into a *List of Politically Unreliable* [80] submitted by Lampeter to the RKFDV on October 17.

The 'self-selection' process was to be according to this list and exclude:

All mixed marriages in which either partner was a Slovene.

All opponents resisting resettlement until after the end of the war.

All opponents of the VGL such as Dr. Arko and other members of the bourgeoisie.

All opponents of the VGL such as priests and teachers.

Broadly, the "List ... " contained all those with inferior non-German blood and those not fully committed to National-Socialism according to the concepts of the VGL, which viewed self-selection as a duty to the Reich. No "politically unreliable" was to be part of the future Gottscheer-German community. All of them were to be resettled to somewhere else or rejected outright from being included.

Initially, all marriages in which one partner was a Slovene were excluded. "The VGL supplied long lists of such marriages to the EWZ" [81] This selection rule was later modified to exclude only those who "did not stand with us or did not join our organization". To be interpreted by the VGL as it saw fit.

The cause for this revision was pressure from the RKFDV office and especially from Gauleiter Uiberreither, the head of the civil authority of the annexed Slovenia, including the part into which the Gottscheer were to resettle. The Gauleiter and the

---

80 *List of Politically Unreliable*. See: http://www.gottschee.de (Archiv-Dokumente).

81 *Die Umsiedlung*, pg. 99.

COMPLETING THE TASK

RKFDV viewed the majority of the Slovene population living there as valuable material to be Germanized and become citizens of the Reich.

The Gauleiter even "…. hinted in a conversation, that he judged the human value of the Gottscheer not higher than those of the Slovene who, for the sake of the Gottscheer, are being expelled". [82] This was not to the liking of Lampeter who resented that his select Aryan Gottscheer were to be reduced to the level of the "inferior Slovene" and live as equals among them in Styria, the area now under control of the Gauleiter.

But the category labeled as "unreliable" extended beyond those that did not measure up to the standards set by Lampeter and his inner circle. This is clear from a letter to the Gauleiter, dated November 2, 1941, in which Lampeter describes the status of the population and his vision regarding its future in the Reich:

"Today there are 2,665 families in the villages and 261 in the City. Of the 2,665, we have designated only 1,201 as fit to run a farm. Of the remaining 1,464 families, 577 have small farms, 364 are workmen with a little land. There are 139 families who are to be excluded from the settlement area, together with another 384 older, no longer capable families". [83]

According to the above, the VGL had decided to deny 577 farmers their equivalent, if small, farm in the Reich. Instead "worthy and capable" young Gottscheer, landless peasants who had never run a farm but were loyal supporters of the VGL, were to become fully landed "border farmers" in the Reich. This is verified by A. Dolezalek, head of the planning staff for the "General Settling Area", in a note dated November 6, 1941. [84]

No wonder that Dr. Stier, on November 13, found the rejection rate so high. And by that time, only 40% of the entire population had been processed and none of the City's residents, most of them resisters and opponents, had been in the train.

No mention is made of how the 577 dispossessed farmers were to be reimbursed or what and where their future in the Reich was going to be. The same applies to the fate of the 139 families who were to be excluded as well as that of the 384 older no longer capable families. And no mention is made of the 261 families in the City, many of them owning their homes, businesses and other non-farming assets.

---

82   *Die Umsiedlung,* pg. 55.
83   *Quellen,* doc. 144, note 7.
84   *Die Umsiedlung,* pg. 100.

The VGL also used the label of "politically unreliable" to settle personal grievances and accounts with opponents of its cause and its methods. By so tagging an opponent or one resisting their leadership role, it was able to exclude from resettling or mark for future action anyone it so labeled. Of course, no one apart from Lampeter's inner circle knew this.

Lampeter's personal "List" included twenty five individuals (and families, all but one living in the City), as those who might purposely give a false report on the VGL. Among them is Dr. Arko, a confirmed National Socialist and one who encouraged doubters to resettle, as well as nine individuals linked to his person. In the "List" is also the lawyer Dr. Ferdinand Siegmund who, according to Lampeter's description, was an individual seeking cooperation with the Slovene. Lampeter is incensed that Dr. Siegmund desired to open a Kindergarten in his village to serve all children including Slovene. Lampeter freely admits in his "List" that to prevent this, he wrote an anonymous letter to Siegmund, saying that if he persisted with his plan, he would not return alive from his next hunting trip to the forest. Furthermore, to quote Lampeter from his List: "The clerics, or Roman-Catholic oriented are to be viewed as a special sort of politically unreliable". He identifies by name the six enclave priests, one teacher and one farmer and dismissively identifies their supporters as: "predominantly old women".

But on November 17, the SS was interested more in demonstrating success of the ingathering process than in the racial purity and political commitment of the ingathered. "All are now allowed to resettle" was the justification for avoiding an embarrassing defeat. And the lists classifying the optants (all methodically prepared by the VGL) can be used at a later date.

And used they were. After the resettlement was completed in 1942, the SS acted on these lists which contained the names of 571 A (Altreich) cases; persons the VGL designated as unworthy to be part of the future community. The A cases were culled out from the temporary quarters in the settlement area and transported to the Reich where they spent the remaining war years in labor camps.

COMPLETING THE TASK

The VGL had administered the racial profiling process according to the directives given them by their SS handlers in Berlin in May 1941. This profiling called "self selection" followed all the ideological guidelines of the SS Ingathering Authority which required that only the racially fit and ideologically committed ethnic Germans be brought back into the Reich and become full fledged citizens. The VGL performed this function in line with expectations, albeit according to their own interpretation which nearly resulted in an embarrassment to the SS.

The SS was more interested in returning as many ethnic Germans as possible mainly to show success of the program. This is clearly obvious with the intervention of Dr. Stier in Gottschee. "Bring them all in; we will purify later. Meanwhile we can use them for their labor" was the motto. This was obvious not only with the Gottscheer A cases, but throughout Eastern Europe with its multitude of ethnic Germans.

The Marschall family was one of 700,000 ethnic Germans living in the northeastern part of Moldavia Romania. All were targeted for return to the Reich. Living in Botosani, Mr. Marschall, a family man and father of the ten year old Anton, succumbed to the siren song and in spite of his wife's resistance, signed up to be resettled into the Reich. He was a successful master tailor in his own comfortable house and surrounding garden. Apart from that there was little to hold him in Romania and the return to the Reich and the promises of a good life there overcame his wife's objections. They left in the spring of 1941.

Decades later, his son Anton remembered how they boarded the train, already crowded with other resettlers for the long ride to camps in the Salzburg region of former Austria. There they were quartered, temporarily, in a processing camp for the purpose of profiling and being sworn into citizenship of the Reich. (No profiling train "Heinrich" came to them). And shortly thereafter, they were to be assigned their final destination in the Reich.

But time passed. Others departed and the Marschall family waited for their turn. Anton's father finally asked an SS officer, with whom he had good relations, why he and his family were not being processed like the others.

The officer explained that the delay was due to the fact that his wife was not racially pure since she was a Polish Slav and therefore not qualified to become a citizen. They were to be sent to a labor camp because his services as a tailor were required there.

The realization that he and his family had become outcasts, second rate human beings with no future other than servitude to the Nazi state, sent him into depression. Anton remembers how he surprised his father at the edge of a cliff and is convinced to this day that he was about to jump to his death. It was only the sight of his ten year old son that prevented the suicide.

Soon after that, they were taken to a labor camp elsewhere in Salzburg province. There, Anton's father was assigned to practice his trade and soon became the preferred tailor for the SS officers in charge of the camp. He became so proficient that he was also sent into other camps where he took measurements for uniforms of SS officers there.

The Marschall family remained in the camp until the arrival of the Americans in April of 1945. They stayed there, but were soon moved out of their relatively comfortable barracks to make room for inmates arriving from concentration camps. After that, the family was moved to a displaced persons camp, formerly a stable for horses and one without toilet facilities. The liberators had identified them as ethnic Germans, formerly sympathetic to Hitler and treated them accordingly. They remained there until their application to emigrate to the US was ultimately granted in 1951. They left for America after having lived in camps for ten years.

The Marschall family was the Romanian version of the Gottscheer A-Case; the processing camp the equivalent of the train on a siding of Gottschee city railroad station. Except that in the ingathering of ethnic Germans of Romania and South Tyrol, the SS performed the profiling on their own. In the case of the Gottscheer, the VGL insisted on doing this dark deed themselves, knowing full well that through this act they were condemning many of their tribe to a life of servitude, if not death.

After the processing of the Masern residents, including our family on November 16, Jaklitsch held several meetings in his large guest room to instruct the villagers on how to get ready for the move.

COMPLETING THE TASK

All movable possessions can be taken. Not allowed were useless items such as dog houses, stones to weigh down sauerkraut, old useless plowshares, old iron, etc.

Furniture and other household items including dry goods should be crated for robust handling. Foodstuffs such as potatoes should be packaged to prevent spillage. Liquid items such as sauerkraut should be in sealed barrels to prevent leaks.

All tools and gear necessary for farming or performing a trade are movable possessions, but must be in a condition for secure transportation. Loose parts of farming gear and tools should be tied together or crated to prevent separation and loss.

A third of the livestock can be taken. Poultry and pigs must be caged. And on the day before departure, the animals should be well fed and the cows milked.

Jaklitsch suggested that boards and lumber be purchased at the lumber mill for making pallets and crates strong enough for transport in trucks and rail freight cars. Nails and other hardware would be supplied by his store.

All should dress warmly for the journey. Enough food should be brought along to last for several days. And he personally would be making inspections to make certain all is done as it should be.

I still visualize the effort of my father to secure his possessions for transport. Every piece of furniture, every farming implement, every tool and every article from his carpenter shop was carefully packaged.

The poultry was gathered into cages and the fattened pig was placed in its own wooden crate. It was going to be slaughtered in a different land. And on the day of our leaving, Sunday, December 7, 1941, the crates were loaded on trucks and the livestock led on to other vehicles standing in line. All was to be loaded into the freight cars at the City railroad station.

For days before our departure, perhaps a week if not more, Paul and I were left with Grandma Ilc so as to get out of the way of the adults. But perhaps the real intent was to spare us the trauma of a home being readied for abandonment, eating marginal meals and sleeping on the floor, the beds and bedding now mostly crated up.

THE BELLS RING NO MORE

Grandma Ilc was very attentive during our final days with her. She found things for me to read, gave me short writing lessons and together we worked on my multiplication tables. Ten times anything was easy, but less so beyond that, about which she was very forgiving. But over and over she made me promise to never stop learning, the key to my future, as it would have been for Alois her oldest son, had he not been killed by the Italians now sitting on her property toward whom she dismissively pointed her chin. But she no longer shooed me away when the aroma from the kettle, in which they were cooking yet another version of what was by now my favorite food, was pulling me helplessly in their direction.

Father, Mother, Mitzi and Yiorgo came to fetch us for the last time on Saturday, the day before our departure on December 7. Grandma cooked a final meal for the family of her oldest daughter, the only one of her children she was in contact with at that time to the exclusion of all others. Angela and her family, only five houses away were not invited, nor were Janez and family living in the neighboring village of Blate. Neither was Jože and his family, but he was living in distant Ljubljana surely too far away, besides she had not spoken to him since he had married without her approval in November 1939 and whose wife she had never met. Franc was in Argentina and she had not heard from him in years.

We said goodbye while it was still light. It had been snowing and the road was covered, perhaps too much so for Yiorgo to find his way home alone in the dark. It was a tearful moment between mother, daughter and granddaughter and perhaps even Father, but that I do not remember. The three year old Paul was bewildered and I was embarrassed by the lengthy embrace from the woman I loved and never saw again.

That night Mitzi and I slept on top of the heated oven for the last time, while the parents and Paul slept on hay that had been brought into the big bedroom from the loft.

The Reverend Alois Krisch of Altlag (Stari log) writes about the final days in his village.[85]

"Now started the resettlement. It began in the second half of November. [He and his village left on December 15.] The news of the disappointment received from our people after they arrived in the settling area was devastating. A murmur

---

85 *Dokumentation der Vertreibung*, pg. 18

COMPLETING THE TASK

but not too loud started among the people, since firstly the depressing reports from the settlers was more than their spirits could bear and secondly the food supply during the past few months was the worst ever and never again so bad until the end of the war. Yes we had food stamps, but little was available. Our own harvest had been sold, as well as the livestock apart from the few we could take with us. Firewood had not been stored since cutting down even in one's own properties was not allowed without permission from the authorities and also one had not planned for another winter. No longer could anything be changed.

"Transports left day after day. The most distant villages left first so that on the way to the train, the people would not have to travel through empty villages". (Two of the more distant villages, Rieg and Göttenitz had passed through Masern before we left).

The Reverend continues:

"Our turn started on December 15 with house numbers 1-12. In the morning the crates were taken by trucks to the station, the livestock was driven there by the people themselves. In the afternoon we were to be taken there on buses.

"Many people were on the village square, all in tense expectation. Had I not known how difficult it is for people to leave their home, I would have seen it on their faces. I therefore took it upon myself to prevent my own crying and tears and postpone any mourning until later. Between neighboring houses stood smaller groups. Nervously individuals move from one to the other. Talks with those leaving tomorrow or the day after provide temporary distraction.

"The buses arrive. Get in! At the final handshake many are laughing, but their expressions show they are closer to crying. Peter Kikel of Number 33 (who is staying) while saying farewell to his neighbors, can not contain himself; he weeps. Others barely maintain their composure.

".... 'Follow soon'. 'Yes, tomorrow, the day beyond, a good journey'. 'Auf Wiedersehen'. And off they go."

The writing of the Reverend describes, more or less, similar scenes taking place throughout the enclave. The Masern departure was not very different. It vaguely resonates in my memory, perhaps only because the excitement of leaving for a promising future seemed to have removed all other sentiments for the moment. Our buses came in the morning and were waiting for us on the village square. Mother held the key with which she had locked the front door, but Father made her go back and leave it in the lock as we had been told.

But I also remember vividly, Jula, Grandma's youngest sister, only a few years older than my mother, standing in the snow just outside Dolenja Vas, at the intersection of the main road to Gottschee City and the road leading to the Hinterland. She had come from Ljubljana to say farewell to her niece and childhood school friend, but had arrived too late. Now she was waving her goodbye with a white kerchief at the intersection of the road forking to the right, the road my ancestors took about 600 years ago to settle in Grčarice (Masern), a place which, seemingly, I was one of the few anxious to leave.

Chapter 14

Our Ingathering – their Deportation

The people of Masern left on three different days; the days of December 7, 9 and 11, 1941. Together, three trains transported the 206 inhabitants, their farming equipment, 87 pieces of livestock and crates filled with their portable possessions.

The village had been divided into three groups in the order of house numbers starting with number 1 and since our house number was 15 of 65, we were in the first group. Jaklitsch at number 11, being the village leader, was in the last group.

The trucks that were to take our goods to the train station in Stara Cerkev (Mitterdorf) had arrived on the village square early in the morning of December 7th. The buses that took us to the station arrived around noon and we arrived there in time to watch the livestock and possessions being loaded into freight cars. The freight cars were at the end of a string of coaches, each prominently marked with the SS symbol, carriages with soft seats that were to take us on the journey to our new homeland, the Third Reich. Only intimates of the VGL knew that this far away place was no more than another part of occupied Slovenia at the end of only 75 miles (150 Km) of track. The straight distance for a crow was about 40 miles (64 Km). A short distance in miles, but for most people on the train, a world away.

Prior to boarding, we lined up outside the station house where uniformed girls served hot stew from the big kettle of a military field kitchen, to be eaten at tables set up in the station waiting room. It was bland compared to the meal cooked by the Italians in the courtyard of Grandma Ilc. After the meal, armed SS men managed and controlled the entry to the coaches and organized the seating within, since everyone wanted window seats. The SS men were part of the security staff that accompanied us on the way. This was in line with an order from Dr Hans Bauer, the Chief of Section III of the Gestapo and Commandant of the Security police for the occupied Lower Styria who, in a letter dated October 6. 1941 passed on to his subordinates a directive from Himmler:

"The resettlement of the Gottscheer Ethnic Germans may result in transgressions by certain Slovene circles. To prevent this, thirty Slovene personalities should be identified who in the event of such transgressions can be arrested immediately. In addition it should be circulated that for every Ethnic German who comes to harm, ten Slovene will be executed." [86]

At the departure of the first resettlement transport on November 14, there was a band that played, among others: "Muss I' denn, muss I' denn, zum Stätelein hinaus, ...". (Must I, must I leave the little city ...."). Now there was only the coughing of the steam engine that accompanied the waving of kerchiefs from those remaining on the station platform. Much had changed in less than one month.

Our train left the siding at Stara Cerkev (Mitterdorf) at 15.00 hrs in the afternoon of December 7 and arrived at a siding in Brežice (Rann) at 2.35 in the morning of December 8. It carried 119 people and 33 animals. At nearly the same time the people of Veliko Mraševo, renamed by the occupier to Gross Mraschau, were being loaded into trucks and deported to make room for us.

The other two Masern trains followed two and four days later.

Our train, the second of three each day, traveled according to the schedule set at a meeting of officials of the "Deutsche Reichsbahn" and "Direzione Ferrovia Lubiana" in Munich on October 23, 1941. The route taken was from Stara Cerkev (Mitterdorf) via Grosuplje, Ljubljana and from there via Litija and Zidani Most to Krško and Brežice, the final destination. It had covered the distance of approximately 75 miles in roughly 11½ hours, after several stops along the way. [87]

The schedule was precise in order to avoid blocking this main rail link to Zagreb which was heavily traveled by the military. At times the train sat on sidings to allow higher priority trains to pass. It sat on a siding outside Brežice until daylight when finally it pulled into the station. [88]

I vividly remember waking up during one of our many such stops. The light from the moon in a cloudless sky lit up the darkened coach, its brightness increased by reflections off the glistening snow on meadows outside. Most people were asleep but some of those awake, including my father were singing, albeit quietly so as not to disturb the others. The conclusion of *Heimat deine Sterne, Sie strahlen mir auch am fernen Ort,......* (Homeland your stars, they shine for me also in a distant place .....) was followed by silence interrupted only by deep, if suppressed, sighs. The song, a popular hit like *Lili Marleen,* was repeatedly played by the Reichsdeutsche Rundfunk for the Wehrmacht soldiers in many occupied and distant lands. But for those in our coach now blowing their noses it carried an unintended message; their

---

86   *Quellen, doc. 141.*

87   *Niederschrift – Deutsche Reichsbahn, Generalbetriebsleitung Süd, München, 25. Oktober 1941, later: Niederschrift.*

88   ibid.

OUR INGATHERING – THEIR DEPORTATION

old Heimat was no longer theirs, the future Heimat unknown. I was not burdened by such reflections and went back to sleep.

The farmer K.R. writes about the start of the resettling:

"After the departure of the first three trains [November 14, 15 and 16] there was a pause. [A 5 day interruption, but he does not say why]. At their departure, these initial resettlers knew not where they were going. Only after their arrival [the following morning] did it become known that this was their new homeland. And a few days after the arrival of these three first trains it also became known in the Gottschee district where this new homeland was. Many did not believe it and said it was impossible that it was." [89]

And the Reverend Alois Krisch [who arrived in Brežice on December 15, one week after us] writes:

"We have arrived. At first we could not leave the train since the people from the Möseler transport [another village], which had arrived before us, were still in the hotel.

"But even before we exited, there came one who arrived two days before and, crying, told how bad it was here, how badly he fared and about the hovel he had received as a house. I was angry but restrained myself from scolding him knowing that he owned nothing at home, where he rented a hovel. When I explained his former condition to the people they calmed a bit. Later, a woman who had arrived some days before came and made it even worse. Reality and all its aspects had come very soon and all too harshly.

"After we exited the train we were taken to the hotel, the formal place of reception. (The Möseler people had been moved to the movie house). The officials who received us there and who for weeks had seen the disappointments experienced by our people and heard their lamentations, tried hard to be welcoming. One official, who was aware that I was the transport leader and a priest, asked me to calm the people and make clear to them that at first they will be assigned only temporary accommodations and that they will all receive their final properties in the spring. He asked me to do this while we were having a good warm breakfast.

"Then a pleasant flicker of hope lit up among the arrivals. This happened when, prior to their departure from the hotel, they were given provisions for the first eight days; bread, butter, flour, meat, coffee, canned food, etc. In addition they received money; 100 RM [Reichsmark] for each family head and an additional 50

---

89 *Dokumentation der Vertreibung.*

RM for each family member. And on the bus to their new village, they laughingly announced: 'This is not a bad beginning'." [90]

I also remember the 'good warm breakfast' and the move into the movie house where we were welcomed by friendly young women in the uniform of the Reichsarbeitsdienst. They led us, mostly children, to the large viewing room where the rows of chairs had been replaced by rows of mattresses. The warm cocoa quickly put Mitzi, Paul and me to sleep, while Father, Mother and most other adults went back to the station to see about their possessions in the freight cars. We were awakened early in the afternoon and together with the adults who had returned we received a meal and the provisions as described by the Reverend. During lunch, we were addressed by an SS official from the Settlement Authority, the DAG (Deutsche Ansiedlungs Gesellschaft). The uniformed officer divided us into groups, each group to be bused separately to Veliko Mraševo (Gross Mraschau) our new village. He also stressed that the assigned house was temporary and that we would move into the final house as soon as all the property details were worked out. Our possessions now being unloaded from the freight cars were to follow in the next few days with the livestock coming first.

The ride to Veliko Mraševo was slow, covering the short distance of only fourteen km (approx nine miles) in about an hour. After leaving the movie house near the train station, the bus traveled through the center of the town to the long bridge at the other end. This gave us the first glimpse of the local administrative center of our new homeland. The town, which predates the Roman era, was known as Rann when the region was under Imperial Austria. It became Brežice after 1918 when Lower Styria became part of the new Yugoslavia. It reverted to the German version, as did Veliko Mraševo and all other names when the region was occupied and annexed to the Reich in 1941.

Brežice (Rann) was a neat little place with its own medieval castle and a high water tower that defined the town's skyline. However it lacked the large square of Gottschee city and its imposing double spired church. Instead of the little stone bridge over the tranquil river Rinse next to the church in Kočevje city, there was a long double arched steel bridge spanning two mighty rivers at the end of the town opposite the rail station. One of the arches was over the wide and swiftly flowing

---

90 *Dokumentation der Vertreibung.*

Sava. Only a short distance beyond that, the second one arched over the slightly slower and narrower Krka (Gurk) which merged with the larger Sava less than 500 meters downstream.

After crossing the Krka, the driver turned right and after 1,500 meters crossed the same river which had made a sharp left again to immediately enter a small, seemingly deserted farming village. It was Krška Vas (Gurkdorf), a village of less than fifty one story houses close to either side of the road; the buildings in the back not much different from those in Grčarice (Masern).

The land beyond Krška Vas on either side of the road was flat, farmland with stubs of cornstalks protruding from the snow. To the left in the distance, beyond the Gurk which had turned away from the road, were the southern high hills that surround the Krško/Brežice plain, from which the Slovene population was still being removed by the SS to make room for the "ingathered" Gottscheer. The bus driver explained that at this point, the hills were the border between Italy and the Reich. Further on, the river Krka (Gurk) would become the border. And to the right of the road the land was flat, the northern hills surrounding the broad Krško/Brežice (Gurkfeld/Rann) valley too far away to be seen.

After three Km we entered Cerklje (Zirkle). But just before we came to this village we became aware of a Luftwaffe airfield on the right from which planes were taking off and landing. It was a training field for Stuka dive bombers which explained the occasional screaming noise in the distance where pilots were practicing their aim. Later, near the end of the war, this airfield and its surroundings became a prime target for Allied planes from their bases in liberated Italy. At the entry to Cerklje, a village much larger than Krško, we noticed the school house on the left, a place where I was to continue my spotty education. A building much larger than the one in Grčarice, this school served all surrounding villages including the one in Veliko Mraševo and was the place where all youngsters of the area would be educated.

As we drove slowly through the empty Cerklje, at least twice the size of Masern, other landmarks appeared. At the only intersection in the village center, the large building on the right was the local Gasthaus. It was to become the new Jaklitsch inn, the replacement for the one left behind. The road on the left led to the church of St. Peter and Paul and to the bridge over the Krka (Gurk) which had again come closer. But after Cerklje, the river again curved to the left to get out of the way of the hills directly in front of us.

Beyond the intersection on the left was the walled in cemetery in which, in the very near future, were to be buried two of my best friends. And further on at the end of the village on the left was the Reichspost, the post office which, like the one in Dolenja Vas, served the surrounding villages. Except that instead of Jula Bojčeva, our postwoman in Masern, a uniformed Reichspost man delivered whatever mail there was to our village on a bicycle. There was never much of it since no one, including our relatives in Dolenja Vas or Brooklyn, New York, knew where we were.

What did come was the mail from the Government which kept sending call up letters to the shrinking pool of eligible men. Later on, when all able bodied men, including the postman and many women were taken into the Wehrmacht, we school children picked up the mail and brought it back with us. And in the winter when the snow was too deep to trek to school, I would shoulder my rucksack and climb on the back of our second horse Shargo, the new companion to Yiorgo, and ride the always good tempered animal to the post office to get the mail for the village. But as we neared the village on our return, Shargo took control, assumed a trot and then a full gallop, all in eagerness to return to the warm stable where a measure of oats was waiting for him in the trough. All I could do was to hang tightly to his mane to prevent falling off. And duck my head as he stomped through the open door of the stable.

Beyond the post office, the last building in Cerklje, there was a straight stretch of 1,500 meters, half of which was a gradual incline to the top of the hill separating Cerklje from Veliko Mraševo. This slope was to become a joy on my bicycle; the accumulated downhill speed making it possible to coast the straight and level part way into the center of the village. Many a test run was made here to determine who had the best bike, the best being the one which coasted the farthest. I usually lost each race in spite of the frequency with which I disassembled the axle of both wheels to clean each of the bearing balls and then carefully returned them into the raceway coated with grease. But nothing helped and I never won a race. Equally frustrating was the return since the bike had to be pushed the entire distance, the gear ratio being far too high to pedal it uphill. Most others could do this on their much older models, disproving my claim that my bicycle, being German made, was the best.

After only a short level stretch at the top of the hill, zigzagging at first to the right and then to the left, the road came to the downward slope giving way to the Mraševo (Mraschau) valley. At the bottom of this much shorter and steeper slope, the bus made a sharp left turn on to a secondary road and just beyond, after a 500 meter stretch of open fields, was Gross Mraschau/Veliko Mraševo, the village destiny had decreed to be our new home.

OUR INGATHERING – THEIR DEPORTATION

At the near left side of the intersection stood a solitary little house, the lower edge of its straw covered roof barely above the heads of the couple standing beneath it. It was the house of the only Slovene and his wife who had been allowed to remain in the village. This we found out in the next few days when we, the new arrivals, especially the youngsters, explored the empty houses in the empty village, the signs of a hasty departure evident everywhere. In the centre of the kitchen table of one abandoned house there stood, surrounded by unused spoons, a bowl of untouched porridge while on the stove the residue of the meal clung to the sides of the pot in which it was cooked.

After the open field, the bus entered the village. The houses, while different, were in many ways not unlike the ones in Masern except that all had much more space between them, including more open ground also between the stables and barns behind the main house. All on the bus admitted to a good initial impression. And when asked what happened to the prior owners, the driver replied that they were all resettled into the inner Reich. This was puzzling since it was us who were supposed to be resettled to the inner Reich. However, the credibility that they were resettled willingly did not last beyond the time it took to see that the prior owners had left in a great hurry since they took with them only the barest of necessities.

The signs that the former owners were forced to leave in a great hurry were elaborated on by the Slovene at the intersection. After classes were started the following spring in Cerklje, I would stop in front of his little house on the way home from school. There I watched him operate his delicate veneering saw, which he worked by pedaling with his feet like a sewing machine, and with which he cut the delicate slivers of wood for a chest he was decorating. He did not mind and since I spoke Slovene he soon, if reluctantly, began to tell me in detail how the village was emptied out by the SS.

This may have been a mistake since I repeated it all to Father who may have passed it on to Jaklitsch. In any event, later that fall of 1942, he and his wife disappeared. Whether they were removed by the SS during the night or they slipped over the border to safety was not known. All the contents within the house, including the little saw were left behind. I am sure he would have wanted me to have it, but soon someone else took it; it was too heavy for me to carry home.

Half way into the village the bus turned right on to a branch road. After passing a few houses on either side it pulled into the courtyard of the house next to the last on that road; our new, if temporary house according to the bus driver who had read our name off his list. He unloaded our hand luggage and the bundles of food we received in Rann before leaving. "We will pick you up early in the morning and take you back to the station where you can sort out your possessions and your animals and bring them back to your house". Then the bus backed out and returned to the center of the village, leaving us standing in the few inches of newly fallen snow.

The door to the house was unlocked and the first thing we noticed inside was the bitter cold. Hardly surprising, this being nearly mid December and the house unheated for days after the prior owners left in a hurry. Signs of this were everywhere, in the unmade beds, the open doors of the half empty wardrobe, the pulled-out drawers of the chest from which most contents had been removed. After a quick look about, we settled in the kitchen where the unwashed dishes of that day of hasty departure were still on the table and the water in one of the pots on the stove frozen to solid ice.

Then Mother took charge. She ordered her silent and deeply distressed husband to inspect the stable and barn and see if there was feed for the animals when they arrived tomorrow. But she did this mainly to spare him his crying in front of the children, something he could do freely outside but tried to hide when I joined him in a little while. Years later, when we talked about that day, he admitted that he was prepared for much unpleasantness but what disturbed him most was the realization that due to us, other people's lives were so profoundly affected.

Mother started a fire in the stove that quickly warmed the freezing kitchen, a space somewhat smaller than the large one in Masern. She did the same in the cavity of the fireplace of the oven heating the bedroom, a corner cube similar to the one in Grčarice (Masern) and which likewise was fired from the kitchen. This oven, like the one in Masern, not only heated the large room that was used as the common bedroom, but with its door open, also the rest of the house. As in Masern, this method for heating was also used in this part of Slovenia.

With the kitchen cleared and the house warming up, Mother and Mitzi prepared the large bedroom for the night. They refilled the mattress sacks of the two double beds with fresh straw from the barn and made them up with clean linen sheets they found in the cupboard. The coarse and heavy horse blankets that had been left behind on the beds would keep us warm until ours arrived. The parents and Paul were in one bed and Mitzi and I in the other.

It was getting dark. Mother lit the kerosene lamp hanging from the ceiling in the still warming kitchen and started to prepare a meal from the provisions received in Rann. The aroma from the meat and gravy of the tin cans soon filled the house.

OUR INGATHERING – THEIR DEPORTATION

And as the temporary chill, brought through the front door by a shivering Father was vanishing, we had our first meal in a house which, even if not final, was now ours but in which we felt like intruders.

During the meal Father told us what he had discovered.

There was some fire wood stacked and drying under the barn overhang. Hardly enough to last the winter. The barn itself was full of hay, enough to feed Yiorgo and our cow until the next harvest. The granary bins in the barn were filled and the below-ground cellar next to the house was full of potatoes and other staples. The empty stable was large enough to house Yiorgo, the cow and several additional animals. It only needed cleaning out. The solidly built but also empty pig pen was ready to accommodate the fattened pig. It was large enough to accommodate several others in the future, Father said. All seemed, at least for the time being, satisfactory. And in the warming bedroom, with its newly made up beds, we all went to sleep. In beds, in which not so very many days ago, others were equally anxious about their future.

The farmer K.R. and the Reverend Alois Krisch each wrote their versions of arrival in the settlement area. [91]

The train of the farmer unloaded in Krško (Gurkfeld) station in the western end of the Krško/Brežice plain, whereas the train of the Reverend (who arrived in Brežice on December 15, one week after us) had made its final stop in Brežice (Rann).

The farmer writes:

"When my turn came, the exodus was nearly completed. I left my Gottschee homeland on January 9. The last transport left two or three days later. [Actually, the last train left on January 22, 1942. But by January 1st, 1942, as many as 9,000, more than three quarters of the total of the Gottscheer had already been moved]. Apart from the furniture and the farming gear, I was allowed to take only one cow. Three other cows had to be turned over to the Italian administration. Three families and a single man remained in the village. One of these three was expelled in 1946. Two families are still there and live on the land they own. The single man lives with them.

"When I, with my family and the others from our village arrived at Gurkfeld rail station, we were welcomed there by representatives of the DAG. For the first night we were quartered in makeshift buildings next to the station house. On the following

---

91   *Dokumentation der Vertreibung*, 1961

day we were registered. The DAG made available vehicles to us to bring our properties to our destined village and place.

"Late in the afternoon I arrived at our assigned farm near Rann. It was a desolate sight. The windows and door were in very bad condition. There was driven snow in the rooms of the house. In the neglected stable where I was to shelter my cow there was no room. A stable for three animals was occupied by five. Two of the animals were removed by the DAG in order for me to shelter my cow. To do so I first had to drain the stable floor and remove the dung. I was also required to assume the care of the other three animals.

"No firewood was on hand; for the first night I fired the ovens with debris from the attic for three hours but the rooms remained cold since they had not been heated for a while.

"The winter of 1941/42 was very cold. Necessary firewood was not available. Most of the houses which the settlers occupied were in a neglected condition. The region was poorer than the one in Gottschee; the houses and farms inferior to those we left behind.

"But most troubling for me, as for the others was the fact that, from this region, the native Slovene population had been forcibly displaced. How could one sleep in houses that had been taken from other people?

"Now it was clear to us why the settlement region had been concealed!"

The Reverend also reports, if with a different perspective, on the conditions and the attitude of the settlers.

"Here the condition of the houses and farm buildings is way below those at home. In fact, the dwellings in the Gottscheer land were much better and roomier.

"Much blame regarding the dissatisfaction rests with the senselessly exaggerated propaganda of the past summer describing splendid homes and farms into which the re-settlers were going to move.

"It was said, 'the resettlement will be from farm to farm. You will leave your house and will be transported by automobile from the train to your newly equipped farm' – now they find hovels and live with the entire family of four, five even six children in a single damp room. It is incomprehensible how the propaganda was able to convert such adverse conditions into reality".

OUR INGATHERING – THEIR DEPORTATION

It seems that the Reverend, one of the two Gottscheer priests who resettled, (there were four who did not), wants us now to think that he, like the simple farmers, was also fooled by the "propaganda". This is unlikely given the fact that the Reverend was an educated man in contrast to his parishioners, most of whom read no newspapers and heard no newscasts on a radio and had never been outside the enclave. He was a vocal supporter of the resettlement and a defender of the VGL who, even after 1945, claims that "Nazis they were not". But now, he justifies himself with the following:

"Many of our people had second thoughts about resettling after it became known that a part of Lower Styria would be forcefully cleared to make room for us. [Word got back to the enclave soon after the first settlers arrived there.] 'To move to a place from which others are being driven out?' This caused our people great difficulty; many talked to me about it!

"In actuality these considerations were a question of conscience; the question being, could one accept a property which became available through such methods? As spiritual adviser I counseled that they should dismiss such thoughts. The entire matter is, for the re-settler, only barter; the surrender of one property for another. And since the intermediaries in this case are two states, (Italy and Germany) the individual re-settler is not responsible, even less so because he neither caused it nor wished it".

The value of the Reverend's spiritual advice may be seen in the following:

"When asked by my bishop in 1941 if I will leave [resettle] or stay I replied: 'I will stay with my people; wherever they go, I will go' ".

Four years later, in May 1945, he is on the road with his people attempting to outrun the approaching Communist liberators. He calls them bandits.

And when he realizes that they are very near, he takes flight. "I decided quickly, took my briefcase and told my housekeeper that I may not return and left. With that I separated myself from the bulk of our people and from all I had wished to save".

Nowhere does the Reverend reflect, as do the farmer, my father and many others, on the fact that from this region the native Slovene population had been forcibly evicted to make room for the Gottscheer! Did he, especially as a priest, sleep peacefully, knowing that the houses his parishioners were now sleeping in had been taken forcefully from other people?

The Reverend also writes that he spoke with many settlers in various villages and learned much, but to obtain a total overview was not possible. He is certain, however, that not all settlers were treated the same and often with wildly contradictory ground rules. Among the lucky and satisfied, the Reverend places those who had little or nothing in the enclave but now were much better off. He also talks about those who did not complain and accepted what they were given. Then there were those who complained bitterly and with good reason:

"There were too many disappointments, much sorrow and many tears, much anger and cursing, most often with good reason and cause. But also in some cases without justification, since they had nothing at all back in the enclave. And it was these who complained the most. They were the people who had shown the greatest enthusiasm for the resettlement and now were the least satisfied. Some believed that they were to get something special, much better than the others. They believed in this but could not explain why".

The answer to the "why" is in the letter Lampeter wrote to Gauleiter Uiberreither on November 2, 1941.[92] In this letter Lampeter states that the VGL had decided to deny 577 farmers their equivalent, if small, farm in the Reich.

Instead, "worthy and capable" young Gottscheer, landless peasants who had never run a farm but were loyal supporters of the VGL were to become the landed "border farmers" of the Reich. This is verified by SS-Untersturmführer A. Dolezalek, head of the planning staff for the "General Settling Area". [93]

But the promise of the VGL to its "enthusiastic supporters" (those who now complain the most) had been confirmed by SS-Sturmbannführer Dr. Stier and Dr. Wollert (the DUB in Ljubljana) when they came to Gottschee on November 9 to reverse the severely lagging enthusiasm for the resettlement. Their decision had been published in the November 17, 1941 issue of the *GZ*. (see chapter *Assignment and Preparation*)

The reason by the VGL for concealing the settlement area to its people is given by SS-Sturmbannführer (Major) Dr. Stier, the Leader of the Resettlement Office in Berlin. He described in his notes the initial planning meeting with the VGL

---

92   *Quellen*, doc. 144, note 7.

93   *Die Umsiedlung*, pg. 100

held at the SS Reichshauptamt (headquarters) in Berlin in May 1941. (see chapter *Assignment and Preparation*)

The Mannschaftsführer had good reason to conceal the region and the conditions there. Lampeter knew that to convince a population attached to their land was going to be difficult. And to tell them that instead of being resettled to the 'Inner Germany', they were to take over the properties of expelled Slovene, would most likely threaten the success of the resettlement. But Lampeter was wrong. This concealment not only jeopardized the resettlement but, ultimately, contributed to Lampeter's downfall and disgrace.

Long before the invasion of Yugoslavia on April 6, 1941, Hitler had decided to annex Lower Styria and Upper Krain, both populated by Slovenes believed to be sympathetic to Germany and therefore willing candidates for assimilation into the Reich. Hitler ceded the Slovenia south of these two areas, which included Ljubljana and the Gottschee enclave, to Italy. (Hitler had communicated his decision to Count Ciano at the conference in Vienna on April 20, 1941).

After the occupation Hitler gave total responsibility for the civil administration of Lower Styria to Siegfried Uiberreither, the Gauleiter of Styria. He formalized this assignment on April 14, 1941 by appointing Uiberreither as the Chief Civilian Administrator for Lower Styria with orders to take directives only from himself. Simultaneously, Hitler gave Gauleiter Kutschera of Carinthia a similar responsibility for Upper Krain. [94]

(The enclave was not occupied for strategic reasons since it was too isolated, geographically too remote in difficult territory and as such presented indefensible borders to the German Reich. Consequently Hitler decided to resettle the Gottscheer to the Save/Sotla area of the de-facto annexed Lower Styria, from which all resident Slovenes were to be removed).

The Marburger Zeitung of April 29, 1941 reports on a speech of Uiberreither:

"On April 28, 1941 the Chief of the Civil Administration of Lower Styria gave a speech in which he told a group of SA-Men from Upper Styria:

"When more than three weeks ago the Führer gave me the assignment to again incorporate Lower Styria into the homeland he said to me: 'Make me this land [Lower Styria] German again!' And when he also said: 'I will place all the power in

---

94   *Quellen, doc. 16.*

that land in your hands', I realized that a heavy responsibility was descending upon my shoulders". [95]

With this assignment Hitler tasked the Gauleiter to prepare Lower Styria for formal annexation to the Third Reich. However, from that day forward the Gauleiter treated the area as annexed, certainly de-facto if not de-jure, which was never to be.

And on April 20, only nine days before the article in the Marburger Zeitung, Himmler had already promised part of this land to the Gottscheer who were told that they would be resettled into the "Reich".

Both Lower Styria and Upper Krain (like the rest of Slovenia) had been part of the Austrian Monarchy until 1918. During this time, the Austrians were successful in their centuries long germanization of these lands, partly because both areas were geographically close to the German speaking part of Styria and Carinthia. During this time, German expressions entered the Slovene vocabulary to such an extent that a large part of the population, especially in the rural areas, now spoke a language that was a mixture of both. The SS Reichsamt called these Slovene "Windische".

The germanization of the Slovene had been especially effective in the main cities of Maribor (Marburg), Celje (Cilli), Ptuj (Pettau). By the start of WW1, they were seen to be German cities. This was also, if to a lesser degree, the case in the smaller cities further south such as Krško (Gurkfeld) and Brežice (Rann).

However, this ongoing "germanization" by the Austrians was challenged by the emerging Slovene nationalism during the 19th century. And when after WW1, Lower Styria (like Upper Krain) became part of Yugoslavia, the new Slavic state decided to negate the effort of the Austrians.

To do this, the Slovene government used the same tactics as it did in the Gottschee enclave. It replaced the formerly German official language with Slovene, turned administrative controls over to loyal Slovene nationals, encouraged Slovenes to move into ethnic German areas and forced the German speaking minorities to learn the Slovene language.

But as in Gottschee, the resident ethnic Germans, the Germanized Slovene elite and many of the Slovene sympathetic to Germany, particularly those in the big cities, actively resisted the 're-absorption effort' after 1918 by joining pro German organizations such as the Kulturbund and the Steirischer Heimatbund. After Hitler

---

95 *Quellen, doc. 17, note 4).*

came to power in 1933, these organizations actively served to promote Nazi ideology. As in Gottschee, they lobbied for annexation to the Reich in the event of German occupation of Yugoslavia. And when in 1941 Hitler agreed to do this in Lower Styria, the leaders of the Steirischer Heimatbund were overjoyed, while their counterparts in Gottschee were deeply disappointed.

The notes on a meeting between the Reichsminister of the Interior and Gauleiter Uiberreither (stamped secret) explain the "Windische" to be in line with the opinion of the Reichsamt:

"The Windische represent a sort of intermediate stage between the Germans and the Slovene. Predominantly they are a rural population, which during the Habsburg Reich was loyal to their German state. They will today strongly welcome the annexation, since they will benefit economically from it. Among them, our germanization policy will fall on fertile ground. Viewed racially, there is hardly any difference between the Windische and the Upper Styrians [in Austria further north]. Among them the German language has remained known since 1918. Via the Steirischer Heimatbund and close contact between the Windische and the Germans at all levels, their re-germanization will occur rapidly.

"In the new territories, the NSDAP [the Nazi party] will not be built up. In its place steps the Steirischer Heimatbund. It encompasses all the Ethnic Germans and the German-friendly Windische. The Heimatbund is organized in line with the [NSDAP] party. The leadership in the Local District Office will be predominantly Ethnic Germans. Their leader, the Bundesführer, shall be an ethnic German, presently the SA-Standartenführer, [Franz Steindl]". [96]

How the Reichsamt itself viewed the population of Lower Styria in 1941 is documented by Dr. Lammers, Reichsminister and Chief of the Reichskanzlei in Berlin:

"In the area of Lower Styria, which contains approximately 550,000 people, there live several hundred thousand "Windische" who represent the majority of the population. The Windische were originally Slovene who, after strong intermingling and centuries long cohabitation with the Germans of Lower Styria, moved closer to 'Germandom' and in doing so adopted the German culture". [97]

---

96   Quellen, doc 13.

97   Quellen, doc 153.

(A more precise later statistic places the total population at 570,000 with a breakdown as follows: Ethnic Germans 35,000, Slovene 135,000 and Windische 400,000.) [98]

The Gauleiter also believed the Windische to be loyal and valuable members of his dominion and was to give them full rights as citizens of the Reich, he now having, according to Hitler "...all the power in that land" in his hands. But this plan would soon lead to serious conflicts with the ingathered Gottscheer who objected to be placed on the same level as the "racially inferior" Slovene and with whom they were now to coexist as equals in the Third Reich.

The process of "assimilating all Slovenes of Lower Styria" was to be through the "Steirischer Heimatbund". "By joining, the Slovene (mostly Windische) will show their intent to become Germans". After they joined, they were issued a green ID card and given all the rights of a temporary German citizen. They would become full citizens of the Reich after a trial period of 10 years. Those Slovene who could prove their lineage was Ethnic German (like the Gottscheer) were given a blue ID card and made citizens of the Reich immediately. [99]

Both the Gauleiter and the SS-Reichshauptamt in Berlin knew that success with Hitler's assignment: 'Make me this land [Lower Styria] German again! ' depended on solidifying the attachment of the Slovene "Windische" to German nationalism. To assure this, all Slovene nationalists who might interfere with this objective had to be removed, their property nationalized. In line with this, SS-Reichsführer Himmler issued the first directive on April 18, 1941:

"Remove immediately the entire Slovene intellectual elite. [Teachers, priests, lawyers, doctors, engineers].

"Remove all Slovene nationals who settled in the area after 1914.

"Remove the entire Slovene population from the Save/Sotla area. [The southernmost border of the Reich].

"Remove from the villages of Lower Styria the inhabitants who display a foreign bloodline.

"The rest of the population, [mostly Windische] remains. As per directive from the Gauleiter, this population shall show its allegiance to Germany by joining the Steirischer Heimatbund". [100]

---

98   *Quellen, doc 319.*
99   *Quellen, doc 153.*
100 *Quellen, doc 23.*

OUR INGATHERING – THEIR DEPORTATION

In line with this directive, SS-Obergruppenführer Heydrich estimates that a total of 260,000 Slovene must be deported. All were to be evacuated to Serbia. [101]

The responsibility for the ingathering of ethnic Germans had been assigned by Hitler on October 7, 1939 to the SS Reichshauptamt under Himmler. This included the clearing of annexed lands of non-German resident population to make room for the 'ingathered'. To deal with both aspects of this assignment Himmler established the office of the RKFDV.

To facilitate this effort in Slovenia, the Reichshauptamt set up an RKFDV Station in Maribor, headed by SS-Sturmbannführer (Major) Laforce. This office was to take and coordinate directions from both the SS Reichshauptamt in Berlin and the Gauleiter in Graz, Styria. Differences, if any, were to be resolved by Hitler himself. The Ingathering into Lower Styria was labeled "Südmark" and placed under SS-Untersturmführer Bliss.

This dual governance led to considerable friction between the two offices. The objective of the SS was to remove the entire non-German population and resettle the land with ingathered ethnic Germans. The objective of the Gauleiter, however, was to follow Hitler's orders: "Make me this land [Lower Styria] German again! " To accomplish this, he wished to keep in place all those Slovenes who were sympathetic to Germany and who had been partially assimilated during the many centuries under Austria. And settle the ingathered Gottscheer among them as equal citizens of the Reich.

At a meeting on May 6, 1941 between the Gauleiter, the SS-Stabshauptamt and the Foreign Ministry of the Reich, the German Military Command in Serbia presents objections to the proposed immediate shipment of 260,000 Slovene to Serbia. It claims that in view of all other demands on transportation at that time, including the war in Greece and the preparations to invade the Soviet Union on June 22, such

---

101 *Quellen*, doc 27.

shipment will impose a severe burden on the rail network. The start of moving the Slovene is therefore postponed to the beginning of July. [102]

In mid May the government of the newly formed Croatian Ustasha state, (now an ally of the Reich), offers to accept the Slovene who were to be expelled providing it can, in turn, expel to Serbia (now occupied by the Reich) an equivalent number of Serbs residing in Croatia. Hitler agrees to this offer on May 25, and on June 4 discussions to accomplish this start in Zagreb. [103]

The conclusion at that meeting was that the population transfer was to occur in three waves.

1. Move 5,000 intellectuals and politically suspect Slovene to Serbia. To be done by July 5, 1941.

2. Move 25,000 Slovene, who had settled in Lower Styria after 1914, to Croatia. To be done between July 10 and the end of August 1941.

3. Move 145,000 Slovene to Croatia. To be done between 15 September and October 31, 1941.

Included in the last wave were 65,000 Slovene farmers from the Save/Sotla area (in part to make room for the Gottscheer) and 80,000 farmers from Upper Krain, the part of Slovenia that was annexed to the Carinthia Gau in April 1941.

In all, the 260,000 of the original plan of May 6, 1941 had been reduced to 175,000.

The following is what actually did occur:

Wave 1: By July 5, 1941, 4,780 of the targeted 5,000 intellectuals had been shipped directly to Serbia. The rest fled beyond reach. In essence this task was accomplished mainly due to careful preparation prior to the occupation.

Wave 2: By August 22, only 7,750 of the projected 25,000 had been moved to Croatia. The initial estimate proved to be far too high. Some of the targeted 25,000 escaped over the border into the Slovenia occupied by Italy. Many others were reclassified as being of German descent, or discovered to be Croatian citizens and, therefore, could remain in place. Additional individuals were excluded due to a shortage of qualified labor in Lower Styria. [104]

---

102 *Quellen, doc 27, 210.*
103 *Quellen, doc 81.*
104 *Quellen, doc 131, 179.*

OUR INGATHERING – THEIR DEPORTATION

(Wave 2 evacuation ceased between August 22 and September 8. This was due to extensive Slovene Partisan activity against the Nazi occupier at the end of July - beginning of August in both Upper Krain and Lower Styria. This action was so serious that Himmler ordered a stop to the evacuation).

Wave 3: By September 22, a total of 9,343 had been moved to Croatia. Another 17,000 moved to Croatia voluntarily. By this date only 26,343 of the 175,000 had been removed. [105]

At a meeting in Zagreb on September 22, the RKFDV projected another 65,000 Slovene to be moved to Croatia, 45,000 from Slovenia and 20,000 from Carinthia.

But the Croatians stated that "due to the political situation it is no longer possible to accept and settle the Slovenes". This was because Partisan activity in Croatia (in response to the expulsion of the Serbian population to make room for the Slovenes), reached such proportions that further acceptance was out of the question. [106]

By September 22, 1941 the Slovenes that were to be deported to make room for Gottscheer were still in place; their resettlement, as ordered by Himmler to start on October 10, was now in doubt. However (according to Article 10 of the Resettlement Contract with Italy), the resettlement of the Gottscheer was required to be completed by November 30, 1941.

Consequently Gauleiter Uiberreither concluded that the Gottscheer resettlement had to be postponed to the spring. As a result, SS-Sturmbannführer Laforce, head of the Maribor RKFDV office, on October 8 requested that the resettlement be postponed until after March 20, 1942. [107]

When the VGL received the news that the resettlement might be postponed, it sent protests to the SS-Stabshauptamt in Berlin and to the RKFDV branch in Maribor. It had good cause to protest the delay since it already had to deal with substantial opposition by the Gottscheer and they feared a further delay would increase this resistance to a point which might threaten the entire resettlement project. [108]

On October 18, however, Himmler did order the deportation of the Slovene population from the Save/Sotla region. But now into camps of Inner Germany, their transfer to Croatia being no longer possible. This decision was announced to the Slovene on October 20 and the removal of 45,000 Slovene from the region started without further delay. The first train carrying Slovene to Lower Silesia left

---

105 Quellen, doc 179.
106 Quellen, doc 133.
107 Quellen, doc 149.
108 Quellen, doc 143, 144.

on October 24, at 10.28 AM. [109] On October 20 Himmler also ordered the start of the Gottscheer resettlement.

The VGL received Himmler's decision on October 20 and it immediately began to carry out the final preparations. The ingathering train "Heinrich" arrived at the Gottschee City station on October 21 to start the "Option" processing.

And on November 15 the SS-Stabshauptamt reported to Himmler that: "The first Gottschee transport left on November 14 for Lower Styria. And by today 20,000 Slovene had already been removed". [110]

But by November 15, 1941, another 17,000 Slovene had still to be removed. This was happening while the Gottscheer were already arriving. It is very likely, therefore, that our train crossed with one going in the opposite direction carrying expelled Slovene. When we arrived in Veliko Mraševo (Gross Mraschau) it was obvious that the former residents had been forced to leave not much more than a few days ago.

The final train carrying re-settlers left Gottschee on January 22, 1942. But some Slovenes were being expelled even long after that. Including the family living in the small house with the thatched roof at the turn-off to Veliko Mraševo.

According to the final SS records of the initially targeted 260,000 Slovenes, only 68,123 were removed from Slovenia; around 37,000 of them to make room for the Gottscheer. The reduced number was in large part due to the effort of Gauleiter Uiberreither who wanted to keep the Slovene in place.

At the end of 1941, the Reich's Ambassador to Croatia, SA-Obergruppenführer (General) Siegfried Kasche sent Gauleiter Uiberreither a report on the resettling of Slovene and Serbs. [111] Part of this report is an appraisal of the political and economic consequences of this resettling effort. Essential excerpts are quoted below:

"Lessons from the Slovene Resettlement.

"Through this Slovene resettlement, the southern border of the Reich was to be cleared of all hostile forces and the national determination of the Slovene destroyed. In fact, exactly the opposite was achieved.

---

109 *Quellen, doc 164.*

110 *Die Umsiedlung, pg. 59.*

111 *Quellen, doc. 179.*

OUR INGATHERING – THEIR DEPORTATION

"By resettling entire villages without considering the political orientation of individuals, even of persons who were already accepted into the Steirischer Heimatbund, the remainder felt uncertain and threatened. Had the deportation been more specific it would have given those remaining a feeling of being secure; but in fact it was expanded and continued sporadically. Consequently, this uncertainty, together with unfavorable economic measures, in effect turned the 70-80% of German-friendly Slovene into bitter enemies of Germany, bringing new numbers to the forces of the bandits. [112]

"While we ruthlessly resettled the Slovene, the Italians [in their part of occupied Slovenia] used a surprisingly different tactic. The Italians accept as valid the Slovene national personality; the Italian High Commissioner even declared, on his arrival in Ljubljana, that he valued Slovene culture and the Minister for Italian national culture created an important Slovene function within the Italian Imperium.

"When the Slovene initially learned that Ljubljana was to be under the Italians, the Ljubljana Slovenes were horrified. (The prior poor treatment of Slovene minorities by the Italians was well known). Today the situation is quite different; the Slovenes see the Italians as their savior. And through the establishment of a Slovene University in Ljubljana, there will doubtlessly emerge a Slovene-Italian center, whose activity will naturally be directed against Germany.

"The Slovene resettlement has also unfavorable results on the rest of Europe since it portrays us Germans in the role of a brutal egotist. The worst being that we could have avoided this label. This label [brutal German egotist] is self evident in the grotesque cases where Slovenes, resettled to Croatia and above all in Serbia, are captured by representatives of the Reich's Labor Ministry and are transported as laborers to Inner Germany. This begs the inevitable conclusion that the resettlement of the Slovenes had no other purpose than to steal their property and use them as ordinary slave laborers.

"The Slovene resettlement also brought substantial economic damage. The Reich lost a large part of the valuable workforce of farmers, craftsmen and ordinary laborers. The Slovenes are a thoroughly qualified workforce.

"As a replacement for the very capable Slovene farmers, the Gottscheer are not an equivalent substitute, firstly because their work methodology is antiquated and secondly, because a part of them have, through their wanderings, lost their farming skills. Through this, some of the fertile lands of Lower Styria will become, if not totally untilled, at least in part under-utilized".

---

112 *Slovene Partisans, at this time still non-communist and independent of Tito.*

THE BELLS RING NO MORE

At the time of this report, Germany's Ambassador to Croatia, SA-Obergruppenführer (General) Siegfried Kasche did not yet know of the severe penalties Himmler was to impose on the once friendly Slovene for their unexpected resistance to the Germans. To suppress this resistance Himmler issued, in June 25 1942, an edict called: *"Befehl für die Unterdrückung der Bandentätigkeit in den Gebieten Oberkrain und Untersteiermark"* (Order for the suppression of bandit activity in the territories of Upper Krain and Lower Styria).

According to this edict, "... all elements of the population who willingly supported the bandits with manpower, provisions, weapons and shelter, are to be rendered harmless. The men of a guilty family, in many cases also those of their clan, are to be executed, their wives taken to concentration camps and their children sent into the Altreich for reorientation." [113]

The first mass action to expel relatives of the executed supporters of the Partisans in Lower Styria according to Himmler's edict, started at the beginning of August 1942. More than 1,000 persons were seized and taken to a collection camp in the Celje vicinity (Teharje). On the 9th of August, the children were separated from the surviving adults and taken (by train) to the re-settlement camp in Frohnleiten (Upper Styria). Anna Rath, the leader of the guards, reports on the abysmal condition of the 430 children on that train. The adults were taken to concentration camps where most of them perished in gas chamber.

"In four other major actions between October '42 and June '43, the children and the surviving adults were taken to various camps of the VoMi in the Bavarian part of the Ostmark. With another edict from the Reich's Security Headquarters in Berlin, dated July 16, '43, further expulsion of relatives of the executed collaborators of the Partisans was stopped. After that date, they were taken to the penal work camp in Sterntal [Sternice] which was set up and run by the Steirischer Heimatbund". [114]

According to a letter dated February 10, 1943 written by SS-Sturmbannführer Klingsporn in Berlin:

"Approx. 600 children from Lower Styria and Upper Krain were, according to directives from the Stabshauptamt, turned over to the 'Verein Lebensborn e.V.' for their care and adoption".[115] The purpose of Lebensborn was to help raising the next Nazi generation.

"In the months of July and August 1942 alone, the German occupier burned eleven villages and leveled them to the ground; shot the entire male population

---

113 *Quellen, doc 256, footnote 2.*
114 *Quellen, doc 251, footnote 2.*
115 *Quellen, doc 292.*

above fifteen years of age and deported the rest of the population. This population had for some time given shelter and support to the bandits". [116]

The reflective Ambassador Kasche could have predicted that Himmler's edict would only turn the once German-friendly population of Lower Styria into hatred for the occupier. In fact, any sympathies the Slovenes retained toward the Germans remained only among the most intimate collaborators of the Nazis.

After the capitulation of Italy in September 1943, the rest of the Slovene territory, until then occupied by Italy, was taken over by Germany. In this part as well, Himmler's edict of June 25, 1942 was enforced mercilessly to deal with Partisan collaborators.

On our second day in Veliko Mraševo (Gross Mraschau), Mother woke us at daybreak and all were up long before the bus arrived. Mitzi, Paul and I were to stay behind while Father and Mother left for the rail station in Brežice (Rann). "You are not to go far and stay out of trouble while we are gone", she said.

The three of us went to look for the others who had arrived with us the day before. But we found only teenagers and children since most of the adults, like our parents, had taken the bus back to the station to take possession of their belongings. And after the young neighbors showed us their new houses, we continued to explore our new surroundings.

The village consisted of about 80 farm houses, all next to one another and most of them along the dirt road that started 500 meters beyond the little thatched house at the intersection and led to the river at the other end of the village. Along this dirt road, two other dirt roads branched off to the right, the first leading to our house and the fields beyond. The second branched off at the apex of a small triangle of space in the middle of the village. This road served another few farms and then also disappeared into the fields.

The triangle of graveled space at the second intersection appeared to be the village square; a space only a small fraction of our large village square in Masern. A space far too small for a troop of gypsies, a traveling circus, the assembly of a fire brigade or the trinket stands set up on the day of the patron saint.

And the triangle was bare. There was no ancient linden tree offering pleasing fragrance in the spring and pleasant shade in the summer to those resting on

---

116 Quellen, doc 238, note 6.

surrounding stone benches. No tree on which to nail important announcements. And along the edges of the square there were no taverns in which to have meetings, have a drink, talk or argue with friends and neighbors. No school. No store for women to buy staples and to gossip.

There also was no church on or near this triangle. Instead there was a large freestanding cross constructed of lumber beams on to which was nailed the carved figure of a thorn-crowned Christ. It stood not on the square but on one side of one of the three roads bordering the triangle.

But there was a church on a raw plot of land at the end of the road leading away from the tip of the triangle, just before the start of the fields. It was dedicated to St. Markus. It was a lonely structure surrounded by neither trees nor bushes; a parsonage nowhere in sight. The main structure seemed complete but it was obvious that the completion process had been interrupted, if not by the war, then by a lack of funds prior to that. The nave inside was empty; its large and spacious floor space lacked benches. The walls were void of any decoration and the bare and unadorned altar a mere shadow of the one we left behind. Also bare was the raised choir space with its entry to the bell tower whose interior was also empty; no stairs or ladders leading upward to a clock platform or a space for the bells. And with no clock or bells to obstruct the view, the raw interior of the steeple disappeared in darkness.

Beyond the base of the triangle, the main dirt road continued through the rest of the village toward the river. Straight and in-between an uninterrupted series of adjacent farmhouses. After about 300 meters of open fields, the road ended in a small sandy beach. The river Krka (Gurk), which had skirted the hills after Cerklje, had swung back again toward Veliko Mraševo (Gross Mraschau). At this point it was wide, deep and dark, its slow waters silently hiding the destiny of my school friend Franz. But further downstream where it curved to the right it narrowed and hurried over shallows, the water rippling over protruding rocks. Here one could wade across as did some of the Slovene in their desperate attempt to escape the SS that was clearing the village only a few days ago.

At this point the three of us were unaware that this relatively young, bland and characterless village would never become a successor to Masern with its 600 year old tradition, its harmonious self sufficiency and interdependence. But we were aware, if dimly, that the river would play a major role also in our future and the future of our new village.

OUR INGATHERING – THEIR DEPORTATION

They returned from the train station in early afternoon. Yiorgo pulling our own farm wagon with Father sitting on the bench up front holding the reins. The light carriage was attached to the rear and to that was roped our cow. Mother followed on foot. They were part of a caravan of wagons bringing the possessions of those of us who had arrived yesterday.

Some of the crates were on our wagon behind Father. The rest, including the crate with the fattened pig was on a second wagon provided by the DAG. The caravan was accompanied by Slovene men the SS had engaged to help with transporting the possessions of the settlers to their destination. They and others had loaded the labeled crates on the wagons, crates which had been placed in the snow on the siding at the station since the train had to return to get other settlers.

In our yard the Slovene unloaded the wagons, taking the most sensitive crates into the big barn. And when the unloading was done and the animals safely in the stables, the Slovene men chatted with Mother in the kitchen as she was giving them something to eat and drink. Whatever went through the minds of these men when they discovered that this intruder was also a Slovene can only be guessed!

After that day, the 9th of December 1941, it took several days to unpack the crates and find a place for their contents. There was much redundancy of items, both within the house and in the farm buildings since the previous owner had been forced to leave all his possessions behind. Much of the existing furnishings within the house, including a complete set of china, were given to Katharina who arrived four days later with far less and was given a house that had very little in it. She had brought little with her, having lost all of her possessions when her little wooden house burned to the ground in 1938. Since then, she, her husband and the two boys had been living in the house of her in-laws. Now she was happy to again have her own place, one far better that the one consumed by flames.

During the following few days, Mother would find time to walk with us three into the village and visit those who like us had come on the 9th of December or thereafter. And while she talked to other women, Mitzi and I wandered off to join other youngsters inspecting the village and the still empty houses in it. Signs of a chaotic and hasty departure were everywhere, all similar to what we had found in our house.

By December 13, all of those destined for Veliko Mraševo had arrived. But not all of the 206 that had left Masern; some were taken to Malo Mraševo (Klein Mraschau), a smaller village about two km further along the Kostanjevica Cerklje road. Two of them we never saw again; our former neighbor Mattl and the incontinent recluse Peinitsch. They had their papers marked "A" and were sent to the ambiguous "Altrcich".

THE BELLS RING NO MORE

I do not remember how the other new arrivals reacted to their new village and their assigned homes. It seems, at least judging from the reports of the Farmer and the Reverend that the people of Masern fared better than many others in different villages. I do, however, remember Father commenting to those who arrived later that the soil of the land was superior to that we left behind.

But I also remember that most kept lamenting the expulsion of the Slovene.

All however, talked nostalgically about the Masern they left behind. "A jewel of a village left for this drab and characterless place of no more than a string of houses on a dirt road leading to a river" was being said. Not the promised place somewhere in the inner part of old Germany, a place of culture and tradition that had been promised us so frequently during the year, a Germany of which we had become especially proud in the last decade. Instead, it was just another part of the annexed Slovenia from which the rightful owners had been forcibly removed. And the possibility that it was to be part of the Third Reich only temporarily and that we too might suffer the same fate, had not yet crossed many a mind. But this was to become apparent all too soon.

Chapter 15

Mission Accomplished

SA Untersturmführer (2nd Lieutenant) Stieger, the Leader of the Rann District Settlement Staff, reports from the enclave on December 12, 1941:

"The news arriving here in the Gottschee enclave from the first settlers [to the Save/Sotla area] is shattering to those about to leave. Enragement has spread throughout the enclave, the people believing they have been universally deceived, especially by Lampeter and his VGL which had purposefully concealed the settlement area, kept the poor conditions there secret and even made unrealistic promises. Some Gottscheer reacted spontaneously and resorted to individual action". [117]The farmer R.K., whose village was among the last to leave the enclave, writes:

"When it became known that our homeland to be was in the German occupied Slovenia on the Croatian border, a large part of the population again actively opposed the resettlement. This, in spite of the fact that the resettlement was already in full swing. These opponents sought ways to extract themselves from the noose, but found no way out and were forced to accept their destiny. There were many cases where the re-settlers brought their property from the rail station back to their original villages at their expense. But the VGL immediately stepped in to frighten these people. They told the re-settlers that they no longer owned their property; neither house nor land, all is now in the hands of the Resettlement Authority which will not return anything. The people were left with no choice other than bring their possessions to the station for the second time".

The anger of the resettlers had turned to despondency. The simple farmers could not stand up to the tactics of the DUG (Deutsche Umsiedlung Gesellschaft – German Resettling Authority) or the VGL.

This was not the case with the bourgeoisie of Gottschee city. This group was not willing to resettle without defined assurances regarding their economic and financial future. And given the disheartening reports from those who had already arrived there, they lost trust not only in the VGL but also in the Resettling Authority and decided to resist.

---

117 *Die Umsiedlung, pg. 123, 124.*

On Jan. 2, 1942, Dr. Redell, the deputy head of the DUB (Deutscher Umsiedlung Bevollmächtigter – German Resettling Plenipotentiary), the Civil Resettling Authority and the Reich's intermediary to the Italians, with his office in Ljubljana telegraphed the SS-Stabshauptamt in Berlin, the German Foreign Office and the RKFDV office in Maribor the news that the "Gottschee City people are resisting resettlement and are prepared to withdraw their agreement if their resettlement is not postponed until March". The telegram also said:

"We made them aware that such a postponement is not possible and since the VGL has not taken a position against their stand, we believe they support these wishes. Believe it urgent that the Reichskommissar impress on the VGL that the German Reich is bound by the Resettlement Contract to the agreed upon dates. I have asked Stabsführer Laforce, head of the RKFDV station in Maribor, to immediately explain the situation to the re-settlers and the VGL". [118]

The above request for help was prompted by a letter of protest from a group of sixty one Gottscheer (of the City) to Dr. Wollert, the head of the DUB. [119] The letter, which was drafted at the initiative of Dr. Arko, explained their position in six specific points:

1. "We had been promised, repeatedly, that the Rann [Brežice] triangle would be an exclusively Gottscheer settlement and that in this area foreign influence will be excluded. Now we have come to realize that we have become a category of second class citizens. All responsible positions there are already occupied by others [Ethnic Germans from Lower Styria] and therefore our interests are not represented as we had wished".

2. "Our larger vested interests may, due to lack of space, be resettled outside the area. But only with a guarantee that this is a temporary arrangement".

The lack of space was verified by a delegation of City Gottscheer which was sent to the two cities, Brežice (Rann) and Krško (Gurkfeld) to investigate. Their report was alarming especially when it became known that there were not enough dwellings in the two towns to accommodate the people of Gottschee city. The fact was that of the 300 dwellings requested by Dr. Wollert, the head of the DUB, only 35 were available.[120] This was according to a report from SA Untersturmführer

---

118 *Die Umsiedlung*, pg. 126.

119 *Nacistična*, pg. 662.

120 This to a report from SA Untersturmführer (Lieutenant) Stieger, dated Dec. 31, 1941 (see *Die Umsiedlung*, pg. 124, note 9 and pg 136, pg 42.

(Lieutenant) Stieger, dated Dec. 31, 1941. Those for whom no space remained were to be settled in Upper Krain or Carinthia. [121]

3. "To assure a secure arrangement, representatives of [our] citizens should be elected. Their nomination should come from the undersigned group".

4. "Businesses and enterprises in the settlement area should be turned over to Gottscheer if they are presently in non-Gottscheer hands".

5. "Of special importance is the sale of the properties in the [Gottschee] City. It would be unacceptable to all of us if these properties were to be sold or turned over to EMONA [the private Italian society handling the purchase of the Gottscheer properties for the Italian government] prior to our departure".

6. "And of special concern is that our Savings and Loan Bank, which we have maintained during our most difficult times of oppression, be fully reconstituted in the settling area as a Gottscheer institution, including its reserves of 400,000 RM [Reichsmark]". [These reserves were to be surrendered to Italy as part of Article 6 of the Contract.]

Given these disheartening reports, the Gottscheer of the City had lost trust in the VGL and the Reich. A Reich that had promised to resettle them as a unit into an area within which they could function as an autonomous group. Now it seemed to them that the Settlement Authority's civil officials, predominantly ethnic Germans of Lower Styria or Windische Slovene, were denying them that promise.

In reaction to the appeal for help on Jan. 2 by Dr. Redell, the official responsible for placing the Gottschee City resettlers in the new area, SS-Untersturmführer (2nd Lieutenant) Bliss and SS-Hauptsturmführer (Captain) Liupold Schallermayer, both of the Maribor RKFDV office, left immediately for the enclave on Jan. 3, to rectify the situation. But on the way there, they stopped to see Dr. Redell in Ljubljana where they also met a representative of the Foreign Office of the Reich and Dr. Knuth, the DUB Resettlement Commissioner resident in Gottschee City. Also present was Josef Schober, the Volksgruppenführer who was the official leader of the Gottscheer. (if in name only)

Both Dr. Redell and the official from the Foreign office explained that the "uneasiness of the Gottscheer resettlers was due to false rumors originating from members of the VGL". Dr. Knuth agreed with this and even identified Lampeter as one of the "rumormongers". [122]

What Schober contributed to this meeting is not known nor why he was there. The German officials, however, learned that Schober was uncomfortable in his role

---

121 *Quellen, doc 239.*

122 *Die Umsiedlung, pg. 128.*

as Volksgruppenführer. He wanted to resign from this position since his functions had been assumed by Lampeter who wished to formally become the leader of the Gottscheer. The officials persuaded him not to resign and he agreed to accompany them to the meeting in the City. [123]

Later that day the four German officials as well as Josef Schober, met with about 100 Gottschee City residents who wished to withdraw their formal request to resettle. Lampeter, who arrived at this meeting late, defended their written protests by claiming that "the allocated houses are worse that those in Gottschee, in the best of them sit Slovenes and officials of the Reich; that the claimed high profits of businesses there are misleading". Bliss countered that Lampeter's claims were rumors and called them "criminal". The assembled Gottscheer were astonished over this dispute by two members of the elite SS formation of the Reich, ending in a public accusation of Lampeter; the beginning of his downfall and disgrace.

Bliss, the head of the SS-Settlement Staff of Lower Styria called "Südmark", had requested the meeting at which he planned to accomplish three important objectives (see *Die Umsiedlung*, pg. 128) to dispel their doubt and restore enthusiasm for the resettlement:

1. Disprove and negate the causes of the written complaints.
2. Restore enthusiasm for the resettlement.
3. Discover the head of the group spreading rumors.

Regarding Point 1. "The Gottscheer were, after his clarifications, deeply ashamed and with tears in their eyes begged him to ignore their despondency. The VGL had failed them totally and it had spread the rumors".

Regarding Point 2. "Bliss noted that after his clarifications, the resettlers themselves explained that the reason for the letter of protest was fully attributable to the rumors spread by members of the VGL which gave them the impression that they would place themselves into an absolutely uncertain existence".

Regarding Point 3. "Bliss concluded categorically that Lampeter was the primary offender".

Bliss, together with his three colleagues and Schober, achieved all three objectives, the most important being Objectives 1 and 2. The Gottscheer were satisfied with his explanations and now agreed to resettle.

In his Objective 3, Bliss included the following comments in his report of the meeting on Jan. 3, 1942:

"Lampeter has, as a result of the various honors bestowed on him for his work in the Ethnic Group, become a megalomaniac and is for further German political

---

123 Nacistična, pg. 624

purposes, absolutely unusable. As an SS leader, I am ashamed to see such a political child in the uniform of the SS and in the rank of a Sturmbannführer. Had I been given his assignment and produced such problems, I would deserve to be demoted and taken to a concentration camp for retraining. The future leaders of the Gottscheer must, therefore, under no circumstances be taken from the ranks of the VGL but must be replaced by activists from the Reich" [124]

This was the political death sentence of Lampeter declared by Bliss, one of the most important officials responsible for the integration of the Gottscheer in their new land.

The report of Bliss resulted in a rapid disintegration of Lampeter's position and stature. The report was seconded by Laforce, his supervisor and head of the Maribor RKFDV station; it was distributed to all relevant officials including Gauleiter Uiberreither, who for many months had been irritated by Lampeter's arrogant behavior.

The process that led to Lampeter's decline and ultimate political demise had actually started on December 29, 1941 after he and his staff leader Richard Lackner visited the Save Sotla area to verify the unfavorable reports arriving back in the enclave. After finding the conditions the arriving settlers were facing there unacceptable "due to neglect by the Settlement Authority", he and Lackner drove directly to Maribor to see Laforce, the head of the RKFDV Station to report on what they found and request that the situation be rectified. Laforce was absent and Lampeter deemed it pointless to discuss the matter with the lower ranking SS-Untersturmführer Bliss.

At this juncture, the impulsive Lampeter lost his patience and, ignoring all formalities of the SS hierarchy, decided to present his grievances directly to the highest authority. He describes this in his memoirs written in February, 1942:

"With a present from the Gottscheer Mannschaftsführer to Reichsführer-SS Heinrich Himmler, the youth leader was sent by the Mannschaftsführer to Berlin on December 29, 1941. There to hand the present directly to the Reichsführer and explain to him the conditions in the settlement region. This was, alas, not to be; the Reichsführer was at the Führer's headquarters".

But on the 5th of January, youth leader Richard Lackner did meet with SS-Gruppenführer (Major General) Greifeld, the highest ranking officer under

---

124 Die Umsiedlung, pg. 129.

Himmler, and explained the unsatisfactory conditions in the settling region. Present was SS-Oberführer Hintze, head of the Expulsion Staff "Altreich-Ostmark" at the RKFDV in Berlin, who supported the (Lackner) report. Greifeld already had other reports which described the poor conditions there. Greifeld told Lackner that this morning he had tasked Hintze to "straighten out the conditions down there". The only news Lampeter received from Lackner in Berlin was on Jan. 6, in which he stated that until Jan. 3, he had accomplished nothing.

After the meeting on Jan. 3rd with Bliss and the Gottschee City people, Lampeter returned to the settlement area. He found the conditions there "worse than before; without the settlement authorities (Bliss, Schallermayer, etc.) attempting to improve the situation".

For the second time, Lampeter took a dangerous leap over the entire SS hierarchy. On Jan. 9 (prior to having met the returning Lackner) he sent a letter directly to Himmler in which he described the progressively deteriorating conditions which "must not be allowed to continue". A copy of the letter was mailed to Greifeld sometime later. Consequently, a copy of Lampeter's letter sent by Himmler to Greifeld was received prior to the one mailed to him by Lampeter directly. Himmler also ordered Greifeld to conduct a full investigation.

Greifeld, the Chief of the Stabshauptamt of the RKFDV, the Ingathering Authority directly under Himmler, was offended by Lampeter's reckless neglect for protocol as was the entire SS hierarchy below Himmler. Greifeld reacted by sending Hintze (now in Maribor) a telegram on Jan. 15, 1942:

"Lampeter, the head of the Gottschee-Mannschaft, in a letter to the Reichsführer SS dated Jan 9, 1942, grossly exaggerates the apparent difficulties [in the settlement region] which seem to be no more than an attempt to acquire for himself the leadership role [of the Gottscheer]".

To Hintze, who, had been sent by Greifeld to investigate Lackner's complaints, this was an order in disguise. He discontinued his investigation and reported that in the settlement area, "all is in order". (This claim was documented by SS-Obersturmbannführer Wagner, dated Jan 25, 1942. See *Die Umsiedlung*, pg 132). Hintze also immediately called for a meeting of all responsible SS station officials, as well as the Gauleiter and the VGL for January 16, 1942.

The five hour long proceedings labeled "Case Lampeter", were conducted by the Gauleiter. It was in effect a trial of the behavior of the Mannschaftsführer. Three separate issues were on the agenda:

The six specific charges listed by Lampeter in his letter to Himmler. All were rejected as inaccurate and dismissed.

MISSION ACCOMPLISHED

The events at the protest meeting on Jan 3rd. Lampeter countered by saying that the meeting had been pointless. "The calming of City people was not necessary since they, having lost their economic basis for survival due to all others having already left, were forced to leave as well". This callous comment was received as being arrogant by those present. And Hintze charged that "by reporting unfavorable conditions he poured oil into the fire instead of exercising his duty as a National-Socialist and persuading the City people to resettle". [125]

Hintze's charge had to do mainly with Lampeter's arrogant deed of twice bypassing the entire SS chain of command. Adding to this was the unacceptable attitude he projected at a Jan. 11, 1942 meeting with the Sturmführers of the villages which had not yet resettled. At that meeting, the contents of which were to be kept secret, Lampeter not only read his letter to Himmler to his subordinates, but also openly criticized the SS Resettling Authority and requested that evidence be collected to further prove its incompetence.

However, six of his Sturmführers, like most of the Gottscheer, no longer had confidence in Lampeter and reported the meeting to the SS. Hintze openly confronted Lampeter: "To the Sturmführers you have, among other things, said: ... "over the head of the Gauleiter and bypassing all responsible SS Stations, I will take my requests directly to Berlin". [126] The 25 year old Lampeter agreed that he said so, claiming his right to intercede on behalf of the Gottscheer at the highest authority of the Reich).

At the end of the hearing, Hintze documented the conclusion arrived at:

"After extensive discussions with Lampeter, I have gained the impression that he is too young and inexperienced for his assigned tasks, as well as the promotion to SS-Sturmbannführer and that he lacks the necessary insight and self discipline such a position requires. I have, therefore, explained to him that I myself will assume the leadership of the Gottscheer militia and wish that he refrain from any further activity in the settlement region.

"This decision also applies to his Staff leader Lackner. More drastic steps may be taken which may be mitigated by his youth which, however, I doubt. In any event, I hold that a further presence of Lampeter in the settlement region is undesirable and that he, regardless of the outcome of further proceedings, be immediately recalled to the Altreich". [127]

---

125 *Die Umsiedlung, pg 134.*

126 *ibid.*

127 *Die Umsiedlung, pg. 135.*

THE BELLS RING NO MORE

Three days after January 16, Hintze informed Greifeld in Berlin of the results of the hearing and his recommendations. But after reading the letter, Dr. Stier, the technical adviser to Greifeld, wrote to Hintze that the removal of the idealistic young leadership be reconsidered since it might affect the allegiance of the ingathered Gottscheer. He suggested that either Lampeter or Sturm remain as leaders to prevent creating an impression that these former fighters are being sacrificed. Hintze replied that no one wishes to remove Sturm, Lackner or Schober, but that the Gauleiter (who had the final word) himself concluded that it would be politically untenable to keep Lampeter in his position. Hintze also added that the leadership of the Sturms has been assumed by Laforce himself.

This conclusion, reached by the members of the RKFDV, terminated Lampeter's leadership of the Gottscheer Germans. "The discrepancy between the conception of discipline and obedience of these SS-men and the unorthodox behavior of Lampeter was so large that a compromise was no longer possible". [128]

The events suggest that Lampeter's behavior played directly into the hands of the Ingathering Authority of the Reich which demanded, as the end result, the termination of the ethnic character of the ingathered groups. This was formulated in 1940 by SS-Obersturmbannführer Dr. Fähnrich, head of the Section I, directly under SS-Gruppenführer Greifeld, Chief of the RKFDV in 1939. Paragraph 5 of the Ingathering Policy states:

"After the Ingathering of an Ethnic Group into the Reich, the Ethnic Group Leadership ceases to exist since over the Ethnic Group stands the Reich.

"The concepts defining the Balkan Germans, the Wolhynian and Bessarabian German, [Gottscheer, South Tyrolean], etc…, must, as quickly as possible, be eliminated." [129]

Greifeld reminded Gauleiter Uiberreither and Deputy of Reichskommissar Himmler of this policy in the letter (stamped Secret) dated October 31, 1941. A copy had been sent also to the Chief of the Maribor branch of the RKFDV, SS-Sturmbannführer Laforce:

"From your letter of October 12, 1941, I see that you are not fully oriented regarding the developments within the leadership of the Gottscheer. I ask you

---

128 *Die Umsiedlung*, pg. 136.

129 *Die Umsiedlung*, pg. 136.

therefore, not to take sides in these intra group quarrels. The present leadership [VGL] should for now remain, since only through a unified and firm leadership is a frictionless resettling guaranteed. This recognition of the present leadership must however not lead to a situation where persons who politically have not kept pace with the others, but have doubtlessly earned great honors regarding the upkeep of Germandom, are vilified. [Those on the "List of politically undesirables", i.e. Dr. Arko, etc.]

"After the resettlement of the Gottscheer to Lower Styria, I ask that care be taken that the Ethnic Group as such ceases to exist and that the Gottscheer, unconditionally, integrate themselves into Lower Styria and into Germandom as a whole.

[signed] Greifeld, SS-Gruppenführer". [130]

It is evident from the above that the "Case Lampeter" provided a convenient set of circumstances for the SS to enforce the Ingathering Policy of the Reich.

The chastened Lampeter, relieved of his function as leader of the Gottscheer Mannschaft, frustrated in his attempt to become leader of the Gottscheer Germans in the Reich, in February 1942 writes his memoir; his own Lagebericht (Situation Report) *"The Gottscheer Ethnic Group, 1930-1942"*. His damaged ego is clearly evident in Part III he called *"Die Letzte Entwicklung"* (The Final Development).

Loosely quoted excerpts from Part III are: (The entire version is available on www.Gottschee.de):

"The VGL is being phased out so that the resettlers can be led according to fundamental principles of the Reich.

"Sturmführers 1, 2, 3, 4, 8 and 10 have been discharged. Among them are some of the best. They are being replaced with those who in the old homeland stood apart; were the strongest opponents of the organized VGF, or who even were Slovenes. Reactionaries such as Dr. Arko are especially favored and one hears that his "Gesangsverein" will be revived under his direction.

"The Gottscheer Germans gravely contemplate these events, since they know both their former leaders as well as their replacements. A confidence in the [SS] Settlement Authority no longer exists. Their inner doubts are thereby reinforced. …. They tell themselves: 'The greatest idealists, the preachers of Germany and its National-Socialism are being cut down and in their place come men who once were

---

130 Gottschee: Das verlorene Kulturerbe der Gottscheer Deutschen. Ljubljana 1993, pg. 35.

their fiercest opponents'. The general mood can, in contrast to the one in the old homeland, be described only as negative. The disappointment they were forced to experience on their arrival in the Reich led to depression and apathy. The Gottscheer faithfully followed the call of the Führer. They believed they were returning to the Reich to enter its orderly existence. In this they were disappointed from the first day on.

"All these avoidable mistakes, none caused by the VGL, produced only scandalous conditions in the settlement region, so that today the negative and the inferior feel comfortable while the capable believe that there is no place for them here and leave for Inner Germany.

"Especially senseless is the attack on the honor of their [Gottscheer] tribe. [He describes a public event at which the Gottscheer dialect was used]. After being asked by a German civilian if they are Gottscheer, the man said: 'Too bad I do not have my pistol on me; I would quickly show you what I think of your Gypsy language'. Generally, the Ethnic Group is referred to only dismissively.

"Depressing is the fact that, here in the Reich, some of the Gendarmes are Slovenes who are disrespectful to the Gottscheer and force them to speak Slovene. Also great concern exists regarding the allocation of properties. Because of their recent experience, confidence in the Settlement Authority does not exist.

"Today it must be concluded that, after a few weeks in the Reich, the Gottscheer Group has been stripped of its bearing which served them so well during the 600 years among the Slovene. The only item which was faultlessly accomplished by the [SS] Settlement Staff was the total annihilation of an organization [the VGL] surely rare in the history of Ethnic Germans and the destruction of their treasured property; the idealism, the initiative and the joyous self-sacrifice. And all this places a heavy burden on the belief in Germany".

As is apparent in the last paragraph above, the disillusioned fanatic does not differentiate the nine year old Nazi Reich from a Germany that for centuries had been proud of its liberal traditions and cultural achievements. A Reich, which had blinded its people with the curse of extreme nationalism and racial superiority. Perhaps he never would; his ideology too deeply ingrained as he describes elsewhere in his memoir:

MISSION ACCOMPLISHED

"In National-Socialism, which found its way into the remote Gottschee only after its assumption of power in 1933, the youth discovered its true life's purpose, the recognized signpost to their aspirations and willingness to act".

The now deeply wounded Lampeter, his ego bruised, his fanatical idealism challenged and his until now unshaken belief in the Reich heavily burdened is, certainly at that point in time, incapable of introspection. Feeling betrayed by those he idolized as the best of the super race, he is incapable of reflecting on his own betrayal; the betrayal of his people from whom he withheld the truth and whom he coerced and pressured to get them to leave their ancient heritage and their lands.

He is also blind to the fact that he and his once loyal subordinates are now being blamed by the Gottscheer re-settlers for the loss of their homeland; for luring them into what they see as something inferior and far less than the Promised Land in which they are now being stripped of what they cherished for centuries; their uniqueness as an Ethnic Group.

But Lampeter and his still loyal intimate circle were not totally discouraged. After all, Lampeter's direct superiors were neither Bliss, nor Laforce, nor Hintze nor Greifeld. It was Himmler himself who had personally promoted him to SS-Sturmbannführer and accepted him as leader of the Gottscheer. Any dismissal, Lampeter believed, would have to come from Himmler himself. Had not Himmler and Hitler promised the Gottscheer in Maribor on April 26, 1941, a closed settlement area including full autonomy after the resettlement ?

It is evident that Lampeter was not aware of Himmler's Ingathering policy as defined by Dr. Fähndrich (see *Die Umsiedlung*, pg. 145):

"After the Ingathering of an Ethnic Group into the Reich, the Ethnic Group Leadership ceases to exist since over the Ethnic Group stands the Reich".

Or of Greifeld's "secret" letter to the Gauleiter dated October 31, 1941:

"After the resettlement of the Gottscheer to Lower Styria, I ask that care be taken that the Ethnic Group as such ceases to exist and that the Gottscheer integrate themselves unconditionally into Lower Styria and into Germandom as a whole".

THE BELLS RING NO MORE

But the presumptuous leaders of the Gottscheer Germans continue to act in a sovereign manner. And Lampeter, who after his dismissal on January 16, 1942 has no formal role behaves as if he still had. All to the great annoyance of the SS officers of the ingathering hierarchy, the Gauleiter of Styria and the officials of the "Steirischer Heimatbund".

In view of Hitler's Ingathering Directives, transformed into policy by Himmler and now being executed by both the Gauleiter and the SS-Staff of the RKFDV, it is clear that the assurance of autonomy the VGL received in Maribor on April 26, 1941 was no more than an empty promise. This must have become evident even to the disillusioned Lampeter who continued to hope for favorable news from Berlin.

But even more troubling to Lampeter, his VGL and other Gottscheer all now citizens of the Third Reich, was the realization that they were now at a level no different than that of the "inferior" Slovenes of Lower Styria, all scheduled to become German citizens of equal rank. SS-Untersturmführer Dolezalek quotes the Gottscheer: "We thought that we were leaving for Germany, but ended up among Slovene bandits. Did we not resettle to get away from them and now we are again surrounded by them?? And even worse; there are now "Windische" and other Slovene in administrative positions giving orders as equals!!" [131]

The makeup of the Rann District (Settling Area A), with the ingathering/expulsion completed, is described by the Berlin Stabshauptamt of the RKFDV on April 13, 1943 as follows:

"Slovene [who were allowed to stay] 8,000, Gottscheer Germans 12,500, Dobrutschka Germans 250, Bessarabian Germans 500, Buchenland Germans 200, South Tyrol Germans 400, Obersteiermark Germans 600. In the Settling Area A, as many businesses remained in the hands of the prior [Slovene] residents as came (or should have come) into ownership of the Gottscheer. In fact, however, the property size of the prior residents is smaller". [132]

The "Promised Land" is obviously neither a closed settlement, nor is it autonomous and controlled by the VGL. Half of its businesses are in the hands of Slovene; the ratio of Gottscheer vs. non-Gottscheer [most of them Slovene] is nearly 1:1, i.e., less than it was in the enclave. And the use of Gottscheer dialect, the only mark

---

131 Nacistična, pg 653.

132 Quellen, doc 304.

MISSION ACCOMPLISHED

of former ethnic identity, is either discouraged or forbidden and the Leader of the District is a non-Gottscheer. [133]

All objectives of the "Ingathering Policy" had been accomplished.

Since there was to be no autonomous Gottscheer-German enclave in Lower Styria, the new arrivals became a part of the Brežice (Rann) District of the "Steirischer Heimatbund". Already on April 24, 1941, its leader, Bundesführer Franz Steindl announced that, "on order of the Gauleiter, the Heimatbund is the sole and total organization of all loyal residents of Lower Styria". The Rann District, like all other districts in Styria was administered by a District Leader [Kreisleiter] appointed by the Gauleiter. In the fall of 1941, Gauleiter Uiberreither had planned to appoint Lampeter as Kreisleiter of the Rann District. But due to Lampeter's unacceptable behavior, especially in December 1941/January 1942, the post went to Adolf Swoboda, a member of the Nazi party, the NSDAP. [134]

In March 1942, the branch of the SS-Ansiedlungsstab called "Südmark", the organization responsible for the now completed "Ingathering" into Lower Styria was disbanded and Bliss its head, transferred out. What still remained to be done was the distribution of the land among the arrivals and the final allocation of residences to the "Ingathered". This was to be accomplished by SA Standartenführer (Colonel) Erwin Seftschnig, with Laforce as his Deputy and SS-Untersturmführer Dolezalek as the officer responsible for surveying the land.

In mid March of 1942, the Gauleiter visited (for the first time) the settlement area. There he discovered that the morale of the ingathered Gottscheer Germans was very low and to improve it, he decided to return some of the members of the former VGL into leadership positions.

For this the Gauleiter created, on May 16, 1942, the "Leadership of the Gottscheer Germans". (Distinctly different from the former "Leadership of the Ethnic Group", the VGL). He appointed Lampeter as its head with Martin Sturm as

---

133 ibid.

134 Quellen, doc 34.

his deputy and placed them both under Swoboda, the Leader of the Rann District of the "Steirischer Heimatbund".

But the "Leadership" had very little of the power and influence it formerly had in the enclave. The majority of the Gottscheer Germans had no further confidence in their former leaders. Even the mass rally, organized by the "Steirischer Heimatbund" at Lampeter's urging and held in late spring of 1942 on the large sport field of Brežice (Rann), did not lift the spirits of the "ingathered". The rally, modeled on those held in the enclave during the summer of 1941, included not only the Gottscheer Stürme and Hitler Youth groups, (I among them), but also groups of the "Steirischer Heimatbund" and units of the local German military. It was an impressive affair but produced little improvement in the general mood of the former Gottscheer.

In the structure created by the Gauleiter, neither Lampeter nor Sturm received much support from the District Leadership under Swoboda. Apart from receiving a salary, they had no office staff and no automobile that would allow them to visit people spread out over a distance of 90 km. And since the new "Leadership of the Gottscheer Germans" was not producing the expected results, Lampeter was relieved by Himmler of his political duties at the end of June 1942 and transferred into the "Waffen SS-Division Frundsberg" in Stalsund, Germany as an ordinary soldier. After training, he was transferred to "Waffen SS-Division Nordland" and sent to the Russian front where he was severely wounded.

After his recovery, he attended officer training school and on August 30, 1944 he was promoted to SS-Untersturmführer [2nd Lieutenant] in the Waffen SS-Reserve. During the next four months he is with a reserve regiment in Buchenwald. From there he was recalled (on Jan 1, 1945) to the SS-Staatsamt in Berlin, (where he still had his title as Sturmbannführer, in the political branch of the SS), and sent to Rann to help build up the Volkssturm and battle the Partisans.

Early in 1942, Richard Lackner was offered the responsibility for the "Windische Youth" in the "Steirischer Heimatbund" of the Rann District, an office which, according to his own admission, he staffed mainly with Gottscheer. In 1943 he was transferred to the "Heimatbund" office in Rann where he got into conflict with Bundesführer Steindl who accused him of being a non-cooperative Gottscheer. He resigned and, according to his own admission, voluntarily joined the SS-Division "Totenkopf", ("Deadhead", the most infamous of all SS Divisions) in which he remained until the end of the war.

After June 1942, Lampeter's position was assumed by Martin Sturm who signed his name as "Leader of the Gottscheer Germans" until the Stabshauptamt in Berlin, on July 28, 1942, forbade him to use this title. As the "agricultural adviser" on matters related to the ingathered, he was henceforth to sign any official document only with his given and family name.

And when at the end of 1942, the "Steirischer Heimatbund" assumed all political matters related to the Gottscheer Germans, all other remnants of the once sovereign and powerful VGL of the Ethnic Group arrived at their ultimate end.

And what about the people of the Ethnic Group? On this, the Reverend Alois Krisch, the once so vocal supporter of the resettlement and defender of the VGL, writes the following in his memoir:

"Now I must say that it was stressed to our people by officials in the Reich, 'we no longer recognize either Slovene or Gottscheer; here we have only Lower Styrians'. Some of these gentlemen tried to suppress our Gottscheer dialect. To which we replied: 'As long as there are other German dialects we will speak ours'. When one time in an air raid shelter a [Gottscheer] mother rebuked her young son in her dialect, a nearby teacher told her, 'here we speak only German'. After I told her ours was a very old German dialect, she remained silent.

"Not all 12,000 Gottscheer came to the Rann/Brežice region. Many were settled 100 km or more away so that they were completely separated from our people. Some, the "A" cases, were sent to the Altreich [inner Germany] and so forever lost to the Ethnic Group. Many to other distant places, business men to other towns, all are no longer part of the community of our people. We have become far fewer.

"Here in each village, there are also Slovene families, more than we had among us before; in Rann they are in the majority. In addition, settled among us are many from South Tyrol and from Bessarabia. The way we are being treated does not give us much hope. Many said even then, that as soon as possible after the war, they will find another place in the world, here they will not stay. A Gottschee community will be no more. Therefore, what readily comes to mind is the thought that we Gottscheer belong to the fairytale:

"Once upon a time ..."!

Chapter 16

Veliko Mraševo

Christmas of 1941 was one to remember.

In spite of having arrived in Veliko Mraševo – (Germanized into Gross Mraschau) only seventeen days ago and the chores of restoring order and continuity burdening every waking hour, both parents were not going to let the lingering turmoil spoil this event for their children.

By now Mother and Mitzi had scrubbed the house clean. Our furniture in place, the pots, pans and cutlery organized in the kitchen, the warm house was, in spite of the bitter cold outside, beginning to feel like a home. In the stable, the animals were comfortable, but Father was worried about the pig in the less well insulated sty. He had already discussed this with a man from the DAG (Deutsche Ansiedlungs Gesellschaft) who had visited the village a few days after all settlers had arrived. The Settling Authority agreed to buy the pig with food stamps and cash since our new house had no smoke room in which to cure the meat after the slaughter. And even if it had one, there was no hardwood available, the nearby woods growing slender birches only. Until then, the sty was to be filled with straw which, together with the pig's thick layers of fat, would prevent the animal from freezing. There was no similar danger to the chickens we brought from Masern and the others who had drifted back after their abandonment; they had their feathers to keep them warm.

There was no shortage of food staples, the ones that we received in Rann were being replenished at the grocery store in Zirkle. Among the items were delicacies, all much too pricy for the 300 Reichsmark, which is all we had at the moment. Of course the sausage and the ham Mother purchased were not as good as those we had made ourselves in the past.

We had greater difficulty in finding a suitable Christmas tree; the flat marshy land around us and the soil of the nearby woods on the hill toward Zirkle were not friendly to pines. There was no shortage of them on the higher hills across the river but that was in another country, out of bounds to us.

Mitzi and I searched in the woods off the Zirkle road and eventually found a proper size fir which we dragged home on the few inches of new snow. (In Masern, by now, there would have been feet of it.) All seemed to be coming together, with this Christmas promising to be not much different from those of the past.

THE BELLS RING NO MORE

Except for one thing. Jacklitsch let it be known that the young women of the Reichsarbeitsdienst (the mandatory national service for young women) would give a gifting party where they would distribute toys to all the children under fourteen. The party was to be on Christmas Day at ten in the morning in the large house on the main road, a short distance beyond the turn off to our new village. (For now the temporary house of Franz Jacklitsch). Instead of the usual apples, candies, notebooks, new pencils, fresh erasers and oversized clothing there might be something different and unexpected this year.

As in the past, the tree was decorated in the late afternoon of Christmas Eve. The fragile glass ornaments had all survived the journey including the silvered star to grace the top. As before in Masern, the tree stood in the corner of the large bedroom, diagonally opposite the oven cube and next to it on the table the unfolded cardboard crèche.

Mother hinted that there would be few gifts under the tree in the morning. This was hardly a surprise, as we had noticed that the store in Zirkle sold groceries only. That evening, after watching the candles brought from Masern burn away their remaining half we all went to bed early. The three of us with low expectation about what we would find under the tree, but full of excitement about the party. As for the parents there was no need to wait for the bells calling to midnight service. They were not to be heard this year nor anytime soon again.

The Jacklitsch house was filled by the time we got there. Not only with kids but also with the adults who brought them there. We were welcomed by good looking young ladies from the Reichsarbeitsdienst, twenty something girls in shapely uniforms and smiling faces. All making an effort to dispel not only the bashful demeanor of the kids, but also the distant reserve of the adults. They were visiting not only us but also other villages, surely mindful that by cheering up the kids, they would improve also the sagging spirit of the adults.

There were chairs for the adults, Jacklitsch having brought them from his tavern in Masern. And when all were seated, the woman in charge gave a short speech. She welcomed us into the Reich and praised our loyalty to the Führer. Then there was something about celebrating winter solstice as the real spirit of Christmas, with duty to the Führer being above all else.

Most of this was directed more at the adults than the impatient kids; we were here for the presents not a speech. But she kept it to a minimum except to say that the gifts were from the Führer whom we should thank individually for what we were about to receive.

The presents were laid out in a corner of the room. On the two walls above, looking down on us was the picture of Hitler. And when called, each of us was to step forward and when asked "what would you like", we were to select one item from the pile. And then say: "Thank you my Führer".

She read our names from a list. But long before being called, I had surveyed the pile of fire engines, cars, guns, dolls, etc. What I wanted was not there.

As usual, my name was at the end of the list. And when she asked what I would like, I said "a story book". And when she looked at me in shocked surprise, I did not hesitate to repeat my request.

"You mean a fairytale book". Not knowing how to make it clearer, I nodded my head. So she turned to one of her colleagues who left the room and came back with a book in her hand. I also looked at Hitler's picture on the wall and said: "Thank you my Führer".

I really wanted a book of stories, not fairytales. At ten I knew the difference. Nevertheless, it was the first book I owned; I kept re-reading it throughout that winter and spring, even in the dim light of the kerosene lamp. Slowly for sure since my understanding of German was limited and nothing else to read could be found in the village.

Shortly after the New Year, Jacklitsch announced a meeting where all adult villagers would be addressed by men from the DAG. They were going to inform the settlers about the final assignment of houses and the allocation of land to each farmer. Among other things.

After the meeting, the parents and a few neighbors, among them our friend Johann Krisch, settled in our kitchen and anxiously talked about what they had heard. I gathered that all was not well but what mattered to me was the happy news that school was to begin in Zirkle in the middle of January. I had not been in a class since Dežman left Masern in the spring of 1941 and the prospect of learning again after so much idleness was exciting, if also daunting. Now all learning would be in German, a language I barely understood, the former Slovene useless and the Gottscheer dialect of little help.

The adults were far less pleased. They were told that the final assignment of houses and property would not take place until all the land was surveyed and divided into parcels. These parcels would, only after the survey was completed, be assembled into units which, together with an appropriate house and associated buildings, would form a self sustaining farm. The units were to be of different sizes so as to match as accurately as possible the property owned back in the enclave. Only then would these units be turned over to their final owners. All this being a large task, taking perhaps a full year, the villagers were asked to be patient. And until this was done, they would continue living in their present houses.

But there was one more item. Until all units were defined and assigned to owners, the land had to be cultivated, planted, tended and harvested. All this was to be done, with guidance and assistance from the DAG, by all able men and women of Gross Mraschau. The villagers were also required to take care of the additional livestock temporarily assigned to them, livestock belonging to former residents. Our household was to get several cows and another horse which, together with Yiorgo and Father as their driver, were to be used for various tasks assigned to him by the DAG.

For their efforts, the villagers were to be paid in Reichsmark; wages with which to buy all necessary provisions. And after finally taking possession of their own farm, the DAG would continue with financial assistance until the next harvest brought self sufficiency and independence.

It had been stressed again to be patient and understanding. After all, the Reich was in a glorious war in which brave soldiers were giving their all for their country. The residents of Gross Mraschau must do no less.

In the next few weeks there was much discussion and grumbling about this when the villagers met with Jacklitsch. "Did we come here to be workers for the DAG?" was a commonly heard question. Jacklitsch, having lost most of his former credibility (and authority) did his best to calm them. Father helped him by explaining the logic of the DAG to those who again came to pass the time in his makeshift workshop on the long and idle winter days as they had done in the past. Except the workshop was now in the large room of the adjacent house which, for the time being, had also been allocated to Father. Here they sat on the benches surrounding the corner cube, their backs against the warm tile. Jacklitsch, and soon also the DAG, became grateful for his help. Recognizing his effectiveness, the DAG provided him with a battery operated radio and every evening the large room of our house was packed with those who came to hear the news at seven in the evening. At other times, the radio was shut off, mainly to save the batteries which were hard to get.

VELIKO MRAŠEVO

The farmer K.R. writes:

"The houses and farms which initially were assigned to us were only temporary. The administration and care of the farms and livestock remained entirely in the hands of the DAG. Even in the spring of 1942 the DAG continued to administer and cultivate the land. In this, the DAG engaged all able resettlers but paid them only undervalued wages as field hands. During this time the surveying and grouping of acreage into farms was in full swing".

In his report "Two Years Later", dated May 4, 1943, SA-Obersturmbannführer Erwin Seftschnig, head of the DAG department at the RKFVD in Maribor, describes the status of the final land assessment at the Settlement area. [135]

Seftschnig writes about the enormously demanding effort to survey the entire Save/Sotla region encompassing approximately 75,000 ha (290 sq miles) within a period of two years. This was completed at the end of 1942 when the territory, until then managed by the Interim Land Administration of the RKFDV, was turned over to the Steirischer Heimatbund (SH) for final assignment and distribution to the ingathered.

The task of the DAG was to divide the territory into parcels which, together with appropriate residences and farming buildings, would form self sustaining farms. The allocation would include arable land, vineyards and forests. Parcels of different land sizes and compositions were defined and three different "Farm Types" were mapped out for assignment to qualified ingathered farmers. The property was to be, roughly, in line with the property owned prior to resettling. Five additional "Non-farm Types" were created mainly for tradesmen, shop owners, laborers and landless residents.

The DAG created 1,275 "Farm Types" and 1,184 "Non-farm Types" for a total of 2,459 residences on 64,431 ha of land. The final report gives the number and details of the allotment to each Type. Placed into a "Reserve" were 10,005 ha of land. Total land = 74,436 ha. [136]

The report also shows that 9,296 ha remained in ownership of 1,215 Slovene families with an average ownership of 7.6 ha. The report does not define these

---

135 Quellen, doc 307.

136 Quellen, doc 301, 307.

families, but it can be assumed that they were "Windische" who were allowed to remain and keep their land.

The Types created by the DAG were as follows:

Farm Types:

Type 1, Farmer: land 30-70 ha, vineyards 5-10 ha, forests 10-40 ha	Qty 42
Type 2, Farmer: land 10-30 ha, vineyards 1 - 2 ha, forests 8-12 ha	Qty 404
Type 3, Farmer: land 7-10 ha, vineyards 1 - 2 ha, forests 4 - 8 ha	Qty 829
	Tot 1,275

Non-Farm Types:

Type 4, Small tradesmen, plumbers, etc: house plus 2-4 ha	Qty 340
Type 5, Small shops owners: house only	Qty 7
Type 6, Farm workers: house plus 1-2 ha	Qty 520
Type 7, Resident: house only	Qty 67
Type 8, Resident: house plus small garden	Qty 317
	Tot 1,184

(Additional details are listed in *Quellen*, doc 301, 307)

The division of the land into Farm and non-Farm Types was broadly in line with information Lampeter supplied to the Gauleiter, in his letter dated 2 November, 1941. However, Lampeter's letter was mainly about adequate land allocation to those he defined as "fit" to run a Farm Unit. To provide for healthy growth and expansion in the future he recommended that the average "Farm Type" be at least 20 ha. In his letter he voices his concern that:

"….there would be a land shortage in the settlement area. Four weeks ago, I gathered from a conversation with the leader of the civilian Land Planning Office, party [NSDAP] member Baier, that there is not enough land for the arriving Gottscheer" and he urges the Gauleiter to make more land available.

The actual numbers of Farm and Non-Farm units created by the DAG vs. those requested by Lampeter is as follows:

	Farms	Non-Farms	Tot	City Units	Others	Overall Totals
DAG	1,275	1,184	2,459	0	0	2,459
Lampeter	1,201	941	2,142	261	523	2,926

It is evident the DAG created the total number of family property parcels more or less in line with the numbers provided by Lampeter. In his letter to the Gauleiter, Lampeter stated that only 1,201 out of a total of 2,665 Gottscheer villagers are fit

VELIKO MRAŠEVO

to run a farm. Among the 1,201 families Lampeter saw "fit" were many of his loyal if landless supporters who needed to be rewarded for their effort in persuading the population to resettle. According to the DAG, all 1,201 families were to receive a Type 1, 2 or 3 farm.

In the same letter, Lampeter identified 941 families as "577 small farmers" and "364 workmen". All of these were placed by the DAG in the non-farm category. The small farmers were to receive at best a "Non-Farm Type 4". The workmen were to get anything from a "Type 5" to a "Type 8".

Of the 1,275 Farm Units created by the DAG, 1,031 were ultimately allocated to the Gottscheer. Of these, nine hundred and ten were accepted and occupied by May 4, 1943. Fifty nine rejected what was offered them and were consequently placed in the Non-Farm category.

The 365 units (the difference between the 1,275 created by the DAG and the 910 accepted by the Gottscheer), were eventually given to resettlers from South Tyrol, Bessarabia, Dobrutschka and Styria Germans.

The 261 City families were to be (according to the VGL) settled in either Brežice (Rann) or Krško (Gurkfeld), the two towns in the area. However, the SS-Ingathering Authority had different plans for this troublesome elite. Their ultimate placement will be explained later in this chapter.

In his letter of November 2, 1941, Lampeter also identified 523 families to be separated from the ethnic group and sent elsewhere by the Ingathering Authority. Of these, 135 were to be excluded for being opponents of the VGL, and 388 of these were to be excluded for being older, no longer capable families.

In the end however, most of the 2,926 families accounted for by Lampeter were resettled to the Save/Sotla area. But for many of the 523, the Save/Sotla area was a transition place only. Their destiny had already been defined by an "O" or "A" mark in the resettlement document on the processing train at Gottschee City railroad station. Only those marked "St", were permanently settled in the Save/Sotla area.

In a lengthy report dated October 1942, SS-Untersturmführer Dolezalek, head of the SS-Planning section, describes the conditions in the area.. [137] Among other items, he states that:

---

[137] *Quellen, doc 272*

"Fundamentally the Gottscheer are satisfied. Naturally, complaints are heard everywhere.... They complain about many conditions and inconveniences but they will, over decades, accept their new homeland..... .

"Above all, one is forever surprised to hear from the settlers that [Gottscheer] Germans are the minority in many, if not in most villages. After careful assessment by myself, I have concluded that the ratio is 1:1.

".. for a desired solution, the settlement area is unsuitable not only in its composition, but also is far too small in its proportions. I must, therefore conclude that a vivisection of the [Gottscheer] ethnic group is unavoidable. This will be very painful for them and is, for other reasons also regrettable, since it would not have been necessary".

The farmer K.R. writes:
"The distribution of the farms started in August 1942. The allocated houses and farms were mostly in a neglected state. The homes and farms were generally in a condition inferior to those we left behind. The area itself is poorer than that in Gottschee.

"Many did not accept the assigned property since it was not equivalent to the value of what they owned formerly. In some cases the assigned farm was barely one third of the property left behind.

"The DAG advised all those who had a legitimate claim to accept the assigned property. It had no legal means for enforcement, but it pressured the resettlers to accept the allocation. Many were led to believe that, should they reject this offer, they would lose the right to be given a place, and subsequently be reimbursed for the land left in the enclave at the lowest possible price. The majority gave in and accepted; they had little choice. This was the case also with me. I refused to accept the assigned property at first, but then accepted another place worth one third of the property I used to own.

"There were some who refused to accept what was assigned to them. These people were taken to a camp for resisting [unwilling] workers in Germany. There they proved they did not resist work, they had been sent there only because they refused to accept a property of inferior value. Found not guilty as accused, they were released and after a few months they returned to the settlement area where the DAG found them housing accommodations".

VELIKO MRAŠEVO

The Gottscheer Zeitung of March 1993 quotes a Gottscheer:

"The officials from the DAG wanted to know why the families Lampeter [another Lampeter] and Michitsch have not yet accepted a property. I was in an adjacent room when the 'visit' [the DAG] arrived and heard my father argue. The debate became heated and Busse, the leader of the Gurkfeld/Krško DAG office threatened with expulsion of the families to a camp in the Reich [Altreich]. Kallinger, another official casually hinted to Father of an assignment to a 999 battalion (a penal battalion). The result: three days in jail for my father."

And the Reverend Alois Krisch writes:

"There occurred many injustices. Some who at home had large well kept farms, received similar properties. Others who also had similar properties at home received places which barely equaled one quarter of what they owned before. Many of them naturally did not accept what was offered. Yet others were offered properties exceeding ten times or more the value of what they owned in the enclave. But some rejected the offer because it included a thirty year mortgage.

"The disappointment was heightened because the people saw there were few good houses and farms. They knew therefore, that only a small part of our people could (in the sense of the former propaganda [on the part of the VGL]) be adequately compensated. This came from those who were still in their temporary housing as well as from those who had already accepted a place. And some of the disappointed moved several times [from farm to farm] but they remained dissatisfied.

"When they refused to accept it was said that people who did not accept what was offered several times would be sent to Poland. [Less than a year ago, the VGL told the Gottscheer they would be sent to Abyssinia if they did not agree to the resettlement]. During the political and racial examination on the train some were defined as A- and O-Cases. They were those who, due to being related to the Slovene or seen as being politically unreliable, were not welcome in the annexed border territory. [The Reverend refers to the 'List of Politically Unreliable' prepared by Lampeter and submitted to the SS-Ingathering Authority at the end of October 1941].

"Sometimes when people declined to accept the assignment, brutal force was used and when they resisted, they were threatened with weapons. A man F. P. from Altlag had a weapon pointed at his chest until he finally gave in.

THE BELLS RING NO MORE

"I know of a young Gottscheer farmer who, after being threatened this way, said: 'Herr St., offer me something that is half or even a third of what I had at home and I will accept it'.

"The lucky ones were those who had nothing, or very little at home. Here they had good wages and benefits, partly because of their many children. Some of them said they never had it so good".

The reason for the injustices mentioned by the Reverend was in large part due to the recommendations of the VGL. Resisters who had large properties at home received inferior ones, if any at all. On the other hand, supporters of the VGL who had little at home were handsomely rewarded.

In the above, both the Reverend and the farmer K.R. report only on the settling of farmers. But the Reverend also writes about the merchants and bourgeoisie of the City who not only gave up their properties in Gottschee City but also lost the community they served and from which they earned their living. On this he writes:

"Many business people were sent to distant places, different cities. They were settled far away, in Maribor, Ptuj and elsewhere and separated from our people more than 100 km away. They no longer counted as being part of the totality of our people.

"It was said there is no more room for them here. Why not? In this 'shortage', some of the nicest houses in the city [Brežice (Rann)] had become offices and single officials lived in luxurious villas".

(The editor of "Documentation der Vertreibung....." comments: "With thirteen examples, the Reverend attempts to highlight the difficulties of the Gottscheer business people in the settlement area". The thirteen cases are however not identified in the book).

But with regard to some of them I personally can add the following:

Father's cousin Franz Tschinkel, Sturmführer of Sturm No 1, the Gottschee City Sturm, from whom Father purchased my bicycle was given a row house on Main Street in Brežice which had on its ground floor a small dry goods store. At home in Gottschee City he owned a huge dealership for bicycles and sewing machines on a large parcel of land on which stood also the very large family villa.

Alois Krauland who married Ridi, the sister of Franz, was an official at the Savings and Loan Bank in the City. He was also editor of the Gottscheer Zeitung for three months before it closed in November 1941. He and his family were resettled to Brežice (Rann) where they were assigned a house they refused to accept. Since the Bank had ceased to exist, there was no similar position for him in either Brežice or Krško and he and his family were moved to Maribor where he found a job. After he was drafted in 1943, the family returned to Brežice but left for the safety of Upper Styria in early 1945.

Alois was very likely among the sixty one City people who signed the Petition sent to Dr. Wollert in December 1941 containing their "Six Demands" [138] including the request that their resettlement be postponed until March. And he most certainly was among the 100 who assembled on January 3, 1942 for the meeting with Bliss and Schallermayer where the two SS-Officers persuaded the City Gottscheer to resettle.

Splitting up the troublesome Gottschee City elite was in line with Paragraph 5 of Himmler's Ingathering Policy which demanded the dissolving of an ingathered Ethnic Group, the Gottscheer included. Making available only thirty five dwellings instead of the 300 requested by Dr. Wollert for the City residents, would certainly break up and disperse the Gottscheer elite and facilitate the planned dissolution of the Gottscheer as an ethnic group. [139]

The reconstitution and maintenance of the Savings and Loan Bank in the settlement area (as requested in Point 6 of their December 1941 Petition) was important to the City elite as a symbol of Ethnic Group continuity, perhaps even more than their concern for the 400,000 RM reserves. It seems clear however, that they were unaware of Article 5 of the Resettlement Contract which (in part) states:

"The entire net wealth of those persons subject to this Agreement will be transferred to Germany". [140]

This included all reserves and deposits in the Savings and Loan bank, until the resettlement the property of the Gottscheer depositors.

Obviously Lampeter and his VGL were aware of Article 5 as well as the rest of the Contract. And to maximize the deposits in the S & L, the GZ issue of September 18, 1941 requested that all resettlers surrender their cash into a special account at the S & L bank. (See chapter "Completing the Task")

It is clear that Himmler's Ingathering Staff not only deceived the resisting farmers but also the resisting elite. The SS was determined to succeed in their assignment and to do so it used whatever deception was necessary. "Get them to resettle first, all

---

138 Die Umsiedlung, pg 126.
139 Quellen, doc 239.
140 Die Umsiedlung, pg 153.

THE BELLS RING NO MORE

else will follow" seems to have been the motto. And at every step in this deception, they had the full cooperation and help from Lampeter and his VGL.

The Reverend Krisch adds what he calls a "dark perspective":

"In addition to O-Cases ["O" was for Ost, i.e.Poland,] there were A-Cases. These were already identified as such on the processing train [EWZ Ingathering train]; their resettling passport stamped "A". They were to be separated from the other Gottscheer and taken to the "Altreich" [the old Germany], therefore the label "A". They were those who were not considered full-valued (apparently according to the racial laws).

"They and their family were taken there and again separated from the others and placed in various factories as laborers, in spite of having had properties and were farmers at home.

"The old and disabled [A-Cases] were taken to assisted living homes. Some we knew were taken to Passau [a city in Austria]. We know that some of them died there soon. Of the others? Was it social welfare or - - ? "

It is possible that the Reverend may have been aware of Paragraph 24 of the Resettlement Contract dated August 31 1941, which states:

"The infirm and those of unsound mind, which are allowed to resettle will, according to prior agreement between the High Commissioner and the German Empowered for the Resettlement [DUB] regarding timing, be taken to the nearest border station and there turned over to the German authorities". [141]

Ludwig Kren, the editor of the *GZ* 1971-1996 reports on this in his April 1996 issue. (The GZ was revived in Klagenfurt, Austria in 1955. Editors were Fritz Högler 1955-1962 and Herbert Erker 1962-1971. Erker had also been editor under Lampeter 1938-1941). Kren had tried, some years after the end of WWII, to find out what happened to the A-Cases with not much success. He writes:

---

141 *Die Umsiedlung*, pg 159.

VELIKO MRAŠEVO

"My efforts to contact such A-Cases and learn about their experiences produced little echo; more to the point, answers were 'our family, our parents, we all have suffered terribly and now wish to be left alone'.

"But one reply was received from the widow Maria Dernič, formerly of Windischdorf, now living in Austria:

'One day the order came 'collect your things'. We were loaded into a train. Destination; Thuringia. Final stop; transition camp Bad Blankenburg. Already there were about 150 families, mostly Gottscheer from all parts of the enclave. It was said they were not 'pure Germans'. Maria remembers Gottscheer Franz Michitsch, who was married to a Slovene woman from Ortenegg and an old married couple from Rain near Mitterdorf. From Windischdorf also Jerlsch Mitse [Maria] with two children. The assigned work place was the mechanized weaving mill Stöckigt in Langenberg, Thuringia.

"On October 27, [1943] she [Maria] received permission to visit a family in the Brežice area. She did not return to Thuringia. In Brežice, she was made to dig tank trenches in the surrounding fields.... After the war she worked on farms and finally found a room in a community residence."

These misled and betrayed Gottscheer, labeled by their countrymen as "A" or "O" Cases, not only lost their homeland; they were also separated from their community. And on November 14, 1941, when the first train left, none knew where they were going and what their future was to be. Certainly not Maria Dernič or the family of Josef Tramposch, the school friend I met after the resettlement and to whom I said goodbye after they were ordered to "collect your things". But more on that in the "Rabbit".

Some, such as the able Maria were destined to work for subsistence next to the Slovene to whose expulsion they unwittingly contributed. The destiny of the infirm and handicapped of Gottschee can only be guessed at. Among them were two men from Masern; our neighbor Mathias Michitsch (Mattl) and the incontinent recluse Josef Peinitsch. They were not heard of again.

The fact that Maria Dernič and other A-Cases responded to Ludwig Kren with ".... we wish to be left alone", was hardly surprising and most likely prompted by their memories which linked Kren to the inner circle of the VGL. They surely remembered him as a close intimate of Wilhelm Lampeter, Richard Lackner and other key individuals who convinced them to believe in Adolf Hitler, coerced them to resettle, only to be cast out later.

Kren officiated with Lampeter and Lackner in many of the big rallies on which Kren reported in the Gottscheer Zeitung (GZ) issues of 1941. At this GZ, Kren was an assistant to Herbert Erker, the editor of the GZ under Lampeter and a member of the inner circle. Erker again became editor of the GZ from 1962 to 1971 and upon his death was succeeded by Kren. (The GZ was re-instituted in Klagenfurt in 1955.) During the decades until his retirement in 1998, Kren continued to deflect, as editor of the GZ, any criticism of his friends with considerable success.

And in 1990, after Lampeter emerged from behind the Iron Curtain, the revived Gottscheer Zeitung under Kren warmly welcomed the former SS-Sturmführer into the various Gottscheer Organizations of the Diaspora.

Not listed as an "A'" case was our family; the family of a man who, in every respect fit the "not full-valued" definition of the VGL as spelled out by Lampeter in his "List of Politically Unreliable". An invalid not fit to operate a farm in the Third Reich and one married to a Slovene woman with an illegitimate child from a Slovene father.

Why we were not among them remained a mystery until recently.

Our resettlement documents, finalized on November 16, 1941 by the officials on the processing train were stamped "ASt". The documents showed that this was a mixed marriage with a Slovene, a woman who had an illegitimate child fathered by a Slovene. (I obtained these documents from the Berlin Documentation Center in 1970).

But the documents also mention that Father was a member of the Kulturbund since 1935, that the spouse and daughter are "fully assimilated and that all speak very good German". This fact and perhaps also his friendship with Sturmführer Franz Jacklitsch were reasons for being marked "ASt" and not simply "A", the marker for casting out the likes of Maria Dernič, Josef Tramposch and all the others. At least not yet!

The papers also mention that my father Johann Tschinkel is an invalid with a missing leg. In spite of this, he was allocated a Type 2 Farm with two houses, 24 ha of land including a large vineyard. Three more hectares than he owned in Masern.

The answer to this mystery is in a Directive from Reichsführer-SS Himmler dated August 10, 1942. The Directive defines, in General Order No. 16/III, the agricultural land distribution to the settlers. According to this order, veterans who sustained injuries as a result of WWI were to receive preferential treatment. [142] Father was recognized as a war invalid which, together with the fact that his Slovene wife and adopted daughter were "fully assimilated", was the key to our acceptance and, very likely, also our survival.

---

142 Quellen, doc 301.

VELIKO MRAŠEVO

We moved into our assigned house and property in the spring of 1943. The house was on the main road just off the triangle in the center of the village. But in the meanwhile, from Dec 1941 to March 1943, many important events took place.

One of these events was the start of school in January 1942. Father and I had been to Cerklje (Zirkle) the week before to register, to get instructions and find out about the hours. I was introduced to the teacher, a very nice Slovene lady named Marija Schroif, who kept asking me questions in German which I understood only in part. Father explained that in the village of Masern we spoke only Gottscheer and at home a mixture of Gottscheer and Slovene and that my education until now had been in Slovene only. He also explained that since my mother was a Slovene and I being the product of a mixed marriage, I was not allowed to take part in any German schooling that was given by Dežman to only the "ethnically pure Gottscheer" of Masern. After hearing all this, she asked me a few questions in Slovene, "just to get to know you a little".

Then she explained that all instruction was going to be in German which I must learn quickly. And that we must speak only German in class or outside and even at home and that all of us must quickly become proficient in this language now that we are citizens of the Reich.

In the above, Frau Schroif was in line with the directive of the Commandant of the Security Police and Security Service of Lower Styria, dated 19 Nov. 1941. This directive states:

"The policy regarding speech is to completely eliminate the Slovene language. In public life, effective immediately, only German is permitted. It is anticipated that in four years German will predominate and that Slovene as a language will have largely disappeared. In school, only German must be spoken, however, a certain level of duality can be used to facilitate learning". [143]

The following Monday, Father took me and a few of the others to school on one of the coldest days of January 1942. There was new snow but neither that nor the cold were enough to bother Yiorgo pulling the sled that came with us from Masern.

---

143 *Quellen, doc 178.*

Father promised to get us after school let out but only if it snowed some more. If not, we should be able to walk the few kilometers home.

The day before I carefully repackaged the small rucksack with notebooks, pencils and erasers, leaving space for the sandwich and an apple Mother was going to give me in the morning as lunch for my first day. The same as on my first day of school in Masern in the fall of 1936.

The teacher's desk was on a raised platform, off center so as not to block the chalkboard. On the wall above was a large picture of Adolf Hitler looking down on the mix of his new citizens. A place where not long ago hung the picture of the King of Yugoslavia. When she entered the room in the morning we all rose to attention. Standing in front of the class she would have us stare at the picture on the wall and with raised right arms, made us repeat after her with "Heil Hitler". Only then would she mount the platform and start teaching.

There were about thirty of us, all grades from one through eight in a room a bit larger than the one in Masern. Benches to the left and right of the center isle, the little ones nearest to the teacher, the higher grades further back; girls on the left and boys on the right. In all, at least in the beginning, a mix of reserved Gottscheer and Slovene pupils eying each other with a combination of curiosity and suspicion which barely hid the underlying dislike.

To the Slovene we were intruders, taking the place of their deported classmates and friends. To us, they represented the racially lesser Slovene who had (as we had been told) tried to assimilate us in our former homeland. So we had moved to get away from them, but here they were again. Why they and their families had not been deported was for us all a surprise, especially to us few from Veliko Mraševo (Gross Mraschau) from which all Slovene families, except one, had been removed.

For them, the surprise was that we not only understood their language but that some of us could even talk to them in Slovene.

With all eight grades in one room, the teacher was busy but managed to teach the different levels in some sort of order. Her first task was to teach us German. Progress was quick for many of us who had our Germanic dialect as a reference to the new language. But learning the German language was much more difficult for the Slovene kids who had never been exposed to German.

However, this common knowledge of Slovene became a helpful bridge for the teacher in her effort to teach us German as rapidly as possible. To help her with her lessons at first, she used Slovene words as a "dictionary" to the Slovene as well as the "Gottscheer German" students. And when after a few weeks, the initial reserve

VELIKO MRAŠEVO

abated and mistrust between the kids gave way to cooperation, the Gottscheer who learned German more rapidly were now helping their Slovene schoolmates.

But as soon as we conquered the rudimentary parts of German, she forbade the use of either Gottscheer or Slovene in her class room. Only German would do. She also told us that the ban was to be observed beyond her hearing and even at home, a prohibition we all ignored.

With eager studies, help from Father and the friendly encouragement of the teacher, I did well that winter and spring in spite of having missed an entire year of schooling. When asking for a show of hands, after a few weeks she asked for mine only as a last resort, something I resented at first. And when at midterm I brought home a certificate with only top grades, Mother did not hesitate to show it around.

A few weeks before the end of the term I became anxious when Frau Schroif asked me to take a sealed letter to Father. But when, instead of a reproach after reading it, he asked me if I wanted to go to the "Hauptschule" (high school) in Brežice (Rann), I was overjoyed. It turned out I was the only one she recommended to leave the "Volksschule" (primary school) for higher education. But I was not pleased at my final term report in which, instead of the expected top grades in all five subjects, she had simply written across all lines only one word; "Hauptschulreif" (fit for high school). And when my proud mother showed the report to Katharina, both Mother and I were disappointed with her dismissive response "what, no grades?" Afterwards Mother consoled me with "What does Katharina know?"

The Slovene man in the little house at the intersection seemed pleased when I mentioned the teacher's recommendation and that I had decided to accept. Pleased perhaps because of all the new German children in his village and in the Cerklje School, only the one with mixed blood in his veins was fit to go.

He then talked about a boy in the village who for four years, rain or shine or snow walked the 12.5 km to Brežice and back. "You at least have a bicycle".

I started the Hauptschule in the fall of 1942 and lasted there until at the end of October when it got cold. I quit, in part only, because of the weather. The main reason was that in this first grade of high school, I was again a persecuted minority. I may have been the only Gottscheer German in class; if there were others, I do not remember.

My antagonists were the twin girls. Perhaps a year or so older but they were in the same classroom since more than one grade was taught simultaneously by the lady teacher, also a Slovene. The twins lived on Main Street in town, not far away from the school house, where the family had some sort of business. Their parents may have been "Windische"; Slovene for sure. They were pretty princesses, intimidating with their "urban" polish, used to getting their way. As it turned out also with the teacher, since both girls were her favorites.

As I was used to, I raised mine when a show of hands was requested. The fact that I was right more often than they put them into state of fury which they held in check only until the next break when the teacher left the room. This is when they pounced on me with ceaseless taunts in which they were very good. Some of it had to do with my clothing which smelled of the farm if not the barn, the sweat from the cycling, my accent, my diminutive size; my person in general. When they realized the misery their taunts caused me, the taunting only increased. And it got even worse when they discovered that I was the son of a Slovene mother who of her own free will opted to become a German. As opposed to their own who had no choice but be subservient to the invader.

Defenseless against the subtle ways of my tormentors and unable to obtain any relief from the unsympathetic teacher, I longed for the stress free days in Cerklje and the friendly tutelage of the Slovene teacher there. My parents knew that I was unhappy and kept asking questions, but I did not let on that a pair of girls was making my life miserable. Instead, I hid behind the evermore unfriendly weather which had turned cold, with snow expected anytime soon to put a stop to cycling and force me to walk the 12.5 km there and back.

But even before the snow, I decided to quit. And it happened after a few especially bitter cold days which made both parents more sympathetic to my repeated hints to give it up.

On a day when the twins were particularly vicious, I swung at them with my jacket just when the teacher came back from her break. She asked for no explanation, neither from me nor anyone in the class; I was judged guilty on the spot. Not allowed to defend myself, which would have been useless anyway, I was ordered to stand in the corner facing the wall. And when, finally, she ordered me back to my seat, it was the smirk of the girls that made up my mind.

VELIKO MRAŠEVO

Since the parents had been expecting it anyway, my decision was readily accepted by Father, especially in view of the present and coming weather, as the reason for my quitting. Less so by Mother who thought I was giving up higher education too quickly. Mindful perhaps of the drive for learning her mother had instilled in at least two of her four sons, one becoming a doctor, the other a lawyer.

But since I was the oldest and in only a few short years would take on the running of a large farm, in Father's mind it was perhaps the right decision after all.

More surprised was the teacher in Cerklje when I again appeared in her class room. She did not believe my explanation and tried to discover the real reason for my return, but I stuck to the weather. If she made an attempt to get to the truth some other way I do not know.

I did not have to explain my decision to the man in the little straw covered house at the intersection to the village. He would have been disappointed. But he was no longer there. He had either escaped across the river or been taken away by the SS to some camp.

Surely the most disappointed would have been Grandma Ilc but I could not tell her; she was now worlds away. Perhaps she would have reminded me to stick to the promise made in early December 1941 that I would never stop learning. But that was a promise which, in spite of this temporary setback, I fortunately was able to keep.

I saw the twins again at the end of May 1945 when we were temporarily in the concentration camp near the railroad station in Brežice (Rann). They were marching proudly through the town at the head of a parade, both dressed in the uniform of the Communist Youth League and wearing the red starred cap, each holding high the Communist flag. To prevent them from seeing me I hid behind some adults until they passed.

The remainder of that term was, at least for me, uneventful. On exceptionally bad mornings Father would harness Yiorgo and take me and some of the others to school or if there was high new snow I simply stayed at home. But usually the small group of us had to make it home on our own, even if it was still snowing.

I was readily accepted back into the class, including by the teacher, my explanation accepted all around. I was challenged by her teaching because it was more according to ability than age. In line with this she gave me the more difficult homework she normally assigned to older pupils, in this way pushing me ahead of my peers. She also had a pile of books in the classroom which those of us who liked to read could take home as part of extra reading assignments. To the pile I added my book of fairytales which quickly became very popular.

Later that spring of 1943 we had a new teacher.

Marija Schroif was replaced by Herr Pfeifer, an invalid SS officer who had lost his right arm on the Russian front. He wore his uniform with all earned ribbons in class, the sleeve of his missing arm folded half way up and tied to the jacket. Marija may have been strict but this man was a fanatic.

Not only did we start the day with the Heil Hitler salute, but he made us sing "Deutschland über Alles …" every morning. He did little teaching other than talk about the glory of Germany and the Third Reich in particular. Apart from Hitler, Bismarck and Frederick the Great were his heroes. He kept our attention by talking about his days at the front and how his unit was on the outskirts of Moscow which, for "tactical reasons", was not taken in the winter of 42/43.

When I asked why Napoleon had taken it, he flushed with anger at first but then explained that occupying the city was a mistake which cost the French the war. I did not ask further questions, knowing well enough that Hitler's armies had lost in Stalingrad and were being pushed further and further back. It would have cost me dearly had I done so. He had already marked me as one who knew too much and lacked conviction in the cause.

He let it be known one morning when we were again singing the National Anthem. With my right hand extended in the salute, I averted my eye from Hitler's picture on the wall and stared out the window. He came off the platform and reached me just after I had turned my head back and looked at him as he, in full fury, struck me with his remaining hand on the right cheek with a force that knocked me down.

The SS officer was our teacher for only a few months. He lived north in a city in Austria and may have been sent to our area only because there was a severe teacher shortage.

VELIKO MRAŠEVO

His replacement was Alois Tscherne, a fifty year or so Gottscheer who, with his wife, moved into the empty teacher's wing of the school. They had a son and daughter who lived and attended High School elsewhere and came home only for holidays and term breaks. His teaching was far more rigorous than that of the friendly Slovene lady or the fanatic Pfeifer. Unlike his Slovene predecessor he did not resort to the "Slovene dictionary" and used Gottscheer only when necessary. He, of course knew Slovene, but if he used it to help his Slovene pupils I don't remember. Besides, it was now strictly forbidden to use either language.

He divided us into grades strictly according to age, which did not suit my level at first. But soon I reestablished myself and he even gave me special assignments after he had a conference with Father.

Tscherne was a stern man, apt to lose his temper. He used his severity, at times complemented with the stick, to keep the unruly in check and the rest of us placid, as opposed to the way of the Slovene lady who accomplished the same objective with a velvet glove and a smile. On one occasion he not only lost his temper, he became enraged and I the victim of his fury.

For lunch he went to his quarters, leaving us in the classroom to eat our sandwiches. He did so near midterm of 1944 but accidentally left his class log, in which he was preparing our midterm grades, open on his desk. Someone noticed it and soon we were all crowding around to get a preview of what our grades were to be. He was heard returning and before he entered the room we were all sitting in our places.

He was very secretive of what our grades were to be. So when he noticed the breadcrumbs from our sandwiches on the open page of the log, his face turned purple and he exploded with "who was up here". He became even more furious when no one raised a hand. And when I finally if slowly raised mine, he stormed off the platform with the stick which he brought full force on to the open palm of my hand.

I was the only one who had raised a hand. After he got back to the platform, he contemplated us while slowly recovering from his rage. Looking at me, still clutching my right hand, he commanded me to stand up. Then he apologized and turning to the class he said:

"Every one of you look at a brave student. The rest of you are cowards".

I did not feel brave, my hand hurt too much. I am certain the others did not think they were cowards, only that I was stupid. But when later I showed the red welt to Father, he agreed with the teacher and Mother said that I was not stupid.

THE BELLS RING NO MORE

Since the incursions from the Partisans across the river were happening more frequently and Allied strafing planes out of Italy were showing up unexpectedly, Tscherne made all of us dig zigzag trenches in the back of the school. But the real reason for this was to provide shelter for the various army units who came to rest in Cerklje and especially on the school grounds. Some of these units included medics with ambulatory trucks and medical equipment. Since they usually stayed only for a few days and there being no doctors in the area anymore, the villagers would line up for free evaluation and treatment.

So did I in the summer of 1944. I injured myself or had perhaps been bitten or stung by an insect on the inside part of the lower right arm just above the wrist. The point of injury grew into a button sized red spot. The poison must have entered a lymph canal and the infection traveled slowly, inch after inch, further up the arm as a reddish blue ribbon. After several days the tip of the ribbon was nearing the elbow.

Since our only medical doctor in the area, with a practice in Krško (Gurkfeld) had been killed by a direct hit bomb from a B17 returning to Italy from a bombing run in the north, Father took me to the medic who was on the school grounds at that moment. By now the ribbon had reached the elbow.

The medic took a look and then reproachfully looked at Father. "Why did you wait so long?" he said.

He worked on the red spot and then gave me an injection. And with a friendly "come back tomorrow" he dismissed me with a smile. He also instructed Father to keep soaking the arm daily in salty water until the streak disappeared.

When I went to see him the following day he looked at the arm and seemed pleased. "Keep soaking the arm" he said. I did and watched the ribbon recede back to its origin and disappear altogether. A few days later I cycled to the school grounds to thank him but by then he had left with his unit. I did not know it then but learned later on that he had saved my arm and very possibly also my life.

Tscherne was our teacher until the spring of 1945. The Archives of Slovenia show that he was so despondent over the defeat of the Reich that he cut his and his wife's arteries, but the attempt was not successful. Both were taken to the hospital and in time they recovered.

I met Tscherne many years later in Brooklyn where he worked as a laborer in a factory. His wife had been born in the US which made her automatically a citizen and allowed her and her family to immigrate right after the end of the war. I met him through his son Robert at the Polytechnic Institute where both of us were engineering students.

As soon as we met, Tscherne said "you are the one who stood up". I saw him often afterwards and I think he was proud of me. Not only because I stood up. Robert and I were among the few teenage sons of countless Gottscheer immigrants, who with their parents came to the US soon after the war and who subsequently graduated from a university.

Chapter 17

The Rabbit

I got to know Josef in the spring of 1943 on the way home from school.

On our way we grouped, as in class, according to age but the older boys walked with the girls. Half way home our paths split, the older group taking the more direct and paved road since they had to return quickly to help their parents with farming chores. We the younger ones preferred paths through the birch woods, to walk along the Krka and jump over streams feeding the river with runoff water from the fields.

Trailing our small group was Josef Tramposch, another six grader in our school. Josef trailed because he was not yet accepted as one of us partly because his family came from some other part of Gottschee and also because his manners, his language and his walk were strange and different. His family had arrived in Veliko Mraševo later than we and was assigned a farm on the edge of the village, some distance from the center. Due to this, the family had little contact with other settlers and kept to themselves. Apart from his parents, Josef had a teenage sister no longer of primary school age. Although clearly with a typical Gottscheer family name, his manner of speaking had a strange accent and his walk a waddling strut.

Early that spring, on one of the walks home and eager to make friends, he bragged about how he caught fish in the stream leading to his house and offered to show me. As we walked along the water he pointed to barely discernible shadows amid the patches of grass growing over the water's edge or below the willow branches hanging over the stream. It was obvious that he had a particularly keen eye for finding fish in places I had not bothered to look before. We agreed to meet later that day with our spears to test our skills.

The streams, as was discovered in the spring following our arrival in the village, were spawning grounds for pike, sharp toothed fish that sought refuge away from the swiftly flowing river. On their journey up the streams they hid in covered spots and rested on their way to a place in quieter waters where they could safely deposit the eggs they carried in their swollen bellies.

This discovery revealed the purpose of the spears hanging on the walls of tool sheds of most houses in the village. Their purpose was for catching the pike and other fish in the streams and the river.

The spear was similar to a hay fork except that the prongs were closer together, each resembling an oversized straightened fish hook with a very sharp point. The fork was mounted on the end of a long, straight and slender wooden pole, smooth and polished for accurate thrusting. Its purpose got around quick enough, but the villagers, who over centuries had become accustomed to red meat, had little taste for white meat full of nasty little bones. And after it became known that it was illegal to spear spawning fish anyway, interest in developing a taste for this kind of cuisine diminished altogether. But not for Father who had acquired a taste for fried filets at the Isonzo front in Italy.

When later that afternoon I met Josef with my spear, the fish we saw earlier had moved, but Josef soon found others hiding elsewhere. I kept missing but after Josef showed me how to compensate for the bent trajectory in the water, my aim began to find the target. It seems Josef, as an eleven year old, had already discovered some of the laws of Physics, laws which I learned only many years later.

After that initial expedition, Josef and I walked along the streams together. On the way home we marked the spot hoping the prey would not move, and returned later with our spears. But I had to ask for permission to go on this always exciting hunt and if allowed to, was told not to bring back more than one catch since catching spawning fish was forbidden. Having Josef, with his keen eye as a companion, made virtually certain this was the case. Nevertheless, many a fish escaped until I learned the proper aim and thrust and how to pull the flailing catch, some two feet long, from the water.

I became proficient and was successful even after the spawning season when other species arrived from the river. These fed on the now abundant harvest hatched from the eggs of those who had previously avoided or escaped our spears. The new arrivals were swifter than those burdened with eggs and required more accurate aim and sharper reaction. But again, Josef had a knack which he patiently imparted to me, though I never learned to be as good as he was.

While fish started our friendship, rabbits brought us closer together. His family like mine raised domestic rabbits as a supplement to chicken and pork, the staples of our rural existence. Rabbits multiplied, grew rapidly and provided us with tender and delicious meat, a succulent alternative to the otherwise monotonous daily fare.

THE RABBIT

Mother would roast them as she would a chicken or boil them with various vegetables and herbs, and the broth, with barley added, became a delicious soup.

Our rabbits lived and multiplied under the feeding troughs of the livestock stable where they romped freely, having learned to stay out from under the hoofs of the towering animals. They fed on the hay and oats overflowing from the troughs above, a diet heavily supplemented with grain, carrots and lettuce or any other available vegetables from Josef and me, their caretakers who also kept their watering dishes clean and full. Together we built shelters for them, wooden boxes that fit under the troughs but were removable for cleaning outside the stable. The box had an opening at one end big enough for a fully grown rabbit to enter and exit. Through the same opening, an arm could pull out by its long ears a resisting occupant hiding at the far end of the box. But the rabbits got to know their handlers and allowed themselves to be lifted and stroked with only minor protest, but when strangers entered the stable, they all scurried for the openings and struggled to get inside.

When pregnant, the females dug tunnels into the soft ground below the feeding troughs where they deposited their litter. The tunnels were big enough for our arms and soon after the female appeared after having given birth, we would count the litter with our fingertips, while the mother next to the intruder stomped her hind legs in protest. When a few days after birth, their naked skin became covered with soft fuzz, the blinking creatures would emerge from the tunnel and learn to drink the cow's milk waiting for them in a dish at the entrance. They soon got used to the outside and to prevent them from wandering under the deadly hoofs, we created a fenced-in safety space around the opening which contained them, at least for a while. But they grew rapidly and with the fence no longer much of a barrier, some of the litter was crushed, but most survived.

As they grew and the cavity at the end of the tunnel became too small, they soon found the boxes, their half way house to maturity.

The abundant litter could easily have gotten out of hand were it not for the demand of Mother's kitchen and the dominant male who never allowed rivals to reach maturity and become large enough for a family meal. He would wound or even kill them as soon as they threatened to become rivals. The females, on the other hand, got pregnant as soon as they became fertile and therefore untouchable for a meal. The only way to stop this was to separate the sexes in separate fenced-in areas under the troughs. This allowed for control of the procreation process by returning only a select few of the females to the dominant male.

Soon after we became friendly, Josef persuaded me to come to his home to see his dominant male called Adolf. This beautiful rabbit with his smooth and shining gray fur was twice the size of any other in any stables of the village. It was fascinating to watch him dominate his flock, his perpetually mounting the females while terrifying subordinate rivals. No male in the village demonstrated equal prowess. Adolf did not mind being lifted up by his long ears and stroked. He especially loved being fondled by his testicles, which made him show his pink penis emerging from its protective pouch.

On this first visit I not only met this beautiful specimen but also Josef's parents and sister. The father and sister were typical Gottscheer, but it was clear that Josef had inherited his unusual features, mannerisms and peculiar gait from his mother. Soon thereafter we would walk home apart from the others, talk about fish and rabbits, meet with our spears to fish or make for the stables to watch Adolf dominate his flock.

Josef did not segregate his females to prevent impregnation and his total population was, therefore, much larger than mine. Adolf was definitely a more virile male, of which there was ample proof in his stable. And when one day Josef suggested that we exchange our dominant males for a while, I quickly accepted since I was eager to increase and diversify my flock.

But we made the mistake of releasing Adolf before we removed my dominant male. In no time there was a bloody turf battle when Adolf starting mounting, in rapid succession, the females of my flock. It took our combined efforts to separate the two frothing males and Josef carried back to his stable my wounded and bleeding male, leaving Adolf behind.

During the next few weeks, we came directly to our house to watch Adolf rule. He tolerated no competition and asserted his dominance by wounding even the immature young males who had to be separated out. All able females became pregnant immediately. Since this reduced the number fit for slaughter, Father soon complained about the reduced frequency of rabbit stew at evening meals and the exchange was terminated.

While the fish and the rabbit brought us together in that spring of 1943, our common difference cemented the friendship during the following summer. This difference was because both our mothers were outsiders. My mother was a Slovene who had married a Gottscheer and who after years of living in Masern, was finally accepted by most of the residents as an equal in spite of her persistent Slovene accent. The acceptance was helped by the fact that she had been allowed to become a citizen of the Third Reich in spite of her Slavic background.

THE RABBIT

But the state had also accepted Josef's mother and made her and her family citizens of the Reich. She, like Mother had also married a Gottscheer, and had been accepted into her village in the enclave. She also had a strange accent, but in the eyes of the state was very different from my mother, the Slovene.

Unbeknown to most, if not all villagers, Josef's mother was a Gypsy.

After the resettlement, the Gypsy caravans that once passed through Masern were no longer to be seen. But in Veliko Mraševo, neither Josef nor I knew of the hierarchy of Nazi racial profiling in which a Gypsy was little different from their "detested Jew", a remark heard so often in the last few years. Neither of us had ever seen a Jew and so the image of a Jew, created for us by VGL officials, was not much different from that of Lucifer painted for us in Sunday sermons by the priest in Masern.

But while we heard that the Jews were a menace and like the Communists, dangerous to the Reich and western civilization, we never heard that Gypsies were useless parasites, unworthy to be among civilized humanity. Therefore, the real reason for their disappearance could not be imagined in the remoteness of our existence and became known to us, as did the reason for the other tragedies, only years later.

The Slavs on the other hand, deemed by the Nazis a cut above the Jews and the Gypsies, were not dangerous to the state but were to be subjugated to provide the manual labor needed by the superior master race. In this, the Slovene Slavs were a unique exception mainly due to the long exposure to Germanic culture of the Austrian bureaucracy which, since the establishment of the Empire in 1273, had dominated their existence. The centuries-long undisguised effort by the Austrian Germans to assimilate the Slovene, the continual mingling and extensive intermarrying of the Germanic and Slavic residents of Carniola and the later Slovenia had produced a racial ambiguity that favored their integration into the Reich.

As a loyal offspring of such intermarriage, I was the typical example, with the indignities heaped on me due to being half Slav now a thing of the past. My inferior half was not visible; I was blond, blue-eyed and indistinguishable from the others. I was accepted as an equal; Josef was not that fortunate.

THE BELLS RING NO MORE

Later that fall, on a day when there was no school, Josef arrived breathlessly, having run the two kilometers from his house, to offer me Adolf since his family had to leave on short notice. I paid little attention to the reasons for their leaving as we ran back to Josef's house. The prospect of calling Adolf mine was displacing any other thought.

This changed as soon as we entered the courtyard of his father's house, where two serious looking men in black leather coats were milling around the open end of a canvas-covered truck, into which Josef's sullen father was loading bulging suitcases.

Another man appeared from the house, and so did Josef's crying mother and sister, each carrying bundles of clothing to the back platform of the truck on to which they climbed via a small ladder. Josef was ordered to join them on the benches and after a teary-eyed handshake he climbed the ladder to sit next to his sister. Yet another Gestapo appeared from the house with Josef's father, who joined his family on the benches. The Gestapo closed the house door, turned the key but left it in the lock. He and his colleague leapt on the truck, the other two closed the swinging gate, got into the cab of the truck and drove off. I waved to Josef as the truck moved away and disappeared, leaving me standing alone in the middle of the courtyard.

But not for long. I had come to get Adolf who was as usual, under the troughs in the stable together with the restless animals who had not been fed that morning and were making their neglect known with audible complaints. Safely holding Adolf by his long ears and clutching his smooth body against my chest, I ran from the otherwise deserted and eerie place that only a short while ago had been the safe and comfortable home of my friend Josef and his family.

Later that day, a man from the DAG administrator's office in Brežice (Rann) came to explain to the villagers the reason for the rapid departure of the Tramposch family. Apparently this family had been negligent in its duties to Germany and therefore unreliable as citizens and guardians of the border of the enlarged Third Reich. The SS man noticed unease among the assembled villagers and talked at length about the importance of reliable border farmers. When asked where they were taken, he explained that they were being resettled into the safety of the "Old Reich" where they were to receive an equivalent farm, and that their possessions were to follow them immediately. He pointed out that while he was speaking, the Tramposch possessions, including their livestock, were being loaded on to trucks which were to follow the family. This apparently was the case since on the following day I found only a few stray rabbits in the stable, and the house, now accessible through the unlocked door, emptied of most belongings.

The effort of the SS man to convince the villagers was only partially successful, as was apparent from the hushed discussions that followed after he left. The rapid

THE RABBIT

departure of the Tramposch family was unsettling and on the minds of many. Some said it was unfair to uproot a family, especially on such short notice, even if the husband had a strange and unfriendly wife.

The event was particularly unsettling on Father who knew that Josef's mother was a Gypsy. The Tramposch departure reminded him of the examination and profiling of all those who opted for resettlement in October 1941. It was now clear to him that it was this examination that revealed to the SS that Josef's mother was a Gypsy and that the children had inherited her features which determined their fate. Father remembered that he and his family had also been processed, examined and profiled, in no way differently than the Tramposch family. His wife, while not a Gypsy was nevertheless an "inferior" Slav, which made him fear that the Tschinkel family might be next on a list.

Father's fear was not without foundation, as I realized later in 1969, when I obtained the complete set of documents of my family as they had been recorded on the processing train. The records I found in the Berlin Archives clearly state that my mother was of the Slavic race, but that for the moment, this fact was not a barrier for citizenship of the Reich. But being a Gypsy had also not been a barrier for the Tramposch family including my friend Josef.

When I discussed all of this with him some years after the war, he admitted that he shared his fears about his mixed marriage with no one, not even with his wife. But his fears were about being resettled again, this time to a "place safer" than the fragile border on the edge of the Reich. Surely, he could not imagine the destiny in store for the Tramposch family when they were moved there on such short notice.

For me, the sudden loss of my friend Josef was in part balanced out by the joyous acquisition of the prize rabbit Adolf. He quickly adjusted to his new environment and flock after his most threatening rival was slaughtered for a meal. The episode of the Tramposch family soon moved into the background as the villagers accepted the explanation given by the man from the DAG office, or suppressed doubts that the Tramposch were not dutiful citizens. In any case, it was unpatriotic or even unlawful for a citizen to verbalize or even to entertain treasonable thoughts.

Doubts if any were fully dispelled by a picture postcard that arrived a few weeks later addressed to me and was passed around in the village. It was from Josef.

All was well and they were happily settled in their new house, identified by a penned arrow on the face of the card showing the residential part of a town. The arrow pointed to a corner house surrounded by a picket fence in what seemed to be a suburban neighborhood, judging from other houses nearby. The card must have been written by the sister, since the handwriting was not that of the eleven year old Josef who, I remembered, had difficulties in forming legible characters, much less words in Frau Schroif's class. As with all postcards, it contained no sender address, except that the postmark imprint identified the mailing post office to be, according to Father, somewhere in Poland. No other mail came and the only reminder of my friend Josef was Adolf, the new master under the troughs of our stable.

But the more likely destiny of Josef and his family emerged only decades later.

It came in the 1960's on reading William L. Shirer's book "The Rise and Fall of the Third Reich". In chapter 27 under "The Extermination Camps", Shirer documents the ongoing process of the Nazis to rid the Reich of Jews, Gypsies and other undesirables. Shirer also describes the selection process at Auschwitz where it was decided, on arrival at the camp, which Jews or Gypsies were to be used for labor and which ones were to be gassed immediately. And Shirer writes: "though there were heart-rending scenes as wives were torn away from husbands and children from parents", none of the victims realized just what was in store for them, as Hoess (one of the camp commanders) testified after the war. Some of them were even given pretty picture postcards showing a town called "Waldsee" to be signed and sent back home saying: 'we are doing well here, have work and are well treated.'"

The above described a likely destiny for Josef and his family after he waved goodbye at me from the back of the truck in 1943. This even more so when my father now confirmed that Josef's mother had been a Gypsy. Having learned that the Nazi exterminators regarded Gypsies no differently than Jews, the likely fate of my friend Josef, his sister and mother was extermination, the destiny of all Gypsies inside the Reich. After reading Shirer, it was now easy for me to imagine the horrible scene where Josef, his sister and mother were separated from their father and husband at some railroad siding inside a Nazi camp.

The fate of Josef's father, the (racially pure) ethnic Gottscheer German who had fallen in love with a pretty and flirtatious young Gypsy girl wearing colorful and billowing skirts, a woman who perhaps came through his village as part of a traveling

THE RABBIT

group as they had in Masern, was less certain. At best, he survived by being allowed to atone in a Nazi labor camp for his sin of polluting his race by marrying a racial outcast, a Gypsy. Perhaps he even survived the war, ending only two years after being hauled out of a falsely perceived security and mercilessly separated from his loving, but in the eyes of the Nazi state, parasitic wife and children.

The fate of Adolf, named by Josef after the leader of the Third Reich, is far less uncertain. It came in the spring of 1945 when a part of the last batch of German troops retreating from the advancing Partisans arrived in our village for an overnight stay and some of their trucks pulled into our courtyard. But contrary to prior regular troops, this lot of very young SS soldiers was hostile, took over the house and announced that they wanted to sleep in our beds. Father was deeply annoyed but Mother was more forgiving and to accommodate them, she suggested that we all sleep that night in the upper hay loft of the barn. Mother's point was that they were tired and had not slept in proper beds for a long time. She became less understanding when she noticed their leering at her twenty two year old daughter who was quickly ordered to keep out of sight.

Like all the other transient troops, they also wanted to be fed, preferably meat. Mother mentioned chicken or rabbits but told them they would have to catch and cook them on their own. They had little luck getting their hands on the free ranging birds who would take to the air whenever cornered. She did not tell them to wait until the late afternoon when they returned on their own to the hen house for the night, where they could be grabbed with ease. Unsuccessful with the chickens, they shifted their attention to the rabbits in the stable and immediately went after the biggest of them, my Adolf.

Clearly, these young SS were city boys, trained to capture and kill humans but not chicken or rabbits. Adolf kept evading them by running in between the legs of the animals and finally through the opening of the stable into the courtyard. They had not bothered to close the door.

They were even less successful in the open courtyard until one of them remembered how they killed enemies. A volley from his submachine gun slowed Adolf but did not kill him. The wounded animal scampered on, dragging his limp and bleeding rear with his front legs, leaving a trail of blood until another volley stopped him all together. He was still struggling when yet another burst partially severed the head from the body and the opened skull spilled the brains into the dirt. A knife separated the dangling head from the rest.

After that they did what was normally done with slaughtered animals. They slit open the belly to remove the entrails, pulled the skin from the body, and washed the carcass with water from the pump at the trough. They cooked the meat in a large pot on Mother's stove.

I was deeply saddened over the loss of Adolf, a constant reminder of my friend Josef. The full impact of his end came only years later, (after having read Shirer's book), in nightmares in which Josef merged into the body of the dying Adolf dragging himself across the dirt. But in April of 1945, I was disillusioned only by the brutality of this group of elite soldiers, the pride of the Reich, toward such a superior animal. I still believed that real Germans did not behave like that. But knowing that all was going bad, the end of the Reich so near and our future so uncertain, I instinctively envied Josef for having been moved into the safety of the inner Reich.

Little did I know!

Chapter 18

Settling In

During the spring, summer and fall of 1942, when the final land apportionment was being worked out by the officials, the farmers tilled and planted the parcels assigned them temporarily by the DAG. This effort was monitored and at harvest time a part of the yield was apportioned to villagers according to need. The rest was hauled away on trucks as state property. For their effort, the "workers" received payment in Reichsmark to purchase other needed staples at the state store in Zirkle. But all were looking toward the allocation of their own property. This started in late fall of 1942 and before the next planting season, most of this was done.

Contrary to the writings of both the farmer and the Reverend describing inequities and injustices in the allocation, similar complaints did not exist in our village. Here there were no Slovene; the entire population was made up of ingathered Gottscheer only. It would seem therefore that our situation was the exception in the settlement program since it does not agree with their reports. But their claims are supported by other available and reliable documentation, making clear that our case was indeed the exception, not the rule.

Little time was needed by the DAG to survey the land since the defining of parcels followed the existing land records. Adjacent parcels were simply combined to satisfy the allocation. This was possible since the village now had only half the number of its prior residents. For this reason most of the settlers who were awarded Type 2 farms received, in addition to the main house and its farming complex, also the adjacent house and its associated buildings. There were no Type 1 farms in the village and Katharina and the others who had little, if any land in the enclave, were given a Type 6. (see Chapter Veliko Mraševo).

Jacklitsch moved to Cerklje and there into the large house at the main intersection which also included a Gasthaus with a few guest rooms. Members of the DAG stayed there as did the Agricultural Advisor of the Cerklje district whose task it was to instruct the farmers in cultivating their land and vineyards. Father consulted him frequently and they got to know each other well. The public room was larger than the one in Masern and there was an upright piano. The Adviser often played it and his lively and sometimes melancholy tunes had us, the music starved youngsters, listening at the door on the way home from school.

THE BELLS RING NO MORE

Schaffer, the former Fire Chief moved into a villa on the hill, some distance from the village center across the Kostanjevica road. In Masern his had been a very nice house, fully restored after the fire in 1934, but this one was even grander. There no longer being a fire brigade, he now had little reason to come into the village. And the village not having a Gasthaus, he had to get drunk at home or at the Jacklitsch place in Cerklje. But when he came home, his wife Maria again came to Mother to escape his temper as she had done in years past.

We moved into our final home in the spring of 1943. Father had accepted a property unit measuring 24 hectares of land which was 3 ha more than he owned at home. Included in the 24 ha were a few hectares of forest and a vineyard of approximately 1.5 hectares in the hills near Krško (Gurkfeld) nearly one hour away.

Our new house was on the main road to the river, just slightly before the triangle in the middle of the village. The buildings of our "Type 2 Farm" were the houses and associated barns and stables of two adjacent former farms combined into one unit and so we now had two of everything. For our residence Father chose the larger and more pleasant house which also needed fewer repairs. It used to belong to a family named Žibert and its house number was 38. In the second house he set up his workshop. And adjacent to that, directly on the triangle, was the house of Katharina.

Across the road, on the second side of the triangle, was the Primosch couple, good friends of our family with their two young sons Josef and Ferdinand. Each soon to be drafted in succession; both of them never came back from the war as was the case with most village men who were drafted into the Wehrmacht or joined the SS.

On the third side of the triangle was the house of Hans Mams and his aging parents who owned the farm but were hardly fit to run it, which in turn kept the 40ish Hans out of the army until early 1945.

Johann Krisch and his mother were in the house next to our immediate neighbor on the road away from the river. To have this long time friend so near was not only fortunate for Father but for all of us as well. He was a powerfully built man who helped us a lot and in only a few years was to save my life more than once. He remained a family friend even after his 1943 request to marry Mitzi was denied. His mother had died recently and both parents believed the 45 year Johann Krisch was too old and mainly wanted a replacement pair of hands. Mitzi was not happy about

SETTLING IN

this decision and tearfully countered that they denied Johann only because they did not want to lose a worker.

The repairs on our house and others in the village were being done by forced labor workers from Czechoslovakia. I stopped by to watch them repair our windows and tried to speak to them but they were neither receptive nor friendly. To house them, the DAG had erected a wooden barracks on a field near the little house at the intersection on the Kostanjevica road. This barracks also housed the Slovene forced laborers assigned to the farmers in the fall of 1942 and who lived there until the fall of 1944.

Already in the spring of 1942, Father had been given another horse we named Shargo. From that time forward, he and his oddly matched team of Yiorgo and Shargo were constantly called upon to contribute to the farming effort carried out by the DAG during that year.

Shargo was in all ways a complement to Yiorgo. Smaller in height but stocky in width, he was a good natured draft horse that unhesitatingly followed commands. His smooth and shiny fur was the color of chestnuts, whereas the gray of Yiorgo was being crowded out by ever larger spots of white, his ultimate color. Contrary to Shargo, Yiorgo had a race horse frame and a temperament to match. Especially when rested, he needed the sharp voice of Father and even the whip to keep him in line.

During 1942, the DAG had also assigned to us (as they had to the Farmer KR) for temporary care-taking, additional livestock from its stores of cows that had been confiscated from the Slovene. These were now permanently ours with the proviso that the expected daily quota of milk was available for pick up every morning.

And to help run the farm, in the spring of 1943 the DAG assigned to us four workers from the pool of forced laborers housed in the barracks built by the DAG. Most of these workers were Slovene from the vicinity of Maribor, but some were from Bessarabia. Two of the Slovene I remember particularly well.

One was Theresika, a young woman of about 20 and a somewhat older young man named Tomaž. Both were "Windische" for whom this assignment was to be their passport to German citizenship. Both knew some German but we spoke to them in Slovene when out of hearing of authority. They worked alongside us, ate with us and were treated as part of the family. But they had to return to the barracks at night.

Mitzi and Theresika became friends and she stayed with us until the fall of 1944. This was not so with Tomaž who kept disappearing but showed up again a few days if not weeks later. When one time he did not return he was replaced, but many of the replacements also disappeared after a while. Not all were cooperative and hard workers in spite of being treated like family.

Essential to running the farm, however, were the various pieces of farming machinery Father received from the DAG via the help of the Agricultural Advisor in Cerklje. Among them was a very modern plow with various attachments for planting and harvesting potatoes, a grass mowing machine with special attachments for cutting and bundling the grain, a hay turner, a hay rake and a machine for seeding. All pulled by either Yiorgo or Shargo or both. There was also a large pressure cooker that cooked potatoes and beets for the pigs in a matter of minutes. Such machinery, which so dramatically lightened the labor of farming, was unknown in Masern, if not in the entire enclave.

Not all farmers in the village were given such equipment, which caused some to complain to the DAG. But the award to Father could not be challenged because it was based on Himmler's directive defining agricultural land distribution to the ingathered. The village did, however, receive for communal use a modern steam engine driven threshing machine and a distillery whose output lightened the mood of the ingathered, even if only for brief intervals in the now progressively deteriorating war situation.

The equipment received was remarkably easy to use. All could be operated by a single person from a seat on the machine needing only direction to a team of horses pulling it. Levers on the machine next to the seat could engage or disengage various features required by the task. The plow however, had no seat but Father soon fabricated one from which he could operate the levers. At first Mitzi, Mother or I helped him with the horses, but soon even this was not necessary.

It was so easy to use that in the spring of 1944 that I, as a slight thirteen year old, did most of the plowing. Not only our fields but also those of some of our neighbors. Tscherne the teacher came by to find out why I was missing his class so frequently to which Father replied that I was needed on the farm to help with the war effort.

The biggest problem in all this was the temperamental Yiorgo. He would, at least in the beginning, get impatient at being directed by a mere boy and would bolt

SETTLING IN

at any opportunity knowing he could easily free himself from the little hands holding the reins. I soon learned to sense his rising impatience, forcefully apply the whip at the proper moment and behave like the master Yiorgo expected me to be.

But until then he behaved foolishly and his high spirits created a number of dangerous situations for himself, the placid Shargo who joined the frolic and anyone else who stood in the way.

There was the time when he, Shargo and I were plowing a field. Seemingly after an agreement between the two, they tore loose and galloped off, the heavy plow flying back and forth behind them. They were forced to slow down only when the plow blade caught the soft earth sending strings of furrows into the air. Ultimately the blade dug in deep which overpowered them and brought them to a halt. There was no damage other than the deep and irregular ruts through otherwise geometrical and orderly acreage and fields.

At yet another time, when pulling a harrow back and forth on a freshly plowed field with me guiding him from the rear, Yiorgo decided to make for the river to get a drink. I again could not restrain him and had to let go of the reins when he started to run and then gallop. He galloped through the village to get to the river on the street familiar to him, the harrow flying from side to side and up and down behind him. The villagers jumped out of the way but caught up with him when he was getting his fill at the river's edge. Having had enough, he placidly allowed a neighbor to lead him back to our stable without any resistance, where Father gave him a whipping and forbade any further oats which, supposedly, had encouraged the rebellion.

But one time he became particularly indignant at his boy master who was about to fool him again and in his fury nearly trampled me to death. This happened after a day in the fields when both horses were fed and as was usual every evening, I individually led each from the stable to the watering trough. Placid Shargo always followed easily, but not Yiorgo.

At times he would tear loose and gallop into the fields behind the barn where he playfully tried to avoid being caught, especially by me. Someone else usually had to get him. But one evening I came to get him with a handful of oats in a tray which I rustled at him. He followed me into the stable where he finally got his reward for being obedient.

But only once. When I tried it again, he followed me for a while as I walked toward the stable. However Yiorgo wanted it now not later. Getting very close behind me, he rose up high on his hind legs and before I could run away, he brought his hoofs down on my back, smashing me to the ground.

THE BELLS RING NO MORE

Fortunately Father, who was nearby and watching, let out a forceful yell which stopped the attack. The excited Yiorgo turned away and raced back into the fields where Johann Krisch finally managed to catch him and bring him back to the stable. There he received a most brutal whipping from Father.

The hit from the iron shod hoof, apart from knocking the breath out of me and from which I recovered quickly, caused no other damage other than a bruise that hurt for a few days. And after this day, Yiorgo received oats only after a hard day's work had him totally exhausted. But I also learned to lower and make more authoritarian the sound of my commands, use the whip more often and harder and the rebellious behavior ceased altogether. I had gained his respect; we got to know each other better.

It was the plowing that finally got me the pocket watch I was promised in 1939 as a confirmation gift.

Johann Krisch had a plot that needed plowing. He also had a pocket watch he never used but which I had been admiring for years. It had been in his family for generations; a beautifully engraved silver piece, whose lid snapped open when you pressed the wind up button. Engraved on the inside of the lid were the elaborately carved initials JK, and both the hour and minute hands, as well as the second indicator, were embellished with handsome curlicues to make each reading of time a delight.

When Johann asked if I would plow his land, for which he offered the watch as payment, Father readily agreed. Johann was well aware of my admiration for the piece and having no son of his own to pass it to, did not mind parting with this heirloom. And with this act, the outstanding promise of my parents would be made good.

The fact that I was to acquire it through my own hard labor, instead of receiving it as the deserved gift was overlooked, but no matter. I was finally getting my watch. It came with a leather strap that could be adjusted for the differing distances between the buttonhole and the breast pocket of a jacket or vest coat worn on festive occasions. However, such occasions were now a thing of the past, but the watch was nevertheless installed properly in my jacket in the closet, ever ready for an important event. In the meanwhile it was frequently retrieved, fondled and shown about as my favorite possession.

SETTLING IN

I owned it for little more than a year. In May of 1945, at the point of a gun, the strap latch was unbuttoned, the watch pulled from the breast pocket of the jacket and taken from me by a grinning Tito Partisan not much older than myself.

The vineyard was on the southern slopes of Libelj near Krško, about 9 km from our village. With its fully equipped cellar, including press and barrels it had been somewhat neglected during the past year and its vines now needing careful pruning.

Since the vineyard of Johann Krisch was next to ours, we joined forces and the two horses brought the big wagon filled with our workers to Libelj in less than an hour. Under Father's direction, all of us turned the soil, clipped the shoots, tied them to the wire between the stakes and sprayed the vine with a copper sulfate solution during spring and summer. The knowledge for all this had been imparted to Father by the Agricultural Advisor from Cerklje and by Theresika who also knew about vineyard cultivation, herself coming from the wine region around Ljutomer. And in the fall of 1943, the vines were laden with bulging grapes.

The vineyard was steep, stone outcroppings in places interrupting the straight lines of the vines. All of us had been warned to stay away from the stones; there were snakes that loved the warm rocks and were vengeful when interrupted in their slumber. And when Theresika let out a yell, we ran to find the crying girl pointing to two bite marks on her leg. Johann quickly found the snake and chopped its head off with a hoe.

I came along on the short ride to Dr. Röthel's practice in Krško, with Father making the horses gallop wherever possible and Mitzi and Johann Krisch trying to comfort the sobbing Theresika. The doctor gave her a shot after having a look at the snake's head Johann had brought along and by the time we returned to the vineyard, the swelling ceased to increase. After a few days, it disappeared altogether; the two teeth marks remaining a little longer.

Had this occurred one year later, Theresika would not have been so lucky.

After the Allied invasion of mainland Italy in September 1943, we fearlessly watched the endless silvery formations of bombers on their way north, but sought safety outdoors when they were returning later and did target practice with their remaining bombs. On Christmas day 1943, when Dr. Röthel was having dinner with his family, his house received a direct hit, killing them all. The doctor may have believed that on this day such acts would not be performed.

THE BELLS RING NO MORE

Since Dr. Röthel had been the only resident physician in our area, any medical attention from now on was available only from military units temporarily in the area. Apart from that, the people living in our region were on their own.

Harvesting the grape was a day of hard labor. Helping were Johann, Katharina, her husband Alois and a few others from the village. My back being too young to carry the heavy buckets of grapes uphill, I was tasked to join others in crushing them with bare feet in a large round wooden tub.

A part of the juice was taken back home but some was left to ferment in barrels behind the locked doors of the vineyard cellar. Also brought home were the remnants of the crushed grapes, there to ferment in open barrels and distilled at a later time.

Unfortunately, later that fall, thieves broke the door of the vineyard cellar and drained the barrels dry. Not only ours but also those of Johann Krisch and many of the others nearby. After that, Father reinforced the door and fabricated an unbreakable locking mechanism to prevent a repeat in the following fall. Nevertheless, after that most of the unfermented juice was brought home to the safety of our house.

While harvesting the grape was toil only, the extracting of alcohol from the now fermented grapes in the barrels was something else. Later, when most farming was done and idleness stretched the day, the communal distillery was fired up in one of the houses according to a prearranged schedule. When it came to us it was fired up in the large room of the empty house, the extraction of the clear and potent distillate pouring out of a nozzle from dawn to dusk.

Again, the Adviser from Cerklje came by with various pointers including on how to control the alcohol content of the emerging distillate. It filled many bottles, most to be sold as brandy to the State cooperative while some others were buried in the grain of granary bins in the attic. I once quietly followed Mother on her trips up the stairs and surprised her taking a swig from one of the bottles. Red in the face and pointing to her stomach, she explained it was for medicinal purposes.

During most of the day, the room contained a half a dozen or so men who came to sample. And later on, many a wife came to retrieve her no longer steady husband who was reluctant to leave, only to return a little later that afternoon.

The still moved from farm to farm, a process that lasted for weeks and eventually a smell of alcohol enveloped the entire village. This was most noticeable as I came home from school or was on the back of Shargo when, after a heavy snowfall, I had to get the mail at the post office in Cerklje.

SETTLING IN

While the soil here produced an ample harvest and the grapes a better wine than what could be had at the Jacklitsch inn, our new village was, unfortunately, not surrounded by a forest. No longer were we in the presence of majestic pines and firs that reached for the sky and filtered the sunlight, encouraging the growth of soft green moss on the protruding rocks keeping moist the carpet of needles underfoot, ensuring a cushioned walk in the cool and shady air. No longer present the strong fragrance of the running sap and the buzz of armies of bees in their effort to harvest the nectar oozing from the cones. This was not pine country.

And whatever forest there was, it was on the hill between Cerklje and Veliko Mraševo. By contrast, all of the higher hills across the river were thickly covered with trees of all kinds. On our side, in addition to a rare conifer, there was only an occasional oak or maple maturing among mostly slender white birch or some other less imposing deciduous tree. And, since the total forest area was small, its allocations were also small. Ours was approximately one and a half hectares.

The immediate consequence was that we no longer had an unlimited supply of firewood. While our predecessors were able to get what they needed from across the river, we had to supplement what was available in our allocated parcel with coal from the store in Cerklje. Mother soon learned to light a coal fire with kindling wood in the kitchen stove. But without adequate firewood it was not possible to heat the big oven and she had to learn to bake bread in the kitchen stove. This was in turn welcomed since we no longer had to sleep in a room in which the heat of summer was increased by the corner oven. There was, however, always enough firewood put aside for the winter and the warmth from this oven, to which we were so accustomed.

Except for the tasks connected with the vineyard, the job of operating the new and much larger farm was not very different from that in Masern. There was much more arable land to be cultivated, but now we had a team of horses and a lot of labor saving machinery. Before, we used only the land we needed for our own harvest and leased the rest to others in return for their labor. Now we had slave labor workers to help us with all that acreage.

Whatever we had produced in Masern we kept for ourselves; cash for the rest of our needs was provided by the ever willing forest silently growing sellable lumber. And if the farm produce became a victim of the whims of nature, more lumber could be cashed in to buy what was lost. Now, our entire livelihood had to come from the sale of the harvest, the forest no longer providing a comforting backup. In this respect, the former farmers of Masern were less well off.

Here in Veliko Mraševo as formerly in Masern, I as oldest son, was destined to become master of the land when eventually the time came. Until then I and others like myself, would continue to plow the earth and grow a harvest while patiently waiting for our turn as generations of our ancestors had done before. Except that destiny had something quite different in mind for all of us.

While much remained the same, the tragic loss to the people of Masern was their centuries old community life. The glue that kept the village of Masern interdependent and constant was absent and could not be duplicated in Veliko Mraševo. It could also not be duplicated for all the other villages of the former enclave in this stolen land.

The farmer K.R. writes:

"The cultivation of the farms is progressing well and the resettlers delivered their obligation dutifully in accordance with the regulations. When I was allocated my farm by the DAG, I also received a pair of oxen and a cow. I tilled the ground carefully, but for me and my family there was constantly an uncomfortable feeling to sleep in a house that had been taken away from its rightful owner.

"In the spring of 1943 the deported owner of the house returned from Silesia for a few days vacation in his former homeland. During these few days here he lived with a resident Croatian who had not been deported and indirectly inquired if he could visit and see his house again. I welcomed him and he stayed some two hours with me. He reported that his son had died in Silesia as a consequence of the deportation and that he had brought the body with him for burial in his native land. He was hopeful for an eventual return to his homeland. I gave him a parcel of provisions for his return journey".

In the fall of 1943 I acquired a new friend and kindred spirit, a much welcomed replacement for my departed schoolmate Josef Tramposch.

SETTLING IN

Franz was the 15 year old son of the Sturm family that moved into the still empty house on the Kostanjevica road, a short distance from the one Josef and his family had so unexpectedly been taken by the SS. The origin of the Sturm family was Masern number 22, the house in which the grandmother of Franz had died in 1939 and where I had helped Father get the measurements of the corpse he needed to make the coffin. She left the estate to her only son who lived in Austria where he married and had a son Franz and daughter Frederike. As heir, he opted for the estate to be resettled and took possession of the awarded property in late summer of 1943.

As with Josef, Franz and I met in class at Cerklje where I now had a serious competitor and for our teacher a choice of two hands held up high with the answer. We got to know each other on the way to school and back and cemented our friendship at his house, since it was the first on the way back and only a short distance from the little straw decked house at the intersection.

During the school year of '43/44, I spent much time at the Sturm house, where his parents welcomed me as a good companion for their son. There we jointly did our homework and read books of which his family had more than mine. They also had a radio where I occasionally got the news that I had to repeat when I got home.

Apart from that we had little contact, he having no interest in raising rabbits and being forbidden to spear fish. Also, his parents seemed to be protective and kept their children near and consequently, we rarely saw them in the village among the other youngsters. My mother thought this was a mistake; children should be allowed to roam and be among others of their age. Events soon proved how right she was. She also believed that I spent too much time at the Sturm house and discouraged me from going there too frequently.

On the way home from school we lingered while taking out of the way treks through the woods and walk along the stream as I had done with Josef. Only to look for fish; not to spear them. Except that after spotting one, I would return on my own, weapon in hand. And if I caught one, he insisted on hearing the description of the adventure and seeing the spot of my conquest.

Not that all walks home were as pastoral or so harmless and serene.

In early fall of '44, the Agricultural Advisor living in the Jacklitsch inn at Cerklje suddenly disappeared. Since he was such a well liked man and a great help to Father and many others in the district, everyone was very concerned. I knew him well from his many visits to our village and to our house in particular. We also missed the tunes he sometimes played on the upright piano at the Jacklitsch inn which made us linger at the door on our way home from school.

Prior to his disappearance, he was reported to be despondent and depressed, apparently as the result of a letter he received from home somewhere up north. One rumor had it that his fiancée, whom he was to marry soon, had left him for someone else. Another, that she was killed in an air raid.

The mystery of his disappearance ended when, after leaving the school house to go home, we heard that his body had been found in the river and was in the charnel house at the cemetery.

Since this was on the way home, I was determined to go see him. Franz was reluctant but then agreed to come with me. The grave diggers in a corner of the cemetery told us not to go there, but we went anyway.

The door of the small house was open with light entering the room through little windows high up on the walls. The fully dressed body was on the boards of two sawhorses, its feet pointing toward the door. Not much to see from here. Was it really him? I had to look. Franz did not want to so I went around to the front of the body myself.

It was a mistake; the fish had been at his face. Much of it was missing, all distinguishing features gone, the hair peeling off the scalp, the protruding bulbous eyes staring at me.

How I got out and out of the cemetery I do not remember. But Franz told me later that I ran and screamed. The horror of that vision stayed not only through the rest of that day and night and the days to follow, but came to me in nightmares for many months to come.

Apparently the news he received had driven him to suicide. They found him after the legs and lower part floated upward, while the upper part of his body remained attached to something in the water. It was his hands that were still clamped on to an underwater root of a willow tree. He was determined to kill himself; he held on to it until he drowned.

No relatives came to claim the body which was buried unceremoniously in the unconsecrated ground of the cemetery.

The people of Masern lost their village square, but they gained a river.

SETTLING IN

Gone was the village square and the three inns that welcomed villagers throughout the year; to go there for refreshments, to discuss serious matters or pass on trivial gossip. Or come for a dance on summer Sundays, outside on raised wooden platforms to the harmonica tunes of Josef Primosch. In warm weather, linger in the shade of the linden or rest on its surrounding stone benches, passing idle time. Watch Schaffer exercising his firemen testing their equipment. Take part in the multitude of events connected with the church on the square. To browse for bargains on trinket stands that filled most of the square on the day of the patron saint. To take part in the procession on Easter Sunday, following the brocaded priest under the canopy and the orderly columns of Schaffer's uniformed fire fighters. All to the festive peal from the bells in the tower.

All of the above, and much more of what mattered, was left behind. But we youngsters now had a sandy beach by the river.

It was not much of a beach, a 15 meter long stretch of small pebbles and sand at the bend of the gently flowing river. The slowly downward sloping road from the village led to it and stopped where the sandy beach began. After the sandy part, the river bent away and picked up speed at the shallower part further down stream.

Young and old were drawn to it; the elders bringing the cattle to be watered and to wash away the sticking dust accumulated during the long day. And later, when the water was finally warmed up by the approaching summer, we all went in for a refreshing dip.

The young were there whenever possible. On any day after school or when no longer needed to help with chores, but always on Sunday afternoons when most adults were resting up for another week. This is when we were joined by them as they came to get their feet wet or just watch or sit in the grass along the embankment.

But what seemed pastoral to the eye turned treacherous under water. The sand continued to slope gradually into the darkening river and at about four meters from the edge, a ten year old child would be submerged only to the chest. But a step or two beyond that the ground would drop to a precipitous depth.

This treachery of the river was discovered the first summer when some of the younger men explored the water. I had already been warned of this by the Slovene in the straw covered house at the intersection, cautioning me not to go in very far while urging me to quickly learn to swim. "Everyone living by the river should know that" was his advice.

None of the new residents knew how. Father claimed he learned to swim in the Isonzo, but since he never gave a demonstration, few believed it. And at the Isonzo he still had both legs!

THE BELLS RING NO MORE

Mother was always reluctant to let me go; the first summer of 1942 only in the company of Mitzi who yelled when I was getting in too deep. Four year old brother Paul was allowed in the water but only while being held by his sister's hand. The following two summers Mother forever made me promise to stay at the water's edge and then was visibly relieved when I reappeared. Father was more sanguine; he only made me promise not to go in unless others were there.

In the spring of 1944 we were again eagerly awaiting the day when the water was warm enough to go in.

There was much discussion about this on the way home from school and Franz admitted that he and his sister had been forbidden to go near the river.

Part of this had to do with the fact that by then, a strip of land along the river's edge had been mined as was the space on which had been erected a three meter wide barbed wire fence. Except at the road to the beach which had a removable gate to give the villagers access to the river. The gate was closed at night and protected by border guards in a nearby bunker.

The village was informed by the guards where the minefield started; the area to stay clear was marked with stakes. But the parents of Franz and Frederike took no chances and used this as the real reason to keep them away from the river.

It was clear that this prohibition was agony to Franz especially when school started after the long summer and on the way home, taunts of being a sissy nearly drove him to tears. On such afternoons, I declined to go to his house to do homework; I would rather go to the river.

Near the end of that hot summer of 1944, a highly excited Franz announced in class the he might finally be able to join us that afternoon. After school he hurried home while we cut through the woods to get to the river as soon as possible.

We were already in the water when he came running and behind the bushes stripped off his clothes. While doing that we paid him no attention.

Almost immediately after that he was flailing in the water. In his excitement, he had run in, but went beyond the shallow part where he slid off the edge and his feet lost contact with the ground. We all rushed forward to help him, but his frantic struggle propelled him only into still deeper waters where we could no longer reach him since none of us knew how to swim. All of us were stunned; none knew what to do. At least for a moment.

SETTLING IN

But off to the side was a light, highly unstable and never used canoe which was quickly pulled into the water. With Anton, the younger son of Katharina, kneeling in the tip and the rest of us forming a chain to the older son Albert holding on to the other end, the little boat was pushed out into the deep. By now however, Franz was in even deeper water where even the outstretched hand of Anton could no longer reach him from the tip of the dangerously swaying boat.

And Albert, already at the very edge of the abyss, would not go further nor let loose of the boat, fearing that the now less frequently reemerging Franz would tip the unstable canoe and also cause the drowning of his brother. And when Franz did not surface again, Albert pulled the boat back in.

As I ran toward the village, men were already rushing toward the river in response to my yells for help. One of them stopped me and said I should run to tell the parents.

Both were busy with some other workers in their farmyard threshing wheat. At first no one paid any attention to me as I stood there all sweaty and exhausted from the long run and afraid to say anything. At least not until I was noticed by Johann Krisch who was among the helpers and asked why was I standing there. And after I stammered that Franz had drowned, he quickly told the parents who dropped their tools and all ran off toward the river. I ran after them but Father stopped me in the village and ordered me to go home; protecting me from yet another set of nightmares.

I forgot, or perhaps did not wish to remember how the body was recovered. It was explained to me two decades later by Karel Žibert, the owner of No 38, the house we lived in for just over two years.

He remembered the afternoon in early fall of 1944 when he and his friends were frolicking in the water on their side. We often saw them diving off the high and steep embankment there. They became aware of the commotion on the opposite side. It was the drowning of Franz.

They watched our efforts to save him and he recalled how some of the older boys got into a boat to row across, seeing that the desperately struggling body had disappeared. And when they got there they dived into the water, found the body and dragged it ashore. After that, they quickly got back into the boat and returned to their side.

THE BELLS RING NO MORE

The body of Franz was laid out in the Sturm house as was, years ago, that of his grandmother. Except that this time Father and I did not take any measurements as we had done then and he did not make the coffin. He also did not allow me to go to see the body nor take part in the funeral at the Cerklje cemetery where Franz was buried.

I never went to the Sturm house again, a place where, most likely, I was no longer welcome.

In the fall of 1944 we took in our second harvest. Now that the food situation in the Reich had become critical, as was apparent from the empty shelves at the cooperative in Cerklje, an inspector determined the amount of the harvest each farmer had to surrender to the state. Voluntary offering was no longer an option.

The inspector was Karl Tschinkel, formerly of Masern 12, the oldest of the three brothers Father had been at odds with for many years. Karl had been given the role of village leader by the Heimatbund, after Franz Jaklitsch was finally called up. In his mid 40's, Karl was unmarried and living alone and was, due his extreme nearsightedness not fit to be a soldier. With no one else around, he was assigned the job, a choice welcomed by the villagers who knew that he might not be overly thorough in his assignment.

One of his tasks was to enforce the requirement that the farmers surrender half of the harvested grain and half of livestock such as pigs, calves and chickens to the State cooperative.

He did this again in the fall of 1944 when he went from house to house with a ledger in which he made his entries. But the villagers were prepared. With most of the grain moved from the bins, some of the livestock from the stables and the brandy on the ready, they waited for his arrival.

The inspection did not start until he was properly warmed up with a few jiggers. He recorded half of what he was shown and after one more glass from the farmer pretending to be exploited, he moved to the next one along the road. This was repeated as he progressed from house to house which soon made him uncertain on his legs. Somewhere along the way he was given lunch including wine and he partially recovered by taking a short nap. But after he resumed, he no longer desired

SETTLING IN

to perform the inspection and asked the farmer to fill in the numbers himself. When he finally completed his round, he was escorted home and not seen for a few days.

That fall, Karl was particularly lenient when Mother showed him around. He grinned when she showed him the half empty bins, pigsties and stables, as if he knew better. Perhaps he was making up for past misdeeds; the cutting down of Father's stately pines and the re-assembly, with help from his brothers, of Father's heavy wagon on the peak of our house when we were away. Nevertheless, the inspection may not have gone so well had Father, instead of Mother, shown him around.

It was rumored, however, that Karl was not as gullible as it appeared. He enjoyed the deference and attention and in return practiced leniency toward his fellow villagers who were reluctant to part with the products of their toil. Had the District Chief become aware of Karl's misdeeds toward the state, he surely would have been severely punished.

In the spring of 1945, little work was done in the fields and there was no attempt to plant another harvest. The forced laborers had not returned to help with the work and the news on the war was frightening. It was now obvious that Germany was going to lose the war and even the much talked about Vergeltungswaffen, the secret revenge weapons, gave us little hope. And since it was now certain we would no longer reap another harvest from this land, why bother.

Chapter 19

Twilight by the River

It is shortly before the hour on the evening of February 2, 1943 and our dimly lit 'big' room is again half filled with neighbors who, as usual, have come to hear the nightly news. Some are huddled around the primitive radio, its exposed vacuum tubes powered with an array of lead acid and dry cell batteries, the glow of the filaments showing the tension on their faces. Others are sitting on the benches around the corner oven, their backs up against the warm tiles. The radio sound is kept at a minimum to save power since a recharge or replacement of the precious batteries is nearly impossible.

For months we had been following with rising anxiety the news from the Russian front and the great battle of Stalingrad in particular. On November 21, 1942, the Soviets had encircled the German Sixth Army under General Friedrich von Paulus, trapping 250,000 German soldiers in the city. Hermann Göring, the head of the Luftwaffe declared: "we will supply the army by air until the ring is broken and the Soviet army defeated".

But for weeks nothing positive on Stalingrad was heard in the news. Lacking encouraging reports, everyone realized that the trapped Germans must be running out of ammunition, heating fuel and medical supplies. And without winter clothing, the situation must surely be desperate. According to Josef Michitsch, our Masern sexton who had been a POW in Russia during WWI, winter temperatures there can reach sub-zero Fahrenheit and night temperatures of -40F are not uncommon.

We all knew of the successes which immediately followed the invasion of Russia on June 22, 1941 when Germany and the Axis powers quickly advanced deep into Soviet territory. The *Gottscheer Zeitung* had been printing glowing reports on these battle victories while we were still in the enclave.

But later that fall, the successes slowed and the predictions of early victory over the Soviets did not come to pass. According to the plan for Operation Barbarossa, Leningrad was to have been captured by the end of July 1941 and Moscow long before the start of the brutal Russian winter. Barbarossa was based on the belief that the entire Red Army would collapse within five weeks. In this plan, the seizure of Moscow was considered the key to ultimate victory over the Communists.

Now, 19 months after the invasion, Leningrad was surrounded but still not captured, all attacks to destroy the city having failed. And when the Germans finally got to within 18 miles of Moscow's center on December 5, 1941, the Soviets started an offensive the following day which defeated the Wehrmacht and pushed it back one hundred miles, denying the Germans their victory. And now the situation in Stalingrad was very discouraging. Promptly at seven o'clock, the somber music stopped and the announcer read the news:

"Hier ist der Reichsdeutsche Rundfunk; wir bringen die Nachrichten". (Here is the Radio Network of the German Reich; we are bringing the news). Then after a pause and without any other preliminary comment, the voice slowly and solemnly announces: Stalingrad has fallen."

Father turned off the radio. Some women started to cry. After this defeat, many in the room had their lingering doubts about a German victory reinforced. All knew that if Germany lost the war, we were doomed. We could not stay on properties stolen from others and as citizens of the Third Reich would not be allowed to return to Gottschee, an integral part of a liberated Slovenia in which we would not be permitted to stay.

I, who was sure of ultimate victory, had no such doubts. But I knew that Father did.

A few days later, the batteries die and now the news is by word of mouth only. We hear that von Paulus, the valiant General in charge of the surrounded Sixth Army Corps, who during the battle was promoted by Hitler to Field Marshal has surrendered and with his surviving troops, is on the way to Siberia.

For months Father had been saying that von Paulus was the Reich's greatest General, a term Hitler himself had used when he announced the promotion only a few days ago. The fact that after his surrender, Hitler called von Paulus a traitor and coward did not get to us until much later but got me into trouble in the meanwhile.

On March 18, 1943, our school is visited by Uiberreither, the Gauleiter of Styria. We are all lined up in front of the school in Cerklje under the nervous supervision and the fussing of Pfeifer our teacher. I am the first in line; a privilege granted me since I am one of his best students. The big cars come and the uniformed Gauleiter approaches, trailed by his uniformed staff, all wearing highly polished boots.

He comes straight at me and asks: "who is the greatest general on the eastern front?" Without hesitation I roar out, Feldmarschall von Paulus.

He stares at me a while as if to make up his mind what to do with me, then looks at the paling teacher. After another look at me he goes down the line asking no more questions.

From that time on I am never again the first in line. Of course my father got a serious reprimand from Jacklitsch, but Father has the right answer: "I didn't know; our batteries went dead ".

The battle of Stalingrad began with heavy bombing by the Luftwaffe on August 23, 1942 causing a fire storm, killing thousands. The sprawling metropolis became a graveyard. In early September, the German Army advanced into the city and Hitler declared in a public speech on September 30, that the German army would never leave it. On November 21, the Red Army surrounded the city trapping 250,000 German soldiers of Sixth Army in the pocket.

Hitler promoted Friedrich von Paulus to Generalfeldmarschall on January 30, 1943. Already on November 30, 1942, Hitler had publicly commanded that the city be held at all cost. He took it for granted that von Paulus would obey his order to fight to the last man and take his own life since no German Field Marshal had ever surrendered.

Paulus disobeyed Hitler after being promoted, saying that as a Christian he could not, in good faith, kill himself. When Soviet forces closed in on Paulus' headquarters on January 31, Paulus surrendered. Hitler was furious and openly lambasted Paulus for being the only Field Marshal in German history to surrender alive. The remnants of the Germans surrendered on February 2, 1943.

The battle of Stalingrad had raged for 199 days and was the turning point in the war. It bled the German army dry and after this defeat, the Wehrmacht was in full retreat.

But already one year ago, after only six months from the start of Operation Barbarossa on June 22, 1941, the strategic position of Germany in Russia had become dangerously precarious. This had been predicted by German supply units even before the operation, should the war be prolonged into the Russian winter, but their warnings were disregarded. Hitler had stated that since the war would be over in five weeks only a few mobile units would be needed to occupy the defeated state. Now, nineteen months later, the Germans were being driven back, not only in Russia but on the other fronts as well. And on December 11, 1941, Germany had declared war against the United States, bringing a new powerful adversary into the battle.

The first time I heard that Germany might lose the war was in the early fall of 1942, at about the time the German Army was taking Stalingrad. I overheard this during a conversation Father was having with a soldier of the German border patrol who in pairs patrolled their part of the river border, a stretch half way between Cerklje and Brod. Brod was a small village of a few empty houses 2 km beyond Veliko Mraševo, a short distance off the Kostanjevica road, its houses nestled around either side of the dirt road leading to the bridge across the Krka river.

The guards lived in a house near the narrow wooden bridge, machine guns mounted in the fortified windows. Bisecting the bridge was a barbed wire barrier that prevented any crossing. There were no corresponding guards on the Italian side. I sometimes stopped at the bridge and watched the off duty guards angling on their side of the bridge with a simple hook tied to a string off a stick, but the fish were too smart for them.

The guards often stopped at our house for a short rest and something to eat and drink. Father was happy to talk to them and hear from them news items not heard on the radio. For them, talking to villagers interrupted the boredom of their posting and the uneventful patrols along the river where nothing ever happened. At least not until then, but this was to change soon enough.

This lone guard was off duty and had come to visit Father whom he had befriended during the past summer on his frequent stops. He was an older Austrian from Vienna who like Father had been a soldier in WWI. The soldier was bemoaning the fact that the Soviet Army had not collapsed in five weeks as Hitler had predicted, that the conquest of Russia was way behind schedule and the unprepared Wehrmacht was now heading into the bitter Russian winter that had defeated Napoleon. He claimed that the strategic position of Germany had become bad because neither the Wehrmacht nor the German military industry was prepared for a long winter war in Russia.

But what upset the Austrian even more was the fact that Hitler had declared war on the United States on December 11, 1941. He believed this had been a bad mistake without first conquering the British Isles which now would offer a secure invasion base for the Americans. A two front war is not winnable, he claimed.

TWILIGHT BY THE RIVER

(The soldier would have been even more upset had he known that Hitler had postponed Operation Barbarossa, the invasion of the Soviet Union, by five weeks to June 22, to subdue a rebellious Yugoslavia. He did this against the advice of his generals who feared that the delay might jeopardize the war.)

I expected Father to counter with a forceful denial, but he maintained a downcast, thoughtful silence which encouraged the doubting soldier even more in his treasonable talk. The man, who knew of our status, told Father to get out of Slovenia in time should his fears come to pass and Germany begin to lose the war.

Afterwards, Father made me promise not to mention to anyone what I had heard; "the soldier did not know what he was talking about and yes, definitely, Germany will win the war". I was, of course assured but did not forget what I had heard.

News of the world, the war or even local news reached us via word of mouth only, and then already days if not weeks old and obsolete. After Stalingrad, our radio was dead due to lack of charged batteries and if there were newspapers they did not reach our village. The Gottscheer Zeitung was no longer published; it had died together with the concept of the Gottscheer as an ethnic group. The last issue had been printed in Gottschee City on December 3, 1941.

Sometimes Father got a news update from Franz Jacklitsch, who had a working radio, when he stopped at his inn in Cerklje on the way home. And on some Sunday afternoons Yiorgo brought Father and me to the movie house in Krško where a newscast was shown prior to the feature film. Usually it showed the Führer, Göring, Goebbels and other Reich dignitaries, either alone or in various combinations visiting the front or giving a victory speech. Most impressive, however, were the victorious battle scenes in Russia describing the advances deep into the country. After Stalingrad and later in 1943 and '44, "repositioning the army" was used to describe retreats, claiming that battling the enemy closer to home was strategically more effective toward victory. And soon after that, newscasts were no longer shown.

For us the war was far away and had only a minimal effect on our daily lives. But on July 7, 1943 it also came to us in the Save/Sotla area in the form of a massive partisan raid from across the river.

We were awakened late at night by Mother who silenced our protests by telling us to be quiet as she was commanding all three of us in a whisper to crawl under their bed. While doing this, I noticed Father standing at the window, staring intently into the still dark outside. Then there were voices in Slovene; distant at first but getting nearer and approaching our house. And after some exchange on the street just outside the fence to our property, the voices receded and disappeared altogether. After quite a while other voices returned but now they were in our familiar Gottscheer dialect, those of our neighbors from across the street. This is when Mother said we could come out from under the bed and all of us went outside. It was getting light. By now all the residents along the street toward the river had come out and were telling their version of what had happened.

The Partisan raid had started with houses nearest the river and worked its way toward the center of the village. There was no resistance since the patrolling of the border at that time was minimal and the border guards at the bridge in Brod were kept indoors by raiders who had surrounded their post. The Partisans knocked at each door with rifle butts and told the person that appeared to stay indoors or be shot. Then they went to the stable and led off the livestock toward the river. In most cases they left behind one cow. It seemed they were only recovering what they believed was rightly theirs; we and all other settlers having been given livestock taken from the Slovene deported in 1941. The animals were crossed to the other side of the river at the shallow part downstream from the beach.

They were about to enter our house but were stopped by their commander only because they were running late. This and much more was explained to me by the Slovene Karel Žibert, the owner of number 38, when I visited the village many years later.

The raid left half the village with empty stables. But it also took the life of Maria Mams, the 56 year old mother of the 30 year old Hans. Maria lived alone in the second of two houses which Hans, as the heir to his father's estate, had accepted as his allocation. Her house was next to that of Katharina, the fourth from ours in the direction of the river. She had moved there after Hans married earlier that year and his new wife took over the household.

Maria, who slept in a ground level bedroom, was awakened by the unusual commotion on the street. At the open window, she heard a noise outside and, apparently yelled "who is there"?

Unfortunately, on the other side of the wall, just beside the window was one of the raiders, a young man, standing guard. Startled by the unsuspected voice, he turned and fired, point blank at the shadow in the window, killing her instantly.

We heard other shots, but from a distance. They came from Brod where some Partisans were keeping the border guards in their bunker. They also came from the solitary house at the intersection of the Kostanjevica road and the one leading to the

Brod bridge. It was the house of Ferdinand Kren, the 24 year old son of our former butcher and inn keeper at the cemetery end of Masern village. The elder Kren had died in 1941 and his son Ferdinand as heir was allocated the house and inn at the Brod intersection.

The raiders were on the way to Malo Mraševo, a village one third the size of ours, the settling place for the people of Grčarske ravne (Masereben), the Masern annex. When they banged on his door Ferdinand did not open but instead started firing at the raiders through windows while his mother was reloading his guns. His continuous firing kept the raiders away from the house.

The confrontation at the Kren house was a nuisance to the raiders since the road from Brod led past the Kren house toward to Malo Mraševo only a short distance away, hampering their main objective. Their purpose was not a confrontation or a firefight, but only to reclaim Slovene livestock now in the stables of the settlers, to feed the Partisans in the hills and forests across the river.

But while a few raiders kept Ferdinand busy firing out of the basement windows toward the road, others led the livestock around the back side of the house. When the raid ended, the Partisans withdrew from the house without casualties and the firing stopped. Both Ferdinand and his mother survived.

The raid of July 7, 1943 was the first and biggest of a number of raids across the border both from Italian occupied Slovenia and the puppet state of Croatia. It brought great anxiety to the settlers and caused the German occupiers to fortify the border. But this produced only marginal success; a full commitment to secure the border and deal with the increasing frequency and violence of the raids was not possible since the available resources of manpower and materiel were more urgently needed at the now faltering fronts. And after their defeat at Stalingrad, the Germans continued to lose ground not only in Russia but in major setbacks elsewhere as well.

May 13, 1943 - German and Italian troops surrender in North Africa.
July 26, 1943 - Italian fascist Government falls; Mussolini arrested.
Aug 17, 1943 - Germans evacuate Sicily.
Sept. 3, 1943 - Allies land on Italian mainland.
Jan. 6, 1944 - Soviet troops advance into Poland.
Jan. 27, 1944 - German 900 day siege of Leningrad broken by Soviet troops.
June 6, 1944 - Allies land in Normandy.
July 20, 1944 - Hitler survives assassination attempt by group of his generals who wish to end the losing war.

Not only were the Germans forced to give up their many conquests, but they were also unable to stop or even control the increasing guerilla activity within the territory they still occupied. Yugoslavia and the annexed parts of Slovenia are prime examples. Even here, the attempts of the Germans to fully suppress the resistance are not only unsuccessful; they are also unable to prevent the resistance from spreading and causing havoc with their movements and supply lines.

Guerrilla activity was also causing problems to the Italians occupying Slovenia. Here, however, the common objective of the factions resisting the occupier was fractured by irreconcilable differences between the communist Partisans and two of their ideological opposites, the anti-communists.

One of these was the "Plava Garda", the Slovene branch of the Serbian Royalist Cetniks. Initially anti-fascist, it was forced, in the absence of any other help, to turn to the Italians for support in battling the communist Partisans, their ideologically common enemy. The Plava Garda's last stand against the far more powerful and better organized Partisans was in Grčarice (Masern) where, on September 10 1943, they were overwhelmed and destroyed by the Partisans now heavily armed with weapons the dissolving Italian army had left behind.

Similarly supported by the Italians in their fight against the communist Partisans was the "Bela Garda", the strongly pro-Catholic Slovene defense force founded in 1941. One of its local founders and leaders in the Kočevje area was the Reverend Karel Škulj, the priest of the parish of Dolenja Vas. On September 11, 1942 he reported to the leadership of the Bela Garda in Ljubljana on the success of the Italians:

"On August 13 [Italian] grenadiers arrived in Dolenja Vas and cleaned it out well. They arrested 32 suspected [communist sympathizer] persons. Of these they released two, they took away twenty-six and four of them were shot immediately. People say - all the right ones - ."

The report continues:

"We have already submitted, three times, a request for arming the village guard, but until now without results. On Saturday came a [Italian] Colonel from Ribnica who promised that the matter will be settled soon. The request has been pending since August 14."

And on pg 563 of "Belogardizem" under "Nastop Oboro ženih Oddelkov" France Saje writes:

"At Skulj's urging, the Italians finally armed the Bela Garda of Dolenja Vas".

Shortly after the capitulation of Italy most of the Bela Garda was destroyed by the Slovene communist Partisans in the battle of Turjak on September 19, 1943.

With an ideological orientation that prevented any reconciliation with the Communists, the remnants of both Bela Garda and the Plava Garda joined the Slovene Home Guard, the Domobranci. They were under the command of General Leon Rupnik, the leading Slovene collaborator with the forces of occupation. This collaborationist militia was formed on Sept 24, 1943 by order of SS General Rösener, the head of anti Partisan warfare in Slovenia. The Domobranci swore allegiance to Adolf Hitler twice, both times in the central stadium of Ljubljana.

The first time was on April 20, 1944 in the presence of Leon Rupnik and SS-General Erwin Rösener. They swore allegiance to Hitler again on January 30, 1945, but present this time was also the bishop of Ljubljana Gregorij Rožman, who stood between Rupnik and Rösener on the reviewing stand.

Rožman was passionately anti-communist and was also a collaborator with the Italians and, after September 1943, with the German occupier. He was friendly with SS General Rösener, who ordered mass executions of civilians, hostages and prisoners of war in line with Himmler's decree of June 25, 1942 throughout Slovenia. Quotes and photos exist that attest to the above.

After the war, General Rupnik was tried by the State for treason, convicted to death and executed. Uncle Jože Ilc was the defending attorney appointed by the Yugoslav State. Bishop Rožman fled to the British zone of Austria but was put on trial in absentia by a military court for treason and other crimes. He was convicted and sentenced in absentia to 18 years imprisonment, forced labor and lifelong loss of citizenship.

After September 3, 1943, the part of Slovenia until then occupied by Italy was taken over by the Germans. The Partisans, re-supplied with the weaponry left behind by the dissolved Italian army, became a major guerilla force throughout this part of Slovenia which the Germans, due to their critical shortage of forces, were unable to suppress. In this newly occupied territory, as was the case already in the de-facto annexed part of Slovenia, SS General Rösener, the head of security in Slovenia, rigidly enforced Himmler's edict of June 25, 1942 on how to deal with Partisan collaborators.

This was demonstrated in Mother's village of Dolenja Vas and witness accounts written in 1945 are in the *Slovene National Archives* under AS 1827, KU 20P, šk 3.

THE BELLS RING NO MORE

"After September 8, 1943, the Partisans were in the village [Dolenja Vas] for six weeks. And with the German offensive later in the fall of 1943 came merciless terror and oppression of sympathizers [of the Partisans]. In the village they hanged two captured Partisans, took away all sympathizers of the O.F. [Osvobodilna Fronta - Liberation Front] who had been identified by a local informer. On January 6, 1944, they burned down the schoolhouse and the parsonage on the hill where some of the Partisans had been quartered. On January 10, they set fire to seven farm buildings where, according to the informer, Partisans had taken refuge".

Details on this were related to me in one of my visits to Dolenja Vas in the 1970's:

In the fall of 1943 the Partisans, temporarily quartered in Dolenja Vas, are barely escaping at one end while the Germans are entering at the other. The Germans park their tanks and trucks and set up quarters in houses and courtyards including that of Grandma Ilc. The commandant takes over part of the Pahulje house as his headquarters because it is central, convenient and large. While his wife Angela serves refreshments, the commandant talks to Janez Pahulje who speaks German.

After the commandant settles in, an informer arrives and presents the officer with a list of Partisan collaborators in the village. The commandant gives the order to round up the men on the list and then leaves the house. Shortly thereafter, German soldiers come and arrest Pahulje who, with the others on the list, is detained in the large room of the village municipal hall.

Later in the afternoon, the commandant arrives in the hall, surveys the arrested men and notices Pahulje among them. He turns to a subordinate; points to Pahulje and gives the order, 'release that one and keep the others. Shoot them if they try to escape'.

Next morning two of the captives are hanged in full view of the villagers. The others were loaded on trucks and driven away. Among them was uncle Janez, the 38 year old son of Grandma Ilc, Pahulje's brother-in-law. The village believes all were to be executed.

According to Himmler's edict, the commandant could have executed all those rounded up and burned the entire village. But instead, he had apparently reported to his higher ups who ordered him to hang only two of the suspected collaborators and to hold the others for pick up by the security police.

After they were taken away, the village gave them up as dead. They believed this until the spring of 1944 when Janez and some of the others returned home on a temporary leave from a labor camp in Austria. It seems that Himmler's orders were no longer rigidly enforced and forced laborers were more useful to the Germans than dead suspects.

TWILIGHT BY THE RIVER

After a few days, uncle Janez returned to his labor camp, but on his way there he took a detour to Veliko Mraševo, much to our surprise. After the end of the war in May 1945, he and the others returned, if emaciated, to their homes in Dolenja Vas.

At the other end of their destiny was Franc Pogorelec, the father of Jacob, husband of Mira, the oldest daughter of uncle Janez. Franc who was associated with the Bela Garda had become a member of the Domobranci. At war's end he was captured by the liberating Partisans and was not heard of again.

In our part of the settlement area, the dividing line between the annexed and the occupied Slovenia remained the Krka and Sotla River, our side now *de-facto* annexed to the Reich. And since the other side of this divide was now virtual no-man's land, the raids of the Partisans into the settlement area became more frequent and more daring, forcing the Germans to fortify the border.

In the fall of 1943, soon after the collapse of Italy, the Germans erected a barbed wire fence all along our side of the river and mined a five meter wide space on the river side of the fence. Between the mined space and the river bank they left a strip of land free of mines to allow access to the water all along the embankment. The start of the mined area was well marked to keep us wandering into it and accidentally tripping a mine.

The fence was a dense, impenetrable barrier the height of a man and at least five meters wide. It crossed the road leading to the river, but two gates allowed access to the beach. The gates were closed every evening by either the border guard or the villagers. A small concrete bunker with firing slits was constructed a short distance from the gate and guarded at night by soldiers from the border post at Brod.

There was one more attempt at a raid from across the river later in the fall of 1943 as if to test the defenses in the bunker. The two guards started firing when they heard the raiders opening the gate. The raid was abandoned but one of the raiders, a bearded man in his 50's, was killed by a bullet from the bunker. The following morning all of Veliko Mraševo came to see the body lying dead in the road leading to the gate. By noon, the blood that had run from his body into a puddle on the dirt road had turned brown and was attracting flies.

Later that day, men from across the river came to claim the body lying in the road. They had appealed to the guards at the bridge in Brod to let them cross and bring the dead man back to his village for burial, a request that was granted by the commandant. Accompanied by border guards, four grim men arrived and loaded the body on the stretcher they had brought with them, all to the hostile stares and murmurs from those standing around and watching, without ever meeting the eyes of their adversaries from the other side.

During the winter of 43/44, the gate was permanently closed and mined. This, the earlier fatality and the establishment of a branch of the Brod station in an empty house in the center of the village may have discouraged further raids; the raiders perhaps reasoning that the risk was too high.

The gate was reopened in the spring of '44 to give farmers, who had arable land within the deep bulge of the river bypassed by the fence, access to their parcels for cultivation. It allowed the farmers to again bring their thirsty, if now considerably fewer, cattle for watering at the river.

It also opened the way for the team of Yiorgo and Shargo to get a drink at the river after again tearing themselves free of my hands and galloping through the village. This time, I and others running after them expected to hear a giant explosion caused by them wandering into the minefield. But water was the only attraction for them and they were led away from the river passive and unharmed.

The opened gate also gave school children and adults again the long awaited access to the welcoming beach of whose treacherous waters the drowning of Franz had made us so tragically aware.

While the mined field and mined gate may have been too risky for the Partisans on the other side of the river to attempt another raid, the mines were a magnet for their teenagers who turned mine retrieval into a sport. In the summer of '44, they swam across the river at a narrower point upstream to disarm a buried mine and take it back to their side. The border guards were aware of this but were unable to prevent it since their patrols were monitored by lookouts posted up and down on the other side of the river when this was being done.

On such a foray by one of the boys, a trip wire, hidden in the grass, was pulled by his foot, setting off a mine. The explosion lifted the body into the air and dropped it, at a forty five degree angle, head down and face up into the middle of the barbed wire web.

The sound of the explosion brought people to the site on both sides of the river. Mitzi and I were among the first to get there, but nothing could be done except watch the teenage boy, suspended in the spikes of the barbed wire maze, die an agonizing death. This included the border patrol that arrived soon and was a discouragement to anyone on either side from attempting a rescue. I remember the boy moaning as he slowly died with blood from wounds running down his face and seeing his own right leg below the knee stripped to the bone, the foot part torn away. After he died, soldiers from the Brod station arrived and with big cutters made their way to the body to free him. As before with the dead raider, the border station allowed members of his family to come across the bridge to claim the body.

During the remainder of our time in Veliko Mraševo, there were no other raids into our village.

But the farmer R.K. in his memoir reports that there were many other such raids elsewhere in the settlement area:

"In 1943 the Partisans were widespread and performed predatory raids. My village was less threatened and had no such visits. To protect against the raids, we were consolidated into a home-guard unit under the leadership of the Gendarmerie. At times of imminent danger we were, group wise, assigned to the border guards as reinforcement for the night watch. At a very vulnerable defense point in the village of Globočice, strong resistance caused the raiders to withdraw from their initial forays with only limited plunder. After that, the population withdrew every evening to less threatened villages nearby and returned in the morning. The home-guard looked after their possessions and properties during the night.

"In the middle of the night some months later there came a larger group of Partisans of several hundred well armed men. The guard discovered the raiders when they were surrounding the village but concluded that any resistance was futile. The guard of twelve men immediately sought hiding places wherever possible. Two men even crept into a pig sty.

"The Partisans now felt secure and no longer concerned themselves with the guards. They loaded the plunder on to the wagons they brought along and took with them all the livestock, horses and pigs when they left in the direction of the Croatian border. The guards survived with only a scare. (That night I was not with them; my turn had been on the night before).

"After that, the re-settlers gave up their farms and moved into safer villages. Some villages even ceased to be inhabited and the surrounding soil was no longer cultivated. The Partisans proved themselves harmless toward the population providing it did not resist. There were however instances where some of ours were abducted by the raiders and did not return. Their names I no longer remember. And in 1944 we all already had the view we were progressing toward a bad future".

The Reverend Alois Krisch echoes the farmer:

"An especially bad chapter was the lack of security of our people near the border; the danger there being theft, plunder, murder and abduction. The officials tried to convince our farmers that it is an honor to be a 'border guard farmer' at the 'estate fence' of the Reich.

"These were wretched farmers who had nothing with which to defend themselves! It was said that they should defend themselves with axes and dung forks (this was told them verbally), while the robbers had rifles, automatic guns, pistols and hand grenades. 'For this honor I should let myself be killed? No thank you, I reject this!' was heard as the reply to this affront.

"Later, our defenders received some rifles. Also [home] guards were ordered for one or two villages consisting of two men, while knowing that the others [raiders] always arrived in large bands. At times a guard unit of three to ten men (for a larger area) was organized. Even such bigger units could not have resisted an overwhelming group of bandits. At best they could have alerted the villagers.

"The bandits often made their plunder raids. On one side they came from across the border, on the other side from the Slovene populated hill areas of the north".

The Reverend then provides a detailed list of these raids including the one into Veliko Mraševo. Contrary to the farmer, he speaks of many killings and repeatedly bemoans the suffering and material losses of the settlers. But while the farmer is capable of some introspection about the motives of the raiders, the Reverend keeps calling them bandits and thieves, "making miserable the lives of the settlers". His lingering political orientation, even years after the end of the war, prevented him from acknowledging the fact that the settlers, as part of the occupier, had taken the property of Slovene and were sitting on their land.

He also describes the reinforcement of the border with barbed wire fences and confirms the establishment of the auxiliary border defense force, a group he deems as "… totally incapable of dealing with the well armed and organized raiders". He claims this is the case because this border defense force, in addition to untrained and under armed men, also included unreliable 'Windische Slovene', whose loyalty and determination was no longer certain.

The recollections of both the Farmer and the Reverend refer mostly to the especially vulnerable Sotla river settlement region bordering on one side the Croatian State and on the other side the mountainous area where the resident Slovene had been allowed to stay. Here Partisan activity was considerably more active than in the Cerklje area including the out of the way Veliko Mraševo and other nearby villages. Confirming and expanding on their observation is the report titled "Security Situation in Lower Styria", sent to Himmler by Ulrich Greifeld, SS-Obergruppenführer and General of the Police. The report, marked "Secret", was written on September 21, 1944 and is a comprehensive listing of various security related events since the beginning of 1944. [144]

The essentials of the lengthy Greifeld letter are repeated below to consolidate and validate with recorded documentation, the recollections of the Farmer, the Reverend and my own memories and thereby provide the broader background of the conditions the settlers were exposed to in these final days of the Third Reich.

Greifeld states that at the beginning of 1944, he had discussed the unrest of the settlers with Gauleiter Uiberreither and he subsequently reported to Himmler, in a letter dated January 15, 1944, the *"Readiness of the settlers to leave Lower Styria"*.

Distress over Partisan activity in the "Settlement A" region of Lower Styria was being voiced by representatives of re-settlers who came from Bessarabia and South Tirol (Gottscheer not mentioned).

Himmler replied on January 28, '44 that: "A division of the Waffen-SS will shortly be transferred into this region and a substantial calming of the situation is expected soon thereafter. The South Tirol resettlers must be allowed to return to their homeland; but only in special cases and with permission granted."

---

144 *The report, including relevant footnotes, is reproduced in Quellen doc. 321.*

The unrest of the settlers was especially high due to the raiding expeditions throughout the region by the 14th Division of the O.F. (Osvobodilna Fronta; Liberation Front) in the first part of February '44. Greifeld met with settler representatives and with the concurrence of the Gauleiter ordered that:

"a. The endangered areas be evacuated,

"b. The properties of the evacuated be moved to secure areas,

"c. The families of the evacuated be given shelter by other settlers in secure areas,

"d. The evacuated properties be cared for by communal effort in which the DAG will participate actively." [145]

The SS Division did not do major battle with the Partisans who withdrew deep into the hills without seeking direct confrontation, as was their mode of fighting. But the SS mercilessly dealt with the supporters of the Partisans in line with Himmler's edict of June 25, 1942, on how to deal with those who for "some duration supported the bandits with manpower, provisions, weapons and shelter". [146] This edict was reinforced with Special Orders for specific cases:

"... the male population over 15 shall be executed on the spot, their bodies thrown into flames. The villages shall be destroyed by fire. The rest of the population shall be deported ..." [147]

A follow up report on the suppression of Partisan activity is provided to Greifeld by SS-General of the Police Rösener on April 26, '44:

"In the German/Croatian border area on the German side there are now virtually no bandit gangs. The whole area is adequately secured by the Police and Gendarmerie as well as units of the 18th SS-Panzer Division Horst Wessel. The evacuation of the Gottscheer from this area can not even be considered since they are, under nearly peaceful conditions, able to perform their [farming] activities."

Greifeld continues:

"As expected, the arrival of parts of the 18th SS-Panzer Division produced a reduction of bandit activity and a calming of the resettlers has occurred.

"End of May 1944, parts of the 18th SS-Panzer Division stationed in A settlement region have been withdrawn without replacement by other Waffen SS-Units. Since then, the bandit gang activity in Lower Styria has increased. In the night

---

145 *Quellen, doc 321 and its footnote 7 on pg 644.*

146 *Micro film in National Archives Washington, T-175, R-140, Ref. 2668306-; Bundesarchiv Koblenz, NO-681.*

147 *Quellen, doc 238:*

of June 2/3, a bandit group of 1000 to 1200 men from the province of Ljubljana forced itself into the area of Billichberg/Polšnik where they plundered three supply bases of the DAG and killed three settlers….. [This was the 15th Division of the O.F. (Osvobodilna Fronta; Liberation Front). It was its second large assault into the settlement area. The first was in the middle of October 1943].

"In August and September of this year the security situation in the Settlement Area A has further sharpened. Especially vulnerable is the Brežice (Rann) area due to a strong bandit group operating in the Wachberg/Bohor region further north. [The Partisan Group 'Kozjanski Battalion,' which had been operating there since February 1944, and in the time from June and September '44 completely controlled the area between the Sava, Savinja and the Croatian border]. The village of Bistrica (Königsberg), settled with people from Dobrudscha and Bessarabia, is totally cut off and the road from Brežice/Rann toward Ptuj and Maribor is effectively closed.

"Similarly, the Brežice (Rann) area is again threatened from the south. In view of these conditions, the settlers in the A settling region are very distressed and some are starting to leave the area with their possessions".

Greifeld refers also to a report of the Gauleiter who is responsible for the DAG:

"The DAG can not, prior to the establishment of security, perform an orderly cultivation of the region. The supply bases of the DAG and the farms of the settlers are continuously exposed to threats from the bandits. The situation burns under my fingernails, but I can do no more than keep asking every few days for help from higher-up SS- and Police leaders."

In the same September 21, 1944 letter to Himmler, Greifeld quotes a report received on August 31, 1944 from the mayor of Bizeljsko in the Sotla area, himself a settler from Bessarabia:

"The stronger the bandits become, the stronger is their support from the local Slovene, not only in the surrounding areas but also in the settlement area itself where they [Slovene] again oppose us as the majority while we, the settlers are in the minority".

The mayor of Bizeljsko, representing the settlers in the Sotla area requests, among other items, the arming and organizing of all able men aged 16-60 into village units, that these men receive military training from the SS, the women and children be removed from endangered villages and settlers from South Tirol be allowed to return home.

"The cause of distressed settlers and the reason for their request to be allowed to move out of the area is the activity of 14th Division of the O.F.".

THE BELLS RING NO MORE

Greifeld, with full concurrence of the Gauleiter, ends his letter to Himmler with a plea to negate the call up of 200 men from the Brežice (Rann) area. "If, in spite of the tense reserves situation, it were possible to leave these men in the area and after adequate arming, use them to protect the exposed villages, a certain reduction of tension would occur".

While, after the attempt in the fall of 1943, we had no further raids from across the river, the worsening situation elsewhere in 1944 also came to us and affected our lives there in one way or another.

In line with the request of the mayor of Bizeljsko, the border guard organized, in the spring of '44, the remaining village men, (i.e., those who had not yet been called up), into a village defense force to complement the official border patrol at Brod. Their base post was an empty farm house on the road from our house to the river.

Units of two fully armed men now patrolled the village during the night. Normally there were two sets of such units out on duty, each patrolling the village street while circulating in opposing directions. They would meet somewhere along the way and after exchanging passwords and status, continue their round. After an agreed interval they met at the station where they were relieved by another set of two units. In the morning they all returned home, leaving behind their weapons in the station house, the ammunition and hand grenades locked away in a closet.

The otherwise unlocked house became a stopover resting place for the guards from Brod patrolling the border. They also passed there in the evening to announce to the home guard the nightly password and during the night stopped there to rest. And when the cold winter of 1944 brought them into the house also during the day, they first stopped in the entry space to stomp the snow off their boots before they entered the warm guard room, bringing with them the clinging cold. After hanging up their hats, rifles, belts and heavy greatcoats on hooks, they stood with backs close to the tiled oven and sped their warming up with a few shots of our schnapps.

The unlocked station house was normally off limits to all except the village home guards which included all males from 16-60 as suggested by the mayor of Bizeljsko. But some of our former school friends, now sixteen years old guards, would let us enter and allow us to fondle the unloaded weapons, the most fascinating of which was a light machine gun, but only until an older guard chased us out while reprimanding those who let us in.

TWILIGHT BY THE RIVER

Access by the young border guards became limited and was totally forbidden to their even younger friends after a serious security breach at the river in the summer of 1944.

I remember the day as a warm Sunday afternoon with boys and girls frolicking at the beach (there were no adults present) and exchanging taunts with the Slovene kids on the opposite side of the river. The epithets on both sides became increasingly more vocal and reached a pitch that was too much for one of the older boys on our side, at sixteen now one of the home guards. He went to get the light machine gun from the guard house which he set up on its tripod at the raised embankment next to the beach and pulled the trigger. He aimed over the heads of the kids on the other side and no one was hurt as our tormentors across the river dropped to the ground or ran for cover followed by our cheers.

The firing quickly brought the official uniformed guard and men from the village to the site. The offending young guard was taken to the guardhouse in Brod where he was kept for a few days.

Soon thereafter an officer from the Brod station gave the villagers, including the very young, a lecture on the seriousness of what had happened at the border and of more severe consequences to all should similar breaches of security happen again. After that, all of us under sixteen could enter the guard house only when older home guards or "responsible adults" were present.

The guard house, in the absence of a Jaklitsch type saloon, soon became the village clubhouse. Not so much to the joy of Father who, while now able to work in his shop undisturbed, began to miss the gossip of the men hanging about, passing idle time and wondering about our progressively bleaker future.

At times I would accompany him to the "Wachstube" or guard room, the large main room of our station house, where he would join the others in discussions to do mostly with latest reports from the fronts. Often, especially later in the fall and winter of 1944 when it got cold outside, a bottle of homebrewed schnapps was passed around which helped to increase the decibels in the room now densely filled with the pungent smoke of homegrown tobacco. The men lingered on until their women arrived with reminders to return home and tend to their manly chores.

But the room became silent when the uniformed men from the "Grenzschutz", the Reich's border guard on their routine patrol, walked in for a short rest. It became silent, mainly because all in the room were eager to hear the latest from these soldiers, they now being the main source of news from the outside world.

But contrary to the soldier, who in the fall of 1942 intimated to Father that Germany might lose the war if the Americans were to land on the continent, these guards always dutifully presented the official "Germany will win" line. The line claimed that we were withdrawing to the homeland only to bring the enemy nearer where he could be defeated more easily. Later on another explanation was added. "As soon as the enemy is close enough, we will use our secret weapons with great vengeance. The enemy will be destroyed and there will be German victory". But Veliko Mraševo was not our homeland and this explanation had little credibility. There were few, if any, in the room who believed it, especially now that the Americans had landed and were deep into France, in Italy half way up the peninsula and in the east, the Soviets near the heartland of Germany.

A frequent visitor was Karl Schaffer, the former fire chief. Now 65 and still in good health, the "Wachstube" was nearer than the Weinstube at the Jaklitsch Gasthaus in Cerklje and a place where he did not have to pay. And in the "Wachstube" he rubbed elbows with his former firemen who still treated him with some of the respect he used to command. Even though here, as in Masern, he often got drunk and Karl, the younger of his two sons, or someone else had to escort him home.

His older son Hubert 36, had last winter had been taken into the "SS-Sonderstandarte Untersteiermark", (SS-Special Group), a type of militia consisting of fifteen separate units formed in the fall of 1943 mainly from men of the former Gottscheer Sturm units. The men of these units were trained by SS officers and afterwards used to reinforce the now meager German forces fighting the Partisans in the Settlement Area "A", the Save/Sotla part of Lower Styria.

With Hubert Schaffer was Josef Primosch, the older son of our neighbor across the street. Both were among the twenty three men from the "Alarm-Kompanie Gurkfeld", one of the fifteen companies of this "SS-Sonderstandarte" that became surrounded by Partisans of the Kozjanski Battalion in a fortification at Kozje (Drachenburg) in Lower Styria, but for a long time did not surrender. After finally forced to give up, all twenty-three were court-martialed and executed on the spot by the Partisans on September 12, 1944. [148]

---

148 *Quellen, doc. 321, 322.*

TWILIGHT BY THE RIVER

Another company, called "Alarm-Kompanie Rann", consisted of former Gottscheer now living in the Brežice region. One of its four squad leaders was a "Tschinkel", possibly Father's cousin Franz who formerly was the Sturmführer of Sturm 1, the Sturm of Gottschee city and its surroundings. At the end of the war Franz mingled with the civilians on the road and attempted to escape to Austria. He had switched out of his uniform but was, nevertheless, recognized by the Partisans and was kept in Yugoslavia as a POW until 1951. [149]

Ferdinand Primosch, the younger brother of Josef had been drafted earlier that year when he became eighteen in January 1944. After training he returned home for a short furlough and after that was sent to the Russian front. He also was never heard of again. While our neighbors Josef and Rosalia had lost both their sons, Karl Schaffer still had his second son Karl to help him and his wife Maria, work the land. The Schaffer farm, like Father's and most others, also had Slovene forced labor as help, but by the fall of 1944, they all disappeared. Young Karl, at 33, was hard of hearing which disqualified him from becoming a soldier.

A saddler by trade, his shop in Masern was in his father's attic where I visited him often and watch him making harnesses and other leather goods as well as horse hair mattresses for our villagers and others in the area. He welcomed my presence partly because I added to his otherwise solitary day and partly because I helped him with some tasks for which another pair of hands was needed.

In Masern some of his visitors were former village schoolmates, now unmarried young men, all lusting after Ivanka, the young Slovene who was the keeper of Riegler's dry goods store directly across the square. The store was a branch of the Riegler store in Dolenja Vas and was open only on weekdays with Ivanka arriving from there on Monday morning and leaving late on Friday afternoon. During their visits to Karl, Ivanka was a much discussed topic which became especially animated when she appeared outside the store, the large attic window providing an excellent view. But Ivanka was immune not only to their approaches but also to those of other men in the village and none could do more than fantasize about her shapely figure.

This included Rudi Tschinkel, her next door bachelor neighbor and owner of both the Tschinkel tavern and half owner of the village saw mill, surely a good catch for any single young woman. But Rudi's mother was vehemently against her son's

---

149 *Axis History Forum, SS-Sonderstandarte Untersteiermark.*

intentions and decided to drive Ivanka and her store out of his life and the village. She appealed to Riegler in Dolenja Vas and when unsuccessful, became determined to drive her out of Masern by making the young woman's life miserable. Among her doings was to coat the sill of the front door to the store with human excrement to keep customers away. Rudi had to send two of his sawmill employees with buckets, soap and disinfectant to wash and scrub clean the sill with masses of water. All this made Ivanka only more adamant in her rejection of Rudi and gained much admiration from other women for her determination to remain in the village.

But it was Jaklitsch who succeeded in shutting down the Riegler store, his only competitor in the village. He not only expanded to carry more of the goods sold by Ivanka but also lowered his prices. And after Yugoslavia collapsed in April 1941, he was able to convince the villagers that it was anti-German to buy goods in the store owned by a Slovene. The Riegler store shut down due to lack of business and Ivanka never again appeared in Masern. The house was totally destroyed during the battle of 1943.

Over time Karl Schaffer Jr. and I became close friends, a friendship that continued into Veliko Mraševo where he, even while hard of hearing, was seen fit enough to become a village guard in the fall of 1944.

One evening just before Christmas of 1944, Karl and his companion left the station house on their patrol starting in the direction of the river. The second unit of two men left, at the same time, in the other direction with Ernst Sbaschnig in charge. Ernst, now thirty three, was the son of Franz Sbaschnig, the roof maker of Masereben and who like Karl had, for some unknown reason, also not been called up but was judged fit to be a village guard.

It was a dark midnight shift, dark because the moon was still obscured by lingering clouds that had delivered fresh snow during the day. And instead of the patrols meeting on the road somewhere in the village, Ernst heard a noise in the back of the courtyard of a farm. Peering into the darkness he saw a man, but after calling out the password more than once, there was no reply. So he kneeled down, aimed and fired, hitting Karl who fell on the spot.

Karl's companion who was even further back in the courtyard where both had gone to investigate, heard the shot and yelled out the password. And when all three ran and got to Karl, he was already dead.

Next morning I went to the site where he was shot. The snow was now trampled and the only traces of his killing were the red spots from the blood where he fell.

The body of Karl, dressed in his Masern Sturm 13 uniform, was laid on a bier in the spare room of the station house where it was guarded around the clock by his fellow guards and the constant presence of visitors. According to Masern custom he should have been laid out in his home, but neither his father nor his failing mother were up to the strain, now having lost both their sons. Both insisted that the body be displayed for viewing in the station house and that he be given a military funeral. The coffin was not made by Father but provided by the border guard headquarters in Rann.

Both the border guard and gendarmerie officials from Brežice (Rann) investigated and concluded that the shooting was an accident due to Karl's poor hearing. But rumor had it that Ernst overreacted and shot without first yelling out the password, something that both he and his companion vehemently denied. The rumors persisted and were supported by Karl's partner who claimed that he, having perfect hearing, also did not hear the password from Ernst.

Karl was buried in the Cerklje cemetery with full military honors. And since the now virtually leaderless Hitler Youth was required to attend in their uniforms, Father had to allow me to attend. (He had not allowed me to attend the burial of my other friend Franz which I bitterly resented.)

Karl received a 21 gun salute from fellow village guards and a drummer led us in singing "Ich hatt' Einen Kameraden, einen bessern findst du nit …." (I had a comrade, a better one you will not find ….)

I had a very difficult time at that funeral. This was the third time in less than three years I had lost a best friend; "…better comrades I would not find … ".

The Reverend Alois Krisch writes:

"On Maundy Thursday April 6, 1944, around four in the afternoon came the first bombs. Until then we only watched them fly over us to the big targets in the north, counting at times 200 to 300 of them. On their return they flew dispersed, no longer in closed formation and sometimes were challenged [by fighter planes stationed at the field in Cerklje]. On St. Josef day 1944 we saw an air fight and watched the burning enemy plane plunge downward after being hit. We had fear since until then nothing had ever happened".

THE BELLS RING NO MORE

The air fight was on April 2, 1944 and I remember it well.

On that cloudless Sunday I had cycled to Krško city to see the two o'clock movie at the cinema. Already on the way there, the bombers were returning from their mission up north. It was only when I got to Krško that German fighters appeared and attacked the enemy planes. I and most of population watched one of the bombers being hit by a Messerschmitt to the cheers of the crowd. And as the plane began to dive, two parachutes appeared in the clear blue sky. We were still cheering when the Wehrmacht soldiers revved up their motorcycles and sped away toward the airmen descending into the nearby hills. But the Partisans in the woods who were also watching found one of the survivors first and helped him to get back to his base in Italy.

It is highly likely that the hit bomber we saw was one of the two described Ray E. Zinck in his book titled "The Final Flight of Maggie's Drawers" published in 1998. In this book, Ray Zink describes the story of Joe Maloney the tail gunner of the B-24 who, after his life saving parachute jump, was rescued by Tito's Partisans who then helped him and others get back to his base in Lecce, Italy. Ray's story of Joe's mission, the demise of his flight and the Odyssey of the return to his base in Italy is also described in part on his website, www.josephmaloney.com.

To the unsettling insecurity of the settlers due to ever increasing Partisan activity was now added the daily threat from the attack planes - not only along the Sotla border to Croatia, but also throughout the rest of the settlement region, especially Cerklje with its Luftwaffe airbase, a prime military target in the area. This airbase had already been visited by the Partisans during the big raid of July 7, 1943 when ground units of the OF attacked and destroyed several planes there.

The ever more frequent air raids started in 1944 when bases in liberated parts of Italy allowed low flying attack planes to reach into Lower Styria and its settlement area. Their major targets, in addition to the airfields, were trains on the major rail lines, their rail stations and convoys on the major arteries.

The planes that were doing this were the feared double fuselage P-38 Lockheed Lightnings, which the Germans called the "Gabelschwanz Teufel" (Fork Tailed Devil). With a range of over 900 miles they were able to reach our area from bases as far south as Foggia in the Italy liberated by American forces that had already taken Rome even further north on April 6, 1944. And the further the Allies moved up the peninsula, the more frequent were their air raids in our area, often twice a day or more, as stated by the Reverend.

A major air raid on the Cerklje airfield was on May 25, 1944, the day the German Luftwaffe was celebrating Armed Forces Day. The day had been declared a holiday and the base was opened to the surrounding local population. Mitzi, Paul and I got there early while our parents stayed at home. The friendly airmen served sweet drinks in the canteen and allowed some of the visitors to peek into the planes.

But even before the sirens reached full pitch, there was machine gun fire from two Lightnings that appeared from over the hills just beyond the Krka. They had hugged the terrain and took the defenders of the base by total surprise, causing mass confusion and panic.

Mitzi, who had temporarily put me in charge of six year old Paul, had left us for a few moments. Fortunately Paul and I were not near the German planes nor the hangars, both the main objective of the raiders. I attempted to drag Paul with me under a nearby farm wagon and covered my head with my arms as we had been taught. There was a lot of rapid gunfire both from the planes and from the ground and the sound of flying and impacting bullets was heard all around. Then there were explosions as some of the hit planes caught fire.

But it was over equally fast; the planes flew away and did not return. The sirens were still howling when I looked up, seeing that some of our planes were burning while the airmen were attempting to control the civilians running about. But Paul, the brother who had been placed in my charge, had disappeared.

Joining the others running out of the airbase and through flowing tears, I kept yelling out his name. Finally somebody said that he was seen running with Mitzi on the road away from the base toward Zirkle. I found them both unhurt in front of the Jaklitsch inn, waiting for me. Mitzi explained that she had just returned when I was crawling under the wagon. She grabbed Paul and together they ran out of the airport with bullets hitting the ground all around them.

We were half way home when the small carriage, pulled by a galloping Yiorgo, was brought to a halt by Father. Both parents were as happy to see us as we were to see them.

Fortunately there were no civilian casualties, but several airmen were wounded and a number of planes were destroyed. In addition to damaging the military, bringing unrest and fear to the settlers had resulted in a successful mission for the enemy.

There was one more major surprise attack on the Cerklje airfield on October 3, 1944, but by then most of the German planes had been sent elsewhere. And the remaining German fighter planes were no match for the Fork Tailed Devils that came in low and fast and did damage before their opponents were able to respond.

During the summer and later in the year, the "Devils" concentrated mostly on rail and road military traffic to and from Croatia which they effectively brought to a standstill, at least during the day. But the attacks on this traffic continued at night by the Partisans in the hills, who from vantage points along the way were equally effective.

As the Reverend writes, another objective of the Devils was to terrorize the settler population:

"The danger from the planes strained the nerves of many people. Twice I was forced to seek refuge in the street ditch to escape the low lying attack planes. At one time, fragments of exploding projectiles from the defending guns whistled overhead, making me think that these [projectiles] are just as unhealthy as those from the attackers. In places where no bombs had fallen people had no fear, but those who had seen the dead, the wounded and the blood, fled day or night when the siren sounded the alarm".

I have a similar story. I had been to see a film in Krško on a Sunday afternoon and had just started to cycle home when the air raid siren revved up. I got off the bike and walked toward a solitary house along the road when I spotted a Devil flying in my direction. I dropped the bike and ran around the corner of the house barely escaping the bullets that were hitting the ground. But then he turned and came back at me again as I was rounding another corner of the same house and again escaped the bullets. He did not come back and soon the all clear was heard.

People appeared, took me inside the house and calmed me down. They also convinced me to stay at least until dusk which was very hard to do. But after that, I never went to the movies again.

The Reverend continues:

"From the day on when the first bombs fell on April 6, it was different. They were the smallest of bombs, but there were hundreds of them. Fortunately most of them hit nothing since many fell into fields and the forest behind us. Nevertheless, they caused much damage, many injuries and many deaths. On Easter Sunday, seventeen victims were buried in a mass grave (according to party rules, I could administer Church benediction only afterwards). Soon thereafter, ten more victims were buried having died from wounds [inflicted by the cluster bombs].

"Later the planes came more frequently; the low flying light bombers twice daily. Most of the attacks were on Dobova [just east of Brežice] which also received heavy bombs causing much suffering and many deaths."

Terror to the settlers came in many forms and from many directions. In the summer of 1944 and thereafter, it also came to Veliko Mraševo from snipers in the hills across the river firing in the direction of people in the fields and traffic on the roads.

When the sniping initially started, we all dropped to the ground and crawled behind some protecting object for safety. No one was ever hurt since the purpose of the sniping seemed to be only to disrupt the working farmers and instill fear, not to hit anyone. The snipers knew that the harvest being reaped by the settlers was to be theirs very soon, so it was not in their interest to prevent it.

And when it was sensed that the sniping was not intended to kill anyone, the work in the fields continued in spite of the sounds of rifle fire and bullets whizzing by. But occasionally the sniper aimed nearer to renew our fear of being hit, causing all to fall to the ground and seek cover. At least until the firing stopped.

There was one particularly annoying sniper in the small white house on the steep hill opposite, high above the river between our village and Brod. From there, the sniper had a commanding view of our valley and the Kostanjevica road but his fire was directed mainly at the military traffic on it. In the absence of such, he did not hesitate to instill fear also into the driver of a lone farm wagon or workers in the fields.

Some of us young fools made a game out of it. Get on a bike and speedily cycle from our village to the intersection at Kren's house and back to draw fire from the sniper. Sometimes he obliged with a few bullets but he soon realized it was better to save the ammunition for the military rather than play games with bravado kids. Of course he could have stopped it altogether with a direct kill, but fortunately never did.

But the military soon got fed up being fired at when driving by with their trucks. A company of Waffen SS and two companies of police had been stationed in Rann in September 1944 to provide some relief to the settlers. [150] They drew fire from

---

150 Quellen, doc 322.

many rifles. Watching from the edge of the village, we could see the flashes from their guns before we heard the crack of the shot.

After one such event, two SS trucks roared into the village and stopped at the triangle near our house. Very young SS men jumped out and demanded that a layer of straw to be spread on the ground in the center of the triangle. This done, they lifted from one truck the bodies of two of their dead comrades, placed them on the straw bed and drove off, angrily demanding that we guard the bodies and bellowing that they would be back very soon.

The two dead SS men on the straw, as young as their comrades, had been killed by snipers in the white house as the small unsuspecting convoy was rolling by. Soon the dead were surrounded by the villagers, all talking in hushed voices and waiting for the trucks to return.

They roared back soon, trailing dust, as they had when they left. Without words, neither from the soldiers nor the villagers, they put their dead comrades back into the truck and sped off. The straw, red from the still bleeding bodies, was gathered up and thrown on to the dung heap of our neighbor Primosch, the now sonless couple across the road.

This was not the end of it, however. Sniping all along the Krka border had not only been a nuisance to the military; it had now resulted in casualties and the SS reacted by first sending out a tank to survey the territory.

I was on my bike on the safe stretch of the Kostanjevica road when there was a deep rumble preceding a gigantic tank, it being either a Tiger or the newer Leopard. From the ditch, I watched it roar by toward Brod, expecting it to start a barrage from the white house on the hill. But nothing happened; the snipers were wisely not tempted to draw lethal fire from the long and accurate 88 cannon of the tank.

But later that day, there arrived a short line of armored cars drawing howitzer cannons. Foolishly, the snipers fired at them as they were rolling toward Brod. At the intersection, the small SS convoy stopped behind the Kren house, where they bivouacked for the night and told us youngsters to stay away the following morning.

In the morning they again drew fire from the snipers. By then they had their howitzers ready and responded while we watched from the edge of our village. We saw the flashes from both the howitzer and the exploding projectile at its target at the same time, while the boom from each reached us a bit later. After only a few shots, the house took a direct hit and blew up to the jubilant outcry of all of us watching.

TWILIGHT BY THE RIVER

The terror predicted in the second part of the pamphlet distributed in the enclave by the Slovene in July 1941, had become reality and was now nearing its end phase.

"…. And when the German imperialism is crushed, the rightful owners of the land on which they want you to settle will drive you out. Others will have settled in Gottschee and you will be empty handed, without land, without money, without homes. Toward such a destiny the agents of Hitler [the Gottscheer leaders] lead you ….."

In addition to the three major battle fronts, already in Germany proper or very near it in September 1944, a fourth one was anticipated to come from the south east through our region. To prepare for this, Hitler ordered the construction of the "South-East Wall" in July 1944. [151]

The Reverend also writes about this:

"It was projected that a war front would also come to our region from Serbia and Croatia. Therefore the construction of a "Stellungsbau" (fortifications) was ordered. All had to join in the effort; the digging of tank traps, troop trenches, ditches and barriers of all sorts were prepared, bridges and streets were readied for blasting. Often, low flying aircraft fired into these groups of workers (many female). It was a wild time and it became more so day after day. One felt the nearness of the front – and still the people were forbidden to leave".

Mitzi and many other young women of our village were required to take part in this effort; there were no more able men in our village to take part. Mother prepared lunch for her daughter which I had to take to her on my bicycle, promising to dive into the road ditch as soon as the sound of a plane was heard.

But before all this was underway, we had already dug our bunker behind the barn. Likewise, trenches were already in place in the back yard of the Cerklje school which we had dug on our ever less frequent days in Tscherne's class.

As written by the Reverend, "we all felt the nearness of the front".

All the while, Veliko Mraševo was a stopover place for Axis troops on their way out of the Balkans. By now these units were a mix of nationalities, either still loyal to their

---

151 *Quellen, doc 322.*

controlling German officers or merely waiting for an opportune moment to escape, for which they would have been shot as deserters. Two of such units I remember in particular.

The first unit, a mix of German and Italian soldiers stayed for nearly two weeks, in part to rest but also to protect the ever more vulnerable settlers. The unit had a mobile workshop that was parked on the grass behind our second house. The workshop was an enclosed truck outfitted with an assembly of tools most of which I had never seen. It included a small lathe and best of all, two tanks of compressed gas used for welding. In charge of the shop was Claudio, a young Italian from Rome.

We quickly became friends; he at first undoubtedly seeing in me a conduit for edible farm products which I could help him to obtain. This soon became the case, in spite of Mother urging me to stay clear of him, remembering as had her mother that he, like the killer of her brother, was an Italian. But she succumbed to his charming ways as had the rest of us and soon he was cooking on her stove in the kitchen.

He also urged me to let it be known that he could perform repairs for the villagers in his shop, providing it would not be too obvious to his superiors who were turning a blind eye. And the officers could also not resist his chicken cacciatore.

Soon he was overwhelmed with requests from women who wished the holes in their pots plugged up, something Father could no longer do because solder was no longer available. Claudio charged four eggs for every hole welded up, a method far preferable to soldering which would melt from the heat of the stove.

It was a nearly tearful good-bye when they left. His emotional hug and a kiss on each cheek, unheard of and in full view of other teenagers, was an embarrassment as was the stammered promise that "Yes", I would look him up when, in the future, I was visiting Roma.

The second unit was a large group of almost purely Italian troops who stayed only for two days, most of them camping in tents in farm house yards, some behind our house. The old village men, the only men still around sneered and remembering the days at the Isonzo grumbled: "With so many Italians, no wonder we are losing the war."

But they were a friendly, if hungry lot who virtually begged for food. Mother obliged freely, now knowing that all would stay behind anyway when we left. They all loved the tasty potatoes cooked in the large steamer normally used to quick-steam vegetables for the pigs. And after getting their fill, they sat around their tents, gratefully smoking Father's home grown tobacco and chanting their ever so melancholy Italian songs.

They left in the morning and there was a noisy bustle to get ready. While doing so they were not very careful with their rifles, leaning them against the wall of our buildings. They were shorter and more compact than the much heavier German equivalent and had a fold-away bayonet permanently attached to the barrel. I desperately wanted to have one and when none of the Italians was watching I took the nearest and hid it behind the cellar door.

But when neither the owner nor his buddies could later find it, he reported to his officer who accused Father of having taken it. He of course denied it and the officer threatened to shoot him unless the rifle was produced. The soldiers continued searching, including in the cellar but never looked behind the door. Finally they had to leave, without first shooting Father dead. Somehow he never believed that he would be shot and later, when they were all gone and I produced the rifle, he said "did you also get ammunition?"

Other German units passed through the village and were always surprised to find friendly German-speaking villagers in the middle of Slovenia after making their way through hostile territory further south-east. After they parked their trucks in our courtyard, they would strike up conversation and inevitably asked Father why we were here amidst this hostile enemy population.

Equally inevitable was their suggestion to leave with them on their trucks to Austria. This came after Father explained how we got here to begin with. "Leave everything, come with us to safety. The war is over. Tito's troops will be here soon and when the Slovene come back and find you here, it is going to be bad for you".

"We are not allowed to leave, by command of the Gauleiter" was the reply.

When they left, usually the following morning, they were shaking their heads while wishing us luck and waving goodbye.

Chapter 20

The Road to Exile

Permission to leave Veliko Mraševo came early in the morning of May 8, 1945. It had been expected with rising anxiety for days, especially after it became known that the Russians were on the outskirts of Berlin and Hitler was dead.

The preparations had started in earnest some weeks before, after one of the meetings held by Karl Tschinkel the village representative of the Heimatbund. They included the assignment of those who were without transport to those who did. Father agreed to take Johann Krisch and his Slovene forced laborer Frantze, the nineteen-year-old Slovene who had been assigned by the DAG to Johann after his mother died in 1943. The two became very friendly and Frantze stayed with Johann even after most of the other forced laborers in the village had disappeared in the past few months now knowing they would no longer be pursued.

On Father's wagon was to be Katharina, her husband Alois and their essentials. Both Katharina's sons were now in the military; Albert had been called up two years ago at sixteen and had not been heard of since. Anton, who became sixteen only a few months ago, was taken into the Volkssturm, the final call-up of the Reich now desperate for anyone capable of holding a rifle. It included all boys sixteen or older, while at the other end of life there was no age limit, providing the man could still walk and not fall down after his crutches were knocked away. Anton was still somewhere in the area, where he was being trained to fire a rifle and operate the German Panzerfaust, a shoulder-held anti-tank weapon similar to the American bazooka.

For days, the wagons had been on standby, ready to be loaded with provisions on short notice. Hoops of slender birch saplings supported the canvas covering, carefully tied at the sides to keep out the rain and the driver's bench dry. At the meeting Karl had recommended rations for two weeks and feed for the animals to last until we got to Austria, about 80 miles north-west. Beyond that only the most essential items: clothing, blankets and some valuables which very quickly produced a row with Katharina, who insisted that her china was valuable. And when permission to leave finally arrived that morning, it took only a little time to get moving.

Our first destination was Krško town and by noon, the slowly moving caravan of horse and oxen drawn wagons was rolling through the fields. But it came to a standstill not long after it reached the paved road and after that it was moving only in short intervals followed by long stops. By late afternoon, we had covered eight of the twelve km toward Krško, a journey which on prior days had taken less than an hour.

Few if any in the wagons now clogging the road had an inkling of what destiny had in mind for us. No one yet knew the war had come to an end and with that our promised future in the Reich. The journey that began in 1941 was now on an unpredictable final stretch toward an unimaginable future. The folly of having pulled up, only three and a half years ago, the anchor to a place established centuries before, was still to become fully apparent in the tumult of the terrifying days yet to come.

It was then that the news, flying from wagon to wagon, reached us. Germany had capitulated, the war was over and the once promised future at an ignominious end. The initial impact of the news, while expected, was a shock not unlike that upon hearing of the death of a loved one who had been dying of an incurable disease. But in such a case the shock gives way, sooner or later, to a returning normalcy and realization that life goes on.

This was not the case here. The brutal reality was one of total abandonment, no longer under the shield of any community, authority or state, now homeless with nowhere to go. The Reich, the state that had tricked us in 1941 was no more and there was no way back. For those of us now sitting in the stalled wagons or milling aimlessly among them, there was no prospect for a future, now a fearful unknown, offering at best survival and possibly death.

In late afternoon, dense black smoke from burning tires of abandoned military vehicles along the roadside and in the fields was playing tricks with the rays of the setting sun. The distant thunder of explosions accompanying the retreating, but yet not surrendered army was getting louder and nearer, adding yet another dimension to the prevalent fear. Men swore, women and children cried as did I, inconsolably and for a long time. "Why did we leave and get into this?" was heard all around. Would it not have been wiser to stay in Veliko Mraševo and wait for our destiny there? The braver went beyond that with "we should have remained in Masern", but this new found wisdom offered no comfort; there was no way back to either place.

THE ROAD TO EXILE

When, eventually, after many starts and stops, we reached Krško, it was dusk with black smoke giving way to black night. But there was no end to the thunder of explosions, nearer now, and the darkening day began to compete with the tracer bullets and flares that were lighting up the evening sky.

Our route beyond Krško was to be the east-west highway along the south side of the Sava river to Zidani Most (Steinbrück). Zidani Most is a little town but a major intersection of road, rail and the place where the Savinja River from the north joins the Sava flowing eastward toward Krško and beyond. Zidani Most took the name from the bridge over the Savinja just before it spills into the larger Sava. It was constructed of stone, hence Stonebridge, or Zidani Most in Slovene. At Zidani Most we were to turn northward along the Savinja toward Celje, Maribor and the Austrian border, then defined by the river Mur.

At Zidani Most all west-east traffic linking Ljubljana with Zagreb via Krško, be it rail or road, branches off toward Maribor and further north. In all of these three directions, rail and road tightly follow the river, each at the bottom of a narrow valley with steep banks on either side. In most places along these parts, the rail-bed hugs the river while the road-bed had been hewed into the steep mountain side high above the railroad tracks, there being no room at the river level.

After about two kilometers downriver from Zidani Most the space widens and the Sava river flows in a wider valley. Since there is more flat space on the south side of the river, a wider, less sinuous road was constructed at the start of the wider part on the south side and a narrow steel bridge was built in the early 20th century to ease the increasing vehicular traffic on the north side. With the wider road now on the south side, the narrow road above the tracks was thereby relieved of major traffic and served local needs only. The railroad tracks along the Sava remained on the north side and continued to be the major rail route.

After 1945 the traffic congestion caused by the narrow steel bridge was relieved by a new, wider and more easily accessible stone bridge about one kilometer further down river. Now, the steel bridge is for pedestrian crossing only, its wooden roadway suspended from a graceful arch, painted a pleasant green.

THE BELLS RING NO MORE

As we approached Krško to get on to the road on the south bank, the reason for our slow progress during that afternoon became clear. All lanes of the wide asphalt highway were packed with mostly German military vehicles of all shapes and sizes, all rushing north-west toward Austria to get out of the Balkans, out of Yugoslavia, ahead of Tito's army of Partisans following the vanquished and now fleeing occupier/collaborator of the past four years. This was the traffic we were to join with our covered wagons drawn by horses and oxen and even cows, to escape the so-called "Communist hordes", urged to do this by those who had kept tight control over the gullible and misguided new citizens of the Reich; citizens, who since 1941, were no longer allowed to call themselves Gottscheer.

Slowly, the wagons merged into this traffic but were, after only a short stretch on it, diverted by a still functioning German military police on to the road leading to the bridge across the Sava to the north side of the river. They were keeping the slow-moving stream of refugees off the main road and directing it out of the way to the inferior road on the other side.

Our wagon, now separated from some of the others, made it across the bridge but got stopped on the rail tracks just beyond. Not far to the right was the station where a parked locomotive was coughing steam at irregular intervals and an apprehensive Father, on the wagon bench but unable to move his team and wagon either back or forward was casting worried glances in that direction. Sitting tightly next to him, a petrified me was getting ready to jump off should the locomotive come our way. Eventually it began to do just that and blew a whistle, as if to tell us to get out of the way. It was only maneuvering to get on to parallel tracks at the station, but how was I to know that!

So I jumped off just as the tired but still alert horses, petrified by the huffing engine and the shrill whistle, strained backwards, pulling with them Johann Krisch who was holding them by the head harnesses up front. As I jumped, the backward motion of the wagon disturbed my balance and I landed under the trampling horses. Johann, who saw the coming disaster jumped to catch and drag me to safety out from under hoofs of the agitated animals and away from the still approaching but now slowing locomotive that came to a stop at a safe distance and then reversed direction. This was the first time this close friend of the family pulled me out of harm's way. The second time, only four days later, I was not so fortunate.

After that we moved just beyond the tracks to the village called Videm and stopped in a meadow already packed with other vehicles, but Johann found a spot where we settled for the night. The horses were uncoupled, watered and fed, a small fire heated soup and the women handed out food. Soon I was asleep as were most others either on the wagon or on blankets spread on the now dewy grass. But few slept soundly that first night away from home. Sleep, if any, was continually disrupted by the endless thunder of explosions arriving from all directions while bursts of light from tracer bullets, rockets and flares lit up the horizon and a moonless sky. Was it the ceaselessly retreating army lighting its way, or the approaching Partisans blasting relentlessly to keep the enemy scared and moving, or perhaps a combination of both?

It was still dark when we started to move again. Paul and I were shaken awake by Mother but were allowed, after protest, to continue sleeping for a while longer. When we were finally awakened by the motion of the wagon, the light of early dawn had replaced the artificial light of war, bringing with it the awareness that the nightmare had not been a dream, but was only continuing with renewed vigor.

The traffic on the wider highway across the river, now mostly military, was flowing more swiftly than that on our side, so heavily slowed by the refugees and their animal-drawn wagons. On our narrower road, the faces of the soldiers jammed into their stalled trucks, all grim and silent and partly hidden by unshaven stubble, had the gray of their uniforms. Some were still clutching their weapons which by now they should have discarded. But in the morning of this day of May 9, all humanity and the surrounding landscape was gray, excepting the brightly colored flares and the streaks of the tracer bullets now being dimmed by the emerging sun.

On either side, however, the traffic was mostly uncovered trucks and half tracks of the German military not yet abandoned at the side of road. Invariably, these vehicles were soon to join the other discards of this no longer retreating but now fleeing army, as soon as they too ran out of gas. The narrow spaces off the road were already littered with field kitchens, workshops, howitzers and the trucks to which they were normally attached. In many places, where there was little or no embankment, these items, as well as machine guns, rifles, handguns, grenades and other similar hardware had simply been pushed or dumped into the river by the fleeing soldiers so as not to be caught armed by the victorious and shot. While on May 9, the density of this abandoned materiel was still relatively light, it increased over the next few days to such an extent that all spaces along the road and in the river near the embankment were filled and soon to be joined by the bodies of animals and human beings, who, for various reasons, could not or would not go on.

THE BELLS RING NO MORE

On our side of the river, the wagons of the refugees were moving again and with less interruptions than yesterday, but at a pace not much faster than those on foot, all carrying bundles of varying sizes, be they soldiers or civilians with bewildered children in tow. All traffic on the still level and not yet overly winding narrow road was in one direction, with the slower, animal-pulled wagons on the right, forced there by the military vehicles on the left.

Our progress during the day of May 9, while slow, was somewhat better than the day before. By late afternoon we had passed Brestanica, a small town, and stopped for the night near the little village of Blanca, in a field just off the road where Johann found a spot amid the already tightly packed multitude of humanity and its belongings.

The distance covered during the day, since we left the field at Videm in the early morning was approximately eleven kilometers, just short of seven miles. This was due, in part, to the relatively straight even if narrow gravel road on mostly flat land along the still unencumbered river and also the still somewhat orderly flow of military traffic. At this rate we were going to reach the Austrian border in approximately fourteen days.

The uncoupled and secured animals were fed and resting and small campfires heated pre-cooked meals. The fire from burning bits of wood collected by men was shared by women from surrounding wagons, each carefully positioning her pot to prevent spillage of the precious contents. Later on, when the cool of the late evening displaced the heat of this unusually hot day, the fires were kept alive until the wood ran out. Again, as the night before, few except the smallest children slept soundly, given the tumult of vast humanity continuously on the move on the nearby road. While the wagons of the refugees filling the valley were camped for the night, motorized traffic, mainly trucks, loaded to capacity with now unarmed soldiers, continued to flow, pressed on relentlessly by tired drivers.

And again, as on the night before, flares and tracer bullets lit the sky while the constant and ever nearer explosions illuminated the horizon like distant lightning. The endless thunder and brilliance from all directions continued, numbing the senses of the bewildered folks from Veliko Mraševo and before then, the peaceful and placid Masern.

On May 10, on the mostly flat road near the river, we covered another eight kilometers. As on the morning before, we started to move before dawn, but had to wait for an opening in the slower right lane of the one way traffic, not inclined to have its progress slowed by vehicles trying to enter the queue. But both Johann and Frantze persevered and finally got us in.

Both lanes were again packed and moving, with the motorized vehicles still trying to move more rapidly in the left lane. The wagons in the right lane were now drawn by horses only; all of those pulled by the slower and less agile oxen or cows had been abandoned and the animals let loose in the fields along the road. The former riders were now walking and carrying bundles, while those unable to walk were taken on by kindly owners of wagons still in motion. Those who still could had joined the ever growing multitude on foot, now including hurried soldiers, many in civilian clothing, all trying to get ahead in the narrow spaces between the lanes or along the side of the road. And later, when the full power of the midday sun had quickened the inevitable fatigue and exhaustion, the quest for a resting space in the shade of a tree on the hillside away from the road was no longer orderly or civil.

But on this second day since the end of war, the military traffic on our road as well as the traffic on the road across the river had slowed significantly, now moving no faster than the wagons of the refugees. In the desperate effort to outrun Tito's Partisan forces which were soon to appear, groups of this military had become increasingly less tolerant of the slowdown caused by the refugees. In this, soldiers of the SS and the Ustashe, the Army of the Croatian pro-Nazi satellite state, established after the occupation in 1941, were particularly brutal.

Their desperate attempt to escape the Partisans was not unjustified. The SS soldiers were part of the SS Divisions "Das Reich" and "Prince Eugen", both having been particularly active in enforcing Hitler's edict of September 6, 1941. According to this edict, 100 civilian hostages were to be shot for every German soldier killed and 50 civilian hostages shot for every German soldier wounded. The Germans resorted to this form of retribution after they realized their impotence, even with their overwhelming forces, in combating the hit, run and hide guerrilla tactics of the Yugoslavs. However, this form of retaliation during the next four years of occupation only helped to increase the hatred of the population toward the Germans and solidified their support of the Partisans.

Both of these SS Divisions were heavily staffed with ethnic German volunteers, citizens of occupied Yugoslavia who were, as such, considered to be traitors by the resistance forces. Even more to the point, the "Prince Eugen" division was formed after the occupation and, except for German officers, consisted mainly of ethnic German-Yugoslav volunteers, technically still citizens of Yugoslavia. Now with the war lost and at an end, these fleeing soldiers, aware of a hatred accumulated during four years of brutal occupation, were not counting on forgiveness and mercy by the victors who considered them to be traitors to their country.

Forgiveness and mercy were even less likely for the Ustashe, the soldiers of the Croatian Nazi Satellite State. Not only were the Ustashe considered traitors by the largely Serbian Partisans; they had also been the enforcers of a brutal anti-Serbian policy practiced by their Nazi Puppet State toward its large Serbian minority and Serbs in general. In the period after the establishment of the "Independent State of Croatia" in April 1941 and the following October, the Ustashe expelled 120,000 of the Serbian minority by ejecting them over the border into Serbia. The Croats also established the Jasenovac Concentration Camp in which nearly 100,000 members of the Serb minority, as well as 35,000 Jews were exterminated in ways that even the SS officers described as barbaric. (Vladimir Žerjavić, UN Expert. See Wikipedia for references.)

In this stream of desperate military were also Slovene anti-Communists, the Domobranci or Home Guard who, on April 20, 1944 and again on January 30, 1945 pledged allegiance to Hitler.

This is not to say that all Croats or Slovene were allied with the occupier.

While the existence of the Croatian fascist state is a historical fact, it is equally accurate that a majority of the deeply nationalistic population never accepted this state which was imposed on them by the fascist allies of the German occupier. They joined, in thousands, the ranks of the anti-fascist Partisans, especially after the brutal edict of executing hostages by the German military was brought also to the Croatian villages in eastern Croatia into which the bulk of the Partisans had withdrawn after the great if ineffective German offensive in the fall of 1941.

The Slovene, at first only hostile to the occupier, soon rebelled against the forced resettlement, forced labor and germanization of the remaining population, countered with armed resistance and increased Partisan activity. This generated a sharp response by Himmler who on June 25, 1942 issued the edict to the German forces battling the Partisans in the territories of Slovenia annexed to the Reich. The edict directed that all captured Slovene male supporters of the Partisans were to be executed, their wives sent to concentration camps and their children sent into the "Altreich" for reorientation and to be raised as good German 'Janissaries'.

In the four years of liberation struggle against the German occupier and its supporters, the State of Yugoslavia suffered immense casualties. According to the U.S. Bureau of Census, war related deaths were 1,067,000.

According to the study by Vladimir Žerjavić, 1.027 million people died; the number of dead being 6.67 % of the total population of the country, in 1938 equaling 15.4 million. Another study by Bogoljub Kočović places the number at 1,014 million; nearly the same. Of these, 446,000 were military and 581,000 were civilian; 67,000 of them Jews. More than 95,000 of them were Slovene.

The total estimated number of killed, wounded and prosecuted (in prisons and concentration camps, displaced and pressed into forced labor) was almost 3.75 million, nearly 25% of the population of the country.

However, on May 10, 1945, none of us knew any of this. Nor did we know that Hitler had tasked Himmler, in addition to giving him the assignment to mass murder the Jews, also with the gradual destruction of the Slavic people through starvation and forced labor. But our prejudice had been shaped by effective indoctrination to believe that the Germans and their allies were resisting the mostly Slavic Communism on its mission to destroy the German defender of western civilization. These defenders, losers now, were trying to escape the vengeance of those they had brutally suppressed over the past four years and to escape the Partisans who were "in the service of Communism controlled by Jews, whose ultimate objective was world domination", as we had so often been told and made to believe.

It was not surprising therefore, that these collaborators, clad in German uniforms with only minor insignia variations to tell them apart, were running for their lives. This included men who had shed their uniforms for civilian clothing and now mingled with and pretended to be part of the refugees.

They all were aware the Partisans considered them to be traitors to Yugoslavia and as such, were likely to be shot if captured. .Knowing that their time was rapidly running out, they pushed any obstacle out of their way and off the road. Unfortunately, these obstacles were, apart from the trucks that had run out of gasoline, the wagons of refugees that had become stuck in the left lane when they tried to overtake a stalled vehicle in front of them whose wheel or horse had collapsed and could not move on.

However, we did not yet know that the Partisans would make little distinction between the fleeing soldiers and the fleeing civilians; all those on the road were enemies, more or less. All this would become apparent soon enough.

Fortunately, our wagon, tended and supported by the able Johann and willing Frantze, remained intact and connected to the remaining few of the others who left Veliko Mraševo as a column two days ago. Staying together was recognized as necessary for moving on since it meant that help was on hand when needed by anyone in the group.

By now, each wagon had discarded all now obviously excess baggage, to be replaced by tired children, the elderly and the infirm. On our wagon, in addition to Father and Paul, was the wounded Anton, Katharina's 16-year-old son. Anton had been hit by a stray bullet after he left his Volkssturm unit on May 8 to look for his parents somewhere on the road to the North. He lost some blood, but had been bandaged up by a medic who said that the wound was not serious. Later in the day when the horses became tired, he too had to join those of us who could still walk. Father was on the bench up front holding the reins; Johann was leading the horses by the bridle while Frantze, Mother, Mitzi, Katharina, her husband Alois and I trailed behind or walked next to the wagon. The seven-year-old Paul at times left his spot near Father and joined us in walking, but usually not for long.

The war had ended two days ago, yet the thunder of explosions continued relentlessly and was getting nearer while endless flares and tracer bullets continued to compete with the sun. The constant starting and stopping in the heat of this again unusually hot day tired the body, while the senses, stretched to the limit by the sharp extremes of sight and sound, surrendered to a translucent perception of the surreal. To the nostrils now clung, ever stronger since this morning, the sweet, never to be forgotten smell of decay from the bodies of animals and humans decomposing in the broiling sun.

Later in the day word spread that the Partisans had arrived. They had been observed in small groups off the road and identified by the red star on their caps and tunic collars of the original Yugoslav army uniform. And, of course, they were heavily armed but apparently not yet ready or in sufficient numbers to enter the traffic and take control of the fleeing masses. They started this in the half-light of the following morning.

Toward the evening of May 10, we passed Sevnica and Frantze found a spot for the night, a night no different from the last two. The sounds of explosions and gunfire continued to dull the senses and the perpetual lighting of the sky kept interfering with the dark of the night. To this was added the numbing fear of the imminent arrival of the dreaded Communists, among them surely those from Veliko Mraševo who came to take revenge on us for causing the brutal disruption in their lives and the loss of their homes, three and a half years ago.

That evening, our now small, but still connected group was confronted with a decision on how to proceed the following morning. Just beyond the village of Sevnica and across the Sevnična, a small tributary to the Sava River, there is a fork in the road. The left continues toward Zidani Most along the Sava, while the right follows the Sevnična into a broad valley more directly toward the north, albeit on a secondary road.

It was decided to continue along the Sava, in retrospect perhaps a mistake since the road on the right along the Sevnična, while unpaved, was not only less winding but also leading more directly toward Austria, our goal. Our group was not deterred by reports that the Partisans had blocked the most constricted part of the road beyond Zidani Most along the Savinja toward Celje and that there was considerable fighting with the Ustashe trying to force their way beyond that point.

So, next morning, the 11th of May, we started on what was to be the most difficult day since leaving Veliko Mraševo. Particularly for Mother who had little sleep, kept awake by constant anxiety and worry about Father and Johann, who were both roaming about and secretly observing the Partisans in the woods off the road, getting ready to take over. Father, with his fluent Slovene, overheard one group discussing their plans. Apparently, he had come away from that with the impression that their plan was to kill all the escapees on the road.

Almost immediately after starting toward Zidani Most, the road began to get narrower as it climbed into the steep hillside above the tracks that hugged the winding river.

And soon after we had climbed a distance on this steep road, one of the reasons for the constant firing and explosions during the past few days and nights and the aftermath of these endless sounds, became gruesomely apparent.

The ever steeper hillside down to the river was littered with wagons, trucks and all sorts of military hardware large and small. Mixed into all this were the bodies of animals and humans in various stages of dismemberment and decay, now adding desperation to the anxiety and fear that was with us in increasing measure since we had left, two and a half days ago. We had entered a stretch of the escape route from Croatia that, due to its geography, was particularly vulnerable and exposed to the Partisans and which had, especially in the last few days, become their unopposed killing grounds.

It was now obvious that we should have taken the other road after all, but how were we to know, some said. It had been known, however, that all rail and road traffic between Zidani Most and Zagreb had, for many months before the end of the war, been hampered and finally shut down by the strafing planes and Partisan activity, particularly on this stretch by simply disabling the steam locomotive pulling a train. But we heard nothing about the traffic on the road. What really had been happening, and especially so in the last few days, now became visible to our eyes. The full extent of this was not apparent until much later when it became known that this killing range extended all along the steep embankments along the Sava to Zidani Most and along the rivers in both directions for miles beyond that.

Years later we learned that during the war and particularly in the days leading up to the end of it, the Partisans had used this approximately fourteen kilometer stretch between Sevnica and Zidani Most to harass the military traffic not only on the rails but also on the roads on either side of the Sava River. On our side, the narrow road, in parts carved into the steep terrain, offered an ideal spot for the Partisans from which to target their defenseless enemy below. From a convenient perch above, this road as well as the one across the river could be strafed at will and if attacked, the strafing party could easily withdraw to still higher grounds from which to pick off the attackers. The Partisans had perfected this tactic in the mountainous terrain of Macedonia and Montenegro where they prevailed against the vastly superior forces of the Germans, including their Luftwaffe air power. But during this final phase of the war, there was little effective resistance from the retreating armies and the only break in the firing occurred when the Partisans ran out of ammunition or decided to take a rest.

In the last few days of the war, the German soldiers and their allies, in a desperate attempt to move on and escape being picked off, resorted to the only option available to them when facing a blockage caused mostly by Partisan fire. They cleared the road by pushing the obstacle, whatever that may be, over the edge of the road, where it continued to roll down the steep slope to be either stopped by a tree or land on the ledge near the tracks.

This was even more so the case in the two valleys of the fork beyond Zidani Most, where the steep slope starts almost immediately at each of the two river banks. This constriction continues for at least ten kilometers in either direction, giving the Partisans total command over the traffic below.

However, we never got to Zidani Most.

Since the morning, we had moved very slowly uphill, all in short bursts of constant start and stopping. And after having climbed to some height above the river, the road leveled out to a constant up and down. To limit the burden on the horses straining to prevent the wagon from rolling either forward or back, Frantze and Mitzi were tasked to block the wheels with stones since it took too long to engage the rim brake by turning the crank.

But now the traffic came to a complete standstill for extended periods. The jam was undoubtedly caused by blockages similar to those of the past few days, except that here was no room to get off the road other than over the precipice.

Now the dreaded Partisans appeared, identifiable mainly by the five pointed stars on their caps and tunic collars. Small groups of them slid down the embankment from above, while others came on horses on the road behind us. Most were quite young, in their mid twenties or less, all heavily armed, ready to shoot at any resistance or obstacle and firing occasionally into the air to get attention. They moved in groups among the civilians and fleeing soldiers most still dressed in their uniforms, clearing the road as they moved by and on, tolerating no blockage in the left lane. Unless room was quickly found in the right lane for a vehicle on the left, the young Partisans, with their assault weapons at the ready, uncoupled the horses and pushed the wagon off the cliff.

Word arrived that the Partisans were shooting resisters, now mostly refugees who were still trying to hold on to their few treasured possessions. But the Partisans were determined to clear the road for their trucks and armored vehicles and keep it that way. To make this stick, they subdued any resistance to their hard-won supremacy with terror and death.

THE BELLS RING NO MORE

This was brought home to us, the remaining group of wagons from Veliko Mraševo, mid morning when the left lane again stopped moving. Johann and Frantze went up front to have a look and I followed at a distance in spite of Mother's command not to wander off. One of the refugees' wagons, not one of our group, had moved out of the right lane into the left one but came to a stop behind the stalled wagon in front of it, also blocked from proceeding further. Immediately, a small group of Partisans arrived and ordered the wagon to be pushed over the edge of the road.

Frantze, who knew the owner of the wagon, began to argue forcefully with one of the Partisans on his behalf, asking for a few moments of delay to get the wagon back into the right lane. The soldier soon discovered that Frantze was a Slovene and obviously on the wrong side of the war. The young Partisan pointed his sub-machine gun at Frantze and pulled the trigger. The burst propelled Frantze, who had been standing near the edge of the road, over the cliff and I watched the body of this simple young man, whose humanity by far outweighed his ideology, tumble down the steep embankment.

There was no further arguing from the stunned family owning that wagon. The horses were quickly uncoupled and the wagon, with the few and only remaining precious possessions of its owner, pushed off the barrier-less road, spilling its contents as it tumbled the distance down to the tracks, coming to rest not far from the body of Frantze.

This was by far the most numbing event since we left Veliko Mraševo and it confirmed all reports of the brutality of the Communist Partisans we had heard so much about in the past few years. How much more of this was waiting for us, vulnerable participants in this nightmare of seemingly unbounded proportion, was still unknown especially since we were still so far away from our destination on such forbidding and dangerous terrain and now under total control of the "brutal barbarians", as described by the VGL. None of us was aware of the even larger scope of such happenings all along the way and in both directions beyond Zidani Most, and that for the young Partisans, this "brutality" was part of their final act of retribution and revenge on the German occupier and his allies. However, it is unlikely that Communism, at least in these young avengers, played the primary role.

How the blockage that resulted in the death of Frantze was cleared, I no longer remember, except that it was cleared rapidly for no one was willing to tempt fate and bullets. Words arriving from front and back, told us that the Partisans were using similar tactics all along the road to clear one lane for the vehicles that were to follow their forward groups. As the day progressed and we inched our way toward Zidani Most, the result of this tactic was clearly confirmed by the discarded evidence; material, animal and human, that was accumulating at the bottom of the precipice adjoining the road. The Partisans had made known their method for clearing the lane, not just in our vicinity but all the way along our road as well as on the road across the river. And after the killing of Frantze, no one wished to become the next victim.

During the remainder of that day, the heat, together with fatigue mostly due to a lack of sleep, food and especially water produced a sense of the hopelessness in which only the strongest and the most determined such as Johann and Mother still functioned with some degree of normalcy. Reports of suicides were becoming more frequent, one of them of a woman from our village. Most affected by this was Father, who had the least amount of sleep since we left. This was not apparent to me but was obvious to Mother who recalled the events of that day in detail later on. For me, the day passed in a sequence of surreal sketches that ended when I fell asleep after we descended the higher terrain. Toward the evening we were commanded by a Partisan to camp on the flat land next to the Sava just before the green steel bridge across it.

But during the day when we were still on the higher part of the road and mostly standing still, Mitzi and I were sent into the embankment above the road with buckets to find water, especially for the horses who were near collapse for the lack of it. Had this occurred, our wagon would also have been sent over the edge by the ever near and watchful Partisans all making sure that no blockage stopped the traffic in the left lane now used by their vehicles only. The two of us were sent because Johann was leading the horses by the bridle up front while Mother was dealing with the brake and the blocks under the wheels during the next two or three meters of forward motion. Father, limited by his crutches and worn out with fatigue could not contribute to any of this and even the horses ignored the tugs and pulls of the reins and no longer responded to the whip.

We did find water, but on one of our returns to a trickling brook, Mitzi was accosted by an armed man who began to wrestle the screaming girl while trying to lift her skirts. Our screams, which brought Mother and Johann, intimidated the attacker who released her and took flight. This time I knew that my sister escaped rape for the second time, the first time being six years ago by the smith of Masern when he accosted her working alone in the fields. Her screams, then as now had stopped the assault.

The steep and wooded, but occasionally field-like grounds above the road were full of fleeing civilians and soldiers bypassing the blocked and treacherous road below. On these open slopes Mitzi and I witnessed many tragic scenes, but one became firmly imprinted on my mind which even many decades could not diminish in clarity.

A solitary elderly woman, in the typically dark and billowing skirts of a peasant, her head covered with a kerchief and carrying on her shoulder a stick to which was tied a bundle, is limping across the steep ravine above the blocked road. Catching up from behind her, but at a higher level, is a soldier leading by the bit a horse pulling a small, two rubber wheeled cart of the type used by the German infantry to transport munitions over rough terrain. The cart, its load hidden by a canvas cover, is barely clinging to the steep grassy slope and very near its tipping point.

I watch from above, mesmerized by a clear perception of the tragedy about to happen. Sure enough, just as the cart is about to pass, it starts to tip over. The soldier and the horse, both pulled backward and down, stop the rolling cart, but only after it rolls over the unsuspecting woman.

The soldier lets go of the horse, runs to the immobile woman now sprawled out on the slope, falls on his knees and lifts her head just as I get close. She seems to be dead but her eyes are open. Holding her head, the soldier, with a pained apologetic expression looks up, burdening me forever, with the indelible impression of two sets of petrified eyes staring at me. But not for long. He lowers her head into the grass, gets up, rights the cart and continues on his way.

It had taken most of the day to get to Breg, a village half way between Sevnica and Zidani Most. From this point forward, the road is no longer hewn into the steep hills directly above the tracks and the river, but follows a less tortuous and more direct path on flat terrain toward Zidani Most a short distance away from the winding Sava and the tracks.

We got near the steel bridge, two and a half km this side of Zidani Most before nightfall. We had covered the distance from Breg in a fraction of the time it took to get to Breg from Sevnica and without further highly dramatic events. The constant thunder of explosions and black smoke from burning tires seemed to have abated somewhat, the nostrils less offended by the pervasive smell of rotting flesh. Or was it that the deepening fatigue had dulled the senses to the point where only survival mattered?

Instead of proceeding into the again-tightening cleft of encroaching and even steeper mountains just beyond the steel bridge, pushing the road up to the tracks and the river, we were directed on to a field alongside the Sava near Loca. From here there was a clear view of the traffic on the steel bridge just ahead and on the other side of the river.

From this vantage point, it soon became obvious that all traffic, on the bridge as well as on the river opposite was now in the other direction, opposite to that during the days and nights until now. Since this traffic included the wagons of refugees, it became plain that our planned escape route to Austria was, if not forever at least for now, closed. Father's impression, gathered when he overheard the camping Partisans the night before that they planned to kill us all, took on a frightening reality.

The memory of that evening and night is the view of the bridge with its curved arch of steel keeping the flat roadbed suspended above the swiftly flowing river. This view, coming into focus with each flash of a new explosion remains clear to this day. Adding to that scene is the pleading of Mother to Johann to find her husband who had disappeared again and was lost if not dead. All this was vividly refreshed when, decades later, I re-visited that very spot.

He still had not returned at dawn of the following day of May 12th, when a frantic Mother sent Mitzi and me to look for him. She was now convinced that he was dead and told us to walk toward Zidani Most; "maybe you will find him in the river on the way there". Johann had already gone to look for him elsewhere.

The two of us walked past the steel bridge and then along the bank of the Sava toward Zidani Most. We stopped often to make our way among all the military debris to the very edge of the river to see if any of the bodies at the bottom of the water was that of Father, but to get back to Mother more quickly, we soon decided to look for a body of a man with only one leg.

At Zidani Most we crossed the stone bridge over the Savinja and walked north along its bank. This is when we were stopped by a very young Partisan. He put his handgun to my head and with the other hand loosened the clasp in the buttonhole of the collar of my jacket. By the leather strap he pulled from the breast pocket my precious confirmation watch and after looking at it, walked away with a grinning face.

Since Mother had cautioned us not to go too far, we turned to get back to our wagon. Along the way, we joined the thickening traffic of orderly groups of disarmed military, escorted by their Partisan guards, all now walking with us in our direction. When we reached the campsite, our wagon was gone, but we heard from the few remaining there that those who left were told to cross the Sava on the steel bridge just up ahead.

On the steel bridge, the wagons of the refugees were again kept sharply to the right, making room for the vanquished soldiers on their left as they were being escorted by their guards in a continuous stream to the other side. The wagons were moving in short spurts between halts and we caught up with ours in the middle of the bridge. Johann was leading the horses by the bridle and to our surprise, on the bench was a disheveled Father who immediately asked me to sit next to him but told Mitzi to join Mother and Paul who had gone on ahead.

I was immensely happy to see him alive but quickly noticed his unusual behavior. Strange talk, flashing eyes, jerky movements; all unfamiliar and frightening. The mostly incoherent talk had great urgency and with unusual conviction in his shaky voice he explained that we were being turned back to be taken to a place where we were to be killed. "I heard this again last night when they were talking about us". ".. the young are to be sorted out and re-educated into loyal Communists", "… you don't want to become a Communist, do you. I don't want you to become a Communist; I'd rather have you dead…"

We inched toward the far end of the bridge where, due to the steep embankment just beyond it, the main road took a sharp turn to the left. The much narrower road to the right was blocked by guards. And when we and the silent prisoners on our left finally reached the end of the bridge, there was no choice but to turn to the left.

THE ROAD TO EXILE

But even before we made that fateful left, proving the first part of Father's contention, he kept up his verbal onslaught, made ever more urgent that he did not want me to become a Communist and that he would rather have me dead.

The distance from the steel bridge to the village of Radeče is no more than a few hundred meters. But just before the houses start, there is a fork in the road with the right leading into the village and the left continuing along the Sava, in effect bypassing the village center. And as it was visible, all the wagons of the refugees were directed on to the village road while the prisoners and their guards took the left fork.

The fact that the refugees were being separated from the military was further proof to Father that we were being led to the place of slaughter and that we should kill ourselves beforehand. He did, of course, not know that he had it in reverse and that it was the prisoners, the captured Ustashe and Domobranci who were being led to slaughter while the refugees were separated out and led to a holding camp in a field just beyond Radeče. On the other hand, how was I to know that Father had reached a state of extreme depression in which delusion overwhelms any logic and coherent thought. Nevertheless, he was persuasive and even before we got to the fork, I had succumbed to his verbal barrage and no longer argued with him.

It happened on the narrowing road into the village just a few houses beyond the fork. Passively, I watched him make the preparations. He reached back to get a section of strong cord, a kitchen knife, the knife-sharpening tool and lastly, a hammer. He was going to kill me by smashing my skull.

The first blow broke the bone and made a shallow dent. He swung again, but I instinctively covered my head with both hands and now the blow fell on my protecting right hand, crushing the knuckle of the middle finger but saving the skull.

Before the third blow reached its target, I was yanked from the wagon. Johann, who was busy with the horses but saw the beginning of the tragedy, raced around to the right side of the wagon and pulled me down and into the gutter just before the third blow connected. I passed out for only a moment and as I recovered, while still lying in the gutter, I saw Father attempting to fasten the noose he had made from the cord to the hoop above his seat. But he gave that up and now was sharpening the knife by crisscrossing it with the sharpening tool as he had in the past before carving a roast. After that, he tried to stab himself and then cut his wrists. I passed out again.

THE BELLS RING NO MORE

I only vaguely remember what happened immediately after that. Apparently, Mother appeared and led me away, covered with blood oozing from the hole in my head. She left Johann to struggle with Father and pull him off the wagon, now seemingly dead. The commotion stopped the wagons behind us, but some Partisans showed up and forced Johann to move on with the wagon insisting that he leave the dead body in the gutter, a not uncommon sight in those days.

All this was too much even for my stoic mother. Not only had she lost her husband, her home, her possessions, her lands, her country, all, and now was walking with a seemingly dying son into the further evolving nightmare. She also reached the conclusion, if for different reasons than Father, that there was no further point to living. I had already been convinced of that earlier and did not protest.

It seemed an easy thing to do. As she led me along the village street, I looked for a means and the first appropriate item I saw among all the discarded weaponry was a hand grenade. I was very familiar with the German version, a cylinder shaped explosive at the end of a wooden handle at the end of which was a cap that had to be unscrewed to expose the cord for pulling to make it explode after five seconds. But I knew nothing about this cross ribbed egg shaped foreign device, a blessing which just a little later saved both our lives.

We left the road and made our way along a house to the rear, the place of stables and barns. We entered a barn and agreed that we would stand close together, face to face, when I detonated the grenade.

Had it been a German grenade I would not be writing these lines now. Facing each other and Mother hugging me loosely, I fiddled with a pin, the only possible item that would make it explode, but the pin would not move. Then, when we heard the voices of Mitzi and Johann calling, I gave up and we left the barn. Johann took the grenade from my hands and put it down gently as we walked back to the street. He had saved me for the third time in less than one week, saved my life twice in less than one hour.

What happened immediately after the four of us got back to the street is not clear and those who could fill in the blanks no longer can. It may be that the depression in my skull had something to do with this. If so, I was indeed fortunate that the effect on my memory was limited only to that short period which in the future we discreetly referred to as the "event". Out of Father's hearing for sure.

Johann said that the Partisans had taken the horses and the wagon. Mother went back to find Father while Johann, Mitzi and I walked with the stream of people to find Paul who had been left with Katharina and her family. We found him and the others in a large field near the Sava, just beyond the village. On this slightly upward sloping field just outside Radeče, the Partisans had set up a holding camp to get the refugees off the road and keep them there. Mother caught up with us after a while and between sobs and streaming tears reported that Father was no longer in the gutter where she had last seen him and she could not find him anywhere. She assumed his body had been moved off the street perhaps to a grave. The Partisans she asked would not give her an answer.

Since orders from the Partisans were being spread around that we were to camp here for some days, the five of us found a spot in the already crowded field. Then Mother and Johann went to find the wagon with the hope of rescuing from it some essential items for our survival. They did find it, a short distance from the village and Mother pleaded with the young Partisan now in charge to let her have the tent, a few blankets and some food. That she was successful in this, is in retrospect amazing since the Partisans, including this one knew that all refugees on the road were, if not intimate supporters of the occupier, now fleeing with them from the liberator. Perhaps this compassionate young liberator, now on the bench and holding the reins, was not a fanatic and in his recent past swore allegiance to the side most likely to succeed in this bitter struggle, if only to survive. Or perhaps because his family (surely he had a mother not very different from the one pleading with him now) survived the hostage-taking by the Germans as a result of compassion from someone on the side of the occupier or his allies. Any number of reasons, but compassion for sure.

After Johann helped us to set up the small tent and spread the blankets, we hid within, partly to avoid the stares of neighbors who heard of our plight and partly to cry in private. Then a kind soul came to clean the now drying blood from my head with disinfectant and cover the area with bandages, a wound judged not as deep as was feared. Not much could be done with the crushed knuckle except to firm it up with a splint and then firm up the entire hand with bandages around a longer splint. Both damages healed rapidly without complications in the next few days and weeks, being looked after by the same kind soul if not another. But I was left for life with an enlarged knuckle and a depression in the skull, evidence for all to see on my right hand or feel below the covering hair of my head. Not visible was the damage to the psyche; the nightmares abating only after years. But the memories of the "event" remained intact.

It was two afternoons later when people came running to tell us that Father was sitting beside the road at the top end of the field. At first we reacted with disbelief, a joke surely, since we all were certain that he was dead. But then we ran up the hill and sure enough, there he was. He had been sitting there a while, suspecting that we were in the camp but either too weak to look for us or afraid to face us when he found us. Of course it was both, the latter obvious in his face which quickly turned from fear to surprise to joy. Our pleasure to see him alive erased any resentment or grief among all of us, now relieved by tears including his, one of only two times I saw my Father cry.

The long sleep that night in the tent helped him to recover his composure and revert to a semblance of his former self. The "event" and its aftermath appeared to have cured him of the depression for there was no more talk of grim foreboding in spite of the gloom still all around us. He and the rest of us who had already seen hell, now accepted our destiny, come what may.

Next morning, the person who had taken care of my wounds, took care of his. The chest wound where he had stabbed himself was superficial and the cuts across his wrists were not deep enough to reach the veins. All were bandaged up and rapidly healed.

What did not heal for many decades was a barrier that appeared between son and father, a son who never completely forgave his father for being a weakling at a time when a rock of strength was required for his family to lean on. "In a time of need he failed us", was justification for this invisible barrier that remained between us until his death in 1969 at the age of 76. This barrier remained with me for three decades after that, when I realized that any rock can crumble from depression, an overwhelming yet invisible force. It was this realization that for the fourth time, saved my life.

I too was crumbled by this force into a pitiable heap of misery, albeit by a matter insignificant to what Father faced in 1945 and which pushed him into the "event" that morning of May 12, 1945. My depression was over a trivial matter, temporary according to the treating physician, to disappear as soon as the matter was resolved. True enough, but until it was over, it was as severe as any depression can be, even if eased and controlled by medication.

Father had no such care or medication nor was the matter, which took him into clinical depression, either trivial or temporary. He had lost everything; all his earthly possessions, all anchors to a livelihood for himself and his family, all prospects for a meaningful future. And on that day on the steel bridge, having been forced into that ominous U turn, he was justified in believing that he was about to lose his family as well as his life.

Yes, "but why not let others do the deed" was my reasoning for decades thereafter. And "others, with similar losses did not despair". This logic crumbled, as did I, pushed over a threshold into mental disturbance by, for me seemingly insurmountable difficulties. And so I had my day on a steel bridge, a night in 2000 actually, when I reached for the bottle of tablets. But at that moment came to mind the "event" and its aftermath and I realized that I could not inflict on my family what he had inflicted on his. This awareness made me pull back and more than anything else, was the reason for my "cure". And had that "event" not been there to remember, I most certainly would, again, not be writing these lines.

Another victim of this "event" was the friendship between Johann and Father and by extension between Johann and the rest of the family. I never discovered the reason for this but I suspect that Johann was disillusioned over the character weakness of his friend, now a tainted man. And that Father was a "tainted person" was made clear to us by those who knew and now shunned us. Suicide, even under such trying circumstances was not looked upon with compassion, especially when accompanied by attempted murder of a son.

So we lost touch with Johann who remained in the camp but kept his distance. We saw him, on and off for the next few weeks among the refugees until we crossed into Austria. After that he, like all others dispersed, free at last to go their own way. I did not see him again until several decades later at a public social event. There he reminded me of some of the painful moments during those four days but I was, unfortunately, not yet ready to listen attentively or seek details. I was not yet ready confront that part of the past.

This came, but again only years later. Mother did not wish to talk about it, Mitzi had blocked it out of her mind as did Paul then only seven years old and not a witness to many of the gruesome details. Of course, I would never discuss any of it with Father, who had survived in spite of it all.

I did begin to think more often of Johann in the late 1980's and the crucial role he had played in our lives and especially in mine and I was getting myself ready to see him. He then lived in a remote part of Pennsylvania, some distance away. Both Father and Mother were no longer alive.

But one night in 1988, I dreamed about him and woke up to an overwhelming urge to talk to him. The neighbor I phoned that morning reported sadly that Johann had had a stroke that night and was alive but unconscious in the local hospital. And no, I could not see him. I tried, unsuccessfully, to contact his wife for several days thereafter to see if I could see him when he regained consciousness. The neighbor reported no progress until I had another dream and awoke the following morning with a similar urge to make contact. The same neighbor told me that Johann died that night. I could see him at the local funeral parlor and that he would be buried two days hence.

When I arrived at the parlor, the coffin was still open and I pondered the deeply lined but kind face of the man who played such a major role in my youth and the awareness that without his intervention my life would have ended fifty-seven years ago. The silent gratitude to him was also a sad reminder that I should have thanked him long ago.

We were kept in the camp outside Radeče for three more days until May 17. We survived mostly from what had been rescued from the wagons, but the Partisans did set up a field kitchen and once a day a long line waited for thin soup and a slice of bread. Mother, clustered by her children, carried a larger cup and usually managed to persuade the Partisan with the ladle to put into it a little more, something for her sick invalid husband.

The reason we were kept in that camp for five days became clear only many decades later.

During the entire stay there, we could see from our slightly elevated vantage point, on the road between the Sava and the camp, a never ending day and night procession of columns of vanquished soldiers, taking up most of the room on the spacious road. All were guarded on both sides by Partisans, weapons at the ready and spaced so as to prevent any of their charges from fleeing. Night and day they walked south-east along the Sava. "POW's being led to a camp somewhere", was passed around.

It was clear, however, that this pitiful endless stream consisted of the very men who only several days ago, desperately and by desperate means, were making their way in the opposite direction, trying to outrun their approaching avengers. But the Partisans, their tactics honed by years of guerilla warfare, appeared from the woods of the steep hills on either side of the escape route along the Sava and Savinja rivers, making any resistance futile and capture certain. Some of the fleeing had, at war's end, put up resistance with the hope of reaching the Austrian border, including a fierce if futile fight further up the Sevnica valley toward Celje. This contributed to the delays, including ours and was part of the distant thunder and flashes of light that we heard earlier during our way toward Zidani Most.

Now the captured SS, Ustashe and Domobranci were being escorted back in the reverse direction, most if not all to their mass execution as traitors, their bodies dumped into mass graves that dot the Slovene countryside. All were part of a brutal policy of the liberator which consisted partly in revenge and partly in the elimination of all opposition to the ideology of the new Communist State that had emerged out of this brutal war.

We, of course knew none of this. We only witnessed an endless uninterrupted flow of vanquished men, many no older than the young Partisan who allowed Mother to take the tent. Surely many in that uninterrupted flow had, like him, chosen or were persuaded to join their side of the conflict except that in their case, it turned out to be the wrong one. There were those who chose that side because they saw in Communism an evil ideology and were willing to do battle to prevent it from becoming their future. However, in doing this they became allied with an equally evil ideology, which had, under the pretense of destroying Communism, invaded their country and brutalized its people.

Securing this stream of thousands, led out of the confined spaces of the two congested valleys along the rivers north and west of Zidani Most, was of prime concern to the liberators. Only when this was more or less accomplished did they turn their attention back to the relatively benign mass of refugees, in our case those languishing on the sloping field near Radeče.

We had been given some notice that on the following day we were to be moved. By now the stream of escorted captives on the main road below had diminished to a trickle. And early in the morning of May 17, open trucks appeared on the narrow road above and Partisans with sub-machine guns started to herd the frightened mass emerging from the tents toward the trucks, allowing only the most minimal possessions to be taken with them. Other Partisans packed each truck to capacity, closed the rear gate and ordered the truck to roll off to an unknown destination. As our truck rolled away we all, including a silent Father, were resigned to our fate, all the more troubling, given the direction along the Sava.

The trucks moved southeast, opposite to the northwest direction only a few days ago and on the opposite side of the river. Now, in contrast to the northwest pace, we were moving rapidly toward where we started from and our fate beyond that.

We reached Krško, a distance of 30 kilometers from Radeče in less than one hour. And, as we did nine days ago at sunset on the 8th of May, we again crossed the bridge across the Sava and the place where Johann saved me from being trampled by the hoofs of our frightened horses. We passed Videm where we camped that first night and continued southeast along the river. After a few minutes and ten kilometers more, we reached Brežice where the trucks stopped inside a camp surrounded by a barbed wire fence enclosing wooden barracks built by the SS after the occupation in April 1941.

We had arrived in Brežice once before, albeit under very different circumstances. The irony in our return did not escape most. The first time we got there was in December 1941. Then we arrived on the comfortable seats of heated railway coaches; not on the hard floors of uncovered military trucks. Then, as now, our destination was uncertain; but then the future was far less dismal and survival more certain. Then we stayed in the Brežice movie theatre cleared of chairs, on comfortable mattresses and fed good meals until taken to our houses in the Promised Land. Now we were behind barbed wire in barracks, the men separated from their wives and children, sleeping on bare floors thinly covered with crumpled straw full of lice, surviving on thin soup and a slice of bread once a day and hoping that we would be sent back to Kočevje where we came from just four years ago. Poorer for sure, but the land had survived and perhaps even the house, more than what awaited our ancestors when they arrived there some six centuries ago.

The camp was guarded by very young Partisan soldiers, local recruits by their looks, behavior and language. Their acting tough did not deter Mother, fluent in their local Slovene dialect, from chatting them up and talking them into letting her leave the camp to visit Veliko Mraševo, her home, for only a short few hours.

After all, she had to come back to her hungry family, hopefully with some food these young guards could not provide. And again, the pleas coming from a woman not unlike their mother were met with compassion and they allowed her to leave the camp.

She came back with bread, sausages and wine, all given to her by the Žibert family that had returned to their home after four years of enforced absence. The sausage, the wine and the grain for the bread had all been left behind on May 8, for which the Žiberts were now grateful and willing to share with the woman who left the house in a condition better than it was when they were forced to leave. They had received her hospitably, showing no hostility to a person who was part of the reason for their expulsion.

Not happy was the woman in the house next to the Žiberts, whose property had also been assigned to us. When she heard that Mother was at the Žiberts she came to angrily confront Mother over the condition of her house which had received only minor repairs and been kept more or less in the condition it was when we took possession of it. Mother's defense was in pointing out that all the rotting windows had been replaced and painted (by slave labor from Czechoslovakia) and that quite a bit of our furniture was left in the house. Also, the grain bins in some of the rooms, which we used as storage spaces, were left half full as was the hay loft which was empty when we arrived. "And you all have your property back but we lost everything, are starving and know not what is to become of us. And we were victims just like you". All that, accompanied by a stream of tears calmed the woman and further helped to convince the Žiberts to be generous on Mother's behalf.

I returned to Veliko Mraševo and the Žibert house mid morning of a Saturday in the summer of 1988. I parked the hired car on the triangle and slowly entered the familiar courtyard of Number 38, only steps away. I was apprehensive, having no inkling of how I would be received, if at all, or simply given the boot.

Immediately apparent was the enlargement of the house and other improvements, the most obvious being the magnificent tractor near the barn. Such a machine, with its vast amount of horsepower, was unimaginable in our time there when its task was being performed by only two horses, our Yiorgo and Shargo. But my contemplation was interrupted by a middle aged woman, dressed in working clothes, coming out of the barn asking what I wanted.

I came to talk to gospod Žibert, I said as I gave my name. "He is not here, but he should be back any moment. I am his wife" and could she help me. I explained that I was the oldest son of the family that lived here during the war and that I now lived in America but came to apologize for being the cause of their expulsion in 1941.

The quickly changing expression on the face of the woman let me know that my fears of not being welcome were without cause. She invited me into the house leading me to the large room fronting the street that in our day was used jointly as the living room and dining room and at night, the bedroom of Father, Mother, Paul and myself, with Mitzi using the spare bedroom. Now it was used as a comfortable living/dining room only, the beds having been moved into other rooms of the enlarged and improved house.

Mrs. Žibert immediately served apple cider and we chatted comfortably until after only a short while, her husband arrived from the nearby Cerkle where he had driven for supplies. I introduced myself again and explained that I came to apologize for being the cause of their expulsion in 1941. He greeted me warmly, thanked me for the effort to seek him out and waved off my apology with a magnanimous: "we were all victims".

Karel Žibert, now in his mid fifties had like me, been forced to leave his home when he was ten years old. As we sat around the dining room table on which a recognizably new red wine had replaced the cider, he described the early morning hours of the fateful day. They were having breakfast in the very room we were in now when canvas covered trucks began to roll past the house and further into the village toward the river. Karel's father guessed the reason for the trucks and together with his wife, Karel and older sister Justa ran into the woods beyond the barn. From behind trees, Karel and his family watched the villagers being rounded up by armed Gestapo civilians and black uniformed SS men and herded into the trucks.

By mid morning, the trucks began to leave. It took less than two hours to empty the village of its roughly 300 inhabitants. During this time, the victims had been allowed to collect only the most essential items of clothing and gather them into small bundles or equally small suitcases. By noon all the trucks, including the one carrying their neighbors were gone.

Shortly before noon, another column of trucks rolled into the village, the drivers and passengers being civilians with some military among them. This time they came for the livestock, mostly pigs and cattle who by now were clamoring for attention. All were, like their owners a few hours ago, loaded on to the trucks, a process taking longer since the animals did not respond to threats as their owners had in the morning. But all was accomplished quickly and by mid afternoon these trucks were also gone.

Karel and his family waited until dark then silently made their way across the fields to a place along the river nearest the Dobrava village, pausing occasionally to listen for German or Italian guards who, even if infrequently, patrolled their respective side of the border. In the stillness of the night, their muted calls across the water were quickly answered. The villagers of Dobrava had witnessed the tragedy as it developed during the day both from the river bank and from the steep hill just behind the village and knew that some managed to escape into the woods and were now waiting for them. Immediately after contact was made, a boat emerged from under the willows and slid silently across to fetch them to the relative safety of a part of Slovenia occupied not by the dreaded Nazis, but by the much more tolerant troops of Mussolini's Italy.

For the next three and a half years, Karel, other escapees and the villagers of Dobrava watched the goings on in the village across the river. After having ascertained the routine of the German border patrol, headquartered near the bridge in upstream Brod, some of the former residents and other brave souls returned under the cover of darkness to retrieve whatever possible from their former homes. Staging such excursions was not a problem since the Italians had few forces in place and did not patrol their side of the border. And when within weeks, they saw the village being re-populated, Germans moving into their houses, they realized the permanency of the expulsion and loss of their homes and their land.

With glasses of wine animating our conversation, Karel and I continued to recall the dramatic events of those years, events we shared but experienced with different perspectives imposed on us by the river, the border and the collision of ideologies. The hatred that in those tragic days had no boundary was no longer present; it had been diffused and softened over the years since and given way to compassionate understanding between the two former enemies, now sitting at the same table sharing wine.

Karel talked about the summer afternoons with school friends in the water on his side of the river, at that point about 60 meters wide, while keeping an eye on the hostile crowd of youngsters on a little beach on the opposite side. He did not know that our parents, like theirs, halfheartedly forbade us to go near or into the river for fear of drowning or, in their case, being fired upon by the guards from across the water. A least they had learned to swim, having grown up along a river, which was not the case with us.

Karel remembered the time when an especially vituperative exchange of epithets with bathers across the water resulted in bursts of bullets fired at them from our side. He also remembered the afternoon in early fall of 1944 when a commotion on the opposite side attracted their attention. It was the drowning of my friend Franz. They watched our helpless efforts to save him and he recalled how some of the older boys got into a boat to row across and help. I do not remember how the body was finally retrieved because I had been ordered by the adults who came running to go and tell his parents. But Karel explained that his older friends had rowed across, dived into the water, found the body and dragged it ashore. After that, they quickly rowed back to their side.

Yes, he not only remembered the huge explosion in 1944, but he was there and saw it all. He and others had watched one of their older friends swim across the river at a narrower point upstream to retrieve a buried mine from the minefield as he had done before. But this time the boy pulled a trip wire hidden in the tall grass with his foot, setting off the mine which lifted the body and dropped it into the middle of the barbed wire web. I recounted to Karel how I watched the boy die.

I asked Karel if he knew of the big raid of July 7, 1943. He not only knew of the raid, his father and some of his older friends were part of it. The Partisan raiders brought along the teenagers to help get the cattle from the village stables, lead them to the river and cross them to the other side. The raiders and all the villagers on their side of the river were fully aware that there was only minimal risk since the patrolling of the border was virtually non-existent by then.

Karel heard about the shot that killed Mrs. Mams who had heard a noise just outside and yelled 'who is there'. He also knew the young man who had fired the gun.

THE ROAD TO EXILE

The group of raiders of which the elder Žibert was a part was about to enter our courtyard when the raid, much to the chagrin of Karel's father, was terminated. I explained to him that at that very time, Mitzi, Paul and I were under the beds in this very room, sent there to hide by our parents, who had been watching the goings on through the windows.

The Žibert family attempted to return after we left on May 8, 1945, but there was some shooting. They came back for good later and yes, they all remembered my mother when she came to beg for food.

I asked if I could see the church and Mrs. Žibert, who had joined us after changing into her Sunday best said she would get the key from a neighbor and take me there. There were still no bells in the steeple, but the outside of the building was in excellent repair, the last coat of paint had not yet lost its luster and the once bare surrounding grounds had been planted with attractive shrubbery. But the biggest surprise was the interior of the church which in our time served as an empty space under a roof, used mainly for storing common farming equipment: the threshing machine and its mate; the wood-powered steam engine with its huge flywheel; the copper boiler of the still and its companion the condensing vessel and a few wagons and plows. Now the space was filled with hardwood benches and the floor sparkled with attractive tile. Even more to the point was the Eternal Light burning over the decked altar signifying the presence of the Host in the Tabernacle. It was obvious this was a functioning Catholic church in a Communist state.

Mrs. Žibert explained how the people of Veliko Mraševo and those of the smaller communities nearby struggled since their return in 1945 to collect funds to complete the church, which they had started to construct in the early 1930's. It had been consecrated to St. Peter and Paul on June 29, 1934 and Mass was held on Sundays by a priest from the Cerkle parish. Before the war, worshipers sat on chairs, the money for the benches not yet raised. And after the villagers came back in 1945, they struggled with collections and finances and except for the lack of bells, were now pleased with their church, the spiritual and communal center they had wanted for so many years. A reminder of the effort of my ancestors in Masern, centuries ago.

After the church, Mrs. Žibert led me through the main part of the village with houses on either side of the road leading to the river. Some had gone to ruin or had become vacant lots, their original owners not having returned from the Nazi labor camps after the war. Occasionally she stopped to introduce me to someone on the street or near their house. However, she always prefaced the introduction by saying that I had come to express my regret for being the cause of their expulsion and that we also were victims of Nazi ideology. No hostility was shown and most expressed their appreciation for my gesture. Some asked me to step inside to have a glass of wine. Unfortunately I had to decline their generous hospitality due to my limited time. "But please visit us when you come again".

We walked to the river, a short distance from the last house. The bunker, the fence and the gate had been dismantled soon after the villagers returned. The little beach was smaller than I remembered but a short pier, with a rowboat tied to it, was new. A similar addition at the other side, now seemingly less far away made for easy crossing, this being the widest part where the water is deep and gentle, holding the reflections of clouds and willows and poplars lining its banks. Here the water flows slowly and peacefully, giving little resistance to a boat being rowed across. A little further downstream the river disappears gradually around a bend into a narrower stretch where it picks up speed and is more of a challenge to those crossing there.

Mrs. Žibert patiently watched me linger on the sloping beach while my mind wandered through images of the past, the most vivid being the drowning of my school friend Franz who with flailing arms propelled himself into ever deeper water. I remembered how, unable to help we watched until he disappeared and the water became smooth again.

On the way back, I asked Mrs. Žibert if she knew what happened to the carpentry tools Father had left behind in the workshop he set up in the house of their neighbor, the house of the woman who had so vehemently expressed her anger at Mother on that day of May 1945. Oh, they all are now in possession of the wine barrel maker at the other end of the village. Would I like to go and see them. She phoned and yes he is home and would gladly talk to me.

This time we walked in the opposite direction, away from the river, on the road leading out of the village. Slowly at first but more quickly past the house of Johann Krisch since it brought up images I was not willing to dwell on at the moment.

Past the house of Karl Mausser who after some years had finally discovered for himself the well-known village secret why his wine became progressively more watery every spring and summer. His wife and two teen-aged daughters all had developed a liking and dutifully replaced every liter of wine taken from the barrels with water from the pump.

Past the house of the smith, the smithy silent after mid 1944 when he, like most of the able men in the village, was called up. His youngish widow was assigned a placid but able Slovene forced laborer and there were rumors.

Past the house of the middle aged spinster sisters who frequently entertained a man or two late into the night. The men would announce their leaving early in the morning by joyously playing an accordion.

Past other houses, some of them still empty but which, like those in the opposite direction toward the river, each had their own history that remained unknown to us in the three and a half years we lived there.

The barrel maker was waiting for us in his shop near the house. He showed me the many tools his father had taken from the workshop Father had set up in the large room of the house next to the Žiberts in 1942. He did this before the owners of that house returned. His father had also been confronted by the same angry woman for leaving the workshop bare. She considered the tools to be rightly hers.

He proudly showed off the different size Yankee brand planing tools Father had brought back from Brooklyn in 1914, just after the beginning of WW I, seventy-four years ago. All were oiled to limit rusting and kept in excellent shape, but he had difficulty getting replacement cutting blades. He said he was fortunate to have them since these precision tools allowed him to make superior barrels. As I fondly fingered a small one, he offered to let me have it as a memento, a touching gesture I was obliged to decline. The plane was useful to his trade and small compensation for the misery brought upon his family by our intrusion in 1941.

A little later, as we sat over a glass of wine in his living/dining room, I told the barrel maker that I had been in this house, in this very room in December of 1941, shortly after we arrived in Veliko Mraševo when I and several other youngsters were exploring the empty houses in the village. In the middle of the table in this very room had been a large bowl of porridge, untouched by the spoons surrounding it, obviously left there by residents forced to leave in a great hurry. He was born after the war, but clearly remembered the tales of his father, describing the arrival of the trucks that were to take them away; how the family ran into the woods and under cover of the following night escaped across the river. They, like the Žibert family spent the following years on the other side of the Krka, in Kostanjevica, a small town some fifteen km upstream. His father was with the Partisans and participated, with Karel Žibert's father in the big raid on the villages along the Krka in the summer 1943.

Warmly we said good bye and he again offered to let me have the small plane. "And if you ever change your mind, just let me know", he said as we were leaving to return to the Žiberts.

Since that summer of 1988, I visited Veliko Mraševo several times, each time enlarging the store of memories of the three and a half years in that village; eventful times that appeared more dramatic and tragic with each passing decade. Why were we there to begin with, how did we get there and why. But it was only years later when I realized the full magnitude of that first visit. That return and others to that village and that country caused the beginning of a personal catharsis, which challenged me to take seriously the notion that there is more than one side to a story. This particularly so when I realized that our Gottscheer history was being written by those who helped to end it, a veiled and distorted view shaped by the bias of a still lingering ideology. Therefore, the expressions "history belongs to those who tell it" and "truth and history are poor bedfellows", both coined by Napoleon Bonaparte, became for me an urge to tell it my way.

Karel Žibert survived the battle for his homeland, his inheritance, his possessions and his hearth, but lost the war to cancer. He died in 2002 at the age of 69. In him, I lost the once bitter enemy I jeered at across the river, who then became a compassionate victor, sharing his meager supplies with my pleading mother and ultimately a treasured friend after so magnanimously accepting my apology.

The generosity of the Žiberts greatly helped the otherwise inadequate subsistence provided by our captors at the Brežice camp. But Mother was now confronted with requests from others to share, especially from families with small children who were starving. Father was against it but she shared some of the bread anyway saying that she would go out again to get more. Others tried to do what she had done but they did not speak Slovene and the guards were not sympathetic to pleas in German, the language of the defeated occupier, in spite of tears.

In the afternoon of May 23, word had it that we should get prepared and ready to leave the camp the following morning. This seemed to become likely since the food ration was a bit more generous that evening and bottles were provided for water. But where to, maybe back to Masern? No one knew and even Mother could not get an answer from the young guards behind the wire fence. Perhaps they also did not know. But they did tell her to fill the bottles.

The rumbling of the trucks began to wake us at dawn the following morning. This was followed by the shouting of the guards ordering us to line up outside immediately. This took little time since we were all sleeping in our clothing, not changed since the 8th of May.

Rejoined by our men from the barracks across the dividing fence, we were ordered again to climb on to canvas covered trucks; destination unknown. This, in a few minutes, turned out to be the railroad station; the very one we arrived at under such different circumstances in December 1941. Waiting for us on a siding was a long line of boxcars, some with gaping doors, others shut tight. At the front end was a connected locomotive, intermittently coughing steam. It was apparent that the train had arrived from the south carrying passengers behind the shut doors and had stopped to pick up others like us.

"We are going home …", was heard hopefully but without much conviction from many; their arrival three and a half years ago and the irony of our present situation being painfully on their minds.

It was difficult to get into the cars, so high up from the coarsely graveled tracks but the threatening submachine guns were an encouragement to help each other. The Partisans monitored the space inside the cars and when packed to mostly standing room only, drove those still outside up and down the train to find room in other cars, the tears shed by the separated being ignored, the order enforced by the barrel of a gun.

Finally the doors rolled shut, the multi-hooked bolt engaged to the fully closed position. The first jerk of the engine caused those standing to pile up against each other, some tripping over those who found room to sit on the boards of the floor.

THE BELLS RING NO MORE

The expected direction of the train, noticed by the location of the locomotive, was confirmed; at least we were not moving East.

The train rolled slowly and even slower over sections that were being repaired, stopping often. Those who managed to peer through the cracks of louvers high up on the wall of the car reported on our progress as we passed known markers along the way. The late May sun began to add to the heat from the packed mass of sweating humanity; the air further fouled by the stench from the open bucket in one corner of the car for the relief of its occupants. The water in the bottles was reluctantly shared.

After some hours the train stopped. The door rolled open, the inrush of fresh air lessened the stench and brilliant sunlight blinded our eyes. The open door also revealed a Partisan, his sub-machine gun aiming at the opening to prevent its human contents from spilling out. This was not likely; all occupants by now fully aware that their lives had value only to themselves.

As the eyes slowly adjusted to the new light, they revealed, beyond the pointed barrel, a stunning sea of yellow flowers in a large field gently sloping downward toward the Sava. Mother asked if she could run down to the river to refill the now empty water bottles, a request firmly rejected by a wave of the gun.

The pastoral moment was very short. One of now two Partisans climbed into the car and with drawn pistol began to search pockets for jewelry, remove watches and strip fingers of rings. And after he noticed some women fiddling under their skirts, he grinningly examined their crevices for hidden treasure. This ended only when his companion began to yell that the train was to about to move again. Mother pleaded with the Partisans to leave the door partly open. Apparently satisfied with their loot, they obliged by using another of the hooks on the swinging latch, leaving an opening of about six inches. Mother's success brought relief, but did not relieve the hostility from some in the car who felt she was, because of her ability to talk to the tormentors, somehow connected with them. This, in spite of the fact, that she too was subjected to the same torment.

Again, as two weeks ago, we were approaching Zidani Most. Through the opening in the door we observed the road traveled, the track crossings crossed, the places camped at. The road was no longer congested, but the curbs were still bulging with the spoils of war. The once pervasive smell of decaying bodies was no longer noticed; the air inside the cattle car too dense with its own fumes to permit others to enter. The place where Frantze was shot point blank was on the opposite side behind the shut door and could not be seen. But across the river came into view the camp at Radeče where Father re-entered our lives and just beyond that the place where he tried to exit his and just a little further on, the steel bridge where he sought to end mine.

The outburst "maybe we are going home" was not unreasonable given the fact that we were on the same tracks, traveling in the direction we had come from three and a half years ago. "We soon will see" heightened the hopeful suspense; with all now knowing that our destiny was in the way the switches were set in Zidani Most, our approaching fork in the road.

That we were not going home became clear when the train, instead of crossing the Savinja bridge and continuing along the Sava toward Ljubljana and from there to Kočevje, continued to hug the steep hill on the right and head north. Many cried while others were consoling. Father seemed relieved knowing we were rolling toward Austria, the place we had made for to begin with, away from the Communists we had so foolishly tried to outrun.

Beyond Zidani Most, the river becomes virtually buried in a fissure barely leaving room for the track and the road both in parts buried in tunnels. This was in a way fortunate for us since at times the roof of our car was shaded from the now high noon sun adding, at least in spots, no further heat to the already unbearable atmosphere surrounding those languishing inside.

The train slowed to a crawl just before Rimske Toplice or Roman Baths, named so for the Roman settlement there nearly 2000 years ago. This was the place where the SS troops, together with their allies, put up one of their final if hopeless stands, the reason for the blockage that slowed us down so fatefully two weeks ago. The tracks were still being repaired by exhausted looking workers, guarded by machine-gun bearing Partisans.

After that, our train made more rapid progress toward Celje, being slowed only occasionally by repair work on the rails all being done by guarded crews. But eventually we pulled on to a siding at the Celje station, a major east-west-south rail intersection, with the eastern direction leading toward Hungary, along the way there branching off to the left toward Maribor in the north and beyond that to the Austrian border.

THE BELLS RING NO MORE

We stayed on the siding in Celje for quite a while, our door never opened beyond the six-inch crack before we moved on. The reason for the delay in Celje had to do with an exchange of passengers on our train, prisoners really, who were behind the doors of the boxcars we noticed shut when we boarded the train in Brežice. These were taken from the train and replaced with others. We did not know that only a few kilometers east of Celje, in Teharje, was a major prison camp, a Partisan interrogation and holding camp, where suspected collaborators and war criminals were culled out from the great mass of ethnic Germans to be expelled from the new Yugoslavia. Those in the boxcars were taken to Teharje and kept there under brutal conditions. The emptied cars, in turn, were reloaded with those that had been there and cleared for expulsion.

But we knew none of this when we started to move again. We also did not know that Teharje had been a major Concentration Camp of the SS. Nor did we know where we were going, the train slowing down frequently in parts where track repair was underway. There was no sense of direction since no one in our car had ever been this way and the station markers, already changed from German to Slovene were of no help and had no meaning.

There was no sense of direction until we were in what appeared to be the outskirts of a place larger than any since Celje. Then someone yelled - Maribor -, which electrified those awake and roused the others who had surrendered their misery of heat, thirst and hunger to the relief of a semiconscious stupor or sleep. All knew that Maribor was Marburg the German equivalent of the second largest city in Slovenia, in the north of the country. All also knew that the city was near Austria and realized that we were on the way there, a journey into exile that began sixteen days ago.

But relief in the minds of many was still tempered by doubt that we were finally going to get there. And if so, what then and what was waiting for us in Austria, was it not occupied by the Russians, Communists worse than the Partisans, "animals used to killing and raping", as we had so often been told? Were the Russians going to kill us, now that it appeared that the Partisans were going to let us live? Were they going to separate out the young and able, send them to Russia or Siberia and kill the rest, the scenario that drove Father to madness on the steel bridge twelve days ago?

Or perhaps, Austria was occupied by the English or the Americans. If so, our suffering was to end after we crossed the border. And especially so 'if the Americans are there, they would help us to contact aunts Johanna and Paula in Brooklyn who would surely take care of us' !

THE ROAD TO EXILE

The train slowed but did not stop. It rolled slowly through the partly bombed out station, then through thinning suburbs and after that through open fields again. Then it stopped.

The bolt was lifted, the door rolled open and a Partisan, standing off to the side yelled; "raus".

The train had stopped at the edge of a broad downward sloping field and then after a flat part, upward toward the road a few hundred feet from the tracks. On the other side of the road was a long, 20 foot high stone embankment, keeping in place the hill into which the road had been constructed.

On the stones of the embankment was written in huge white capital letters, plain to all spilling from the boxcar to see:

"Wir Danken Unserem Führer"

Plain for all to contemplate, in silence, the four words of now bitter irony, words we had been made to utter so often in mass rallies during the summer of 1941 and the years after that without really knowing why.

The Partisan motioned with his gun to cross over to the road and move on it to the right. The spring grass on the field in front of us was trampled flat telling us that we were not the first to do so. But Mother kept asking "where to" until one of the Partisans grumbled "meja" which she translated as border to others who passed it on. This field apparently was a major drop off point for people being expelled, the trampled grass and the intentional display of mockery on the embankment attesting to that. The now emptied train reversed direction, most likely to pick up another load of humanity marked for exile while being held captive somewhere.

It was now apparent that we were only a walking distance away from the Spielfeld bridge, the bridge crossing the Mur, the river border between Yugoslavia and Austria. This was now only a fraction of the entire distance of sixteen kilometers from Maribor, most of which we had traveled on the train. As we trotted along in the late afternoon sun, it soon became obvious why they had not taken us the few extra miles. The tracks alongside the road had not yet been repaired; twisted rails and deep cavities in the rail bed attesting to bombardments in a recent past. This rail, a major link used by the occupier not too long ago and decades before that, had been a major north/south connection. It was now idle, its repair postponed in favor of more urgent priorities.

THE BELLS RING NO MORE

On our road there was no traffic other than the stream of hurrying refugees now on their final stretch. For the five of us, it soon became a very slow walk; Father not yet fully recovered having tired very quickly and was now struggling on his crutches. Mitzi, Paul and I would impatiently walk ahead then sit on the grass and watch others hurry by until our parents caught up with us.

It was now late in the afternoon with nightfall soon to come, yet the border was still nowhere in sight. At some point there was a cluster of people on the road in front of us which dissolved to pass on as we got nearer. But from within this cluster emerged the thirteen year old Irma Jaklitsch, my one time Masern play-mate, my first girlfriend. In one of her arms she held the remaining half of a huge loaf of bread, while the other hand held a knife with which she had been cutting off slices for those passing by.

We had not eaten since the day before and the liberal slice Irma cut from the loaf for each of us was gratefully acknowledged. It is not far to the border Irma said, and if you hurry, you will get there before nightfall. So we walked on and away since others had arrived and were now crowding around the girl with the shrinking loaf. What caused this teenager to perform this act of generosity, where the bread had come from and the whereabouts of her parents remains a mystery. But I suspect that nearby, out of sight, her father was behind this; he having been the major driving force in Masern to convince the villagers to switch love of God and homeland to love of the Führer and agreement to resettle. As the Nazi trained village leader, he had performed his task to perfection getting all except a few families, undesirables for sure, to leave their homes for the Reich. But now prudently hiding, realizing that those he once controlled and so skillfully deceived might react violently to his sight.

It is also possible that Franz Jaklitsch, the former Sturmführer of Masern, now seeing that his former fanaticism had led the entire village into disaster, merely wanted to share his loaf of bread with those he had so willfully misled. If such a humbling acceptance of the total failure of Nazi ideology was indeed in the mind of this man, he certainly was the exception among so many others who have not done so to this day.

THE ROAD TO EXILE

We walked on, slowly, now the only stragglers on the road; the others of this drama having passed us by. Dusk was rapidly extinguishing the last glow of the sun that had set a while ago as we approached and entered a totally darkened village. No longer able to continue, partly because of the dark and partly because Father had reached the limit of exhaustion, we turned right into the courtyard of a farm house abutting the street. In the back we made for the stable, fortunately empty of its usual inhabitants and fortunately also filled with welcoming straw.

Mother woke us at dawn and with Father having recovered some of his energy we walked through the empty street at a reasonably rapid pace. We knew that we had not far to go but knew not what was waiting for us at the border and beyond that.

The border was the river, the crossing point a bridge to the unknown. On this side, the sleepy and sullen Partisan border guards, emerging from a newly erected shack, casually motioned us on to the bridge as they had motioned to others in days past. But on this day of May 25, 1945, we were the first to arrive and the first to cross, a distinction not up-most in the minds of this small group of five.

The first rays of the sun, markers to a new day and to a new future, were not yet visible when we got to the other side. There, the Austrian border guards, in different uniforms and caps no longer displaying the five-pointed red star, mumbled a courteous "guten Morgen" as they too, waved us on.

Bibliography

Sources

Arko, H., *Gedächnisschrift*, 1941, (see www.gottschee.de).
Auction Records 1911, (družinski arhiv družine Pogorelec, Dolenja vas, Ribnica).
Colanetté, F., *Alphabetisches Verzeichnis der Gemeinde Masern im Jahre 1825*. (Arhiv Republike Slovenije,Ljubljana).
Dokumentation der Vertreibung der Deutschen aus Ost-Mitteleuropa, Band V, Bundesministerium für Vertriebene, Flüchtlinge und Kriegsgeschädigte, Oskar Leiner Druck, K.G. Düsseldorf, 1961.
Ehrenbuch der Schüler zu Niederdorf, 1876 - 1880, (Zgodovinski arhiv, Ljubljana).
Franciscejski kataster, Grčarice, (Arhiv Republike Slovenije, Ljubljana).
Gottschee, Ao 1568, Blagay Vrbar, (Arhiv Republike Slovenije, Ljubljana).
Hitler, A. *Reichstag Speech*, 6. October 1939, (www.hitler.org/speeches).
Grčarice, *Jožefinski kataster*, , (*Arhiv* Republike Slovenije, Ljubljana).
Lampeter, W., *Die Gottscheer Volksgruppe 1930–1942*, s. l., 1942, (www.gottschee.de).
Ledgers on Births, Marriages and Deaths, Masern, 1773-1896, (Nadškofski ordinat, Ljubljana).
Mittheilungen, Deutscher Schulverein, 5 November 1882, (Department of History Swarthmore College, February 1993).
Nüremberg Documents, *Nazi Conspiracy and Aggression, Vol. VI*, (see Google: Hitler's most catastrophic mistake.)
Posnik, Johann, *Tabulation of Grčarice population in 1877*. (County Records, Ribnica).
Raktelj, L. *župnija zopet oživljena*, (Nadškofski ordinat, Ljubljana).
Terezijanski kataster, 1752, (*Bekantnuss Tabellen, Unterkrain,. Dritter Viertl Herrschaft Gottschee, Dorff Maschern, (23 April 1752)* (Archiv Republike Slovenije, Ljubljana).
Urbar Register der Stadtt Gotsche, Anno 1564, (Arhiv Republike Slovenije, Ljubljana).
Vrbar Register des ambts Riegkh, /.../ Anno 1498, (Arhiv Republike Slovenije, Ljubljana).

The Air Bombing of Belgrave, Center of Military History, United States Army, Washington, DC. (see Google: The German Campaigns in the Balkans, Part Two, The Yugoslav Campaign, Chapter 9).

Quellen zur nationalsozialistischen Entnationalisierungspolitik in Slowenien, 1941-1945, Tone Ferenc, Obzorja, Maribor 1980. Documents (on: www.karawankengrenze.at) : 13, 16, 17, 23, 27, 131, 133, 141, 143, 144, 149, 151, 153, 164, 179, 201, 238, 239, 251, 256, 292, 301, 307, 319, 321, 322, 585.

Literature

Diakon, Pavel, *Zgodovina Langobardov,* Obzorja, Maribor 1988.
Ferenc, M., *Gottschee: Das verlorene Kulturerbe der Gottscheer Deutschen.* Ljubljana 1993, 35.
Ferenc, M., *Kočevska pusta in prazna. Nemško jezikovno območje na Kočevskem po odselitvi Nemcev,* Modrijan, Ljubljana 2005.
Ferenc, T., *Nacisticna raznarodovalna politika v Sloveniji v letih 1941-1945,* Obzorja, Maribor 1968.
Ferenc T., *Vprašanje priključitve zasedenih slovenskih pokrajin k nemškemu rajhu.* Prispevki za zgodovino delavskega gibanja, 1974, Number 1–2, pg. 157–201.
Frensing, H. H., *Die Umsiedlung der Gottscheer Deutschen. Das Ende einer südostdeutschen Volksgruppe,* Oldenbourg, München, 1970.
Hösler, J., *Slowenien. Von den Anfängen bis zur Gegenwart,* F. Pustet, Südosteuropa-Gesellschaft, Regensburg, München, 2006.
Judson P., *Class, Ethnicity and Colonial Fantasy at the Margin of the Habsburg Monarchy,* Department of History, Swarthmore College, February 1993.
Kočevski zbornik, Družba sv. Cirila in Metoda, Ljubljana 1939.
Kočović, B., *Žrtve drugog svetskog rata u Jugoslaviji,* Svjetlost, Sarajevo 1990.
Kumanudi, Dr., *Decree, School Ministry of Yugoslavia,* 25 November 1927.
Loser, H., *Masern in Wort und Bild,*: Gottscheer Kalender 1931.
Macartney, C. A., *The Habsburg Empire, 1790-1918,* Macmillan, New York 1968.
Oražem, M., *Grčarice skozi preteklost. Utrinki ob 500-letnici imena Masern,* samozaložba, Ribnica 1998
Oražem, M., *Grčarice, zgodovinski kraj. Ob 60. letnici padca plavogardistične postojanke,* samozaložba, Ribnica, 2003.
Petschauer, E., *"Das Jahrhundertbuch": Gottschee and its People Through the Centuries,* Gottscheer Relief Association, New York 1984.
Požar B., *Anastasius Grün in Slovenci,* Maribor 1970.

BIBLIOGRAPHY

Saje, F., *Belogardizem*, Slovenski knjižni zavod, Ljubljana 1952.

Savich, C. K., *Projekat Rastko*, 2001, Google: Projekat Rastko Carl Kosta Savich – *"Prince Eugen SS Division..."*

Shirer, W. L. *The Rise and Fall of the Third Reich*, Simon & Schuster Inc. New York, 1959.

Steininger, R., *South Tyrol. A Minority Conflict of the Twentieth Century*, Transaction Publishers, New Brunswick, London 2003.

Štih, P., Simoniti, V., Vodopivec, P., *Slowenische Geschichte*, Leykam, Graz 2008.

Trdan, V., *Življenje kočevskih Nemcev med 1850 in 1918*, Ljubljana 1999, magistrsko delo.

Valvasor, J. V., *Die Ehre des Hertzogthums Crain*, Nürnberg 1689.

Vodopivec, P., *Od Pohlinove slovnice do samostojne države*, Modrijan, Ljubljana 2006.

Widmer, G., *Urkundliche Beiträge zur Geschichte des Gottscheerländchens. 1406–1627*, Verein der Deutschen aus Gottschee in Wien, Wien 1931.

Zinck, R. E., *The Final Flight of Maggie's Drawers*, Turner Publication Co, Nashville, Tennessee 1998.

Žerjavić, V., *Yugoslavia – manipulations with the number of Second World War victims /.../ Jugoslavija – manipulacije žrtvama drugog svjetskog rata*, Hrvatski informativni centar, Zagreb 1993.

Press

Gottscheer Bote .... (1904 - 1919).
Gottscheer Zeitung .... (1919 - 1941, 1955 - to date).
Marburger Zeitung .... (1941).
Naprej .... (1919).
Slovenec .... (1919, 1936).

Made in the USA
Lexington, KY
06 July 2014